BURROUGHS WELLCOME IN THE USA
AND THE WELLCOME TRUST

Burroughs Wellcome in the USA and the Wellcome Trust

Pharmaceutical Innovation, Contested Organizational Cultures, and the Triumph of Philanthropy

Roy Church

CRUCIBLE

Burroughs Wellcome in the USA
and the Wellcome Trust

First edition

Published in 2015 by Crucible Books
an imprint of Carnegie Publishing Ltd
Chatsworth Road,
Lancaster LA1 4SL
www.carnegiepublishing.com

British Library Cataloguing-in-Publication data
A catalogue record for this book is available from the British Library

Softback: ISBN 978-1-905472-07-9
Hardback: ISBN 978-1-905472-04-8

Designed, typeset and originated by Carnegie Publishing
Printed and bound by Page Bros Ltd, Norwich, NR6 6SA

Contents

Acknowledgements ix
Dramatis personae xi
Abbreviations xv
Archives and locations xvii
List of figures xx
List of tables xxi
List of illustrations xxiii

Introduction 1

PART ONE: **From subjugation towards independent policy-making**

1. The origins of Burroughs Wellcome & Co. in the US, 1906–1924; the New York sales branch of a British pharmaceutical company 7
2. Burroughs Wellcome (USA) Inc., British subsidiary company from 1924: manufacturing at Tuckahoe, the origins of RD&M, and the Americanisation of Burroughs Wellcome & Co., in the US 21
3. Adapting to peacetime markets after World War II: planning for productivity and hoping for product innovation 10
4. Empirin, a dominant leader in the US market for analgesics from the 1940s to the 1970s and its decline 51

PART TWO: **The pursuit of new products, management crises, and intervention by the Wellcome Trust**

5. Is the doctor in? Product development and the "detailing" of doctors in the market for prescription drugs 65

6. Anglo-American relations between Burroughs Wellcome & Co. (USA) Inc., the Wellcome Foundation Ltd, and the Wellcome Trust, 1924 to the 1960s 75

7. Burroughs Wellcome & Co. (USA) Inc. and the Wellcome Trust: conflict, crisis, and the end of a presidency 89

8. Drug discovery at Tuckahoe and networks of innovation, 1942–1970: pathways to Purinethol, Imuran, and Zyloprim 100

9. Investment in RD&M, laboratory reorganisation, and the FDA Drug Amendment Act of 1962 112

PART THREE: **Relocating the company and remaking corporate image**

10. Relocation from Tuckahoe to the Research Triangle Park: North Carolina and the creation of a corporate identity 127

11. Reorganization, management recruitment, corporate image, and the transformation of marketing 139

12. Septra: product innovation and the expansion of consumer marketing 157

13. The Wellcome Trust, Wellcome Foundation Ltd, and Burroughs Wellcome & Co.: personalities, policies, dividends, and Anglo-American relations 166

PART FOUR: **The transforming impact of antivirals: sexually-transmitted diseases, market development, and problems of management turbulence in the US and the UK**

14. Zovirax, blockbuster drug and the expansion of Burroughs Wellcome & Co. at Research Triangle Park and Greenville 183

15. Management by textbook: McKinsey's review of Burroughs Wellcome & Co. 200

16. Clashing cultures: intra-and inter-organizational conflicts at Burroughs Wellcome & Co. and Wellcome Foundation Ltd 213

17. Lancing the boil at Beckenham: A. D. Little's management review of Wellcome Foundation Ltd, recommendations, and consequences 225

18. The turning point: policy innovation at the Wellcome Trust, the formation of Wellcome plc, and the first public share issue in 1986 236

PART FIVE: "What price is life?" Profiting from AIDS, and responding to public outrage

19. Breakthrough: Burroughs Wellcome & Co., AZT-Retrovir, and the AIDS epidemic 251

20. The economics of AZT; the supply, costs, and pricing of Retrovir, the AIDS drug 265

21. Public and political backlash 273

22. Marketing Retrovir and rebuilding trust through public relations 283

PART SIX: City businessmen and bankers, the Wellcome Trust, and Wellcome plc

23. Management renewal and a reversion to core activities at Wellcome plc 293

24. A global integration strategy 307

25. The second share issue in 1992: a pathway to corporate revival or nemesis for Wellcome plc? 318

26. Ethics and economics, betrayal or moral obligation? The Wellcome Trust, the sale of Wellcome plc, and the formation of Glaxo Wellcome plc 330

PART SEVEN: Epilogue

27. Themes and Perspectives 341

Managing across MNE borders: a study in semi-detachment of a dominant subsidiary 341

A delicate balance: the scientific ethic and commercial imperatives 344

Organizational culture and networks of innovation 346

Drug discovery and drug development 349

Government, business, and pressure groups: price, politics, and public relations 351

Marketing pharmaceuticals: selling, detailing etiquette, and education 353

Inter-related institutional governance and policies: lessons from history 354

Promotion, prices, profits, and principle: Wellcome corporate ethics 358

Appendix: The Burroughs Wellcome Fund 365
Notes 368
Bibliography 400
Index 407

Acknowledgements

I am pleased to acknowledge the funding support from the Burroughs Wellcome Fund in the US and the valuable administrative assistance from Rolly Simpson, Senior Program Officer, and staff at the office of the Fund in Raleigh throughout the project. The Burroughs Wellcome Fund originated from an initiative undertaken by the President of Burroughs Wellcome & Co. in the US who in 1955 secured an initial endowment from the Wellcome Trust in London which depended heavily on dividends drawn from profits of the American company. The Burroughs Wellcome Fund has no affiliation with any corporation. Policy and management have remained completely independent of both the Trust and of the Wellcome companies; the decision made in 2005 to commission a history of the American company was independent of both the Wellcome Trust and of Wellcome plc and its successor companies. Consequently the research and writing of this book has been constrained neither by limitations on resources nor concern regarding scope, content, and editorial considerations.

This project initiated in the US was facilitated greatly by funding provided by the Wellcome Trust in the UK in 2000–2001 for the preparation of an oral history of the business activities owned by the Trust. The research project consisted of interviews with a large number of former leading figures, chairmen, presidents, directors, managers, and others, hitherto employed in the British and American companies and previous directors of the Wellcome Trust. The coinvestigator in this collaborative project was Professor E. M. Tansey. Under her supervision and that of the present author, most of the interviews were conducted by Drs Mike Collins, Gerald Connolly, and Jason Burton. The value of their contributions is attested by the prolific use of the transcripts recorded in the numerous references to contemporary accounts of aspects of the companies' history between 1940 and 1995. To those who agreed to be interviewed (only one declined), thanks are due for their patience and, almost without exception, their willingness for the interviews to be used in full and quoted for publication. Interviewees edited transcripts before agreement to vest copyright in the Wellcome Trust. Sadly, several of the most important interviewees in 2000–2001 are now deceased. Among these was Frederick Coe Jr, for whom his wife acted as transcriber of his personally edited diaries between 1945 when he joined Burroughs

Wellcome (USA) Inc. until 1980 which marked the end of his twelve year presidency during a decisive period in the company's history. I am most grateful to Peggy Coe for the existence and access to this valuable primary source.

The archival and library staff of the Wellcome Trust have provided expertise and support, especially Dr Richard Aspin, Amanda Engineer, Amelia Walker, Crestina Forcina, and Simon Chaplin. Without the agreement of GlaxoSmithKline to loan archives relating to the post 1940 period to the Wellcome Trust Library, and in the US to the library of the Burroughs Wellcome Fund, the book could not have been written. Thanks for effecting the arrangements required are due to Chris Campbell at GlaxoSmithKline in the UK, and in the US to Dorothy Dale Pollock, Glenn Burchett, and Kelly Eubank.

In her capacity of research associate funded by the Burroughs Wellcome Fund during the first year of the project, Dr Viviane Quirke's valuable contribution as a historian of medicine was to provide an important dimension on which to build. Professor Derek Oddy and Dr John Malin were constructive critics of early drafts, as was Professor Geoffrey Tweedale, who read a penultimate draft. I am grateful to each for assistance and advice. I am also greatly indebted to my wife Wendy for her critical attention to the text of successive drafts and for the advice which she has delivered with remarkable patience for far too long. Nobody from the Wellcome Trust or from GlaxoSmithKline has read the manuscript either in draft or in publication form. At Carnegie Publishing I am especially grateful for the assistance of Lucy Frontani and Rachel Clarke in the preparation of the manuscript for publication.

Dramatis personae

CHAIRMEN OF THE WELLCOME TRUST

Sir Henry Hallett Dale (1936–1960)
Lord Piercy of Burford (1961–1965)
Lord Franks of Headington (1965–1982)
Sir David Edward Charles Steel (1982–1989)
Sir Roger Gibbs (1989–1999)
Sir Dominic Cadbury (2000–2006)
Sir William Castell (2006–)

THE WELLCOME FOUNDATION/WELLCOME PLC

Chairmen, general managers, managing directors and CEOs of Burroughs Wellcome & Co. and of the Wellcome Foundation Ltd/Wellcome plc (UK)

Henry Wellcome (partner, 1880–1896; Governor/owner, 1897–1936)

George Pearson (Deputy Governor and General Manager, 1905–1936; Chairman and General Manager, 1936–1940)

T. R. G. Bennett Chairman and General Manager (1940–1948)

H.E. Sier. Chairman part-time (1948–1953)

C. G. Oakes and Dr F. Wrigley (Joint Managing Directors (1948–1955)

Sir Michael F. Perrin Chairman (1953–1970)

D. E. Wheeler and Dr. F. Wrigley, Joint Managing Director (1955–1967)

D. E. Wheeler, Deputy Chairman and Group Director (1967–1970)

Dr. F. Wrigley, Deputy Chairman and Group Director (1967–1974)

A.A. Gray Chairman (1970–1977)

Sir Alfred J. Shepperd, Chairman and Managing Director (1977–1990)

Sir Alistair Frame, Chairman (1990–1993)

John Robb CEO (1990–1993); Chairman and CEO (1993–1995)

Presidents of Burroughs Wellcome New York branch, Burroughs Wellcome & Co. (USA) Inc., and BW&Co.

Thomas Nevin (1911–1944, and general manager)

Guy Dunbar (1944–1945, and general manager)

William N. Creasy (1945–1968, and general manager)

Fred Coe Jr (1968–1981, and CEO)

William M. Sullivan (1981–1986, and CEO)

Theodore E. Haigler (1986–1989, and CEO)

Philip Tracy (1989–1995, and CEO)

Heads/Administrators/Directors of The Experimental research Laboratories (Tuckahoe) and the Wellcome Research Laboratories at Research Triangle Park, NC. USA (Research and Development; and Research, Development, and Medical)

Dr Clifford S. Leonard (director R&D), 1928–1935

Mr Howard B. Fonda ("supervisor of laboratories") 1935–1938

Dr Lazlo Reiner (director R&D) 1937–1938

Prof. Carl J. Klemme ("R&D administrator") 1938–1942

Dr Edwin J. de Beer (acting director RD&M) 1942–1943

Dr Erwin E. Nelson (director RD&M) 1943–1946

Dr Edwin J. de Beer (acting director, RD&M) 1946–1961

Brigadier General Dr John R. Wood (vice president and manager of laboratories) 1955–1960

Dr John Burns and Professor George H. Hitchings (joint directors RD&M) 1961–1968

Prof. George H. Hitchings (RD&M director, vice president, and board member) 1968–1975

Dr R. M. Cresswell (director of development) 1972–1981

Prof. Pedro Cuatrecasas (RD&M director, vice president and board member) 1976–1986

Dr Howard J Schaeffer (RD&M director, vice president, and board and WFL main board director) 1986–1989

Dr David Barry (research vice president, and main board director, UK) 1989–1991

Heads/Directors of Research and Development at Wellcome Foundation Ltd and Wellcome plc.

Dr C. K. Wenyon, 1924–1944 (main board director, 1938–1944)

Dr C. H. Kellaway, 1944–1952 (main board director)

Dr R. Trevan, 1952–1953 (main board director)

Dr K. Adamson, 1953–1973 (main board director)

Dr J. R. Vane, 1973–1986 (Group and main board director)

Dr Ronnie Cresswell, 1981–1985 managing director of Wellcome Biotechnology Ltd, 1985–1987 group director R&D and main board director UK)

Dr Howard Schaeffer 1987–1989 (group R&D director located at RTP and main board director, UK)

Dr Salgado Moncada, 1986–1991 (research director UK)

Dr Trevor Jones, 1987–1991 (group development and main board director)

Dr David Barry 1991–1995 (group R&D and main board director located in the UK)

Abbreviations

ACT UP	AIDS Coalition to Unleash Power
AIDS	Acquired immune deficiency syndrome
ARC	AIDS-related complex
AVR	Antiviral representative
AZT	azidothymidine
BMA	British Medical Association
BWF	Burroughs Wellcome Fund
BWFL	Burroughs Wellcome Fund Library
BW&Co.	Burroughs Wellcome & Co.
CDC	US Centres for Disease Control and Prevention
CEO	Chief executive officer
CIBA	Chemische Industrie Basel
CMR	Committee of Medical Research of the Office of Scientific Research and Development
CMV	Cytomegalovirus
CM&R	Cooper, MacDougall & Robertson
DSMB	Data and Safety Monitoring Board
DDD	Drug Distribution Data
FDA	US Food and Drug Administration
FMD	Foot and mouth disease
GLAAD	Gay and Lesbian Alliance against Defamation
GMHC	Gay Men's Health Crisis
GSK	GlaxoSmithKline
GSK/WF	Wellcome Foundation and Wellcome plc Archives, GlaxoSmithKline, London and Research Triangle Park, Raleigh Durham, NC, US
GWHC	Glaxo Wellcome Heritage Archives, GlaxoSmithKline, Research Triangle Park, Raleigh Durham, NC, US
HIV	Human immunodeficiency virus
HMO	Hospital Management Organisation
HSV	Herpes simplex virus

ICWU	International Chemical Workers' Union
IMS	Intercontinental Medical Statistics
IND	Investigational New Drug Application
MMAG	Medical Marketing Advisory Group
MOU	Memorandum of understanding
MRC	UK Medical Research Council
NCI	US National Cancer Institute
NDA	New Drug Application
NDI	New Drug Indication
NIAID	US National Institute of Allergy and Infectious Diseases
NIH	US National Institute of Health
OTC	Over the counter medicines
PCP	Pneumocystis carinii pneumonia
PSS	Professional sales skills course
R&D	Research and development
RD&M	Research, development, and medical
RTP	Research Triangle Park, NC, US
TIPS	Territorial Information Planning Systems
TRC	Therapeutic Research Corporation
UCL	University College London
UN	United Nations
UNRRA	United Nations Relief and Rehabilitation Administration
USP	United States Pharmacopoeia
VMAG	Veterinary marketing advisory group
WA	Wellcome Archives, Wellcome Library, London
WCRL	Wellcome Chemical Research laboratories
WBL	Wellcome Biotechnology Ltd
WFA	Wellcome Foundation Archives, Wellcome Library, London
WFL	The Wellcome Foundation Limited
WHO	World Health Organisation
WPB	War Production Board
WPRL	Wellcome Physiological research Laboratories
WT	The Wellcome Trust Archives, Wellcome Trust, London

Archives and locations

The main archive collections which provided the sources for this book are those of the Burroughs Wellcome & Co. and its successor, the Wellcome Foundation Limited (WFL) in the UK, Burroughs Wellcome (USA) Inc., and from 1986, when all Wellcome companies were consolidated into a single organization, of Wellcome plc, which are located in the UK and in the US.

WF: The records of the UK company's history before 1940 are located at the Wellcome Trust. This is also the location for transcripts of a series of interviews of senior figures relating to the history of both the company in the UK and in the US and of the Wellcome Trust. The interviews undertaken in 2001–2002 were conducted by Drs Michael Collins, Gerald Connolly, and Jason Burton under the supervision of Prof. E. M. Tansey and the author of this study. This collection also contains transcripts of the diaries of Fred Coe jr between 1944, when he joined BW&Co., until the end of his presidency in 1980.

GWHC: Glaxo Wellcome Heritage Archives are located at GSK at Research Triangle Park, North Carolina US. They relate only to the US business since 1907. They contain extensive annual reports of the President and an almost complete set of issues of the internal company newsletter and journal, Wellcome News. Transcripts of interviews include one undertaken by Jan Tanner of Burroughs Wellcome (USA) Inc. with Gertrude Elion in 1979.

An important chronological continuous source for the history for BW&Co. is an internal publication entitled *Wellcome News*. Originating in 1944 as a vehicle through which to communicate news of people and social events at the company in Tuckahoe to enlisted former employees, by the 1960s business and scientific developments became the principle focus. As a result of changes in editorial policies, between 1984 and 1986 references consist of volume, issue number and page reference. Thereafter references are to month followed by page number.

BWFL: A small collection of private papers is also held by the library of the Burroughs Wellcome Fund, also at research Triangle Park, North Carolina, USA.

GSK/WF: Business records of the UK and American Burroughs Wellcome/Wellcome companies relating to the period after 1940 were acquired by Glaxo after the takeover of Wellcome plc in 1995. Since merger to form GlaxoSmithKline (GSK) in the year 2000, the records have been held in store in Hertfordshire. These archives include board, directors' committees and other ad hoc committee minutes, annual reports, profit and loss accounts and other financial data, reports of management consultants, and business correspondence.

Reference to the business records of the Wellcome Foundation from 1940 and of Wellcome plc since 1986 has presented some difficulty in sustaining consistency. The problem is attributable primarily to repeated reclassification since most records were transferred from premises owned by Wellcome plc to locations belonging to Glaxo Wellcome and subsequently to those of GSK. At the time when they were consulted beginning in 2007 re-classification remained incomplete. All Wellcome Foundation records under the current administration of GSK have been prefixed with GSK/WF/ and of Wellcome plc with GSK/Wellcome plc./. These records were not available for public consultation at the time of research.

WA: The life of Sir Henry Wellcome, of his laboratories and his museums, are the principal subjects of a collection of papers catalogued as Wellcome Archives. They include audio archives (see below).

WT: The records of the Wellcome Trust are on deposit at the Wellcome Trust, Euston Road, London UK. They also contain interviews with chairmen of the Wellcome Trust and of other trustees.

A series of audio and visual interviews with Wellcome trustees and selected directors of WFL were conducted by Dr Peter O. Williams (administrative Director of the Trust until 1991) at the behest of the Trust in 1991, and in 1996 in conjunction with Dr Max Blythe of Oxford Brookes University, UK. Like the 2001 series of interviews, these were passed to the author by Dr Peter Williams for the purpose of preparing this history. Interviews form part of the Medical Science Video Archives at the library of Oxford Brookes University. Interviews also form part of the Moving Image and Sound Collections and are part of the Wellcome Foundation Archive Video-recordings held by the Wellcome Trust. These are to be found under WA (see above). Many of the 1996 series of interviews, however, remain uncatalogued and are not yet available to researchers.

Other relevant oral history sources based on interviews by Victoria A. Harden and Caroline Hannaway with, among others, scientists and clinical researchers at the National Cancer Institute and the National Institute of Health are to be found at http://history.nih.gov/NIHinourownwords, "NIH researchers recall the early years of AIDS."

Since the research project begun in 1999 which led to the publication in 2007 of the first volume dealing with the history of Burroughs Wellcome between 1880 and 1940, the Wellcome Foundation archive held by the Wellcome Library has been catalogued in detail with archive references replacing older classifications (WF). This affects primarily chapters 1 and 2 of the current volume which summarize several chapters in the earlier book in order to provide a historical background to the early years of the American company and its relation to the business based in the UK. Therefore, scholars wishing to explore original sources further may need to consult the Wellcome Library online catalogue to look up current archive file references.

List of figures

2.1 The Structure and Organisation of the Wellcome Foundation Ltd, in 1940. 36

3.1 The Corporate Structure of Burroughs Wellcome (USA) Inc., 1924–1970. 41

6.1 The Wellcome Foundation Ltd Organisation Chart, 1948–1970. 78

9.1 Organisation of RD&M at Tuckahoe, NC, 1955–1968/7. 114
9.2 Organisation of RD&M at Research Triangle Park, NC, 1970–1987. 121

11.1 Organisation of Burroughs Wellcome & Co., 1970–1987. 144
11.2 Organisation of Marketing at Research Triangle Park, NC, 1970–1987. 147

13.1 Growth through formation of subsidiaries and acquisitions by Burroughs Wellcome & Co. in the UK and the Wellcome Foundation Ltd, 1880–1995. 168
13.2 The Structure and Organisation of the Wellcome Foundation Ltd/ Wellcome plc, 1969/73–1987. 172

List of tables

2.1 The New York branch and BW&Co. (USA) Inc., sales and trading profits ($000). 27
2.2 BW&Co (USA) Inc. transfers and dividends to WFL, 1924–1939 ($000). 27

3.1 BW&Co. Sales, Marketing and R&D Costs, 1946–1970. 42

4.1 New products from Tuckahoe, 1949–1959. 53

5.1 Major products sold by BW (USA) Inc. 1960–1972 (%). 66
5.2 BW&Co. field sales representatives and laboratory employment, 1945–1990. 67
5.3 BW&Co. expenditure on sales and marketing, advertising, and RD&M as percentages of total sales, 1946–1975. 68

6.1 BW&Co., sales, profits and dividends 1946–1960 ($million). 79

7.1 WFL Sales and financial analysis 1960–1970 (£million). 91

9.1 BW&Co. total employment: RD&M, sales and marketing, and production, 1960–1980. 120

11.1 BW&Co. Marketing expenditure and RD&M expenses as percentages of sales, 1970–1981. 141

12.1 BW&Co. Sales, Profits ($million), and RD&M as percentages, 1970–1981. 163

13.1 WFL group sales and financial analysis 1960–1970 (£million). 170
13.2 Wellcome Trust income; principal categories and WFL profit, 1971–1984 (£million). 177

14.1 WFL/Wellcome plc sales of principal products, 1982–1987 (£million). 197
14.2 Zovirax sales by methods of administration ($million). 197

15.1 Products (including variants) introduced into the US market by BW&Co. 1970–1989. 203
15.2 WFL rate of return on investment. 1977–1982. 203
15.3 BW&Co. Sales, Profits, and RD&M ($million), 1982–1994. 212

17.1 WFL/Wellcome plc R&D as percentage of sales and profit after tax, 1980–1990. 226
17.2 WFL sales and financial analysis, 1970–1984. 226
17.3 Numbers employed at BW&Co., WFL/Welcome plc, 1946–1994. 234

18.1 WFL net profit, capital employed, and rate of return, 1980–1985. 238
18.2 WFL profits after tax and dividends (£million), 1970–1981. 238

19.1 WFL/Wellcome plc R&D as percentage of sales and profit after tax, 1980–1990. 252

20.1 Initial estimated costs and revenues relating to Retrovir. 271
21.1 International comparative estimates of annual price of treatment with Retrovir, Zovirax, and combination in the US and Europe in 1988 (£). 278

23.1 WF/Wellcome plc sales by therapeutic market area as a percentage of group sales, 1984–1990. 297
23.2 Wellcome plc sales, net profit, capital employed, and rate of return, 1986–1994. 297
23.3 WFL/Wellcome plc dividend per share (£million) and times covered and return on shareholders' equity, 1981–1994. 298
23.4 WFL/Wellcome plc trading profits (£million) by location of company, 1981–1994. 299
23.5 BW&Co. Sales, Profits and RD&M ($million), 1970–1994. 303
23.6 BW&Co. Sales and Profits, 1970–1994 ($ million adjusted by price index for prescription drugs in the US: 1982–1984=100). 304

24.1 Wellcome plc sales of Actifed/Sudafed, Zovirax, and Retrovir, 1987–1994 (£million). 308

25.1 Wellcome plc share price highs and lows, 1986–1994. 321
25.2 Wellcome Trust income; principal categories and WFL/Wellcome plc profit, 1985–1992 (£million). 321
25.3 Wellcome Trust income; principal categories and Wellcome plc profit, 1992–2000 (£million). 323
25.4 Net worth of the Wellcome Trust, 1990–2000 (£billion). 324
27.1 Wealthiest Charitable Foundations in 2012. 364

List of illustrations

Silas M. Burroughs, partner of Burroughs Wellcome & Co., London, UK, 1880–1895. 8

Henry S. Wellcome, co-founding partner of Burroughs Wellcome & Co., London, UK, 1880–1895. 9

Burroughs Wellcome & Co. exhibit at the Chicago Exposition, 1893. 11

Burroughs Wellcome & Co. exhibit, St Louis Exhibition 1904. 12

Thomas Nevin, general manager and subsequently president of Burroughs Wellcome & Co. in the USA, 1911–1944. 14

George Pearson, general manager of Burroughs Wellcome & Co. London, UK, 1905–1940. 15

Kepler cod liver oil with malt extract advertisements. 18

Burroughs Wellcome & Co. offices and showroom, New York. 22

Burroughs Wellcome & Co. Chemical and Galenical Works at Tuckahoe, New York. 23

First aid kits which contained various Tabloids. 28

Tabloids Empirin and Three Bromides Effervescent advertisement. 29

William N. Creasy, general manager at Tuckahoe in 1943. 32

Sir Henry Solomon Wellcome, creator of the Wellcome Trust. 33

Wellcome Trustees *c.* 1938. 34

Denis Wheeler, joint managing director WFL, 1948–1955, and deputy chairman and group WFL director 1967–1970. 41

Frederick A. Coe Jr, joined Burroughs Wellcome & Co. in the US in 1944. 43

Empirin with Codeine advertisement. 58

Lanoxin advertisements. 60–61

H. H. Sier part-time chairman of the Wellcome Foundation Ltd, 1948–1953. 76

Professor Sir Henry Hallett Dale, chairman of the Wellcome Trust, 1938–1960. 80

Sir Michael F. Perrin, chairman of WFL 1953–1970. 83

The Wellcome Trustees in 1962. 90

Dr George H. Hitchings. 103

The new Chemical and Development Laboratories at Tuckahoe, 1966. 118

Ronald Cresswell. 122

Topping out at Research Triangle Park. 135

Research laboratories and offices at RTP. 136

Peter Howsam and Clealand Baker. 142

Theodore E. Haigler. 143

Sudafed advertisement. 145

Cortisporin advertisement. 146

Empirin advertisment. 148

Zyloprim advertisement. 150

The employees shown in the company's advertisements. 153

Septra advertisement. 160

Advertisements for Septra were directed towards the treatment of children's infections and of urinary tract infection. 161

Lord Franks. 167

A.A. Gray. 171

Sir Alfred J. Shepperd. 174

Sir John R. Vane. 178

Pedro Cuatrecasas. 180

Professor Howard J. Schaeffer. 186

Zovirax advertisements. 195–96

William M. Sullivan. 201

Actifed advertisements.	209–10
William Shirra in making television commercials for BW&Co.	211
Group R&D management meeting in the UK.	217
Sir James Black.	220
William F. Castell.	233
Sir David Edward Charles Steel.	237
Sir Roger Gibbs.	239
AIDS awareness poster.	253
David Barry.	259
George Hitchings and Gertrude Elion.	266
Gabriel Cipau.	267
Philip Tracy.	284
Retrovir advertisement.	285
BW&Co. advertisement.	286
Sir Alistair Frame.	294
John Robb.	296
James Cochrane	301
John Precious.	302
Trevor Jones.	309
Wellbutrin advertisements.	314–15
Sir Richard Sykes.	328

Introduction

During the twentieth century the international pharmaceutical industry came to be dominated and led by large corporate multinational companies which were driven by rising costs of R&D and the pursuit of economies of scale and scope in research.[1] The history of Burroughs Wellcome (USA) Inc., an American company which began as Burroughs Wellcome & Co. in 1906, the small New York sales branch of the medium-sized Burroughs Wellcome & Co. in London, UK, bucked this trend until it merged with Glaxo in 1995 to become a part of Glaxo Wellcome, the world's second largest pharmaceutical manufacturer. This became a part of GlaxoSmithKline in 2000. From 1936 until 1986, the entire Burroughs Wellcome business organisation was owned by the Wellcome Trust which retained a controlling interest until 1995. Although technically administered by the board in the UK, successive presidents managed the American business, essentially along quasi-family/entrepreneurial lines, almost independently from the business in the UK.[2] Researching the history of the American company necessitated investigating the interfaces between it, the British parent company, and the Wellcome Trust. Burroughs Wellcome (USA) Inc. can be understood only within an exploration of this tripartite relationship in relation to the pharmaceutical industry, to the history of medicine, and to the process of wealth creation which, during the late twentieth century, enabled the Wellcome Trust to become one of the world's largest charities, thus fulfilling its founder's aim by funding biomedical research dedicated to the improvement of human and animal health.

In several respects, the history of the American company justifies a claim to a role in the industry in spite of its size. Two of its senior, long-serving research scientists between the early 1940s and the early 1980s, George H. Hitchings and Gertrude B. Elion, jointly received the Nobel Prize for physiology or medicine in 1987. Their awards were in recognition of "their discoveries of important principles for drug treatment."[3] Building on the research of Hitchings and Elion, succeeding American scientists proceeded to develop blockbuster drug treatments for the sexually transmitted diseases, genital herpes and AIDS. On all of these counts, the virtual absence of the history of Burroughs Wellcome (USA) Inc. from narratives relating to the international pharmaceutical industry more than justifies a detailed account and analysis of the company which allows its achievements, setbacks, and their explanations to be placed in the wider contexts.[4] The framework adopted is intended to highlight the contributions this study offers to a greater understanding of the history of the business of medicine: the concept of the firm as a resource-based organisation affected by inherited resources. Within that framework the focus is upon principal concerns prompted by scholarly discourse: the history of multinationals and management across borders; organisational networks and drug discovery; the history of medicine, especially antivirals; business and managerial culture; business and government in the pharmaceutical industry, the marketing of pharmaceutical products; and corporate governance. Conclusions are presented in the epilogue.

This study examines the changing nature of the dynamics, causes, progression, and consequences of interactions between these three organizations. The London business was formed as a partnership in 1880 by Silas M. Burroughs and Henry S. Wellcome, two American pharmacy graduates. They transferred their academic knowledge of pharmacy and their experience as salesmen from the US (where they sold ethical drugs to physicians) to the UK where such an approach was unknown.[5] Based on the production of sera and vaccines before and during World War I, the parent company, henceforward to be referred to as Burroughs Wellcome & Co. (UK)) became the largest, the most influential, and the most significant ethical pharmaceutical company in the UK, though during the early years of the twentieth century, it was to lose strong leadership and momentum.

The New York branch, the main focus of this study, henceforward to be referred to as Burroughs Wellcome & Co. (USA), added manufacturing to the sale of drugs during World War I and was later registered in the US as Burroughs Wellcome (USA) Inc. in 1924. In the same year, the Wellcome Foundation Ltd was formed, henceforward to be referred to as WFL, an umbrella organisation which included Burroughs Wellcome & Co. (UK), Burroughs Wellcome (USA) Inc., and other subsidiary companies registered in their respective countries. Four years later, in 1928, the American company opened a laboratory for research and development in the US. Thereafter, the degree of independence secured by the American subsidiary, begun during Word War I, became an increasingly contentious issue between the American and UK directors; their organisational cultures, aims, and strategies followed different paths. Tension mounted as innovation and effective marketing strategies saw the US company's sales and profits grow. These began to offset the effects of a corporate sclerosis which had produced the flagging commercial and financial performance of the parent company in the UK. A further complication in the relationships between the two groups was introduced in 1936 on the death of Sir Henry Wellcome. Silas Burroughs, the co-founding partner of the business in London, had died in 1895 and sole ownership had passed to Henry Wellcome (as he then was). When Sir Henry died in 1936, ownership of all his companies passed into the hands of the Wellcome Trust, which he had created shortly before his death in order to perpetuate the advancement of the human condition through the funding of medical research by dividends from the business.

In its early years the American company's growth had depended primarily on the effective marketing of malt extracts, laxatives, elixirs for coughs and stomach complaints and, especially after World War II, Empirin headache pills (the US market leader) – all simple and primarily ethical medications. The expansion of laboratory research in the US, led from the 1940s by George Hitchings, eventually transformed the product base of both the US and UK companies. Following the development of several antibiotics during the 1950s, Septra (Septrin in the UK), a broad spectrum antibiotic, achieved substantial commercial success during the 1960s and 1970s. Later, Actifed, an anti-histamine decongestant, became the leading prescription drug in the market for cold remedies in the US during the 1980s, when fortuitous opportunity enabled the company to advertise the drug as the medication chosen by the astronaut Walter Shirra to accompany him into space. In 1986, the American and all other subsidiary companies were re-formed into the single UK company, Wellcome plc.

By 1993, in a scholarly comparative analysis of *The World Pharmaceutical Industry* by James Taggart, Wellcome plc was described as a multinational company which, though still relatively small, had become, since its foundation as Burroughs Wellcome & Co. (UK) in 1880, "one of the world's most highly respected research-based pharmaceutical companies."[6] Taggart drew attention to the developments in its US subsidiary company (especially after World War II), which explained why the multinational could be described as possessing a "broad range of products ... almost all the result of internal innovation."[7] The development and marketing of Retrovir, "the AIDS drug," in the 1980s had encountered controversy, ushering in a period during which the company secured a high profile, but for a while, was held in low esteem in the world pharmaceutical industry. Taggart praised Wellcome plc for having invested in genetic engineering, which was believed to herald "the first major ethical product to emanate from the new technology."[8] A recent compilation of significant therapeutic discoveries (not all of which resulted in marketable drugs) between 1945 and 1995 suggests that WFL, though mainly derived from the American subsidiary company, was one of the most innovative in the world. Six contributions from WFL gave it top ranking, followed by ICI (four), and Schering, Lilly, and Myers Sqibb (two each). Yet three of the contributions from the laboratories of Burroughs Wellcome & Co. (USA) before 1970 occurred at a time when, measured by sales, the company and the R&D resources at its disposal were small.[9]

This business history analyses the scientific research and product innovation in which, in contrast to the parent company, the subsidiary in the US excelled by way of the discovery and development, during the 1980s, of the antiviral drug, Zovirax for the treatment of herpes, and the antiretroviral, Retrovir. The company's pricing of the life-prolonging Retrovir prompted unfavorable reactions from medical professionals, the public, journalists, and politicians and culminated in confrontations at hearings held by a Congressional Committee convened to investigate the issues. The President of the American company was summoned for cross-examination, and the ethical arguments raised and hostility experienced by the company led to a shift in corporate procedure. Pricing policy was revised and a public relations initiative launched. This was intended to recapture the long-established trust prevailing within the business which, until the early 1980s, had been promoted by the American Company which used the slogan "research is our only stockholder," an obscure reference to ownership by the Wellcome Trust which implied a distance between profit-making and research.

The Trust was overseen from its outset primarily by a number of distinguished academic medical research scientists whose aspirations coincided absolutely with those set out in Sir Henry's will. The fulfilment of these aims, however, depended on dividends. Until the 1980s, they were severely limited by the poor financial performance of the parent company in the UK. The effects of a lack of investment and managerial failures were exacerbated by manifestations of the long-standing culture divide between commercial managers and scientists. Divisions also existed among the company's most senior scientists, including the two British Nobel Laureates, Sir John Vane and Sir James Black. Differing perceptions of priorities hampered organisational and policy reforms. One consequence was the evolution of increasing differences between the UK and the US companies in their approaches to marketing, innovation, and R&D. These resulted in superior levels of scientific, commercial, and financial achievement in the American company, which successive management consultancy reports regarded as a model which the UK directors should replicate.

The evident failure of the UK company in each of these areas led to reluctant, intermittent intervention by the Trust into the management of the business in both countries, a role not initially foreseen by the early Trustees but which, at times of finanacial and managerial crises – 1939/40, 1944–48, and 1965–68 – chairmen had felt it necessary to adopt. Until the 1980s, the Trustees remained reluctant to step in, limiting action mainly to resolving those management crises involving the removal of American company presidents and chairmen of WFL and the appointment of their successors. The complex interactions and sometimes turbulent relationships between the parent company, the American subsidiary, and the Trust during the years from 1936 to 1995 resulted in a transition from one culture in the Wellcome Trust created in 1936 by distinguished medical academics to another in the 1980s. The dominant influence of leading businessmen in the city of London culminated in two public share issues and finally, in the outright sale of Wellcome plc to Glaxo plc in 1995 to form Glaxo Wellcome plc, the UK's largest pharmaceutical company. Five years later, following the merger of Glaxo Wellcome and SmithKline Beecham (SB) in 2000 to form GlaxoSmithKline (GSK), the Wellcome name disappeared from the world of business. The wealth which Wellcome's companies had created, however, ensured that the future lay with the Wellcome Trust which continues to perpetuate the name of its founder (as does the Burroughs Wellcome Fund in the US[10]), and to fulfil his philanthropic ideals in the twenty-first century on a scale which he could not have envisaged when the Trust was formed in 1936 and which, in the 1990s, emerged as the largest funder of medical research in the UK and one of the world's three wealthiest charitable foundations.

PART ONE:

From subjugation towards independent policy-making

CHAPTER 1

The origins of Burroughs Wellcome & Co. in the US, 1906–1924: the New York sales branch of a British pharmaceutical company[1]

The origin of the American firm of Burroughs Wellcome & Co. was the New York sales branch of Burroughs Wellcome & Co., a British multinational pharmaceutical company in London. The parent company had been formed in London in 1880 by two American pharmacy graduates, Silas M. Burroughs and Henry S. Wellcome. Silas Burroughs, was aged thirty-four when the company was formed in London. His father was a prosperous merchant who became a Congressman. After graduating from the Philadelphia College of Pharmacy, the young Burroughs had worked as a sales representative for John Wyeth & Bro., a small but innovative Philadelphia firm of drug manufacturers, the success of which was based on the invention and patenting of machinery for producing compressed medicines in the form of pills. Burroughs's task was to promote the new medicines to general practitioners in their surgeries and hospitals. This new approach to selling drugs was commonly referred to as "detailing" and its practitioners as "detail men." The unique attribute claimed for the new pills was the delivery of an accurately measured single dose, resulting from strict control of content and purity in their manufacture. Reliability, durable preservation, and easy solubility were other features emphasized by advertising copy. Impressed by Burroughs's effectiveness as a salesman (though less tolerant of his capacity to irritate his employers by a characteristic unwillingness to follow instructions or accept advice), the Wyeths dispatched Burroughs to England to represent their company and to develop a market for Wyeth's compressed pills. Armed with historical, practical, and theoretical knowledge of compressed medicines (the subject of his college inaugural essay) and optimistic regarding the opportunities for selling the new products overseas, Burroughs departed for England in the spring of 1878. Shortly after his arrival in London in June, with the Wyeths' agreement, he created S. M. Burroughs & Co., the sole agency for the sale of Wyeth compressed medicines in all countries outside the US. Almost from the beginning, relations between the ambitious but

Silas M. Burroughs, co-founding pharmacy graduate partner of Burroughs Wellcome & Co., London, UK, 1880–1895. Wellcome Library, London.

abrasive Burroughs and the Wyeths deteriorated. Relations worsened after Burroughs added agencies for selling the products of other American drug manufacturers. He also became managing director of the newly-formed Kepler Malt Extract Company, a business which was to loom large in the history of Burroughs Wellcome and Co. in the UK and of its American subsidiary until the 1930s.

Burroughs's diversifying business interests led him to seek a partner, though another motive was to escape from the day-to-day production and financial management required in the business. He was impatient with detail and confinement to office and factory, preferring the freedom and excitement offered by international travel and the exercise of his selling skills. In seeking a partner in whom he could trust, possessing skills and knowledge of the trade matching his own, he turned to an acquaintance in the US, one Henry S. Wellcome, aged twenty-six, seven years younger than Burroughs, and with whom Burroughs had been on congenial terms for some time. He was familiar with Wellcome's early reputation as a knowledgeable and gifted salesman and corresponded with him for more than a year before Wellcome finally left New York for London in April 1880. In September 1880, Burroughs Wellcome

Henry S. Wellcome, co-founding pharmacy graduate partner of Burroughs Wellcome & Co., London, UK, 1880–1895, subsequently sole owner-manager and subsequently chairman and of the Wellcome Foundation Ltd, founder of Burroughs Wellcome & Co. in the USA in 1906, and creator of the Wellcome Trust in 1936. Wellcome Library, London.

& Co. was created under a partnership agreement between Silas M. Burroughs and Henry S. Wellcome.

In contrast to Burroughs's urbane middle-class background, Henry Wellcome hailed from an impoverished farming family in rural Wisconsin though, like Burroughs, he was a graduate of the Philadelphia College of Pharmacy. He, too, had been employed as a sales representative in the US in the 1870s when he worked for McKesson & Robbins, a long-established and highly reputable drug manufacturing and wholesaling company in New York, the self-styled "greatest drug house in the world." The new partnership of Burroughs Wellcome and Co. began to advertise compressed tablets, the change in nomenclature from pills to tablets reflecting Burroughs's discovery that, at least among the medical profession and reputable pharmacists in Britain, pills tended to be associated with the disreputable patent medicines trade. In 1883, the company began to manufacture its own compressed tablets using machinery imported from the US in rented factory premises in London. After the termination of an agreement with the Wyeths (suppliers of the original compressed medicines), the tablets were marketed under the "Tabloid" trade mark. A larger factory was acquired for the purpose in Dartford, Kent, in 1889. During the 1880s and 1890s, the range of Tabloids was expanded from chlorate of potash, dialysed iron, and pepsin to include bismuth, quinine, cocaine, and ipececac Tabloids.

The second largest product line was Kepler malt extract and its variants. This originated in the predatory entrepreneurship exercised by Burroughs and Wellcome during the first year of their partnership. In the summer of 1879, the chairman of the Condensed Beer Company, based in Jersey, a small island off the south coast of England, had invited Burroughs to become the managing director of the separate, newly-formed Kepler Malt Extract Company. The formula and mashing apparatus used in the manufacture of this new product were protected by patents owned by the inventor, who was one of the new company's directors, a chemist who had also developed the extract. The arrangement with the Jersey company involved the use of the London premises of S.M. Burroughs & Co. A plot to take control of the original Kepler business was conceived by Burroughs (who was overseas at that time when Wellcome assumed the role of general manager in the UK), but both partners were fully involved in implementing the plan. Using Burroughs's position as the initial wedge, the two partners succeeded in securing financial control of the company by acquiring shares from other directors and in 1881, forced the original founders to sell out altogether. Almost from the beginning, Kepler products became one of the parent company's two strongest lines. By 1895, when Burroughs died unexpectedly at the age of 49, Tabloids and Kepler products had firmly established the company among the leading British pharmaceutical businesses. By that time, the company employed over 600 people, recorded sales of about £120,000 (c. $800,000), and possessed a continuous history of profitable activity, the rate of return on capital averaging roughly 20 per cent since its foundation.

The company's commercial success was based on the partners' achievement in establishing a high reputation among the medical profession for the quality of its extensive range of trade-marked Tabloid compressed medicines and solutions and for Kepler cod liver oil and malt extracts. This successful record was achieved in part by Burroughs's selling activity overseas, but primarily because of the young Wellcome's effective management of the manufacture and marketing of trade-marked products in the UK. However, the achievement occurred *despite* a seriously dysfunctional relationship that prevailed almost from the beginning. The increasing intensity of disagreement about their respective responsibilities and the financial implications of the original partnership agreement led to a breakdown in relations between the partners. Until Burroughs's untimely death in 1895, there was continuing discussion of incorporation as a limited liability with public shareholders and also of a possible dissolution of the company. Finally in 1898, at the age of 46, Wellcome succeeded in purchasing the deceased partner's share of the business (legally a first option included in the 1890 partnership agreement). Wellcome became the sole owner-manager of the private company which continued to trade as Burroughs Wellcome & Co., part of the Wellcome Foundation formed in 1924, until his death in 1936.

Burroughs Wellcome & Co. exhibit at the Chicago Exposition, 1893. Henry Wellcome appears in the background on the left wearing a hat. Wellcome Library, London.

The replacement of agencies by branches began in 1886 in Melborne, Australia, a policy for which from 1897 George E. Pearson became responsible. He was born in Bradford, England in 1868, served an apprenticeship in a retail pharmacy, and became a counter assistant. He joined Burroughs Wellcome & Co. in 1885 as a travelling salesman working in London. Once in charge of overseas activities, Pearson proceeded to travel, taking a special interest in the task of expanding sales in Australia, South Africa, and North America. A review of management personnel and organisation led to changes. The Australian branch was relocated to Sydney in 1898; a branch was opened in Cape Town, South Africa in 1902 and another in Montreal, Canada in October 1906. The New York branch of Burroughs Wellcome & Co. (USA) was established in December 1906. Wellcome regarded the operation of the American branch and a permanent presence in the American market as superior to an agency in defending the Tabloid trade mark in the US where it was under attack from competitors.

Under local management directly answerable to Pearson (since 1901 head of a new overseas sales department in London, members of staff were recruited locally to package, market, and distribute imported goods within a system of budgetary control

Burroughs Wellcome & Co. exhibit, St Louis Exhibition 1904. Wellcome Library, London.

also exercised from London. Direct penetration of the US market was not, however, a wholly defensive strategy. Wellcome was convinced that, in addition to defending the growing trade in Tabloids, the quality of Kepler cod liver oil products, especially for Kepler Solutions, offered opportunities for expanding sales. Kepler Solutions were available with added beef and iron extracts, iron and quinine extracts, and with pepsin, phosphorous, or cascara sagrada.

In 1905, the senior of two salesmen based in Canada was redeployed to Philadelphia to lead a campaign to push Burroughs Wellcome products, especially Kepler malt extracts and cascara sagrada and sodium salicylate Tabloids,. Wellcome Brand Chemicals, which were also supplied to the American company from Britain were limited to quinine and chloroform; although their quality was high, they struggled to compete with chemicals supplied by the much larger companies of Squibb and Merck.

Premises leased at 310–14 Hudson Street in 1907 provided boat dock facilities and nearby freight terminals. Here, goods imported from the parent company's factory at Dartford, Kent were prepared (put-up) and packaged, ready to deliver to the New York house for distribution to wholesalers in the American market. Three years later, larger premises were leased at 340–42 Hudson in addition to more prestigious office and warehouse premises at West Twenty-third Street, close to Fifth Avenue, more suited to greeting buyers and other members of the trade. The responsibility in London for the overall and day-to-day businesses in North America lay with Pearson assisted by G. Leslie Moore, the influential chief accountant who presented the annual accounts and reports to both Wellcome and Pearson. Local management of distribution was conducted initially and temporarily by the manager of the Montreal depot, pending the relocation of Thomas Henry Moore (no relation to G. Leslie Moore), formerly manager of the Cape Town depot, to manage the New York branch early in 1907.

Recruitment of staff presented a problem from the outset, partly because of a reluctance to relocate trained and experienced travelling salesmen from Britain. Thomas Henry Moore was advised to search, either for "energetic young Canadians"[2] (whom Wellcome perceived to possess superior ability and business qualities to the average American), or for graduates of Philadelphia College, of which both Burroughs and Wellcome were alumni. He was supplied with multiple copies of a booklet to be distributed to travellers which detailed the dire consequences of consuming alcohol; he was also advised to speak privately with two new recruits whose habits were soon identified as a route to failure and dismissal. The quality of the early sales staff was a matter for concern; the first set of trading accounts submitted to the London office for scrutiny in 1908 was described by G. Leslie Moore, the chief accountant, as unreliable and he left London "largely in a state of ignorance so far as the profit-earning capacity … is concerned."[3] The lack of local control to which he attributed these failings Moore explained as a consequence of "restrained resentment" bordering on hostility shown by the New York staff towards managers in London. He also criticized excessive expense claims by travellers, especially those claims entered under the headings "gratuities and entertainment."[4] After an investigation of the branch in 1911 the manager of the American business, Thomas Moore, resigned.

His successor was Thomas Nevin, a future president of the business in the US. After qualifying as a pharmacist, he worked in a dispensary in Belfast, Ireland until 1904 when he became an assistant sales representative for Burroughs Wellcome & Co. in Ontario, Canada. In 1904 he relocated to Philadelphia as assistant. In the light of Nevin's pivotal contribution to the growth and development of the company in the US during the next 40 years it is pertinent to refer to his initial recruitment which began with an application to senior salesman in Canada, D. L. Kirkpatrick who had appointed Nevin without referring to the London office. Confirmation was withheld pending receipt of reports from four referees and a report by Kirkpatrick after a probationary six week period. Kirkpatrick chose not to wait and dismissed Nevin forthwith – again without consulting London. However, when the referees' reports were eventually received in London, Nevin was contacted directly and invited to attend coaching in that city to prepare him for the role of sales representative. His conduct during the training period so impressed Wellcome that he predicted a successful future for the young man, "if Nevin works with enthusiasm and vigor and British pluck."[5] This initial impression marked the beginning of a personal relationship between the two men

Thomas Nevin, retail pharmacist, general manager and subsequently president of Burroughs Wellcome & Co. in the USA, 1911–1944. His close relations with Henry Wellcome who extended tacit and financial support enabled Nevin to build an enduring American manufacturing organisation and establish a research culture attuned to the US commercial environment. *Wellcome News*, Wellcome Library, London.

based on mutual respect and trust, a relationship which was to prove a determining factor in the medium-term future of Burroughs Wellcome & Co. in the US. Within months of Nevin's reinstatement, Kirkpatrick relocated to Philadelphia accompanied by J. S. Lang, a new assistant (later manager of the Canadian branch). Nevin assumed the role of senior salesman for Canada, but following Kirkpatrick's resignation in March 1906 became manager of the new depot which opened in Montreal in the October of that year. When Nevin succeeded Thomas Henry Moore as manager of Burroughs Wellcome & Co in New York in 1911, he faced serious financial and production problems associated with the low morale of the staff.

From the outset, accusations of financial mismanagement and inefficiency had been directed against Thomas Henry Moore and his senior accountant. Whereas inefficiencies and mismanagement were amenable to tangible problem-solving in New York, Nevin was presented with a more fundamental problem: the prevailing philosophy underlying a policy which dictated the role of the American company in New York in relation to managers in London. The philosophy and the policies consistent

George Pearson, retail pharmacist, subsequently general manager of Burroughs Wellcome & Co. London, UK, 1905–1940, deputy chairman of the Wellcome Foundation and *de facto* managing director, whose relations with the American management of Burroughs Wellcome & Co. in the USA was problematic. Wellcome Library, London.

with it did not originate with Wellcome, even though he was owner-governor and in effect general manager of the entire international Burroughs Wellcome organisation after 1895. By World War I, his immense creativity, energy, attention to detail, and vision for the business had seen the company become the largest and most progressive pharmaceutical manufacturer in Britain. However, in 1905 Wellcome created the post of deputy governor to which he appointed Pearson to act as his personal deputy. The creation of the post of deputy governor in 1905 formalized Wellcome's largely hands-off governorship (increasingly *in absentia*) and signalled further withdrawal from day-to-day management. Lengthy periods away from Britain were spent in indulging his new enthusiasms for motoring, collecting, and large-scale archaeological projects. Pearson became *de facto* the primary decision-maker after 1905 in London where management proceeded without a properly functioning board of directors and with an owner whose role was limited to occasional (though critical) interventions at crucial moments, especially affecting the American company.

Pearson's elevation to personal deputy also increased the influence of G. Leslie Moore. Between 1907 and 1914, his annual reports presented to Pearson and Wellcome included unremittingly critical assessments of the new American subsidiary which his accounts showed losses reported in every year, increasing after the introduction of a 30 per cent tariff on imported supplies from London in 1909. The annual reports were unusual inasmuch that in addition to commentary on the accounts, Moore included annual and accumulating figures for the opportunity cost on investment in the US business. This was a calculation of the revenue which the American business had foregone which might otherwise have been invested in securities. The application in 1914 of a 5 per cent imputed notional interest to accumulated losses since 1907 produced a figure of £225,687 for the sales department, less profit of £37,988 from the works and less £186,42 profit from the sale of goods supplied from London. The total net accumulated deficit shown since 1907 was £169,237. Referring to the accounts and to these calculations, Moore's 1914 report concluded: "... if they represent an attempt to do a profitable business in the US they are not encouraging ... It is difficult to find any indication whatsoever that the New York business can be placed on a profitable basis ... A very large sum has already been expended in the building up of the business and it appears that a further large sum will be required in the immediate future to maintain the business."[6]

Apart from the judgments based on his opportunity cost estimates, Moore's reports do not explain why the sales operations of the New York business should have been consistently returning losses. The explanation is that the sales of imported products and products put-up after dispatch from London were required to conform to the London list prices, plus freight costs and duty. The intention was to prevent price competition with direct exports from London. This approach was consistent with G. L. Moore's prejudice against local manufacture, an attitude shared with Pearson and which probably points to the original authorship of this perverse pricing formula that continued to be applied after Wellcome's disengagement from the business.[7] When Nevin became general manager he had urged Pearson to remove the discriminatory pricing formula, but Pearson refused to discuss the issue.[8]

Both Moore and Pearson believed that the relationship between subsidiaries and the parent country should be conducted in accordance with the assertion that "the tendency must always be for local works to be at best ineffective producers of profit and possibly producers of loss."[9] By duplicating plants and by the hiring of more expensive, experienced workers who were difficult to recruit, local manufacture would increase costs. Costs at Dartford would also rise as a result of a diversion of manufacturing away from Dartford to overseas locations, thereby reducing economies of scale; additional costs would also result from supplying raw materials, information, and other supporting activity to overseas subsidiaries. Nevin agreed that the key to profit was the scale of output and sales of the firm's branded products, but whereas Moore and Pearson believed that retrenchment was the solution, Nevin was convinced that the future of the American company in the long run lay in vertical integration to include full scale manufacturing. Nevin also felt that whatever progress had been achieved in expanding the volume of sales, the London managers deserved no credit.

Although no contemporary evidence of Wellcome's doubts has survived, a letter he wrote to Pearson in 1927 reveals his own rationale for the policies adopted under Nevin before and after 1914. In a thinly-veiled criticism of the chief accountant, Wellcome noted: "In all business undertakings it is a sound principle and always an essential practice for the sake of security to keep under close observation and continuous check the question of profit and loss as well as the account of sales, expenses, and taxes, etc. However, an accountant's view that immediate profits are the all-essential points for consideration in promoting the development and best interests of the business may not prove to be the most practical policy in building up a successful business, especially in pioneer fields …[10] He explained that he had adopted "the principle of spending freely but with deliberately considered methods of effectual propaganda."[11] Wellcome attributed the early problems faced by the company in New York to the transfer from selling through the Fairchild agency to distribution from the newly-formed American business. Without mentioning Thomas Moore, Wellcome was critical of the local management and the sales representatives employed whom he believed to have been "inexperienced in the customs, methods, and usages of the medical trade in America," men who "held narrow and prejudiced views which lessened their influence and usefulness." Although retrospectively, Wellcome referred to the importance of "moderated prices,"[12] the policy was not changed until the late 1920s.

Events, however, were to alter transaction costs which, in time, reduced the bias against the American company imposed by the pricing policy. The adverse effects of the 1909 tariff on imports from London were not considered to be sufficient to justify reforming pricing policy. However, Wellcome did reject Pearson's proposal, advanced in 1913, that in view of the falling rate of sales since the tariff, the price of Kepler goods charged in the US should be increased in order to raise the rate of profit to levels achieved by the Sydney branch. Wellcome's response was that prices were already very high and should be lowered if possible. He added, "I am not discouraged in the least, but we must spur on the manager."[13] The effects of the First World War on the business led to serious consideration of local manufacture in New York. The British government banned chemical exports which threatened sales of Tabloids which then accounted for 50 per cent of the American company's sales. The resources of the parent company were diverted to the production of anti-toxin sera and other biological products supplied to the British army vaccine department. The supply of malted barley used to produce malt extract, which accounted for one-fifth of BW&Co.'s sales, posed a similar threat to sales of Kepler malt extracts. In 1915, therefore, local supplies of raw materials were secured for the manufacture in New York of both Tabloids (using second-hand tabletting machinery) and Kepler malt extracts. Three Bromides Effervescent, a sedative for which multiple (including dubious) claims were made, was the third largest selling product.

In 1917, Wellcome asked Pearson to consider carefully the question of further developing Burroughs Wellcome & Co. in the US by extending manufacturing and "productive propaganda in such a way that the firm will share in whatever commercial prosperity is before us in the USA during and after the war."[14] He predicted that by building on the parent company's reputation for its ethical medicines, for Tabloids and Kepler products especially, and by expanding operations in New York in an efficient manner, America would become the most productive and profitable field of operations. A sceptical, if not hostile, Pearson argued for delaying any decision on the extension of manufacturing until after the post-war presidential election which he anticipated would result in a Coolidge victory followed by a boom.

Kepler cod liver oil with malt extract was one of the two main products of Burroughs Wellcome in the UK which pre-dated the American company which commenced manufacture in New York during World War I.

A policy of delay, however, risked missing an opportunity when in 1915, the British government suspended the Bayer's Aspirin patent, thereby ending the German company's monopoly. Hitherto, Burroughs Wellcome & Co. had sold acetyl salicylic Tabloids in Britain and overseas, the same as those available for sale by the American company, but after suspension of the Bayer patent, Tabloid Empirin was added to the price list. The new name was intended to conceal the aspirin content of Tabloid Empirin, even though its purity and that of Bayer's Aspirin were identical. The intention was to signal to retail chemists, druggists, and general practitioners (among whom self-medication was a sensitive issue), that the company did not seek to encourage such a practice. The simultaneous marketing of acetyl salicylic Tabloids and Tabloid Empirin in the British market appears to have caused confusion both among sales staff and the public and soon led to the withdrawal of Empirin from the London price list.

The history of Empirin in the US was entirely different. The monopoly enjoyed by Compbayer's Aspirin in the US continued unaffected until 1917 when the patent

expired. Nevin perceived an opportunity resulting from the introduction of Tabloid Empirin in London two years earlier. The concept of Empirin as a brand and its availability to the American company from 1915 gave the company a head start in the American market. In 1917, an advertising campaign supported an immediate attempt to compete with Compbayer's aspirin in the US market. Tabloid Empirin became the analgesic which was to accelerate the transformation of the American business from a sales branch to a fully manufacturing enterprise. As yet, however, because of Wellcome's acquiescence to Pearson's preference to delay a decision on further local manufacturing, the full profitable benefits to the American business of a resounding success of the sales campaign lay in the future. The qualities claimed for the new product were: purity, reliability in therapeutic action, accuracy of dosage, portability, duration of preservation, convenience, taste, and compatibility. It also removed the necessity for weighing, measuring, or eliminating waste. The launch of Empirin was timely, for the influenza epidemic in 1918 catapulted Empirin into the position of market leader in the US, a result assisted by a prevailing hostility within the pharmaceutical industry towards Combayer's aggressive advertising which unprecedentedly was aimed directly at the public. Whereas in the US, Burroughs Wellcome required the branch to adopt ethical advertising, Combayer's policy provoked criticism and condemnation among the medical profession and editors of medical journals. Empirin maintained market leadership throughout the 1920s until the 1960s when it remained one of the "super highways" of the business, together with Kepler extracts and Tabloid effervescents.

Wellcome acquiesced to Pearson's preference for a deferred decision on the issue of American manufacture. Within this constraint, Nevin proceeded to plan a reorganisation of the works with a view to improving productivity and requested permission from London to employ a suitably qualified person to implement his plan. Pearson sent an employee from Dartford who proved a complete failure. Dismayed by his lack of experience and adverse impact on labor relations, without consultation with London Nevin dismissed him within weeks and replaced him with a local employee whom Nevin designated as acting works superintendent. Pearson objected but Nevin's representation of the situation to Wellcome received his support by confirming the appointment of the American supervisor. Emboldened by Wellcome's firm support, Nevin urged Pearson to reopen discussion with Wellcome over his proposal regarding the future structure, organisation, and scope of Burroughs Wellcome & Co.'s operations in the US with a view to securing a final decision before 1924. Perhaps not coincidentally, while Nevin was preparing for a reorganisation of the American business, Henry Wellcome was contemplating a restructuring of the entire international Burroughs Wellcome organisation, his principal motivation being to secure tax advantages in the US. One consequence, which appears not to have occurred to Pearson at the time, was to advance Nevin's aspiration to secure increasing independence from London.

CHAPTER 2

Burroughs Wellcome (USA) Inc., British subsidiary company from 1924: manufacturing at Tuckahoe, the origins of RD&M, and the Americanization of Burroughs Wellcome & Co., in the US

The Wellcome Foundation Ltd (hereafter WFL) was created in 1924, a unique, portmanteau organisation comprising Burroughs Wellcome & Co. (UK) and overseas subsidiary companies. Each of the company's branches (some registered in the country of location) and depots across the world were also included. Wellcome's library and museum, created and initially personally funded by Henry Wellcome, also formed part of WFL, though managed separately from the business. Within WFL, the American company became Burroughs Wellcome (USA) Inc. and registered in each state in which the company conducted business. The board consisted of Wellcome as president, Pearson as deputy president, and Nevin as vice-president and general manager. Quoracy consisted of a single board member; consequently in the absence of Wellcome, and also of Pearson except at occasional board meetings, Nevin commanded day-to-day control of the business.

Even though Wellcome had accepted Nevin's case for reorganisation and investment in manufacturing, the American company was required still to conduct activities in accordance with general policy guidelines issued from London. Thus, the newly-formed American company was required to pay WFL a percentage dividend based on net sales of goods, put-up or manufactured in the US (though none was distributed until 1926/7). All existing and future proprietary rights and trade names remained with WFL. The parent company would decide which products, hitherto supplied from London, should be manufactured in the US. Those manufactured in the US would have to be produced employing formulae, recipes, and processes used in the UK and would be open to inspection, sampling, and testing by British scientists. Any proposals for patenting or trade-marking inventions developed by Burroughs Wellcome & Co. (USA) Inc. would have to be communicated to the parent company.

Burroughs Wellcome & Co. offices and showroom, New York. Wellcome Library, London.

These provisions essentially codified existing practices which, in the past, had produced tensions between London and New York, manifested in the discordant relations between Nevin and Pearson.

The formation of Burroughs Wellcome (USA) Inc. appears to have strengthened Nevin's resolution to transform the company through a policy of Americanization and expansion based on manufacturing. Despite Wellcome having distanced himself from the management of the business in the UK after 1905, increasingly close personal relations between Wellcome and Nevin enabled the manager of the American company to exercise influence on major policy decisions. In 1925, Nevin persuaded Wellcome to invest to acquire a much larger factory outside New York City which could accommodate new machinery and substantially higher volume manufacture. Wellcome secured the purchase of a 3.5 acre site which included a factory formerly occupied by the Hodgson Rubber Company at Tuckahoe, New York State, though still within easy reach of New York City. The factory had employed 1,200 employees at a time when no more than 300 worked for the company at the Hudson Street premises and was indicative of Wellcome's ambition. In addition to the factory located on the Hudson River, office and showroom space was acquired in the prestigious twelve storey building on East 41st Street in Manhattan. Wellcome was involved not only in planning the works and negotiating contract prices, but also in designing the refurbished facades of this grand building. After 1924, within the new manufacturing regime, firmly opposed to this development, Pearson and Dr A.D. Jowett, production manager of the Dartford factory in the UK, showed a determination to perpetuate strict control from London in conducting future relations with the newly-constituted Burroughs Wellcome & Co. (USA) Inc. Nevin was informed that new products, even those specifically intended for the US market, would continue to be initiated in the UK, as would any improvements or alterations in manufacturing processes.

However, emboldened by his success in enlisting Wellcome's support over freedom to recruit whomsoever Nevin chose, he proceeded to challenge the Pearson-Jowett

Burroughs Wellcome & Co. Chemical and Galenical Works at Tuckahoe, New York. Wellcome Library, London.

insistence on otherwise complete control of the American company from London. Conflict occurred over three issues: commencement of the manufacture of Kepler malt products using modern machinery and local raw materials, which Pearson sought to prevent by prevarication; the introduction of Three Bromides Effervescent, a bromide which Nevin believed to be particularly suited to the American market but dismissed by Pearson as contrary to the Burroughs Wellcome tradition of strictly ethical medicines; pricing policy, of which Nevin had been critical from the outset; and another policy which was to have the most far-reaching consequences for the company: to establish a research laboratory with a view to developing the company's own ethical medicines, a development which he knew would be opposed not only by Pearson but also by Burroughs Wellcome's scientists in the UK.

The issues around Kepler and the new bromide were resolved by Wellcome in 1926 in response to complaints relayed to him by Nevin, whom he accused of timidity and urged him to "show more initiative ... carry suggestions through."[1] Wellcome outlined his vision for the American company's future, which was in complete agreement with that of Nevin:

> This is the psychological moment for us to put faith in our utmost endeavours to greatly extend the value of our business by practical ethical propaganda most favorable to our particular work [and] materially increase our list of products for this market by adding items likely to command large and steady demand, suited to the views, usages, and fancies of the medical profession in this country. This would include distancing the company's products sold in

> the US from association with Britain by removing references to English origin from advertising and labels … I believe that this is the opportune moment to reconsider the whole question of policy in respect of our American business by adapting more to the requirements of American ideas without lessening our ethical standards.[2]

Whereas Nevin's previous requests for a revision of the pricing formula adopted in London had fallen on deaf ears, when Wellcome attended the Lister Centenary and Clinical Congress in Detroit in 1927 he was assailed by physicians who, while praising the quality of Burroughs Wellcome medicines available in North America, complained of excessive pricing and cost for patients. On Wellcome's visit to Montreal, J. S. Lang, manager of the Canadian company, reinforced these criticisms and recounted the negative responses which he had received from Pearson on this matter in the past. During his review of the relevant correspondence between London and Montreal, Wellcome discovered a memorandum written either by Pearson or possibly Moore, the accountant: "… actuarial reckoning shows that it is customary for the curve of increase [in sales] to fall when following a period of exceptional rise," against which Wellcome noted: "responsible management reports of definite concrete facts of injury caused by high prices and urgent necessity of prompt action to prevent further losses are of far greater weight than actuarial theoretical curves."[3] Wellcome issued the same advice to Lang as he had to Nevin; that he should manage the Canadian business more independently. When Wellcome returned to London, finally convinced that the historic pricing policy was damaging, he berated Pearson because other American companies were promoting their products in the Canadian market just as good at half the price compared with those of Burroughs Wellcome & Co. (USA) Inc., a situation which Wellcome feared laid the company open to a charge of profiteering. As a priority, Wellcome insisted on a revision of current prices by reforming Moore's eccentric accounting system. Wellcome finally acknowledged that by giving all the advantage to London and Dartford, the system had contributed to undermine his own philosophy in which high volume production, low cost, and low prices were essential for growth and sustainable profit. He rejected the accountant's view that immediate profits were essential for the development of a business which, especially in pioneer fields, he believed could be problematic, hampering the process of building up a successful company.

Wellcome took the long view, as did Nevin whose vision went beyond the transition of the American company to a self-sufficient, if not independent, larger scale drug manufacturer. He envisioned a reduction of the company's dependence on products sold over the counter (OTCs), enabling it eventually to become more than merely (in his own words) "a tablet-making outfit,"[4] thereby distancing the business from the dubious activities of the sellers of proprietary medicines on the periphery of the industry. This was the most important issue yet when Wellcome's support for Nevin against Pearson was vital for the company's future, for central to this strategy was the introduction of research and the development of science-based ethical drugs at Tuckahoe. Sensitive to the differences between the pharmaceutical industry in the US and the UK, Nevin explained to both Wellcome and Pearson that his strategy for making a greater impact in the American market was by entering into competition with highly-respected American ethical pharmaceutical companies. He believed that a necessary condition for achieving this goal was to establish a reputation for ethical medicine among the American medical profession and universities, where most medical research took place. He aspired to establish a reputation at Tuckahoe independent of that inherited by WFL in the UK.

Since 1894, the Wellcome research laboratories in the UK had successfully pioneered scientific research as a basis for the commercial development of drugs. By 1927, several of the leading American pharmaceutical manufacturers also possessed research departments. Nevin's view was that a research department was necessary to achieve his goal, not only because of the reputation with which research laboratories were associated, but also to enable the company to respond rapidly to sudden changes in treatments which he had observed the American medical profession was prone to make. A further justification was the introduction of government restrictions and legal requirements which affected the trade in prescription drugs in the US. Nevin's argument for independence was to be strengthened by the "buy American First" campaign triggered by the Great Depression which placed a premium on supplying products unambiguously manufactured in the US.

Pearson was unimpressed by Nevin's proposal and opposed any further transfer of functions, particularly pure research, from the UK. Wellcome took the opposite view and connived with Nevin during 1927 to plan the Tuckahoe Experimental Research Laboratories. Privately, he agreed a budget, approved a salary, the nature of a future director's duties, and the direction research should take, as well as resources for staffing the laboratory. In 1928, in accordance with normal procedure for the appointment of new staff at Tuckahoe, Nevin sought Pearson's permission to appoint Dr C. S. Leonard, Assistant Professor of Pharmacology and Toxicology at Yale, though mention was made neither of a research laboratory, nor his precise role as director of research, nor additional research staff yet to be appointed. Neither was there mention that all staff would be expected to pursue pure research and publish results in learned journals on the model created by the Wellcome research laboratories in England. Nevin's submission to Pearson for permission to appoint an additional staff member described Leonard as an expert chemist who possessed the capability "to ensure that the works' standards were maintained to a degree in every respect comparable to the Chief Works' standards."[5] Leonard's familiarity with the requirements of the US government was regarded as a valuable asset that would enable him to suggest product improvements in line with those requirements. Pearson's reply suggested that Leonard's specialist training in pharmacology and the salary proposed connoted a more senior role and responsibility than merely product control in the works and that his record suited him more to pure laboratory-based research of the academic kind than to the routine duties implied in Nevin's briefest of job descriptions.

In fact, Pearson received Leonard's *curriculum vitae* only after the appointment as research director had been settled. Further surprises awaited Pearson. In June 1929, he read the announcement in the *Chemist & Druggist* of the appointment of Dr J. S. Buck, formerly Professor of Chemistry at Duke University, who was to join the staff at the Wellcome Experimental Research Laboratory opening at Tuckahoe in September. No mention was made of the appointment of Dr L. Reiner, who was responsible for preparing and setting up the laboratory under the guidance of Wellcome, Nevin, and the new director. Pearson remained in the dark until he discovered a new item, research expenditure, in the American accounts. When Pearson objected to the entire project, the resources committed, and decisions on staffing made without his permission, Nevin informed him that during the previous two years Wellcome had been fully consulted and had advised on the project. Wellcome had been coauthor of the director's terms of reference and those of other scientific staff. Nevin explained that Wellcome had insisted that "the apparatus and atmosphere of these laboratories must be thoroughly scientific and ethical but at the same time thoroughly practical,"[6] and in preparation for the project, on Wellcome's instructions, Nevin had visited the best-equipped research laboratories in the US to assess requirements in equipping the Tuckahoe laboratories.

In 1929, Leonard proceeded to assemble his team of senior researchers. D. Lazlo Reiner, of Hungarian origin, was a physicist, chemist, and M.D. who enjoyed a high reputation at the Rockefeller Institute; Dr Johannes S. Buck, an Englishman who had worked with Sir William Perkin, professor of organic chemistry at Oxford, was associate professor of chemistry at Duke University. Dr Axel Hjort, a biologist, and Dr Julia B. Paton, a bio-assayist, were appointed in 1930. Paton, who was formerly an associate of D. Casimir Funk, the internationally-renowned vitamin researcher, was enlisted to assist with the development of new malt extract preparations.[7]

The Wellcome/Nevin strategy for expansion based on volume manufacture and competitive prices and, eventually, laboratory-based research and ethical medicines began during a period of growth in the American economy. G. L. Moore's estimated accumulated deficits, resulting from London's underwriting of American losses, diminished sharply during the 1920s. Between 1922 and 1929, the company's sales rose from $1.1 million to $2.6 million; pre-tax profits increased from $181,481 to $492,094. Profits as percentages of sales reached their postwar peak during the late 1920s, averaging 17 per cent between 1922 and 1929 (see Table 2.1). The major investment in Tuckahoe required large balances to be transferred from London; consequently, not until 1931 did the American company pay its first dividend of $0.5 million to WFL (see Table 2.2). Sales stagnated during the 1930s and the rate of profit dropped sharply from levels not obtained again until World War II, when in most years dividends fell below half the distribution made in 1931.

Throughout the interwar period, growth in sales depended principally on product lines first sold by Burroughs Wellcome & Co. (USA) Inc. before World War I, though

Table 2.1 *The New York branch and BW&Co. (USA) Inc., sales and trading profits ($000)*

	Sales	Trading profits before tax	Profit as % of sales		Sales	Trading profits before tax	Profit as % of sales
1919	696	4	0.6	1930	2,399	227	9
1920	907	144	16	1931	2,363	309	13
1921	1,015	129	13	1932	2,148	246	11
1922	1,131	181	16	1933	2,000	200	10
1923	1,332	229	17	1934	2,085	159	8
1924	1,550	242	16	1935	2,204	140	6
1925	1,786	267	15	1936	2,502	277	11
1926	2,045	328	16	1937	2,756	362	13
1927	2,176	392	18	1938	2,553	203	8
1928	2,399	431	18	1939	2,689	250	9
1929	2,525	492	19	1940	2,967	384	13

Source: GWHC, BW&Co. (USA) Inc., 107.07/11, Public affairs, "Brief analysis."

Table 2.2 *BW&Co (USA) Inc. transfers and dividends to WFL, 1924–1939 ($000)*

1924	158	1932	161
1925	0	1933	252
1926	0	1934	293
1927	0	1935	71
1928	0	1936	149
1929	0	1937	339
1930	0	1938	201
1931	505	1939	219

Source: Church and Tansey, *Burroughs Wellcome & Co.*, p. 425.

from the mid-1920s most were manufactured in the US, for example, Tabloids, Kepler malt extracts, and Three Bromides Effervescent. After the war, each encountered increasing competition from other drug manufacturers possessing far more financial, research, and marketing resources than the New York business. Sales of Kepler cod liver oil and malt products peaked in 1928/9, the result of the coincidence of a booming economy with an influenza epidemic and a related intensive marketing campaign. Already, however, companies employing scientists engaged upon vitamin research had begun to challenge Kepler products. In 1928, Parke Davis & Co., and Squibb advertised the scientific benefits of vitamins A and D in their concentrates in the popular, as well as professional medical publications. Lilly, Abbott, and Upjohn also entered the market for dietetic foods during the 1930s when "vitamin wars" began to undermine the market for traditional dietetic foods.[8] In 1932, Kepler haemoglobin

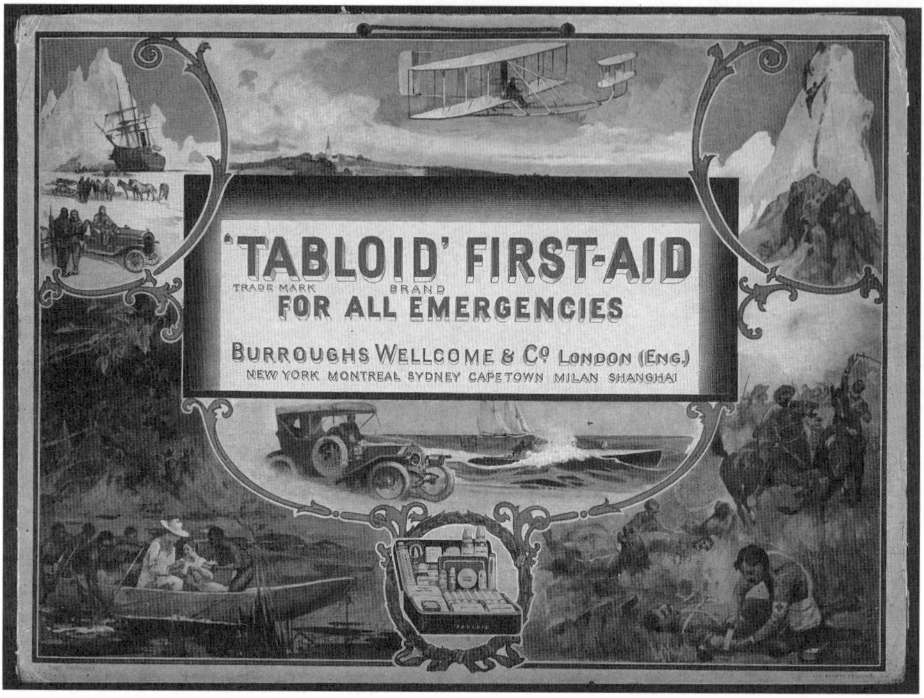

First aid kits which contained various Tabloids, one of two main product lines manufactured by Burroughs Wellcome in the UK since the 1880s were later adapted for the American market. Wellcome Library, London.

with Malt Extract and Cod Liver Oil (B vitamin fortified), was marketed as Kepler HMOV. However, the Kepler line continued to decline in the face of costly publicity campaigns mounted by the leading vitamin manufacturers advertising such brands as "sunshine vitamins" and "bottled sunshine" direct to the public.

In response Nevin sought to develop the small but growing niche market for dietary foods as adjuncts. Dexin was a milk-water-carbohydrate product, a repeat item developed at Tuckahoe launched in 1932 which received strong endorsement by a leading paediatrician. A promotional campaign presented Dexin as suitable for infants and convalescing adults suffering from diarrhoea, persistent vomiting, or weight loss. Another new product was Tannafax, a tannic acid jelly the unique advantage of which was that it could be applied on the spot to prevent the absorption of toxin produced by burns.

Newly-defined markets were also sought for Tabloids, though initially through innovative marketing strategy of existing products. Tabloids first aid kits, introduced to the US market in 1927, consisted of boxed containers of relevant combinations of existing Tabloids (calomel, rhubarb and colocynth), and Empirin, Phenofax, and Menthofax bandages and dressings, all of which were already included separately in the price list. Kits were first marketed to railway companies, gasoline stations, government utilities, corporate organizations, hotels, and schools, and to transportation, fire, and police departments. Pocket first aid kits were designed for domestic use. In 1930, kit

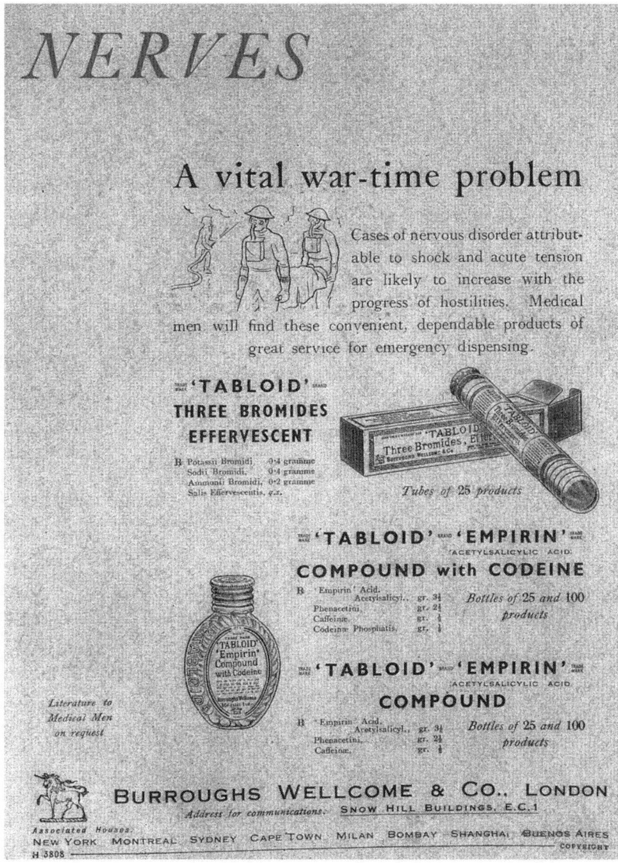

Tabloids Empirin and Three Bromides Effervescent were products originally manufactured in the UK but became important products produced at Tuckahoe after World War I. Wellcome Library, London.

contents were increased to include Tabloid Adhesive Boric Compress, an early form of the later ubiquitous band-aid, which were marketed to hospitals, clinics, and first aid departments in industrial plants, as well as to public service organizations, a task helped by a vigorous national public safety campaign in the US.

Selling more complex preparations supplied from the Wellcome research laboratories in England proved to be a more challenging task for the American salesmen. Nevin viewed specialities, such as Ernutin, Epinine, Infundin, and Ethidol (all adrenal and pituitary extracts) and Wellcome Brand Tincture Digitalis as "an entering wedge" to gain access to American hospitals. Those salesmen who lacked the level of scientific knowledge required to explain to physicians the therapeutic value of such products were urged to prepare themselves thoroughly. They were advised to read excerpts from scientific journal articles reprinted in the monthly circular in order to undertake regular campaigns described as educational. They were also urged to make physicians aware of the research that lay behind the company's specialities. However, sales of oral gland products remained relatively small at a disadvantage when leading science-based American companies, Parke Davis, Lilly, Upjohn, Abbott, and Squibb, introduced a range of potent hormone products during the 1930s.

Insulin supplied from England continued to be included in the American price list, but during the 1930s, Reiner, Searle, and Lang, embarked on an independent research project at Tuckahoe. Their intention was to develop a therapeutic agent which slowed the rate of absorption of insulin sufficiently to allow diabetic patients to increase intervals between doses. On the initiative of the research director at Tuckahoe (and contrary to instruction from London), Globin Insulin was patented. Production commenced in 1938. Although the potential market was not large. from the standpoint of Tuckahoe scientists the development of Globin Insulin for the first time signalled to medical practitioners and to the industry the presence of significant research activity at the tiny Tuckahoe laboratories.

However, the process of integrating laboratory research within the commercial organisation presented serious problems of management. Nevin soon lost confidence in Leonard, the research director, whom he believed had placed his own research and the extension of the laboratories above other company priorities relating to the need for product innovation; Leonard had also created division among the research staff. Nevin was forced to admit that (as Pearson had warned at the time of his appointment) Leonard was more suited to a university career. Sir Henry Wellcome (knighted in 1932) had accepted this judgment and agreed to Leonard's resignation. Nevin promoted Howard B. Fonda as a supervisor of the laboratories. Fonda was not a scientist. He had joined the company after a period as salesman, had taken charge of the office, managing the important Tabloid first aid and medicine case department.[9] Nevin looked to Fonda's proven administrative and organisational skills to stabilize the laboratories by managing their staff more effectively. His brief was to organize and manage the scientists and "to make these laboratories successful in the development of new products."[10] In 1937, Reiner (a leader of the Globin Insulin research team) was appointed director of research. Within a year, however, again Nevin detected too much commitment to pure research rather than to product development,[11] was dissatisfied with his lack of management skills and with his inability or unwillingness to exert authority over staff which he perceived to have deleterious effects on efficiency in the laboratories.[12]

In 1938, Nevin proceeded to promote Fonda from laboratory supervisor to works supervisor. Nevin also appointed an administrator who was both a scientist and had administrative experience managing other scientists. He was Carl J. Klemme, Professor of Pharmaceutical Chemistry at Purdue University and acting dean of faculty. Nevin explained the logic for making this appointment: "I purposely selected a man with pharmaceutical leanings because in my opinion one of the mistakes Sir Henry made when he opened the laboratories was to give the group the impression that they would be allowed to operate as pure research staff. We have gradually forced them to spend more of their time on applied work … when it is so essential to develop new products."[13] The appointment was endorsed by Bennett, Pearson's successor as managing director in London, who expressed the view that because the market for pharmaceuticals in the US was more volatile than that in the UK, the balance between pure research and opportunistic policies justified a higher proportion of applied research at Tuckahoe compared with that existing at WFL in the UK. Nevin's attempt to control the balance between pure and applied research by the appointment of an overall administrator backfired. Senior scientists Reiner, Hjort, and Buck resigned, leaving the issue unresolved.

The Great Depression precipitated a sharp fall in American sales, in response to which Nevin's policy, with Wellcome's support, was to spend the company's way out of the slump. The number of sales representatives increased from sixty-two in 1929 to eighty-two by 1936, while advertising expenditure rose by roughly one-third between 1932 and 1933. More evidence that the depression had not blunted ambition was Wellcome's agreement to fund a large exhibit entitled Century of Progress to form part of the Chicago exposition in 1933. The exhibit was located in the Hall of Science, one of the most spectacular buildings on the site, and described in the official exposition journal as "one of the most thrilling displays we have ever seen."[14]

At a meeting of all departmental heads and twenty-four salesmen Nevin articulated the message implied in the company's exhibit: that scientific research had important *commercial* significance within the overall marketing strategy. He emphasized the vital revenue-generating importance of OTC products, among which Kepler HMOV and Dexin were regarded as the fast-moving products most likely to secure sales in volume. Products with a long history, such as Hazeline Snow cosmetics, Wellcome Brand Toilet Lanoline, and Tabloid Tea were believed likely to benefit from increased advertising and greater effort applied by salesmen in the field. Nevin also stressed the indirect role of the science-based products; even though they were unlikely to grow beyond narrowly circumscribed demands, they fulfilled an important function by reinforcing the company's claim to be regarded as an ethical pharmaceuticals manufacturer possessing a reputation worthy of trust.

By raising its national profile, enhancement of reputation enabled the company to intensify promotional activity to two categories of institutions of rapidly growing importance: hospitals and government departments, which accounted for an increasing proportion of the company's business. Reputation was equally important for securing the status of a recognized bidder for government contracts at a time when expenditure by several government departments on public health services was rising sharply. An opportunity occurred in 1934 when the federal government introduced decentralizing reforms intended to open up the process to new bidders. Although small and new to the arena created by government contracts, Burroughs Wellcome & Co. (USA) Inc. proved to be adept in exploiting the resulting opportunities for drug orders in volume. The company's revised price list was accepted for inclusion in the general price list issued by the US Treasury Department; this enabled the company to solicit direct orders from separate government departments. Sustained, targeted circulation of advertising literature to potential purchasers, direct mailing to every US administrative facility, regional office, and supply depots, proved to be successful. The contract with the buying department of the Post Office in Washington, the company's largest, was

William N. Creasy, pharmacy graduate and retail pharmacist appointed as sales clerk in 1930, becoming sales representative and subsequently general manager at Tuckahoe in 1943. He was president of the company between 1945 and 1968. *Wellcome News*, Winter, 1945. Wellcome Library, London.

for the supply of Empirin compound to post offices nationwide. Through the state procurement office of the US Treasury, tens of thousands of Tabloid first aid kits were distributed in every state. In 1937, the company benefited from its ability to supply Wellcome Bismuth Salicylate preparations to the Department of Health and to state and municipal authorities to assist the Surgeon General's national campaign to combat and control syphilis and gonorrhea.

Another important innovation was the creation in 1934 of a business and statistics department which heralded the emergence among Nevin's management team of a future, long-serving president of the American company. William N. Creasy was born in Bournemouth, England, raised and educated in Ontario, and graduated from the University of Toronto College of Pharmacy in 1929 before working briefly in a retail pharmacy in Ottawa. He had joined the company in 1930 at the age of 22. His initial application to become a sales representative had been rejected by Nevin because of his age, but he was offered a temporary clerical position, checking and pricing orders. Weeks later, Nevin showed sufficient confidence in the new recruit's maturity to send him out on the road, first to work the Brooklyn sales territory and later to San Francisco. His brief was to survey opportunities for developing business in hospitals along the entire west coast which proved so successful that Nevin promoted Creasy to assistant sales manager in the New York office where Guy Dunbar was sales manager. In this capacity Creasy was responsible for managing and writing advertising and publicity copy. He introduced a systematic training program for all new sales representatives and also revised the company's price list which adopted alphabetical ordering of products, an innovation adopted worldwide throughout WFL.[15]

In 1936, Sir Henry Wellcome was again in the US. At that time, the American sales were $2.5 million, roughly one-third of the total sales of WFL. 522 people were employed at Tuckahoe, roughly 15 per cent of all WFL employees. Sales and profits had returned to a slowly rising trend; yet profits accounted for roughly two-thirds of those of WFL. Sir Henry's visit was not a business matter. Serious health deterioration brought him to the US for consultation with his American physicians in 1934 and he underwent surgery for prostate cancer at the Mayo Clinic in 1935. He returned to England in June 1936 and died on 25 July 1936 at the age of 82.

Sir Henry Solomon Wellcome, creator of the Wellcome Trust. Wellcome Library, London.

The demise of Nevin's long-time supporter, whose personal commitment and willingness to exercise authority had been crucial to the transformation of the business in the US since the 1920s, threw open its future. Ownership of the entire WLF passed to the Wellcome Trust, set up in accordance with the terms of Sir Henry's will. However, his will also nominated Pearson, Sir Henry's personal deputy, as his successor as chairman of WFL and governing director of the business. Wellcome's appointment of Pearson as his successor is not easy to understand. Museum curator and friend of Wellcome, Captain Peter Johnson-Saint, told a relative of Nevin that in February 1936 Wellcome had praised Nevin's genius, hard work, and success and that on his return to London intended to retire Pearson and replace him with Nevin.[16] Nevin also appears to have believed that this change was about to take place.[17] Such a step would have been wholly consistent with Wellcome's dismissal of Pearson's approach to the American company and with Wellcome's unwavering support for Nevin. Pearson was aged seventy in 1936; Nevin was fifty-nine. Failure to implement such a change is almost certainly attributable to Wellcome's illness. His reluctance to take such a step long before, however, is probably explained by a sense of obligation. Pearson had joined the company in London in 1891 since when demonstrating complete loyalty to his employer.

Wellcome Trustees *c.* 1938. Standing from left to right: Martin Price, accountant, and J. E. K. Clarke, secretary to the trustees; seated: Launcelot Claude Bullock, solicitor, Professor Sir Henry Hallett Dale, FRS, Nobel Laureate, formerly director of the Wellcome Physiological Research Laboratory, 1906–1914, subsequently chairman of the Medical Research Council, President of the Royal Society, and chairman of the Wellcome Trust between 1938 and 1960, and Thomas Renton Elliott, FRS, formerly a colleague of Dale at the WPRL and subsequently Professor of Medicine at University College London. Wellcome Library, London.

Pearson's elevation was a personal blow to Nevin. It seems that, at least during Pearson's brief interregnum in the immediate aftermath of Wellcome's death, Nevin's role was downgraded[18] though his title of president remained until 1945 when Pearson's successor in London replaced him and promoted Creasy to the presidency. In July 1936, therefore, the American company faced uncertainties: one was immediate and arose from the potential consequences of the elevation of Pearson who had evinced relentless antagonism towards the American subsidiary. Uncertainty was also created by Sir Henry Wellcome's will and the ambiguities contained in supporting documentation of how it should be implemented through the Wellcome Trust. Under the terms of his will, the Wellcome Trust became the new owner of WFL and of his personal fortune; in that capacity, the Trust was charged with administering Wellcome's legacy. However, the will was unclear with respect to the precise relationship between trustees and the directors of WFL (and therefore between trustees and the directors of the American company). Ultimate powers of hiring and firing the chairman and directors of WFL and the president of Burroughs Wellcome & Co. (USA) Inc. rested with the trustees. The chairman and directors of WFL were responsible for managing the business as a commercial enterprise. Consistent with the authority vested in the Trust, the company's activities were open to scrutiny, though limited to an annual report and accounts at yearly general meetings chaired by the chairman of the Trust and attended by the WFL directors.[19] The Wellcome trustees were responsible for administering the entire set of activities embraced by the Foundation, including those of the businesses, research laboratories, a library, a museum, scientific and archaeological collections, and other ventures. However, the appointment and remuneration of all employees, including those in the research laboratories, museums, and the library were under the control of the governing director of WFL and therefore a charge on the company's resources.

The initial composition of the Trust when it was formed in 1936 consisted of either former employees or business associates (though not businessmen) and friends of Wellcome. Following the death of George Lyall, the first designated chairman, barely a year after the Trust was set up,[20] he was succeeded by one of the first trustees to have been appointed. Then aged sixty, Sir Henry Dale F.R.S. was a distinguished physiologist, a former chairman of the Medical Research Council and, since 1936, a Nobel Laureate. He had led research at the Wellcome Physiological Research Laboratory in London between 1904 and 1914 when he had displayed an unusually advanced approach to the development of constructive interaction between pure and applied science and commercial activity. This was the model pioneered by Wellcome since 1894. The other trustees were: Professor T. R. Elliott, F.R.S., aged sixty-eight, a close friend of Dale; Martin Price aged seventy-three, the company's chartered accountant for many years; and Claude Bullock, the company's long-standing solicitor, aged fifty-seven.[21] Although they were the owners of the business (which was accountable to the Trust), when first appointed, the trustees had assumed that they would concern themselves primarily with charitable functions, encouraging and supporting medical research, as laid down in Wellcome's will. Indeed, Dale had agreed to become a trustee only on condition that he "should have no personal interest in or responsibility for the business or its conduct."[22] Even after clarification of Sir Henry Wellcome's wishes by the High Court, ambiguities regarding the relationship between the business and the Trust, contained in the will, remained. At the outset, the trustees interpreted their role as one of non-interference in the policies pursued by the business "except under quite abnormal conditions." The Trust was deemed to possess the power of "last resort." In effect, the trustees were designated as "an immortal self". In the event of differences of opinion between the Trust and WFL, the Trust possessed the power of final decision.[23]

The trustees could not have envisaged that within two years of its formation the Trust would invoke the power of last resort. This followed an internal report on the company requested by Sir Henry Dale, the Trust's forceful chairman, in 1938. The report was presented by Martin Price, the trustee whose profession as an accountant equipped him to evaluate the performance and management of the business in the context of the Trust's financial liabilities. Sir Henry Wellcome's personal fortune, accumulated earlier in his career, had dwindled. High personal expenditure combined

Figure 2.1 *The Structure and Organisation of the Wellcome Foundation Ltd in 1940*

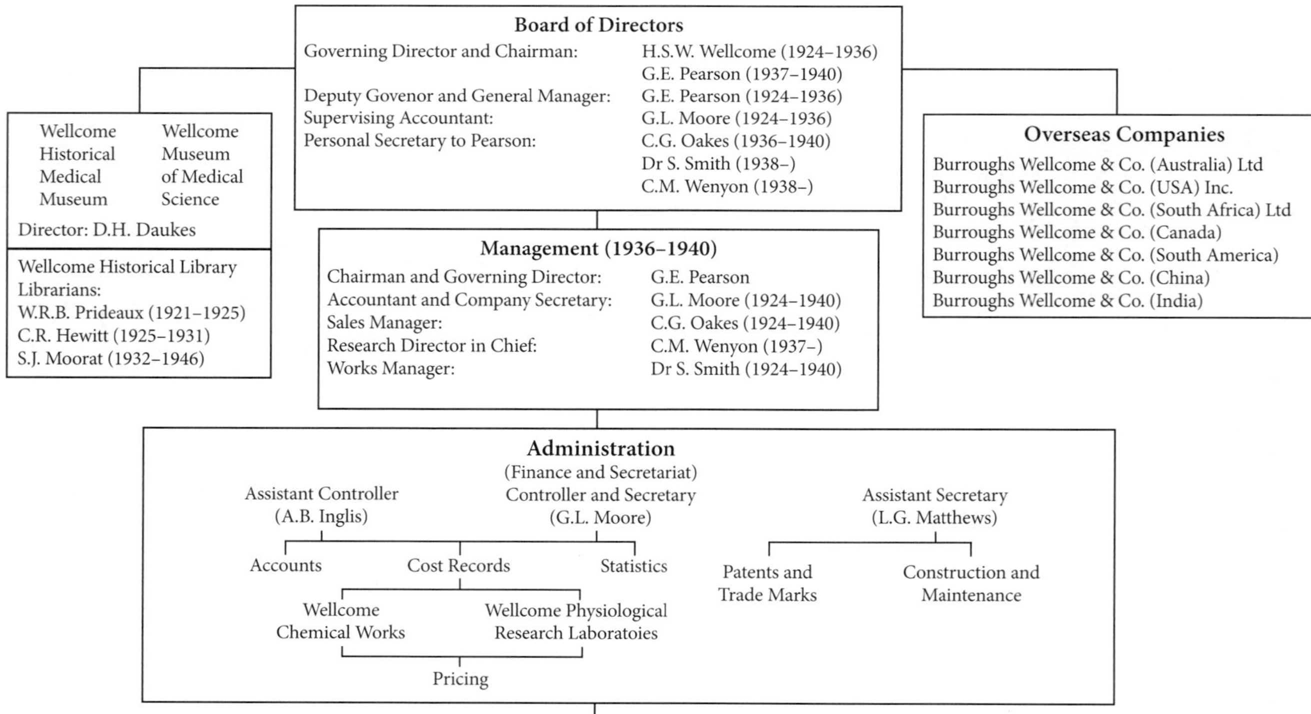

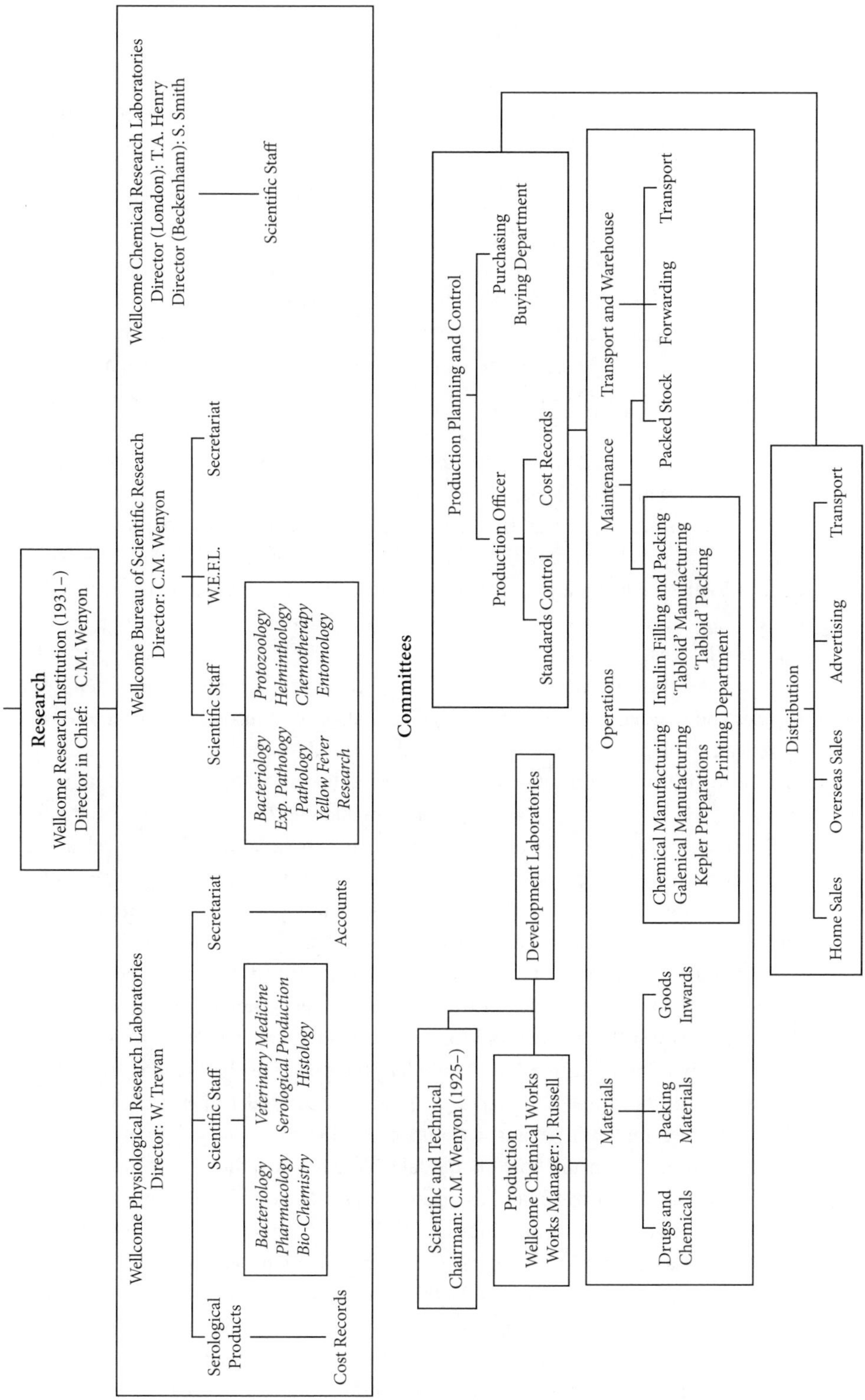
Research
Wellcome Research Institution (1931–)
Director in Chief: C.M. Wenyon
Wellcome Physiological Research Laboratories
Director: W. Trevan
Serological Products
Scientific Staff
Secretariat
Bacteriology
Pharmacology
Bio-Chemistry
Veterinary Medicine
Serological Production
Histology
Cost Records
Accounts
Wellcome Bureau of Scientific Research
Director: C.M. Wenyon
Scientific Staff
W.E.F.L.
Secretariat
Bacteriology
Exp. Pathology
Pathology
Yellow Fever Research
Protozoology
Helminthology
Chemotherapy
Entomology
Wellcome Chemical Research Laboratories
Director (London): T.A. Henry
Director (Beckenham): S. Smith
Scientific Staff
Committees
Scientific and Technical
Chairman: C.M. Wenyon (1925–)
Development Laboratories
Production
Wellcome Chemical Works
Works Manager: J. Russell
Production Planning and Control
Production Officer
Standards Control
Cost Records
Purchasing
Buying Department
Materials
Drugs and Chemicals
Packing Materials
Goods Inwards
Operations
Chemical Manufacturing
Galenical Manufacturing
Kepler Preparations
Insulin Filling and Packing
'Tabloid' Manufacturing
'Tabloid' Packing
Printing Department
Maintenance
Transport and Warehouse
Packed Stock
Forwarding
Transport
Distribution
Home Sales
Overseas Sales
Advertising
Transport

with a decline in the company's profits followed by death duties left the Trust with inadequate funds with which to achieve his ambition for the Trust as a significant funder of medical research. The financial outlook faced by the Trust therefore, dependent upon dividends from an ailing company, was bleak.[24] The trustees decided that the abnormal conditions criteria should be invoked with a view to improving the company's future prospects and ensuring at least continuance of a small funding stream for the Trust. Their first step was to ensure that voices other than that of Pearson should prevail on the WFL board. The trustees used the Trust's power of appointment to add directors to the existing diminutive board. They were Charles Wenyon, long standing head of the Wellcome Bureau of Scientific Research, aged 60; Phillip Oakes, formerly head of the sales department but currently Pearson's personal assistant, and Sydney Smith, scientist and works manager at Dartford, both of the same generation. They participated in the Trust's subsequent investigation into the business in preparation for planning its future.

The outcome in 1939 was the Trust's insistence on Pearson's removal from the governorship of WFL, though he remained briefly as chairman of the more widely defined Wellcome Foundation Ltd (an indication that the Foundation existed as little more than a shell).[25] In 1940, on Price's recommendation with strong support from Elliott,[26] the trustees finally replaced Pearson with T. R. Bennett whom they appointed as both managing director of the company and chairman of WFL. His experience was in sales and marketing, first with the British branch of Johnson & Johnson, the large American manufacturer of proprietary toiletry products, and later with the British firm of management consultants, Urwick Orr & Partners Ltd. In responding to the trustees' early invitation to assess the company's strengths and weaknesses, Bennett criticized a lack of knowledge of modern methods of organisation and control applied to production and marketing, the absence of young executives, and the existence of an ageing sales force. He believed the priority was a thoroughgoing reorganisation of the business, especially a reform of the management of sales and marketing.[27]

Recognizing that the relationship between the Trust and WFL required codifying, specifically the rights and duties of the trustees, a memorandum of agreement was drawn up between the trustees and the company directors in 1941. In it, the trustees claimed responsibility, in the last resort, for "the policy of the WFL as framed and adopted by the directorate …"[28] They envisaged that, in order to ensure the approval of the trustees for WFL's plans for future development and for its major policy decisions, "friendly consultation" should take place between the two parties.[29] Barring any further need to invoke the last resort option to remedy abnormal conditions beyond the annual general meetings at which the chairman of the board presented the accounts and reported the year's events, consultation between trustees and the board was anticipated to be limited to those occasions when changes in membership of the board would be required. The immediate preoccupation of the trustees, each of whom possessed substantial professional commitments outside the Trust, was the disentanglement of Wellcome's non-business activities, the management of the

Wellcome Historical Museum and Library, and the selective disbursement of the funds available annually for medical research. The resulting hands-off relationship (as envisaged by Sir Henry Dale initially) adopted by the Trust also seemed to be appropriate when wartime conditions saw governmental regulation become the major factor in determining decisions on policy and production.[30] With the impressively qualified Bennett now in place, the trustees retreated to the non-interventionist posture which they preferred.

Bennett found himself in command of a business in decline and lacking strategic direction. In Tuckahoe, difficulties arising from conflicting priorities between Nevin and laboratory staff persisted though investment, reorganisation, and focused planning continued to move the American company onto an upward financial trajectory. Wartime demand and government controls in Britain and in the US ensured that the divergent pathways followed by the two companies since the 1920s would be reinforced and perpetuated throughout the second half of the twentieth century.

CHAPTER 3

Adapting to peacetime markets after World War II: planning for productivity and hoping for product innovation

For two reasons, Burroughs Wellcome & Co. (USA) Inc. emerged from the war stronger than it had been when the US entered the war on December 8th 1941. Firstly, the imperative to control costs under war conditions in order to compete for government contracts stimulated improvements in labor productivity. When the war ended, the company employed almost 1,000 workers, roughly twice the number it had employed in 1941. Secondly, success in securing government contracts had generated modest though reliable profits from which the expansion of production capacity and the maintenance of plant and equipment had been made possible. The company was not, however, well prepared to achieve the planned-for postwar expansion necessary to utilize an enlarged production capacity in competition with the much bigger pharmaceutical enterprises that had gained even more from wartime contracts. In 1946 at the end of the war, the volume of sales by Squibb, Merck, and Parke Davis & Co. exceeded those of Burroughs Wellcome & Co. (USA) Inc. by at least sixfold, those of Abbott Laboratories by fivefold, and those of Sharpe & Dohm and Mead Johnson & Co. by more than twofold. [1]

At first, Creasy was left largely undisturbed by Bennett and his successor in London. Fred Coe Jr. (a future president of the company) described Creasy's approach to managing the business during the 1940s and 1950s as having been characterized by a willingness to listen to advice from his co-directors and managers, though essentially "he pretty well ran it."[2] As under Nevin, the management style under Creasy's presidency was entrepreneurial and personal rather than professional and bureaucratic. Postwar planning remained firmly in the hands of Creasy and his American managers. Howard Fonda, works superintendent since 1938, had become vice president in charge of production in 1942 and was elected to the board in 1944; he became the senior vice president in 1945. Earl Rigg, who was responsible for marketing (which included selling, advertising, and promotion), was also a member of this small executive committee which in 1948 was formally designated by London as a local board of management.[3] In 1946, WFL's representation on the American board was reduced to two directors: C. G. Oakes and A. B. Inglis. Bennett's personal assistant in London, D. A. Wheeler, described the relationship thus: "The American subsidiary is virtually autonomous in research as in other matters and it would be contrary to the Foundation's wishes or practice to impose restrictions upon its activities."[4] Such a situation had evolved from the unique relationship (defined by Wellcome and Nevin) between London and New York. This high degree of independence conceded to the American company which the war had further reinforced, began to be contested after the war when WFL began to experience increasing financial difficulties which caused a recurrence of strain in the Anglo-American relationship.[5]

Denis Wheeler, joint managing director WFL, 1948–1955, and deputy chairman and group WFL director 1967–1970. He was one of the principal architects of WFL's product diversification and geographical expansion.

In 1944/5, in anticipation of the ending of government contracts and the emergence of a sudden gap in demand, a planning group began to reorganize the operational functions of the business at Tuckahoe.[6] The American directors assumed that the products which had sold well before the war would experience a resumption of demand on its termination. In any case, finding new products immediately after the war did not seem to be feasible. The initial plan, prepared before the war ended, was to install new plant for producing Kepler malt products and to construct a new Dexin building. However, the plan for a new Kepler plant was dropped in the face of intense competition from Upjohn's Unicap multivitamin cod liver oil capsule, which together with a similar product made by Squibb, quickly

Figure 3.1 *The Corporate Structure of Burroughs Wellcome (USA) Inc., 1924–1970*

Table 3.1 *BW&Co. Sales, Marketing and R&D Costs, 1946–1970*

	Sales ($000)	*Rep's salaries and expenses (%)*	*Advertising Expenditure (%)*	*R&D and RDM (%)*
1946	8,821	8	6	3
1947	10,546	10	5	3
1948	10,741	10	5	3
1949	10,718	10	5	3
1950	11,604	9	9	3
1951	12,738	8	8	3
1952	14,379	8	8	3
1953	15,983	8	8	4
1954	16,691	8	9	4
1955	18,347	8	8	4
1956	19,325	8	10	4
1957	20,188	8	9	6*
1958	21,346	9	9	6
1959	22,732	11**	9	7
1960	24,826	12	6	6
1961	25,865	12	9	6
1962	28,172	11	9	6
1963	29,654	11	9	6
1964	31,608	11	8	7
1965	34,230	9†	8	7
1966	38,948	9	7	6
1967	42,605	9	8	6
1968	48,665	9	7	6
1969	57,027	8	7	5
1970	60,164	9	8	7

* Hereafter includes Medical Department (RD&M) and also marks the termination of research funding (including researchers' salaries) from the Charles F. Kettering Institute subsequently funded internally.
** Introduction of car purchase scheme.
† Hereafter excludes expenses.
Source: GWHC, BW&Co.(USA) Inc., 107.01/02, President's annual reports and accounts.

dominated the postwar market for vitamins.[7] Avicap (advertised for those "seldom sick but never well"[8]) was a new multivitamin capsule possessing higher vitamin content than the traditional Kepler line. This continued to be advertised strictly to physicians as a capsule most suitable to be prescribed daily for a rational multivitamin therapy.

Frederick A. Coe Jr, engineering graduate, manager at the Seth Clock Company and United Steel before joining Burroughs Wellcome & Co. in the US in 1944. After successive executive roles as board director, he was chosen to become president of the company from 1968 when the Trust enforced his predecessor's resignation. Coe planned the relocation of the company from New York to the Research Triangle Park NC. where his patient support of RD&M began to bear fruit in the form of commercially significant new products as he approached retirement in 1980. *Wellcome News*, Spring 1969, Wellcome Library, London.

Avimal, described as a polyvitamin preparation in a nutritious malt extract suitable for children and expectant mothers, was another replacement for Kepler, but neither succeeded in compensating for the decline in demand for the Kepler line.[9] After the war, therefore, products from volume sales were to be limited to Dexin and Tabloid Empirin Compound (with and without Codeine).[10] As maintaining cash flow was the immediate concern, the construction of a new research laboratory, approved in principle, was accorded a lower priority. Expenditure on salaries and advertising compared with that allocated to RD&M show that between 1946 and 1970 sales continued to depend primarily on selling rather than on research.

Despite dissent from Ralphs, the finance director who cautioned against expenditure on the scale envisaged, the board endorsed $500,000 expenditure on a Dexin plant.[11]

Fred Coe Jr. too, had reservations, but at first, as a newcomer, did not express them. Coe is an important figure in the company's history. He grew up in Mechanichville, N.Y. and after high school had spent a year working in the control laboratories of the West Virginia Pulp and Paper Company where he was soon promoted to be in charge of the industrial alcohol department. After graduating in industrial administration at Yale University he spent two years at the Seth Thomas Clock Company in Connecticut where he became a pipe fitter's assistant, subsequently gaining wider experience as a foreman in the electroplating department, in the time-study department, and in the production planning department. In 1940, he joined Carnegie Illinois Steel (which was to form part of US Steel), rising quickly to became head of the industrial engineering department in a mill that produced tank armour during World War II. On the insistence of his employers, he continued to occupy this strategic position until the war ended. In search of experience in another industry, he judged an appointment at Burroughs Wellcome & Co. (USA) Inc. as an industrial engineer to be "a good opportunity."[12]

When he joined thc company in November 1945, Coe was directly responsible to the president, reporting to him alone and requiring only his approval for the way in which he interpreted his role as industrial engineer. Because of this free-floating position, he enjoyed freedom from the limitations inherent in a departmental structure. His initial brief was straightforward: to improve productivity. On his arrival at Tuckahoe he was appalled at the primitive methods of manufacturing: "... I really came into an old-fashioned outfit."[13] He attributed the prevailing methods to the dominance throughout the business of pharmacists whose experience was the production of drugs in small quantities and whose mind-set excluded notions of large scale continuous production. He also believed that poor organisation, even in the manufacture of the products with the largest sales, nullified the potential for technological efficiency.

His doubts regarding the Dexin project arose from a careful consideration of the extent of the market that would be required to ensure demand for the volume of Dexin production planned by Fonda. Coe reckoned that, on the basis of a proposed new building, a new production line, and brand new equipment, output would double or even triple, yet he discovered that outside the manufacturing department where the expansion plan had originated there had been no discussion of demand projections before the board had endorsed the proposal. Coe's fresh perspective led the board to reverse the decision and accept instead, Coe's engineering solution which required much-reduced capital investment justified on the basis of his more realistic future demand estimates.[14] Improvements were made to the plant which affected existing assembly lines for both Dexin and Empirin, but at the centre of Coe's plan was the flexible use of plant and machinery involving re-arrangement and a relocation of processes. Coe's success in reversing the radical, capital-intensive policy recommended by the manufacturing department under Fonda was soon shown to have been justified. Following a period of steadily weakening demand, Dexin production was finally abandoned in 1954.[15]

Dexin was not the only product to face declining postwar demand. During the closing stages of the war, the company had become one of five distributors of penicillin supplied by Pfizer and from 1947, also for streptomycin. When the war ended, sales of penicillin and streptomycin (both of which the company purchased in bulk) were the second and third largest selling products after Empirin; insulin ranked fourth. Between 1946 and 1949 sales of penicillin almost collapsed. The decline followed important developments in the antibiotics industry during and immediately after the war. In 1941, the US government formed the Committee on Medical Research (CMR) of the Office of Scientific Research and Development. The War Production Board (WPB) was created in 1942. The CMR was responsible for enhancing research directed towards the development of antibiotics; this involved inter-firm cooperation and knowledge transfer. The WPB's role was to facilitate the production of penicillin (and later streptomycin) and to raise productivity among a selected number of producers (eventually 20) chosen to receive contracts. Burroughs Wellcome (USA) Inc. was not included among the elite group of antibiotics manufacturers which as a result of the contracts consolidated their positions as the leading pharmaceutical manufacturers in the US. The American company was at a special disadvantage in bidding inasmuch that underlying the large wartime expansion of capacity based on economies of scale was the technology of deep fermentation in tanks whereas until 1945, British companies (including WFL) had remained committed to surface culture still using flasks and producing at half the scale of American companies.[16]

Thus, although in several respects Burroughs Wellcome & Co. (USA) Inc. was stronger in terms of production, organisation, and sales when the war ended, the effects of two wartime developments placed the company at a disadvantage in the American industry. One consequence was the consolidation, through government intervention, of the leadership of the existing largest and most scientifically advanced companies in the US. The other was the failure of the parent company in the UK to match the technology and scale of penicillin production adopted in the US. The American company was at a disadvantage, not only because it sold rather than manufactured antibiotics, but also because the parent company was in no position after the war to supply the American subsidiary with antibiotics which would be competitive in the American market.

In postwar markets for other products, competition from several smaller pharmaceutical firms which succeeded in securing sales to the Army and Navy also had an adverse impact on large ethical suppliers, notably Squibb, Lilly, Sharp & Dohm, and Upjohn, as they did on Burroughs Wellcome & Co. (USA) Inc. Prices set by the new competitors were reported to fall below actual works costs.[17] Between 1947 and 1949, the company's sales of antibiotics fell from $1.2 million (16 per cent of total company sales) to $0.7 million (7 per cent); in 1950 they represented less than 1 per cent. The percentage profits on both of the antibiotics (gross profits of 19 per cent for penicillin and 20 per cent for streptomycin in 1947) were lower than for other regular lines and contributed only marginally to a fragile cash flow. The overall profit/sales ratio fell to single figures between 1944 and 1947. The decline represented a serious setback in the context of a rapidly expanding demand for antibiotics which has been referred to as "the most spectacular therapeutic advance of medical history" before the 1980s.[18] During the 1940s, penicillin quickly became the most frequently prescribed drug in the US. In June 1943, 425 million units of penicillin were manufactured, compared with 646 billion in 1945. One contemporary observer in 1945 described it as "a spree;" intensified by an "antibiotic abandon" among physicians.[19] Burroughs Wellcome & Co. (USA) Inc. was to be locked out from the most important sector of the pharmaceutical industry.

In 1947, however, the company's precarious position in the market was transformed dramatically when a completely unexpected source of substantial profit emerged. The first of a series of orders received from UNRRA, the organisation in Washington responsible for arranging financial aid to promote international postwar recovery and reconstruction was for quinine, benzyl benzoate emulsion, and other chemicals and amounted to no more than several thousand dollars. Moreover, contracts for these items were discontinued when the organisation was disbanded in June 1947. However, it was through UNRRA that the company tendered for a major contract to supply Neostam for the treatment of Kala-azar in China to combat the fatal tropical disease spread by the sand fly. The decision to tender saw Creasy at his most opportunistic. Neostam had been sold by the American company during the early 1940s, though it is not clear whether the drug had been supplied from London or produced in the Chemical Manufacturing Department at Tuckahoe. Creasy later referred to the Neostam contract as having been a highly risky venture, which suggests that either London had been the source of supply in 1943 and Neostam had been merely sold by the American company, or production at that time had been so small (for sales of between 40,000 and 50,000 grams per year),[20] that the sheer scale of the contract put out to tender in 1947 required calculations relating to volume production of a much greater complexity. Later, Creasy was critical of WFL for providing inadequate guidance on a working formula that would enable the American company to manufacture Neostam on a large scale, a vital dimension in the strategy. However, after Tuckahoe scientists refined the UK formula the company's bid won a contract with the Winthrop Pharmaceutical Company. Scaling up for manufacturing was completed within a year and expanding manufacturing capacity for Neostam from 5,000 to 50,000 grams per week to deliver the first order of 1.5 million grams to UNRRA. The substantial orders that followed in 1947/8 generated sales of $2 million; the effect was to enlarge total company sales by roughly 10 per cent. Moreover, even though the product was priced competitively, Creasy could describe the contract as sufficiently lucrative to allow a gradual implementation of the company's longer term plan "a brick at a time."[21] The company's profit/sales ratio rose from 10 per cent in 1947 to exceed 20 per cent between 1947 and 1950 continuing throughout the 1950s and early 1960s; between 1965 and 1970 the average was 26 per cent.[22] From total sales amounting to $6.5 million, the plan was to increase sales from $6.5 million to $43.5 million within ten years which was estimated to be necessary to generate sufficient profits to finance investment internally.[23]

Preparatory to this development Creasy embarked on a systematic rationalization of the company's business. The sale of the three and six storey buildings on 41st Street in New York City contributed to the release of funds for investment. The consequent relocation of employees was accompanied by a reduction in the number from 909 in 1947 to 740 by 1950. During that process, measures were taken to ensure that the organisation was functionally effective on the reduced scale. The functions and responsibilities of jobs at all levels began to be defined, while managers and supervisors were encouraged to recognize that an important part of their role was to take decisions where authority to do so was theirs. The effect of such a measure is impossible to judge. It is certain, however, that the introduction of triple shift working, which the Neostam contracts necessitated, was a key factor enabling a rapid expansion of production to take place.[24]

Measures to ensure cost control were also introduced. The responsibility for drawing up the budget was a newly formed forecasting group which included marketing, sales, and planning staff who met quarterly While not immediately affecting the final cost of products in the majority of lines, the introduction of a new cost system on a departmental basis revealed scope for cost reductions to be made.[25] A new procedure was introduced to make departmental heads more conscious of the cost of running their departments. Each was provided with detailed information on cost breakdown followed by an interview with the plant manager with a view to securing cost reductions.[26] In 1947, cost control of inventories was tackled by introducing an annual distribution budget.

Following recommendations by the forecasting group in 1946 Creasy embarked upon a sweeping rationalization of the product range which excised 250 products from the price list employing the criteria of limited sales and lack of profitability; they included first aid kits, hypodermics, diagnostic agents, medical chests, an extensive photographic line, and all glandular products with the exception of thyroid.[27] Evidence of the impact of the rationalization of products was a doubling of the rate of return on capital employed between the mid-1940s from roughly 20 per cent to exceed 40 per cent by the early 1950s.[28] After the rationalization of the product range, among those products which remained on the list, the largest selling lines were the well-established Empirin Compound, followed by Kepler goods, Dexin, and Wellcome Globin Insulin. Other surviving products of less commercial significance which had been introduced in the 1930s were Elixoid cough syrup, Timofax (an ointment and powder treatment for athlete's foot and similar fungicide infections), Menthofax, for the relief of muscular pain, and Borofax, a lanolin-based preparation to treat skin irritation. Tubarine injection was a long-acting muscle relaxant which originated in the Wellcome Research Laboratories (WRL) and in 1936 was the first pure crystalline d-tubacurarine product. None sold in volume.[29] Creasy acknowledged that these were stopgap products. In the short term, new product development took the form of modifying existing products and stretching their application to different uses. Tabloid Empirin Compound with the addition of Codeine Phosphate was another product seen to be a stopgap which Creasy had persuaded a reluctant Hitchings (the company's leading scientist who was more concerned with medical research[30]) should be added to the product range, one which proved to be a vital, if modest innovation that captured a large slice of the American market for analgesics between the 1940s and 1960s when Empirin became the market leader.

A new round of product rationalization commenced in 1950 under the direction of the newly promoted advertising manager, Clealand Baker with a view to concentrating a limited advertising budget on a few products. Evidence showed a relationship between advertising expenditure and the sale of products and return on capital invested in marketing convinced Coe (by this time head of distribution) who then persuaded Creasy to accept Baker's proposal. Advertising was to be concentrated primarily on twelve products, though one-third of the total expenditure supported Dexin and Wellcome Globin Insulin with Zinc, both of which were in decline and within four years phased out altogether. Enlarged budgets for advertising brought expenditure up to 5 per cent of sales.[31]

Another element in marketing strategy was the recruitment of additional salesmen. Their numbers increased from 108 to 147 between 1945 and 1950, though this brought the level to no more than roughly one quarter of the numbers typically employed by the company's main competitors in the US. The comprehensive postwar marketing strategy introduced in 1945/6, which supported a narrower product range with an expanded sales staff, was accompanied by a new approach to advertising which, during the war, had focused mainly on the trade. Advertising in medical journals and the direct mailing of advertisements to the medical and allied professions assumed an unprecedented scale. From fifty-eight pages of advertisements in nine medical journals, the numbers rose to six hundred and one pages in sixty-nine journals. To a lesser degree, increased advertising was placed in drug, nursing, hospital, and consumer journals.

In 1946, the emphasis shifted from journal and direct mail advertising to the distribution of free samples to medical professionals, a policy which Nevin had pursued successfully before the war. A special quarterly sales brochure was introduced which was intended to improve detailing and selling activities by providing advice on detailing points and selling approaches. At the suggestion of some of the sales representatives, these included the offer of gimmicks for the use of physicians. For example, the plastic demonstrator used in detailing Tabloid Empirin Compound with Codeine Phosphate was offered as a paperweight; the Dexin Infant Feed Calculator was another functional detailing tool, as was the Globin Insulin plastic clock, "a calculator type of gadget which demonstrated the intermediate action of Globin Insulin coordinated with a clock device to indicate the time of day."[32] In the absence of substantial new products rather than incremental adjustments for the purpose of introducing novelty as a selling point, a limited number of changes were made in packaging, including redesigned labels, cartons and outer-covering, bottle shapes to facilitate more efficient packing, and the introduction of improved tubes, droppers, and other applicators.

Another innovation was the launch of a systematic, enhanced mobile exhibition program to be held in booths at medical meetings and, by arrangement with hospital superintendents or managers, in hospital staff rooms. The displays lasted for one or two days, initially in hospitals in the metropolitan New York area. Measured by the number of contacts with physicians directly, the experiment proved so successful that the program was implemented on a national basis.[33] A review of the new national policy conducted after ten months showed that 614 presentations held for 868 days generated more than 33,000 interviews, two-thirds of which involved medical practitioners, as well as residents, interns, nurses, dieticians, and pharmacists. A rate of roughly forty "good interviews" with medical staff per day became the acceptable return on such exhibitions.[34] Through attendance by the company's increasing number of sales representatives, the company was represented at almost all important national and major State medical conventions. In December 1947, a branch office and warehouse opened in San Francisco resulting in a fall in trans-shipment time from Tuckahoe from two weeks to one or two days.[35]

Beginning in 1946, all sales representatives were required to undertake an upgraded training program.[36] Information and ideas were passed on from the sales office national sales programs were planned to regional meetings of sales mangers and representatives in the field. Another educative process, designed to bolster the morale of the representatives on the road and to be instructive both for them and for the office staff, was the introduction of regular visits by all representatives to office and factory. At the same time a complete reorganisation of the sales division involved the appointment of four district sales managers and ten supervisors. Expert input from the medical department staff took place at sectional meetings of representatives which were held in five major cities where they were apprised of new product developments and those in the pipeline.

The return of intensive promotional work with hospitals, both private and government, after 1945 included a special focus on the Veterans Administration, the importance of which stemmed from its management of 120 hospitals containing a total of 120,000 beds. The approval for use of Tabloid Empirin Compound with Codeine Phosphate spearheaded a drive to sell other therapeutic products which Creasy regarded as the key to future commercial success.[37] Repeatedly, he expressed a conviction that in the medium and long term the route to new product development, yielding products possessing high market potential and profit, was through laboratory research. He was, however, well aware of the uncertainty surrounding science-based product innovation. In 1948, de Beer, the acting research director, acknowledged that even if the scientists synthesized 1,000 compounds, after screening, no more than four or five had a possibility of leading to the development of a marketable product that would both gain FDA approval and sell in volume.[38]

Scientists were hampered throughout the immediate postwar years when the highest priority was maintaining cash flow through investment in modernizing manufacturing facilities. A freeze on research appointments was one consequence; another was a constraint on space which followed the relocation of those employees remaining at 41st Street to Tuckahoe.[39] Despite these limitations, beginning from a low base, the number of new compounds synthesized at Tuckahoe increased to an unprecedented 250 in 1947/8.[40] However, successive annual presidential reports contained expressions of appreciation for important scientific developments during the 1950s[41] and regularly alluded to the crucial role of research and development leading to achieve product innovation. Creasy's observation in 1960 was typical: "Unfortunately, the fates did not see fit to crown the efforts of the research staff with the discovery of products that could be added to our list of goods for sale … There is every confidence that the constant industrious search by our research staff will eventually provide useful medicinal agents to present to the medical profession."[42] Discontinuance of the production of Dexin and of Kepler products in 1954 marked the end of the company's trade in dietetic food, a decision taken on financial grounds. Coe recalled that the American directors "all hoped that research would come up with something, because the only answer in our business … was a really brand new product that would do something for somebody. Not just a product that you could sell but one that would do something … We wanted to have a research-based business, and we wanted to have products out of research that were unique to us and had good markets."[43] By planning investment, improving productivity, assiduous marketing, and energetic selling by the sales staff, the directors were attentive to those areas of activity over which they had control; but for a fast-selling product innovation to emerge from the laboratories they felt that they could do little more than hope that their approach to the management of the unexpected would succeed.[44]

CHAPTER 4

Empirin, a dominant leader in the US market for analgesics from the 1940s to the 1970s and its decline

The failure of R&D to generate new products of sufficient commercial importance to satisfy Creasy's ambitions for the company left it increasingly dependent upon sales of Empirin from the end of the war until the 1960s. At their peak, Empirin Compound and Empirin Compound with Codeine accounted for 60 per cent of total sales. Empirin underpinned the company's financial viability. During the 1950s, average profit on Empirin Compound sales was roughly 70 per cent, and 50 per cent on sales of Empirin Compound Codeine Phosphate (percentages described by Coe as much below the company's definition of "normal profit").[1] Annual average pre-tax profit as a percentage of total sales at that time was 20 per cent. Still outwardly optimistic, Creasy expressed confidence in the policy of "holding the line" until research staff achieved a breakthrough.[2] Meanwhile, Empirin Compound samples were used as "door openers." Empirin was offered to receptionists and nurses as a method of gaining access to doctors to enable sales representatives to push other products.[3]

During the 1940s and early 1950s, the highest selling products consisted almost entirely of combinations of new forms of existing products. Creasy's policy could be described as one of interim innovation, awaiting drug discoveries and entirely new products to emerge from the laboratories at Tuckahoe. The most promising area for research with a potential for developing products which might secure volume sales and profit after World War II was that of multiple broad spectrum antibiotics. The origin of these new types of antibiotics was the discovery, among many medical practitioners, that under certain conditions when using large doses of penicillin or streptomycin involving more than a single organism, effective antibiotic therapy presented a serious risk of causing toxic effects. Under conditions where a strain of micro-organisms developed a resistance to a particular antibiotic, or when bugs were only moderately sensitive to one antibiotic, the use of broad spectrum antibiotics was considered to be desirable. Such products began to enter the US market in profusion in 1951 when sixteen manufacturers marketed twenty-one different products.[4] All of these companies were among the twenty who had participated in the WPB productivity program and most had also been involved in the Committee of Medical Research of the Office of Scientific Research (CMR) initiative created in 1942.[5] Doubtless cognizant of the furious pace of growth in the market and perhaps also alarmed at the speed with which firms were exploiting it, Creasy's intuitive sense for commercial opportunity led him in the same direction.

Unusually, in this instance, drug development was initiated not by scientists but by Creasy, though he depended on scientists, primarily those employed in de Beer's laboratory, to implement his plan. The parent company's history of antibiotic production had left it far behind other British, let alone American, manufacturers. None the less, WFL's scientists' previous research in this area enabled BW&Co. to insert itself into the highly competitive American market. Polymixin B, a large molecule polypeptide, had begun to attract attention among scientists in the late 1940s. Scientists at Beckenham had initially expressed confidence in the drug's potential for successful development for use in the treatment of typhoid fever or whooping cough. However, according to Creasy, although the board of WFL continued to express optimism regarding the future development of polymixin B, Beckenham scientists accorded it a low priority among other R&D activities and "pretty much gave up on the drug."[6] The American company secured the assistance of Pfizer, for whom BW&Co. had ceased to distribute penicillin shortly after the war. More assistance was provided by several investigators in American university laboratories who undertook further research and testing of polymixin B. In 1952, the (FDA) approved the company's parental (intrathecal) aerosporin, though for extremely limited application restricted to pseudomonas meningitis.

Creasy was not deterred by this partial success. His view was that, should it be possible to secure FDA approval for wider uses of the drug, the American company would be able to gain access to the greater commercial possibilities offered by the burgeoning antibiotics field. He sought further advice from the leading expert in the field, Dr Jawetz, who was also one of the academics involved in the testing program at the University of California.[7] Jawetz was asked how it might be possible to extend the number of uses for the drug in order to make it commercially worthwhile to manufacture. Because poor absorption and distribution would prevent the drug reaching the infections, Jawetz dismissed the suggestions made to Creasy by the British scientists regarding its suitability for the treatment of whooping cough and typhoid fever. He maintained that searching for treatments for whooping cough and typhoid would be to follow a false trail and advised pursuing development of the drug for a different purpose. He recommended incorporation into topical preparations for use in body cavities such as ears, eyes, bladder, and skin pores. Specifically, he suggested exploiting the drug's high potency by incorporating it in a number of suitable vehicles; for example, propylene glycol for the ear, light petroleum base for the skin, and aqueous solutions for the eye and other infected areas.

Creasy outlined the process by which, through R&D, the Sporin range had been created and developed. Following a strategy first adopted in the 1940s with the launch of Lanoxin, direct contact with medical specialists was the key; "... we were able to seek out and obtain excellent help from a few outstanding dermatologists, ophthalmologists, otologists, and others to quickly try these preparations to help us get them approved and on the market."[8] Initially, Polysporin consisted of polymixin incorporating bacitracin. When bacitracin proved to be unstable it was replaced by gramicidin, though that too was superseded by neomycin and even later by a steroid. Through the iterative process involving scientists from Tuckahoe and a network of university researchers, the company entered the US market for antibiotics with Polysporin, Aerosporin, and Cortisporin, each receiving FDA approval in 1952.[9]

Table 4.1 *New products from Tuckahoe, 1949–1959*

	Brand name	*Drug*	*Application*
1949	VASOXYL Hydrochloride	Methoxamine Hydrochloride	vasopressor
1950	SYNCURINE	Decamthonium Bromide	muscle-relaxing agent
1950	PERAZIL	Chlorcyclizine Hydrochloride	long-acting anti-histamine
1951	ANECTINE Chloride	Suiccinylcholine Chloride	muscle-relaxing agent
1952	DARAPRIM	Pyrimethamine	antimalarial
1952	AEROSPORIN/ CORTISPORIN/ POLYSPORIN	Polymixin B Sulfate products	antibiotics
1953	PURINETHOL	6-Mercaptopurine	leukemia treatment
1953	ANTEPAR	Piperazinne Citrate	anthelmintic treatment
1954	MAREZINE	Cyclizine	motion sickness
1957	CARDILATE	Nifedipine	angina treatment
1957	SUDAFED	Pseudophedrine Hydrochloride	decongestant for the common cold
1959	ACTIFED	Tripolidine Hydrochloride Pseudophedrine	decongestant for sinusitis/ hay fever
1959	EMPRAZIL	Caffeine Tripolidine Hydrochloride Pseudophedrine	Decongestsnt, analgesic, anti-histamenic, and anti-pyratic drug for common cold/flu

After launch, sales of these products remained among the top half-dozen products sold by the company throughout the 1950s and 1960s. From 11 per cent in 1958, sporin sales rose to 17 per cent in 1962, second only to Empirin. Creasy described the various sporin products containing polymyxin as high profit products.[10] In 1959/60, sales totalled $3.8 million and generated profits of $2.5 million.[11] This paralleled the growth of antibiotics occurring in the US market. The years between 1950 and 1957 saw a sevenfold increase in the sale of antibiotics in the US which compared well with a doubling of the sale of other pharmaceuticals.[12] This reflected a general growth trend in the consumption of prescription medicines. A survey conducted by Abbott laboratories (the first of a series of annual reviews) valued the total prescriptions at $603 million in 1948; by 1958 the figure had risen to $2,043 million. A commentator, writing in the *American Druggist,* attributed this trend to a rise in the volume, novelty, efficacy, quality, and resulting expense of drugs,[13] though inflation also contributed to the rise. Other relevant factors were a 15 per cent increase in the number of physicians and a rise in the average prescriptions which they issued.[14] Anti-infectives accounted for 19 per cent of all prescriptions, sedatives for 15 per cent, cardiovasculars for 7 per cent, and analgesics, dermatologics, and antispasmodics for 6 per cent. Cough preparations, metabolics, and anti-allergics each accounted for 5 per cent.

The development of antibiotics mitigated the company's heavy dependency on Empirin and enabled Creasy to persist with the wait and see attitude to Tuckahoe scientists which rendered the company vulnerable once the larger companies possessing substantial advertising budgets entered the market for analgesics. Bufferin and Anacin began to compete with Tabloid Empirin Compound. Darvon and Zactirin competed with Tabloid Empirin Compound Codeine Phosphate which was claimed to be as potent as Codeine yet completely non-addictive. Darvon aroused special concern when in 1957, Lilly's preparation entered the market. This, Creasy feared, offered dismayingly great promise and posed a serious threat to the Empirin business. In an unusually specific appeal to the scientists, Creasy urged them to discover "a useful, simple, non-narcotic analgesic to protect the annual $10 million Empirin Compound business; a useful therapeutic agent to be used prophylactically in the treatment of angine pectoris; a useful oral antihypertension agent; and perhaps a tranquillizing agent that would enable the company to invade this highly profitable market."[15] Action took the form of assembling a team of six working on analgesic research under Dr John C. Seed who embarked on a program to reactivate analgesic screening and to undertake a further search for superior analgesic drugs. The team met every two weeks to exchange data, analyse results, and plan further work. Screening and testing were carried out in a search for a non-addictive analgesic which might deter Lilly from pressing on with the launch of Darvon.[16]

Creasy also sought to discredit Lilly's drug by using evidence from the listing by the WHO Expert Committee on Narcotics which included propoxyphane (an ingredient in Darvon) among addictive drugs. Lilly sought to secure the removal of propoxyphane from the WHO list and at the same time lobbied the State Department against the Karsten Bill which included a provision banning addictive substances. On the Bill's return to Congress, Burroughs Wellcome & Co. (USA) Inc. lobbied in its favor. Creasy arranged an addiction study conducted by Dr Nathan Eddy, pharmacologist and secretary of the Narcotic Committee of the National Research Council who was also a member of the WHO Expert Committee. The purpose of the study was to determine the relative addictive properties of Empirin Compound with Codeine compared with Lilly's Daran, Wyeth's Zactirin, and Ende's Perodan. A similar comparative study was conducted by Dr Lasagne of Johns Hopkins Medical School.[17] The results were inconclusive and the Bill failed to pass through Congress, heralding a period of intense competition in the market for analgesics, though during the 1960s Empirin was presented with an even more serious legal challenge to codeine-based products.

Just as Creasy's capacity for identifying opportunities and his use of networks had been instrumental in the development of the sporins, his sensitivity to market possibilities and networks also proved to be important in the development of relatively commercially successful antihistamines and decongestants used as treatments for respiratory illnesses. The development of antihistamines had been disappointing. In 1954, Marezine, a type of antihistamine motion sickness drug, had received FDA permission to be sold as an OTC product through retail pharmacies. The lack of advertising support comparable to that with which larger companies had marketed their competing products, left Marezine below 3 per cent of sales in the market throughout the 1950s and 1960s.[18] The origin of these antihistamines contained elements of serendipity. Hitherto, pseudoephedrine had been manufactured at Dartford in the UK, and was sold as an unbranded preparation in the US by the American company When WFL decided to cease production of the drug, Coe (at that time head of the distribution unit), recommended dropping antihistamines from the company's price list. He argued that the dominance in the market, already established by Schering and Chemische Industrie Basel (CIBA), limited the company's capacity to expand from the current small sales base. Staff in the research and medical departments concurred.

However, expressions of concern by sales staff in California (where virtually all of the company's antihistamines were sold) led Creasy to consult Dr Shirley Baron in San Francisco. He was the principal prescriber of the drug, regarding the probable consequences of discontinuing the supply of Marezine. His view was that the company "hadn't scratched the surface of its wider potential,"[19] either used alone or in combination with other antihistamines; his firm belief was that dropping the drug would be a mistake. This view, in conjunction with his discovery of the extent of sales in the region, prompted Creasy to disregard Coe's recommendation to end antihistamine-related R&D. Creasy's proposal to the board was that clinical trials of the combination antihistamines should be initiated as a matter of urgency. Subject to satisfactory outcomes from clinical trials on combination antihistamines conducted through leading allergists, the company should then proceed with production by the chemical manufacturing department. In the event of a successful outcome, additional sales would provide the plant with much needed additional throughput. Creasy proposed that whichever preparation under trial should be chosen for production, the distribution unit should arrange for branding prior to marketing nationally. The board accepted his proposals and the trials went ahead. The result was the selection of pseudoephedrine combined with Perazil and Actidil brand Triprolidine Hydrochloride, an exceptionally potent antihistamine first developed in 1951. Sudafed

Tablets and Syrup entered the market in 1957. Actifed (another combined drug containing Actidil and Sudafed) followed in 1958. These too were prescription drugs, with the exception of a 30mg Sudafed, a sugar-coated red pill which was sold over the counter. By 1961/2, these products accounted for 7 per cent of total company sales compared with shares of 17 per cent by the sporins; the share commanded by Empirin products (60 per cent in 1953) was 41 per cent, in relative decline but continuing to dominate the company's fortunes.[20]

Stagnating Empirin sales from the mid 1950s reduced the proportion to 33 per cent during the 1960s. This was partly attributable to competition and the erosion of fair trade agreements which until that time had enabled the company to require wholesalers with exclusive contracts to sell Wellcome's products to maintain retail prices determined by the company.[21] However, the proliferation of sales outlets for drugs (notably chain stores, discount houses, variety stores, and buying clubs) introduced on the West Coast where the company's sales were growing the fastest, created an increasingly competitive market in which price-cutting posed a threat to traditional drug stores and to pharmaceutical manufacturers. Between 1951 and 1955, successful challenges in the State legislatures on the unconstitutional basis of Fair Trade in its treatment of non-signatories[22] led a rapidly increasing number of State courts to nullify their local fair trade acts.[23] The consequences were immediate. In 1955, finding that price-cutting sellers were unwilling to yield to threatening letters, the sales department introduced a 40 per cent margin for retailers at Fair Trade prices on the company's entire product range.[24] Costly legal challenges met with no success. In 1962, Fair Trade was deemed to be effective in only nineteen states.[25]

The decline of price maintenance affected Empirin's profitability (and that of other products), rather than sales, whereas the threat presented by the FDA challenged the very existence of the product. This occurred at a time when the pharmaceutical industry generally was subjected to increasing public scrutiny, criticism from government, and a loss of trust among the public. Evidence given at hearings, begun in 1959 and organized by the Senate Sub-Committee on Anti Trust and Monopoly, received widespread publicity and attracted extensive condemnation of the industry. The Thalidomide tragedy of 1961 caused public outrage after the sedative drug, introduced in the late 1950s, was discovered to have resulted in serous life-changing birth defects in children of mothers for whom it had been prescribed. Withdrawal of the drug from the market in 1961 neither quelled public outrage nor removed prevailing apprehension regarding the industry. It was in this climate that Congress was discussing a bill, proposed by Senators Kefauver and Celler, aimed at tightening regulation of the industry. It had seemed likely that the proposed restrictions would be diluted by agreement between the Senate Judiciary Committee and the Pharmaceutical Manufacturers' Association which had lobbied hard. However, President J. F. Kennedy intervened to rule out compromise after which Senate passed the Bill unanimously, enabling the original Kefauver-Harris Amendments to the Food, Drug and Cosmetics Act to become law, effective from October 1962.[26]

This marked the beginning of a continuous process in which Federal control over the industry's activities in inter-state commerce was strengthened, clinical trial procedures reformed, and companies obliged to adapt and conform to the new regulations with immediate effect. Evidence of effectiveness for drugs proposed for regulatory approval and marketing under the 1938 statute, hitherto requiring only notification, was replaced by a requirement of substantial evidence (meaning adequate and well-controlled) prior to pre-market approval. The requirement for good manufacturing practices when combined with federal government inspection was another important innovation. As a prerequisite to human studies, adequate preclinical toxicity studies were mandatory and extensive record-keeping imposed. Health and Human Services, which appointed the FDA commissioner, was empowered to remove from the market any drug regarded as constituting an immediate hazard to the public. Drug advertising was also the subject of tighter regulation.[27] The immediate impact of the new amendments on the company was the implication for the production and marketing of Empirin products.

The specific challenge to Empirin originated in ongoing investigations into drugs that might possess potential for serious adverse side effects, into which category were placed those containing acetophenetidin. After European physicians had suggested that excessive use might produce kidney damage resulting from phenacetin nephritis, members of the medical bureau of the FDA pressed for strong warning notices to be included on labels for Empirin and similar preparations. Although many other researchers remained sceptical, newspaper and magazine articles appeared in which unqualified assertions conveyed a general impression that phenacetin was indeed dangerous. In anticipation of harmful effects on sales, should such a perception gain ground among physicians and the public, the company mounted a strong educational campaign in defence of analgesic combinations such as Empirin Compound. With the company's encouragement, the WHO arranged a meeting of investigators from several countries to discuss the issue. Their conclusions were wholly sceptical of the link, each beginning with the phrase "It is not known if …" For two years, Creasy deployed such evidence in letters he wrote to everyone connected with the FDA.[28]

Although members of the FDA advisory committee were divided over the evidence on renal damage attributable to phenacetin, none the less in 1963, the labelling of all such products was required to contain a specific reference to the possibility that liver damage was possible. Adverse publicity, reinforced by the label warning, began to affect sales of the Compound, although overall sales of Empirin (which included Empirin with codeine phosphate) did not fall. In 1964, the company issued a four-page statement that appeared in the *American Druggist* drawing attention to conclusions reached by the company's scientists after consultation with experts in renal physiology and renal diseases. A brief report of their review of all relevant international studies undertaken since 1953 concluded with a systematic rebuttal of the claims.[29] Providing dosage was in accordance with instructions on the labels, they maintained that Empirin Compound and its combination with codeine phosphate were "reliable,

Empirin with Codeine was one of the most popular variants of the aspirin-based analgesic in the US during the 1950s and 1960s. *JAMA*. Wellcome Library, London.

effective, and safe analgesics for the relief of pain and headache."[30] Copies of the critical review and a comprehensive bibliography on analgesic abuse were made available to the medical profession and to the public.[31]

Nevertheless, sales of Empirin products stagnated during the 1960s. One reason was the company's inability to reassure prescribers, pharmacists, and patients; the other was competition from Bayer aspirin, Bristol Myers' Bufferin, American Home Products' Anacin, and Tylenol produced by a newcxomer to the analgesics market.[32] Johnson & Johnson, the leading consumer pharmaceuticals company mounted a multi-pronged assault on the market applying large scale manufacturing combined with a comprehensive, high cost marketing strategy. The campaign began with a successful legal action to undermine the monopolistic pricing policy imposed by the Mallinckrodt company which supplied the trade with gum opium, the critical ingredient in codeine. Johnson & Johnson succeeded in securing a license to import gum opium and to manufacture its own codeine. One incidental result was a reduction in the price of gum which was also of potential benefit to Burroughs Wellcome & Co. (USA) Inc. Johnson & Johnson's competitive pain medication product, branded as Tylenol, was reformulated by replacing phenacetin with paracetamol, trumpeted in advertisements as a less noxious formula. Johnson & Johnson's intensive marketing program was aimed at persuading potential consumers that, whereas taking aspirin was dangerous, Tylenol (albeit virtually an identical product) was safe, an approach strengthened by an article published in the *New England Journal of Medicine* which linked aspirin (given in the form APC and codeine to relieve pain) with internal bleeding.[33] Finally, at the frontline of sales, retailers received an introductory 15 per cent discount on Tylenol orders.[34]

The view of senior scientists at Tuckahoe who advised Creasy and Coe, was that aspirin was no more damaging for ulcers than Tylenol was for liver complaints. Another difficulty facing the company in defending Empirin was an inability to demonstrate that phenacetin and caffeine (the other ingredients additional to aspirin) contributed to the effectiveness of the compound as required by the new FDA regulations on efficacy, part of the legislative amendments introduced in 1962. This was not immediately demonstrable because no such studies had been carried out – and time proved to be critical in enabling Johnson & Johnson to establish Tylenol as the new market leader.[35] Throughout his presidency, Creasy resisted reformulation and although, by the time Coe became president in 1968, a large majority of board members still supported Creasy's policy, Coe exercised his presidential veto.[36] The introduction of new specifications for the company's analgesics would take time to achieve. Meanwhile, as a proportion of the company's sales, Empirin fell from 40 per cent in 1960 to 26 per cent in 1970, a decline to which the original Empirin Compound containing phenacetin was mainly attributable, though rising sales of broad spectrum antibiotics was also a factor.[37] Whereas in 1960, sales of Empirin Compound and Empirin Compound with codeine phosphate were roughly equal, by 1970, the original compound accounted for 9 per cent compared with 17 per cent for the newer product. The short term response to competition took the form of advertising campaigns and promotions with prizes that included automobiles intended to persuade the medical and allied professions to continue to prescribe or recommend Empirin Compound while pharmacists were offered higher discounts to encourage them to increase stocks.[38] A national sampling program intended to reach fifty-five million people failed to stem the steady erosion of Empirin's position in the market.

When a new formulation was introduced in 1977, advertisements adopted a more defensive tone. Empracet with codeine was described as a new-non-aspirin/codeine analgesic for modest to severe pain and packaged containing warnings and contra-indications for those sensitive to acetaminorphen or to codeine. A survey carried out by the *American Druggist* in the same year revealed that for headache relief, 31 per cent of retailers normally recommended Percogesic, 18 per cent Tylenol, and 11 per cent Empirin. Phenacetin was finally removed from Empirin for sale over the counter in 1979. In 1980, Empirin with codeine was advertised as "no longer contain[ing] phenacetin and caffeine."[39] Desperately hanging on to the brand, the company continued to market a phenacetin-containing analgesic, Tabloid brand APC with codeine, aimed at physicians who continued to prefer to prescribe this combination.[40] The final attempt to rescue the Empirin brand failed in the face of competition. By the late 1970s, the clear market leader to emerge from this competition was Tylenol which was manufactured by the McNeil Laboratories supported by the huge investment and marketing skills of Johnson & Johnson. William Sullivan, who joined the company in 1973 as general counsel and later became president,[41] concluded that the sheer weight and brilliance of Johnson & Johnson's marketing campaign had been the key factor in capturing the US market for headache remedies.[42] Reformulation and renaming proved to be too late. Empirin had ceased to be one of the most instantly recognized national brands in the pharmaceutical trade.

Replacing Empirin as the company's brand leader, was another veteran product, Lanoxin (digoxin), which, though remaining unchanged in four decades, was widely regarded to represent a standard to which competitors must aspire. Lanoxin was

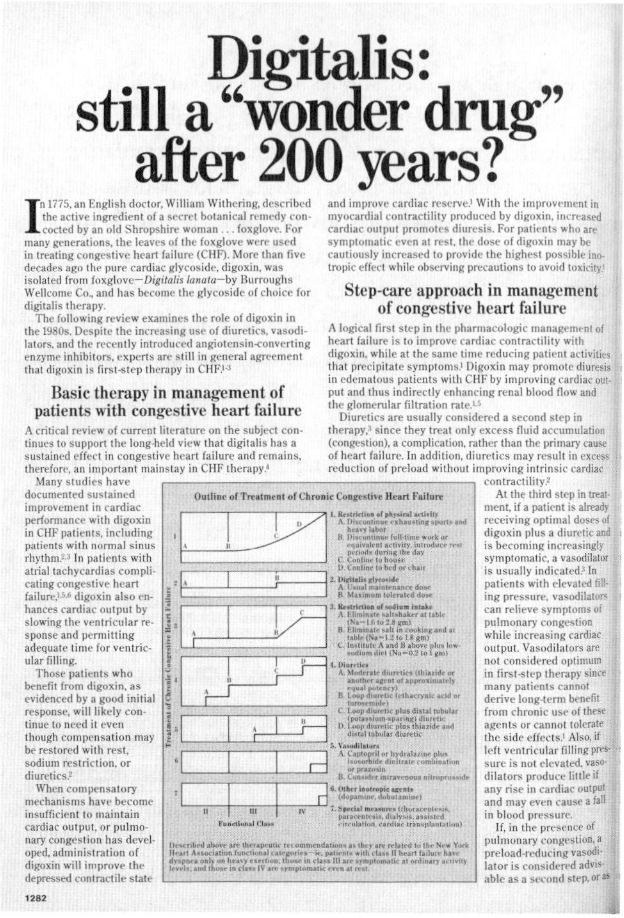

Digitalis: still a "wonder drug" after 200 years?

In 1775, an English doctor, William Withering, described the active ingredient of a secret botanical remedy concocted by an old Shropshire woman . . . foxglove. For many generations, the leaves of the foxglove were used in treating congestive heart failure (CHF). More than five decades ago the pure cardiac glycoside, digoxin, was isolated from foxglove—*Digitalis lanata*—by Burroughs Wellcome Co., and has become the glycoside of choice for digitalis therapy.

The following review examines the role of digoxin in the 1980s. Despite the increasing use of diuretics, vasodilators, and the recently introduced angiotensin-converting enzyme inhibitors, experts are still in general agreement that digoxin is first-step therapy in CHF.[1-3]

Basic therapy in management of patients with congestive heart failure

A critical review of current literature on the subject continues to support the long-held view that digitalis has a sustained effect in congestive heart failure and remains, therefore, an important mainstay in CHF therapy.[4]

Many studies have documented sustained improvement in cardiac performance with digoxin in CHF patients, including patients with normal sinus rhythm.[2,3] In patients with atrial tachycardias complicating congestive heart failure,[1,5,6] digoxin also enhances cardiac output by slowing the ventricular response and permitting adequate time for ventricular filling.

Those patients who benefit from digoxin, as evidenced by a good initial response, will likely continue to need it even though compensation may be restored with rest, sodium restriction, or diuretics.[2]

When compensatory mechanisms have become insufficient to maintain cardiac output, or pulmonary congestion has developed, administration of digoxin will improve the depressed contractile state and improve cardiac reserve.[1] With the improvement in myocardial contractility produced by digoxin, increased cardiac output promotes diuresis. For patients who are symptomatic even at rest, the dose of digoxin may be cautiously increased to provide the highest possible inotropic effect while observing precautions to avoid toxicity.[1]

Step-care approach in management of congestive heart failure

A logical first step in the pharmacologic management of heart failure is to improve cardiac contractility with digoxin, while at the same time reducing patient activities that precipitate symptoms.[1] Digoxin may promote diuresis in edematous patients with CHF by improving cardiac output and thus indirectly enhancing renal blood flow and the glomerular filtration rate.[1,5]

Diuretics are usually considered a second step in therapy,[3] since they treat only excess fluid accumulation (congestion), a complication, rather than the primary cause of heart failure. In addition, diuretics may result in excess reduction of preload without improving intrinsic cardiac contractility.[2]

At the third step in treatment, if a patient is already receiving optimal doses of digoxin plus a diuretic and is becoming increasingly symptomatic, a vasodilator is usually indicated.[3] In patients with elevated filling pressure, vasodilators can relieve symptoms of pulmonary congestion while increasing cardiac output. Vasodilators are not considered optimum in first-step therapy since many patients cannot derive long-term benefit from chronic use of these agents or cannot tolerate the side effects.[1] Also, if left ventricular filling pressure is not elevated, vasodilators produce little if any rise in cardiac output and may even cause a fall in blood pressure.

If, in the presence of pulmonary congestion, a preload-reducing vasodilator is considered advisable as a second step, or as

Outline of Treatment of Chronic Congestive Heart Failure

1. **Restriction of physical activity**
   A. Discontinue exhausting sports and heavy labor
   B. Discontinue full-time work or equivalent activity, introduce rest periods during the day
   C. Confine to house
   D. Confine to bed or chair
2. **Digitalis glycoside**
   A. Usual maintenance dose
   B. Maximum tolerated dose
3. **Restriction of sodium intake**
   A. Eliminate saltshaker at table (Na—1.6 to 2.8 gm)
   B. Eliminate salt in cooking and at table (Na—1.2 to 1.8 gm)
   C. Institute A and B above plus low-sodium diet (Na—0.2 to 1 gm)
4. **Diuretics**
   A. Moderate diuretics (thiazide or another agent of approximately equal potency)
   B. Loop diuretic (ethacrynic acid or furosemide)
   C. Loop diuretic plus distal tubular (potassium-sparing) diuretic
   D. Loop diuretic plus thiazide and distal tubular diuretic
5. **Vasodilators**
   A. Captopril or hydralazine plus isosorbide dinitrate combination or prazosin
   B. Consider intravenous nitroprusside
6. **Other inotropic agents** (dopamine, dobutamine)
7. **Special measures** (thoracentesis, paracentesis, dialysis, assisted circulation, cardiac transplantation)

Described above are therapeutic recommendations as they are related to the New York Heart Association functional categories—ie, patients with class II heart failure have dyspnea only on heavy exertion; those in class III are symptomatic at ordinary activity levels; and those in class IV are symptomatic even at rest.

1282

Originating from digitalis purpurea used for congestive heart failure since the eighteenth century, Digoxin was a standardized substitute marketed by WFL from 1934. Lanoxin was the trade name for the drug: "Still a wonder drug after 200 years?" *JAMA*. Wellcome Library, London.

a branded substitute for digitalis (hitherto extracted from the foxglove) which originated in the Wellcome research laboratories at Beckenham before World War II. After 1929 digoxin became the drug of choice to treat heart failure. However, after World War II WFL ceased producing digoxin, a retreat from the market which at Tuckahoe was regarded as an opportunity. Refinements and improvements in methods of extraction and purification enabled BW&Co. to promote the product as new and improved. The trade name Lanoxin was acquired from the parent company and deployed in an advertising campaign and a new strategy for development and marketing was introduced.[43] Unlike the model adopted to promote Globin insulin which left detail men to contact GPs and interns, the new approach involved scientists connecting with cardiac specialists located in 15 "centres of influence", an approach which allowed for both education and a more subtle method of promotion. Similarly the launching of Syncuine and Anectine in 1950–1951 involved cultivating relations with key anaesthesiologists.[44]

The linking of the final stages of a product's development to promotion through appropriate influential medical elites was applied to the launch of subsequent

a component of an initial regimen, such therapy will be more compatible with the action of digoxin than the effects produced by a diuretic.[1]

Digoxin hemodynamics in patients with CHF

Digoxin provides direct-acting inotropic action to maintain pump function in the failing heart. It also indirectly produces generalized vasodilation in the CHF patient, in contrast to the vasoconstriction seen in normals.[1,6] Vasodilation is a result of the increase in cardiac output, which produces a reflex decrease in sympathetic tone.[5]

Digoxin also reduces myocardial oxygen consumption in the CHF patient by 1) reducing heart rate, 2) reducing heart size and intramyocardial tension, and 3) reducing afterload.[1,6]

Among the other hemodynamic effects of digoxin: reduction of the left ventricular end diastolic pressure and pulmonary capillary wedge pressure; reduction of pulmonary congestion; improvement of renal function by improving renal blood flow and glomerular filtration rate; and reduction in the tubular reabsorption of sodium.[1]

The role of digoxin in patients with ischemic heart disease and CHF

Despite the increase in myocardial oxygen demand caused by the increase in contractility, digoxin decreases such demand in the patient with angina and congestive heart failure.[1,6] By reducing heart rate and heart size, myocardial oxygen demand is decreased, more than compensating for the oxygen-consuming effect of improved contractility. And digoxin further reduces myocardial oxygen demand by decreasing intramyocardial tension through a reduction in left ventricular end diastolic pressure.[1] Digoxin also has been found to improve coronary perfusion in patients with left ventricular dysfunction and congestive heart failure.[1]

Now digoxin is better than ever

Lanoxicaps® (digoxin solution in capsules) provides state-of-the-art digoxin delivery. Bioavailability is virtually the same as with IV administration (90%-100%). It is well known that the more completely a drug is absorbed, the less will its absorption vary among patients and in the same patient with time.[7] Accordingly, the more rapid and more complete absorption of digoxin from Lanoxicaps results in more consistent serum concentrations of digoxin and increased safety for many patients. These same principles also apply when considering the effects of concomitant therapy with any of the many drugs known to interact with digoxin. The enhanced bioavailability of digoxin administered as Lanoxicaps minimizes such interactions and provides less variable serum concentrations and greater safety in patients on coadministered drugs.

References

1. Smith TW, Braunwald E: The management of heart failure, in Braunwald E (ed): *Heart Disease: A Textbook of Cardiovascular Medicine*, ed 2. Philadelphia, WB Saunders Co, 1984, pp 503-559.
2. Spann JF, Hurst JW: Treatment of heart failure, in Hurst JW (ed-in-chief): *The Heart: Arteries and Veins*, ed 4. New York, McGraw-Hill Book Co, 1978, pp 580-606.
3. Smith TW: Digitalis in the management of heart failure. *Hosp Pract* 1984; 19:67-92.
4. Storstein L, Taylor SH: New and old inotropic drugs: Controversies and challenges, Oslo, Norway, May 21-22, 1982: Reflections on inotropic drugs: A personal commentary. *Clin Cardiol* 1984;7:119-124.
5. Agents used to treat congestive heart failure. *AMA Drug Evaluations*, ed 5. Chicago, American Medical Association, 1983, pp 601-609.
6. Sloan RW: Digitalis glycosides. *Am Fam Physician* 1983;28:206-216.
7. Koch-Weser J: Bioavailability of drugs (second of two parts): Therapeutic importance of bioavailability factors. *N Engl J Med* 1974;291:503-506.

Lanoxin became one of BW&Co.'s flagship products widely accepted among the medical profession as meeting the highest standard thereby boosting the company's reputation. Lanoxicaps solution in capsules introduced in the 1980s offered cardiac patients an increased rate of absorption. *JAMA*. Wellcome Library, London.

drugs. The potential for generics to penetrate the market based on lower prices was considerable, as long as efficacy proved to be comparable to that of Lanoxin. Competition from generics did, however, necessitate similar pricing for Lanoxin. When a study initiated by the Federal Drug Administration (FDA) revealed that some hospitals were encountering trouble when using the generics (normal dosage failed to produce comparable effectiveness to the Wellcome product), hospitals turned to Lanoxin. Medical schools had long acknowledged the instant effectiveness of the drug, though there was a narrow range of control existing between toxicity and therapeutic value, but Lanoxin was perceived to be a safe drug because dosage could be easily and speedily varied in treatment. Lanoxin became the drug of choice for cardiac conditions in the 1960s, by which time the company had secured 90 per cent of the heart failure market.[45] In branded or generic form, it was advertised in 1974 as the preferred treatment for cardiac conditions, having had "no recalls for thirty-eight years of uniform potency and persistent effect."[46] The drug did not, however, generate substantial profits.

PART TWO:

The pursuit of new products, management crises, and intervention by the Wellcome Trust

CHAPTER 5

Is the doctor in?
Product development and the "detailing" of doctors in the market for prescription drugs

Although the degree to which the company relied on a single product may have been untypical, the high degree of competition in the industry and the forms which it took suggest that the pressure for innovation experienced by Burroughs Wellcome and Co. (USA) Inc. was not unique. The number of new drugs, introduced into the market annually, rose steadily between 1940 and 1962. Between 1951 and 1955 the figure was forty-two, rising to fifty-two between 1956 and 1960. The regulatory legislation in 1962 resulted in a fall in averages by more than one-half during the remainder of the decade, falling further during the 1970s.[1]

Although the rise in the number of new drugs during the 1950s might suggest a highly innovative industry, a contemporary analysis of new drug introductions published annually in the *American Druggist* between the 1950s and 1960s reveals subtle differences in the character of innovation. The study draws distinctions between the discovery and introduction of completely new chemicals and (a) duplicates of drugs already in the market, (b) combinations of compounds of previously marketed ingredients, and (c) new dosage forms. Almost without exception, between 1955 and 1962, duplicates of existing drugs exceeded the number of new chemicals introduced into the market by roughly one-half. New dosage forms of drugs were twice as high as new chemicals, though the difference diminished sharply after the 1962 legislation. The greatest contrast, however, was between the number of new chemicals introduced and the number of combination compounds of previously marketed ingredients; these were between three and five times as great as the number of new chemicals, a ratio which persisted, though at lower absolute levels, after 1962.[2] The figures suggest the importance of novelty and ingenuity (much of it revolving around antibiotics during the 1950s), rather than basic science as the dominant influence on the competition in the industry during this period.

While awaiting the emergence of commercially significant drug discoveries from the laboratories throughout the period, the company relied heavily on the introduction of combination compounds, the manufacture of duplicates of competitors' products,

Table 5.1 *Major products sold by BW (USA) Inc. 1960–1972 (%)*

	Empirin	*Lanoxin*	*Anectine*	*Sporins*	*Sudafed/ Actifed*	*Zyloprim*
1959/60	45	4	3	16		
1960/1	44	5	4	18		
1961/2	41	5	5	19		
1962/3	38	6	5	18		
1963/4	36	6	5	17	11	
1964/5	36	7	4	20	10	
1965/6	33	7	4	22	13	
1966/7	31	7	4	21	12	
1967/8	28	6	3	21	12	10
1968/9	27	6	3	20	15	12
1969/70	26	6	2	20	15	14
1970/1	24	6		21	17	15
1971/2	23	6		21	19	16

Sources: GWHC, BW&Co. (USA) Inc., 107.01/02, President's annual reports.

and revised dosage forms. In part, as an attempt to counter substitution (and even counterfeiting) in the market, the company became one of a growing number of pharmaceutical manufacturers to establish brand identification through shape, size, and color, or special markings on products.[3] In the absence of significant drug innovation yielding new products, improvements in sales organisation, advertising, and promotional activity resumed their central importance in the company's commercial policy shortly after World War II ended.

Although Coe was recruited as an engineer with special responsibility for time and motion analysis and adaptation of the production systems, he was also given responsibility in 1951 for overseeing the reorganisation of distribution, the recruitment of more detail men,[4] and reforming training for sales staff. Much of the actual design and implementation was delegated to T. R. Holmes, a graduate of Connecticut School of Pharmacy and one of the company's former detail men. He became the manager of a new market research department in 1943 where his prime role was to develop contacts with medical institutions in order to assess their respective sales potential.[5] The field representative staff had increased from 106 in 1945 to 143 in 1950, almost doubling between 1950 and 1960 to reach 278 (27% of the total number employed (see Table 5.2).

However, stringent financial circumstances and a shortage of experienced detail men limited numbers to below the level to which Coe aspired.[6] Within these constraints, he sought to improve the selling performance by existing staff, beginning by convening conferences attended by regional and district sales managers, field

Table 5.2 *BW&Co. field sales representatives and laboratory employment, 1945–1990*

	Total	*Field reps*	*%*	*RDM*	
1945	930	106	11		
1950	740	143	20		
1960	1040	278	27	106	10
1970	1377	462	34	242	18
1980	3403	591	17	854	25
1985	4,088			1,058	26
1990	(4,773)	(1000)*	21	1,200	25

*Estimates, *Economist*, 318, 2 March 1991, p. 74.
Sources: GWHC, BW&Co. (USA) Inc., 107.01/02, President's annual reports; Data supplied by Fred Coe Jr, by fax, 9 May 2002.

supervisors, and representatives from which emerged a redefinition of their respective roles. Each district manager was given responsibility for between ten and twenty field representatives, teaching them sales skills, checking their expense accounts, and ensuring that they "stayed legal," neither misrepresenting products to clients nor misreporting their activities to district managers. District managers also had powers of dismissal.[7] The role of sales supervisors was to monitor and evaluate annual reports that representatives were required to submit before a semi-annual appraisal and salary review. A quarterly analysis of products sold in each district and of average sales for each representative was the basis of a ranking exercise described as a useful and incentive-promoting analysis.[8]

After redefining managerial roles, attention turned to efforts to improve individual's sales performance both by providing support from the sales office and through improving selling methods. Once in the field, at the start of each quarterly promotional program, sales representatives received samples (free of charge) for distribution to physicians and other appropriate gatekeepers. A continuous flow of information, prepared by the customer service department that included sales reports and records of the volume of products sold in each district, was communicated to salesmen while in the field. These data became the basis for choosing which products should receive special promotion in each subsequent quarter.[9] A revised pocket-sized detailing and selling brochure set out the promotional program for each quarter. A supplement containing "inspirational material" consisted of extracts from medical journal articles and actual reprints considered to be of particular relevance to therapeutic developments in the laboratories. Passages from these were intended to equip salesmen with suitable quotations while detailing physicians; other suggestions (more propagandist than inspirational) were more relevant for use in selling to the trade. Armed with a leather detail bag containing drug samples and typically weighing between fifteen and twenty lbs, on an average day a detail man visited seven or eight doctors and made between thirteen and seventeen calls. Interviews of more than a few minutes were discouraged, though within that time a general principle underlying detailing was described by Baker, the advertising manager, as the more you tell the more you sell.[10]

The company's detailing strategy became increasingly focused during the 1950s and 1960s in response to an increasing trend among state, county, and city hospitals to set up purchasing departments. Hitherto, each representative had been allocated a geographical territory, hence the term territorial sales. The new approach involved designating some sales representatives as specialists in selling to hospitals and to government institutions within or across overlapping territories, but in 1951, acknowledging that the volume was beginning to grow, the company issued a brochure entitled *Selling the Hospital.* This outlined suitable approaches to this particular segment of the market.[11] Representatives attended fifty-four medical conventions and conducted twenty-five thousand interviews with physicians,[12] activities which expanded hugely over the next two decades.

During the 1950s the number of sales representatives doubled to reach four hundred; expenditure on representatives' salaries and expenses averaged 10 per cent compared with 5 per cent spent on advertising. Between 1950 and 1959, advertising expenditure and selling costs were roughly equal between 8 and 9 per cent. An approximate parity resumed until 1972, when the introduction of Septra was supported by heavy advertising cost which was reflected in the higher proportion of total marketing expenditure throughout the rest of the decade.

Table 5.3 *BW&Co. expenditure on sales and marketing, advertising, and RD&M as percentages of total sales, 1946–1975*

	Sales ($million)	*Sales and marketing*	*Advertising*	*RD&M*
1946	10,741	8	6	3
1950	11,604	9	9	3
1955	18,347	8	8	4
1960*	24,826	12	9	6
1965**	34,230	9	10	7†
1970	60,164	9	8	7
1975	142,834	6	10	12

*Includes automobile purchase scheme.
** Salaries only.
† Includes Medical Department.
Sources: GWHC, BW&Co. (USA) Inc., 107.07/11, Public affairs, "Brief analysis"; Data supplied by Fred Coe Jr, by fax, 9 May 2002.

The rapid growth of the industry produced a shortage of sales representatives possessing both training and experience, partly because of a high turnover in the industry as the rapidly expanding retail pharmacy trade proved a preferred occupation for young pharmacists.[13] In 1955, a national recruitment campaign was combined with a program intended to improve staff retention by enhancing the career prospects of existing representatives. On the basis of annual appraisal rankings and an assessment of management potential, selected members of staff were seconded to the sales office for further training and administrative experience.[14] Sales manager D. Donelson, who led the campaigns, was critical, however, of the company's traditional resistance to higher remuneration for high fliers, which he believed rendered the company vulnerable to competitors who did. Likewise, he regretted the absence of commissions and bonus payments based on an individual's sales. These policies were partly a matter of principle, but were also a consequence of the company's traditional restriction of distribution to wholesalers which meant that only records of representatives' average sales could be documented. performances[15] Donelson failed to secure reform, the practices remaining until the appointment of a new marketing director in 1970.

One aspect of the traditional approach to recruitment, however, did begin to break down during Donelson's national recruitment campaign. During the early 1950s, qualified pharmacists had accounted for slightly more than two-thirds of all representatives, including thirty licensed pharmacists of whom three were graduates of Philadelphia College, the *alma mater* of Burroughs and Wellcome. Although pharmacy graduates continued to be preferred after 1954, henceforward other suitable science graduates regarded as acceptable included biologists and zoologists, especially those who had worked their way through college.[16] Changed circumstances in the labor market and in the composition of the company's sales force required a rethinking of the training program. The architect of a new training course at Tuckahoe was Charles Singler, a graduate of the Cincinnati College of Pharmacy, who had trained at Tuckahoe. He had become a field representative and subsequently was seconded to head office to chair a detailing and selling committee responsible for the preparation of brochures for use as "the rep's bible."[17] Classroom and fieldwork training alternated in a sequence of four weeks. During four weeks of induction, staff from the medical department familiarized trainees with the scientific and technical backgrounds and therapeutic uses of the company's products. They were introduced to the functions of production, financial services, the secretariat, research and development, and selling and advertising. After training, each spent two weeks at head office followed by two to four months working in the field, returning for another two weeks at head office. The final stage consisted of two more weeks spent shadowing an experienced representative in the field before the new recruit was assigned to a territory.[18] Refresher courses were also introduced when specific problems arose relating to products. Around a dozen participants at a time were chosen to ensure diversity of experience in territories in order to ensure fruitful exchanges within the group. The refresher sessions took place in Tuckahoe for the purpose of enabling field workers to meet office staff.[19]

Sales training at Tuckahoe was an aspect of the company's approach to marketing which most impressed the consultants from Urwick Orr on their brief visit to Tuckahoe in 1966 as part of their overall review of WFL activities. They believed that the Americans' general approach to marketing was a key to explaining the contrasting records of sales and profit achieved by the company in the UK and its American subsidiary which, they concluded, would provide a model from which the entire group (though especially directors, managers, and other staff in London) had much to learn.[20] They recommended to the WFL board that senior staff from London and overseas companies should visit Tuckahoe for training, paying particular attention to the methodology employed in the design of the American training program. Singler was summoned to London to explain the system to the WFL directors and to senior marketing staff.[21] Coe recorded an account of the visit given by Singler on his return to Tuckahoe, "... it was hilarious. Guys were brought from all over to hear about our training program and then asked what they would do about it with their own staff."[22] The exchanges revealed the contrast in business culture and marketing practises. Singler's visit does not appear to have led to reform in the UK where all aspects of marketing continued to attract criticism.[23]

In a new recruitment drive, begun in 1967, letters and circulars were dispatched to twelve hundred college placement directors and one thousand private employment agencies.[24] Between 1967 and 1971 the number of representatives increased from 402 to 501 (accounting for 23 per cent of all employees) plus seventy-eight internal staff in the sales department. They included four regional sales managers, twenty-nine district sales managers, and at least ten field supervisors.[25] Among the enlarged sales force were new categories of employees who were recruited in response to President Lyndon Johnson's national crusade against discrimination and poverty. The directors announced a commitment to the national equal employment policy of non-discrimination and declared their intention to promote the recruitment of qualified minority groups to fill positions in the company at all levels. In accordance with a program of active recruitment from disadvantaged groups introduced by the National Alliance of Businessmen, the directors also approved a scheme for offering employment to twelve youths from among the long-term unemployed and summer employment to sixteen. Both groups were provided with special training. Within the year, several minority group members joined the field sales staff as did the company's first two women representatives.[26] Coinciding with the renewed recruitment drive, the entire training program underwent further reform. The previous field and introductory elements were replaced by a basic training conducted on the trainee's own territory. A new training course was devised to instruct sales representatives (chosen by district and regional sales managers) as to how to supervise those undergoing the new basic sales training programme.[27] A refresher course for veteran representatives was conducted at Tuckahoe to be attended every fourth year.[28]

The post of government sales coordinator, created in 1960, occurred in preparation for a promotional campaign intended to increase sales to the US government.[29] In the absence at that time of designated sales representatives responsible for securing government contracts, the coordinator oversaw initiatives undertaken by five special representatives assigned to medical centres in their respective territories. The main objective set for each representative was to secure a sufficient number of "physician support letters" directed to state Medicaid administrators to convince them that they should approve a product for listing on the state formulary and thereby qualify for financial compensation. Compensation was possible only if a product appeared on the formulary of the local hospital. Detailing the hospitals, therefore, continued to be as important as dealing with Medicaid administrators.[30] In 1966 representatives, in whose geographical territory government installations were located, were issued with a comprehensive brochure entitled Selling to US Government Installations, followed by a US government sales bulletin to emphasize the importance of developing this segment of the market and to provide detail advice on sales methods required to secure contracts.

The company had supplied drugs to the Veterans' Administration since World War II, but even by 1961, drug expenditure by the organisation accounted for barely one-quarter of the government's total expenditure on drugs, though that was to rise during the war in Vietnam.[31] During the 1960s, the company paid increasing attention to the various programs included in the Welfare Medical Assistance Program which was funded mostly by federal grants supplemented by matching funds by states. The estimated market for drugs created by the entire program (worth more than six billion dollars) was between 5 and 10 per cent of that figure. Information on the most important of these programs (Medicare; Medicaid; Office of Economic Opportunity Health Program; and Maternal, Infant, Child, and Youth Health Projects of the Department of H.E.W.) was supplied to field staff in fifty-five memoranda and bulletins. Direct promotional mailings to government institutions were increased from twenty-six to forty-two. Feedback on the campaign at the end of the year was reported to indicate progress in all areas.[32]

Another development was the expanding role of the medical department during the 1960s whose physician members assumed an increasing role in supporting all sales staff by providing specialist therapeutic information to assist in the promotion of the new products emerging from the laboratories. The model for this approach was a successful pioneering campaign in the 1950s to promote Anectine, a muscle-relaxant. At the outset, the role of the medical staff had been to enlist the interest, first of anaesthesiologists and then of dermatologists and ENT specialists. When Fedrazil was introduced in 1960, the medical and sales divisions combined in a program designed to "cultivate carefully" the friendship and interest of physicians specializing in allergy. Other programs, in preparation along similar lines, included the cultivation of neurologists with respect to the development of antihistamine products and synthetics.[33] In 1962, in conjunction with sales and advertising departments, the medical department prepared a medical news magazine, issued at six weekly intervals, entitled *Clinical Trends*. This was aimed at specialists in the fields of ophthalmology, otolaryngology, and allergy. The magazine was informative on the most recent developments in those fields, regardless of institutional or corporate origin, though usually it included a half-dozen advertisements featuring relevant products manufactured by Burroughs Wellcome & Co. (USA) Inc.[34]

A special program, set up to arrange pre-convention contacts between representatives with physicians who were scheduled to present papers of possible interest was judged a success; contacts led to references to the company by some speakers and elicited positive responses from convention participants.[35] After receiving approval from college deans, the sales department targeted medical and pharmacy schools, distributing brochures, reprints, and other material relevant to the company's products. Medical department staff visited important centres of influence, primarily university teaching hospitals, throughout the US where they could respond to inquiries from other physicians, interns, and medical students.[36] The view in the marketing department was that by informing professors in such institutions about the company's new products, dissemination among colleagues and students would provide beneficial results. Faculty responses complimented the "conservative, non-commercial presentation" which the company had followed.[37] In addition to assisting representatives with a large volume of inquiries from physicians, the department was responsible for the accuracy and suitability of all technical information supplied in literature, journal advertising, packing circulars, and label copy. They also gave presentations on therapeutics to representatives' training and refresher classes.[38]

In 1967, the introduction of the clinical exhibit concept was indicative of the changing balance within marketing between the long-established products, notably analgesics, and the new therapeutic medicines emerging from the laboratories. Hitherto, almost all exhibits had been confined to product-oriented displays and commentary, although a special Hitchings scientific exhibit had been a forerunner and was the first to incorporate clinical panels into medical convention units.[39] The first of a series of clinical exhibits focused on diseases and conditions was *The Story of Gout,* built around Zyloprim. The exhibit contained information on the incidence, diagnosis, and complications of gout and on the pharmacology, indications, dosage, therapeutic results, and patient benefits of Zyloprim.[40] In the early 1960s, the company turned to specialist market research service organizations, beginning with a contract with Gosselin (National Prescription Audit Services, Inc.) which specialized in prescription medicines, and another with Koehnlein & Keating which specialized in providing data on hospital medicines. The data supplied related to monthly sales of all the company's products in comparison with the record of ninety-one other pharmaceutical manufacturers' prescription and non-prescription sales, giving percentage market shares by product, both nationally and by census regions, for the purpose of producing five-year forecasts.[41]

All advertising material was prepared within the sales and advertising department by a copywriter, an artist, and a photographer, in cooperation with one of America's largest ethical advertising agencies, William Douglas McAdam. Each advertisement was examined by the medical, legal, marketing, and sales departments well in advance of final approval by the vice president in charge of distribution. The aim was to produce informative, attractive, and tasteful advertisements of the highest quality. Advertisements for direct mail to doctors were also prepared by the company's art and copy group and until the 1960s, appeared either in blue and black or purple and black.[42] Special promotion programs, intended to call attention to a particular product, sometimes involved promotional devices. *The Lanoxin Heart* was developed by an outside supplier working closely with the advertising and medical departments. The result was a moulded, pliable, plastic reproduction of the heart presenting details of valves, arteries, and veins and identified by an explanatory card on the base both as a subtle reminder of location and identity and as a teaching aid for students and nurses.[43] The favorable response from recipients led to similar reproductions of the ear and eye. The free issue of personalized loose-leaf notebooks presented to junior medical students and to senior dental students also found favor.[44] Another promotional innovation introduced in the 1960s was the showing of medical films at medical educational institutions.[45]

One of the fastest-growing activities during the 1960s was customer service resulting from expanding demand for increasingly detailed information and more rapid data delivery. Data-processing equipment enabled the company to speed up the dispatching of orders and to analyse invoices and credits by product, by district, and by territory. In 1965, Univac 60 was replaced by Univac 1004 making possible a computerized perpetual inventory control of finished goods and packaging materials, superseding manual card operations in the planning department.[46] However, these improvements did not solve the problem produced by the time lag between receipt of orders and direct dispatch and delivery to customers. The solution was part of an important shift in distribution policy that began in 1969. Other developments which the reform was intended to tackle, resulted from the large expansion of drug dispensing conducted in hospital out-patient clinics and from the effects of Medicare and state welfare programs which were eroding the traditional distinctions between profit and non-profit institutional and retail drug dispensing.[47] Hitherto, both the company and its wholesalers serviced profit and non-profit hospitals, clinics, government facilities, and industrial accounts under prices which varied according to the classification of the particular account. Henceforward, the company adopted a single price policy.

Beginning in the 1960s, as product innovation slowed, competition in the drug industry saw two new developments. Competition from a new source began to appear as a consequence of the emergence of an increasing number of manufacturers developing and marketing low-priced generic drugs. The market for generics was still small, accounting in 1966 for 6 per cent of all prescriptions, rising to 9 per cent by 1970.[48] This growth was attributable mainly to generic forms of hitherto highly-priced antibiotics and steroids, especially tetracycline which had entered the market in 1967, followed by ampicillin, penicillin, and phenobarbitol.[49] The expansion of generics was attributed to the absence of new branded products produced by pharmaceutical manufacturers constrained by the stricter legal regulation of drug research and development imposed by the FDA in 1962.[50] The rise of generics was also a response to the adoption by hospital and public authorities of policies designed to minimize costs. Invitations to bid, issued to potential suppliers by state, county, and city purchasing departments, began to specify generics for certain categories of products which thereby challenged established branded products.[51] Notable among the several major companies entering the generic drug field in the 1960s were Squibb, Upjohn, Pfizer, Lederle, Bristol Myers, Wyeth, and Parke Davis.[52] Although Coe expressed considerable apprehension about competition from generics, the company manufactured and sold one of the most successful measured by prescription market share. In 1972, digoxin-branded Lanoxin accounted for 90 per cent of the market when the drug was described in the *American Druggist* as "setting the standard for the rest of the world to match."[53] The company's share of total generic sales, however, was no more than 2 per cent.

The second new trend was the decision taken by many manufacturers of ethical drugs to enter or expand the production of proprietary drugs. In 1964, sixty-two companies operated a total of seventy-nine such enterprises, though mostly distanced from their parent companies by name. These included acquisitions made by Schering (Pharmaco), Merck (Quinton), Abbott (Lake), and SF (Menley & James). Geigy formed a proprietary section, and Myers created two, as did Warner & Lambert.[54] A different direction for diversification was represented by Upjohn which acquired Homemakers Inc., a company employing one hundred thousand people providing home and other health services.[55] Coe's vision for the future, however, remained fixed on the company's becoming a leading manufacturer of ethical medicines only. Such an objective conflicted with that adopted by the board in London where a new management regime which favored product diversification and overseas acquisition as the parent company's flagging sales due to an absence of innovation in the UK resulted in financial difficulties which became a serious matter for concern on the part of the Trust. As perceived from Tuckahoe, the American company's relative commercial success attributable mainly to relative independence from managers in London needed to be protected from solutions devised in London to solve the problems of the Wellcome Foundation.

CHAPTER 6

Anglo-American relations between Burroughs Wellcome & Co. (USA) Inc., the Wellcome Foundation Ltd, and the Wellcome Trust, 1924 to the 1960s

After its formation in 1936, important changes occurred in the relationships between the Wellcome Trust and the Wellcome Foundation Ltd (WFL) which were to have significant implications for the history of Burroughs Wellcome & Co. (USA) Inc. In 1939, the Trust had exercised the "last resort" power to ensure Pearson's resignation and had installed T.R. Bennett as chairman of WFL and managing director of the company in London. Immediately thereafter, the inclination of the trustees had been to leave the apparently well-qualified Bennett to manage the organisation.

The relationship between the Trust and WFL began to change in August 1944. In order to pay excess profits tax WFL was compelled to request approval from the Trust to extend an existing bank loan. The Trust's agreement was conditional on receipt from the board of directors of quarterly statements and reports (in addition to the annual report presented face to face with the trustees) on the state of the business; the duration of this arrangement was for as long as indebtedness to the bank exceeded £0.5 million, the figure indicated in the articles of association. The company faced a rapidly deteriorating financial position. As in the US, insulin and penicillin production in Britain had increased during the war in accordance with the demands of the Ministry of Supply. Those requirements necessitated heavy capital expenditure in new buildings and plant by WFL and by other companies that entered the field, one of which was Glaxo. Bennett was both chairman and managing director of WFL as well as being chairman of the Therapeutic Research Corporation (TRC), the cartel charged with responsibility for organizing the national supply of penicillin. In his TRC role, he had invited Glaxo to commence penicillin production in 1941, for which further new investment was required. When government contracts came to an end on the resumption of peace, demand and supply were left to market forces where it soon became clear that the production capacity of WFL was to be a serious liability because Glaxo had invested in superior production methods and achieved higher productivity.[1]

H. H. Sier senior partner of the accountancy firm of Viney, Price and Goodyear, initially a consultant adviser who subsequently became part-time chairman of the Wellcome Foundation Ltd, 1948–1953; he was largely responsible for rescuing WFL from bankruptcy.

Added to the disadvantage sustained in the postwar market for penicillin was a further decline in the company's major pre-war lines. The Kepler range of cod liver oil and malt products did not find favor with consumers after the war, a trend which had originated in the late 1920s. This contrasted with Glaxo's dietetic food, notably Ostermilk. The WFL's trade in compressed medicines, which had continued to be relatively buoyant in several overseas markets, also received a setback resulting from the disruption to international trade during the war. The subsidiary companies in Australia and South Africa operated at a loss, while those in India and China had disappeared altogether.[2]

Bennett's postwar strategy was based on his immediate objective to cover overhead costs. He decided to accumulate stock with which to supply a market which he estimated would have to increase by about 50 per cent after the war if the company were to generate sufficient output from the enlarged capacity. The implied assumption that demand would meet supply proved to be flawed. No such surge in sales occurred. This intensified the financial pressure to cut back on all activities. In 1945, the Midland Bank agreed to extend the existing loan limit to £1million, doubling the permitted level. Again the Trust approved the loan. When, however, in 1946 the company's indebtedness rose above £2 million prompting the board to request a further extension to £2.75 million, to which the Midland Bank had agreed, the trustees became alarmed by the charge on assets demanded by the Bank; the stipulation was that the company should underwrite the loan by mortgages and floating charges on assets. The trustees approved these arrangements but insisted that the quarterly statements should be replaced by monthly accounts. This marked another turning point in the relations between WFL and the Trust.

Having approved the crisis measure to avert an immediate prospect of insolvency, the trustees initiated an independent and urgent investigation into WFL's finances. The investigator chosen was H. H. Sier, formerly a senior partner in the accountancy partnership of Viney, Price, and Goodyear. He was a director of many companies and his expert command of financial and business analysis was therefore well-known to the trustee Martin Price. Soon after the company's accounts went into the red in 1947, Sier's report not only presented a damning indictment of the accounting system, but also expressed serious criticism of a woeful lack of managerial control.[3] In a desperate bid to secure his position, Bennett proposed his own solution. He proposed that WFL should be replaced by a new company to be called Burroughs Wellcome (Holdings) Ltd. This would exclude financial commitments arising from ownership of the WFL building, the non-business related activities revolving around the Wellcome Research Institution building which also housed a museum and library. These would be transferred to the Trust which would take over responsibility and continue to fund from dividends paid to the holding company. This divestment of non-business activities (and by implication of a research organisation viewed as separate from the business) proved too radical for the trustees. They rejected the proposal as contrary to the provisions of Wellcome's will. Instead, in January 1948, Sier became a member of the WFL board where he played a central role in developing and implementing proposals for reform. On the request of the trustees, Sier conducted a second, more detailed review of the finances and management of the business. In March, he attended a meeting of the Trust, chaired by Sir Henry Dale to discuss these matters. This ended in an agreement to recommend to the WFL board that Bennett should be asked to step down. A further recommendation was that in future, the roles of chairman and managing director should be seperate.[4] Bennett resigned in May 1948 to make way for Sier as part-time chairman of WFL. D. E. Wheeler (Bennett's personal assistant) and C. G. Oakes (who had returned to England after managing the Australian company) became joint managing directors. A new finance director, Dudley Robinson, was appointed to assist Sier in his task of reforming the accounts.[5] The structure and organisation of the Trust, WFL, and the overseas subsidiaries remained virtually unchanged between 1948 and 1970 (see Figure 6.1).

As indebtedness to the bank approached the £2.75 million limit, Robinson's first priority was to eliminate debt. In June 1948, Sier convened a special three-day meeting of the board of WFL (to which Creasy was invited from the US) to discuss the growing financial crisis. The board resolved that all subsidiary companies should allocate substantial dividends forthwith. However, conscious that the American company would have to provide by far the most, the board agreed that the views of the directors of the American company should be borne in mind in determining the size of the transfers, particularly "their views as to what proportion of their profits should be retained by them as working capital for their own development."[6] On Creasy's return to New York, the directors of the American company agreed to issue a dividend of $140,000. While the WFL board appears to have accepted this without demur, the Midland Bank objected. A close scrutiny of the accounts of the American company revealed that the profit declared in 1947 was $970,530 (on sales amounting to $10.75 million), prompting a challenge to WFL's own description of the dividend as large: "… the bank does not consider this to be an adequate distribution and in view of the national need for US funds I shall be obliged if you will inform your customers that if a further dividend has not been declared and paid since the date of the balance sheet, the bank will wish to see a further distribution of $280,000 …"[7] In 1948/9, a cash

Figure 6.1 *The Wellcome Foundation Ltd Organisation Chart, 1948–1970*

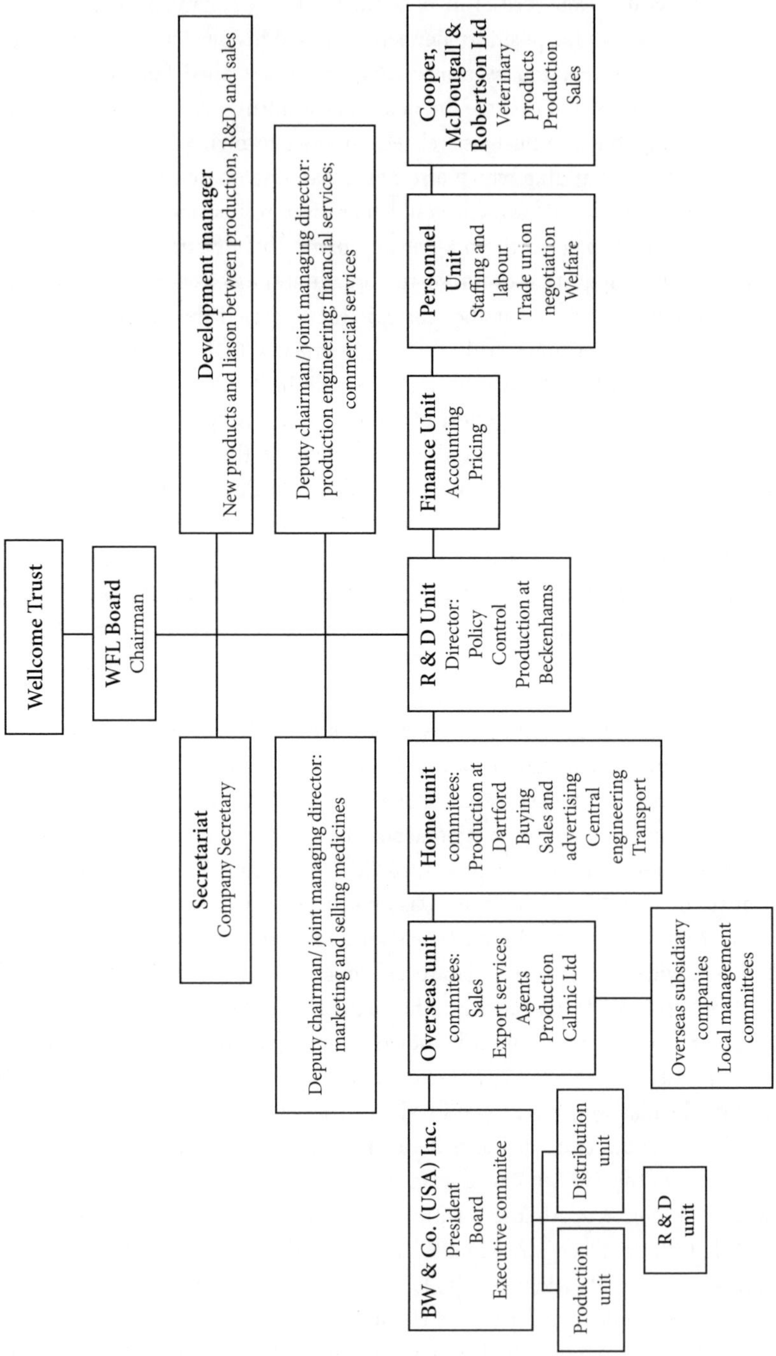

dividend of almost a further $1 million was paid to WFL in addition to a stock dividend amounting to a further $0.6million.[8] The WFL board rejected the bank's suggestion that the Montreal subsidiary should be sold, though it agreed to dispose of property elsewhere. In October 1948, Creasy was elected to the board of WFL,[9] at which time Sier urged him to release "as much cash as possible in the form of dividends" to avoid dire consequences.[10] Extraordinary dividends continued to be distributed during the war with Korea, even though the American company's sales and profits were reduced sharply in 1951 and 1952, partly as a result of the reinstatement of an excess profits tax.[11] From the mid 1950s, both sales and profitability rose as Creasy's reforms and Coe's reinvigoration of the company's sales efforts began to bear fruit.

Table 6.1 *BW&Co., sales, profits and dividends 1946–1960 ($million)*

	Sales	*Pre-tax profit*	*Post-tax profit*	*Dividends*
1946	4.5	0.8	0.4	0.7
1947	5.9	1.6	0.9	0.1
1948	5.8	1,5	0.9	0.4
1949	6.3	1.9	1.2	0.9
1950	7.2	2.4	1.5	1.1
1951	7.7	2.5	0.9	0.8
1952	8.7	2.8	0.9	0.3
1953	9.5	3.4	1.1	0.8
1954	10.8	3.9	1.6	0.4
1955	11.7	4.7	2.2	1.7
1956	13.2	4.8	2.4	1.9
1957	13.0	4.3	2.0	1.3
1958	13.5	4.4	2.1	2.1
1959	13.9	5.2	2,500	2.0
1960	15.0	5.7	2,731	2.2

Source: GWHC, BW&Co. (USA) Inc., 107.07/11, Public affairs, "Brief analysis."

From the beginning, Creasy took his responsibility as a member of the WFL board seriously, winning the appreciation of Sier, and equally important in view of Bennett's fate, of Sir Henry Dale, chairman of the Trust. Correspondence between Creasy and Sier reveals the American's perceptive critique of the UK business. He criticized the excessive number of office staff in London and urged a substantial reduction to permit resulting savings to be applied to increase the pay of remaining staff to motivate them towards securing higher productivity. Creasy noted that London appeared to inventory everything from canteen provisions to postage stamps, involving calculations wasteful of clerical and other effort; he also urged streamlining the cost accounting system. Sier conceded that the accounts drawn up by his assistant accountant "on lines hallowed by

Professor Sir Henry Hallett Dale, FRS, physiologist, Nobel Laureate, chairman of the Wellcome Trust, 1938–1960. He was appreciative of the development of the American company which he visited several times, and was influential in the creation of the Burroughs Wellcome Fund in the US. Wellcome Library London.

the Wellcome tradition"[12] did not help management to gain a true interpretation of the strengths and weaknesses of the company or contribute to informed decision-making for the future and offered Creasy reassurance that reform would take place in time.

Creasy suggested that the prices charged for insulin and digoxin were too low. He noted that sales of surgical equipment yielded a return of barely 4 per cent gross profit which had caused discontinuance of the line at Tuckahoe several years before. In effect, Creasy advocated adopting an American solution to the company's problems: to postpone large capital projects, limit research expenditure, increase production to reduce costs, and focus on expanding sales. To achieve a company-wide improvement in productivity, he proposed reducing staff numbers in each department and holding each director responsible for meeting those targets.[13] He condemned the failure to build a strong medical or clinical department at the research laboratories in Beckenham and urged immediate action.[14]

Creasy's critique and recommendations were based on a detailed investigation of WFL accounts carried out by Ralphs, the finance director at Tuckahoe. Ralphs's analysis showed that, even after eliminating the assets represented by libraries and collections, the capital tied up in fixed assets in the UK was roughly double that at Tuckahoe. As approximately one-third ($300,000) of the value of the Wellcome Research Institution building in London was devoted to a museum and library and $1.2 million devoted to the actual collections, the trustees might realize that approximately $1.5 million of the capital of WFL was employed to carry out the wishes contained in Sir Henry Wellcome's will but did not advance the operation of the business. Ralphs suggested that, if for the record, the trustees wished to receive a dividend from WFL, the dividend could be made by transferring the ownership of the museum and libraries to the trustees, an added advantage of which would be the removal of the asset from the balance sheet and to give a more accurate picture of the business. Creasy acknowledged privately that these specific proposals for restructuring assets might have been "out of order,"[15] exceeding Ralphs's brief, and that they had no chance of receiving sympathetic consideration by the Trust. None the less, Creasy had included Ralphs's suggestions in his report to Sier because privately he thought that "there may be a germ of an idea to the suggestion."[16] Creasy correctly anticipated the board's response which was the same as that given to Bennett's proposal for a similar solution to the crisis shortly before he had been dismissed by the trustees. The board ignored the suggestions both for restructuring assets and for curbing dividends, preferring a less radical solution altogether which consisted of gradual and diffused economies and improvements – a policy which Creasy's assessment of the company almost ten years later revealed to have been beyond the board's capacity to effect.[17]

During that period, discussion of Anglo-American relations had arisen with regard to several specific issues. Since the height of the financial crisis in 1948, the topic assumed greater prominence because of the increasing financial support extended from Tuckahoe to WFL and the highly vocal and increasingly assertive presence of Creasy as a director of the board in London. A greater awareness among the WFL directors of the American company's success may have prompted a proposal, initially made by the trustees, that the American company should take over the Montreal branch and should also assume responsibility for the Shanghai trading subsidiary. Creasy expressed a willingness to undertake some administrative responsibility and to exercise a degree of supervisory control, but advised retaining the *status quo* in Canada as a separate branch. He dismissed the Shanghai proposal completely.[18] The board accepted Creasy's advice and authorized him "to make any decisions and take any action he considered necessary."[19]

Ownership of the American company also became an issue. Continuing pressure from the bank to reduce the overdraft in 1948 led Sier to propose raising cash by offering employees the opportunity to buy shares in the American company. The Trust does not appear to have opposed this, though Creasy and his board did; Sier did not press the issue.[20] A year later, through Linklaters, the London law firm, WFL received an overture from the Schenley Distillers' Corporation, an American firm possessing large interests in the antibiotic field which showed interest in acquiring Burroughs Wellcome & Co. (USA) Inc. After discussion with the trustees, the WFL directors decided not to pursue this possibility. A second approach, which came from Pfizer in 1950, was taken more seriously.[21] After the Trust reported the inquiry to WFL, arrangements were made for a visit from a senior Pfizer representative which was reported to the WFL board on January 9th. Creasy was asked to prepare a response to the board on behalf of the American company (referred to in the quotation below as BW&Co.). This was to be in the form of replies to a series of questions dispatched by airmail in anticipation of a response by telephone before 13 January.

> Was there any reason why a negative response (WFL's position in the past) should be different? Do the directors and managers at Tuckahoe favor further consideration of the proposal? Do you find Pfizer's approach at all attractive? Would the pooling of knowledge and financial link with Pfizer be an advantage for BW&Co.? Do you as a member of our parent Board consider that sale for cash would enable us to develop policy superior to that of holding your company's shares? Would sale of a half share of your company be a satisfactory arrangement for us to develop? Do you think that the dividend we should receive on a possible holding of stock would match the profits of BW&Co. as it develops and expands? Would you regard the provision by the New York House of distribution facilities for Pfizer as a satisfactory alternative? Do you foresee harm to BW&Co. by having a link to Pfizer if Pfizer was able to dictate the policy to be pursued by BW&Co.?[22]

Creasy conveyed the board's unanimous view that a link with Pfizer of any kind would not be in the company's interest.[23] In view of the evident weakness of the parent company, this robust response implies a corporate self-confidence reflecting rising sales and profits at Tuckahoe which might explain a proposal made by the board of the American company two years later to delete "USA" from the company's name. The intention was to remove external perception of the company as merely a foreign subsidiary, but the proposal was rejected as contrary to the traditional Wellcome subsidiary nomenclature "as designated by the founder in 1924,"[24] (another example of the continuing influence on the trustees of the "hallowed Wellcome tradition").

Historically, Anglo-American collaboration had not been a feature within the relationship between London and Tuckahoe. For several years before Wellcome's death until the end of Pearson's interregnum as chairman of WLF in 1940, the relationship between scientists in the laboratories in London and Beckenham with those in Tuckahoe had caused concern for Nevin and his research director. Although initially Bennett had signalled a need to improve relations and begin collaboration between the two companies, the war intervened and Bennett resigned shortly after it ended. The prevailing attitude at WFL to the research conducted at Tuckahoe was typified by the disinterest shown by Dr C. M. Wenyon, Director of the Wellcome Bureau of Scientific Research from 1923 who, from the beginning until his retirement in 1944,[25] had opposed the establishment of research laboratories at Tuckahoe. From the perspective of American scientists, war brought the company a higher degree of independence. De

Sir Michael F. Perrin was appointed by the Trust as chairman of WFL in 1953, despite his lack of experience in business management. On the basis of a detailed critique of the management of WFL from BW&Co. largely accepted by the trustees, Perrin accepted the defence of his senior managers and endorsed their strategy of geographical and product diversification.

Beer, acting director of research at Tuckahoe, extended the higher degree of freedom to other research teams.

The appointment of Wenyon's successor in 1944, Dr C. H. Kellaway, formerly head of the research laboratory of Burroughs Wellcome & Co. (Australia), heralded a brief period of constructive dialogue between scientists in the US and the UK until his death in 1952. In the past, annual reports on research prepared at Tuckahoe had been submitted to WFL and copied to the research director. While Wenyon had been director, no further communication occurred. Kellaway's innovation was to visit Tuckahoe annually to discuss each year's report, to outline research in the UK, and to review the overall research activity within the organisation. Creasy and the scientists at Tuckahoe valued Kellaway's active interest and support regarding research at Tuckahoe, but his premature death in 1952 aroused uncertainty regarding the future. Creasy's concern was that financial difficulties in London might adversely affect the company's plan for long-term investment in research-based innovation. He feared that in Kellaway's absence, research at Tuckahoe might fall victim because of the lack of progress in the delivery of commercially valuable products from the laboratories, though that applied to both companies. The retirement of Sier from the chairmanship of WFL created further uncertainty as he had valued Creasy's judgment in relation to WFL and had supported him on the board. The year 1953, therefore, saw the appointment of both a new chairman and a research director at WFL. Their arrival held the key to future Anglo-American relations.

When Sier retired, the Trust decided that regardless of the opposing view shared by the two managing directors, the position of chairman should become full-time. Sir Henry Dale and Lord Piercy (acting on behalf of the Trust) took advice from the chairman and the research director of ICI who recommended Sir Michael Perrin. He was a scientist whose first career at ICI was followed by membership of the Atomic Energy Commission, after which he returned to ICI in 1952 as general research adviser. Although Lord Piercy thought that Perrin's lack of familiarity with business would be a handicap, the trustees were unanimous in recommending his appointment to the board as full-time chairman of WFL. Perhaps influenced by Dale's strong views, the minute recorded that the Trust believed Perrin's valuable scientific experience and connections outweighed a lack of knowledge of the world of commerce and business finance.[26] On the advice of Sir Henry Dale, Perrin appointed Dr D.W. Adamson, formerly head of a small research unit in Burroughs Wellcome & Co. (Australia), as the new research director.

Shortly after his appointment in 1953, Perrin persuaded the trustees of the necessity of investing £2 million over the next four years and that this would require continued dividend restraint with consequent adverse effects on the Trust.[27] This was necessarily the case because, other than re-investment from current profits, alternative sources of finance for long-term capital expenditure available to other companies were denied to WFL. Under the terms set out by the trustees in accordance with Wellcome's will, WFL was denied access to the capital market. Such a handicap might explain why tentative inquiries regarding possible merger with another drug company had failed.[28] Perrin's plan to modernize the business in the UK which included expansion of the Wellcome Research Laboratories[29] rang warning bells in Tuckahoe, since the American company was the source of a large percentage of WFL profits. Although the Trust had agreed to (continue to) accept lower than a normal percentage of gross profits in dividends, the need for additional capital for the business remained and the US would continue to be the only source. Evidence of the embarrassment caused by the degree of London's financial dependence on Tuckahoe is apparent in the discussion of the WFL directors as to whether to publish the annual accounts and chairman's report (for which, as a company wholly owned by a charity, there was no legal obligation). The two advantages perceived to be gained from publication in the financial press were to reveal the extent of WFL's business operations and to attract capital. On the advice of the managing directors, disclosure was not pursued for two reasons. First, the publication of the American company's turnover of $15 million compared with WFL's turnover of $33 million was so significant that it might have adverse effects on the image of WFL; second was the possibility of "repercussions," perhaps by attracting predators' attention to the scale of the American company's business. Another concern expressed was that, once set in motion, annual publication would be difficult to discontinue.[30]

Under the circumstances in which a new chairman and a new research director were beginning to review options in a context of financial crisis, Creasy and Fonda mounted a bullish assault. Creasy's presidential report in 1953 expressed optimism and urged patience. Referring to the continued progress of research conducted by the Tuckahoe scientists, he observed "though it may not be considered of value to the commercial side of the business, the work has been highly regarded by scientific and medical groups throughout the US and has added to the prestige of the company."[31] Reinforcing Creasy's message, while deputizing for Creasy at a WFL board meeting in London in 1953, Fonda (senior vice president in charge of production) underlined the board's loyalty to WFL, at the same time emphasizing the value that he and his co-directors attached to the unique independence enjoyed by the American company. In his opinion, the managers "did not favor merger for merger's sake," (a reference to the current wave of mergers proceeding in the US).[32] Fonda explained that it was the directors' intention "to direct the company's entire focus towards the market for medical products as the route to further growth in sales."[33] Fonda was more specific regarding research. He described the level of communication between the laboratories in the two countries as too infrequent and of insufficient duration and argued, more generally, that in order to ensure WFL was "an organized and unified outfit," frequent and well-planned visits between London and New York should take place "at such levels and of sufficient duration to allow discussion of fundamental problems as well as of the more day-to-day technical and administrative problems common to both."[34]

Fonda's contribution appears to have had some effect as the new research director embarked on relatively frequent visits to Tuckahoe, as did researchers at a less senior level. Three years later, Adamson's overall review of research described increased levels of collaboration in screening and improved coordination between London and Tuckahoe. In 1954, a tumor screening program was introduced at Tuckahoe, similar to those conducted by Dr S.R. Bushby in Beckenham and by the Sloan Kettering Institute and the Cancer Chemotherapy National Service Centre in the US.[35] Movement of scientists between the two countries, another innovation, offered learning opportunities. However, Adamson admitted that the research culture he and his fellow scientists had discovered at Tuckahoe was absent from the laboratories in London and Beckenham which lacked "the contacts with the professions and academic institutions which we should have, and this problem must be deliberately attacked."[36] He was impressed by the "extra-mural" pharmacological and clinical research conducted through networks established by the Tuckahoe scientists.[37] These were comparable with those pre-war networks which had existed in the Wellcome Research Laboratories in England before World War I, but had since disappeared. Creasy called for a sympathetic understanding of each other's views and interpretations across the laboratories. He also expressed concern at the slow progress towards innovation and discovery translatable into commercial returns. He told Perrin:

I still feel that Research has not been able to make any major contributions (with respect to Tuckahoe sales) for several years, and there is no doubt in my mind that you are very much aware of the importance and significance of research in the future of the company. I have every confidence that the research and development groups will eventually make some highly worthwhile items and that in addition to the material contributions the research people will make a number of highly worthwhile contributions to medical and scientific knowledge.[38]

At the same time, the American directors were planning for capital expenditure amounting to between $3.5 billion and $5 billion over five years in a program which included a research building costing $1.5 billion. This ambition appeared to be threatened in 1955 during the negotiations about the company's annual dividend payments. Although WFL had finally eliminated heavy bank debts, Robinson, the finance director, requested that Creasy should secure agreement from the American board to a payment of £2 million. Creasy's strong reaction reflected a worry that the company's own plans for expansion would be undermined.[39] He underlined the central importance of research and a new building to accommodate the planned growth in staff and future expansion of the business in the US.[40]

Burroughs Wellcome & Co. have a unique opportunity to be of service to mankind. Because our organisation is constituted along unusual lines, in that it does not have private stockholders, it is different from most companies. This does not mean that there is any less forceful spirit to advance and improve, but rather a company with aims such as ours has extra inspiration and a most exciting incentive to strive doubly hard to discover, develop, manufacture and sell pharmaceutical products at a suitable profit, for in so doing the wherewithal is provided to make our enterprise more dynamic, and at the same time to enable the Trustees to execute the altruistic purposes of the Will of the Founder.[41]

The American directors agreed a maximum dividend of $1,575,000. When the WFL board met in January it endorsed Robinson's demand, placing on record reassurances that the WFL directors acknowledged the American company's need for adequate financing. However, Robinson explained that, for tax reasons, such a payment would maximize the benefit for the Trust shareholders.[42] The agreed final figure was represented as 75 per cent of the American company's net profit after tax.[43] In 1956, the definition of surplus was agreed and it was decided that dividend payments should be paid in quarterly cash balances.[44] When Robinson proposed to reallocate overhead costs associated with research throughout WFL across all subsidiaries, Creasy maintained that the US tax authorities would be unlikely to allow such a charge.[45]

Creasy was similarly defensive when the WFL board sought to reinforce a long-standing requirement for overseas subsidiary companies to purchase drugs in bulk *only* from London. This requirement, increasingly honoured in the breach, had not applied hitherto to the New York or Montreal businesses. Again, Robinson's argument was based on the ability of the trustees to recoup the maximum amount of tax on dividends, though the effect would also be to generate additional revenue for the parent company. His logic was that, as it was necessary for dividends to be paid solely out of the profits earned by WFL's direct trading activities, steps would have to be taken to increase the profits of the parent company even if the profits of subsidiaries were diminished as a consequence.[46] The sale of bulk drugs by London to the American company in 1957/8 merely amounted to £21,000 whereas local purchases totalled £2.25 million. Not only were the American drugs cheaper, Creasy maintained that their quality was superior, a view he expressed forcefully to WFL managing director Wheeler in 1959.[47] Creasy's position was that the American company was willing to pay the highest possible price for English goods provided that his company was advised of the English profit (information which WFL was unwilling to divulge). He also demanded that WFL should inform the American company of the cost (which it would not, or more likely was unable to provide). This would reveal the extent to which the price could be reduced to meet competition.[48]

A further source of friction was a growing interference in the management of the American company. When Oakes, the WFL joint managing director responsible for the American company because of his seat on the board retired in 1955, the responsibility passed to D. E. Wheeler, who was one of the two WFL managing directors. This coincided with an issue over authority. Creasy wished to replace de Beer, the existing acting director, who had worked at the Tuckahoe laboratories almost from the beginning.[49] Adamson, Creasy, and Fonda had discussed the candidate, Jukes, who was a research director of another company, and had expressed their approval. However, after the decision to appoint was made by the American directors, the appointment was vetoed in London. An angry Creasy wrote to Perrin accusing his board of challenging his authority as president, and offered his resignation.[50] Almost immediately, Perrin replied, criticizing the WFL board for a veto which should not have been exercised.[51] According to Coe, Perrin was "completely backing down." Relations between Creasy, on the one hand, and Wheeler, Perrin, and Robinson, on the other, deteriorated thereafter. Creasy despaired of Perrin's willingness to take decisions or provide leadership for WFL,[52] and described Robinson as "a little less than honest."[53]

Creasy was especially irked by the prospect of any destabilisation of the company's strategy by WFL's financial demands.[54] Such a threat was received in 1957 when Wheeler was replaced on the American board by Fred Wrigley (formerly of CIBA and newly-appointed sales manager at WFL). Wrigley was a pharmacist and qualified medical practitioner who had first worked for Roche in Canada. Contemporaries described him as aggressive, "a dynamo" who had been head-hunted to manage WFL's commercial side of the business.[55] In the absence of new products in the pipeline, Wrigley was a forceful champion of a policy to broaden the product base through acquisitions and global diversification, both of which he pursued as a matter of urgency and which led to a proliferation of overseas operations. As the second director with a seat on the American Board,[56] Wrigley perceived an opportunity to apply his strategy for achieving commercial success within a reorganized WFL which would inevitably affect the American company. This concern figured in Creasy's annual address in 1958 when the American president warned, "It cannot be over-emphasized that the future success of the company depends on the discovery and medical exploitation of new products, and though it is recognized that research cannot be hurried, the future position is precarious unless the research and medical staffs in Tuckahoe and London can provide at least two or three useful therapeutic agents that can be sold in volume."[57]

CHAPTER 7

Burroughs Wellcome & Co. (USA) Inc. and the Wellcome Trust: conflict, crisis, and the end of a presidency

In October 1957, Tuckahoe was visited by three trustees from London, ostensibly for the purpose of gathering information about the Wellcome group of companies after the future of WFL and its subsidiaries had become a focus for discussion between the chairmen of the Trust and of WFL. Two were original members of the Trust designated by Sir Henry Wellcome before his death in 1936. L. C. Bullock was a solicitor and formerly chairman of an insurance company and Martin Price was a chartered accountant who had played a major role in evolving relations between the Trust and WFL and who had been instrumental in the removal of both Pearson and Bennett from the leadership of the parent company. The third was Lord Piercy, CBE, who had been a trustee since 1948 when he had first visited Tuckahoe, accompanying Sir Henry Dale (whom Piercy was to succeed as chairman in 1960). Formerly a Director of the Bank of England, Piercy was also chairman of the Industrial and Commercial Finance Corporation.[1] Before the trio had left London, Dale, then aged 82, had suggested that while they were in New York the visiting trustees should invite Creasy "to discuss frankly" his view of the business of the Wellcome group as a whole and to express his own personal opinions on all matters affecting it. There seems little doubt that Dale was already aware of Creasy's views. The two shared some family history. As a boy, Dale had been a playmate of Creasy's father when their respective families spent holidays together in the south of England. During the 1950s and 1960s, the Dale and Creasy connection was renewed. Dale was a frequent visitor to North America, travelling across the US and Canada to visit eminent university scientists in their laboratories.[2] On these occasions Creasy spent time, sometimes travelling with him, but always arranging for Dale to visit Tuckahoe to ensure that he was aware of current activities and future plans.[3]

Bullock, Price, and Piercy met with Creasy and his senior managers and also privately with Creasy. At the end of the visit, Bullock's verdict was that "If Sir Henry were alive today, he would be delighted with the advances of Burroughs Wellcome & Co. [USA Inc.] Sir Henry's ambitions were unlimited and they have met

The Wellcome Trustees in 1962, described by Lord Franks after he assumed the chairmanship in 1965 as senile and heralded an accelerated process of retirement and replacement.

with success."[4] The sequel was Bullock's report to Sir Henry Dale and the other trustees, followed two months later by a special meeting convened by the chairman of WFL to which the Trustees were also invited. All, including Sir Henry Dale, attended. The single agenda item, "The Wellcome Foundation Ltd [WFL] and its subsidiaries: general policy," consisted of a memorandum which was essentially a report prepared by Bullock based on the informal meetings between the trustees and Creasy.[5] Circulated with the memorandum before the meeting were data showing comparative current R&D costs and expenditure, home and export sales, and a breakdown of employment, each separately for the parent company and Burroughs Wellcome & Co. (USA) Inc.

In introducing Bullock's memorandum, Perrin drew attention to three main issues raised by Creasy, "that the American company employing only some 800 people contributes 70 per cent of the profits, whereas the Foundation, employing 2,500 people, contributes only 9 per cent of profits for the Foundation in the UK; that the Foundation employs an unnecessarily large number of people; that the Foundation is producing too many products, some of which must be unproductive."[6] Lord Piercy summarized Creasy's general argument by pointing out that WFL's profit was inadequate in relation to the size and complexity of its organisation and the capital employed. Perrin conceded that each of the issues raised had to be explained in such a way as to persuade the trustees that the directors were aware of problems and were in the process of solving them by applying policies which the trustees (he hoped) could accept or endorse. In effect, Perrin left the WFL managing directors to respond to Creasy's critique. A preliminary commentary included with the data that Bullock had also provided signalled the defensive approach that Wheeler and Wrigley had adopted, taking as the starting point Bullock's introductory qualification that "It cannot be too strongly emphasized that direct comparison between one company in the pharmaceutical industry and another can be grossly misleading, and particularly as between one country and another."[7] Bullock highlighted the disparity

Table 7.1 *WFL Sales and financial analysis 1960–1970 (£million)*

WFL group	*Sales*	*Pre-tax profits*	*Post-tax profits*	*Dividend*
1960	28.1	3.5	1.8	0.5
1961	29.6	3.7	1.8	0.5
1962	30.5	3.8	1.9	0.6
1963	31.7	3.9	1.8	0.7
1964	33.8	4.3	1.9	0.9
1965	36.5	4.6	2.0	0.5
1966	43.8	5.7	3.2	1.4*
1967	50.5	6.4	1.6	1.5
1968	62.5	7.7	3.6	1.6
1969	75..1	9.6	4.7	1.85
1970	85.7	8.8	4.8	2.1

*Payment under covenant.
Sources: GSK/WF/SCS/798, WFL and Wellcome plc accounts and annual reports

in the volume of export business conducted by the two companies; 40 per cent of the parent company's total sales were sold in 135 countries, whereas American exports were almost non-existent. Wheeler argued that export sales were vital, though he conceded that they "added complexity to the business." He maintained that exports provided an important offset against the effects of price controls imposed on the home market by the Ministry of Health. Wrigley reported that between thirty and forty countries were important consumers and that while demand in the remainder of the 135 countries was small, it did not add greatly to the burden on the sales organisation. He expressed confidence in the potential for the future development of these markets to increase sales.

Evidence of the complexity to which Wheeler referred may be inferred from the employment of 208 staff in the sales department at the London office in addition to only forty-one sales representatives. At Tuckahoe, sixty members of staff were employed in distribution supported by 185 sales representatives. This reflected contrasting approaches to marketing, a feature of which was a decline in the innovative emphasis on pro-active roles for sales representatives employed by the parent company compared with the period before World War I.[8] Complexity also resulted from the range of products sold and the practice of selling through 16,500 separate retailers' and wholesalers' accounts, whereas the American company sold only through a small number of wholesaling accounts. Wheeler conceded that the American model of distribution was superior and would be adopted "at the appropriate time … possibly when the company had an outstanding new product which every retailer had to stock"[9] (and which by implication would require little marketing effort and minimum commitment of resources). Wrigley admitted that the number of representatives was too small and reassured the trustees that steps would be taken to increase their number to forty-eight, while adding that none of the pharmaceutical companies in Britain employed more than one hundred. The contrasting levels of administration support Creasy's conviction that the London office was overstaffed. Non-production and non-research staff (excluding those in finance) amounted to 25 per cent compared with 7 per cent of staff at Tuckahoe. Wheeler's replies were platitudinous, "It should be remembered that the prosperous subsidiaries in the United States and Canada would not now exist if the decision had not been taken many years ago to start operating in those countries."[10] His responses ignored the possibility that the policies adopted towards overseas trade, wherever it might be found and regardless of the potential for effective demand, might not have been worth the costs resulting from complexity. The figure estimated to have been spent on "overseas development" (managing executives' time) was £60,000.

Both Bullock and Piercy were critical of an excessive number of products and packages listed in WFL's price catalogue by comparison with those of the American company. WFL offered 500 different products sold in 1,400 packs bearing foreign language labels: the comparable figures in the American catalogue were 84 and 188. Wheeler's defence was that the diversity was a consequence of the British company's wider range of activities and that the degree of variety in packaging and labelling was therefore appropriate. Wrigley declared that the product range was reviewed regularly, but that reduction of the range awaited the introduction of new products yet to be discovered. For the Trust, Price reiterated Creasy's criticism that a review of product range was far too slow and questioned the wisdom of a policy of placing a higher priority on maximizing sales rather than on profitability. Price accused the directors of a preoccupation with covering large overheads which arose from supporting a huge bureaucracy.

Wheeler counter-attacked by criticizing the high degree to which the American company was dependent on sales of Empirin to the value of $10 million which represented 50 per cent of sales. The memorandum revealed that half of the company's output came from about twenty production workers utilizing continuous production methods and extensive mechanization (made possible by the volume of sales), a statistic which Wheeler interpreted as a contributory explanation for a disparity in levels of employment in the two companies, rather than an indictment of the inferior level of mechanization and production methods prevailing at Dartford. Wheeler referred to a general view among his co-directors that the American business was too narrowly based, not only in its range of products, but also in the company's unwillingness to undertake veterinary business in the US and to develop sales in South America. As a member of the board, he would have known that the American company's single-minded concentration of resources on developing human medicines for the rapidly growing market in the US was based on assessments of comparative profitability. A comparison of production costs showed significantly higher average overheads and wages for the parent company in which "production profit" was less than one half of that of the American company. The parent company's profit to sales ratio was 5.6 and 6.4 on capital employed, which compared with 21.4 and 41.9 per cent. Bullock ascribed the inter-company differences to the existence of long-established and elaborate buildings, plant, and equipment needed for WFL's more diverse business and to higher stockholding demanded by the pattern of business at home and overseas. Lord Piercy asked the board whether they agreed that a 6.4 per cent return on capital employed was unsatisfactory; the board agreed unanimously.

Coe recorded Creasy's description of the minutes of the meeting with the directors and the trustees as "whitewash with half truths."[11] Creasy wrote to Perrin at length in a series of intemperate letters in which he reacted against the criticisms that had been leveled against the American company. One consequence of the special meeting was a request that Creasy attended every third WFL board meeting in London. However, his attendance became increasingly rare, making it clear, according to Coe, that "He doesn't care too much for those people."[12] Fonda attended in his place. Another outcome of the special meeting was that Wrigley should attend every third meeting of the American board in Tuckahoe. His presence did not improve Anglo-American relations. Coe's first impression of Wrigley, before he had joined WFL, had been to distrust him.[13] Wrigley's approach at early meetings in Tuckahoe gave the impression of a self-important figure who saw his role as overseeing the American company. His attempt to persuade the board to sell Saxin by radio and television advertising, which conflicted with the company's aspirations in the therapeutic medicines market, irked Creasy and contributed further to uneasy relations between the two.[14]

In 1958, Perrin asked Creasy to prepare a document to be considered at a special meeting of the WFL board in London to take place in January, 1959, to review the role of the American company in the context of a new strategy of expansion through diversification and acquisition. The lengthy document and accompanying charts and statistics plotted the history of Burroughs Wellcome & Co. (USA) Inc. from its formation, but focused mainly on performance and progress during the years since World War II. Perhaps in anticipation of a possible rationalization of research that would involve consolidation in the UK or possibly a change in the American company's status in order to release capital for acquisition, Creasy emphasized that the future of the American company depended on the research side of the business at Tuckahoe; he expressed confidence that despite disappointing commercial results it would provide "some worthwhile products to produce and sell."[15] The outcome of the review of the American company did not disturb the research activities at Tuckahoe. Perrin and his co-directors believed that the future of WFL depended on a policy of modernization of plant and equipment in Dartford and Beckenham and expansion of the business through diversification and acquisition.

The new policy first affected the American company when in 1959 WFL acquired the private veterinary enterprise of Cooper MacDougall and Robertson Ltd (CMR) for £1.75 million. This represented a modest expansion but met Wrigley's aspiration towards product diversification by bringing insecticides into the WFL portfolio.[16]

The directors of the American company had strongly opposed this acquisition. They conceded that it might be desirable from a London perspective because North America constituted the largest veterinary market in the world and initiatives there would be necessary if the policy to achieve expansion were to be effective. However, when the WFL board had proposed that the American and Canadian companies should spearhead developments in their respective countries, the American directors expressed no interest in becoming involved, either as producers or distributors of veterinary products. Creasy had emphasized that the American policy was to concentrate on the market for human medicine which the directors believed to be in the interests of the company and also in the best interests of WFL.[17] In London, Creasy had cast the single dissenting vote against the acquisition. Reviewing the information supplied by CMR before and after the transaction, Coe observed that the profitability of the company was even lower than the directors had been led to believe during discussions prior to acquisition.[18] Involvement in production and distribution was imposed on the American company which, as Creasy and Coe predicted, would be seen ultimately as a diversion from a strategy of innovative research and development focused on human medicine and a constant drive to increase efficiency and reduce costs. Creasy's outright opposition to the diversification policy was the culmination of his growing dissatisfaction with the activities of the board of WFL. He expressed this opinion forcefully in private (as Coe's diaries reveal), and increasingly in public. This created growing tension in Anglo-American relations and in the following decade led to intervention by both the board of WFL and by the Trust, with significant consequences for the history of the American company.

Although in denial regarding his deteriorating health, Creasy acknowledged the need to prepare a successor to lead the company, someone whom he trusted to assist in formulating future strategy and ensuring effective implementation. Fred Coe Jr. had joined the board of directors in 1952 when he was appointed vice president in charge of distribution. With Perrin's agreement, in 1955 the additional responsibility for production was transferred to Coe from Fonda who showed no wish, after thirty-eight years with the company, to retire at the age of fifty-nine. In 1960, finance had been added to Coe's portfolio as had his new position of executive vice president, in effect as Creasy's deputy. Four years later, and again with Perrin's wholehearted approval, Creasy transferred the chairmanship of the executive committee of the board to Coe, thereby formalizing Coe's position as the most influential figure in the company. Creasy remained as president and chairman of the board (to which the executive committee reported) but without executive responsibilities or powers. This arrangement proved to be unstable because Creasy ignored his constitutional position as non-executive chairman by continuing to interfere in research and medical matters. In 1964, after only two years in post, both the head of toxicology and the director of medical affairs resigned, their letters of resignation accusing Creasy of "trying to run everything with a little knowledge in some areas."[19] Both were new to the company and unprepared to allow intrusion into their respective departments.

Their resignations were followed shortly by that of Dr John Burns, another recent recruit and an even more senior figure, who had joined the company in 1960 as vice president and, with George Hitchings, as joint director of research. Burns left to lead 800 investigators, scientists, and physicians at Hoffman La Roche, a multiple of the number of scientists and medical staff employed at Tuckahoe.[20]

Increasingly, Creasy's own co-directors, senior managers, and senior scientists felt unable to conceal dwindling confidence in their president who, by the mid-1960s, was not only treating the board with contempt, but verbally abusing senior managers, including Coe.[21] Creasy's dictatorial attitude, manifested in a disregard for the committee structure and combined with increasingly erratic behaviour, led to deteriorating relationships with colleagues.[22] As early as 1953, the vice presidents had failed to persuade him to spend time away in a clinic for rest and recuperation.[23] By 1960, Coe believed that increasing absentmindedness and a seeming lack of interest was undermining Creasy's authority both in Tuckahoe and in London. He speculated as to whether Creasy's characteristic egocentricity might have turned into megalomania.[24] Relations between the respective boards of the two companies remained fragile. The 1965 annual negotiation of dividends precipitated fierce exchanges between Creasy in Tuckahoe and Robinson and Perrin in London when, once again, a level of dividend was requested which Creasy regarded as excessive.[25] This time his objections were fuelled further by Perrin's suggestion that WFL should reduce contributions to the Wellcome Fund, the charitable body which Creasy had persuaded the trustees (though Sir Henry Dale particularly) to set up in 1955.[26] Again Creasy wrote to Perrin threatening to resign, and again Coe restrained him from an irrevocable exit from the company.[27]

The increasingly infrequent attendance at WFL board meetings in London, either by Creasy or Fonda, resulted in the withdrawal of American membership. Henceforward, responsibility for Burroughs Wellcome & Co. (USA) Inc. was effected entirely from London by a director who became responsible for all overseas subsidiary companies.[28] In 1966, unknown to Creasy, Perrin and the two managing directors, Wheeler and Wrigley, had identified Coe as future president of the American company and began to prepare to remove Creasy from office. In September 1966, Wrigley had approached Coe privately and suggested that he should spend three or four months in London to prepare for such a transition. Aware of Creasy's repeated threats to quit and referring to WFL directors, Wrigley observed, "They might take up his threat some day."[29] This invitation followed Creasy's final loss of credibility which precipitated his departure.

The occasion was the visit to Tuckahoe by three consultants employed by Urwick Orr & Partners, a leading firm of management consultants in the UK who, on the Trust's request, had been commissioned by the WFL chairman to investigate the structure, organisation, and management of WFL in a brief which included a visit to Tuckahoe.[30] On arrival in Tuckahoe, Creasy met them with ridicule and, despite attempts by Coe and Dowling to persuade him of potential benefits from the review, refused to cooperate with the consultants or participate in the proceedings in any way.[31] Instead, Creasy instructed Coe to be responsible for managing the exercise. He was deputed to prepare a five-year strategy which included significant input from Hitchings who presented a vision and a plan for investment and implementation. They reflected both aspirations based on increasingly confident expectations that the R&D in progress would deliver product innovations and took account of the impact of the 1962 legislation and subsequent decisions made by the FDA which had led to an increase in laboratory staff at Tuckahoe.[32]

In Creasy's absence, Coe, Pressel (production director), and Dowling (company secretary and legal adviser) took part in the interviews arranged by the Urwick Orr consultants.[33] Creasy was also absent from the de-briefing after the consultants' departure, but he met Coe and Dowling and intimated his intention to resign at a special meeting of the board which he asked Dowling to convene forthwith. Unknown to Coe or Creasy, it appears that immediately after Wrigley presented a report of the consultants' catastrophic visit to the WFL board in London, it was agreed that should Creasy offer his resignation (which he had already threatened to do at least three times[34] and was, by now, a fairly predictable event), the board should accept.[35] Many months later, Perrin told Coe that from April 1966, only the process by which Creasy should be removed had been in doubt. In January 1967, without Creasy's knowledge, three of the directors of WFL were to visit New York for no declared purpose. Only Coe and Dowling, who received instructions from London to convene a special meeting of the board on April 7th, knew about the impending visitation beforehand. They feared a disastrous outcome and expressed the hope that it would "not upset Creasy too much."[36]

On the evening preceding that meeting, Wrigley referred to previous letters in which Creasy had threatened to resign. Wrigley asked him when he wished to do so; Creasy replied "tomorrow."[37] The mission of the London directors was revealed to the board the following day. It was agreed that Creasy should issue a notice announcing the further transfer to Coe of all responsibility for the medical department, research, and the secretariat. Creasy accused the London directors of firing him, refused to announce his retirement, and was abusive towards Wrigley. Coe and Dowling urged the local directors to support them in trying to dissuade WFL from dismissing Creasy, but received less than unanimous support.[38] Pressel expressed the view that Creasy's departure would probably be for the best, adding "now maybe the business could move ahead."[39] In letters to Perrin and to Sir Henry Dale, Creasy denied that he had asked for severance and insisted that the minutes should record that he was asked to resign.[40] When Dale (by this time superseded as Trust chairman by Lord Piercy) replied to a letter from Creasy in which he had sought his support and simultaneously accused Perrin of moral cowardice, Dale's reply was equivocal, leaving Creasy without hope for a retreat either by WFL directors or by the trustees.[41] Even Creasy's hope of retaining the titular chairmanship of the board was disappointed. In December, Perrin instructed Coe to notify all Tuckahoe staff of Creasy's resignation.[42] At a meeting in Tuckahoe in January 1968, Perrin informed the board of his intention to recommend strongly to the Trust that Coe should become president; the decision was finally taken at a general meeting of WFL and the Trust.[43] Born of a lengthy friendship and an exasperated loyalty shown by Coe to Creasy, Coe succeeded in persuading Perrin to agree that the board minutes recorded involuntary resignation (which would be to Creasy's financial benefit). Perrin also agreed to Coe's suggestion that Creasy should continue as chairman of the Wellcome Fund, though Perrin insisted that Creasy should occupy an office distant from the Tuckahoe premises.[44]

Coe became president on 1 April 1968, heralding a new phase in the history of Anglo-American relations. Changes to the organisational structure of research included the formation of designated committees which included representatives from both Tuckahoe and Beckenham.[45] The beginning of Coe's presidency coincided with challenges resulting from a reorganisation of WFL in the course of implementing the recommendations contained in the report issued by Urwick Orr & Partners. Based on scrutiny of the board's activities and on interviews with the chairman, directors, and other executives and managers in London, Dartford, and Beckenham, the report and recommendations focused mainly on the business in the UK. The American company was peripheral to the investigation (though the consultants' visit to Tuckahoe in 1966 had proved to be a catalyst precipitating a change to the presidency).[46] None the less, the report offers a carefully prepared independent basis on which to compare approaches to business in the UK with those in the US.

Whereas Creasy's criticisms of WFL in the 1950s were leveled at ineffectual leadership in London, the consultants' report emphasized a fundamental weakness of structure and organisation. The report described the aims of WFL as understood by both directors and senior managers to be little more than general intentions. Neither overall objectives nor policies had been formulated explicitly for WFL. In the absence of effective delegation, those omissions had also undermined detailed planning with time scales. The result was an organisation in which duties and responsibilities remained undefined and staff lacked a sense of urgency. While the board received accounts which encompassed the operations of the entire organisation, managers at departmental level were unable to provide the investigators with data relating to sales, capital expenditure, costs, profits, or cash flow relating to their own activities; none was aware of the contribution made by his own department on the ultimate profitability of WFL.

Confusion regarding objectives had resulted in extensive duplication of effort. In addition to Urwick Orr's criticism of structure, the consultants identified a flawed management culture. They discovered that managers below director level believed that each should take action only after checking that any initiative would be in accordance with "the mind of the centre" of the organisation,[47] an abstraction conceived by the consultants to describe an organisation which was so bureaucratic and at the same time so hierarchical that managers operated without clearly defined functions and roles. One seriously damaging conclusion was that board members to whom managers deferred were "too involved in day-to-day affairs due to a reluctance of the next level of management to take decisions,"[48] resulting in widespread frustration. The Urwick Orr consultants concluded that such an organisation could not succeed if increased central control continued to reside in the hands of a dysfunctional board and that it was essential to call for a clearer line management structure within which powers and responsibilities were defined precisely in order to achieve an efficiently functioning organisation.[49] Although the laboratories were not central to the review, the consultants discovered an alarming omission of commercial considerations in determining R&D expenditure and evaluating outcomes in the UK. They concluded that the WFL board was ineffective in formulating strategy and ensuring implementation; it was little more than a progressing body preoccupied with excessive and undigested detail supplied by the finance department. The data were unhelpful in the formulation of long-term aims and appropriate policies which the directors found difficult because, except for the chairman and managing director, all board members were also full-time departmental managers. They were absorbed in the routine duties of departmental heads to the exclusion of corporate aims and objectives.[50]

Four years later (before implementation of the recommendations had been completed), an international survey of corporate images attributable to major international pharmaceutical companies dealt a further blow to WFL. Based on the responses of physicians across the world, the perception of WFL was that of an old-fashioned organisation which produced high quality products and high quality research, but which at the same time, also possessed a poor record of developing new products and marketing existing products. The organisation was perceived to be fragmented, a conclusion with which the company's directors and younger managers concurred. They agreed that the image of WFL had been neglected and should receive attention.[51] The contrast between the history of the management of the companies in London and Tuckahoe is extreme. The structure and organisation put in place by Creasy in the 1940s was designed to achieve rationalization and reveals the application of a completely different business philosophy which, until his final few years as president, lay behind his approach to the formulation and implementation of long-term aims. This included the definition of functions and responsibilities at all levels – executive, managerial, and supervisory; the formulation of relatively detailed ten-year plans, regularly reviewed; the introduction of a costing system; the establishment of a forecasting group whose forecasts were based on systematic and comprehensive sales and accounting data; and the elimination of unprofitable products from the company's price list. In opposition to chairmen in London, Creasy had also established that the ultimate aim of the company was to be a leading manufacturer of therapeutic medicines.[52]

The success of such developments affecting management since the 1940s had enabled the American company to move away from an immediate postwar priority of retrenchment to an emphasis on product innovation (though cost control continued to be important throughout the 1950s and 1960s). An expanding sales force and the introduction of reformed marketing strategies applied to existing products had enabled the company to remain profitable during a period when basic research failed to deliver commercially important drugs. The 1960s brought problems of growth, but also presented challenges. This weakness began to be remedied as investment in RD&M began to expand in order to support the efforts of senior researchers at Tuckahoe, where a policy of extensive recruitment and a reorganisation of laboratories began to deliver products possessing therapeutic significance and a route to growing profitability as envisaged by Nevin and Sir Henry Wellcome from the 1920s, embraced by Creasy from the 1940s, and furthered by Coe during the 1960s and 1970s.

CHAPTER 8

Drug discovery at Tuckahoe and networks of innovation, 1942–1970: pathways to Purinethol, Imuran, and Zyloprim

Beginning in the late 1950s, the research infrastructure at Tuckahoe underwent significant transformation in scale, direction, personnel, and policy. Nelson's research leadership from 1943 to 1946, had ended in conflict with Creasy when their respective perceptions of priorities could not be reconciled. Nelson had believed that senior staff in the laboratories should be charged primarily with conducting the research agreed among themselves in consultation with him.[1] Evidently he wished to secure a similar degree of independence to that enjoyed by WFL scientists in the UK. He was irked by the suggestions which Creasy was prone to offer to senior scientists to stimulate their interest in exploring commercially productive research.[2] Nelson's departure in 1946 brought the return of de Beer as assistant director until a future director was found. The expansion of the medical department following Nelson's resignation is an indication of Creasy's insistence that the role of the scientists at Tuckahoe should be product, as well as research oriented. The expanding role of the medical department in close collaboration with research and development was to prepare and manage new drug applications delivered to the FDA, arrange clinical investigation of new and existing products, assist with the preparation of the company's literature, and deal with professional correspondence.[3] The discovery by de Beer of the antihistaminic properties of chlorcyclizine hydrochloriede (brand name Perazil) introduced in 1950, represented a major advance which enabled the company to introduce a line of products for the treatment of hay fever and allergic rhinitis which would make a significant contribution to diversification. Perazil was a piperazine, rather than a conventional ethylenediamine compound and relieved allergy symptoms for between twelve and twenty-four hours which was more rapid than other antihistamines and had milder and less frequent side effects.

Under de Beer's leadership as acting director, building on the work of Buck and Hjort in the 1930s, further research resulted in the development of Vasoxyl, a long-acting vasopressor. The historical origin of this product, launched in 1950, lay in a long pre-World War I history of curare preparations at the Wellcome Research

Laboratories in the UK. After World War II, Squibb had set the pace in using curare preparations to develop a muscle relaxant which it introduced into the American market. This was a cause of personal frustration at Tuckahoe; Creasy perceived Squibb to have upstaged WFL and to be set to gain the commercial advantage of many years of pioneering research by the British company. When Kellaway, the research director at WFL learned of Creasy's sensitivity towards this development (Creasy was in London for a board meeting at the time), Kellaway drew his attention to recent literature published in British medical journals which had reported the discovery of the myonaural blocking action of decamethonium bromide which was of relevance to muscle relaxants. He suggested that Creasy should contact academic scientists (whom he named) working in the field with a view to assessing the current state of research and exploring future possibilities. Creasy was successful in securing their cooperation, evidence of which was the publication of several studies in rapid succession, pharmacological and clinical, which were helpful to de Beer and his co-researcher, Castillo, at Tuckahoe. In conjunction with Searle, Jaros, and Pollinger of the medical department they advanced the research and development of Syncurine brand decamethonium bromide, the first muscle-relaxant of its kind and the company's first synthetic product. Kellaway's intervention, therefore, was the proximate origin of a research and development process which resulted in the first completely synthetic product to emerge from the Tuckahoe laboratories at the marketable product stage.

The same research group, led by de Beer, was also responsible for developing a second muscle-relaxant in the form of Anectine brand succinylcholine chloride. They were introduced into the US market in 1950 and 1951. Creasy considered three aspects of these developments to have been important. First was the commercial potential for Anectine on which the profit margin was 80 per cent (though sales were barely 5 per cent of the company's total sales ten years later); second was the achievement of producing a drug which quickly became the acknowledged leader in the field of skeletal relaxants; and third was the construction of a network through "careful cultivation of the anaesthesiologists" which provided a model for the future. With Creasy's encouragement and assistance, de Beer and other scientists at Tuckahoe "sought out and established excellent relations with some of the country's academic anaesthesiologists."[4] Creasy considered this process of creating a network to be of major significance in establishing the company's reputation as "more than a mere tablet-making business."[5] The skeletal muscle-relaxant Anectine brand succinylcholine chloride was also the result of research led by de Beer with extensive collaboration with scientists outside the company.[6] None, however, resulted in a therapeutic commercial product commanding substantial sales.

Achieving this objective was the work of appointments made by Nevin during the early 1940s which were to transform research in the Tuckahoe laboratories and effected a revolution in pharmacology at the American company. The first appointment was Dr George H. Hitchings, who in 1988 was to become one of the company's two Nobel Prizewinners; the other was Gertrude Elion (who was to share the prize with Hitchings). She joined him at Tuckahoe two years later. Hitchings was born in 1905 and graduated from the University of Washington. He completed his PhD in biochemistry at Harvard in 1933 where he was a teaching research fellow and demonstrated an early interest in measuring the purine base constituents of nucleic acids. He described how for nine years he had experienced "a period of impermanence, both financial and intellectual."[7] Temporary teaching appointments at the Huntington Laboratories of Harvard in cancer research, at Harvard School of Public Health in nutrition research and at the Medical School of Western Reserve University, altogether a period of twelve years severely limited his capacity to publish.[8] This was to begin to change when he left academia for an appointment at the BW&Co. (USA) Inc. Experimental Laboratories at Tuckahoe in 1942 where his role was to direct a team of biomedical researchers in a continued search for new compounds directed towards a slowing down in the growth of cancer, viruses, and bacteria and in so doing, to adopt a new approach to chemotherapy.[9]

The timing of Hitchings's move into industry is significant, for until 1941 the role of pharmacologists in the industry had been consultative or as participants in collaborative research agreements with some of the leading companies, notably Eli Lilly, Parke Davis, Merck, Squibb, Upjohn, and Abbot.[10] The principal explanation for the reason why pharmacologists (at least American-trained pharmacologists) were largely absent from the laboratories set up by these companies during the 1920s and 1930s was that "industrial pharmacologists" were precluded from membership of the American Society for Pharmacology and Experimental Therapeutics. Research undertaken inside company laboratories was regarded as practical rather than contributing to the development of fundamental science, which was the justification for excluding practitioners from membership of a narrowly-defined scientific profession.[11] The growing practice of companies retaining university scientists as consultants on long-term contracts eventually led to successful pressure to remove the ban in 1941. Hitchings, therefore, was among the first of a wave of academic researchers who were attracted away from university laboratories to become fully employed as research scientists in industry while still enjoying the status of those remaining in academia.

The organisation of research, development, and medical activities at Tuckahoe remained largely unaltered between 1945 and 1955. De Beer was associate research director of pharmacodynamics, Hitchings associate research director of chemotherapy, and Beale was director of pharmaceutical and chemical development. The medical department was headed by Searle. Each head reported to an administrator, the senior vice president, Fonda until 1957, and thereafter Brigadier General John R. Wood. The departments were separate, unlike the two main functional units of production and distribution. Hitchings's research concentrated on nucleic acid biosyntheses. He described his exploration of enzymes and metabolic pathways by means of antimetabolites as an approach to chemotherapy at a time when it was "in limbo."[12]

He believed that it was unfashionable to such a degree that "it was necessary to defend its importance before one could present a paper on nucleic acids." It seemed

Dr George H. Hitchings, biochemist, formerly professor at the Medical School of Western Reserve University who was appointed as leader of a small research team at Burroughs Wellcome & Co. at Tuckahoe in 1942. He recruited Elvira Falco (in the background) as research assistant in 1943 and Gertrude Elion in 1944. Hitchings and Elion worked in collaboration for 31 years. Allopurinol was their earliest important discovery which heralded the company's first medicines to treat childhood leukaemia, gout, malaria, bacterial infections and to facilitate safe organ transplantation; together with Schaeffer, Elion was also a leader in the development of the herpes virus. Hitchings and Elion were awarded the Nobel Prize for Medicine in 1988 for their method of rational drug design and their contributions to medical science (circa 1948).

to him that it was unlikely that any university would support research.[13] However, an equally important influence on his decision to move to a commercial laboratory was his view of research as a means to an end achievable through the development of marketable drugs. He regarded research and development as a continuum which, a colleague observed, Hitchings pursued with a passion. The creation of a product was the principal source of his satisfaction. In the 1960s, when Hitchings attracted numerous prizes and honours, he explained why he still preferred to work in a company rather than in an academic setting: "I can go to Harvard tomorrow and I can take my entire group … but Harvard doesn't provide me with all the facilities I need to get a drug developed and put on the market."[14] The opportunity to convert pure science into commercially significant drugs which would enable their use to treat their patients was an important initial attraction which took him from academe to BW&Co. in 1942. The laboratories at Tuckahoe were small and researchers few in number. On the other hand, on the model established by WFL in the UK and by its American subsidiary with which it seems likely Hitchings was familiar, pure research had been given support in the past and an increasing number of scientific publications from the scientists employed, both in the US and the UK, was evidence of this. None the less, in view of Nevin's expressed concern regarding the balance between pure and applied research, it is perhaps surprising that Hitchings was allowed to start his own research program and adopt a novel approach which would involve other research staff, without reference to a need to target a likely product outcome in the short or long term. Hitchings contrasted this with conventional industrial research:

> Much of the basic research supported by industry is, in a sense, retrospective. As semi-empirical discovery of a useful drug provides the stimulus for deeper probing into how and why it works, and thus to a deeper understanding of the underlying disease. This, in turn, may give rise to new concepts and new discoveries. The marketing of the initial drug provides not only this stimulus but also the funding that makes its pursuit possible. Our programme differed from this pattern in a number of aspects. It was untargeted in the usual sense; its primary purpose initially was to participate in a major area of developing chemical knowledge. At the time this work began, chemotherapy was largely in the hands of empiricists, with academia in general standing apart. The prevailing view was that there was insufficient fundamental knowledge to support the rational approaches to problems of infections, let alone neoplastic disease. The discovery of Prontosil and the rapid rationalization of its action with enunciation and illustration of antimetabolite principles opened the door, we thought, to an approach that could reconcile the dichotomy through participation in both basic research and its application'.[15]

At Tuckahoe Hitchings found "a quiet place to work on problems that others did not yet see as important."[16]

In 1943, Hitchings recruited Elvira Falco, a chemist formerly in the bacteriology department whom he held in high regard, as assistant in chemotherapy research. The following year, he hired Gertude Elion.[17] She was born in 1918 and received a chemistry degree from Hunter College in 1937. While training to become a school teacher she taught chemistry, physics, and general science in a New York City high school to fund an MSc. in chemistry at New York University awarded in 1941. At that time, women were rarely appointed as laboratory staff, but a wartime shortage of male chemists had enabled her (and indeed Falco) to secure employment. Initially, Elion took a job as an analytical chemist at the Quaker Maid Food Manufacturing Company until the spring of 1944. After six months of employment at a laboratory owned by Johnson & Johnson in New Jersey, her application to become research assistant to Hitchings was accepted.[18] In addition to Falco, other members of the original team were Doris Lorz, Dr Marion B. Sherwood, and the bacteriologist H. Van der Werff. The entire staff of biochemistry was housed in a single large laboratory.[19] A further significant appointment in 1947 was that of Peter Russell. He was a former graduate of Cambridge University, UK, though at the time when he was recruited he was an academic at Harvard; Hitchings rated highly his competence in organic chemistry, valuing especially his intuitive association with medicinal chemistry.[20] Falco's contribution to purine research was such that she "participated in everything from bacteriology and animal feeding to organic chemistry."[21] Elion's expertise in the field of purine metabolism justified her central role in the "thiation" of hypoxanthine and the subsequent work on other compounds and agents that followed from the 1950s onwards.[22]

The group explained their research aims and methodology in 1950 in a reflection on eight years of work since Hitchings alone had embarked on his initial study conducted at Tuckahoe. The research explored relationships between chemical structure and the ability of certain pyrimidine derivatives to serve as precursors for acid synthesis or as modifiers. The starting point was Hitchings's belief in the possibility of discovering fundamental knowledge of the role of pyrimidine and purine bases in growth and an understanding of the part played by folic acid in the synthesis process. Since parasite tissues in general were seen to depend for survival on a more rapid growth, hence a more rapid synthesis of nucleic acid than host tissues, he entertained the possibility of discovering new chemotherapeutic agents. As this hypothesis applied equally to bacterial, viral, rickettsial, and neoplastic diseases, Hitchings observed that "in a sense one might say we have been searching for a philosopher's stone, the universal panacea of the ancients."[23] Thus, from the initial basic science prompted by the current antimetabolite theory, Hitchings's group adopted a biochemical approach to chemotherapy. They shared aspirations to discover agents with known mechanisms of action from which, it was envisaged, multiple drugs could result which could treat several unrelated clinical indicators as well as introducing medically important applications. This approach offered the potential for the simultaneous development of several alternative treatments.[24]

Few tools and techniques, such as iron and paper chromophotography, existed for the study of purines in the early 1940s. Knowledge, however, was available in the form of antimetabolite theory developed to explain the action of sulphonamides; Hitchings hoped that a biochemical approach to chemotherapy would lead to the discovery of agents with known mechanisms of action.[25] Elion later described the knowledge which they lacked when, in 1944, she applied the theory to purine metabolism by examining purines as substrates or inhibitors of the enzymes guanase and xanthine oxidase. The latter was one of the few catabolic enzymes which had been purified successfully. Even so, when the studies began the researchers did not know "how the chemicals would work, how they would get into the nucleic acid; how they would interfere with function if they did." Elion described these as "big open questions" to which they had no answers, but on reflection, "the exciting thing was that as we began to unravel what the compounds did, we could deduce what enzymes were there even before we knew that the compounds existed."[26] This leap into the almost unknown by the biochemistry department took place because of the freedom which

Creasy allowed the scientists at Tuckahoe – a degree of independence which they acknowledged. Elion recalled the value attached to the absence of corporate direction, even to an apparent disinterest shown by senior managers towards research activity until disclosure of a potentially important (and from the commercial standpoint, useful) compound at the end of a long development process which had sometimes lasted several years. By 1947, the study of purine metabolites absorbed the attention of six of the company's researchers (almost all) who by that time, according to Hitchings, had found the therapeutic agents and needed "... only to find the diseases in which they will be active."[27] The next phase in development required a substantial increase in synthesizing and testing, for which laboratory space was inadequate, facilities for screening against animal tumors did not exist, and research and medical staff were too few.

The potential for further development, however, did not escape the attention of C. P. Rhoads who was the director of the Sloan-Kettering Institute owned by the wealthy entrepreneur Charles F. Kettering. A scientist and self-promoting businessman who had invented the self-starter for automobiles which was the basis of his fortune, Kettering's philanthropy took the form of funding cancer research for which he had provided a hospital, clinic, and research facilities where, in addition to a core staff of investigators, academic clinicians could work pursuing their own studies in collaboration with other researchers. Impressed by the progress being made at Tuckahoe, Rhoads visited the laboratories at Tuckahoe in 1947 and urged that many more compounds should be tested. Once he was apprised of the physical and financial limitations which ruled out the immediate investment that would be necessary, a proposal was forthcoming from the Institute for a collaborative arrangement with the company: Hitchings's research group would have access to all of Sloan Kettering's facilities. Moreover Kettering himself would fund additional researchers who would join the group under the direction of Hitchings and his team at Tuckahoe. All would share information, not only among the enlarged group, but also between it and other academic clinicians working at the Institute. Such an arrangement also enabled Tuckahoe's scientists to observe patients in the Institute's clinic. The agreement (for an unspecified period which, however, lasted for ten years until 1957) marked the beginning of a flow of compounds forwarded to the Institute to be screened for activity; between 1949 and 1951 more than 100 purines underwent testing. In 1949, Falco synthesized p-chloro-phenoxy-2, diaminopyridine, and together with Russell, pyrimethamine, a new kind of folic acid. Testing took place of 6-mercaptopurine (6-MP; Purinethol) and 6-thioguanine (TG), both of which proved to be active against a broad spectrum of rodent tumours and leukemias and provided evidence of efficacy, crucial to securing FDA approval. In 1952, Hitchings and Elion obtained a patent for 6-MP, the company's first anti-leukemic drug.

A year later, Kettering scientists' studies with humans recorded several months' remission in children suffering from acute leukemia and caused fewer side effects.[28] Until a meeting convened by Sloan Kettering to share the information with other clinical investigators and therefore the public, neither medical nor marketing departments at Tuckahoe had been aware of the discovery, a situation indicative of the "hands-off" approach of Creasy and his senior managers alluded to by Elion.[29] In 1953, the FDA approved 6-MP for clinical use and it entered the market in 1953 as Purinethol brand 6-Mercaptopurine.[30] This achievement received wide publicity beyond the medical journals, thanks to Walter Winchell, the immensely popular gossip-writer and newspaper columnist for the *New York Daily Times,* who highlighted the small company's role in making an important medical breakthrough. The company, which ranked fifteenth among producers of prescription medicines, featured in a series of articles published in the *American Druggist* devoted to "leading drug companies"[31] whose discoveries were listed together with the products they supplied.[32]

De Beer's discovery of the antihistaminic properties of Perazil lay behind the development of Marezine, introduced in 1954, an antihistamine intended to relieve motion sickness. This product had achieved limited success, so too had the decongestant-antihistamines.[33] Actidil brand tripolidine hypochloride, one of the most potent antihistamines produced hitherto, had been synthesized at the Wellcome Research Laboratories in Beckenham.[34] Symptoms were relieved within four hours and the duration of relief was delivered within roughly twelve. However, these attributes appear not to have been translated into success in the UK market. A more successful commercial exploitation of the compound occurred at Tuckahoe where it led to the development of new combination antihistamine products (see Table 4.1). Sudafed was the first, the result of studies carried out in the research laboratories at Tuckahoe by Dr de Beer working in collaboration with Dr D.M. Avadio of the University of Pennsylvania. Clinical trials under the supervision of Dr Whitman in the medical department showed no side effects. Sudafed was launched in 1958 in tablet form. It was an oral decongestant intended to provide complete respiratory relief rather than limited local relief and was advertised as "total therapy for relief symptoms of the common cold and 'flu."[35] Actifed, another improved combination antihistamine, followed quickly and within five years of the launch, sales accounted for 8 per cent of total company sales; Sudafed claimed 2 per cent. By 1970, Actifed sales accounted for 14 per cent of total sales; the combined antihistamine total was 19 per cent.

When in 1957, the arrangement with Sloan Kettering was terminated by mutual consent, the annual subsidy to the company was $75,000 which accounted for roughly one-quarter of all expenditure on RD&M at Tuckahoe which included one half of the company's own research staff. The subsidy accounted for 10 per cent of an enlarged research budget at Tuckahoe when it was withdrawn. However, improvements in the company's finances from 1947 allowed the absorption of the hitherto subsidized additional researchers into the company's own staff establishment.[36] Friendly and collaborative arrangements with the Institute continued.[37]

While Sloan Kettering had provided valuable screening facilities in New York, testing also took place in the Wellcome Tropical Research Laboratories in London with compounds supplied from its American subsidiary. Pyrimethamine, the first therapeutic pay-off from Hitchings's program, was subjected to screening and testing by scientists in London, Dr L.G. Goodwin and I. Rollo. Their interest was in identifying anti-malarial rather than anti-leukemic activity. Quinine for use as an anti-malarial treatment had figured in the parent company's price list since the nineteenth century. When, during World War II, a demand arose to meet the needs of armed forces serving in the tropics, a quinine shortage triggered a search for a substitute with reduce side effects. Military personnel on duty in the Pacific had been issued with Atebrine, the favored treatment at the time, which was bitter-tasting, turned skin yellow, and could cause gastric upset. The development of the substitute Daraprim grew out of researching the role of nucleic acids in cell multiplication by Hitchings and his team.[38]

The result was a new drug possessing strength several hundred times greater than that which it was to supersede. The advantages of Daraprim over Atebrin, to which Daraprim would present competition, were threefold. The first was that Daraprim, potent but non-toxic, was estimated to be 1,000 times more powerful than Atebrin; the second was that the drug was more suitable for mass production and was cheaper than Atebrin; the third was that Daraprim could be administered three times per week compared with the three times per day required for Atebrin.[39] The potential market for the product derived from a calculation of three million annual deaths from the disease which was reckoned to be sufficiently big to justify large-scale production both at Tuckahoe and Dartford in the UK. However, initial contracts that were received showed that few countries intended to use Daraprim as a prophylactic, thereby limiting potential demand on which marketing assumptions had been made.[40] A possible association of side effects with a risk of abortion contributed to levels of uncertainty sufficient to undermine sales of Daraprim and led to its withdrawal.[41]

After the Daraprim failure, collaboration with the Wellcome laboratories in the UK was limited and sporadic. However, although the long term arrangement with Sloan Kettering ended in 1957, the Tuckahoe researchers were soon in collaboration with scientists elsewhere. At the New England Medical Centre where William Dameshek was chief of haematology, Robert Schwartz, a clinical scientist, embarked on a study of immune response for which he required agents, one of which was 6-MP supplied privately on request from Tuckahoe. In 1958, evidence of activity prompted Schwartz to seek collaboration with Hitchings and Elion which involved the latter developing an animal model for testing immunosuppressive activity. However, Hitchings maintained that as another of the company's compounds, azathioprine, possessed immunosuppressive qualities in rodent models, it was a more promising agent for further study. As investigation progressed, an additional figure appeared on the stage. Dr Roy Calne was a pioneer in transplantation visiting from St Mary's Hospital in London who, in 1960, occupied a year's fellowship at the Peter Bent Brigham Hospital in Boston, the location for most human renal transplantation. Calne visited Tuckahoe where Hitchings and Elion encouraged him to experiment with their purine and pyrimidine analogs (including azathioprine) with which they supplied him. In

Boston he discovered that azathioprine could modify renal transplant rejection in human patients with kidney grafts. Hitchings and Elion promptly filed to patent the compound. In 1963, successful transplantation of kidneys in unrelated human donors was achieved with the drug. By 1965, Imuran was described in *Science* as the drug which is used throughout the world for immunosuppression, though FDA approval was not received until 1968, after which it became essential for liver transplants in the US.[42] The drug was also used widely on an experimental basis in most heart transplant operations, including the successful breakthrough operation carried out on Philip Blaiberg by Dr Christian Barnard, when it was one of the chief drugs administered to keep the patient alive until he died 82 weeks later.[43]

Meanwhile, the therapeutic success of Imuran led to an intensification of a program of testing at Tuckahoe in search of superior immunosuppressives as well as anti-tumour compounds for the treatment of auto-immune diseases.[44] The biochemistry department had investigated several hundred purine and pyrimidine derivatives during the 1940s and 1950s. These included an examination of purines as potential substrates for and inhibitors of xanthine oxidase, an enzyme which metabolizes purines in uric acid. By 1956, Elion's group had found that the pyrimidine which proved to be the strongest inhibitor and a substrate for the enzyme was the hypoxanthine analog known as allopurinol. As yet, however, the precise utility of the drug was not known and awaited the outcome of clinical trials while further investigations continued at Tuckahoe. These developments attracted the interest of researchers at Duke University where R. Wayne Rundles was researching the haematological effects of purines, pyrimidines, and folic acid metabolites in patients suffering forms of anemia. After meeting Hitchings and Elion at a conference held in Tuckahoe, Rundles began to incorporate the results of their research into his own, while knowledge gained from Rundles entered into the investigations of Hitchings and Elion. The next step was collaboration between Elion's group and Rundles's team to carry out studies with humans which began to point to the use of allopurinol as an agent to reduce uric acid. Independent clinical investigations confirmed both the safety and effectiveness of the drug.

Simultaneously, Creasy set a recently appointed head of a new chemical development department, Ronald Cresswell, two tasks.[45] Although trimethoprim and allopurinol had been discovered in 1956, neither molecule had been synthesized to meet sufficiently high standards of purity to secure commercial application. Cresswell's small team succeeded in developing new chemical processes, one of which established allopurinol as an axanthine oxidase inhibitor. Investigation into toxicity of the drug was carried out with the cooperation of two physicians at Mount Sinai Hospital in New York, Drs Gutman and Yu, whose group of stable, arthritic patients had been crippled by gout. The improvement in their condition was so swift and effective that Gutman made a strong representation to the FDA, insisting that the drug must be made available. The FDA fast-tracked the approval for entry into the US market; meanwhile in 1967 Hitchings and Falco secured the patent for Zyloprim for the treatment of hyperuricemia, most commonly in the form of gout.[46] Hailed as a new concept in the treatment of gout and other disorders caused by excessive uric acid in the blood, Zyloprim received FDA approval and entered the US market in 1968.[47] Perhaps less dramatic compared with the publicity accorded to Imuran in relation to transplant surgery, Zyloprim was to prove commercially equally significant for the American company. The profitability of the drug was a consequence not only of patent protection but also of the FDA's unexpectedly rapid decision to approve the drug for marketing. For a time unprepared, this necessitated the company using a production process which, though new, was both expensive and still in the course of improvement by Cresswell's small team. The production of early batches created allergic reactions among staff which gave urgency to replacing the process with a superior method. The replacement technique offered the advantage of greater purity but also a substantial reduction in costs compared with those of the initial batches which had been priced in accordance with the initial cost and profit margin. As the second process reduced cost by roughly 70 per cent the profit margin increased. This explains the substantial profits obtained in the US and subsequently (as Zyloric) in the UK and Continental Europe.[48]

By 1970, the company's researchers had established a relatively small but strong base from which subsequent discoveries were to generate large sales and profits as well as kudos within the international scientific community. Hitchings had received international recognition which he believed was accorded him for his "approach to research, rather than for specific drugs";[49] he was also at the centre of an extensive network of researchers. The results of his research had contributed much to a transformation of the chemotherapy area and by 1970 had begun to be recognized formally through honours and awards bestowed by professional associations and international institutions and organizations. In 1968, he had been honoured by the American Association for Cancer Research, received the Gairdner Foundation award, and the George Mendel award. In 1969, he was awarded the Passano prize for his achievement in chemotherapy, specifically for the discovery of mercaptoputine (Purinethol), pyrimethane (Daraprim), and azathioprine (Imuran). In 1971, he received the Purkinje Medal Society award, followed by the American Chemical Society's honour for achievement in medical chemistry in 1972. He was honoured by Edinburgh University in 1973 for achievement in practical therapeutics and modern medicine. In 1974, he was elected to the small elite comprising foreign membership of the Royal Society in London. By that time, he had authored 185 journal articles and held 85 US patents.[50] The Mullard award by the Royal Society in London in 1976 acknowledged his outstanding contribution to the advancement of science and technology, the first American to receive the award.[51] In the same year he received a National Academy of Sciences honour, regarded as one of the highest that could be accorded to an American scientist.[52] A biographical article appeared in *Modern Medicine* entitled "The man who made immunosuppressive drugs a clinical reality."[53] A Nobel Prize came twelve years later, awarded jointly with Gertrude Elion.[54]

The history of drug innovation at Tuckahoe underlines the significance of networks and interaction between the researchers in the corporate laboratories and those working in other institutions, notably universities. The network into which Hitchings's predecessors had inserted the laboratories at Tuckahoe from the outset, and which he had assiduously expanded, had enabled this small company to achieve a record of innovation of high quality that could compare favorably with that of other much larger laboratories of big pharmaceutical companies. The period between 1947 and 1957, when Sloan Kettering funded one quarter of the company's RD&M budget and made available state-of-the-art facilities to its scientists, was crucial in bridging the gap between the financially difficult postwar years and the revenue and profit generating Empirin years between 1957 and 1970. In the case of each product resulting from the basic research originating in the 1940s, external clinical researchers were influential in the vital transition from the laboratory to clinical use by transforming a scientific possibility to therapeutic application. This process, which was vital for success in the pharmaceutical industry, was about to come under scrutiny. It was subjected to further regulation by the FDA during the 1960s when tragic events surrounding Thalidomide and the widespread public concern that followed, resulted in the intervention of the Kennedy administration to ensure urgent legislative action to secure the greater safety of drugs which was to affect all pharmaceutical manufacturers.

CHAPTER 9

Investment in RD&M, laboratory reorganisation, and the FDA Drug Amendment Act of 1962

The 1962 Drug Efficacy Amendment to the Federal Food, Drug, and Cosmetics Act required manufacturers to provide proof of the safety and efficacy of drugs before approval. Disclosure of side effects became mandatory for labelling and advertising. Clinical trialling also became subject to closer regulation. By compelling companies to collect and report adverse reactions to new drugs prior to entering into a revised approval process, the FDA presented a serious challenge to those manufacturers unprepared to meet the new requirements.[1] However, at Tuckahoe reform and reorganisation had already begun in this direction during the directorship of Brigadier General Dr John R. Wood who was appointed as a vice-president in 1953 and leader of both the pharmaceutical and clinical departments.

Wood had graduated with an MA in chemistry and biochemistry from Columbia University and was director of medical research at Edgewood Arsenal, Maryland during the war.[2] He was chief of the medical division army chemical centre between 1945 and 1950. Prior to becoming commandant of the Walter Reed Army Institute of Research, from which he was recruited to Burroughs Wellcome & Co., (USA) Inc., Wood had been chairman and research director of the medical research board at the office of the Surgeon General.[3] After conducting a review of the company's research laboratories in 1957, Wood concluded that while the increasing number of new compounds researchers had been synthesizing was important, the chances of successful discovery were limited by the tendency towards adopting a single-purpose focus and to filing away the results without further action. His view was that the history of research was replete with accidental discoveries and seeming failures being turned into dramatic successes. With this in mind, he advocated a broader pharmacological assessment of the preparations produced by chemists. To achieve this, he introduced reforms intended to systematize, expand, and intensify the screening process. He also took steps intended to remedy a perceived lack of adequate communication between chemists and pharmacologists.[4]

Alongside production and distribution units, Wood reorganized separate research, development, and medical departments into a third major operational and functional unit, RD&M. The pharmacodynamics department was led by de Beer, chemotherapy by Hitchings, pharmaceutical and chemical development by Beale, and the medical division by Searle. Both pharmacodynamics and chemotherapy departments included dedicated sections of organic chemistry, biochemistry, and pharmacology. The distinctive sections within pharmacodynamics were clinical pharmacology, parisitology, and pathology. The distinctive groups within chemotherapy were biology, microbiology and bacteriology. This organisation of RD&M remained between 1955 and 1961. Wood's reforms were followed by an immediate increase in the rate of activity. Whereas 275 new compounds were synthesized out of 436 screening, toxicity, and pharmacology studies in 1955/6, comparative results in 1958/9 were 455 new compounds from 1,733 studies. This reflected especially well on productivity in the medical division and in the development laboratories.

Following the death of de Beer and Wood's retirement in 1961, the board decided that RD&M should be managed under a joint directorship. Hitchings was director of chemotherapy while the newly-appointed Dr John Burns assumed the directorship of pharmacodynamics. Burns was formerly deputy chief of the laboratories of chemical pharmacology at the National Heart Institute. He brought with him Dr Allan Conney whose role was to lead biological pharmacology at Tuckahoe, and two more former NHI senior researchers, Drs Kuntzman and Salvador.[5] Other important appointments were intended to strengthen the medical department where new government regulations introduced in 1962 rendered the provision of extra resources devoted to toxicological and clinical studies even more of a priority than before. Henceforward every pharmaceutical company would have to strengthen toxicology to meet stringent FDA requirements before approving products for release and marketing.[6] In October 1962, the company appointed Dr Jean Weston as director of medical affairs who, in collaboration with Hitchings and Burns, would devise methods of studying the therapeutic usefulness and toxicology of newly-discovered drugs. Weston's wife, Dr Kathleen Weston, joined Searle's team to lead toxicology (also reporting to Burns). A biostatistician, Ronald Gauch, was another of several appointments related to the perceived need to meet the new FDA requirements; his expertise was intended to benefit medical and research staff across all departments.[7]

The achievements of RD&M during the 1960s owed much to Creasy's enduring support for Hitchings and his team. This took the form of major investment in buildings, equipment, and increased recruitment of personnel in the laboratories. Only some of these developments were a consequence of the new legislation. By 1957, the board had prepared plans and cost estimates required for a major investment plan for which, until that time, resources had not been available due to the financial demands of WFL. Having eventually secured agreement with WFL over dividends, the company's major five-year investment plan began to be implemented in 1957 in an intensified drive to discover and develop new therapeutic medicines. This also meant provision for improved clinical evaluation through human toxicity and clinical studies prior to submitting drug applications to the FDA.

Figure 9.1 *Organisation of RD&M at Tuckahoe, NC, 1955–1968/7*

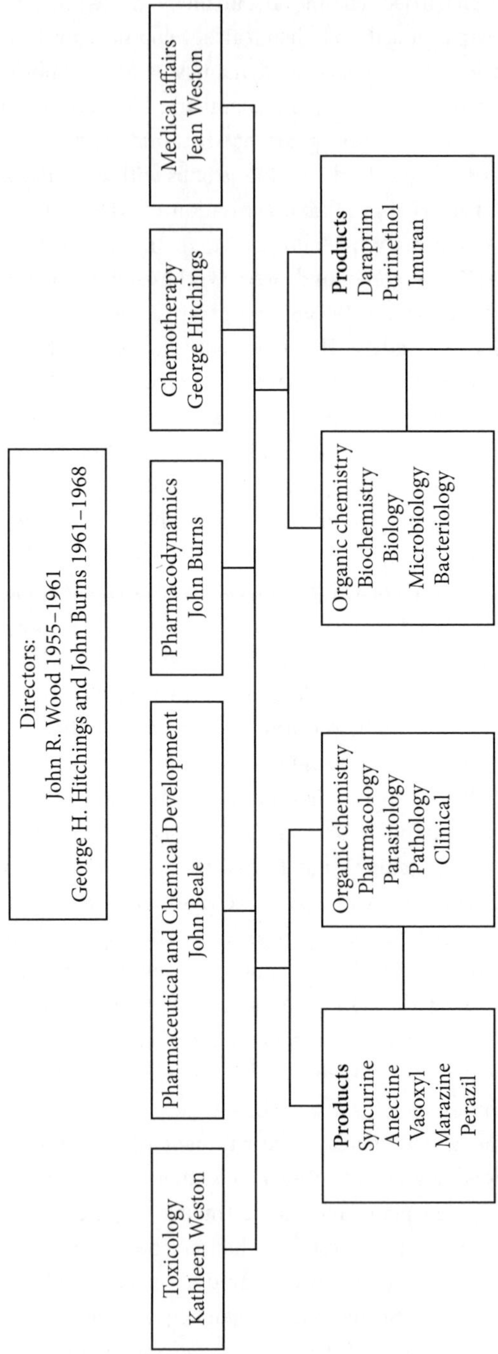

In this respect, Hitchings and Creasy anticipated some of the principal changes introduced as requirements under the regulatory system following the amended legislation of 1962. Creasy's 1960 presidential address had drawn attention to the current weakness in the industry which was an inadequate regard for the importance of improved clinical evaluation. Creasy accused many other companies of having used insufficient animal and human pharmacology before issuing a drug, "We and other pharmaceutical companies are coming to a realization of the necessity for doing thoroughly responsible clinical studies of drugs and from such studies to provide the profession with factual information on clinical usefulness, toxicity, side-effects, dosage, precautions and contra-indications."[8] These sentiments, even the language, were wholly consistent with views expressed before the Senate Subcommittee on Anti-Trust and Monopoly in 1959. Creasy condemned the failure of companies to insist upon satisfactory experimental designs before proceeding with clinical investigations. One consequence of inadequate studies was a scarcity of sufficient pharmacological and toxicity data to present to medical staff. Further problems were shortages of patients available to take part in clinical trials and the overloading of those physicians known to be competent to conduct studies of high quality. In order to tackle these problems and "to get the best out of the research … being done by our chemists, biochemists, pharmacologists, and others,"[9] the company's policy had been to expand the medical unit which by 1960, employed sixteen staff, compared with the same number in the development laboratories and ninety-six in the research laboratories divided between pharmacology and chemotherapy.[10] A physician trained and experienced in the cancer chemotherapy field was appointed to guide clinical trials and develop connections between chemotherapy researchers and appropriate clinical centres across the country. The expansion of laboratory space, increased staff numbers, and departmental reorganisation were accompanied by the creation of new roles, all part of the investment program aimed at achieving the company's long-term goal, originally set out by Nevin and embraced by Creasy, at the centre of which was the discovery and manufacture of therapeutic medicines of the highest quality

The greatest immediate impact of the 1962 Act was the demand for more resources to implement stringent requirements for an obligatory, detailed *documentation* of research, clinical trials, of production methods and procedures, and the packaging and labelling of all new prescription drugs prior to submission for approval. This exercise involved several senior researchers, medical staff, and lawyers at the company spending hundreds of hours studying and interpreting the regulations with respect to clinical investigation and the introduction of new drugs.[11] Existing products, including Marezine, Actidil, Perazil, Alcopara, and Empirin Compound were required to undergo toxicology and mechanism-of-action studies. All phases of production were affected by the regulations. Modification of formulations became necessary, as did the revision and reprinting of a high proportion of labels and packing circulars, and the preparation of analytical control data to certify, for the first time, every batch of antibiotic products. Revisions were approached with caution because the new regulations were imprecise and long production runs were discontinued, resulting in interruptions and costly overtime.[12] New regulations on packaging and promotion were intended to abolish past practice which had relied excessively on medical testimonials and clinical impressions, rather than hard evidence based on well conducted and carefully designed clinical studies. To meet the new standards, packaging, labels, and all other promotional literature had to be reviewed and revised where necessary in order to ensure disclosure of information relating to indications of use and dosage, contra-indications, and side effects. Although the exercise was completed within months, it was carried out only by a substantial diversion of the company's personnel to carry out the process.[13]

The 1962 amendments were followed by further regulations and "policy orders," one of which was issued in 1964 requiring records and extensive reports on every product covered prior to June 1963, each accompanied by a completed New Drug Application (NDA) or Antibiotic Certification form. Regulations which had applied before 1964 were deemed by the FDA to be insufficient to justify approval, therefore each drug currently sold, to which the regulations applied, required an "efficacy report" in addition to the pre-1964 report of evidence of safety. This new order presented a particular threat to antibiotic preparations, the most frequently prescribed drugs in the US accounting for 14 per cent of all prescriptions during the early 1960s.[14] Antibiotics represented 20 per cent of the company's sales.[15] In 1966, the company received a policy order which threatened removal of all batches of major antibiotic preparations from the market. In 1966, the new drug commissioner, Dr James L. Goddard, summarily ordered the removal of all of the company's antibiotic sporin products from the market, banning the introduction of further batches until efficacy of the drugs had been proven, an instruction not open to appeal. Hitherto, Creasy had supported regulation which he believed to be necessary to deal with competition from companies unwilling or unable to conduct R&D along ethical lines. However, as an unanticipated recipient of the FDA's new powers, Creasy now became a fierce critic of the FDA's methods. His characteristically robust response was to describe the FDA as "a capricious and unpredictable dictatorship which demands of industry instant obedience yet in its own performance is often incredibly slow, inconsistent, and confused." He accused Goddard of being guilty of targeting individual companies "without prior notice, sometimes without supportable grounds and with maximum publicity."[16]

Apart from the difficulties created by the 1966 order relating to existing products, in most other important respects the overall impact of the 1962 Act on the company was less than that experienced by many other pharmaceutical companies. The expansion of facilities and staff begun in 1957 ensured that only marginal additional resources were required to meet the FDA's newly defined "adequate" preclinical toxicity studies which became a pre-requisite for human studies; henceforward, all New Drug Indications studies (NDIs) must receive informed consent prior to permission to proceed. The distribution of an experimental drug under these procedures involved the acquisition of the written agreement of nominated investigators to supervise administration of the drug to patients, and an undertaking to refrain from distribution to other investigators. However, other than the increased demand on the company's resources to arrange greater numbers of trials and to provide more extensive documentation conforming to the FDA's detailed instructions, none of these provisions in the statute had a major impact on current practices.[17]

This was because, since the opening of the experimental research laboratories at Tuckahoe in the 1920s, the essential methodology employed in research and development was along ethical lines, typified from the 1940s by the work and achievements of de Beer and Hitchings and their respective teams.[18] The FDA requirement that companies must "exercise due regard for the professional ethics of physicians and the interests of patients" and ensure "good manufacturing practices"[19] did not present the company with a problem. That part of the new statute which had a serious impact on the company and led to a further surge in investment and recruitment was the ending of mere notification that a drug was safe. This was replaced by a requirement that "substantial evidence" of extensive, well-controlled clinical investigations to demonstrate safety must be presented as part of the pre-market approval process. Henceforward the evidence was to be judged by independent experts engaged by the FDA for the purpose. Other significant amendments extended automatic approval of new drug applications (NDAs) in the absence of a response by the FDA from 60 to 180 days.

Future requirements laid down by the FDA had influenced the contents of Hitchings's five-year plan, drawn up for Urwick Orr in 1966 to include a doubling of the space available for research and clinical work and increased spending on research, the medical division, and the chemical and pharmaceutical development laboratories. It included renovation and expansion of improved animal quarters, necessarily more complex because of the greater variety in testing required by Congressional legislation. He also proposed increasing annual expenditure on RD&M from between 6 and 7 per cent to at least 10 per cent of sales revenues.[20] Although marginal to the consultants' UK based review, Coe's overall five-year plan for expansion of the company which incorporated Hitchings's contribution attracted criticism from the investigators from Urwick Orr consultants who described it as unrealistic. Coe's predicted sales growth estimates based on existing and new products in the pipeline were not questioned, neither were the estimates of production and investment levels required. The criticism focused on a perceived underestimate of the space required to meet the targets and of a failure to recognize that the scale of expansion of modern manufacturing and warehousing in addition to R&D facilities envisaged could not be accommodated at Tuckahoe.[21] Nonetheless, an unchanged plan for growth was incorporated into proposals to the WFL board in London in 1967 based on the claim that new products with large commercial potential were beginning to enter the pipeline and justified WFL support.[22] The board accepted the plan, including levels of investment. The space issue remained unresolved.

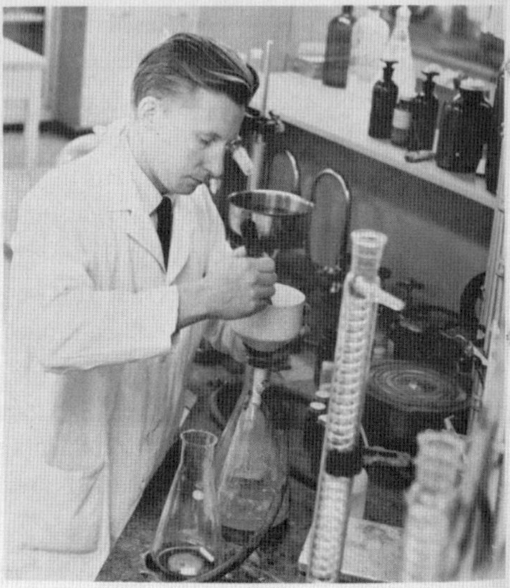

The new Chemical and Development Laboratories at Tuckahoe, 1966.

The FDA legislation had strengthened the case for protecting the American company's profits for re-investment in RD&M at Tuckahoe. Added to an improved infrastructure, new appointments enhanced the reputation of the laboratories and staff at Tuckahoe. Among recent appointments, Burns enjoyed a national reputation and had established links with various influential bodies across the scientific community.[23] Also like Hitchings, Elion, and others in the laboratories at Tuckahoe, he was a member of editorial boards and important industry and government committees. Through prolific publication of papers in leading scientific journals (listed in annual reports of the research committee) a reputation was established for the company's laboratories comparable to those of other pharmaceutical companies in possession of far greater resources. Creasy was conscious of the significance of the company's senior researchers despite the long wait for new, commercially significant products. He described Hitchings, Elion, and Burns as experiencing constant pressure to speak at scientific and medical meetings in all parts of the world.[24]

The addition of the extensive networks established by Burns to those which de Beer, Hitchings, and Elion had created provided the basis for a policy which went beyond a simple expansion of staff during the 1960s. Reputation within the scientific community attracted outside investigators from across the US, Canada, and Europe, each spending

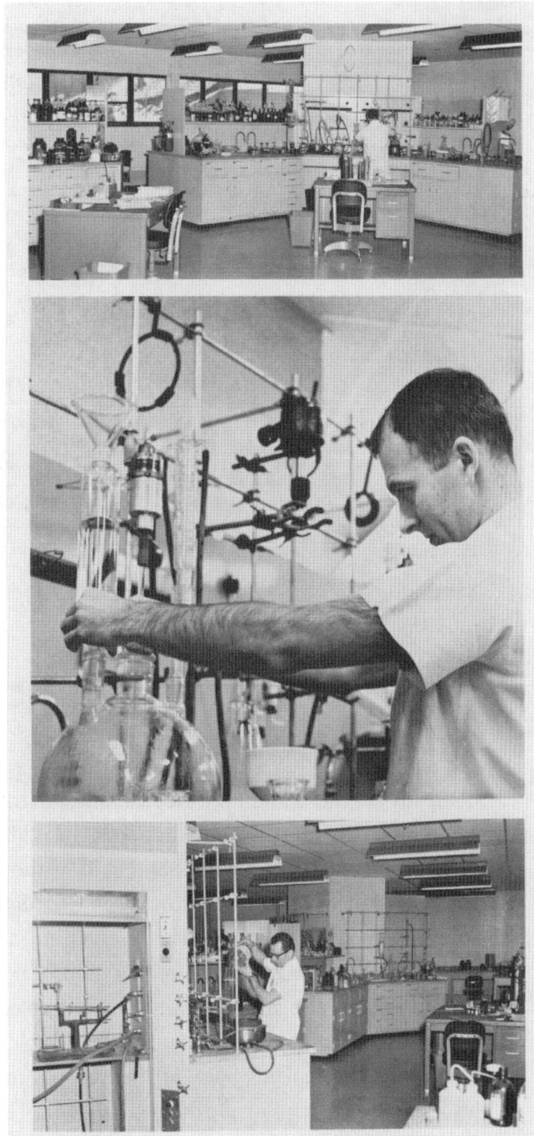

periods, often several months, at Tuckahoe to work on aspects related to drug action, metabolism, and the interaction of drugs.[25] Creasy alluded to such benefits in his 1963 presidential report when he praised senior research staff at Tuckahoe, "When they have drugs that are promising or of interest they have no trouble persuading investigators at the National Institute of Health, in medical schools, and clinics to place our compounds under study."[26] The resulting network facilitated collaborative programs associated with cross-licensing agreements, some initiated with other companies and others with university schools and departments, with NIH research groups, and with other scientific organizations.

The implications for all pharmaceutical companies of the new regulative legislation introduced in 1962 accelerated the growth of the medical department. The general shortage of scientists adequately trained in clinical pharmacology presented a problem in the industry; less than one-third of medical schools in the US were believed to possess clinical pharmacology departments judged to be highly competent.[27] Partly as an attempt to alleviate this problem and partly because of the general sudden expansion of demand for such people following the 1962 legislation, in 1966 the board endorsed a strategy which had emerged out of the inter-active networks previously established. Hitchings and Burns were encouraged to seek medically- qualified members of staff who possessed training and experience in fundamental aspects of biochemistry, pharmacology, or toxicology. The new members of staff were to work on a part-time basis in the laboratories and selected medical centres where they would be expected to develop close contacts with specialist medical investigators working in collaboration with the

Table 9.1 *BW&Co. total employment: RD&M, sales and marketing, and production, 1960–1980*

	1960	*1972*	*1974*	*1976*	*1978*	*1980*
Research		241	283	313	368	396
Development		105	130	255	324	370
Medical		23	35	53	65	86
RD&M	**106**	**369**	**448**	**621**	**757**	**852**
Marketing		68	81	95	105	103
Sales representatives		497	543	591	589	591
Sales and marketing	**278**	**565**	**624**	**686**	**694**	**694**
Production		**606**	**678**	**764**	**846**	**963**
Total Employment		**1,709**	**1,983**	**2,325**	**2,618**	**3,403**
Percentages						
RD&M		22	23	27	29	29
Sales and marketing		33	31	30	27	24
Production		18	34	33	32	33

Source: Data supplied by Fred Coe Jr, by fax, 9 May 2002.

company on the initial toxicological and pharmacological studies of newly-developed compounds in animals and humans. In addition to valuable interaction between external medical investigators and staff of the medical department at Tuckahoe was the provision of technical information and data for use by research staff. To ensure feedback, members of staff were expected to maintain close contact with the medical division in the process of the preparation of reports on products for the FDA.[28]

Other staff also moved in and out of university science departments and medical schools, for example Dr Stata Norton Ringle who, after several years working in laboratories at the University of Kansas, was re-employed as research pharmacologist at Tuckahoe. After Burns resigned in 1968, Hitchings was appointed vice president RD&M with a seat on the board, the first time, Creasy reported, that "scientific opinion and guidance" would begin to contribute directly to executive decision-making and company policy.[29] These developments resulted in a threefold increase in the numbers employed in RD&M between 1960 and 1972 which compared with a doubling of the size of the sales and marketing departments. This trend continued during the 1970s when further expansion of the numbers of RD&M employees outstripped those in sales and marketing. Hitchings proceeded to reorganize research, integrating the two hitherto existing divisions to form a unified multi-divisional structure which both eliminated overlap between sections and maximized opportunities for interdisciplinary research and development. In 1967, a new department of experimental therapy was opened under the direction of Gertrude Elion.

Figure 9.2 *Organisation of RD&M at Research Triangle Park, NC, 1970–1987*

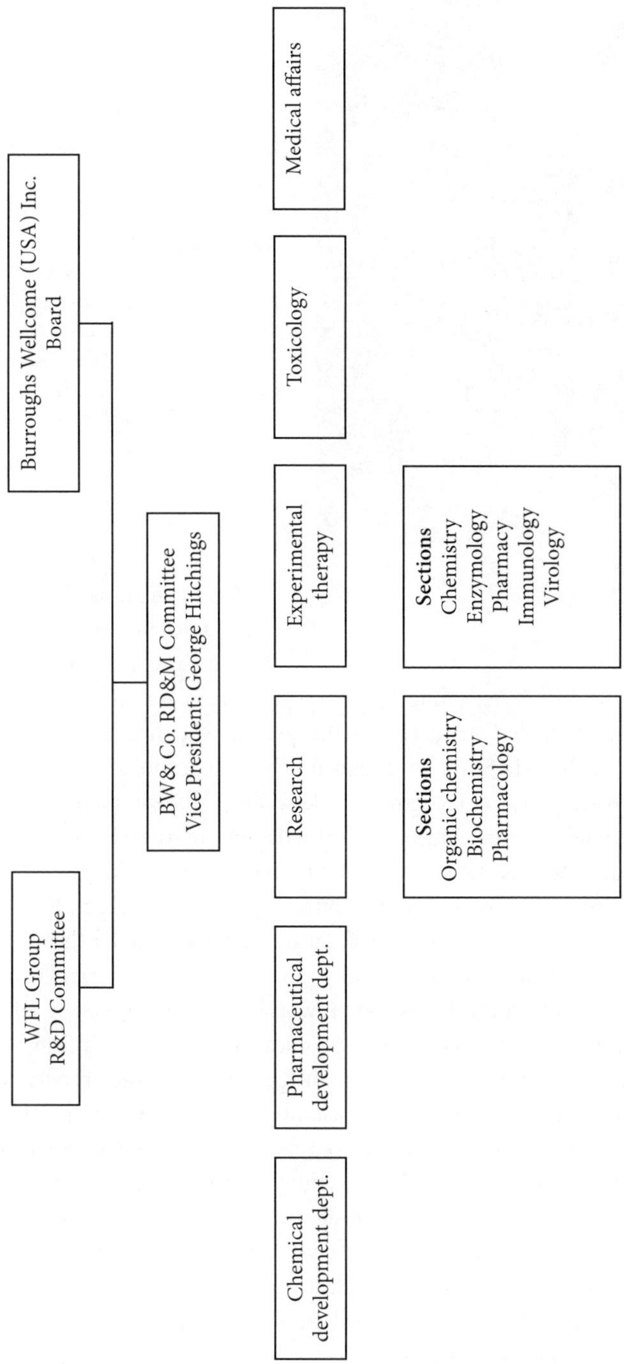

Ronald Cresswell was born in Scotland but recruited to BW&Co. in 1962 by Hitchings as a biochemist. He became head of development research, technical and development director, and subsequently managing director of Wellcome Biologicals Ltd and main board director of WFL. After playing a critical role in transforming drug discoveries into products suitable for production on a commercial scale, he resigned from Wellcome plc in 1987, finally admitting defeat in his attempt to reform and integrate a fractious R&D organisation in the UK which he believed necessary to a strategy intended to create a functionally effective multinational company partly by adopting best practice at BW&Co. in the US. *Wellcome News.*

On the margin of reorganized unified multi-divisional structure of RD&M was Ronald Cresswell. Later, Hitchings would lend support to his becoming his successor. Theirs was not always a harmonious relationship, though Hitchings was the person who had appointed him in 1962. Cresswell was born in Scotland, attended Whitehill School in Glasgow, and graduated from the University of Glasgow. While a PhD student there, he was invited to a CIBA conference to contribute to discussions of the chemistry and biology of purines with other participants amongst whom were Hitchings and Elion. In 1960, Cresswell's research took him to the Sloan Kettering Institute in New York where, at a meeting of the American Chemical Society, he encountered them again. Cresswell had surprised Hitchings by successfully synthesizing 2-imino riboflavin (an analogue of vitamin B2) which Hitchings had previously admitted to having failed to do more than twenty times even though he was a leader in Cresswell's field of research into pterididine and purines. The outcome of their meeting was an offer to Cresswell of an appointment as a senior biochemist working with Hitchings. This he accepted, declining a similar offer he had received from ICI.[30] Soon Cresswell's sense of being excluded from the long-established tightly knit group of researchers surrounding Hitchings led him to the point of resigning to join ICI after all. However, Creasy's high regard for Cresswell's potential[31] outweighed a risk of continuing friction should Cresswell stay. In 1964, Creasy's radical organisational solution to avoid alienating Hitchings was to disengage Cresswell from Hitchings by inventing a new position as head of development research. Cresswell's one-man department was intended to work in parallel with the research of Hitchings, though Cresswell would work from a laboratory, shortly to be built, specifically dedicated to drug development.

Following Cresswell's sideways promotion, Hitchings appointed Dr Krenitsky, formerly a biochemist at Yale Medical School, to lead the biochemistry department while Burns appointed Dr Kozma, formerly Professor of Pathology at Central University of Venezuela, to head pathology and toxicology, and Dr Robert Maxwell, formerly of Vermont Medical School, to lead pharmacology. The latter was joined by Dr Cervone from Downstate Medical School and by Dr Sigg, formerly with Geigy. Donald A. Knight was appointed to coordinate and prepare investigations prior to drug submissions and applications[32] and to take charge of regulatory affairs by assisting in all matters pertaining to FDA regulations. Among the most important appointments of all was that of a pioneering chemist, Howard Schaeffer, in 1970. Formerly a professor at Texas University, he was to have a major impact both as research leader and directly on the company's financial performance in succeeding decades.

These were significant new appointments, but the replacement of an ailing, unpredictable Creasy by Coe as president was also of huge significance for the future of RD&M and the company, both in the short and longer term. Creasy's resignation coincided with the imminent fruition of the basic molecular pharmacological research which he had encouraged with patience since the 1940s and was about to result in commercially successful products.[33] Several important therapeutic advances had been made since the early 1950s, but not until the late 1960s did new products commanding sales in volume enter the pipeline. Zyloprim brand allipurinol, the result of research conducted by Hitchings and Elion, was launched as a treatment for gout in 1968 and represented 6 per cent of sales by the end of the first year in production. This compared with Empirin (31 per cent), and the sporin line of products (18 per cent). This compared favorably with the combined sales of Sudafed and the recently introduced Actifed (12 per cent), and Lanoxin (7 per cent). A rise in Zyloprim sales from $2.6 million to $8.5 million took sales to 14 per cent of total sales by 1970. The ranking of the other main products in 1970 were: Empirin (27 per cent), the Sporins (18 per cent), and Actifed and Sudafed (15 per cent). Although the Sporins and Actifed and Sudafed had reduced the company's overwhelming dependence on Empirin for sales and profits, the scientific breakthrough, which would secure a scale of commercial success which Creasy had awaited with a mixture of frustration and rising apprehension since the 1940s, materialized only as he was on the point of resignation. Septra was launched in the US after he had left the company.

This raises the question as to why Creasy and the American board of directors showed such patience, continuing to invest in the project for so long without commercial result. The absence of new products irked Creasy. He was concerned about the opportunity cost of Hitchings's insistence on pursuing research in the unfashionable direction of nucleic acid and establishing the company's reputation within the wider scientific community (though he later came to value this). Contrasting temperaments heightened the tension between the two, especially during the last ten years of Creasy's presidency which were marked by his increasing lack of self-control. Creasy was ebullient, expansive, a highly sociable person motivated by the constant pursuit of profitable business, whereas Hitchings was reticent, thoughtful, and dedicated to scientific research, though also occasionally unpredictable in relationships with colleagues.[34]

Perhaps Creasy's background as a pharmacist gave him an appreciation of the contribution pure research offered mankind, but he was well aware that profit was vital to sustain continued investment in research. Elion later attributed Creasy's patience with the team for so long as a consequence of his own ignorance of research to which he felt he had nothing to contribute and therefore reluctant to interfere. Creasy respected the opinions of Dale and the two research directors, Kellaway and Adamson, who all appreciated the value of the research carried out at Tuckahoe. Elion also attached special importance to Kettering's interest in the work of Hitchings and his team. Dale, Kellaway, and Adamson were scientists, whereas "... the fact that someone as brilliant and money-minded as Mr. Kettering had so much faith in it led to a feeling of 'well you know, here he's got this prophet [Hitchings] on his own back doorstep and maybe he'd better look again'."[35]

In effect, for many years, Creasy's patient support of the biochemistry department was a matter of faith, validated by that shown by others in whose judgment he trusted.[36] Creasy later reflected on how vital for the company's survival and long term growth was his persistence in encouraging scientists at Tuckahoe to develop combinations of drugs originally discovered in the UK, development of which had been either discontinued or discarded before entering the market. Creasy described how they enabled the company "patiently to keep ... researchers going ... by scratching along with some shake-'em-up-and-mix-'em preparations which turned out to be useful, profitable, and able to keep not only the US show on the road but also the Foundation and its subsidiaries."[37] Those products were not difficult to develop and market, though he emphasized the requirement for "just a little initiative, imagination, and a lot of faith." Innovative primarily in a commercial sense, they attracted scorn amongst the purists. Creasy observed later that several people remaining with the organisation in the 1970s were "still basking in the profits and glory of these preparations."[38] By the time he left office, a sufficient assembly of creative research staff and accumulated research momentum existed at Tuckahoe so that the new president could emulate a confidence in the company's scientists comparable with that which Creasy had shown hitherto. The new president matched the ambition shown for the company by his predecessors. From the outset Coe showed a determination to project the company as research-based, innovative, and capable of competing with the leading large pharmaceutical manufacturers in the US. In order to realize this ambition, any major development had to be subject to approval by the WFL board in London. Coe envisioned a dramatic relocation of all of the American activities from the cramped conditions in New York to rural North Carolina, and the construction of buildings of stunning architectural design that would herald a significant transition projecting a national, modern, corporate image.

PART THREE:

Relocating the company and remaking corporate image

CHAPTER 10

Relocation from Tuckahoe to Research Triangle Park: North Carolina and the creation of a corporate identity

When, in 1967, the American company's case for expanding production and research capacity was presented by Creasy to the WFL board it was accepted in principle. He was invited to explore possible alternatives for securing sufficient space to sustain expansion on the scale implied by the company's five-year plan.[1] Creasy delegated this task to Coe who was to be assisted by Dowling, vice president and general counsel and Pressel, personnel manager. The firm of Lockwood Greene & Associates, engineering and architectural consultants, were commissioned to conduct a cost benefit comparison between expanding capacity either on the Tuckahoe site or at possible alternative locations.[2] Since 1925, activities had become scattered across six parcels of land traversed from east to west by a major street and bisected from north to south by the Hudson River. Additional constraints on physical expansion were imposed by the adjacent Penn Central Railroad, the Bronx River Parkway, and long-established businesses and residential housing. The factory, offices, and workshops comprised thirty-three separate buildings of varying heights up to six stories. Options were limited further by the absence of adjoining property available for purchase. The consultants advised that, in order to meet the requirements for future growth in production (which had been doubling every five years since the 1950s), the site at Tuckahoe would need to be redesigned completely. This would involve expensive reconstruction which, even on completion, was predicted to be inadequate to meet the target for output and an expanded work force to be met within ten years. The consultants concluded that Tuckahoe had outgrown its location and that a new site should be found. Initially, Coe and his colleagues showed caution and submitted a planning proposal to the Tuckahoe mayor's planning board for permission to elevate a building to five stories. When the proposal was rejected, Coe drew the mayor's attention to the only option open to the village's largest employer which was to leave Tuckahoe altogether after forty-three years.[3] In January 1968, Fantus, a consultancy firm specialising in identifying locations for businesses, was engaged to identify sites which met economic criteria specified by the company, regardless of geographical locations. Fantus was to explore costs and benefits of relocating to: (1) a new site within a sixty mile radius of Tuckahoe, (2) a site in New England, and (3) any site east of the Mississippi River. Coe and Dowling visited two sites for which Fantus expressed preferences, one in Connecticut the other in North Carolina. The preferred option on cost grounds was the southern state because land and real estate costs in Connecticut were roughly seventy times higher than in North Carolina where industrial sites were on offer at $1,200 an acre; building costs were also substantially lower than in the north eastern state.[4]

Before describing the process of final decision-taking and the process of relocation, explanation for the removal from Tuckahoe to North Carolina deserves consideration. Tanner, an assistant manager in the public affairs department and the author of "The American Story" that appeared in the house journal "Wellcome News" in 1981, explained the move as necessary because the company had "nowhere to grow."[5] This explanation was consistent with the rhetoric of public relations that surrounded the issue outside the company at the time. Physical limitation was certainly the important consideration which necessitated expanding space, not least to avoid the frequent overtime (a cause of friction) required of production workers to meet rapidly growing demand. However, in addition to physical and planning constraints, cost reduction and a reform of labor relations were equally important motives, though mention of these appeared neither in Tanner's account nor in contemporary public pronouncements by company spokesmen.

The Taft-Hartley Law, introduced in 1946/7, led to a more bureaucratic approach to labor relations after the war. Creasy established a personnel department which, unlike the previous industrial relations department, included non-production workers. The new department developed a system of procedures which was published in bulletin form to explain how to proceed on matters involving hiring, separations, dissemination of personnel information, safety, disciplinary action, records, recreation and entertainment, transfers and promotions, and a general statement concerning employee relations. A handbook was issued to all new employees in which was contained an address from Creasy. This included a brief history of the company, an outline of the organisation, and full information on personnel policies and procedures. The president's annual report for 1948/9 praised the personnel department for efforts "to encourage in departmental heads and supervisors whose employees are Union members a feeling of importance of working with the Union and not as its antagonist. It has been emphasized to all that the initial cooperation of the Union in any problem will accomplish the task at hand almost every time. The Union people desire to be a part of the Company and to be treated as members of the team."[6] Creasy emphasized that harmonious relations would make for improved production and raise understanding of the company's problems among employees. War and a shortage of labor resulting from the draft into the armed forces had energized trade unions. The first potential postwar crisis occurred in the company's new San Francisco branch office in 1947 when the company was threatened with strike action. An agreement between management and union was signed with the Warehousemen's Union Local 860.[7] The most important contract to secure, however, was that struck with the International Chemical Workers' Union Local no. 7, A.F. of L. which represented hourly-paid production workers.[8] Contracts reached with both were of two or three years' duration. Progress on another front was achieved with the recruitment of John Sciarpelletti, formerly president of the Production Workers' Union, to the personnel department in 1947 where he became supervisor of the job training and safety section.[9]

Creasy was the driving force behind the company's policies designed to promote employees' welfare. These consisted of a successively reduced working week, enhanced sickness and accident leave, retirement, insurance, and vacation and holiday entitlement.[10] A pension scheme which benefitted both salaried and hourly-paid employees, and provision of medical (including hospital) care was favorably compared with those at IBM. All were improved progressively until his retirement in 1968. With the intention of ensuring high morale among employees and to contribute to greater job satisfaction, he introduced a program of formal orientation for all new employees. This was intended to encourage identification with the company; an employees' safety committee and an employees' education fund completed the welfare structure. Creasy also introduced management training programs designed to instruct supervisory staff as to how to apply currently perceived sound human relations practices.[11]

Company policy was spelled out in a statement of its aims regarding labor relations with respect to the role that supervisors should adopt. The company's aim was: "To give suitable employment to all workers, to remunerate them well, to promote their welfare, to assist in providing for their future, and to ensure that all employees in their respective grades are treated equitably."[12] A contemporary recalls that Creasy, who lived on site at Tuckahoe, knew everyone in the company and their family circumstances and made a habit of walking round the factory and the laboratories exchanging remarks with staff at every level "from supervisors to bottle washers … he was very opinionated. A very likeable man, but obviously very much … a nineteenth century patriarch."[13] Employees who had worked for the company for up to four decades described the culture of the company which they had joined in the 1940s and 1950s as displaying the characteristics of a second family in which everyone was friendly. Not until 1960 did the numbers employed at Tuckahoe exceed one thousand.

For most of that period when in his prime, the provision of a single cafeteria ensured interaction between managers and monthly and hourly-paid workers.[14] A Christmas hamper and turkey were distributed to all of the company's employees. Creasy knew people by their first names and was informal when speaking to employees, passing the time of day as well as expressing interest in the work being done by individual workers. Creasy was also reported to have been an enthusiastic participant in the inter-plant softball league, "pitching … in there down and dirty with the rest of the fellows."[15]

In 1961, the committee and the union had agreed a new contract which included wage increases of 5 per cent and 4.5 per cent in the two subsequent years, an increase in shift bonus, an additional holiday entitlement, and improvement in vacation and sick pay policies. Shortly after the successful negotiation, the election of a completely new and inexperienced group of union officers aroused apprehension among members of the company's negotiating committee who resolved to adopt a flexible approach to future contract negotiations. Production supervisors were instructed to show patience in handling an anticipated increase in complaints and grievances In 1966, a new three-year contract approved by the International Chemical Workers' Union gave production employees an annual 5.5 per cent wage increase, a more liberal vacation entitlement, and a gradual reduction in the working week from 40 to 37.5 hours. The negotiating committee expressed a hope that "a generous and cooperative settlement by the company would lead to more mature and constructive labor relations."[17] It is probably no coincidence that the feeling of unease occurred at the same time as the local union established closer ties with the International Office and engaged an attorney as a consultant. A source of apprehension among members of the negotiating committee was their sense that the new union leaders had emasculated shop stewards with whom relations in the past had been peaceful and constructive, by concentrating power of negotiation within a small executive committee. Other matters for concern were large increases in the numbers of requests for time off in which to conduct union business and pressure for shared partnership with managers in determining the outcome of any individual's grievance. These demands were symptomatic of a new, forceful approach by the union towards the limits of managerial control. From the standpoint of the negotiating committee, the local union was challenging managerial responsibility for supervising workers.

The context of these developments was the growth of union activism in the US and the policy of the federal government. The first was manifest in a general tendency among unions to challenge company rights and privileges without offering practical solutions. This was attributed to the encouragement of a militant attitude among workers by the international office of the International Chemical Workers' Union (ICWU). The second arose from the uncertainty arising partly from decisions of the Supreme Court and lower courts which were perceived to have favored "liberal interpretations" of the labor laws, and partly from decisions made by the National Labour Relations Board and also from arbitrators' opinions.[18] It was against this background that labor relations had reached a nadir at Tuckahoe by 1967, evidence of which was an increasing number of unresolved grievance cases submitted by the union. Pressel accused the union executive committee of persistently exaggerating grievances of a kind which hitherto had been resolved at departmental level, but which the new officials took to the fourth and final stage of the grievance procedure.[19] For these reasons, Coe, who was leading the exploration of options for relocation but also attended negotiating committee's meetings, saw that plant relocation on space and land cost considerations might also afford an opportunity to leave the company's labor difficulties behind. Privately, Coe recorded that the principal attraction of establishing a non-unionized plant was the termination of twenty-five years of operating the production unit "under the duress of a Union contract" and the protection of the line managers' prerogative in implementing policy and handling an individual's grievance. A diary entry underlines his thinking: "the only way to get this straightened out would be to move away and to hope to get rid of the union."[20] He was also swayed by the two million dollar annual savings which the consultants predicted would result from the lower labor costs gained by moving to the south.[21]

From London, Wrigley and Adamson, who were kept informed of Coe's plan, visited the proposed sites in North Carolina. Greenville in Durham County had been a prosperous tobacco manufacturing town but was now in decline and suffering from unemployment. For this reason, the consultants advised that Greenville would offer ample opportunities to recruit roughly five hundred production workers (Coe's estimated requirement) on arrival. One hundred miles west was Raleigh, located within three miles of three major universities – Duke University and the Universities of North Carolina and North Carolina State – which between them possessed two medical schools and a school of pharmacy. As a result, the center of the southern state possessed the highest concentration of PhDs in the entire US.[22]

The special attraction of Raleigh was the Research Triangle Park (RTP) situated close to Raleigh airport and unique in the US. The park had originated in a concept advanced in 1936 by Howard Odum, chairman of the Institute for Research in Social Science at the University of North Carolina, who had envisaged a public research institute where scholars could meet for conferences and workshops from which academics and society might benefit. Later, Romeo Guest, a local builder, conceived a plan to reduce the state's overdependence for employment on lowly-paid tobacco, textile, and furniture manufacturing and its reliance on supplementary income generated by educating out-of-state students. Developing Odum's research park idea, Guest envisaged the formation of an industrial park which would be able to exploit the expertise concentrated in the region's academic research complex and which would also attract research-oriented, hi-tech businesses, retain well-qualified graduates in the region, and thereby revive the economic fortunes of the State of North Carolina. The Triangle Foundation, composed of both academic and business leaders, was set up in 1956 to assist the three major universities to create a joint research institute which would act as a magnet to attract out-of state companies whose success in business depended on knowledge creation. One of the principal roles of the Triangle Foundation was to promote the concept of a potential synergy resulting from geographical proximity of business activity and research and to persuade business executives to sign up to the plan. In 1959, the universities created the Research Triangle Institute, a non-profit making body dedicated to developing and encouraging pure and applied research for use by firms active in diverse business activities and by government bodies. The institute was a wholly-owned subsidiary of the three universities and undertook contract research in a variety of fields for clients located both in the park and outside. Faculty benefited by becoming external consultants whose earnings supplemented their salaries. This proved an attraction to other academics from outside the State. Businesses benefited from the pro-active encouragement by the Park Foundation to utilize university facilities and from reciprocal faculty involvement in business-oriented R&D. By the time that Coe came to explore the park in 1968, those employed by the institute numbered nine hundred including 250 faculty. The corporate occupants included IBM (the largest employer in the Triangle), Data General Corporation, Monsanto, Becton Dickinson, Hercules, and other pharmaceutical firms, though only their non-manufacturing activities were allowed in the Park. Non-business occupants included the permanent headquarters of the Environmental Health Sciences, the Environmental Protection Agencies, and of the Chemical Industry Institute of Toxicology.[23]

On behalf of WFL, Wright, its managing director, and Adamson, its research director, approved Coe's executive committee's proposal that Greenville should be the site for a factory and Raleigh for offices and laboratories. Hitchings agreed to the removal of production to Greenville but pressed strongly for retaining research and administration in Tuckahoe (as did Elion who feared a threat to her regular attendance at the Metropolitan Opera). Leaving RD&M and/or administration in New York, of course, would have negated the synergistic benefits that Coe anticipated from the move to RTP. Although from the sideline, Creasy supported Hitchings and Elion expressing reservations, Wrigley assured Coe that the board of WFL would endorse whatever decision his executive committee reached; the cost of the plan to WFL would be zero. In effect, this gave the green light for Coe to opt for the North Carolina solution.[24] The thirty million dollar finance required to acquire 450 acres of land and the construction and equipment of buildings was to be raised locally by the American company. This paved the way for implementation of the five-year plan, prepared in 1966/7 at Urwick Orr's request and of which the consultants had approved, subject to provision of adequate space.[25] Implications of this included not only substantial growth in investment and production in the US, but also in RD&M expenditure on fundamental research the bulk of which was also to be undertaken in the US.[26] Perrin explained to the Trustees in 1970 that such commitments would ensure that "the right scientific reward would be forthcoming."[27] For the first time, WFL committed itself in principle to eliminating some research groups in the UK regarded as no longer effective.[28] The ascendancy of the American company, achieving efficient production in crowded conditions and high quality fundamental research in the equally cramped laboratories at Tuckahoe, was finally acknowledged in London, though it proved to be shortlived with the appointment of a new research director at WFL in 1973.

The recommendation by the executive committee of the American company to relocate to North Carolina was accepted by both boards and was conveyed first to all supervisory level employees in January 1969. The negotiating committee informed union officials the following day. An immediate response was the formation of a coalition consisting of Tuckahoe villagers and local government and union officials to campaign against the move. Coe hired public relations consultants Myers Infoplan International Inc. to advise on every aspect of how employees and communities might be affected and formulate policies to minimize effects. The most urgent decision consequent upon relocation, however, concerned buildings. Coe perceived an opportunity to change the company's national profile and image. Attitude surveys had shown physicians to have regarded the company as a manufacturer of high quality reliable products, but at the same time, they perceived it to be a stodgy and old-fashioned business.[29] In choosing the RTP as the precise location, Coe hoped the proximity to innovative and dynamic companies already situated there would affect the company's image which would become associated with these more modern characteristics.

New buildings of modern design and fine architecture which would provide employees with a pleasant environment would emphasize a corporate modernity. Coe took personal command of the commissioning of design and construction in which he was advised by Fantus, the consultancy firm which had identified the new location from which he chose from a shortlist of some of the most prestigious architects in the US. The board accepted Coe's recommendation of Paul Rudolph, already known to Coe as a fellow Yale graduate. Rudolph was known for creating unique designs from which his firm constructed exceptional buildings. However, presented by his drawings for the new building at RTP which showed an elevation at 22.5 degree angles, Coe agreed that a modernist appearance was conveyed but the building would be exceptional only inasmuch as it resembled "a chicken hut."[30] None the less, expressing confidence in Rudolph's fresh and exciting vision,[31] the board proceeded to raise the projected thirty million dollar cost of land, buildings, and site development through a loan from First National City Bank & Trust Co. of North Carolina.[32]

Commissioning the building and solving the financial problem proved straightforward; more difficult was persuading employees that the move was in their interest and necessary if the company were to grow. A public relations department was formed to implement Infoplan's strategy. Personal letters were sent to non-union employees from the company inviting them to relocate. The same invitation was sent to a few carefully chosen union members among those paid a salary or an hourly rate with a view to establishing a skilled, experienced, and reliable core of workers capable of supervising the introduction of manufacturing at Greenville. A key figure among this group was George Barry, a former president of the union at Tuckahoe, whom Leslie (who had replaced Pressel as personnel manager) regarded as a good employee known not to see eye to eye with some other union members. He was appointed as a supervisor in the chemical manufacturing department.[33]

Negotiating the relocation of production workers to Greenville presented the major challenge because of strong union involvement.[34] An initial problem arose because the contract with the ICWU gave the union all rights of negotiation on behalf of production workers; this prevented the company from dealing with employees directly. The initial position adopted by the international union representative was encapsulated in a declaration attributed to him, "Nobody will move there to the dismal swamp. We want the most for the mostest."[35] The union demanded generous severance pay and special pension benefits. The company agreed in principle. Only a small number of those who took severance pay subsequently applied for non-union jobs in Greenville.[36] Before decisions affecting those who were undecided were made, however, the company embarked on an elaborate consultation process. All supervisory, technical, and professional salaried employees and their spouses, and other salaried and (significantly) non-union hourly workers were offered visits to North Carolina at the company's expense; most took advantage of this. After the visits, the public relations department conducted a survey to gauge the likelihood of relocation after visiting. Among administrative, supervisory, professional, and clerical employees, 68 per cent opted to stay with the company after relocation.[37]

This was an indication of the favorable terms offered or arranged by the company for those who decided to move. The terms included all removal costs plus a month's additional salary to cover incidental expenses. Through the mortgage brokers, Homequity Inc., movers were offered assistance in selling their homes at favorable market prices. The company negotiated with two local savings and loan organizations to extend mortgages on favorable terms to the company's employees. The Wachovia Bank in Raleigh agreed to allow employees to borrow a month's salary to fund house purchase deposits. In preparation and during the process of relocation in association with InfoPlan, the public relations department distributed a monthly newsletter entitled "On the Move" to keep those affected fully informed of the progress of building construction, the plans for moving, and all other all aspects of the transition. The public relations department assumed responsibility for issuing Wellcome News, hitherto produced by the advertising department twice a year. To ensure adequate space in which to report the major and rapidly changing developments affecting all staff, the journal became a monthly publication and remained as such, following the move to North Carolina.

The plan to establish a non-unionized plant at Greenville was explicit from the outset. The personnel department was instructed to provide "all possible assistance and guidance in seeing that the Greenville plant is managed in a fashion that will make unionization unnecessary in the minds of our hourly workers ... Constant vigilance in regard to the effect our policies, fringe benefits and human relations efforts have on our employees will be required on a continuing basis."[38] Line managers were urged not to "pass the buck" to the personnel department when employees expressed dissatisfaction regarding the effects of decisions made on the basis of company policy, a tendency which had posed a problem at Tuckahoe in the past.[39]

The establishment of a new plant was accompanied by an extensive reorganisation of staff involving the appointment of new department heads and group leaders, a process not completed until 1972.[40] All production and supervisory workers who decided to move to Raleigh received training to cope with anticipated cultural changes. This included methods of handling hourly workers in the rural South as compared with

Topping out at Research Triangle Park, Mr Dowling (vice president), Dr Nichol, Dr Hitchings (research director), and Mr Rudolph (architect). *Wellcome News*, Wellcome Library, London.

those in New York. Supervisors were trained to adjust to the differences in operating a non-union plant compared with a unionized work force and they were introduced to ways of discouraging unionism and entrenched working practices.[41]

Labor difficulties at Tuckahoe encountered during the transition proved to be less serious than had been anticipated. This was largely a consequence of the election of new union officers. The new local president, Larry Trotte, showed a highly cooperative attitude, applying himself to reconciling differences between supervisors and employees, and tackling long-standing problems left by the previous union administration. Both before and after the announcement of the proposed move to Greenville, relations remained harmonious. A collaborative company-union placement office was set up, intended to assist employees who did not wish to relocate to find alternative employment. An improved grievance procedure was introduced. A permanent arbitrator, mutually approved by the company and the union, was appointed to adjudicate on issues relating to severance pay, health insurance, and related matters affecting those employees who had been laid off.[42] Among the hourly-paid (unionized) production staff, five hundred and thirty-seven were let go before the move.[43] Yet despite the hostile response of the union officials at the time of the announcement, the transfer of production from Tuckahoe was not accompanied by serious disruption.[44]

Most of the hourly paid staff needed to fill positions at Greenville had to be

Research laboratories and offices at RTP which attracted architectural awards and provided a corporate image of modernity employed in the company's publicity.

recruited locally in and around the town and given rapid training. Between September 1969 and March 1970, personnel staff processed five thousand applications for five hundred vacancies. Some were sent to Tuckahoe for training on the job, most others were trained by company supervisory staff, partly subsidized by the State of North Carolina and assisted by Pitt Community College. Potential new recruits were familiarized with production lines by watching film shot in the Tuckahoe factory which showed exactly what would be expected of them once production began. Once hired, each received four hours training before joining a line. In the absence of a union, cultural differences in the workplace posed an early problem for managers and supervisory staff. Compared with workers in New York, some of the new recruits showed a less disciplined approach on the factory floor by smoking and especially by disregarding safely rules and regulations or when safety considerations required implementation of established policy carried over from Tuckahoe. A new policy decision to prevent racial difficulties, hitherto not a problem in New York, was to insist that once an employee entered the workplace there was no "color line." Objectors would have to leave.[45]

Although the movement of manufacturing to the Greenville site was relatively smooth, major disruption was caused by the inevitable discontinuity in production caused by the move from Tuckahoe. The first products were shipped from the new factory in April 1970, though not until the summer of 1972 could the factory be described as effective as an operating unit.[46] The relocation to Raleigh also proved problematic, though the difficulties arising were architectural rather than staff related. A series of errors in design, faults in construction, and alterations (several on the insistence of senior scientists) caused delays which were costly to the company and disrupted research. Coe exercised patience and persistence in trying to assuage the doubts expressed by Hitchings and Elion who insisted they would be unable to function effectively unless alterations and adaptations were effected to provide sufficient and a suitable configuration of space.[47] Elion reckoned that between six and twelve months' research was lost as a result of the move. Office and science staff left Tuckahoe in August 1970 but could not move into the building at the Triangle until December 1972.[48]

However, the move also produced some positive developments. Until the much enlarged research laboratories were completed, occupation was a gradual process, relieved by offers of space in the laboratories of neighboring universities. Hitchings and his team had long been involved in collaboration with scientists at Duke. Consequently, it is not surprising that on arrival at RTP he was invited to become an adjunct professor by Duke, as was Elion by the University of North Carolina (UNC). By 1972, four more senior scientists became adjunct professors at the medical schools of Duke and UNC and another at UNC School of Pharmacy.[49] Such close collaboration between company scientists and academics had long been company policy. Physicians on its staff were encouraged to continue academic involvement by being permitted to spend up to 40 per cent of their working week, not only on research, but also teaching students. Teaching necessarily involved seeing patients which enabled the company's physicians to be familiar with current developments in their respective fields. Professors acted as consultants and spent sabbaticals working with the company; post-doctoral research also involved university-company cooperation and sometimes collaboration. The company's library became part of the universities' inter-library exchange, while financial contributions made by the company to the pharmacy and medical schools was indicative of a policy to integrate thoroughly the company with the scientists and physicians in organizations within a few miles radius of RTP.[50]

Alterations and adaptations to buildings contributed to an upward revision of the costs of the futuristic "chicken hut" (widely praised both nationally and locally as an architectural success). An initial estimate of $12 million in 1969 rose to $19 million by 1971, and costs continued to rise after a grand opening of the completed building which took place in April, 1972 when termites were discovered eating the concrete beneath the skin coating applied to the building. Replacement of the entire coating cost $2 million, though a realistic comparison of costs and a feasible recoverable award led the board not to proceed with legal proceedings.[51]

The opening of the new building coincided with the re-registration of Burroughs Wellcome & Co. (USA) Inc. into Burroughs Wellcome & Co. (hereafter referred to as BW&Co.) as a newly-created North Carolina corporation with a stock value of $24 million, a victory won by the board against a history of opposition by WFL. Apart from the financial advantages of re-registering in the state, Coe believed that, regardless of the legal reality of the relationship between BW&Co., WFL, and the Trust, the removal of the suffix USA would project the image of a US national company rather than as a foreign subsidiary. Coe and the board hoped that the juxtaposition of a building of striking design and leading American companies would reinforce the impression of a progressive organization with the highest aspirations. In his first report as president, Coe declared his ambition "to encourage Burroughs Wellcome & Co. to become one of the top US pharmaceutical companies."[52] In his new capacity, he expressed his approach to the company's future in characteristic style, "we can no longer fly by the seat of our pants. Careful forward planning for the best deployment of resources must be done."[53] With his predecessor's style of leadership fresh in mind, Coe committed himself to transforming the company "from one based on strong personal guidance to professional, managerial leadership and management by objective."[54] This did not, however, herald a transition from an entrepreneurial to a managerial culture. Though adopting a contrasting, more consensual style to that of his predecessor, Coe's personal guidance was central to a transformation of the image and of the substance of the company's achievements during the 1970s.

CHAPTER 11

Reorganization, management recruitment, corporate image, and the transformation of marketing

Coe's promotion to the presidency of the American company, announced on 1 April 1968, marked the beginning of a transformation of the company. The first major step towards realizing his vision was his radical approach to relocation which he regarded as a necessary condition for expansion as a manufacturer of ethical prescription drugs. The second was to obtain knowledge and experience of the policies and practices of large corporate pharmaceutical firms by appointing new personnel to undertake key roles at the most senior level. The third was a structural reorganization of the company that involved a re-definition of management functions in a re-arranged committee structure. The relocation to RTP enabled Hitchings's five-year plan to be fulfilled. More space facilitated reorganization of research, development, and medical functions within a newly-consolidated division. At the apex of the division was Hitchings as vice president responsible for research, to whom a newly created vice president (medical) reported. This was Dr Ronald Cresswell whose new role included responsibility for both chemical and pharmaceutical development and also for technical development and quality assurance in a division which assumed increasing importance to accommodate progressively burdensome requirements imposed by the FDA.

At the same time, Coe addressed the problem of the human resources required to fulfill the potential of the new facilities. After an investigation of the activities and staffing levels of competitors' medical departments, in 1972 the company embarked upon "a hiring binge of MDs" able to cope with monitoring the rapidly expanding volume and scale of clinical studies required by the FDA.[1] This had led large manufacturers of ethical medicines to expand, establish, or acquire clinical testing facilities. Upjohn initiated a national network of regional clinical laboratories to provide rapid blood and chemical tests to doctors and hospitals.[2] Abbott purchased two companies deeply involved in the clinical and diagnostic laboratory work, while Roche acquired the Kings County Research Laboratory, a clinical and diagnostic facility serving doctors and hospitals in New York; Smith, Klein, & French (SKF) purchased the Leary Laboratory of Boston which possessed expertise in clinical and nutritional chemistry, endocrinology, enzymology, immunological testing, and toxicology.[3] In part, this development was another consequence of FDA requirements. However, whereas hitherto, the College of American Pathologists had enjoyed a stranglehold over clinical testing, a successful legal action instituted in 1966 led to the issue of an anti-trust decree by the Justice Department. Henceforward, chemists and other non-MDs were permitted to operate laboratories which would be allowed to exhibit and advertise. This change, to which was added the prohibition of any boycotting of commercial laboratories and of price-fixing, had the effect of opening up the field of clinical testing to commercial competitors.

Advanced, automated, and highly accurate technology was another factor contributing to the trend towards increasing commercial clinical initiatives among the larger companies concerned to ensure state-of-the-art testing and control over the rising costs of laboratory analysis.[4] Creasy and Coe were alert to the increasing importance to ethical drug manufacturers of dedicated in-house testing facilities. Clinical testing facilities had hardly existed at Tuckahoe where medically qualified staff had been few; those at Beckenham played a minor role in supporting American scientists. Until the 1970s, toxicological and pharmacological testing had depended primarily on external contributions from a network of specialized medical investigators in medical centers in a network established by Hitchings and Burns through close personal contacts and collaborative research. A lack of medically-qualified staff and the space necessary to accommodate the greatly enlarged number and variety of animals required to meet FDA testing requirements[5] was a constraint on development and expansion until the company's relocation to RTP in 1970. The relocation made it possible to provide state-of-the-art clinical testing facilities to meet the new stringent requirements and the installation of advanced equipment appropriate for the expanded capacity. The relocation also saw a reorganization of the research, development, and medical functions within a newly-consolidated division beginning in 1972.

The proportion of resources directed towards research, development, and medical activities rose steadily throughout the 1970s. Employment in sales and marketing including advertising rose by 33 per cent compared with an increase of 130 per cent in personnel employed in RD&M. Salary expenditure on RD&M rose from 16 per cent of total salary costs to 19 per cent whereas sales and marketing including salaries for those employed in advertising fell from 39 per cent to 29 per cent.

Under the direction of Dr Chesney Goodall, the medical department was incorporated into the research laboratories within which sections were reorganized, each being allocated special responsibilities for clinical investigations, for marketed products services, and for regulatory affairs. A clinical pharmacology unit was created in collaboration with Duke University Medical School.[6] Thereafter, virtually all testing of compounds prior to the IND stage, typically conducted over a period between two and five years, took place at RTP. During the next stage, clinical testing

Table 11.1 *BW&Co. Marketing expenditure and RD&M expenses as percentages of sales, 1970–1981*

	Sales ($000)	*Rep's salaries and expenses (%)*	*Advertising Expenditure (%)*	*R&D and RD&M (%)*
1970	60,164	9	8	7
1971	68,066	9	7	9
1972	78,555	8	9	10
1973	95,352	7	10	11
1974	110,896	6	12	10
1975	142,874	6	10	10
1976	157,141	7	9	11
1977	184,106	7	10	12
1978	201,975	6	9	14
1979	237,687	6	9	15
1980	262,006	6	9	16
1981	274,227	6	9	17

Source: GWHC, BW&Co.(USA) Inc., 107.01/02, President's annual reports and accounts.

occurred at selected sites around the US in the clinics of experts who performed the studies in collaboration with the company's scientists. The reputations of Hitchings and subsequently of Schaeffer, Cuatrecasas, and others enabled the company to enlist experts' agreement to work with experimental drugs and to choose the most qualified investigators.[7]

Among the most important new appointment in 1970 was that of Peter Howsam. He was first introduced to Coe by Wrigley, vice chairman of WFL and director of BW&Co. Wrigley had been employed by CIBA in Montreal where he had met Howsam, a Canadian, who was working for SmithKline & French.[8] After leaving Harvard with an MBA in 1948, Howsam joined SmithKline & French, initially helping to build the business in Canada. During seventeen years with the company he accumulated wide-ranging experience in the US, the UK, Europe, and Australia. This included pioneering the introduction of over-the-counter pharmaceutical sales for SmithKline. In 1965, he was appointed vice president and general manager of The Canadian Warner Chilcott division Warner-Lambert, a manufacturer of pharmaceuticals and diagnostics. Within a year he became executive vice president of the Canadian company and vice president of Warner-Lambert International with responsibility for marketing worldwide. Although Wrigley was joint managing director of WFL and occupied a seat on the board of BW&Co., he did not have the power personally

Peter Howsam (left) and Clealand Baker appointed vice presidents. Peter S. Howsam, business administration graduate, vice-president of Warner-Lambert International responsible for marketing worldwide. In 1970 he was appointed to the board of BW&Co. as director of sales and marketing whose reforms drew on his experience of best practice in a large American organization. Clealand F. Baker was a pharmacy graduate who since 1941 had filled successive managerial posts responsible for sales and advertising. On Howsam's appointment he assumed responsibilities for corporate planning in relation to new drugs and conducting public relations with Washington. Both became vice presidents in 1971. Howsam remained with the company until 1985.

to recruit Howsam, though he persuaded Coe to interview him which he did at length twice in one day. Even though no post was available and Coe had not been seeking to recruit another manager, he offered Howsam an appointment as director of sales and marketing immediately, removing the incumbent to the new position of director of personnel, created especially for him.[9] Another post was created for Clealand Baker, hitherto head of marketing and advertising, who became responsible for special assignments, attending to relations with Washington and building the clinical and commercial case for new drugs prior to proposals submitted to the FDA. Charles Singler became head of sales and W. S. Adams became head of marketing services, coordinating the company's sales promotions plans, product development, packaging, market research, sales analysis, and sales forecasting. Parrish, formerly Baker's assistant responsible for advertising, was appointed to the newly-created post of director of advertising.

Howsam's arrival at RTP coincided with another important appointment from another large company in New York. Born in North Carolina, Theodore Haigler was a finance director when he had been approached by Arthur Clark, financial controller since the 1930s, who was about to retire from BW&Co. and believed Haigler would be

Theodore E. Haigler was appointed financial director of BW&Co. in 1972 and president in 1986. He soon became the central figure responsible for managing the launch of Retrovir and orchestrating the company's defence against the critical onslaught from AIDS activists, Congress, medical practitioners, and the media, which included accusations of monopoly price and profit exploitation and a demonstrable lack of moral responsibility. Although hampered by the largely unsympathetic attitude of the board in London, anxious to recoup heavy R&D investment, Haigler's policy intended to recover a loss of trust in the company was to concede price reductions and simultaneously to create a strategy involving participation of AIDS activists.

a suitable successor. In 1972, after an interview with Coe, Haigler agreed to accept the post of financial comptroller.[10] A third incomer, Thomas E. Kennedy, joined the board in the same year. He was an experienced sales representative at SmithKline & French, though his most recent role had been as vice president in charge of administration at Geigy. Coe appointed him as his personal assistant, but on Pressels's unexpected death, responsibility for engineering and production also passed to Kennedy who also became a vice president. Howsam, Haigler, and Kennedy were added to the board. In 1973, led by Coe, the new board of directors replaced the executive committee with a management coordinating committee whose responsibility was to organize three functional committees (sometimes referred to as divisions) each chaired by a vice president. These were the research committee, chaired by Hitchings; the distribution committee, chaired by Howsam; and the production committee, chaired by Kennedy. A patents committee, chaired by L. A. Nielson, was regarded as a specialist service unit, rather than one of the major functional committees.[11] Although the vice presidents were given corporate responsibilities, they did not form part of a corporate structure; the process of executive decision-making described by Kennedy continued to be effected on a personal basis, "management was not a one man band" but Coe was universally respected within a "fluid management structure including lots of consultation."[12]

This incomplete reform of the management structure did not prevent substantial change being brought about by the new vice presidents. The new position of office manager was charged with the task of standardizing administrative, secretarial, and clerical services.[13] Greater standardization and control were also important elements in Haigler's reform of finance. When Howsam had joined the company in 1970, he was critical of a lack of departmental financial accountability to head office, a

Figure 11.1 *Organisation of Burroughs Wellcome & Co., 1970–1987*

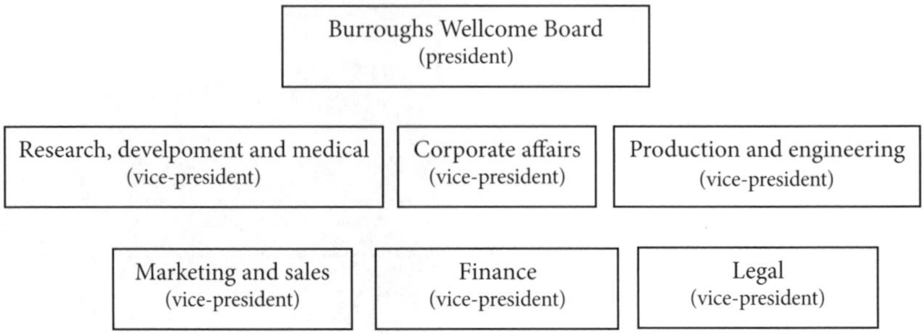

culture which he contrasted with the "numbers … and profit-oriented" ethos that had prevailed at Warner Lambert.[14] Haigler overhauled the costing system, introduced computerization, and raised levels of financial accountability and control in all parts of the organization to produce an environment of a kind with which Howsam had been familiar at Warner Lambert International and Kennedy at Geigy. Another reform introduced by Coe, with advice from management consultants, was that of career development and management training, part of his drive towards professionalization and improved motivation among an expanding staff at RTP.[15]

Howsam had also expressed concern over a poor record of product innovation, the lack of a formalized product planning system, and the use of outdated methods of market research.[16] The company regularly employed two marketing organizations specializing in analysis of the pharmaceutical market. The National Prescription Audit Services Inc., (Gosselin) provided a monthly audit of new prescriptions for all of the company's products and of all competitors, together with re-fill data from which an estimate of total prescriptions could be constructed. This survey data charted monthly prescriptions for twenty-eight products compared with those of ninety-one competitors. Davee, Koehlein & Keating supplied a monthly audit of hospital sales of the company's products and those of all competitors. A quarterly report compared these with those of competitors. However, while these data were informative, because the data were supplied on a national basis and showed results for census regions only,[17] they did not relate to actual sales at regional and district level, thereby limiting the scope for detailed measurement and analysis of sales performance product by product or by individual sales staff. BW&Co.'s approach to marketing may not have impressed Howsam, but by comparison with that of the parent company, policy and practice were far in advance, particularly in the employment of outside agencies to assist with marketing. This was the verdict of a collaborative report on WFL and its subsidiary companies conducted by two firms of consultants, MIPAL, a British consultancy and Lea Inc. in the US in 1972.[18]

Sudafed was a popular nasal decongestant. *JAMA*.

Howsam expressed admiration for the quality, enthusiasm, and commitment of the field sales staff which numbered five hundred and one in 1970, including fifteen female representatives and forty-six from ethnic minorities. He considered them to be more competent and better trained than those employed by Warner Lambert, though hampered by inadequate support from sales staff at RTP who, he believed, accorded insufficient priority to an informed use of statistics.[19] The absence of computerization before 1972 meant that market data were not subjected to sophisticated analysis; for the same reason, budgeting and auditing in relation to marketing was primitive compared with best practice in the industry.[20] His plan was to match detailed information of sales, product by product, district by district, with profit. Howsam's thoroughly professional analysis of the company's problems and his plans for reforming marketing methods soon impressed even Hitchings whose invitation to join the research committee he accepted with alacrity and pride.[21]

The personnel in Howsam's departments remained unchanged, leaving him in a role which he compared to that of a new coach brought in to invigorate an existing team.[22] He did, however, transform the entire structure and organization of all aspects of marketing. He ended the separation of responsibilities between one vice president for sales, promotion, and training from another responsible for marketing and advertising. All of these responsibilities were merged into the single role of vice president (sales and marketing) who presided over four departments, each managed by a director: sales and sales promotion, advertising, marketing services, and training. A marketing policy committee, composed of the four directors and chaired by Howsam

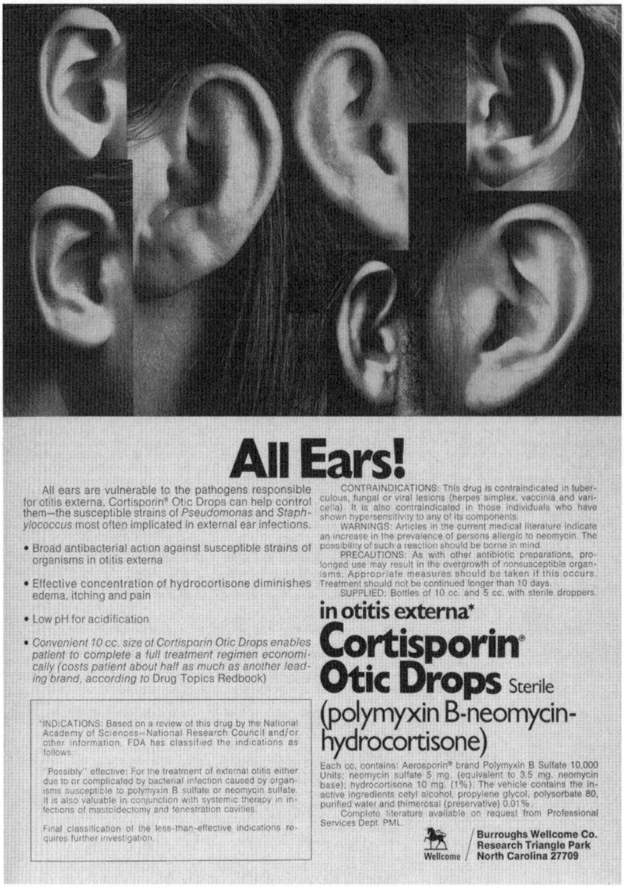

Cortisporin was an antibiotic. *JAMA*.

as vice president, took decisions on all matters relating to marketing.[23] All proposals, regardless of the substance, magnitude, and departmental origin of an initiative required approval from the marketing policy committee. Distribution of the minutes of its meetings allowed all departments to be informed of decisions taken.[24] This reorganization was consistent with Coe's philosophy of allowing managers to manage as long as they produced results.[25]

Howsam embarked on a radical reappraisal of the company's policy with respect to the range of products contained in the price list and the resources allocated to support each product in their respective markets. In 1970, nine products generating 80 per cent of sales, "the big nine," each generating annual sales of a minimum of $1 million. These were: Empirin compound with codeine and Empirin compound, Zyloprim, Actifed/Actifed-C, Sudafed, Neosporin, Cortisporin, and Anectine (see Table 7.1). Henceforward, expenditure from a total marketing budget that remained the same was concentrated on these nine products while the remainder were placed in the hands of an advertising agency and restricted to journal advertising and other low cost promotion.[26]

Figure 11.2 *Organisation of Marketing at Research Triangle Park NC, 1970–1987*

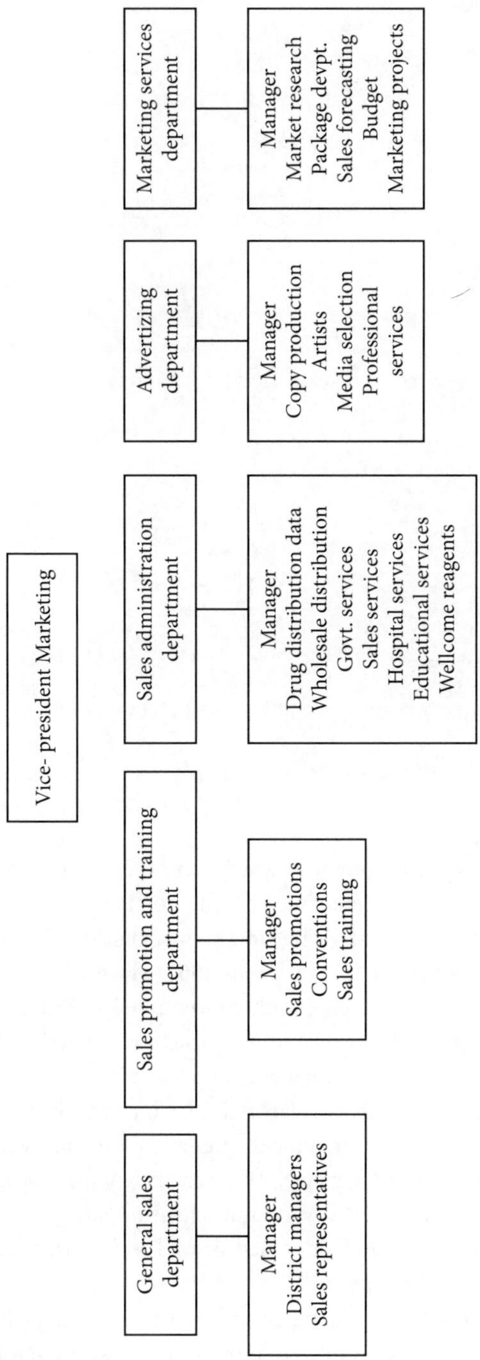

Empirin. In response to questions regarding the safety of the company's largest-selling product and increased competition in the market for analgesics, the company's "Eyes on Empirin" campaign included a competition for dealers. *JAMA*.

Two of the "big nine" products which were the first to benefit immediately from Howsam's early reforms were Empirin, the company's longest-established product dating from the 1940s; and Zyloprim (known outside North America as Zyloric) which entered the market in the US in 1966. Howsam believed that sales should be higher and could be achieved with concentrated attention and resource support. Empirin sales stagnated in an expanding market for analgesics, though they accounted still for 23 per cent of the company's sales in 1970. Coe's insistence that attempts should be made to re-establish market leadership, which had suffered from public concern regarding phenacetin content, presented Howsam with a challenge. In the 1960s, on advice from the agency N. W. Ayer, the company had experimented briefly with radio advertising in New York and television advertising in Houston, but the increase in sales volume and value had proved to be insufficient to cover the costs and the project was abandoned.[27]

Instead, in 1971, a new campaign to boost sales of Empirin compound took the form of a promotional deal directed to physicians, nurses, and dentists for which the prize was a Ford Pinto automobile. The invitation to compete included encouragement to all health professionals to "... give our men a leisurely hour or so of your time to talk about Empirin Compound."[28] In 1974, a "fiddle free" cap was introduced to appeal to potential customers such as the handicapped and the elderly who were unable to cope with child-resistant closures.[29] The same year saw a massive sampling program which was to reach fifty-five million people.[30] This long-established method of promotion was reined in from 1975 when the company's sampling program was cut by half. The reduction was in accordance with a policy agreed by all members of the Pharmaceutical Manufacturers' Association, a voluntary response in anticipation of Senator Edward Kennedy's proposed measure intended to prohibit the sampling of prescription drugs to physicians.[31] The reduction in sampling, however, proved to be for three years only as the threat of legislation receded.

Zyloprim resulted from Hitchings's research over several decades and presented Howsam with a different kind of challenge to those of Empirin. Although Zyloprim had been acclaimed by medical practitioners as a breakthrough in the treatment of gout in 1966, since its introduction, despite high profit margins, annual sales had failed consistently to produce levels even approaching the accumulated costs of RD&M. Howsam's concern was that the company "had this magnificent patent, a best drug, based on the Hitchings concept of shutting off something as opposed to just blanketing. It was a targeted concept, a unique product as a treatment for gout."[32] Yet sales of $8.5 million (14 per cent of total BW&Co.'s sales in 1970) were below the share contributed either by Empirin or by Neosporin, the company's principal broad spectrum antibiotic.[33] Because the efficacy of Zyloprim remained uncontested, Howsam diagnosed the problem as the company's inability to persuade general practitioners that the drug would not produce side effects. A new promotional campaign combined public relations and educational initiatives aimed at specialist groups of medical professionals. Contracts for this campaign were placed with MEDCOM Learning Systems, an organization which specialized in the preparation of educational films and printed brochures for advertising and promotion to the medical profession. In 1968, medical films were prepared for distribution to medical, nursing, and pharmacy schools, a measure intended to inform the younger generation of the company's research activities and to familiarize them with its products. In 1970, MEDCOM undertook to design, prepare, and deliver "a total gout learning system," which included the preparation of an eighty-four page monograph with color illustrations accompanied by a thirty-minute documentary film on gout involving the participation of several leading gout authorities from the US and the UK. Within eight months of completion in 1972, the film had been shown to twenty-five thousand physicians, and forty-nine medical schools had approved it for inclusion in the curriculum.[34]

This approach to promoting Zyloprim was extended to other drugs of the same high quality for hospital use. Beginning in 1971, the film *Clinical Trends in Anesthesiology* was mailed six times a year to medical professionals as were *Clinical Trends in Urology* and *Clinical Trends in Family Practice in 1973*.[35] By the mid 1970s, eight such special in-house pamphlets were distributed to discrete groups of specialist

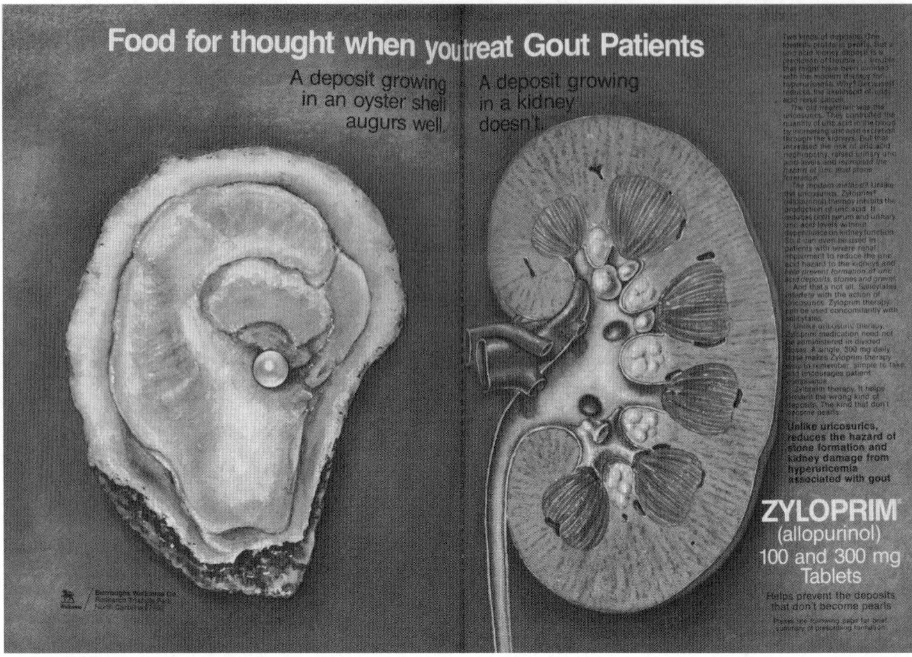

Zyloprim was a treatment for gout. *JAMA*.

physicians who comprised an increasingly segmented market sympathetic to the form of educational promotion exemplified by the clinical trends film series.[36] From 1975, despite disapproval in London, some of the material was used to promote Zyloprim within the MEDIX television series.[37] Between 1970 and 1973, sales of Zyloprim rose from $8 million to $14 million. By 1980, the share of company sales held by Zyloprim was 18 per cent, followed by codeine analgesics (a reformulated generic replacement for Empirin introduced in 1979) which recorded 11 per cent, Sudafed 9 per cent, and Neosporin 8 per cent.

Having selected those which should receive budget support, Howsam devised a new product-planning strategy by adapting the product manager system common to many large companies to fit within the company's existing resources. Adaptation was necessary because of the difficulty in recruiting experienced product managers to rural North Carolina but the objective was the same: the removal of central control of product development by senior management and the transfer of responsibility for budgeting, a product's target consumer market, the content, frequency, and placement of advertising, and finally, resource allocation based on measurement of expenditure against profitability to dedicated product managers drawn from all marketing-related departments and field staff. In the absence of professional product planners,[38] RTP staff selected for this role continued to fulfil their functional responsibilities in their respective departments. Among the fourteen selected by 1975 were six young field sales representatives who were expected to progress to executive management level. They were participants chosen as part of the company's management development

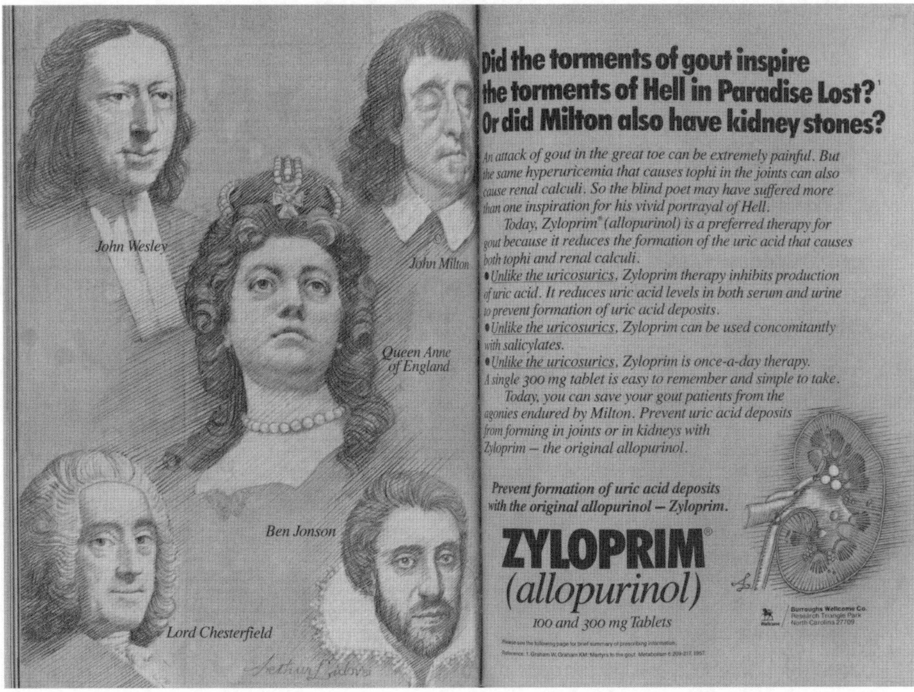

program introduced in 1971. They were seconded from field sales to undergo two years of rotation between the various departments involved with marketing. Howsam explained the philosophy underlying a new management development scheme intended to prepare aspiring managers for the product-planning role, "what we do is encourage our young people to come up with ideas but then the old dogs have to review them."[39]

Training was provided by a marketing consultant from UNC School of Business whose text was a handbook distributed to trainees. Assistance was provided by marketing services personnel whose expertise in, for example, government sales, direct mail, hospital promotion, or market research might be relevant to a particular product. The company's advertising agency was also a source of statistical information and advice. The experience and knowledge of regional managers and field sales staff was available through arrangements for liaison with product planners. They were trained to operate the myriad computerized compilation of the Intercontinental Medical Statistics (IMS) services into which the marketing research department fed monthly data on the company's products and those of competitors to form a data base. Product books which consisted of detailed histories of each product formed the basis for discussion between the marketing policy committee and each of the product planners during the course of the annual (and later quarterly) product review when product plans were formulated for the forthcoming year.[40] Each planner presented a product plan at meetings of the marketing policy committee, first through informal discussion before drawing up an overall product plan at a formal meeting which recommended the proposal for approval by the board. The product planner's responsibility after that was to monitor progress of the specific product assigned.[41] As well as offering opportunities for career development, Howsam maintained that the strength of his system lay in motivating all participating staff to realize a plan they had helped develop. This emphasis on encouragement and motivation in the context of product planning and development was consistent with the larger management preparation program among marketing and sales staff which included access to a new college training option planned by Coe and Howsam which enabled office staff to take an MBA or a science master's degree to become a qualified manager.[42]

The introduction of product planning and product champions carried implications for the advertising department and the relation between the company and advertising agencies. Hitherto, transactions had been conducted on a business to business basis in which BW&Co. placed contracts for the placement of advertisements in media outlets. For forty years the William Douglas McAdams advertising agency, a well-respected organization specializing in the promotion of ethical drugs, had received the company's contracts.[43] Henceforward, other agencies became full partners in the planning process before decisions on how much, in what form, and where advertisements should be placed which involved reciprocal communication between company and agencies of confidential, commercially sensitive information based on trust; thus, agency outsiders became insiders.[44] Another innovation, introduced in 1971, was the use of external services to test new advertisements before placing any major contract with an agency.[45]

These important changes in policy were accompanied by a reallocation of advertising contracts. Requiring a wider range of services, Howsam arranged new contracts with Deltakos, the specialist medical communications agency owned by J. Walter Thompson, because in addition to advising and developing advertising campaigns, the agency undertook to provide computerized market analysis. Coe described the agency as "more physician/product/indication-oriented."[46] The advertising accounts for Empirin compound, Lanoxin, and Zyloprim were placed with Deltakos. Because of a conflict of interest, the Empirin compound advertising contract was placed with the Rosenthal agency formed by Rolf Werner Rosenthal, a former employee of the McAdams agency.[47] These organizational changes intended to introduce a greater professionalization into advertising did not end the practise whereby employees assumed the roles of models. A professional adviser selected and photographed selected employees from various departments. Suitably attired, whether as knowledgeable scientist, blushing bride, or elegant ballerina, they represented the ordinary Joe or Josephine suffering from headaches, colds, coughs, urinary tract infections, gout, or other afflictions for which the company offered remedy or relief.[48]

The innovations were aimed at improving the level and quality of support for representatives in the field. Howsam persuaded the management committee to abandon past practice by ending exclusive dealing through wholesalers and introducing an incentive scheme.[49] The move to direct sales in 1970 facilitated the introduction of a new payment system for field staff, as did the use of territorial information planning systems (TIPS).[50] TIPS made it possible to record the professional calls made by

The employees shown here were appearing as amateur models in the company's advertisements. *JAMA*.

representatives and provided an objective method of ascertaining the best selling performances among sales representatives (rather than the fastest talkers).[51] The new system could be used to identify the most productive doctors measured by the number of prescriptions issued for the company's products and the volume and value of sales attributable to each. This program was superseded by STARS which in 1975, further refined the process of identifying high-prescribing doctors.[52] Just as TIPS informed the sales and marketing staff, the installation of drug distribution data (DDD) provided important intelligence for the directors because the program measured sales by comparison with those of competing companies down to the zip code level.[53]

A further element in the reforms affecting sales staff was an upgrade in instruction which formed part of Coe's broader new management training scheme. In his capacity as head of the management training program and in consultation with Howsam, Singler introduced the employment standards program which included modules advising on how to approach different categories of organizations and professionals, the conduct of interviews, and role play related to attendance at medical conventions. Beginning in 1975, the entire field staff received a Professional Sales Skills course (PSS). This was a three-day course intended to teach verbal skills. The course was presented first to the office-marketing personnel and regional managers who, in collaboration with the training department, became responsible for disseminating the process among managers at regional and district levels. Thereafter, the course formed part of the initial basic training for new sales personnel. The PSS techniques were incorporated in a bi-monthly issue to field staff of the selling plan containing the promotional agenda and tactical approaches to be employed.[54]

Sales representatives received Howsam's reforms with enthusiasm. Regan welcomed the sharing with field workers of more advanced statistical data which related sales to profit as "a breath of fresh air" because it would enable them to avoid "wasting time spending hours promoting things … on which little money was being made."[55] This step together with the introduction of product planners enabled people to feel involved; "… Howsam took us out of the Dark Ages of marketing."[56] External validation of the new system was also forthcoming in 1974 by an independent marketing consultant who observed that, "In comparison with most companies, Burroughs Wellcome's marketing planning is well done." Particular praise was directed to a broad base of involvement, outstanding written feedback from planners, and high quality market-research based sales and promotional information available to the planners."[57]

Radio and television advertising had been tried briefly in the 1960s without success and the experiment had been abandoned. The return to television in the early 1970s was in response to a collaborative report commissioned by WFL on its corporate image (which also included subsidiary companies) prepared by two consultancy organizations, MIPAL in the UK and Lea Inc. in the US. The 1972 report was based on surveys of doctors' perceptions and concluded that both the British and the US companies possessed poor records in product innovation. It also revealed that only 12 per cent in the US rated research reputation highly; an overall favorability rating ranked the American company twelfth in the US.[58] One suggestion contained in the report was that a possible approach to improving the American company's image among doctors in the US would be to plan a campaign to disseminate information to familiarize them with research achievements and activities and with its corporate structure.

The conclusions and recommendations of this report to a reinvigorated board prompted an immediate public image offensive. In 1972, under vice president Howsam's chairmanship of the distribution committee, which dealt with all aspects of marketing from product planning to delivery,[59] the medical and advertising departments collaborated in preparing a new booklet for distribution by representatives in the field and a slide/tape presentation for use at medical conferences and trade meetings; the image of the new building was used in both. With the advice of the Rosenthal agency, advertisements were placed in fourteen medical journals under the heading "Research is our only stockholder," a reference to the altruistic aims of the Wellcome Trust which allowed clients to infer that profits from the company's products would not finance dividends destined for the pockets of commercial investors. The advertisements described the company's support for medical research through the Wellcome Fund and the Trust and contained a colored photograph of the new building at RTP. The advertisement was intended "to give physicians a reason to 'choose' BW&Co. if all other things are equal in their selection of medication."[60] An approving account of the campaign in *Product Management* highlighted the illustration of the futuristic premises at RTP as conveying the company's commitment to a progressive modernity.[61] Howsam accepted the logic of conveying to potential prescribers that, assuming equal quality, "they should prefer to be instrumental in sending the dividends to charity rather than to the capitalist stockholders of such companies as SKF and Warner Lambert." However, Howsam expressed reservations based on his experience at Warner Lambert where "everybody worried about earnings per share," a state of mind which acted as a spur to effort and efficiency. He feared that that the stockholder caption might convey the wrong message to employees by implying that they inhabited a "comfortable culture", a culture alien to those among the company's large corporate competitors.[62] Creasy articulated a similar concern that the company must overcome any inertia that might result from ownership by a charitable body rather than by an organization "pressed by hungry stockholders."[63]

BW&Co.'s advertising policy was cautious compared with those of the major advertisers. During the early 1970s, manufacturers of "therapeutic strength" vitamins, insulin syringes, and hydrocortisone creams introduced direct advertising to consumers through magazines and television.[64] In 1972, a teaching film entitled *I am Joe's Heart*, an examination of heart disease, was produced to be screened in 1973, the strategic thinking behind it being the indirect projection of the reputation of the company's Lanoxin. The film originated in one of a series of articles jointly prepared by the medical and advertising departments and which had been published in *Readers' Digest*.[65] In embarking upon television advertising in 1972, the company was a latecomer. By 1970, companies such as Pfizer, Bristol Myers, SKF, and Merck, were already spending roughly 60 per cent of advertising expenditure on television and were among forty-three advertisers of drugs and products in allied fields which figured in the top corporate advertisers in the US.[66]

Much more ambitious than "Joe's heart", though similar in purpose, was a national television initiative intended to establish the company's image as a modern research-led manufacturer of ethical medicines. This stage of the campaign consisted of sponsoring a series of health educational films. Because the company sponsored the series, each of the films was accompanied by a corporate advertisement which included the image of the RTP building. The MEDIX films were produced by Dave Bell Associates, an organization which, in 1972, had pioneered an award-winning health awareness program prepared in association with the Los Angeles County Medical Association, the initiator of the project. The association provided ideas, medical know-how, and advice to the producers for each of a series of thirty-minute programs presented in documentary format filmed on location showing surgical procedures in progress. The primary intention was to encourage people to learn about health and medicine and to persuade them to take responsibility for their own health before they became sick.[67] Relevant pamphlets, made freely available to the public on request after each program, proved popular. Far from compromising BW&Co.'s reputation for ethical medicine, which had initially been a concern for Coe, association with a high quality and popular television series conveyed an image to the public of a company of integrity which was at the center of medical research which had practical implications for public health. The brief appearance of the image of the RTP building also linked the company with the prize-winning awards and commendations bestowed on MEDIX by television critics, and the medical press. Medical societies and associations with special interest in one or more programs also praised the series; they included those concerned with heart, kidney, lung and eye disease, epilepsy, alcoholism, plastic surgery, and highway safety. The series also received an Emmy award.[66] The MEDIX series was screened nationwide reaching 60 per cent of the national television audience. One employee voiced a widespread view shared by staff at RTP and Greenville, "It's good for us to let people know who we are and what we are doing."[68]

Another element, part of the public image strategy, was the Pharmacy Education Program introduced in 1974. Within ten years the program had attracted 43,000 pharmacists to participate across the US. The prize awarded to each of the one hundred and fifty-six winners of a national competition included a grant valued at one thousand dollars which each winning pharmacist could direct to any pharmacy for funding scholarships and loans. Between 1974 and 1984, BW&Co. contributed $1.4 million.[69] By that time the company ranked fourth in delivering total prescriptions in the US, third in the number of new prescriptions, and had risen from twenty-second to fourteenth in dollar sales volume by US pharmaceutical companies.[70]

CHAPTER 12

Septra: product innovation and the expansion of consumer marketing

Septra was the company's first new product to which was applied Howsam's product planning system and his other marketing reforms. Septra had originated in research conducted by Hitchings and Elvira Falco at Tuckahoe between 1952 and 1956 when they had synthesized numerous benzyl pyrimidines. One group of compounds (diaminopyrimidines) was sent to Dr Stanley Bushby at the tropical medicine laboratories in Beckenham where he tested the compounds for anti-malarial activity. From these tests conducted in 1956–57, Bushby developed structure-activity relationships out of which Hitchings, Dr Barbara Roth, and Elli Katsikis developed Daraprim, an anti-malarial product. Hitchings and his team, experts in metabolic studies, built upon the research of Bushby and his colleagues who had identified anti-bacterial properties of pyrimideine compounds in Beckenham, in the UK. The result was the discovery of a series of compounds which culminated in trimethoprim.[1] Though impressed by the new antibacterial, scientists at Beckenham feared toxicity causing blood dyscrasias. Acknowledged at the time was a risk under certain conditions to a patient contracting Stevens-Johnson syndrome, of an idiosyncratic allergic reaction requiring rapid diagnosis of symptoms to avoid more serious damage, even death.[2] In accordance with Cresswell's assessment of the culture of absolute risk avoidance at Beckenham, despite Hitchings's plea to Adamson in 1962 to allow perseverance with trimethoprim (on which the American company had secured a product patent) and to "to give it a chance," the decision was taken not to proceed with further work on the compound.[3]

Hoffman La Roche had been a major producer of sulphonamides since their discovery in the 1940s. However, by the early 1960s they were considered to be at the end of their lives. Roche held a license from the Japanese pharmaceutical manufacturer Shionogi for sulphamethoxazole from which Roche sought to develop a new compound to compete in the same large anti-infective market as the ageing sulphonamides. Both Roche and BW&Co. (USA) Inc., therefore, were in search of new compounds to compete in the same important market, a competition of which Hitchings was well aware and which compounded his frustration with the decision made by the WFL board to discontinue work on trimethropin. He responded by becoming the secret architect of an alternative solution which would not depend on scientific input from the laboratories at Beckenham- but which would eventually require WFL's permission. There were two elements in his solution. One was the question of how to reduce the risk of toxicity of the drug; the other was the engagement of another corporate partner with whom to collaborate at the scientific level and who would be prepared to agree with the parallel commercial exploitation of any product developed from joint RD&M contributions.

While collaboration with scientists from other non-corporate institutions had long been a feature of RD&M, joint agreements with corporate partners (other than the rare instances within WFL) had not. The exception occurred in 1952, when Eli Lilly initiated negotiations with a view to incorporating tricyclamol, a chemical compound covered by US and UK patents, in a new product under development and also to sell the compound on a royalty basis. The agreement licensed Lilly to produce tricyclamol and to sell the new product of which it was an ingredient, but required the company to divulge clinical, pharmacological and other data relating to its product. The joint agreement provided for the companies' joint marketing of Tricoloid.[4] Although the commercial impact of the agreement was insignificant, it is possible that Hitchings may have been reminded of what had happened in 1962 when he began to seek a solution to the problem presented by WFL's imposition of a block on the further development of trimethoprim. Secretly, Hitchings travelled to Basle, where he approached his counterpart at Roche to explore the possibility of collaboration. He believed that a combination of sulphamethoxazole, which Roche produced on license from Shionogi, with trimethoprim might lower its toxicity, thereby satisfying marketability.[5]

Creasy was furious when he discovered Hitchings's initiative but stopped short of opposition when Wrigley, whose support for any proposal was crucial to securing WFL approval, was enthusiastic at the prospect of partnership with one of the world's largest and most reputable companies.[6] On his recommendation, the board in London agreed to the proposal. Dr S. Bushby, head of chemotherapy at Beckenham who had collaborated with Hitchings at Tuckahoe in the 1950s, and his colleague Dr Fowle, a clinical researcher, relocated to RTP to assist Hitchings and his counterpart at Roche proceeded with the development of a combination compound. The outcome was a cross-licensing agreement. BW&Co. (USA) Inc. owned a product patent on trimethoprim, an antibacterial, while Roche, which was a major producer of sulphonamides, held a license from Shionogi which supplied sulphamethoxazole. The reason why the companies collaborated in the preparation of a joint submission to the FDA was that each possessed reservations regarding their respective products. Roche's sulphonamides were considered to be at the end of their lives. The production of a compound consisting of both trimethoprim and sulphamethoxazole offered Roche access to a new product (to be called Bactrim). At the same time, scientists at Tuckahoe and WFL could avoid the risk of excessive toxicity which, at that time, was believed to be associated with trimethoprim. However, joint research showed that the trimethoprim content (and therefore its potential for toxicity) could be reduced which made it possible to produce a lower but adequate dose of the compound.[7] Together the two companies' scientists sought to develop an antibacterial combination of trimethoprim and sulfamethoxazole superior to both.[8] All bench work research was carried out at the Tuckahoe laboratories to which Bushby relocated to continue his earlier role in the project; Roche conducted clinical testing. The joint agreement with Roche made provision for the development and production of a single compound for which a joint submission would be made to the FDA for a new drug application (NDA). This would be the first test of BW&Co. (USA) Inc.'s capacity to meet the extensive requirements for clinical studies and testing introduced by the FDA earlier in the decade.

First, however, the company sought appeal in the UK, where standards and restrictions were less rigorous than those imposed by the FDA in the US.[9] Shortly before the launch in 1968, Bushby expressed confidence that "No other drug will prove right first time in such a high proportion [80 to 90 per cent] of cases of urinary tract infections or bronchitis."[10] Fowle emphasized its broad spectrum and drew attention to the drug's unusual capacity for killing germs rather than merely inhibiting their reproduction.[11] Shortly after the launch of Septrin (the trade name in the UK), the *Journal of Clinical Pharmacology* described it as a major discovery.[12]

Superior therapeutic attributes explain why Septrin immediately became a powerful competitor with anti-bacterial preparations already entrenched in the market. While initially introduced in tablet form as a treatment for urinary tract infections, the prospects for widening indications and securing an enlarged market for the compound promised growth for the company's business on a scale which, apart from Zyloprim, other therapeutically significant but less commercially rewarding drugs had yet to achieve.[13] Directors in London acknowledged that Septrin marked a new era "not only for medicine but for the Wellcome group itself."[14] At the annual general meeting of WFL in 1970, Wellcome trustees Sir John McMichael, F.R.S., and Prof. Barcroft, F.R.S., both distinguished academic research scientists with special interests in medicine, agreed that already Septrin was achieving widespread recognition as a major advance in treating kidney infections.[15] WFL's chairman, Sir Michael Perrin, predicted that Septrin would become the company's largest selling product within five years.

The new drug was also significant in other ways. First, it was the fruit of the first substantial and successful research collaboration between Wellcome scientists under Hitchings at Tuckahoe and Bushby at the Wellcome Research Laboratories in Beckenham. Second, Hitchings maintained that Septrin was the latest in a series of discoveries which had resulted more from a *method* of working than from a pre-selection of targets. "The method is now a way of life at the Wellcome research laboratories [at RTP] and the creative young people who are now contributing to our efforts assure you that there will be an unending series of exciting discoveries."[16] Hitchings was referring to the creation of a drug development programme. Hitherto, the review of research projects was reserved by the research committee. Henceforward,

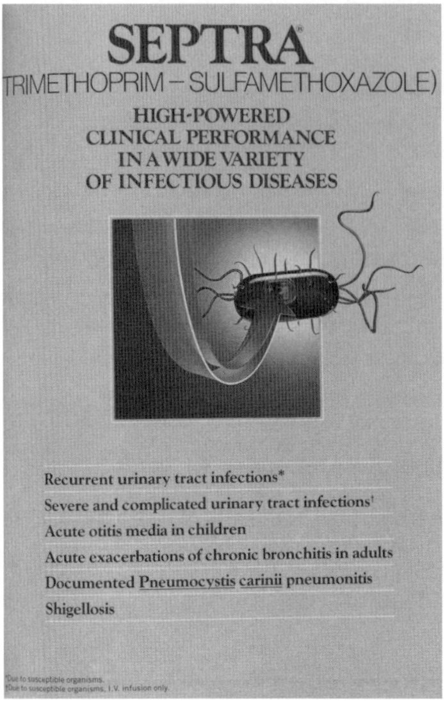

Septra, a combination antibacterial treatment. *JAMA*.

once a drug entered a phase III trial, responsibility for reviewing projects passed to a newly-formed development-marketing committee chaired by Cresswell.[17] Another dimension of the significance of Septra, the American trade name, approved for launching into the US market in 1973, was that it carried implications for the future strategies of the company to exploit the massive scale of potential demand in the existing market for anti-bacterials. The task of effective exploitation presented BW&Co. with a major challenge to its marketing organization, strategy, and manpower.[18]

Because of more onerous requirements to present evidence of efficacy and safety, approval for the US market took a further five years after Septrin was launched in the UK. This gave BW&Co. an advantage over Roche which, under the joint agreement, could also market its own product resulting from the collaborative research program between the two companies. Between 1968 and 1973, Septra and Bactrim (the trade name for Roche's product) competed to be first into the US market. During the five years since Septrin was launched in the UK and in forty other countries in which WFL possessed trading subsidiaries or commercial links, valuable information was accumulated on product, markets, and marketing which informed BW&Co.'s preparations for a renewed application to the FDA. The greatly enlarged medical department at RTP prepared twenty-eight volumes of pre-clinical raw data, discussions, and conclusions for submission. This was followed by accounts of the design, inception, and monitoring of a large series of human studies. After sufficient data had been generated to demonstrate the efficacy and safety of Septra for use in patients suffering urinary tract infections, an NDA consisting of one thousand pages was prepared for submission to the FDA. Final approval was announced in August 1973 when the company declared a SEPTRA PINK DAY. Buildings at both Greenville and RTP were festooned with posters and streamers and free lunches were offered to all employees. The editor of Wellcome News pronounced, "There will never be another day quite like Septra launch day."[19]

The launch assumed particular importance because anti-infectives formed the largest segment of the pharmaceutical market. However, marketing the same compound (different only in trade name) head to head with one of the largest and most respected pharmaceutical companies in the US presented a daunting challenge to BW&Co.

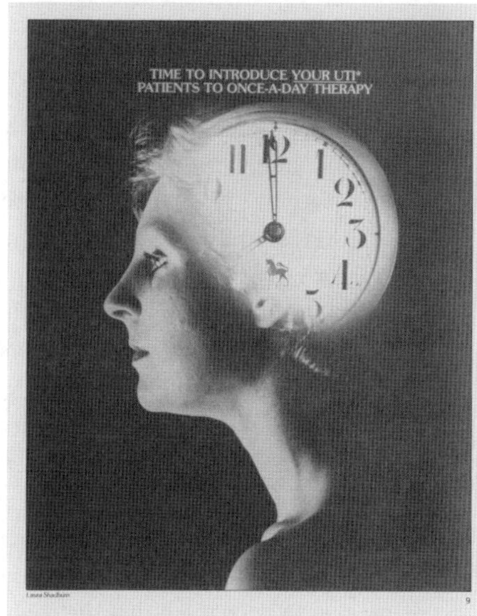

These advertisements for Septra were directed towards the treatment of children's infections (left) and of urinary tract infection. *JAMA*

Roche, a Goliath in the industry, outsold Wellcome many times over, both in the US and in Continental European markets. Moreover, the William Douglas McAdams agency, formerly BW&Co.'s long-standing agent, held the Bactrim account for Roche, whereas in 1972, BW&Co. placed the Septra contract with the small new Rosenthal agency, the terms of which required Werner Rosethal to collaborate closely with the company's marketing, sales, advertising, and market research services departments.[20] The campaign began by medical staff conducting in-depth interviews with general practitioners, internists, pediatricians, and urologists in two cities in an attempt to establish the extent and character of the renal and upper respiratory markets. The first decision concerned product specifications. Instructions from London specified the application of an identical formula used in the production of Septra, a white tablet containing a commonly-used liquorice flavor, the model which Roche followed. However, market research in the US indicated a preference among children for either cherry or grape flavors. London was ignored and Septra appeared as pink and cherry flavored.[21] Coe, Howsam, and Adams, the trio in charge of the launch, agreed that it was important to be first in placing the product in volume in the market ahead of Roche as soon as the FDA communicated its approval.[22]

This presented a challenge to the recently appointed head of chemical and plant development and of engineering, Gabriel Cipau, who graduated in chemical engineering and physics, continuing to complete a PhD related to RD&M, and had joined BW&Co. in 1970 when he became project engineer in command of the process of relocating plant and production from Tuckahoe to Greenville. Once the basic plant had reached full working capacity at Greenville, his task was to solve the problems of development and scaling up production to meet the anticipated volume of Septra sales. Under his direction, the company's first fully-automated, computer-controlled, small-scale reactor was in place by 1973.[23] A speedy delivery of Septra after approval, insisted upon by the marketing committee, required production to precede the FDA's decision which was the signal for immediate selling to begin. Even though production coincided with a plant closure for vacation, none the less, volunteers ensured that the packaging line was fully staffed, enabling commercial shipments of Septra tablets to leave the Greenville plant twenty-five minutes after the official word had been received.[24]

Other policy decisions were taken after attempting to anticipate those which Roche would make. BW&Co. employed these assumptions in setting price and deciding methods of advertising, promotion, and selling. Coe, Howsam, and Adams decided on a price of $21. The trio also agreed that it was important to be first in placing the product in the market.[25] Two months after the launch, intelligence provided by representatives revealed that the company's price was not competitive with the actual offers being made by Roche's representatives in the field. Discounts to wholesalers further complicated the problem. Although Roche's published price was close, small differences in prices charged to volume purchasers, hospitals, and chain stores prompted Coe to lower prices to a competitive level.[26] Sales representatives in the field were made ready for a vigorous (less subtle) approach to the campaign. Howsam urged field staff to "Sell Septra while the other man eats! Sell Septra while the other man sleeps!" His message, conveyed through the Wellcome News, was that the first few weeks and months would be critical in establishing the drug as the antibacterial of choice and that sustained intensive detailing would be the route to success in selling.[27]

The immediate outcome of the head-to-head competition between the David and Goliath in the US market for anti-infectives at the end of the first year was that sales of Septra were twice those of Bactrim.[28] By 1978, however, sales by BW&Co. and Roche were equal, together accounting for 33 per cent of the market.[29] The verdict reached by an independent observer of the industry quoted in *Product Management* in 1974 was that the intensively projected corporate image of BW&Co. since 1971 had contributed directly to the company's ability to match Roche in the battle between Septra and Bactrim.[30] Product-related promotional campaigns also attracted praise; for example, in 1976, a crystal glass Steuben owl used to advertise Septra received the Palshaw award for the most outstanding medical advertisement to appear in the journal *Current Prescribing*.[31]

Between 1970 and 1980, Zyloprim had risen from 15 to 18 per cent of sales to secure first place; Codeine Analgesics (a reformulated generic replacement for Empirin introduced in 1979) recorded 11 per cent, Septra sales had reached 11 per cent by 1980, followed by Sudafed (9 per cent) and Neosporin (8 per cent). The overall expansion of the company's sales and profits, together with the increasing expenditure on RD&M reflecting the nature of the new products, is shown in Table 12.1. This also shows a deceleration in the rate of profit as the decade of the 1980s began.

Table 12.1 *BW&Co. Sales, Profits ($million), and RD&M as percentages, 1970–1981*

	Sales	*Pre-tax profit*	*Profit/sales*	*RD&M*	*RD&M/sales*
1970	60	12	20	7	12
1971	68	16	24	9	13
1972	79	19	24	10	13
1973	95	26	27	10	11
1974	111	27	24	11	10
1975	143	37	26	14	10
1976	167	44	27	18	11
1977	184	37	20	23	12
1978	202	45	22	28	14
1979	238	46	20	34	15
1980	262	33	13	43	16
1981	274	34	12	46	17

Sources: GWHC, BW&Co. (USA) Inc., 107.01/02, President's annual reports; Data provided by Fred Coe Jr, by fax, 9 May 2002; GSK/WF/SCS/798, WFL and Wellcome plc accounts and annual reports.

Even rapid sales growth since the 1960s, however, had not enabled the company to approach the size of competitors. Rapid growth in total sales during the 1970s was attributable mainly to an expansion of prescription medicines, although the sales of OTC prescription products, principally Empirin and increasingly Sudafed, rose from $11 million in 1971 to $54 million in 1981 when they represented one-fifth of the company's total sales.[32] Howsam's previous experience in the sale of OTC drugs had convinced him of the potential for growth of the company on a scale that would enable it to achieve sufficient size to rank among the industry's leaders, Coe's declared ambition. After reviewing existing products, Howsam identified Actifed, a combined decongestant and antihistamine which had been in the price list since the 1930s, as a prime candidate for the OTC market. The history of the drug began with pseudoephedrine, a decongestant developed by researchers in Beckenham and sold first in England in 1934 and then in the US in 1936.

In 1951, K. Adamson, then director of research at Beckenham, developed the antihistamine triprolidine (the only new product to result from his research). Further work by de Beer, pharmacologist at Tuckahoe, combined the decongestant with the antihistamine which resulted in the product Actidil.[33] In 1959, Actifed was approved as a prescription drug. When it was launched into the highly competitive US market for the treatment of sinusitis, colds, and hay fever in 1960, thirty-four similar products were introduced at the same time. The principal competitors, who dwarfed BW&Co. (USA) Inc., were Schering with the product Coricidin, SKF with Ornade, and

Upjohn with Pyrroxate.[34] Two years later, in the wake of the thalidomide tragedy, an amendment to the Food, Drug, and Cosmetic Act included a requirement that not only *new* drugs must be shown to be safe as well as effective, but that drugs already on the market should also be investigated. A review panel involving the National Academy of Sciences/National Research Council set up by the FDA responsible for the Drug Efficacy Study of Implementation devised four categories of drugs: effective, probably effective, possibly effective, or lacking substantial evidence of effectiveness.[35] Securing approval for Actifed, however, was accorded a lower priority during a period when concern for the future of Empirin dominated the concerns of senior managers until Howsam's arrival at BW&Co. in 1970.

After reviewing the company's product portfolio, he became influential in changing the policy towards Actifed and in embarking on the process of obtaining FDA certification of effectiveness which included clinical studies. In 1972, the submission of an efficacy study resulted in the award of an advisory rating of only "probably effective" and limited to use for seasonal and perennial rhinitis. This rendered the drug liable to compulsory withdrawal from the market unless the submission of additional data for review and evaluation by the FDA itself led to approval. Further uncertainty about the future of the brand resulted from concerns expressed by the Pharmaceutical Society and by police over risks associated with the codeine content of the syrup. Protecting the brand became a priority from 1977, following a meeting of the marketing committee attended by Coe which, as a matter of urgency, set up an investigation of close substitutes as a method of countering the criticism directed towards the drug.[36] A team was recruited to investigate alternatives and also to commence a bioavailablity study working in parallel with a new decongestant products group. An NDA submission for Actifed to be upgraded to fully effective status required an adequate number of clinical studies and trials which were completed in 1979, having cost $0.75 million since 1970. The rating as "effective" by the FDA in 1981 was followed by a product launch as an OTC drug. Hitherto, Coe had ruled out advertising prescription medicines except to medical practitioners. This policy was still in place in 1978 when the marketing services manager at BW&Co. explained the logic behind the strategy in an interview with a reporter from *Advertising Age*, "While there is growth potential for OTCs there is no sure success largely because while a profit margin might conceivably be higher than on an ethical drug, a consumer goods company could easily come along, knock off the product and undercut the price … The cost of promotion is considerably higher than on ethicals with no great return on immediate sales … Burroughs Wellcome intends to stick in the long run with what it knows best – prescription ethicals. They are more stable and that is where our experience is."[37] Evidence existed to justify a degree of caution before proceeding with this form of advertising. A survey of physicians carried out by *American Medical News* in 1982 discovered that roughly two-thirds objected to advertisements pitched to patients.[38]

Howsam's marketing innovations were intended to advance the company's aspiration to expand to achieve at least medium size. However, his experience at

SmthKline and Warner Lambert led him to conclude that growth on a substantial scale was unlikely to be attained through complete reliance on internally generated product innovation. Before joining BW&Co., Howsam had enjoyed the freedom to negotiate licensing arrangements the like of which he was confident could make a contribution to widening the company's product range. However, this was the single dimension of marketing which he failed to introduce at BW&Co. Coe was persuaded, and so too was Cresswell, who displayed a special interest not only in the development potential of research, but also in the wider possibilities available from inter-firm collaboration. Wrigley, the British director on the BW&Co. board with overall responsibility for WFL group marketing, had also expressed approval of licensing in principle. A major qualification was an insistence that any licensing arrangements negotiated by BW&Co. must cover the entire world. From the Americans' perspective, this appeared to be a blocking tactic by WFL which would uphold the Wellcome tradition which had been wholly opposed to licensing.[39] Howsam attempted to secure licensing arrangements with Allen & Hanbury, Boots, Beecham, and Fisons but was not surprised that all refused to concede worldwide licenses. Unsurprisingly, none was prepared to license against itself in the UK. The effect was to deprive the American company (specifically Howsam and Cresswell) of the opportunity to negotiate licenses for the US and Canada exclusively and to deploy in support of licensed products the best group of salesmen (in Howsam's opinion) in the US. Howsam believed that this was a major strategic error resulting from a decision made in London where the British directors showed a concern to adhere to an ethically-rooted historical precedent while completely disregarding both the potential of the North American market and the interests of BW&Co.[40] A further restraining influence on the potential for growth was a failure to emulate other major companies which, from the late 1960s, began to market drugs for which the patents held by the owners of the original trademark had expired.[41] Although WFL directors had acknowledged that product innovation was necessary for expansion, they had concluded that the alternative to achieving it through RD&M in the company's own laboratories was diversification through corporate acquisition. By excluding the possibility of adopting an innovative marketing strategy that included licensing, once again the American company's aspirations were threatened by being undermined in the UK.

CHAPTER 13

The Wellcome Trust, Wellcome Foundation Ltd, and Burroughs Wellcome & Co.; personalities, policies, dividends, and Anglo-American relations

During the two decades following World War II, the financial difficulties facing WFL had been the major influence in determining the Trust's perception of an appropriate dividend policy for the business. Under Sir Henry Dale's chairmanship of the Trust until 1951, outstanding mortgage and bank loans had prohibited any distribution and throughout the 1950s, annual dividend payments rarely exceeded £0.5 million.[1] Dale's successor as chairman in 1960 was Lord Piercy who had been a trustee since 1948. Formerly a managing director of a company in the timber trade, chairman of the Industrial and Commercial Finance Corporation, and a director of the Bank of England, he was described by the secretary of the Trust as "an academically-based city financier."[2] He continued Dale's dividend policy throughout his chairmanship until 1965, accepting the constraints suffered by WFL's continuing financial difficulties, even though they were relieved increasingly by the profits and dividends received from the American company.[3]

A new chairman was appointed in 1965. He was Sir Oliver Franks (Later to become Lord Franks). An academic philosopher, a diplomat, a civil servant, and between 1954 and 1962, chairman of Lloyds Bank,[4] he was thought by Peter Williams, secretary of the Trust, to be universally regarded as a brilliant chairman of meetings, regardless of content or context.[5] During his period as the Trust chairman, he limited his role to presiding over the annual meeting attended by the company chairman, his directors, and by the trustees as the sole shareholders, and to agreeing dividends with the board through private discussions with the finance director and chairman. One director's account of an annual meeting called shortly after Franks assumed the role of chairman is illuminating. Board members generally regarded the trustees as naïve with respect to business. However, encouraged by Franks to participate (an innovation at such meetings), the trustees promptly "skewered" the directors by asking "devastatingly simple questions" about the business to which the directors

Lord Franks a formerly diplomat, subsequently chairman of Lloyd's Bank, and chairman of the Wellcome Trust between 1970 and 1982. His reforming initiative to replace the trustee gerontocracy which he had inherited lowered the average age and introduced a highly successful business leader as his successor as chairman, the first of three trustee chairmen possessing similar business and financial experience. He also began to introduce a more questioning approach to relations between the Trust and the board of WFL. This heralded the end of many years since the threat of bankruptcy had passed since the 1950s when relations consisted of amicable routines. of the trustees, Wellcome Library, London

had no answers.[6] This occasioned hilarity at the time (even among directors), but in retrospect, it was a worrying reflection on the state of the company which may have prompted Lord Franks to seek expert advice from Urwick Orr and Partners, a leading firm of management consultants which, in 1966, began a review of the structure and management of WFL.[7] The investigation took place at the end of twelve years during which a higgledy-piggledy process of worldwide diversification had imposed strains on a management structure which had remained largely unchanged since World War II.

The effect of this policy, driven by Wrigley and Wheeler, which took the form of geographical expansion and acquisitions since the 1950s had led to a proliferation of entities within WFL which rose from eleven in 1956 to forty-two by 1966. Few of these predominantly small overseas subsidiaries possessed manufacturing or research capacity. The American company was exceptional in these respects, both in its scale of manufacturing and of RD&M; both were present in Australia but not at significant levels. Most other overseas activities were essentially trading enterprises. Diversification was not accompanied by substantially higher profitability for WFL which remained consistent at around 13 per cent of sales throughout the 1960s.

Figure 13.1 *Growth through formation of subsidiaries and acquisitions by Burroughs Wellcome & Co. in the UK and the Wellcome Foundation Ltd, 1880–1995*

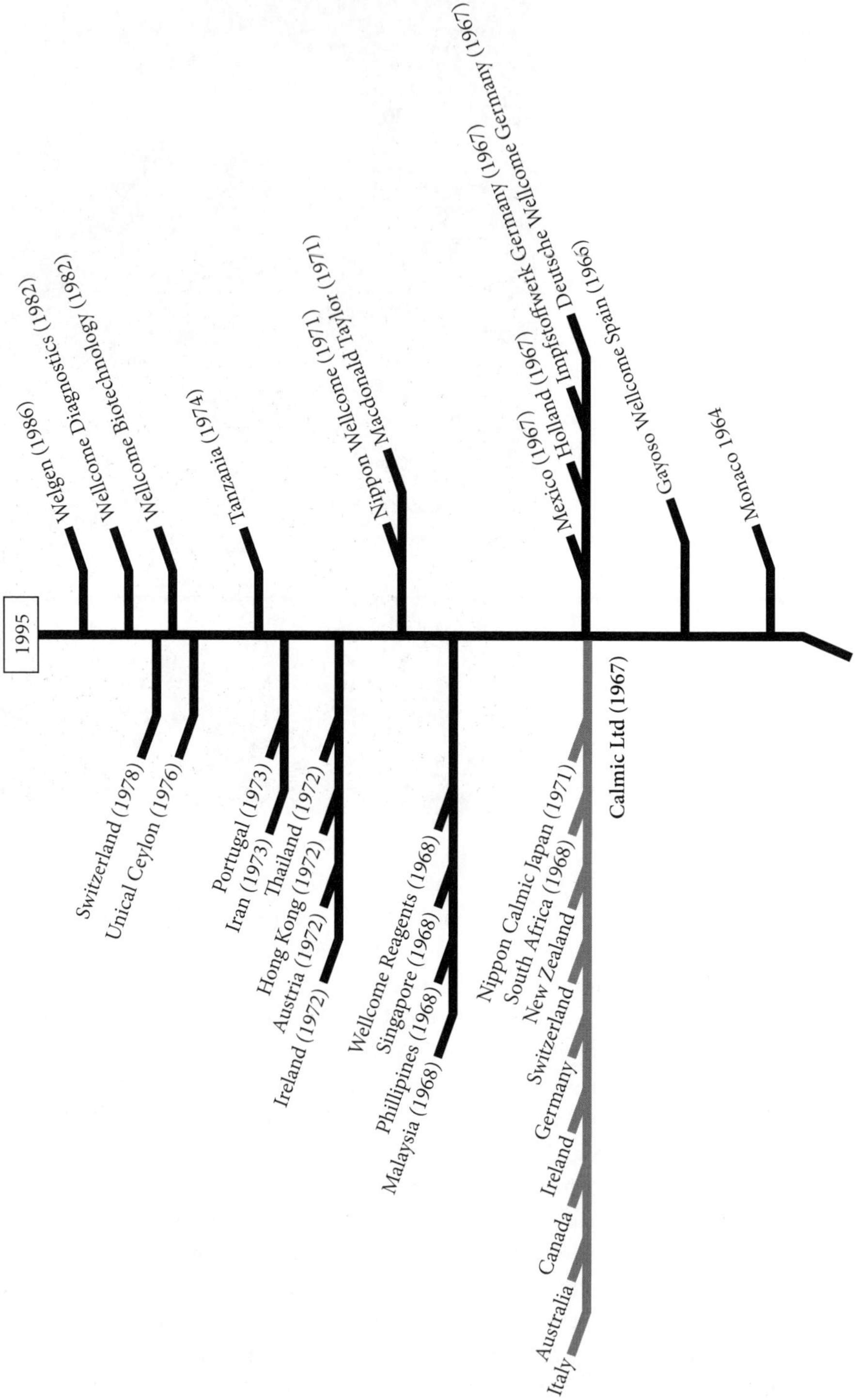

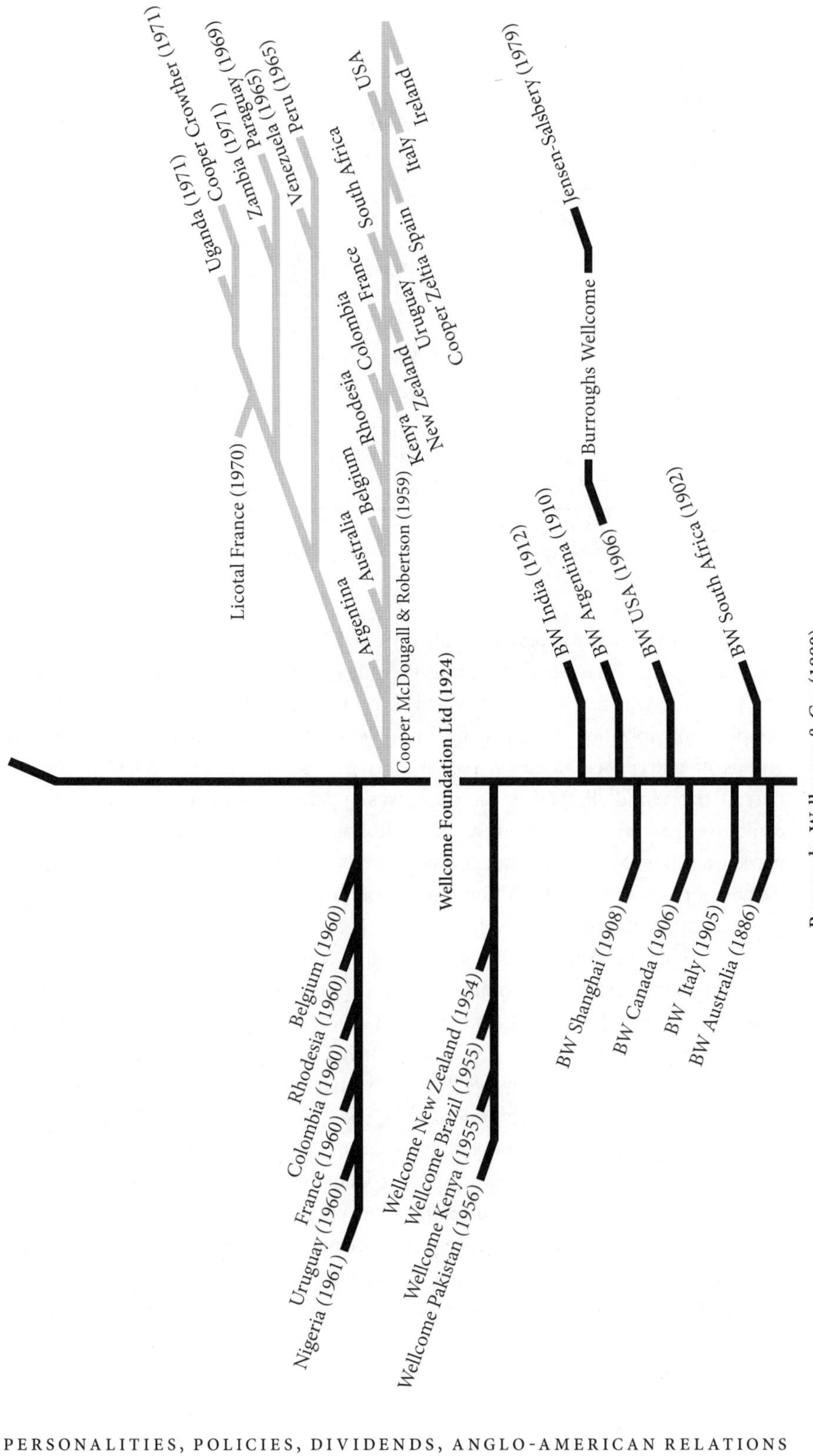
Burroughs Wellcome & Co. (1880)
Wellcome Foundation Ltd (1924)
BW South Africa (1902)
BW USA (1906)
BW Argentina (1910)
BW India (1912)
Burroughs Wellcome
Jensen-Salsbery (1979)
BW Australia (1886)
BW Italy (1905)
BW Canada (1906)
BW Shanghai (1908)
Wellcome Pakistan (1956)
Wellcome Kenya (1955)
Wellcome Brazil (1955)
Wellcome New Zealand (1954)
Nigeria (1961)
Uruguay (1960)
France (1960)
Colombia (1960)
Rhodesia (1960)
Belgium (1960)
Cooper McDougall & Robertson (1959)
Argentina
Australia
Belgium
Rhodesia
Colombia
France
South Africa
USA
Kenya
New Zealand
Uruguay
Cooper Zeltia Spain
Italy
Ireland
Licotal France (1970)
Uganda (1971)
Cooper Crowther (1971)
Zambia (1971)
Paraguay (1969)
Venezuela (1965)
Peru (1965)

Table 13.1 *WFL group sales and financial analysis 1960–1970 (£million)*

	Sales	*Pre-tax profits*	*Post-tax profits*	*Dividend*
1960	28.1	3.5	1.8	0.6
1961	29.6	3.7	1.9	0.6
1962	30.5	3.8	1.9	0.6
1963	31.7	3.9	1.8	0.7
1964	33.8	4.3	1.9	0.9
1965	36.5	4.6	2.0	0.5
1966	43.8	5.7	3.2	1.4*
1967	50.5	6.4	1.6	1.5
1968	62.5	7.7	3.6	1.6
1969	75..1	9.6	4.7	1.9
1970	85.7	9.1	4.5	2.1

*Hereafter includes a payment under deed of covenant.
Source: GSK/WF/SCS/798, WFL and Wellcome plc accounts and annual reports.

In 1968, the WFL board accepted in entirety Urwick Orr's recommendations. They were endorsed by the Trust which approved the implementation of the changes proposed. The most fundamental reform intended to centralize control was to reconfigure the rambling organization by replacing multiple individual business enterprises with groups of enterprises based on regions: Britain, Europe, North America, and the Rest of the World (ROW). A chairman was appointed to each group management committee responsible for the three main functions: financial accounting, R&D, and marketing, thereby creating an additional layer of management and multiplying the number of committees. Each committee was left to define precise objectives and methods of functioning effectively.

Apart from the formation of regional groups, functional management committees, and changes in titles, progress towards implementation of the detailed recommendations were delayed until the appointment of Perrin's successor as chairman of WFL in 1970. The Trust considered all three deputy chairmen as candidates, though Wheeler, who had been temporarily responsible for the management of R&D since Adamson's death, was ruled out on health grounds. The energetic extrovert, but abrasive Wrigley who was responsible for the marketing function and who was the WFL presence on the American board, received little support from either his colleagues on the board of WFL or the trustees.[8] Without enthusiasm on the part of the board, A. A. Gray was appointed to succeed Perrin. He was a chemical engineer and formerly a senior production manager at Unilever in the UK until he became deputy chairman in charge of production at WFL. His personality was a complete contrast with that of Wrigley; Gray was withdrawn, an uncharismatic figure who would prove to lack both leadership qualities and the ability to motivate others. Yet as chairman of

A.A. Gray was a chemical engineer who had joined WFL in 1954 from Unilever, where he had been the UK production manager. After becoming deputy chairman of WFL in 1967, he was appointed chairman in 1970 until retirement in 1977. His chairmanship was marked by delegation and drift, failing to ensure implementation of the recent management consultants' recommendation which had been endorsed by the board.

WFL he became responsible for acting on the consultants' recommendations and initiating fundamental reform of the business. After an initial flurry of decisions "in principle," however, Gray delegated the task of implementation to subordinates and allowed the process to drift.[9] His first attendance at the BW&Co. board meeting in the US was remembered by the American directors for his display of evident boredom throughout the proceedings which prompted two of them to express despair that he was their new leader and to wonder whether they should quit. Coe described Gray as "innocuous".[10] Gray's intimation in 1972, that Coe was too old to join the board of WFL[11] also revealed a serious lack of judgment as to the potential value to WFL of a clearly effective leader.

Beginning in 1972, power in WFL was concentrated in the hands of three deputy directors who reported to the chairman. These were Wheeler, in charge of group production, engineering, and financial services; Wrigley, responsible for group marketing and selling human medical products; and Gray, chairman, but also responsible for group marketing and selling veterinary medicines and animal nutritional products.[12] Within this overarching structure, each of the constituent functions within each of the deputy chairmen's portfolios was represented by a director who was also a member of the parent board: Adamson, director of R&D; Robinson, director of finance; Lomas, director of production and engineering; and Falder, director of personnel and sales. Within the global group structure, Coe became group chairman for the region comprising North, South, and Central America. Unlike other regional chairmen, on his insistence, he was also allowed to remain as president of BW&Co.

As part of the reorganization of WFL, seven new directors were appointed in 1971/2. Two had been Wellcome employees since 1953. J. H. Peter Upton was appointed as a legal adviser, became company secretary and subsequently overseas manager responsible for managing activities in Africa and Asia. Australia was added to his area of responsibility when he became regional director within the new group structure in 1972. By that time he had also succeeded Gray as chairman and managing director of Cooper, McDougall & Robertson, the UK veterinary business

Figure 13.2 *The Structure and Organisation of the Wellcome Foundation Ltd/Wellcome plc, 1969/73–1987*

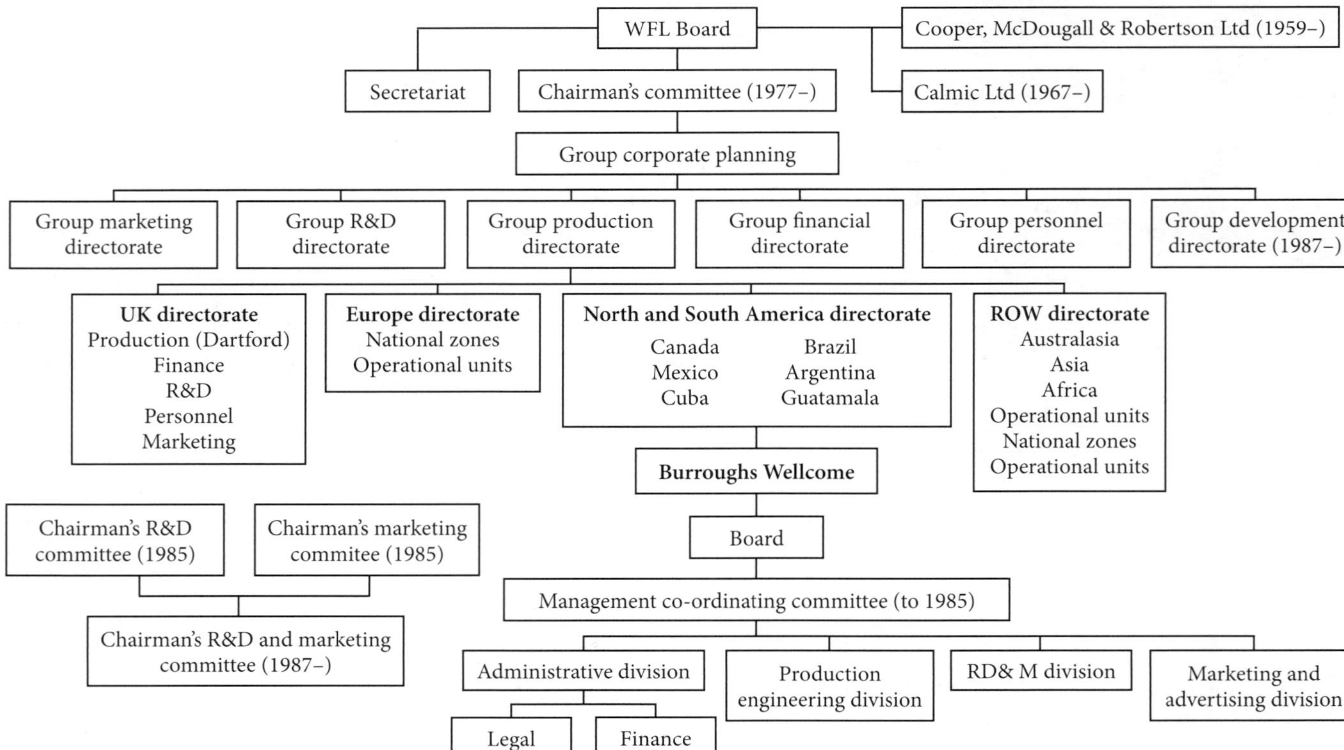

acquired by WFL in 1959/60, subsequently renamed Coopers Animal Health Ltd.[13] Upton's immediate contemporary, R. C. Devereux, was an industrial engineer in the pharmaceutical division of WFL who became chief engineer and deputy production engineer, until in 1967 he was dispatched to Australia as head of Calmic, the newly acquired, highly diversified consumer-product company whose main activity focused on supplying industrial hygiene equipment. In 1972 he was appointed to the board as group production director.[14]

David Godfrey took his place at Calmic and also joined Devereux on the board. Godfrey was a pharmacist who after graduating in 1951 embarked on a career in retail pharmacy before joining WFL in 1956 as a medical representative. He left the company after five years when he became a commercial director at Sterling Winthrop, returning in 1966, becoming managing director of Calmic in the following year.[15] Five years later Henry Copestick, a chartered accountant previously employed at ICI joined WFL who in 1967 became the manager of European activities. In 1971, however, he was given the leadership of a newly created corporate planning group which gave him a seat on the board of WFL.[16] His successor in Europe was Claude Matons, who was Italian and a lawyer by profession who accumulated administrative experience in the American pharmaceutical industry during the 1950s where he was employed at Johnson & Johnson and Sterling Winthrop, and at Organon, a pharmaceutical company in the Netherlands. When he joined WFL, he assumed command of the Italian subsidiary company which at Pomezia possessed the largest pharmaceutical manufacturing facility outside the UK in Europe. He became the director responsible for activities in the European region in 1971.[17] Other new members appointed to the board in 1971/2 who had no previous experience of WFL were P. K.Brewin, formerly with the management consultancy of John Tyzack and partners, who joined as personnel officer, and Dr Arnold Worlock who became group marketing director. The fourth and most important appointment was that of finance director, Alfred Shepperd, whose career with the company lasted almost twenty years and included the roles of managing director and subsequently of chairman and chief executive of Wellcome plc.

An economics graduate from UCL, he had spent thirteen formative years in a financial role with the Rank Organization under the autocratic chairmanship of Sir John Davis. A brief period spent with textile and engineering companies was followed by six years as managing director of Kayser Ullman Industries Ltd.[18] He left that organization in 1972 to become finance director of WFL. In 1975, Coe was influential in persuading Gray to recommend to the Trust that Shepperd should be promoted to deputy chairman. When Gray retired in 1977, Shepperd became chairman and managing director, remaining in that role until his retirement thirteen years later. Although the composition of the board of WFL had changed substantially during Gray's seven-year stint as chairman, changes had been structural rather than fundamental. However, although the restructuring had occurred on paper, the reality was that the group-based plan had failed and the flawed management culture of WFL, identified by Urwick Orr, remained unaffected. In a meeting of the chairman's

Sir Alfred J. Shepperd, Finance director of WFL between 1972 and 1977 and chairman and managing director between 1977 and 1990. Wellcome Library London.

marketing committee in 1977, chaired as usual by Shepperd, Worlock, the chairman director of group marketing, admitted that, since its formation in 1972, the group had even failed to agree upon objectives.[19] Regional meetings where "frank and friendly exchanges" occurred were described by Worlock as useful, even though they had failed to establish any basis for cooperation.

After a series of complaints in the past to which no response had been forthcoming, three members of the chairman's committee: Coe, Godfrey, and Matons, expressed serious criticism of the lack of progress. Coe criticized the long delays in responding to new product proposals (principally originating from BW&Co.), the poor caliber of staff sent to RTP to visit the US and other subsidiaries, the hindrances placed on local management rendering local efforts counterproductive, insufficient dissemination of information across the global organization, and excessive time spent by senior managers in travelling overseas which had adversely affected the performance of their departmental tasks.[20] Coe had no confidence in Worlock whose interference in the negotiation of a licensing contract between BW&Co. and Upjohn over Tribissen, a veterinary product, had jeopardized the joint project.[21] Following one meeting of regional directors, Coe recorded that all of them believed that Worlock was "a disaster."[22] Worlock's response was a proposal for the formation of two marketing advisory groups – a medical marketing advisory group (MMAG) and the veterinary marketing advisory group (VMAG) – each responsible for discussing strategies and needs and advising on group marketing. The composition of these advisory groups consisted of senior marketing representatives from major markets (roughly a dozen), who met quarterly, thus supplementing the annual meeting of the group marketing committee which would consider their advice. Shepperd was enthusiastic because he saw each of the marketing advisory groups as "an excellent vehicle for the US to contribute its experience," an explicit acknowledgement of the superior marketing record demonstrated by BW&Co. in the US.[23]

Worlock, however, was not the only weak link among the directors. A private late evening conversation left Coe with the impression that Shepperd believed that almost all of the board of directors he had inherited in London, was (as interpreted by Coe) "a bunch of jerks."[24] As the post of director of WFL group's corporate planning in 1972 was one of the few recommendations made in the critical Urwick Orr report in 1967 to be implemented fully, the approach of Copestick and his fellow directors is significant in explaining the lack of progress towards rationalization during the 1970s and 1980s. In an interview published in the Foundation News he commented on the reduction of staff, "It is fundamental to understand that a large international group cannot change course rapidly ... It is not in the Wellcome tradition. " This essentially passive approach to rationalization is revealed by his description of the corporate plan introduced in 1975 which emerged as the result of a process in which plans were submitted by sixty or so reporting units across the world, fed into a computer, and tested for errors, "the computer produces a consolidation which is, in effect, a corporate plan."[25] He told his interviewer that the "ever-increasing demand for pharmaceuticals meant that the company would benefit from a guaranteed expanding market and the scientific base to exploit it ..." and referred to the "huge strength" conferred by the "unique organization and unique constitution" under which the company operated. However, he conceded that in the past, some had claimed that WFL had been "less than dynamic in the red-blooded commercial sense," but that this was offset by "the company's reputation for good medicine, integrity in dealing with people, and care in making claims for products." The corporate ethos had enabled the company "to exercise unchallenged leadership within the industry" on which he believed the company could capitalize[26] – a remarkable and complete delusion expressed by Copestick. The account of computerized planning was mirrored in the factory at Dartford where the group production director was R. C. Devereux who perceived his role as that of quality control, ensuring that each product proposed by subsidiary companies for manufacture met criteria set in the UK. He admitted that one consequence of this decentralized reactive approach was the production of "very large numbers of products with very small runs."[27] However, Upton insisted that "variety was a source of strength."[28] These views expressed by senior directors seven years after the critical Urwick Orr report explain the frustration expressed by Shepperd shortly after his appointment as finance director, and even more fervently by Coe.

In a confidential conversation with Coe in March 1977, shortly after Shepperd's appointment as chairman and managing director, Shepperd revealed that he was considering how relations between the Trust and the board might be reconstituted in a way which might facilitate changes to the composition of the board.[29] Changes in the chairmanship, personnel, and policy of the Trust also presented further uncertainty affecting Anglo-American relations because as the main source of profits, BW&Co. was as vulnerable to a change in dividend policy by the Trust as WFL. Consequently, the composition of the Trust was a matter of vital interest to both Coe and Shepperd. Shortly after assuming the chairmanship, Franks described the trustees as "senile and squalid"[30] and embarked on a policy of radical reform. First, he plotted the rapid retirement of the gerontocracy he had inherited; second, he took the resulting Trust vacancies as an opportunity (regardless of Wellcome's will) to reform both the composition of the Trust and its procedures. The result was an enlarged body increased to seven members. He replaced a solicitor and an accountant by scientists who, by bringing their number to five, increased their potential influence on Trust policy.[31] However, these changes meant that the presence of a "man of business," as specified in Wellcome's will, disappeared from the body. Franks may have believed that his own experience as chairman of Lloyds Bank qualified him in this respect. Technically, this may have been true. However, Peter Williams described him essentially as an academic, philosopher, and diplomat,[32] lacking experience of substantial involvement in a business organization or of a manufacturing business. Franks's chairmanship took the form of complete dominance in decision-making which was facilitated by the long-standing Trust convention, established by Sir Henry Dale, that voting had no place in conducting its affairs. Hence, between the 1950s and the mid 1970s the overwhelming influence of the relationship between two dominant chairmen who determined the financial relationship between the Trust and WFL.

When Shepperd became finance director he sought to strengthen the company's financial position by maintaining the low dividend arrangements under previous Trust chairmen. Even before Shepperd succeeded Gray as chairman of WFL, he had cultivated a congenial relationship with Franks, producing a period of complete harmony between the Trust and the business. The cozy relationship between Franks and Shepperd is well illustrated by the description offered by Peter Williams, secretary of the Trust at that time, of the process by which WFL annual dividends were determined. Franks would meet Shepperd who would tell Franks the figure which he considered that the business could afford, after which Franks would not challenge him and would subsequently inform the trustees of the agreed figure. No objection was ever raised by trustees; they were simply in awe of Franks, whose conduct made them feel "like being with the headmaster … if we challenged him he would give us six of the best."[33]

In 1974, with an eye to retirement from the chairmanship, Franks invited Sir William (later to become Lord) Armstrong to become a trustee with a view to succeeding him as chairman. Like Franks, his experience of business was tangential rather than central to his distinguished career; again like Franks, he had become chairman of the Midland Bank after a brief spell as a director. His long and outstanding career had been in the Civil Service, of which he had become head in

Table 13.2 *Wellcome Trust income; principal categories and WFL profit, 1971–1984 (£million)*

	WFL net profit after tax	*WFL dividend and covenant payment*	*Trust income from deposits, and interest*	*Wellcome Trust income*
1971	4.5	2.1	0.3	2.4
1972	4.6	2.1	0.4	2.5
1973	6.4	2.5	0.4	2.9
1974	9.3	2.6	0.3	2.9
1975	10.8	2.9	0.5	3.4
1976	11.0	3.2	0.2	3.9
1977	19.7	3.7	0.7	4.4
1978	25.0	6.8	1.0	7.9
1979	30.9	6.6	1.1	7.7
1980	31.9	7.4	1.1	12.2
1981	37.1	10.0	2.1	13.6
1982	33.0	10.5	3.0	16.2
1983	36.9	13.0	3.2	16.4
1984	38.1	13.0	3.4	15.9

Source: GSK/WF/SCS/798, WFL and Wellcome plc accounts and annual reports.

1968. However, although Armstrong's sudden illness, followed by untimely death, saw Franks continue in post until 1980, the newcomer's relatively short period as trustee heralded a new era in the relations between the Trust, WFL, and potentially therefore, BW&Co. In attendance at early meetings, he detected an accumulation of a "head of steam" among the scientific members who felt frustration that ambitions for the Trust were constrained by the financial limitations resulting from WFL's dividend policy jointly agreed by Franks, whose authority remained unchallenged on the committee, and Shepperd.[34] Armstrong shared this concern that the Trust was unable to conduct even a limited research funding exercise, particularly because by the time he joined the Trust, WFL was generating profits (notably those supplied by the dividends received from an increasingly profitable BW&Co. in America). As a preliminary to agreeing the 1974 dividend, Franks invited Armstrong as his chosen successor and Shepperd (then finance director representing Gray) to a private dinner, the usual occasion when the recommended dividend was agreed between the two chairmen. Ignoring whatever Franks's reaction might be, Armstrong "ambushed" Shepperd who reluctantly conceded to his request for a personal undertaking that, between 1974 and 1976, WFL would increase annual dividends to the Trust from £1 million to £4 million.[35] The average dividend between 1971 and 1976 was £3 million. A covenanted supplement as part of the arrangement for dividend restraint raised the level marginally again in 1977.

Sir John R. Vane, pharmacologist, formerly professor of experimental pharmacology at the Royal College of Surgeons, University of London (and later a Nobel Prize winner), who joined the Wellcome Foundation in 1973 as group research director until 1986. Wellcome Library, London.

This change in dividend policy imposed by the Trust underlined the urgency for WFL of developing new products. The acquisition of products by taking over other companies would require financial resources which were now under threat from the Trust. Gray's response as the new chairman of WFL was to declare his intention to explore raising funds from the overseas subsidiary companies to fund the revival of the business, possibly by selling equity. This first required agreement of the Trust.[36] As the profitability and rapid growth of the American company seemed to make the American subsidiary, BW&Co., the only part of WFL that might interest investors, Gray's declaration justified apprehension among staff at the board to support, in principle, an increased investment in R&D at Beckenham where the recent record of product innovation had been limited to the antihistamine, Actidil, in 1960. Relations between the two research directors, Adamson in charge of Beckenham since 1953 and David Long, director of clinical research at Euston Road laboratories in London since 1959, were not harmonious.

Their disagreements at board level over WFL's research policy resulted in both being replaced in 1972 by Professor John R. Vane who became group research director beginning in January 1973.[37] Vane was a pharmacologist who, following postgraduate work in Oxford, was assistant professor at Yale for two years where he also spent time as a consultant for Squibb. He returned to the UK in 1955 to join the department of pharmacology at the Royal College of Surgeons, London University where he was appointed Professor of Experimental Pharmacology in 1966. There he developed a bioassay system for measuring the release and fate of a group of hormones known as prostaglandins which led, in 1971, to an understanding of the link between prostaglandins and aspirin. He left the Royal College to join WFL as research director in 1973, together with colleagues with whom he had been working at the Royal College, and formed a prostaglandin research department. In recognition of his research he would be made an FRS in 1974.[38] Vane's assumption of the leadership of R&D at WFL followed a preceding period during which rifts had occurred between research directors. Issues regarding research policy, competition for resources, and control and status, had culminated in the resignation of three senior figures. Creasy believed the origins of the feuds were attributable to Adamson's lack of leadership as research director, his office-bound approach having shown little interest in encouraging his staff.[39] Vane's presence at WFL soon revealed evidence of a robust, even abrasive approach which did not bode well for future relations, either with his staff in the laboratories, or with fellow directors in the boardroom, or with anyone at RTP.

His relations with American managers and scientists were markedly different from those of Adamson who had shown support, but not intervention.[40] On Coe's first meeting with Vane, he was left with an impression that the new research director was aware that he faced problems relating to research organization, strategy, and personnel in the UK. Discussions in an early meeting with Vane in London aroused Hitchings's suspicion that Vane was trying to take over, seeking to use his authority as group research director to establish new priorities in the company, the first of which was a greater share of the group's resources for scientists in the UK.[41] From the outset, relations between Hitchings and Vane had been infused with suspicion compounded by clashing egos. With few exceptions, Hitchings had long held a generally low opinion of the scientists at Beckenham, a view which derived not from their undoubted levels of education and knowledge, but based on their failure to produce research resulting in commercially worthwhile projects.[42] Hitchings's immediate fear was that Vane would impose a research director upon the American company, regardless of the views of the American board. Coe sought to reassure Hitchings, expressing a misplaced confidence that because Vane would not have to work with Hitchings's successor he would be most unlikely to rule out any candidates favored by the American directors.[43] It soon became clear, however, that unlike his predecessor, Vane intended to intervene in BW&Co.'s research appointments and policy.

Coe succeeded in dissuading Vane from appointing Bushby who had a record of successful collaboration with American scientists, but whom neither Coe nor Hitchings regarded as a suitable leader at RTP. However, their preferred candidate did not obtain Vane's approval. He was Ronald M. Cresswell, head of development research. By the 1970s, the preceding uneasy relationship that had prevailed between Hitchings and Cresswell in the 1960s had been replaced by one of mutual respect. Hitchings reaffirmed Cresswell's qualities as a scientist and acknowledged that, since his appointment in 1964, he had been an effective manager of development research. Although Coe and the board of BW&Co. supported Hitchings's recommendation, Vane disagreed.[44] Vane regarded Cresswell's record of pure, rather than developmental research (from Vane's standpoint a distinction of the utmost significance) to be insufficient to justify his appointment at that level of seniority. On Vane's insistence, the vacancy was advertized both in the US and in the UK, reinforcing Hitchings's fear of a plot by Vane to appoint a candidate of his own.[45]

Privately, Coe and Hitchings sought a suitable alternative among American scientists from outside the company, eventually deciding upon an informal offer to Pedro Cuatrecasas, formerly Professor of Chemical Pharmacology at Johns Hopkins. In 1972, in recognition of his discovery of how insulin regulates the functioning of cells in

Pedro Cuatrecasas, formerly professor of chemical pharmacology at Johns Hopkins university, appointed as director of research, development and medical division and vice president of BW&Co. between 1975 and 1986. Under his directorship of RD&M, the SKUNKWORKS project concealed continuing research into antivirals from the board of BW&Co. and led to the development of AZT. Wellcome Library, London.

the body, he was awarded the John Jacob Abel award in pharmacology. A highly respected expert in metabolic diseases, most recently he had been carrying out clinical work in endocrinology at the National Institute of Health where he had developed a scientific process technology called affinity chromatography.[46] After he visited RTP to deliver a lecture, Coe agreed with Hitchings and Cresswell to support his appointment, though initially Cuatrecasas had considered and declined Coe's provisional offer which was subject to the agreement of the WFL board. Coe and Hitchings revived Cresswell's candidature which Vane vetoed again.

After almost two years of prevarication by Vane and tortuous negotiations between Coe and Cuatrecasas in 1975, he was appointed as director of BW&Co.'s RD&M (research, development, and medical), a division consisting of almost one thousand scientists and MDs to which he appointed a new head of organic chemistry and a sizeable new research group working principally in an area of neuro-pharmacology. Cuatrecasas also became a vice president of the American company. On his initiative in 1975, in an attempt to promote closer Anglo-American cooperation, six scientists from Tuckahoe and Beckenham met to explore how relations might be improved and collaborative work undertaken.

The initiative was short-lived, no doubt partly because the fractured relationship between Hitchings and Vane was replaced by an equally sour relationship between Vane and Cuatrecasas. Even though researchers at RTP were in sight of a major breakthrough following the successes of Zyloprim and Septra, Cuatrecasas was not invited to join the WFL board, thereby protecting Vane's superiority as overall group research director as well as director of research in the UK. Cuatrecasas soon complained to Coe of persistent harassment from London.[47] Thereafter, for two years communication between the two was limited to mail, rather than telephone.[48] Relations between them deteriorated further when Shepperd steered the WFL board towards a diversion of an increasing proportion of group expenditure on R&D to support the development of science-based innovative products at RTP. In June 1981, dismayed by this perpetual friction, Shepperd held a private meeting with Coe to discuss "how to get John Vane and Pedro to stop acting like children."[49]

Although postwar tensions affecting RD&M at the American company emerged during the 1970s, another source of friction dated from the 1960s. Tension between

London and RTP also resulted from the diversification policy pursued to compensate for a lack of product innovation. This had been imposed on a reluctant board in the US. Since the 1950s, joint managing directors, Wrigley and Wheeler, had negotiated small, principally trading acquisitions across the globe. The most significant acquisition affecting the American subsidiary was the firm of Cooper, McDougall & Robertson (CM&R) in 1959, a long-established British company possessing a high reputation as a manufacturer of veterinary medicines. CM&R also owned a small subsidiary in the US, The Denver Serum Company, where two-thirds of the world's market for veterinary products existed and where WFL wished to make a major impact through the exploitation of its renowned immunological research and vaccine technology. Based on what were subsequently revealed to be misleading reports on recent and current profit levels, the board in London expressed optimism regarding the additional cash flow expected from the company.

Neither Creasy nor Coe was persuaded by the financial case for purchase; they regarded such an acquisition as a distraction that might weaken American managers' focus on human ethical medicines. Although the WFL board was apprised of these reservations, they had not been conveyed to Dale and the trustees who, in 1964, in ignorance of the divided views, gave permission for the purchase of the entire capital of the company of £82,000. The trustees did, however, indicate that the Trust was in no way committed to assisting with the financing of any deal.[50] BW&Co. was required to guarantee a loan to the re-named Coopers (USA) Inc. to enable the American veterinary company to buy the Denver Serum business which they had acquired in 1967.[51] The owner and managing director of the Denver laboratories remained with Coopers until 1971 when, as part of the relocation strategy, Cooper's veterinary products plant was removed to NC. This new organization became the Animal Health Division of BW&Co. which in 1973 assumed complete managerial responsibility for the animal health business.[52]

This rationalization policy aimed at developing animal health products internationally was driven from London, following a provisional decision taken by the WFL board, that both human and veterinary biologicals should receive further development through R&D, a policy endorsed after further discussions in 1972. The policy received strong approval from Vane and Gray. Historically, WFL had possessed a long-standing reputation for veterinary medicine among the international scientific community since between the wars. Beckenham scientists insisted that pursuing biological and chemotherapeutic routes would bring advantages that justified continued investment in vaccines.[53] On financial grounds, however, Wrigley had argued that it would be unwise to invest further in one of the "less fruitful sectors of the company's business."[54] The commercial case against investment was based on the problem of covering overheads, let alone "of earning a proper return." This was partly due to the unpredictability of the demand for vaccines which depended on sudden outbreaks of disease. The uncertainty which surrounded production was exacerbated by the insistence on the part of national governments (which were the principal sources of demand) on participation in the control of the production of certain vaccines.[55] However, Vane persuaded the board that withdrawal would adversely affect relations with the UK government, that optimism for the future of immunology was justified, and that a commercial pay-off could be expected in the long-term, an argument which secured further capital investment in R&D at a laboratory at Berkhamstead in 1972. This failed to deliver the confidently predicted commercial reward, either in the UK or in the US. The Denver business, for which BW&Co. was responsible, also proved to be a loss-making enterprise.

In 1979, in accordance with WFL policy, in a bid to offset the continuing losses made by the Denver Serum Company, the directors decided upon the acquisition of Jensen-Salsbery Laboratories (Jen-Sal) from Richard Merrill Inc. in Kansas for $21 million in cash. Again, this ignored the opposition of Coe and the directors of BW&Co. which had been reported to the WFL board.[56] Although veterinary sales increased by 50 per cent, losses doubled.[57] Two years after the Jensen-Sal takeover, the completion of a systematic investigation of the accounts led BW&Co. to propose a complete managerial and financial restructuring of the business and the subjection of the company to probationary status.[58] Further diversification occurred in South and Central America, again involving BW&Co. After World War II, the American company operated through agents in Mexico, Colombia, Panama, Venezuela, Puerto Rico, the Philippines, Chile, Argentina, Brazil, and Cuba, though because of currency shortages, tariff, and other restrictions, as well as political volatility, export sales to these countries remained minimal throughout the 1950s and 1960s. The American company's largest single export market (though only in relative terms) was Mexico, though in 1965, the introduction by the Mexican Government of prohibitive duties on imported pharmaceuticals prompted the directors to establish its first foreign manufacturing subsidiary in South America in 1967. Coe became more involved with the business from 1971 when he was appointed as president of one of the WFL's newly-created regional management structures, in which his own responsibilities included the US, Canada, and all of South and Central America. From the perspective of the board, these forms of diversification based on regionalization represented a diversion of management resources away from competition in the US.

As in the case of licensing policy which was to frustrate BW&Co.'s plan for growth,[59] the imposition of veterinary medicine as a part of the American company's responsibilities was contrary to the American directors' perception of optimal business strategy focused entirely on human medicine. Such interventions by directors in London were manifestations of an historic ambivalence towards the American subsidiary from the beginning which manifested as a reluctance to listen and an insistence on control. Those who evoked the Wellcome tradition in justifying policies contrary to the wishes expressed by the American directors overlooked the history of personal, unwavering, unqualified, and resourceful support extended to the American company by its founder between 1906 and 1936.

PART FOUR:

The transforming impact of antivirals: sexually-transmitted diseases, market development, and problems of management turbulence in the US and the UK.

CHAPTER 14

Zovirax, blockbuster drug and the expansion of Burroughs Wellcome & Co. at Research Triangle Park and Greenville

The distribution between resources invested in marketing and those in RD&M during the 1970s reflected change in the balance of the company's activities. Most striking was the declining percentage of sales representatives employed compared with scientists and clinical staff. As a percentage of total employment in 1970, sales representatives accounted for 35 per cent compared with 18 per cent in RD&M. By 1981, the comparable figures were 17 per cent and 24 per cent, indicative of the changing balance between scientific research and selling (see Table 9.1). Patterns of expenditure reveal a rising proportion of marketing costs attributable to advertising, though not until the end of the decade did expenditure on RD&M reach the same level as marketing expenditure (see Table 9.2).

Three important additions to the scientific staff were made during the 1970s. BW&Co. were in competition with Merck and SmithKline for the first, Prof. Howard Schaeffer from the University of Buffalo in 1970. Hitchings had recruited him following their first acquaintance at an international conference in the Netherlands where both were speakers. Days later, Hitchings had invited him to become head of chemistry in the Tuckahoe laboratories.[1] Hitchings's reputation for the research which he and colleagues at RTP had conducted into purines was the clinching factor that led Schaeffer to opt to join the smallest of the competing companies. Schaeffer's work at Buffalo had concentrated on an enzyme for purine nucleosides known to possess anti-cancer activity.[2] The second appointment was that of Pedro Cuatrecasas MD in 1975,[3] formerly professor of Pharmacology and Experimental Therapeutics at Johns Hopkins University School of Medicine (described in the preceding chapter). The third recruit was Dr David Barry, appointed by Cuatrecasas in 1977. He was a Yale graduate in medicine whose principal interest was viral vaccine and antiviral research which he was chosen to lead at RTP. Previously employed at the NIH where he had first encountered Cuatrecasas, he had also spent five years with the FDA where he had met more BW&Co. scientists (some of whom were later to become colleagues)

Professor Howard J. Schaeffer, formerly professor of medicinal chemistry at the University of Buffalo appointed as head of chemistry at BW&Co. in 1970 who in 1986 succeeded Cuatrecasas as director of research, development and medical division and vice president. The discovery of acyclovir which led to the development of Zovirax is largely attributable to him and his team. *Wellcome News*, Wellcome Library, London.

before joining the FDA's Bureau of Biologics, subsequently the Centre for Biological Evaluation and Research.[4]

At different times, all three recorded their appreciation of the legacy of organization and culture already established at the company's laboratories. The most detailed is that given by Schaeffer who described the fluid, iterative, non-prescriptive approach adopted by Hitchings which he had first established at Tuckahoe. This was subsequently embodied in the systems and processes of RD&M at RTP: "We were all in the same building where … scientists would meet regularly, some from chemistry, some from pharmacology … and have informal conferences and group meetings and really work out how to attack certain types of research problems. There were times when I wanted to have certain projects worked on … I would talk to certain people and see who might be interested in doing it. It was very seldom I had to assign a project to someone, mostly they'd say 'I like that idea, I'd like to work on it.' And so it wasn't forced so much on anybody … they would volunteer to do the work."[5]

Newly-recruited young scientists were given ideas to work on for about five years, after which each was encouraged to formulate his or her own proposals. According to Schaeffer, almost invariably the authors of such ideas received resources and the liberty to pursue and develop them. The price of support, freedom, and openness enjoyed by all scientists at RTP was working in a climate where the prevailing expectation (albeit at the back of their minds) was that their research would lead to a material that could be developed into a drug. At Beckenham, where the laboratories were commonly referred to as the "University of Beckenham", prestige was associated with pure research and publication. Achievements resulting from applied research and development leading to product innovation and profit were not regarded as an important objective.[6] Schaeffer believed that the distinctive difference between the laboratories in the UK and those in the US was the ethos which Hitchings created at Tuckahoe and perpetuated at RTP, where "... in one sense there was freedom; in the other sense there was dedication to try to develop something that was very useful ... it wasn't strictly a university-type atmosphere ..."[7] One characteristic of Hitchings's personal and management style was to show that " he was interested in what you were doing but he didn't want to interfere ... he gave everybody an awful lot of leeway as to what they wanted to do, again with the idea that what you work on should lead to something of some value, or should at least open up some new ideas."[8] Underlying this approach to managing science was Hitchings's philosophy which, as demonstrated in the 1970s in his own research, moved closer to the notion of rational drug design. Hitchings claimed that his approach to research throughout his career had been purposeful, rooted in a cumulative pragmatism: "Pure empiricism is self-limiting. The purposeful exploration of enzymes, metabolic pathways and cell receptors leads to increasing competence. Competence accumulates and so does one's confidence that the future will bring the solution to many problems that at present seem difficult or insoluble."[9]

Schaeffer described the benign management regime that prevailed in 1970 when he joined the company. Although the president had expressed concern from time to time over the absence of product innovation and the hope that something would turn up "pretty soon," scientists were not subjected to actual pressure.[10] Responsibility for the overall organization of research lay with the small research committee which had its origins in the early years at Tuckahoe under Hitchings's leadership. Schaeffer believed that the committee understated its role which he perceived to be a "very potent and valuable organization," a project-type committee which was also concerned with medical as well as research issues and problems.[11]

The structure and functioning of this committee, which remained largely unaltered under Hitchings's two successors for more than two decades, provided a degree of stability which Schaeffer regarded as crucial to the company's eventual success and which culminated in the hugely commercially successful anti-virals.[12] Although the structure remained largely unchanged, one significant development in 1974 was a widening of the committee's scope, possibly influenced by Howsam, who joined at Hitchings's invitation. Hitherto, deliberations had been informed by scientists and medical staff represented on the committee. Shortly after Howsam, chairman of the marketing committee, became a member, product managers passed quarterly reports to committee members to keep them informed of progress in their respective creative strategy sessions. Ultimately, the research committee was the most influential body in affecting board decisions as to which compounds should proceed to the stage of actual product development.[13] The next modification of the research committee's activity was initiated by Cuatrecasas after 1980 when he introduced an even greater degree of interdisciplinary exploration in the development of compounds.

When Dr David Barry was appointed to BW&Co. in 1977 as the head of virology,[14] his impressions of the company and of the laboratories at RTP were similar to those formed by Schaeffer seven years earlier. Barry was equally impressed by the continuing existence of a shared research philosophy among senior scientists at RPT. He found himself working in a liberal management culture which enabled research groups and individuals to enjoy a considerable degree of independence as well as the support and encouragement of colleagues. He found Hitchings inclined to be critical and less forthcoming with advice to younger researchers than Elion, though Schaeffer and later Cuatrecasas were described as being stimulating and "wonderfully supportive to research colleagues and their work without a trace of arrogance."[15] He described the culture at RTP as "gentlemanly" where scientists were not interested in the seniority of authorization of published papers. He found the collegial culture in the laboratories at RTP and that which he had experienced at the Rockefeller Foundation to be benign, completely different from the "cut throat" relations between scientists whom he had encountered while employed by the FDA.[16] These accounts of the culture in the laboratories at RTP contrast with that described by Leslie Walton who had experienced working both at RTP and the Wellcome research laboratories of WFL in the UK. He was a member of the chemotherapy department under Stanley Bushby who, he recalled, had informed him that he was not paid to think but only to work. Staff continued to be addressed by titles, never by first names, and nothing could be done without permission "from the next level up." Walton encountered a completely different culture when he accompanied Bushby to RTP to join the RD&M division for the purpose of developing and preparing Septrin for the British market. His recollection was of an environment in which Hitchings and Elion (who displayed a willingness to spend time and "to talk normally" with all staff) were addressed as George and Trudy.[17] On the subject of Anglo-American relations, he observed that both companies regarded information as privileged, though he detected a considerably greater reluctance among scientists at Beckenham to share information with counterparts at RTP than the other way round.[18]

In 1979, the principles underlying the project system initiated in RD&M at RTP and replicated in the company's product planning system shortly after were repeated at Greenville. By this time, following his success in effecting the Greenville production transfer, Gabriel Cipau, a chemical engineering and physics graduate whose doctoral thesis explained aspects of R&D, had joined BW&Co. in 1970, soon becoming head of chemical and plant development and of engineering, reporting to Cresswell as technical director. Cipau's demonstrable capacity for embracing an inter-disciplinary approach across production and RD&M had equipped him particularly well to the tasks, first of integrating activities across the new plant and second, of applying the principles underlying the project system to production and engineering units. Each project team included between ten and fourteen members from a wide range of departments, the leader of each chosen on the basis of relevant specialist knowledge or experience. However, they were not given formal authority over other members although the leader was responsible for guiding the general direction of progress. Cipau used the same model for tasks involving major formulations, packaging changes, equipment and facilities evaluation, and development of large data processing information systems. Six quality circles on the Japanese model were formed at Greenville in 1981, each involving workers in problem-solving in the area of production. Thus, between 1970 and 1981, the introduction of a project-based and problem-solving system throughout the company resulted in an organized, yet non-bureaucratic system, a corporate infrastructure well-prepared for the scientific innovation, efficient, and subsequently large-scale production of the company's first blockbuster anti-viral drug.

The renewed impetus to anti-viral research dated from 1970 and followed the appointment of Schaeffer.[19] Initial conversations with Hitchings shortly after joining BW&Co. gave Schaeffer cause for concern. On Hitchings's invitation, Schaeffer had submitted proposals for his future research for which he would require resources and funding. Essentially, Schaeffer intended to extend and enlarge his previous investigations seeking to develop anti-viral, anti-cancer, or anti-bacterial agents. In a typically acerbic evaluation of Schaeffer's proposal, Hitchings had expressed the view that viruses were untreatable, because once infection had occurred the presence of symptoms meant that the virus had already done the damage and that therefore, it was too late to be treated (implying that Shaeffer's proposal was seriously flawed).[20] Despite these reservations, however, Hitchings agreed that whatever resources Schaeffer required, they would be forthcoming. Temperamentally more sympathetic to colleagues, Elion was the most approachable mentor among members of the research staff and not only engaged with Schaeffer's plans, but also volunteered to become the project leader, taking the work forward in cooperation with the various departments with which she had long-established relations. This research required a new laboratory to accommodate virologists and oncologists who would study the action mechanism of the compound. Hitchings's promise to fund the project was fulfilled.

Profit generated by the company's ballooning sales of anti-bacterials was an important source which Coe successfully removed from the view of the WFL board in two ways. One was the historic practice of adopting a high depreciation rate; the other was the more dubious (undisclosed) tactic, following a "session with a bunch of financial guys trying to figure out how to keep our profits down,"[21] the effect of which was to conceal the true state of the American company's cash flow. In 1977, Coe described Shepperd as being "upset because our profit before tax is $6 million below last year and he doesn't believe we can make it up."[22] Added to the success of these measures was Shepperd's own commitment to ensure that Schaeffer, Elion, Cresswell, and Cipau received the necessary resources to meet rapidly rising expenditure on the project. Shepperd continued to limit dividend distribution to the Trust (on an artificially reported American profit base). Even so, rising expenditure on RD&M imposed a strain on financial resources. Between 1970 and 1983, aggregate RD&M costs incurred by the company doubled from $14.5 million to $33 million. These costs were attributable directly to the development of the new antiviral drug and excluded both manpower costs in the UK (though minimal) and, more importantly, overhead costs plus investment in RD&M during the eight years since the compound had been discovered.[23]

Expenditure on this scale became a matter of concern for WFL directors who, in 1981, had raised the issue of cash flow for debate. Shepperd insisted that despite protestations from Vane, the group research director, until new products entered the market and the future of the company was secured, research budgets must be cut and staff numbers in the UK reduced.[24] Among a total staff reduction from 7,400 to 6,600 between 1979 and 1981, research staff numbers fell by 235,[25] which Shepperd defended by pointing to high research costs at Beckenham. The absence of new products from the Wellcome laboratories was raised again in 1981 at a joint meeting of the WFL board and the trustees, when the directors and two trustees, the distinguished pharmacologist Sir William Paton FRS, and Prof. W. S. Peart FRS, also remarked on high levels of overall research expenditure at Beckenham and questioned the criteria used to prioritize research projects.[26] Vane's response was evasive, couched in generalities. Coe, however, was quick to explain that at RTP, priorities were assigned according to the length of time that particular projects were likely to take and to their perceived chances of commercial success; he expressed his confidence in the outcome of anti-viral research at RTP[27] where the search for new products was gaining momentum.

The biochemistry department had discovered purine analogs with anti-viral activity in 1947, but a perception of high toxicity and therefore doubtful clinical applicability explains why investigation was discontinued until 1968. The single result of this line of inquiry was the introduction in 1962 of the drug Marboran for use in the prevention and treatment of smallpox. However, renewed enquiry was prompted by Schabel's discovery that arabinosyladenine inhibited growth of DNA and RNA viruses. This finding stimulated Elion who hypothesized that purine analogs could be developed successfully as antiviral agents. During the later 1960s, her group's new studies led to the discovery of antiviral activity in several synthetic analogues, though not until 1968 had the synthesis of a compound (2,6-diminopurine arabinoside) led to a program of antiviral screening intended to isolate a therapeutically applicable compound. In the absence of animal screening facilities at Tuckahoe, the task had been undertaken by Dr John Bauer at the Wellcome Laboratories in the UK (who after screening facilities became available at RTP in the mid-1970s relocated to where his experience and expertise could be applied.)[28] He found the diaminopurine arabinoside Ara-DAP to be active against both herpes simplex virus (HSV) and vaccinia virus.[29] However, once again further development in this direction stalled.

From 1970, Schaeffer led investigations into anti-virals while Elion assumed a broader responsibility as head of the new experimental therapy department formed in 1967. His approach differed from that of Elion's group and, as in the case of earlier drug innovation, Schaeffer's initiative was in response to an approach from outside the company, this time by Dr Charles Heidelberger, holder of an American Cancer

Society Fellowship at the University of Wisconsin, whose own research into cancer treatment had resulted, in 1960, in the synthesizing of trifluride. This was a chemical which, in the light of research begun by Hitchings at Tuckahoe and continued at RTP, also touched on ophthalmics which, Heidelberger believed, provided a basis for further research into the development of a treatment for corneal lesions caused by herpes. Schaeffer, with Elion's support, agreed to collaborate with Heidelberger in this research and enlisted Lillia Beauchamp, a former colleague, whom he described as a superb chemist. She assisted in the analysis of a mass of data which Schaeffer had accumulated while at Buffalo. Roughly twenty compounds were selected for further investigation. Elion's group studied the mechanisms of action, enzymology, and in-vivo metabolism.

However, for expertise in animal studies Schaeffer turned to Dr John Bauer, a respected scientist at Beckenham who had been instrumental in the development of Marboran for the treatment of smallpox. Both he together with Dr Peter Collins, another Beckenham scientist, were experienced in screening antivirals and conducted the tests in search of antiviral potential at the Wellcome Laboratories in the UK.[30] These compounds included one for an acyclic nucleoside known as acyclovir which so impressed the two British scientists that they telephoned Schaeffer to declare that in their entire laboratory experience acyclovir was the most active compound they had ever encountered. They concluded that not only was acyclovir a compound many times more active than any other anti-viral developed hitherto, but also that it displayed a remarkably low toxicity.[31] Cuatrecasas described the breakthrough in antiviral chemotherapy as heralding a new era comparable with that associated with penicillin.[32] The company's successful application for an Investigational New Drug (IND) was followed in 1980 by FDA approval, though as yet, use was limited to topical acyclovir in the treatment of herpes eye infections. Viroptic Ophthalmic Solution (in which trifluride was the key ingredient) was the first marketable product resulting from this research.

Largely following Vane's advice, the WFL board had approved of pressing ahead to market Viroptic, a product unlikely to become significant commercially; however, managers and scientists at RTP had their eye on a potentially more rewarding market. During the 1960s, the Centre for Disease Control (CDC) had identified a possible link between herpes II and sexual transmission. This had attracted little public attention at the time; unlike gonorrhea and measles, genital herpes was not classified as a notifiable disease in the US.[33] In 1973, the *JAMA* reported an article written by Dr Marvin S. Anstey that appeared in *Family Health* in which he observed that since the late 1960s the genital herpes virus appeared to have risen among the civilian population, though empirical evidence on more than a local scale had yet to be gathered to substantiate his impression.[34] Concern among professional health workers grew during the 1970s which made medical and marketing managers believe that a drug directed towards the treatment of sexually-transmitted diseases would enter an expanding market. Following FDA approval of acyclovir for the treatment of herpes eye infections, a procedure was devised at RTP for providing American sales representatives with training in virology to prepare them for their role following the hoped-for FDA approval of Zovirax, the trade-marked product intended for use in the treatment of both herpes I and II. Although the new anti-viral drug was not a cure, it was found to reduce symptoms in initial infections and to shorten episodes of genital herpes. A notable characteristic of Zovirax was that it attacked herpes viruses while leaving normal cells unharmed, evidence of a low toxicity which rendered the drug suitable for extended and repeated use. Zovirax was ineffective against recurrent genital herpes and could not be applied to vagina, cervix, or mouth. The importance of the drug derived not from the danger that herpes presented to sufferers (syphilis and gonorrhea were more dangerous), but from the incurability of the disease. Its sales potential lay in safety for extended and repeated application and it was approved for marketing in ointment and powder forms as a treatment for herpes I in March 1982.

By that time, the rising concern among professionals and practitioners during the 1970s had been transformed by an explosion of publicity surrounding the disease during the early 1980s. The front cover of the April 1982 issue of *Newsweek* carried the headline, "The Herpes Epidemic" and contained a leading article entitled "Herpes: the VD of the 80s."[35] "Herpes breaks out" was the title of a report in the journal *Science* which referred to the announcement by the Centres for Disease Control that the disease had reached epidemic proportions.[36] Such publicity contributed to a growing public consciousness of a widespread vulnerability among the population. This was because the infection was prone to be recurrent. The *Newsweek* article that appeared one month before the launch of Zovirax for the treatment of herpes II in May 1982, highlighted changes in contemporary social and sexual behavior which enlarged the potential impact of a treatment, let alone a cure, for sexual diseases.

The self-evident potential for Zovirax as a treatment for a widespread medical condition was not matched by an obvious method of marketing the product. The critical questions facing the company were those to do with estimating the size of the market, determining the scale of production, fixing prices, and deciding on forms of distribution. Because, hitherto, no effective treatment had existed and therefore no control measures had been available, government had not considered official and legal surveillance of the disease to have been justified. Herpes was not considered to be a notifiable disease in the US. A tentative conclusion, based on sampling conducted by CDC, was that in 1982 perhaps 20 million people suffered from herpes and that the rate of new infections fluctuated annually between 300,000 and 500,000.[37] US government estimates suggested that between 1960 and 1979, a nine-fold increase had occurred in those afflicted with the disease. Even at an early stage of clinical trials, Cresswell, director of development since 1972 and from 1978 a vice president, had predicted large sales. He believed that together with other products in the pipeline (the company obtained an NDA for its first anti-depressant drug in 1981), Zovirax had equipped the group with the potential for sales volumes that would enable it to "take on the giants" – a reference to Merck and Roche.[38]

Howsam was less convinced by Cresswell's optimism and, through the marketing committee, sought to gather more reliable figures pertaining to the possible extent of the market from external research organizations which used national mail and telephone surveys, as well as personal interviews. None proved to be satisfactory, mainly because respondents proved reluctant to answer questions about genital herpes or sexual lifestyles. Those who answered did not always answer truthfully. Questionnaires distributed to physicians who were known to treat herpes patients yielded useful information, but little relating to the incidence of the disease. Further evidence was assembled through focus groups which included interviews with physicians and sufferers together. None of the resulting data sets was statistically robust, but the process of gathering the information was valuable. It enabled the company to identify influential figures within the medical community whose work with herpes patients essentially defined the market and was valuable in assisting with formulating marketing strategy. Otherwise, CDC estimates remained the only reasonably reliable aggregative evaluation of the size of the market which, from an economic and marketing perspective, Howsam regarded as a disappointingly "pretty small number." He concluded that despite the unique character of Zovirax and the public perception of the existence of a nationwide herpes epidemic, a large market for the drug was unlikely because of the taboos and sensitivities associated with sexual disease. He believed that the development of a significant market for the drug would depend on securing approval for the treatment of other conditions, notably shingles or cold sores (possibilities which researchers were already pursuing).

In 1981, even at the project pre-product stage, Cresswell, Cuatrecasas, and Howsam had begun to address the problem of turning potential clinical need into effective demand through several initiatives managed by a newly-formed symposia committee. Among its early responsibilities were the arrangement of major scientific and clinical symposia aimed at health professionals, the organization of roundtable discussions, and the production of an educational film about Zovirax. Because Howsam was cautious with regard to the initial level of demand, he persuaded Coe to give priority to organizing effective distribution rather than maximizing production prior to the launch. He argued that the level of prescriptions issued would be irrelevant unless the 50,000 drugstores in the US could be persuaded to stock the product. By mid-June 1982, no fewer than 90 per cent of retailers had received at least one tube of Zovirax ointment on the assumption that if pharmacists witnessed the drug being prescribed, the result would be further orders. Simultaneously, samples were distributed to doctors to enable them to begin treating the disease on diagnosis for effectiveness of the drug depended on the commencement of early treatment. The assumption was that by demonstrating the efficacy of early diagnosis and treatment, those used to treating herpes would induce confidence among other doctors which potentially would be a powerful basis for promotion.[39]

The Rosenthal agency which handled the Zovirax account ensured that no information was released before the launch, either to the medical or lay press.[40] From the outset, heavy expenditure on promotional literature, advertisements in professional journals, tele-conferences, symposia, lecture programs, medical conferences, video tapes, and seminars were the methods adopted to educate medical professionals about the herpes simplex virus. In May 1982, a seven page advertisement aimed at more than a million physicians appeared in numerous professional journals, among which four specialized in obstetrics, three in urology, three in dermatology, one in surgery, one in internal medicine, and seven were multi-specialty publications. Publicity on the same scale was repeated within the year. This took the form of mailings of a patient information pamphlet to the target audience of physicians. A herpes alert center was set up in response to queries about the benefits and limitations of the product from physicians seeking an introduction to the new science of sexually transmitted diseases.[41] Supplementary updated information was contained in a sexually transmitted diseases newsletter intended for physicians. Information and advice at an appropriate level to promote understanding among the lay public was offered through a herpes information center.

Other training material was used to prepare the five hundred and twenty-five salesmen chosen to sell Zovirax. They were instructed to avoid overselling the drug and to avoid "hard selling." Howsam described their task as one of educating doctors, pharmacists, and public health officials about the disease and the drug. He stressed that in order to gain their trust and willingness to believe in the drug when introduced in more effective forms in the future, each of the groups must be made to understand fully the limitations as well as the benefits of the treatment on offer.[42] The strictly ethical overture represented by Howsam's approach to sales representatives, however, was not reflected in some of the advertisements issued by the Rosenthal agency. In 1983, advertisements for the company's new herpes drug appeared in the *Washington Post* and were judged by *Medical World News* to have crossed the line into direct advertising to the public.[43] An advertisement which declared "Help for herpes is here" attracted criticism and a call for restraint from Dr Hal Strelnick, spokesperson for the Health Policy Advisory Centre, a non-profit group based in New York. He criticized the advertisement as "headline-grabbing" because it contained no reference to the failure of the drug to accelerate healing (except in a minority at an early stage of diagnosis) or to prevent recurrence of the condition. He maintained that the optimal method of informing most sufferers of the disease was through package inserts for patients.[44] The company's filmed advertisements for Zovirax, presented by Ann Landers, a popular newspaper advice columnist, attracted further criticism.

Neither ethical nor controversial methods of promoting the drug succeeded initially in creating a high demand. Sales performance was monitored from the outset by tracking the number of prescriptions issued weekly and classified by prescribers' medical specialties. Sales volume was judged to be less than satisfactory during the first three years to 1985, thereby vindicating Howsam's caution and falling even below his own conservative sales estimates. The explanation for the difference appears

Zovirax was the first effective widely accepted treatment for genital herpes. *JAMA*.

to have been the making of two assumptions before the launch, both of which had proved to have been misplaced. One was that Zovirax would be prescribed for use prophylactically for patients undergoing chemotherapy treatment in order to avoid herpetic lesions. The other was that sufferers from herpes genitalis would be admitted to hospitals where the drug would be administered. Neither proved to be the case. When these errors of judgment were reported to the board in London, Vane showed neither understanding nor sympathy. His characteristically acid observation was that the disappointing record was attributable either to the American company's misjudgment of the market or to a failure to educate doctors;[45] he offered no constructive suggestions.

The perceived failure, however, was short-lived, thanks to improvements in production, variation of the forms in which the drug could be administered, and a successful application for FDA approval for extended uses for Zovirax. Simplification of the production process began immediately after the launch. At the time when the synthetic pathways from the basic research laboratory were established in 1974, the process yield in producing the drug had been 14 per cent. Cipau's scaling up for commercial production involved the installation of computer-controlled central technology applied to the distillation column and volume freeze dryer; Cipau described this development as "a quantum leap" in technical complexity. By 1982, the yield from bulk chemicals had been raised to 70 per cent, a fivefold increase in the yield from raw materials which substantially reduced production

"You have Herpes," an advertisement indirectly intended to assist doctors to prescribe Zovirax by offering advice on how to manage the act of diagnosis. *JAMA*.

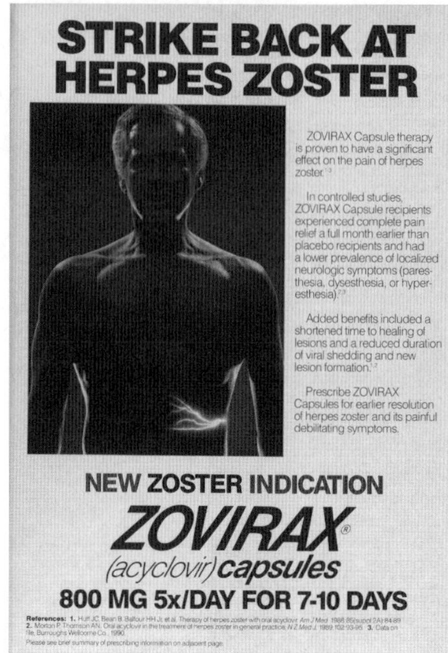

Zovirax capsules introduced in 1985 heralded widespread use, achieving blockbuster proportions for the company's sales. *JAMA*.

cost.[46] With a view to developing intravenous administration, studies were carried out at John Hopkins University, where patients with herpes encephalitis faced a death rate of up to 75 per cent. Unusually, half-way through a double-blind placebo-controlled intravenous study, the principal investigator halted the process after discovering that one-half of the patients recovered almost 100 per cent while the rest were becoming progressively more ill. The placebo group was given Zovirax intravenously immediately. FDA approval for this form of administration followed soon after.[47]Clinical testing of an oral form of administration took place at one hundred major US medical centers with the participation of one thousand patients afflicted by initial and recurrent herpes The results produced were sufficient to justify the FDA approval of Zovirax capsules early in 1983, described by Barry, head of the company′s clinical investigation and virology department, as the first safe and effective therapy for all forms of genital herpes. Alleviation of the effects of a recurring affliction could be achieved by repeated prescriptions which made it possible to manage the disease. A leading article in *Drug Tropics* welcomed the addition of capsules in the "war on herpes," referring to the US Department of Health's estimate of the annual increase in the numbers of Americans suffering from genital herpes at 300,000.[48] By 1983, Zovirax for intravenous use exceeded the topical form of the drug which rose threefold between 1984 and 1985.

Table 14.1 *WFL/Wellcome plc sales of principal products, 1982–1987 (£million)*

	Group sales	*Sudafed/Actifed*	*As %*	*Zovirax*	*As %*	*Retrovir*	*As %*
1982	593			5	1		
1983	674			15	2		
1984	806			27	3		
1985	1,004	142	14	62	6		
1986	1,005	135	13	153	15		
1987	1,132	127	11	248	22	25	2

Source: GSK/WF/SCS/798, WFL and Wellcome plc accounts and annual reports.

The most significant boost to sales, however, came from oral capsules; by 1987/8 capsules accounted for 38 per cent of sales, intravenous for 35 per cent, and topical for 22 per cent.[49] Within two years of FDA approval of oral formulation, Zovirax sales exceeded $150 million, catapulting the company into the elite group of the large blockbuster drug manufacturers.

Table 14.2 *Zovirax sales by methods of administration ($million)*

	1981/2	*1982/3*	*1983/4*	*1984/5*	*1985/6*	*1986/7*	*1987/8*
Ophthalmic Ointment	<2	1.5	3	3.9	9	12	16
IV	>2	9	11	27	52	94	135
Oral		<1.5	3	26	56	95	148
Topical	7	12	16	23	39	62	84
Suspension				<2	<2	<2	<2

Source: GSK/WF/SCS 1585, Chairman's marketing and R&D Committee, 1989.

Because overhead costs were not recorded in financial data produced by the company, only the direct costs associated with RD&M and testing are available. Between 1983–84 and 1988–89, "internal manpower costs" directly attributable to RD&M relating to Zovirax amounted to $33 million plus external grants and contracts of $18 million. These were in addition to accumulated internal manpower costs of $14.5 million between 1970 and 1983 when external grants and contracts, mostly for clinical testing, were $6.9 million. Cost did not, however, present patients with a major problem. The price for the treatment of an average herpes condition consisted of five daily capsules taken for five days and implied a total expenditure of between $15 and $18, though suppression of the disease in patients suffering recurrent outbreaks might cost up to $60.[50] The cost to patients outside the US would become considerably higher, notably in the UK and Europe when they became significant markets. Although the incidence of herpes was not on a scale similar to that in the US, the higher dosage levels specified by physicians in those countries offered greater returns to the manufacturer. Compared with the price of regular treatment dosages prescribed in the US expressed as 100, the ex-Wellcome price index figures in the UK were 336, in Spain 329, in Germany 315, and 224 in France.[51]

The high expectations surrounding anti-virals were matched by similar optimism as regards the progress made by the longest-running project group led by the medical division's psychiatry section. Research into bupropion had begun in 1966 under the leadership of Dr Nari Mehta in the company's organic chemistry department at Tuckahoe. An IND had been filed with the FDA in 1970 when the drug was assigned project status. It was synthesized in 1975, the year of Cuatrecasas's appointment as vice president RD&M. The drug marked the company's first attempt to enter the therapeutic area of psychiatric illnesses. After assessing the drug's potential, Cuatrecasas assumed responsibility for the next stage of development, testing, and the preparation of an NDA for Wellbutrin which was filed with the FDA in December 1981.[52] This was anticipated to be the company's second blockbuster drug after Zovirax at a time when work which would eventually result in Retrovir, had hardly begun.[53]

Skeptical of the market prospects for "yet another anti-depressant," marketing executives at RTP had shown little support for the development of the drug; even greater doubt was expressed in London.[54] Cuatrecasas had persisted with the project none the less. In 1982, a highly complicated scaling-up process was transferred to a pilot plant at Greenville, while the pharmaceutical research and development laboratories undertook preparations to proceed to clinical trials.[55] An unprecedented degree of collaboration was planned between Greenville and Dartford in the UK. The entire supply of active chemical ingredient was produced in the UK; the drug was formulated in Greenville and supplied to Dartford.[56] FDA approval was secured in 1986 and plans for marketing Wellbutrin swung into action. In March 1986, more than 600 members of BW&Co.'s staff assembled in Phoenix for a national sales launch, an event at which the program comprised professional briefings and presentations (though not all related to Wellbutrin) and modeled on the launch of Zovirax in Dallas in 1985. However, Haigler cancelled the launch of Wellbutrin on the night before the meetings began. The reason for cancellation was the late receipt of a report that a clinical trial which had involved the use of Wellbutrin in experimental studies had resulted in four out of fifty suffering seizures. Although Wellbutrin was to be marketed for use specifically with patients suffering from depression (and not from bulimia), and in the absence of any expression of concern by the FDA, it was decided that the company should await further information and consider the implications.

Reactions of staff assembled in Phoenix in preparation for the immediate major launch were recorded later in Wellcome News. Despite disappointment, representatives acknowledged the wisdom of the decision which, it was believed, would strengthen the company's public image as one of a professional, ethical, and caring organization.[57] After advice from the FDA, a further three thousand patients were involved in clinical trials which took three years, at the end of which the drug was found to have adverse side-effects *only* on bulimic patients who, it transpired, had comprised the initial trial. This explained the alarming effects of the drug.[58] The opportunity cost of the postponed launch was high because in 1987 Eli Lilly had received FDA approval for Prozac which, like Wellbutrin, was intended as a treatment for those suffering from depression. By the time the Wellbutrin trials had been completed, Prozac so dominated the market for anti-depressants that it was already the industry's best-selling drug. As far as the anti-depressant Wellbutrin was concerned, the costs of related RD&M expenditure, investment in production capacity, and the preparatory marketing program could never be recovered.

Coe had been president throughout most of the period during which he had supported the RD&M which led to Wellbutrin. The collapse of hopes for the new drug occurred after he retired from the company at the end of 1980. This followed a decade of unprecedented success when Zyloprim and Septra began to generate substantial sales. Coe's period of office also coincided with the culmination of path breaking anti-viral RD&M led by Hitchings, Elion, Schaeffer, and Cresswell, bringing the company to the verge of launching its first blockbuster drug; under his presidency, the first steps were taken to prepare for the consumer marketing of OTC proprietary drugs of which Howsam was a strong advocate. Howsam's reform of the company's marketing strategy was well advanced and he, Cuatrecasas, and Cipau had developed and introduced a reformed project system across the company. Coe's contribution throughout his presidency was to exercise an approachable but decisive "fluid" style of management. Within a sound human relations culture, he was equally at ease motivating engineers, marketing and sales personnel, scientists, and others. Coe was president for 12 years beginning in 1968. However, he had been a board director and Vice President responsible for distribution since 1952, to which were added responsibility for production in 1955 and finance in 1960. In 1964, he also became executive Vice President, chairman of the executive committee of the board, in effect Creasy's deputy President. These transfers of responsibilities occurred during a period when Creasy's erratic behavior had intensified since 1953, when the company vice presidents had failed to persuade him to attend a clinic "for rest and recuperation."[59] For nearly 30 years, therefore, Coe, protected Creasy from exasperated chairmen of WFL, the trustees (and from himself), at the same time emerging as the figure who commanded the loyalty and respect both of his colleagues and employees. From his appointment in 1944 until 1980, Coe was the figure who achieved most in shaping the history of Burroughs Wellcome & Co. His corporate legacy was to come under challenge by the new regime about to be introduced by his successor.

CHAPTER 15

Management by textbook: McKinsey's review of Burroughs Wellcome & Co.

The responsibility for choosing a successor to the presidency of the American company lay with the Trust, though historically on the recommendation of the chairman of WFL and in the past had not presented problems. Although Creasy's elevation had been sooner than Nevin might have expected, Creasy had established his position as the dynamo and proved to be a popular choice with colleagues. The same was true regarding the pivotal position occupied by Coe whom Creasy had groomed as his successor (though he had not anticipated Coe's premature promotion to the presidency by the Trust). As Coe's retirement approached, privately Coe and Shepperd drew up a shortlist; Peter Howsam, marketing director (Coe's first choice), Theodore E. Haigler jr., finance director, and William M. Sullivan, executive vice president and chief operating officer (favored by Shepperd). Shepperd prevailed, arguing that his legal expertise would be required in an increasingly litigious industry.[1] Lord Franks and the Trust accepted the recommendation;[2] Sullivan's appointment as president and chief executive officer of BW&Co., at the age of forty-seven, took effect immediately after Coe stepped down in December 1980. Phil Tracy, another in-house lawyer and future president, succeeded Sullivan as general counsel.

Until 1965, Sullivan's experience had been as a specialist in corporate financial affairs at a New York City legal firm and subsequently, as assistant general counsel and director of the legal department within the chemical and pharmaceutical divisions of the Ciba-Geigy Corporation which was also in New York. He had joined BW&Co. in 1973 when he succeeded Dowling as general executive counsel and director of the legal department. Coe's reservations about Sullivan, which he had expressed to Shepperd in the strongest terms, were not only concerned with his abilities as a corporate lawyer or his limited experience of business and having managed in a department of only fifteen (a weakness which Sullivan acknowledged to his co-directors when the appointment was agreed).[3] Even though Sullivan had been with BW&Co. for several years, Coe believed his personality was ill-suited to the prevailing culture at RTP.[4] He regarded Sullivan to be aloof, projecting an image that contributed to a widespread feeling of

William M. Sullivan was formerly director of the legal department at the Ciba-Geigy Corporation who was appointed as general executive counsel at BW&Co. in 1973. He was president of the company between 1981 and 1986. This portrait shows the president in an ironic pose in a laboratory environment where he was at odds with scientists at RTP. *Wellcome News*, Wellcome Library, London.

apprehension among his colleagues and other staff at RTP.[5] Coe had warned Shepperd against appointing Sullivan because his business experience beyond legal matters was limited. The announcement of his appointment at the board meeting, heard in "utter silence", stunned the directors who were unanimous in regarding it to be disastrous for the company's future.[6]

Sullivan later admitted that his early impression of BW&Co., the small pharmaceutical company in rural North Carolina, was that of a comfortable, old-fashioned family-oriented business in which directors, managers, and departmental heads at different levels appeared to enjoy harmonious relations both inside and outside the office or laboratory. This included socializing in their homes.[7] This was an accurate assessment. Since 1968, Coe had continued the paternalist tradition inherited from Nevin and Creasy (and, of course, from Wellcome himself during the early years at the parent company in London and Dartford). Each had demonstrated his own entrepreneurial and personal approach to leadership. Coe had developed firm views on strategic policy which he was always prepared to explain, argue about, and justify to his co-directors and managers, believing that a consensual approach was imperative for effective management. This had enabled him to re-build the corporate culture of BW&Co., originally established by Nevin, which Creasy's increasingly erratic behavior and that of the unions during the 1960s had threatened to undermine. In all of these respects, BW&Co. was indeed completely different from the metropolitan, large, bureaucratic corporate culture of Sullivan's former company in New York.

In preparation for his new role, Sullivan attended a young presidents' program at Stanford, designed to prepare executives to fill the most senior executive roles in corporate America and to equip them with the latest managerial jargon. Sullivan had returned to RTP especially impressed with the importance of corporate structure and organization and by the "windows of opportunity" concept.[8] On his return to RTP, one of his first initiatives was to create a new corporate affairs department responsible for human relations, public relations with health centers, and lobbying politicians both at State level and in Washington. Tom Kennedy (Coe's personal assistant throughout the 1970s and acting vice president, production and engineering) was appointed vice president responsible for corporate affairs. Also, within the first six months of his presidency, and prompted by his experience at Stanford, he engaged the McKinsey firm of management consultants at the Atlanta office to review the functioning of the company and to report in 1982. The final report, which was presented to the board at RTP and subsequently to the directors in London, described the company as a business "doing well with an ageing product line while investing in the future."[9] Product developments about to come to fruition in the 1980s were described as heralding a new strategic era which would require "a greater sense of urgency aiming higher and based on a continued level of research investment."[10] A list of products (including variations) introduced into the market between 1973 and 1985 reveal this transition.

Such an approach was vital according to McKinsey because the industrial environment facing BW&Co. was becoming increasingly challenging. One effect of government regulation through the FDA had been to reduce the introduction of new drugs in the industry and to lower the period of protection offered by patents to an average of eleven years. These developments contributed to the emergence of an increasingly competitive market in which large companies dominated innovation; size assumed increasing importance for effective competition. McKinsey estimated that the cost of developing a new chemical entity was $87.5 million. By the early 1980s, measured as a percentage of sales revenue, BW&Co. was investing 17 per cent in RD&M, which compared with 8 per cent at SKF and 9 per cent at Merck, Searle, Upjohn, and Lilly.[11] This was interpreted as another indication of the cost burden of innovation borne by a relatively small company.

The growing use of generics which by 1981 secured 15 per cent of the market, was a further factor causing perturbation in the industry by altering the terms of competition. BW&Co. was beginning to experience high rates of substitution of Actifed, Zyloprim, and Lanoxin by generics. McKinsey's overall verdict on the company's position within the industry in 1982 was that it was in survival, rather than challenging mode in a highly competitive industry. A troubling historical and comparative trend in financial performance was the main justification for this conclusion. McKinsey explained a declining trend rate of return on investment to levels below the annual average for the industry as a consequence of a sharp rise in the RD&M investment to sales ratio.[12] The rate of return on capital employed at WFL reveals a similar downward trend following the rise during the 1970s.

Table 15.1 *Products (including variants) introduced into the US market by BW&Co. 1970–1989*

	Prescription drugs	*OTC products*
1970		
July 1973	Septra tablets	
September 1976	Imuran injection	
February 1976	Cortisporin otic solution	
November 1976	Empracet	
December 1976	Septra DS tablets	
January 1979	Sudafed DS tablets	Empirin tablets (reformulated and with Codeine)
July 1979	Septra suspension	Sudafed plus tablets and syrup
		Wellcortin cream, lotion and ointment
April 1980	Viroptic ophthalmic solution	
May 1980	Proloprim tablets	
June 1981	Septra IV infusion	
April 1982	Zovirax ointment	
September 1982	Lanoxicaps	
August 1982	Wellcoverin tablets	
October 1982	Zovirax sterile powder	
October 1982	Wellcoverin injection	
September 1983	Zovirax tablets	
November 1983		Actifed tablet and syrup
1983		Actidil tablet and syrup
1984	Tracrium injection	Actifed with Codeine cough syrup
February 1985	Zovirax capsules	Actifed 12 hour capsules
March 1987	AZT/Retrovir	
July 1989	Wellbutrin	

Source: GWHC, BW&Co. (USA) Inc., 107.07/01, *Wellcome News*, 15 May 1984, p. 16; *Chemical Marketing Reporter* 7:239, Feb. 1991, p. 19.

Table 15.2 *WFL rate of return on investment. 1977–1982*

1977	44
1978	48
1979	55
1980	34
1981	28
1982	22

Source: GSK/WF/SCS 461, Board minutes, 3 Nov. 1982, McKinsey, "US strategy study."

In presenting the results of the McKinsey study to the WFL board in London, Sullivan drew attention to the American company's ambition to become the premier research-based company in the US. He emphasized that a necessary condition for achieving this was the more rapid development of potentially important medicines "for which the magnitude of the need is great" at lower average cost, and through more effective marketing. An assessment of the company's organizational capabilities concluded that routine execution was satisfactory, though it criticized a lack of focus: "Cross-functional opportunity identification and execution" was perceived to be especially weak for which the remedy advised was the development of "a cadre of managers."[13] Building on the criticisms contained in the report, Sullivan also expressed his own serious personal reservations regarding ownership of BW&Co. by the Wellcome Trust.

He believed that the Trust's charitable status and the absence, therefore, of the public reporting of accounts had weakened the exercise of the market discipline which otherwise would have ensured that profitability was the main aim of the business. While he conceded that Coe had regarded profit as fundamental to the success of the business, nevertheless Sullivan also felt that Coe had shown a more relaxed attitude to the trade-off between research and community benefits, perhaps favoring a policy closer to the philanthropic spirit contained in Wellcome's will by not requiring the degree of profit-driven discipline that Sullivan regarded as necessary. McKinsey's analysis of pricing gave some credence to this view by referring to an historical under pricing of certain drugs, notably Lanoxin and allopurinol, both of which were known to be the physicians' preferred prescriptions for the treatment of heart and gout conditions. Both were products possessing a long history during which prices had remained unaltered regardless of inflation, though Sullivan conceded that the Kefauver hearings during the 1960s and the critical climate which they generated, may also have contributed to Coe's reluctance to increase prices.[14] Acknowledging that one new important drug was in the pipeline and that high and rising RD&M expenditure was unavoidable in the short-term, the report emphasized that the immediate priority for the company was to find ways of funding the development, testing, and launching of the new drug. Two methods of expanding revenue to ease potential cash flow problems were recommended. One was a revision of the pricing of existing products with a view to maximizing profit; the other was a reform in the management of product development with a view to accelerating the process of introducing new drugs.

The starting point for reforming pricing policy was a decision to rule out price rises for products in competitive markets while giving serious consideration to raising the prices of products that could be shown to enjoy monopolistic advantage in their niche markets. In 1982, Lanoxin (sales of $19 million) held 95 per cent of the prescription cardiac market. In other similarly specialist markets, Cortisporin Otic ($18 million) held 76 per cent and Zyloprim ($44 million), 65 per cent; Neosporin ointment ($18 million) held 48 per cent. Despite the near monopoly held by Lanoxin, since its introduction its price had been only marginally higher than that of generic aspirin;

this meant that any potential advantage to be secured from branding and from the company's reputation remained unexploited. A rise in the price of Lanoxin initially caused consternation among the medical fraternity, but careful management through public relations enabled the company to obtain a multiple increase in sales revenue. A similar logic was applied to the price of Zyloprim with respect to competition from generic allopurinol, and to Neosporin and Polysporin.[15] The relative market positions of other products were Septra solid dose ($28 million) which held a 9 per cent share; Codeine Analgesic ($22 million), 14 per cent; and Sudafed ($23 million), 14 per cent. At the time of the review, Actifed's share of the market was 5 per cent ($11 million).

McKinsey drew attention to the potential offered by exploiting long-standing ethical prescription products in the OTC market as a method of compensating for the relative lack of new products and as a hedge against the uncertainty surrounding those in the pipeline. The report recommended the preparation of the decongestant and antihistamine, Actifed, to be advertised direct to consumers through an extensive national campaign. This recommendation strengthened Howsam's case for a policy which he and Parish, head of advertising, had advocated in the past. They had already persuaded Coe to move the company in this direction with OTC Empirin in 1979, Sudafed cough syrup in 1980, and Wellcortin cream, lotion, and ointment planned for consumer marketing in 1981, though stopping short of national television advertising.[16] Distribution was extended from retail drug stores to include specialist food shops willing to meet minimum purchase agreements.

Another McKinsey recommendation was a reform of the product management system introduced by Howsam during the previous decade in which product planners performed dual functions. Sullivan was impressed by McKinsey's account of the product management system in place at Proctor & Gamble in which each professional product planner was entirely responsible for a single product, once it had emerged from RD&M.[17] In order for the new system to work, Sullivan believed that Howsam, vice president and architect of the existing system, should be replaced by someone from another company familiar with the Proctor & Gamble model of product planning. Surrounded by speculation and supposition among Howsam's colleagues, the mystery surrounding his departure is dispelled by a secret minute of the January 1983 meeting of the board of WFL in London, where Sullivan alleged that Howsam "was not equal to the task of marketing new products and developing OTC sales," and that he lacked "analytical marketing skills and the ability to inspire and lead 600 people in a team."[18] The trustees accepted Sullivan's recommendation that Howsam should be dismissed, but rejected his proposal for a successor. The nominee, whom Sullivan claimed possessed the potential to become a future company president, was a recently-appointed (unnamed) sales representative working the Kansas territory whose claims to become vice president of marketing did not impress the trustees.[19] Howsam's record of achievements during the 1970s belies Sullivan's judgment.

After Howsam left the company in 1983, Sullivan proceeded to introduce a new product planning system around three groups: OTCs, anti-infectives, and Zovirax with all other prescription products, to each of which was assigned a product manager. In charge of this restructuring was Douglas Rieff, the new vice president of marketing appointed by Sullivan "to help determine appropriate projects into which development resources were channeled."[20] The objectives were to ensure an efficient selection of compounds for project status, shorter development times, and speedier approvals of new products. A marketing research group was strengthened with the intention of creating an independent and highly professional group of market researchers.

In 1984, Rieff was demoted from the positions of vice president and acting director marketing and sales, but he remained as marketing director. The new vice president was Peter Reckert.[21] He possessed considerable experience in operating within a product management system such as Rieff had designed. During his previous career, Reckert had also been involved in marketing twenty different types of pharmaceutical products, from vitamins to beta blockers.[22] After employment with Syntex, he had worked for Stuart Pharmaceuticals, managing the agency side of the business as vice-president/general manager of a subsidiary of J. Walter Thompson. Reckert's brief in 1983 was to implement continuing reform of the project product development system and devize a marketing strategy in response to trends in the drug market, originating in the 1970s but accelerating, in which both the character of demand and the roles adopted by institutions were changing. The introduction of Zovirax, Tracrium, and Actifed also posed questions regarding marketing strategy: Zovirax tablets had just begun entering the market and would soon be followed by capsules; Tracrium, an intermediate-acting muscle relaxant for use during surgery, which offered greater safety and more rapid recovery than existing drugs, gained FDA approval for the US market in 1983. Both products required marketing effort directed towards hospital usage and, at the same time, greater efforts were needed to penetrate the OTC market with Actifed (as recommended by McKinsey) for which it was to obtain FDA approval in 1984.[23]

In addition to the new products entering the market, the changing market environment to which the company responded was a pressure on the costs of drugs which led both government and hospitals to seek ways of reducing them, partly by the greater use of generics and partly by institutional reorganization. In 1980, generic substitution for a list of approved drugs drawn up by the FDA became mandatory in forty-seven states.[24] By early 1983, the government met more than one-third of the nation's health bill, health expenditure having risen to being second only to that spent on defense. Limits were introduced on government contributions to Medicare, one effect of which was to motivate hospital managers to exercise greater economy on drug expenditure. One response was the growth of Hospital Management Organizations (HMOs). These had originated during an earlier period of inflation during the 1940s, though they remained insignificant until after the 1973 Health Maintenance Act which had provided funds to promote methods of controlling health care costs. The benefit associated with HMOs was their ability to exploit size advantage in purchasing drugs. The concentration of health care provision led to centralized buying and the replacement of the single physician by a purchasing organization or buying group;[25] committees and officers assumed increasingly important roles in negotiating with pharmaceutical companies at a time when generics offered increasing opportunities for hospital managers to reduce costs.[26]

These developments ended the dominance in prescribing and purchasing drugs by a single physician, a local hospital, or an independent neighborhood pharmacy. Whereas in 1980, 75 per cent of physicians were in private practice, 2 per cent in group practices and 3 per cent in HMOs, the comparable percentages in 1990 were 29, 57, and 14. Because HMO's charged recipients flat predictable fees, companies encouraged their employees to enroll,[27] 6.3 million of them by 1977 rising to 15.1 million by 1984.[28] Two HMO's, American Healthcare Systems and Voluntary Hospitals of America, included more than one thousand hospitals and represented 20 per cent of the nation's hospital beds. A similar trend towards concentration occurred among the nation's fifty thousand pharmacists, 40 per cent of whom formed part of large chains, while thirty-four retail co-operatives purchased in bulk on behalf of ten thousand independent pharmacies. Hospitals and government bodies accounted for an increasing proportion of BW&Co.'s sales during the 1980s.

By setting therapeutical equivalence as the minimum requirement and reducing a seven-year clinical trial process that applied to branded drugs to between six and eighteen months, the Waxman/Hatch Act in 1984 was to add further impetus for HMOs to specify cheaper generics. It represented a compromise, balancing greater patent protection for manufacturers with quicker public access to lower-priced generic drugs. The Drug Price Competition and Patent Term Restoration Act widened the opportunity for generic drug manufacturers to secure rapid approval from the FDA and offered a strong incentive for the entry of firms manufacturing. By 1985, the number of manufacturers of generics had reached four hundred.[29] These developments explain why, just as specialization in manufacture was growing rapidly during the early 1980s, the selling of drugs underwent a similar process. This assumed immediate importance for BW&Co. because several new products approved by the FDA and entering, or about to enter, the market (Wellcoverin injection tablets, Leukaran, Tracrium, Zovirax, and Septra extensions), were expected to be sold almost entirely to hospitals. The strategy adopted in response to these changes was a reorganization of field staff into specialists assigned to one of three divisions: professional product, hospital, and government, and a residual division described as street representatives.

A specialist OTC sales department was formed in 1983 in preparation for the Actifed sales campaign for which food chain stores and supermarkets were added to the list of outlets. The fastest growing OTC sales were those of chain drugstores; they accounted for more than 60 per cent of the drugstore market. Prices and cash discounts were the same for all sales outlets. The introduction of a new telephone-marketing system was intended to secure more low- to mid-volume accounts.[30] The decision to sell non-prescription products through supermarket chains marked the introduction of a national broker program. To manage this segment of the market, eleven key account representatives were appointed to report to area broker managers.[31] Five area brokers supervised fifty local brokers (each representing the company's OTC product line to food chain stores) whose objective was to secure maximum shelf space filled by BW&Co. products.[32] These developments were strengthened in 1986 when the department was transformed by the creation of a consumer products division led by the general manager, Terry Stevens, who was appointed vice president of the division two years later.[33]

Initially, like his predecessor, Sullivan was wary of committing the substantial resources necessary to mount a national television advertising campaign, as recommended by McKinsey, to promote Actifed. Before taking any decision, he ordered test marketing as a basis for cost benefit analysis from which he required convincing statistical evidence that national television advertising would be a worthwhile investment.[34] When it became known that BW&Co. was considering entering the consumer drugs industry, Gillette (the large consumer products company) proposed combining in a joint venture to harness their respective experience and expertise in consumer marketing and pharmaceutical innovation. Instead, the company built up its own infra-structure designed to effect the transition from prescription drug and ethical promotion to marketing a consumer product. Kinelski, formerly of the McNeil Laboratories associated with Johnson & Johnson, was recruited to manage the project within the company. He possessed the knowledge and experience from building the sales of Tylenol as a consumer product (which involved winning a major share of the market formerly supplied by Empirin) which Sullivan believed to be vital for success with Actifed.[35] Ross Roy/Compton was the advertising agency chosen to advise on the re-launch and jointly to develop the subsequent marketing strategy. Until 1984, Actifed had been available in syrup and tablet form. The range was completed in that year when the FDA approved a twelve-hour formula of the product in capsule form. Hitherto, Actifed had not competed in this segment of the market which was worth $170 million in 1982 and which, during the first year, generated the largest revenue of the company's entire range of drugs.

Howsam's advocacy of national television advertising reflected a well-established trend among the large pharmaceutical companies. Other companies had introduced "patient advertising" of OTCs in family magazines and on prime-time television. This had begun in the early 1970s when they had carried advertisements for drugs which had moved from prescription to OTC products such as "therapeutic strength" vitamins, insulin syringes, and hydrocortisone creams. The trend extended to prescription drugs, beginning in 1982 with Merck's promotion of Pneumovax (a pneumonia vaccine) in *Readers Digest*.[36] Pfizer, makers of Procardia for the treatment of angina and hypertension, advertised in *Time, Newsweek, New York Times, and Washington Post*. Lederle advertised Pnuimune as a vaccine to treat "the disease that won't die" in a series of full-page advertisements which a spokesman denied were advertisements but insisted that they were "paid-for public service announcements."[37]

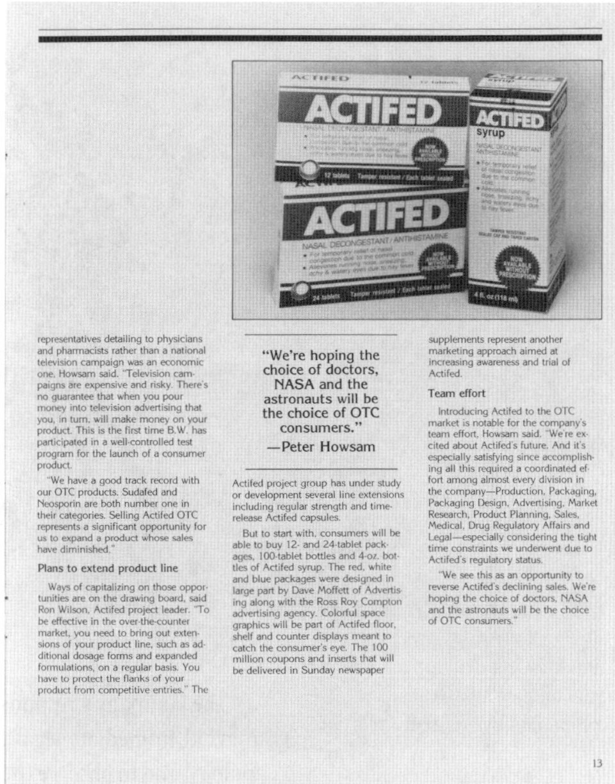

representatives detailing to physicians and pharmacists rather than a national television campaign was an economic one, Howsam said. "Television campaigns are expensive and risky. There's no guarantee that when you pour money into television advertising that you, in turn, will make money on your product. This is the first time B.W. has participated in a well-controlled test program for the launch of a consumer product.

"We have a good track record with our OTC products. Sudafed and Neosporin are both number one in their categories. Selling Actifed OTC represents a significant opportunity for us to expand a product whose sales have diminished."

Plans to extend product line

Ways of capitalizing on those opportunities are on the drawing board, said Ron Wilson, Actifed project leader. "To be effective in the over-the-counter market, you need to bring out extensions of your product line, such as additional dosage forms and expanded formulations, on a regular basis. You have to protect the flanks of your product from competitive entries." The Actifed project group has under study or development several line extensions including regular strength and time-release Actifed capsules.

"We're hoping the choice of doctors, NASA and the astronauts will be the choice of OTC consumers." —Peter Howsam

But to start with, consumers will be able to buy 12- and 24-tablet packages, 100-tablet bottles and 4-oz. bottles of Actifed syrup. The red, white and blue packages were designed in large part by Dave Moffett of Advertising along with the Ross Roy Compton advertising agency. Colorful space graphics will be part of Actifed floor, shelf and counter displays meant to catch the consumer's eye. The 100 million coupons and inserts that will be delivered in Sunday newspaper supplements represent another marketing approach aimed at increasing awareness and trial of Actifed.

Team effort

Introducing Actifed to the OTC market is notable for the company's team effort, Howsam said. "We're excited about Actifed's future. And it's especially satisfying since accomplishing all this required a coordinated effort among almost every division in the company—Production, Packaging, Packaging Design, Advertising, Market Research, Product Planning, Sales, Medical, Drug Regulatory Affairs and Legal—especially considering the tight time constraints we underwent due to Actifed's regulatory status.

"We see this as an opportunity to reverse Actifed's declining sales. We're hoping the choice of doctors, NASA and the astronauts will be the choice of OTC consumers."

13

Actifed, a nasal decongestant antihistamine, was up-rated by the FDA in 1981 as an effective treatment for rhinitis and was re-launched in 1983/4 in which the company's national advertising campaign included reference to NASA. *Wellcome News*, Wellcome Library, London.

For the first time in BW&Co.'s history, the marketing campaign included not only national television advertising direct to consumers, but also full distribution for sale by food and variety outlets, in addition to drug stores.[38] Actifed was at the center of this development which was timely because in 1980 it had featured in a list of *Pills that Don't Work*, a book (of which more than 200,000 copies were sold) promoted as "a consumers' and doctors' guide to over six hundred prescription drugs that lack evidence of effectiveness."[39] The study resulted from conducted by the Health Research Group which had been founded by Dr Sidney Wolfe with the consumers' campaigner Ralph Nader.[40] In February 1982, Actifed was once again a specific subject of adverse comment by the principal author when he appeared on a popular television program and declared that nobody should be taking Actifed.[41] In fact the allegation of a lack of efficacy was based on information which was out-of date. The source was the list of drugs drawn to the attention of the Drug Efficiency Study Review Panel set up by the FDA following the new regulations introduced in 1962 for the purpose of testing existing prescription drugs to establish efficacy as well as safety in order to retain prescription status. Following Actifed's first rating in 1972 as "probably effective" additional clinical studies were carried out at RTP which in December 1981 had resulted in an upgrading to the FDA's "effective" category for the treatment of rhinitis.[42]

CONQUERING THE HOSTILE ENVIRONMENT OF SPACE

The hostile environment of space has been conquered by Neil Armstrong, Edwin 'Buzz' Aldrin, and Michael Collins, whose Apollo 11 landing on the moon brought pride and wonderment to the millions who watched from earth.

We at Burroughs Wellcome & Co. (USA) Inc. are proud to have played a part in that successful mission. As in several previous Gemini and Apollo flights, our products were among those chosen by physicians of The National Aeronautics and Space Administration for use in the astronauts' on-board medical kit.

Marezine® brand Cyclizine Injection, Neosporin® Ointment, and Actifed® Tablets were among the eleven different brand-name pharmaceuticals contained in the 5 - by - 8 - inch medical kit filled with products carefully chosen for use in a possible in-flight emergency.

Dr. Charles A. Berry and his medical team in the Manned Spacecraft Center in Houston carefully monitored the astronauts' heartbeats and respiration, to prevent fatigue which could have caused a fatal accident. The ground physicians also stood ready to advise the astronauts on which pills or injections to use, if needed.

Since the NASA physicians couldn't advise liquids and bed rest for astronauts Armstrong, Collins and Aldrin, and couldn't directly observe them, drugs had to be pre-tested on the astronauts. This involved using the drugs during pre-flight training, under conditions approximating those of the mission as closely as possible.

All of us at Burroughs Wellcome & Co. can feel a sense of pride that our products were carefully tested and selected to share a place on man's first journey to the moon.

14

A line drawing depicting space-conquering astronaut accompanied by Actifed. *Wellcome News*, Wellcome Library, London.

The company's response to the adverse publicity was to avoid immediate legal action, to seek retraction and apology, and to observe the effect on sales. The coincident preparations for a major new advertising campaign, however, offered the opportunity to counter the harmful publicity by employing a spectacular award-winning television campaign, arguably one of the most arresting in the history of advertising. This did not originate from expert advice or from a committee decision but from a casual observation heard by Parrish, director of advertising, that the astronaut, Wally Schirra, had taken Actifed into space. Parrish contacted Schirra at NASA and persuaded him to participate in a series of advertisements promoting both Actifed and Sudafed. Once rumors of the forthcoming advertisements became known, Schering-Pugh, whose own decongestant, Drixoral, was also about to come off prescription, filed a complaint alleging untruth in advertising, though BW&Co. provided evidence to the contrary thereby undermining the attempt to spoil the campaign.[43] The advertisement – showing an image of Schirra, clothed in his space-suit outside the shuttle, clutching a container of Actifed and extolling its benefits – was tested by "pulse advertising" before commitment to a major investment The product and the advertisement were placed in distribution outlets in certain localities to test reactions which revealed roughly a two-week lag between transmission and a surge in local sales. The television advertisement was also featured at the 1984 national medical convention when Schirra hosted the BW&Co. exhibit to which physicians flocked in large numbers, eager to meet him.[44] Schirra became the public face of the company.

For more than ten years, Actifed had been the nation's leading prescription nasal decongestant antihistamine with sales amounting to $14 million in 1983. This

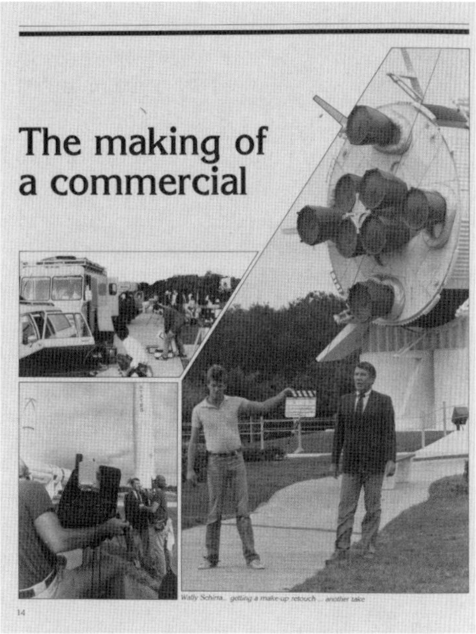

The astronaut William Shirra engaged in making television commercials for Burroughs Wellcome & Co. *Wellcome News*, Wellcome Library, London.

compared with the cost of the campaign to promote Actifed ($12 million) which had been planned in 1984/5. This amount divided the board, but was approved. A significant decision was to proceed without seeking permission from the board in London, even though the switch to consumer advertising was a fundamental change in policy.[45] The re-launch of Sudafed was given similar advertising support as an OTC product. By the end of the first year's campaign, doubts expressed by some members of the BW&Co. board were confounded. Intensive and imaginative advertising had catapulted Actifed into the top position in the cold tablet market with sales of $45 million.[46] Sudafed was second.[47] In 1985, *Advertising Age* reported that sales of Actifed and Sudafed in 1984/5 together commanded 19 per cent of the cold remedy market worth in total $750 million.[48] In the same year, the American Marketing Association awarded the company a prestigious "Effie", in recognition of the highest achievement in marketing.[49] The campaign included newspapers and television advertisements with a photograph of Shirra and news of a sweepstake in which the winner was promised a $25,000 US Savings Bond and an expenses-paid trip to the next shuttle lift-off. The appearance of these advertisements, however, was marred by the Challenger tragedy of 28 January 1986, when the campaign was aborted immediately on receiving the news of the spacemen's deaths, all Actifed advertisements were cancelled.[50] Subsequently, sales fell below forecast figures.[51]

The thirty-year-old antibacterial product, Neosporin, was another chosen for re-launch in 1984. Until then, Neosporin had been a component in the company's first aid kits and had received virtually no dedicated promotion. Beginning in 1984, the Neosporin product manager secured agreement with the medical department for a clinical study to support a claim of faster healing as a marketable attribute. A comparative clinical study between the leading antiseptic products in the market was planned, organized, and carried out by scientists at the University of Pennsylvania. The study showed a 60 per cent faster healing property of Neosporin for minor abrasions compared with competing treatments. This finding was translated by an advertising company into a thirty-second commercial advertisement emphasizing "Neosporin, it's the one." A successful outcome of a pilot exercise conducted in two cities was followed by a major investment in a comprehensive national advertising campaign and a special promotion involving incentives for retailers.[52]

The combination of successful product innovation and adjustments to marketing strategies resulted in a rapid expansion of sales and rising profits and rate of return during the 1980s.

Table 15.3 *BW&Co. Sales, Profits, and RD&M ($million), 1982–1994*

	Sales	*Pre-tax profit*	*Profit/sales*	*R&D*	*R&D/sales*
1982	310	24	8	54	18
1983	429	48	13	62	18
1984	415	78	19	72	17
1985	581	136	23	82	14
1986	665	141	21	105	16
1987	765	221	29	126	16
1988	891	401	45	140	16
1989	974	425	44	151	16
1990	1186	524	44	209	22
1991	1242	575	46	212	17
1992	1304	690	53	230	18
1993	1516	749	49	269	17
1994	1,366	759	56	282	21

Sources: GWHC, BW&Co. (USA) Inc., 107.01/02, President's annual reports; Data provided by Fred Coe Jr, by fax, 9 May 2002; GSK/WF/SCS/798, WFL and Wellcome plc accounts and annual reports.

The influence of McKinsey is clear in Sullivan's reforms to product development and marketing, in particular the introduction of specialist sales divisions and entry into the OTC market supported by national television advertising campaigns. For the implementation of these innovations he recruited specialists from outside the company, an approach much more difficult to apply to a reform of RD&M. McKinsey had emphasized the importance of sustained investment but also a need to introduce a greater urgency surrounding the process of transforming research into products intended for profitable markets. The attempt to achieve this objective precipitated a clash between the recently-appointed practitioner of contemporary managerial philosophy and the inhabitants of laboratories where a scientific culture was rooted in decades of academic experience and internationally-recognized research achievements. Sullivan's initiative to implement McKinsey's recommendations for reforms to RD&M proved a significantly more difficult task compared with those successfully executed in the areas of administration and marketing and would precipitate a crisis of management of major proportions.

CHAPTER 16

Clashing cultures: intra- and inter-organizational conflicts at Burroughs Wellcome & Co. and Wellcome Foundation Ltd

The McKinsey recommendations were applied to organization, human relations, and all aspects of marketing and were carried out relatively smoothly without significant opposition to Sullivan's plans at board level. This was not the case, however, with respect to recommendations affecting the management procedures and conduct of RD&M. Hitchings referred disparagingly to the McKinsey organization as "McMouse" and even before the review had begun, the company's scientists expressed their resentment towards an intrusion into the laboratories to investigate activities.

The starting point of the review that led to justification for reform was the unimpressive history of product innovation at BW&Co. which, before 1982, had resulted in only a single completely new product since Zyloprim in 1966 (Septrin/Septra was a combination antibacterial). The report reaffirmed the quality and central importance of high spending on research and confirmed the external reputation of the company's scientists.[1] However, it also concluded that the recent rise in expenditure on RD&M was excessive and had resulted in a halving of the rate of return on investment between 1977 and 1982 from 44 per cent to 22 per cent, well below the industry average. This failure, as McKinsey perceived it to be, was attributed to a lack of control over RD&M within a prevailing laboratory culture which did not focus sufficiently on the aims of the business. Instead of the "gentle, light-handed"[2] approach followed by the research committee so valued by successive scientists working within the ethos that had evolved from the laboratory culture initiated by Hitchings in the 1940s, McKinsey favored centralization and a transfer of power which could make RD&M more accountable. The report recommended that decisions regarding prioritization of research should be removed from the laboratories to the boardroom and that the chairman and the board of directors should exercise managerial control over RD&M as it did over other functions.[3] It was suggested that the company should aim to initiate five new projects annually, from which one should obtain an NDA, a target which implied the need to identify potential blockbuster drugs to ensure "a continuous stream of new medicines."[4] This was to be achieved through the introduction of a higher level of accountability on the part of the company's scientists who should be required to defend proposals for the extension or termination of projects. The chairman and the board, rather than the research committee, should adjudicate within the context of the overall financial and strategic aims of the company.[5]

Although Sullivan had been aware of the existence of RD&M before he became president and CEO, his knowledge of the organization of RD&M and of scientists' procedures and conduct was extremely limited and was one reason why the McKinsey findings were so important in influencing Sullivan's approach to corporate policy. The report allayed his doubts regarding their reputation among the research community but confirmed his suspicion that expenditure on RD&M was too high. He was also impressed by the McKinsey perception of a mistaken assumption among the scientists that the current research focus on basic cellular metabolism would lead to a higher rate of product innovation than a policy which concentrated expenditure on developing drugs for one or a limited number of diseases chosen by applying the criteria of market opportunity, volume sales, and profit.[6] An even more fundamental criticism, articulated by Sullivan, was that the entire company was rooted in a philosophy alien to achieving business objectives. He believed that the slogan coined by Coe as part of the re-invention of the company at the time of the move to RTP, "research is our only stockholder," had encouraged the company's scientists to continue to believe that the principal purpose of selling the company's drugs was to fund their research, rather than research being the primary route to selling marketable products; their philosophy, which he described as "letting the flowers grow," ran counter to achieving sound, strategic, and financial objectives.[7] In an interview printed in Wellcome News he challenged the attitude prevailing in the past which he characterized thus, "Wait for research to come up with the products and everything will be fine. It isn't as simple as that. We do need to come up with products … What we haven't done well in the past is to maximize our product opportunities after the introductory period and develop families of product once a specific new chemical entity is introduced."[8] Sullivan accepted the McKinsey analysis wholesale, interpreting it as a justification for ending what he perceived to be a laissez-faire approach to research at RTP.[9]

In 1984, two years after the report had been received, Sullivan claimed that considerable progress had been made in implementing the review recommendations, specifically in "instilling into our organization the kinds of values which should permit us to achieve our overall strategic objectives."[10] During that period, a corporate affairs department had been introduced, the vice-president director of marketing had been replaced, sales and advertising had been reorganized and a new product development system had been created along the lines favored by large consumer goods companies. In these respects, Sullivan's reforming strategy had gained momentum. However, ample evidence exists to show that there had been no substantial re-orientation of the company's corporate culture, especially in the laboratories. Transforming the systems, philosophy, and approaches of the RD&M scientists presented a more difficult problem, generated opposition, and eventually, created a crisis for the management of BW&Co. and for the president himself.

Highly skeptical before the review had begun, scientists dismissed the report as methodologically flawed since the conclusions lacked scientific foundation. At a general level, they criticized the consultants' grid approach in their analysis of research activities. Specifically, they also rejected the conclusion that research into anti-virals was unlikely to lead to the invention of drugs possessing the potential to generate maximum profits by treating a common disease, such as hypertension and Alzheimers. None the less, Sullivan proceeded with an attempt to implement changes aimed at securing improved focus and to prioritize projects in accordance with the McKinsey recommendations. This micro-managerial interventionist approach, completely alien to the traditional culture and relationships between management and RD&M, was bitterly resented by Cuatrecasas, Hitchings who no longer managed a laboratory, and Schaeffer who described their respective relationships with Sullivan as resembling those "between cats and dogs."[11]

The most striking example of outright defiance was that perpetrated by the vice president of research, Pedro Cuatrecasas, who rejected the blockbuster model and decided to ignore Sullivan's insistence that research should be re-directed away from current lines of investigation towards efforts to invent a drug for a common disease. Instead, he created a secret unit pursuing a research agenda in selected areas deemed to be at risk should the Sullivan strategy become officially and effectively operative. The model applied by Cuatrecasas in close cooperation with Barry, the principal investigator,[12] was based on the SKUNKWORKS concept which had its origins at the Lockheed Corporation in Burbank California where it had been instrumental in securing significant innovative breakthroughs in aviation. The philosophy underlying the system was a belief in the creativity of parallel "alternative" forms of project initiatives and management. The project was funded from a separate budget set outside normal corporate accounting limitations. A chief engineer had been given charge of a group of selected engineers who were allowed to work on one or two projects of their own choice outside the company's general strategy. In response to Sullivan's threat to Barry's antiviral research, Cuatrecasas told him "I'll cover for you, work on it but be quiet."[13] In the version of this model devised by Cuatracasas, a shadow project was created as cover to protect Barry's ongoing work. Supported by a team of chemists who, again unknown to Sullivan, carried out basic research, Barry assumed the principal role by screening a series of non-compounds believed to possess the potential for activity. Within months, the alternative project achieved a breakthrough with AZT which offered the prospect of another new drug entering the market within a few years.[14] It is not surprising, therefore, that Schaeffer later observed that the McKinsey report had had minimal impact on research and researchers, despite Sullivan's best (or worst) efforts.[15]

Concealed from Sullivan, the work of Barry and his co-researchers had received protection while other scientists were exposed to the methods which Sullivan had adopted to achieve another objective: that of reducing RD&M expenditure. A critique of the initiative was contained in an open letter addressed to the president composed by Morton Harfenist, group leader in the organic chemistry department at RTP. The letter appeared in a 1985 issue of the Wellcome News in which he criticized the diversion of time from the advancement of RD&M's primary goal of researching and developing new drugs. This was because the bureaucrats required staff to complete multiple forms, respond to surveys, prepare cover-all-contingency plans, and attend a proliferating number of meetings, none of which contributed to the achievement of Sullivan's stated aim for BW&Co. which was its transformation into a leading company. Harfenist also expressed concern that those among the RD&M staff who played down the importance of completing and submitting "pieces of paper" ran the risk of being perceived as uncooperative by those who dominated the bureaucracy. While he accepted the need for strengthening the means by which premier status might be achieved, he condemned the way in which they were being implemented with bureaucratic disregard for the effects on the research staff. Sullivan's reply, contained in the same issue, conceded that one outcome of a recent senior management conference had been the formation of a task force to explore ways of reducing red tape and simplifying paperwork. He expressed concern that Harfenist referred to the existence of differences in ways of thinking between "business-oriented" and "research-oriented" staff (a dichotomy which Sullivan did not deny) and declared his intention to eliminate such an outlook by finding ways to establish more common ground between the two groups.[16]

Cuatrecasas believed the gap between Sullivan and the scientists was unbridgeable, an incompatibility the evidence for which is contained in an article written by Cuatrecasas entitled "Dilemmas in contemporary drug development." The article first appeared in print through the University of Rochester Medical Centre for the Study of Drug Development but was reprinted in Wellcome News in 1983. It appeared a few months after an interview with Sullivan which was published in the *Pharmaceutical Executive*[17] in 1982. Sullivan's interview was one of a series intended to elicit the opinions of the CEO's of the leading (almost all the largest) pharmaceutical companies of the state regarding their respective industries, their experiences, and their business philosophies. Raising the profile of the company, still a relatively small enterprise within the industry, the interview was prompted by the rapid approval and recent launch of Zovirax. The article written by Cuatrecasas referred to the industry generally and expressed his serious concern over the decline in drug innovation since the 1960s which he believed was, to a large extent, the result of a decreasing commitment to the fruits of research. He was critical of a decline in the proportion of corporate resources devoted to basic research within an environment of government regulation which had a stifling effect on drug discovery. He was also critical of the growing pressure on scientists to become involved in premature value decisions at stages inappropriate for

The group R&D management meeting in the UK shows group R&D director, Dr John Vane (seated, second right), and group technical director, Dr Ronnie Cresswell (seated right). Seated from left are Dr James Black and Dr Pedro Cuatrecasas. Standing from left: Drs Howard Schaeffer, Mr Win Singleton, George Lyon, Drs John Beale, Douglas Munro-Faure and Mr Warwick Dench. Wellcome Library, London.

sound predictions and conclusions, "This is the real 'drug lag' of substance … there are many potential medicines which are not being discovered at all, or even worse, are not being developed or pursued once discovered at the bench." He emphasized the importance of major innovations resulting from extensive research and experience with patients. He advocated a reorientation by pharmaceutical companies away from a preoccupation with immediate return as the criterion for investment in technology and research, "… an innovative industry cannot afford to be dominated by accounting principles … Future strengths are eroded when business is guided by the spirit of the budget." He concluded, "Internal discovery and entrepreneurship must be fostered, since the complexities and pressures of corporate organizations lead toward bureaucratic and rigid policies that maintain institutional orderliness."[18]

While his criticism and analysis were couched in general terms at the level of the industry, the tenor of his remarks on drug innovation and research priorities implies a fundamental divergence between his values and understanding of the nature and role of research and those of Sullivan. Creasy and Coe had appreciated and accepted, to a degree, the Cuatrecasas philosophy as articulated by Hitchings since the 1940s. For decades the presidents of the American company had allowed Hitchings and his team creative space within the organization which enabled the evolution of a corporate culture in which cooperation between scientists and business managers (sometimes difficult) proved to be successful in the long-term. Sullivan showed less sympathy for the established corporate culture in which his predecessors had finessed successfully the potential conflict between profits and basic research through pragmatism and patience.

During his nine years as a BW&Co. executive, Sullivan had views on aspects of the business culture that he had been part of since joining the organization. He was not comfortable with the family feeling attested by employees at all levels of the company. Whereas the approaches of Creasy and Coe had been those of inclusion and were essentially intuitive in their relations with colleagues and other staff, Sullivan was withdrawn, distant, and cerebral. An example was his instruction that managers must read "*In Search of Excellence*" the current best-selling publication which captured the attention of elites in the boardrooms and management schools across the US and, though briefly, influenced management thinking.[19] Sullivan's unwillingness to visit departments and to be introduced to staff was a common criticism among managers, as was the lack of support he showed towards staff.[20] The appearance of a door on the hitherto open plan fifth floor at RTP closing off a newly-arranged president's office from other executives was interpreted as isolating him both symbolically and physically from others in the organization.[21] Unlike Coe, Sullivan appeared to favor micro-management, regardless of his lack of understanding, for example, of RD&M or IT.[22]

It was only a matter of time before the incompatibility of Cuatrecasas's approach to research with that of Sullivan led to a final rift. However, a difficult relationship with Sullivan was not the only consideration, for as American research director, Cuatrecasas came into conflict with Vane as WFL group research director. One consequence of Sullivan's appointment in 1981 was to increase the amount of time spent by Cuatrecasas trying diplomatically to avoid major conflicts with either Vane or Sullivan. The culmination of five years of effort in this regard was the resignation of Cuatrecasas in January 1986 (seen at least by one senior colleague as virtually forced upon him).[23] Tension also existed between Sullivan and Cresswell after Cresswell relocated from RTP to London to become WFL group technical director with a brief to secure greater integration of RD&M within the WFL group. Anxious to preserve the high level of independence from the board in London, Sullivan had withheld cooperation between BW&Co. and WFL.[24]

Added to the difficulties facing Sullivan at RTP were those which he discovered in London when in 1981, in his capacity as the new president of BW&Co., he began to attend meetings as a member of the WFL main board. Cresswell was also a main board member from 1981, after having been recruited from RTP by Shepperd to become group technical and development director located in the UK with special responsibility for biologicals across WFL. In 1977, Shepperd had persuaded the board that acquisition of a competitor was the solution to the problem of renewal of the product range, but the company's liquidity position ruled out financing acquisitions by borrowing. The alternative was to sell assets which implied changing the capital structure of WFL for which the Trust's permission was required. Shepperd had raised the possibility with Lord Franks in 1977 when he adhered to the view held by his predecessors that the Trust should not issue shares in the company because this would not be in accordance with Sir Henry Wellcome's will.[25] Discussion of the same proposal by directors in 1981 (by which time Sullivan and Cresswell were present) ended without consensus. This was at a time when the chairmanship of the Trust was about to change, giving Shepperd the hope that a new chairman might bring a more sympathetic view to the company's problems.[26] In 1980 a highly critical internal reported on all activities relating to RD&M, production, and sales of Foot and Mouth Disease vaccine (FMD), anti-malarials, interferon, and other biologicals in the early stages of development.[27] Sullivan and Cresswell brought an American perspective to bear on the problems and became severe critics not only of the management failures affecting biologicals, but also across the organization. Even before the crisis in 1980/81 which focused on biologicals, the board in London had expressed increasing concern about WFL's stagnating profits while R&D expenditure was high and rising.

The background was unprofitability of the production and sale of biologicals; annual sales amounting to £10 million were regarded as unsatisfactory by the board which had decided to initiate an internal review of the activities of the biologicals committee. It is significant that, in 1976, neither the chairman of the committee, James Black, nor the director of research, John Vane (both fellows of the Royal Society) was involved in carrying out the investigation. This is explained by the rapid deterioration in relations between the two from 1977 when Vane had persuaded Black to leave University College, London (UCL), where he was professor of pharmacology, to pursue his research at WFL's laboratories. In effect, Black's appointment implied an acknowledgement by Vane (who was under pressure from the board) that researchers at Beckenham had failed to introduce commercially valuable innovations. The result of Vane's own research into prostaglandins had resulted in thromboxane synthetase inhibitors which proved to be neither more nor less effective than aspirin. The cost of producing prostacyclin prevented it from competing with the low price of aspirin; consequently none of the inhibitors found their way into the market.[28] By contrast, Black's record of research and discovery had resulted in the development of spectacularly successful drugs. While employed at the ICI Pharmaceuticals Division between1958 and 1964, he had been pivotal in bringing the first beta-receptor antagonist to market. Propranolol, the first beta-blocker to be successful in the treatment of cardiac conditions, notably angina, was launched as Inderal in 1964. Within six more years, while employed by Smith, Kline & French, his histamine project, modeled by analogy on the beta-adrenoceptor project, resulted in the development of cimetidine and entered the market as Tagamet in 1976. The effective treatment for peptic ulcers rapidly became the highest selling prescription drug ever.[29] This record prompted Vane to refer to him as "the world's best discoverer"[30] and to persuade him to join a research culture at Beckenham comparable with laboratory environments commonly found in universities, but where he promised Black that ample research funds would also be made available.

In the event, relations soured from 1978. Vane's hopes received a setback as soon as Black joined the company. Shepperd asked Black if he could provide another H2 blocking agent or a beta blocker for angina, to which Black's response had

Sir James Black. Before he joined WFL in 1977, Sir James Black had already established a reputation as an outstanding discoverer of drugs which was later recognized in the award of a Nobel Prize. While employed by ICI he had developed beta-blockers for the treatment of angina, and as the senior scientist at SmithKline & French enabled the company to place an effective treatment for peptic ulcers on the market, a drug of huge commercial significance,. In anticipation of Black's continued creativity, Sir John Vane persuaded him to join scientists at WFL to remedy the company's poor record of innovation in the UK. Soured relations between the two knights quickly undermined the plan, ending with Black's departure in 1985 to pursue his own research independently – funded by WFL. Wellcome Library, London.

been "Not interested at all. I want to do something new."[31] However, Vane was not blameless. Even though Black's record appeared to justify respect for his judgment in the discovery of safe drugs, Vane rejected Black's first request for funds for clinical trials of lamotrigine, an anti-epileptic discovered by Wellcome scientists at Beckenham. Black believed he could meet safety requirements by reducing toxicity. Dr Munro-Forbes, Vane's close co-researcher in charge of the medical department, disagreed with Black and advised Vane against funding the trials.[32] Cresswell adduced this episode as an example of an ultra-cautious mindset among Beckenham scientists. Munro Forbes suggested that his role as a research scientist was to do no harm and to protect the good name of Wellcome, to which Cresswell replied that his role should be "to put new drugs on the market that do good to people," a philosophy prevalent among scientists at RTP.[33] A clear illustration that justifies Cresswell's observation is the subsequent history of the compound. Following the departures of both Black and Vane, pre-clinical studies were completed and clinical trials were conducted in the US and Canada. The resulting product, Lamictal, received approval in the UK in 1991 and in the US in 1993.[34]

At a time when the board was becoming increasingly concerned about the relationship between research expenditure, innovation, and profit, the introduction of a budget to meet the costs of Black's research resulted in even more competition between research groups, among whom resentment already existed because Vane was perceived as having allocated greater resources to prostaglandin research than was justified.[35] This was the context in which a clash of personalities contributed to divisions and a worsening of morale among research and other staff at Beckenham. In 1980 an internal report on biologicals drew attention to "basic inadequacies in … management systems involving cost measurement, cost control, asset management, and continuity of product supply."[36] Imprecise research priorities required better definition and audit; financial planning needed more clearly defined goals for sales, profits, and return on capital. Some marketing input and commercial planning was required in anticipation of hoped-for new product development and entry into the market.[37] The fundamental weakness was found to be a complete lack of control. This implied the failure of both Black as chairman of the biologicals committee and Vane as director of research to provide leadership and effective management.

The board's discussion of the report focused on the two areas of activity which absorbed most resources. Dr Arnold Worlock, employed at WFL in marketing since 1970 and widely regarded by board directors as an incompetent, none the less group marketing director since the adoption of group organization in 1973, expressed his dismay at the failure of the biological committee to relate products to the potential value of markets. He observed that vaccines and anti-malarials were in greatest demand in countries least able to pay or to provide an infrastructure to handle them.[38] Lord Greenhill, a non-executive director and former chairman of BP, was critical of the use of outdated methods to produce interferon and feared that the company's lag in the development of genetic engineering technology was such that it was too late to catch up.[39] Vane rejected, on principle, the cost/benefit criteria for research expenditure, and in the case of interferon admitted that he did not expect marketable products in the foreseeable future, while insisting that it would be significant even if it had limited applications as an anti-cancer agent.[40] The report proposed a consolidation of all biological activities into a single group directorate which should be represented on the main board and be responsible for formulating financial goals and ensuring management accountability; it was envisaged that biologicals R&D should continue to be responsible to the R&D directorate of which Vane was chairman.[41]

Unconvinced that internal reform was likely to be effected by current managers, in 1981 Shepperd persuaded Cresswell to move from RTP to Beckenham with a brief to transfer the American approach to development and apply it to the R&D organization in the UK. His immediate task was to focus on biological R&D from which new products were badly needed if it was to be financially viable. Cresswell embarked on a new biological review, necessarily working with Vane as R&D director whose resentment of the American's intrusion into the development area was made clear from the start.[42] Joint recommendations confirmed the findings of the previous internal report, supplemented by results from Cresswell's own inquiries, and set out a plan for reform along lines which Black had failed to achieve. Cresswell later described his experience at Beckenham within an environment created and defended by Vane since 1973 as "an emotional roller-coaster … the division I took over … was remarkable for its traditional, conservative ways and feudal structures." The frustration of what he described as his "reformists efforts," he attributed to entrenched attitudes which presented him once again with his "recurring dilemma between corporate commercial needs and personal scientific ambitions."[43]

Cresswell's plan was to create a single business entity which "should form the basis for recreating purposive research and development and motivate those associated with the venture to overcome the 'Cinderella complex' from which the biological business suffered."[44] It recommended the formation of a separate enterprise possessing a group structure; this was the origin of Wellcome Biotechnology Ltd. in 1981 (Wellcome BioTech Ltd). The memo emphasized the need for integration, prioritization, cost-effectiveness, and managerial control through accountability; the business-oriented tenor of the plan is indicative that Cresswell was the originator and was strongly influenced by his experience at RTP. Vane had given up on Black whom he described as "unmanageable,"[45] leaving Cresswell to attempt to implement reforms to an organization which included R&D in addition to the production of interferons, vaccines (including FMD), sera, and immuno-globulins. Vane appears to have been more concerned by the steady increase in numbers of research staff at RTP and the growing research expenditure secured through direct approval from Shepperd which would exceed that in the rest of WFL for the first time in 1983, a trend which would continue. In 1982, Vane had expressed apprehension regarding the possibility of "a further slide in power base should a major new product emanate from the American unit."[46] Vane continued to argue for a check on the upward trend of research expenditure allocated to BW&Co. but was overruled by Shepperd. At the same time, Vane concentrated attention on retaining his power to allocate all other research budgets. This brought him into further conflict with Cresswell who (unlike Black) possessed effective management experience and a seat on the main board whence he challenged Vane directly. He insisted on the creation of a separate R&D biologicals directorate to ensure an independent supply of clinical resources for Wellcome Biotechnology. Opposition within WFL towards Cresswell's attempt to reform biologicals proved especially difficult, for in addition to opposition among scientists at Beckenham was a lack of cooperation from Sullivan, now president at RTP and also main board director, who showed no interest in the development of biologicals.[47]

The increasing contrast between the historical record and future outlook of BW&Co. and the parent company was the background against which, in 1982, the WFL board decided to hold an international strategy meeting entitled "US strategy study." The two-day conference, chaired by Shepperd, was held in Singapore and was the first of its kind to review long-term strategy; it was also the first time that the directors from both the main board and the board of BW&Co. had participated in such an exercise. The discussions ranged widely, directors expressing views not only on the relationship between WFL and subsidiary companies, but also on their perceptions of the underlying problems of the UK organization. Deep divisions surfaced as directors felt free to air their views outside the usual time and other constraints imposed by a formal board agenda. Godfrey criticized the central structure of the WFL group, describing it as an anachronism which had resulted in a proliferation of factories constructed overseas for political and legal rather than for economic reasons and most of which were showing losses. He also advocated rationalizing R&D by relocating more to the US to alleviate group cash flow and to address "the inability of the UK business to meet costs."[48]

Beginning in the mid 1970s, the numbers employed by the American company rose steadily, continuing throughout the 1980s. By 1982, research scientists at RTP outnumbered those in the UK, 986 compared with 895. RD&M expenditure, on developing products in the pipeline in the US was £31.5 million, which compared with £38.8 million in the UK where no new products were in prospect for the foreseeable future.[49] Vane countered the criticism by arguing that whereas RTP was almost completely focused on human therapeutic research, scientists in the UK were also pursuing research into biological animal pharmaceuticals (FMD), and other vaccines (none of which was profitable). Each project, therefore, was conducted on a smaller scale and at higher cost. He argued that should a further shift in resources favor RTP, his ability to control the group R&D directorate would become even more difficult. Shepperd reassured Vane that as group director he would continue to issue instructions which would prevail.

Sullivan disputed Shepperd's stance as inconsistent with his own presidential authority and insisted that as RD&M vice president at BW&Co., Cuatracasas was answerable to him as president of that company. Should a disagreement between Vane and Cuatrecasas remain unresolved, then the WFL chairman should rule, a response which prompted Vane to ask who, in the event of "differences in ideas" between him and Sullivan, would set priorities? In fact, the absence of clear processes for setting priorities was a common theme expressed by several directors and aimed not just at the R&D directorate but across the entire WFL organization; development, product extensions, and marketing were similarly criticized for excessive centralization. Repeatedly, several key concerns emerged during the two-day discussions when Lord Greenhill, Sullivan, and Cresswell were among the fiercest critics of the extensive and complex committee structure of the entire organization which lacked either clearly-defined responsibilities or functions. Other senior managers expressed concern that directorates were constantly at odds with each other due to personal conflicts. At lower management levels, a widespread uncertainty was attributed to an absence of clear definitions of managers' responsibilities resulting in a lack of understanding of the contribution which they might be expected to make to the company's objectives. This was attributed to a lack of communication between the directorates and senior managers who did not meet and it was suggested that consultation meetings between the two would improve matters.

Unbelievably, Shepperd described the prevailing absence of consultation as a strategy to avoid "an unhealthy speculation, lobbying, and apprehension that this would generate." Instead, he encouraged directors to "discuss among themselves without putting anything in writing and then to submit individual views to him in writing." Another proposal, advanced by Sullivan and Cresswell which received support from other directors, was that WFL in the UK should undergo a thoroughgoing open investigation process similar to the review recently completed by McKinsey in the US. Shepperd conceded the wisdom of mounting a review, though he expressed skepticism of the value of "outside consultants with particular points of view." His preference was for an investigation limited to the use of internal resources which excluded consideration of the company's relationship with the Trust and the possibility of issuing public equity. From his perspective, such a review was preferable because it would not require external consultants. Sullivan disagreed strongly, arguing that the American experience showed that only external consultants could provide a truly fresh look at the business.[50] Privately, Shepperd was more concerned about the clash between two major scientists which he believed was the explanation for the company's problems, rather than the fundamental issues regarding structure, organization, communication, and policy raised at the conference.[50] He opposed a McKinsey-type investigation because he was not prepared to expose the serious discord that existed at Beckenham in the UK.

Although Vane and Black were aware of Shepperd's anxiety not to publicize the difficulties in the laboratories, within months of the conference Shepperd acceded to their joint request to enlist external intervention with a view to resolving their differences by recommending concrete measures through some form of reorganization of the laboratories.[51] Shepperd turned to the A. D. Little management consultancy. In August 1983, this firm was asked to investigate and advise how best the chairman might resolve the problems caused by the continuing and intensifying personal clash between the "prima donna scientists,"[52] and to recommend reforms that might be necessary to establish an effective and commercially productive R&D organization. Shepperd set up a steering committee consisting of himself, Vane (as research director), and Faulkner (the principal investigator for Little). Shepperd's attempt to limit the investigation to R&D with a view to finding a solution to unstable personal relations in the laboratories failed. The significance of the Little review and report had much wider implications for the future of the entire Wellcome organization which, coinciding with a change in the leadership of the Wellcome Trust, heralded a radical change in relations between WFL and the Wellcome Trust.

CHAPTER 17

Lancing the boil at Beckenham: A. D. Little's management review of Wellcome Foundation Ltd, recommendations, and consequences

The Little report on WFL was damning. Sales and profits had increased well above inflation, however, profit as a percentage of sales had declined (see Table 17.1).

The intended fundamental reorganization of the company into regional groupings on the model recommended by Urwick Orr in 1968 had failed to solve the problems identified in its report sixteen years before (mainly because implementation of operational organization and management within an ostensibly regional structure remained incomplete). The exception was the North American group which contributed 45 per cent of global sales and generated 73 per cent of WFL's profit, yet employed only a quarter of the number of WFL employees. Whereas the UK industry average rate of return was 17 per cent, that for WFL was 11 per cent which compared badly with rates of return for Glaxo and Beecham of 27 per cent and 24 per cent respectively. Between 1979 and 1983, as a percentage of WFL sales, R&D expenditure rose from 23 per cent to 33 per cent which was high compared with other companies in the UK.[1]

The report linked poor performance to defective organization especially of R&D, the diversity and complexity of which created problems of control and accountability. The spread across eight therapeutic areas (comparable with the world's largest pharmaceutical companies) resulted in most of them being underfunded. The report concluded that the funding of those substantially smaller programs and projects initiated in the UK was unlikely to result in major innovation in a commercially productive area and placed the business at a competitive disadvantage.

Lines of responsibility were unclear, as was research strategy which appeared to be non-existent. As group research director, Vane was responsible for clinical and biomedical research and administrative divisions, yet the therapeutic unit within the biomedical division for which James Black was responsible, was subject only to nominal control and was expected to provide services to other research units on site at Beckenham. Another organizational anomaly was Cresswell's role as technical

Table 17.1 *WFL/Wellcome plc R&D as percentage of sales and profit after tax, 1980–1990*

	R&D/sales	*R&D/profit*
1980	11	150
1981	10	158
1982	11	180
1983	12	212
1984	12	201
1985	12	188
1986	13	216
1987	13	146
1988	13	124
1989	13	110
1990	15	112

Source: GSK/WF/SCS 798, WFL/Wellcome plc accounts and annual reports.

Table 17.2 *WFL sales and financial analysis, 1970–1984*

	Sales	*Pre-tax profits*	*Profit as percentage of sales*	*Post-tax profits*	*Dividend plus payment by deed of covenant*
1970	85.7	9.1	11	4.5	2.1
1971	96.5	10.0	10	6.4	2.5
1972	113	11.7	10	6.4	2.5
1973	140	19.6	14	9.4	2.5
1974	274	24.0	9	12.4	2.8
1975	213	28.7	13	13.5	3.0
1976	290	41.4	14	19.8	3.7
1977	350	46.7	13	21.7	5.6
1978	382	51.1	13	23.6	7.0
1979	412	51.6	13	28.8	8.0
1980	442	48.1	11	35.9	9.0
1981	500	50.1	10	33.1	10.5
1982	593	55.1	9	37.1	13.0
1983	674	61.2	9	37.9	14.0
1984	806	89.5	11	48.5	17.0

Source: GSK/WF/SCS/798, WFL and Wellcome plc accounts and annual reports.

director responsible for development. Formally, he had reported through the R&D director to the main board. However, he was also managing director of Wellcome BioTech Ltd. which was being developed as a free-standing supply organization to WFL and thus qualified him to sit on the main board. Employing roughly five hundred people, including one hundred and fifty research staff, this body was not required to report to the R&D group director. Thus tension was built into the organizational relationships between Vane, Black, and Cresswell. The contradictions were compounded by interpersonal difficulties and resulted in a senior management team described as "damagingly split." Open conflict contributing to low morale among staff was interpreted as evidence of a "poorly operating organization."[2]

The complex committee structure included overlapping membership, functions, and roles and was inconsistent in its reporting procedures. The resulting diffusion of responsibilities and the lack of executive arms to ensure action provided a disincentive to personal commitment to ensure particular lines of action were pursued, "Discussion replaces, rather than precedes, executive action." The report described the executive as having no clear idea of what it was trying to achieve regarding cost or time-scale. This appeared to be the case with the absence of management control over research projects. Project control committees conducted reviews regularly, but their approach to each project was uncritical, devoid of adequate management, and rooted in "inertia and a reluctance to chop to keep it alive even if the results are disappointing." No system existed for prioritizing R&D strategy. This was compared adversely with the procedures at RTP where RD&M activities were recommended by the research committee and decisions made independently by the board. Collaboration between scientists at Beckenham and RTP was limited to *ad hoc* coordination and cooperation on some programs and projects. Cuatrecasas repeatedly complained of duplication, an example of which was Vane's vigorous push for investment into the provision of facilities for anti-viral chemotherapy at Beckenham in 1984, a time when scientists at RTP had forged ahead with anti-viral research.[3] Another aspect of organization that occasioned Little's concern was the lack of communication between levels of management, a complaint "expressed forcefully by subordinates" which "bordered on contempt for the lack of direction and control exhibited from the top of the organization."[4] The report was critical of the absence of an adequate forum for informal communication or exchange of ideas between scientists. Inter-divisional and functional committees forced senior managers from different areas to work together to some extent, if only to deal with committee agendas. However, interdepartmental contact between scientists below this level was limited. This was attributed to a wide dispersion of buildings on the Beckenham site and reluctance among senior managers to use social facilities.

In addition to the organizational weaknesses, the Little report highlighted a lack of management skills (characterized in part by the absence of "management by walking around") especially at senior levels, but at other levels too. The overall verdict was that WFL suffered from systemic management failure Recruitment policy and the nature of the annual reviews of scientists' performances were considered to explain in part, systemic management failure. Annual reviews conducted within the R&D directorate by immediate superiors were based solely on scientific contribution to research as indicative of "scientific excellence" (a phrase attributable to Vane); achievements in time and personnel management received little credit. Interviews with senior managers provided the evidence of managerial incompetence. One maintained, "When I arrived my sole direction was to build a center of excellence. In the 18 months since I arrived no further advice or direction has been forthcoming." Another commented, "Dr Vane is rarely seen at all outside the mansion", and yet another, "Contact with the director is related to personal standing rather than the job. Certain senior personnel have access whereas others do not." A senior scientist observed that, "... the way some people behave, you'd think the company got its money from an annual flag day."[5] Defamatory comments such as these led Shepperd to fear a libel suit from Vane, should the remarks appear in the report.

In addition to defective organization, a fundamental problem underlying poor management was perceived to be the prevailing culture at Beckenham where the imperative of commercial performance had not been reconciled with that of scientific endeavor. The report observed that unlike their counterparts in the US, scientists at Beckenham enjoyed the opportunity to "free wheel" and to "pursue their own scientific interests with no requirement to account for their time in any rigorous manner" and with "no concern for the financial interests of the company and its commercial survival."[6] The jibe about the "University of Beckenham," was found to be justified. Remote from the economics of the marketplace exacerbated by poor communications between group marketing and group R&D a lack of dialogue contributed to a general lack of appreciation by scientists of the importance of market forces."[7]

Criticism aimed at the complexity of the R&D organization, the dense, sclerotic bureaucratic committee structure that stifled managers' capacity and motivation to exercise effective management was, by implication, extended to the entire organization. The group committee was criticized for lacking clearly stated strategies with respect to R&D and for the resulting inadequate input to the procedure for turning research into development and ultimately marketable products. Market forecasts were merely extrapolations unhelpful to policy makers.[8] Little's final recommendations addressed the need "to strengthen and revitalize top management structure" by appointing a "managerially-commercially-oriented experienced" UK director of R&D (who should not necessarily also be a research scientist or a main board member and who would continue to be responsible to Vane who would continue as the group R&D director). This would relieve both Vane and Black from day-to-day management functions at Beckenham. Three research streams should be created in distinct organizational units: therapeutic (Black), biomedical (Cresswell), and prostaglandin (Vane's own area of research which Faulkner admitted was a personal concession to Vane, though objected to by Sullivan because of a lack of "a prior market analysis.)"[9] A separate research services division (outside Black's responsibility) was needed to serve both research and development, as was a planning coordination unit.

The project management system was seen to be a key flaw, being in some cases under the very loose guidance of the project control committees; it lacked any budgetary accountability. Little strongly recommended that this emphasis should be reversed, "Line authority should be strong on scientific control and project teams should be strong on budgetary discipline." The report also recommended reform of payment systems with a view to providing incentives and rewards for measurable performance based on revised cost benefit criteria. The committee structure should be simplified and the operating environment improved to assist with restoring morale and stimulating motivation. Little also urged the establishment of a clear worldwide strategy, including much greater integration of R&D activities in the UK with R&D in the US.[10]

At the meeting of the board in January to consider the report, a letter from Steel, the newly-appointed chairman of the Trust,[11] was tabled to inform Shepperd and the board that the trustees hoped that "no serious loss of personnel will occur," a thinly-veiled reference to Black (knighted in 1981) and Vane (knighted in 1984), though they understood that "without flexibility by those concerned the trustees find it difficult to see a workable solution being achieved without such a loss." The letter referred to the need for the board to adopt "a not overlong time limit … for devising a scheme for improving the management of the R&D directorate acceptable to the chair and the board which should be implemented and duly evaluated."[12] With the intention of maintaining secrecy, the board had resolved not to acknowledge the letter formally.

Reactions to the report were strongly expressed, not least by the non-executive directors. Lord Greenhill described it as containing a damning indictment of company management and of the R&D directorate in particular. He pleaded with the protagonists for a reduction in tension, urging cooperation in the company's interest. Another non-executive director, Jeremy. W. Lever, QC, Fellow of All Souls, who had been appointed in 1983 to bring to the board his expertise in European Union (EU) and competition law, conveyed profound concern over the findings of the report (widely shared by the other directors), particularly over the lack of innovation from high levels of R&D expenditure in the UK, the failure in managing R&D leading to low rates of return, and damage to the business globally.

Both non-executive directors, Greenhill and Lever, underlined the impatience evident in the statement circulated from the Trust. Greenhill believed the Trust's concern was perfectly proper and that it was fortunate that, because the company was not quoted, it should be possible to tackle the problem without being exposed to public criticism from shareholders.[13] Shepperd agreed, adding that the board was right to worry that the Trust might wish to begin taking over responsibility for what must be management decisions.[14] Lever was even more explicit regarding the implications of the report, "Within the next three years, had we been a public company we would be ripe for takeover. Even so, the Trust has, I believe, given a clear warning that unless the unacceptable state of affairs is remedied speedily the task is liable to be passed to others. If we can demonstrate to the Trust that we are tackling the problems seriously they might be willing to grant us breathing space for the fruits of reform to show. Otherwise ... the Trust is likely to intervene quite soon one way or another." He proposed that the group R&D director and a new director of UK R&D should be asked to produce a detailed report within six months of taking office, detailing the steps which had been taken to remedy the defects identified by Little and future specific steps to be undertaken.[15]

Sir John Vane, recipient of a Nobel Prize in 1982 and whose knighthood was conferred on 1 January 1984, remained in denial, rejecting the allegation that R&D in the UK had failed to develop new products and dismissing the charge of a lack of coordination between Beckenham and RTP and opposing the reforms proposed by Little. Lever urged the formation of a task force to implement the recommendations and also to address the question as to the future of the company's commitment to insulin and tropical medicine, both identified as loss-making activities. In response, Vane invoked the long-standing interest shown by the Trust in tropical medicine. This meant that the Trust should be consulted before decisions which might affect research in that area.[16] On the subject of Black's future, Vane reported that he had reassured him that "the board would be distressed if he left, but changes were needed."[17] Vane had offered him three possible solutions; first, the Little solution, was to appoint Black formally as head of the therapeutical research division; Vane believed this would still involve interaction between Black's research and that of others and therefore present difficulties. The second was for Black to join another organization, and the third was to create a separate project for Black with a team of his own choosing, the composition of which was to be determined by Black himself, funded by a research budget, and conducted "on a small site away from Beckenham." Black was expected to respond within ten days. Sullivan expressed concern that alternatives two and three would have a major impact in the scientific world. If, as Vane's description implied, Black should remain supported financially by the company but "exempted from the commercial rigors of R&D strategy," Sullivan argued that the plan was inconsistent with the Little recommendation that structure and process were needed which subjected R&D to integrated control. Lever was similarly worried by public perception should Black leave the company; his preferred option was number three.[18]

Vane rejected the appointment of a senior manager from outside R&D to be involved in planning its reform. Instead, he proposed setting up a task force reporting directly to him and to a steering committee of his own choosing."[19] When apprised of the probable composition of the task force, Cresswell expressed incredulity (as did the central shop stewards' committee).[20] Lord Greenhill, with support from other directors, had proposed that Dr Howard Schaeffer from RTP should lead the task force, Vane resisted, claiming that "staff at Beckenham would not take kindly to an American coming to sort out their problems."[21] The board resolved to set up a task force which excluded Vane, but also included Schaeffer on a temporary secondment to Beckenham from RTP. Dr P. H. Bentley represented Little, and the task force was chaired by Dr D. S. Freestone, an associate of Vane from Beckenham.[22]

The specific recommendation made by Little, the creation of the post of director of R&D UK was carried out forthwith by the board. However, disagreements among the senior scientists regarding the precise authority and role of the new director, as well as the type of person suitable for the appointment, continued throughout the year following the report. Vane insisted that control should lie with him. Schaeffer strongly disagreed before resigning from the task force and returning to RTP.[23] At a private meeting of executive directors in January 1985 (to which Vane was not invited), Shepperd reported that Vane had defended his resistance to the specifics of the reforms by insisting that he "had been conned into accepting the original Little Report because of the power struggle going on." Shepperd admitted to his co-directors that if at an AGM a trustee should ask whether the board was satisfied with the management of R&D he would be unable to give an affirmative answer. This was the unanimous opinion shared by other directors.[24]

Discussion led to broad agreement among the directors that as long as Vane remained in post it would not be possible to appoint a UK director as recommended by Little and therefore Vane should resign. However, Shepperd proposed a compromise, offering Vane an undertaking that the company should reorganize only "more or less" along the Little lines on condition that Vane withdraw from executive responsibility for R&D in the UK (while retaining his role as group director R&D). Also, in accordance with Little's recommendations, a new post of UK director of research at Beckenham should be created to which should be appointed a person acceptable to the board (rather than a Vane appointee). In fact, Vane successfully resisted an external appointment and filled the post by promoting Dr Trevor Jones, a pharmacist rather than a research chemist or biologist, whom he had previously recruited from Boots to head development at Dartford. This arrangement implied continuing control by Vane of UK research regardless of the reorganization and contrary to the intentions contained in the Little report. In line with advice from the trustees who endorsed Little's recommendation, a chairman's R&D committee was set up to monitor the effectiveness of the new arrangements and to be involved in the formulation of R&D strategy and resource allocation at an early stage-in effect, a mechanism for controlling Vane. In future, the R&D committee would report to the chairman's R&D committee which made recommendations to the main board.[25]

Meanwhile, in April 1985, Black left WFL and soon, through the Rayne Institute (a funding vehicle set up by WFL) relocated his research group at King's College Medical School, to pursue independent research.[26] Vane also resigned one month later, explaining that in his role as group director of R&D he felt he had "too little direct involvement with science and too many managerial responsibilities" which limited his academic commitments.[27] Cuatrecasas was believed to have had an ambition to become a member of the main board in London (which Sullivan almost certainly would have opposed). However, despairing of the dysfunctional character of R&D and the board Cuatrecasas accepted an offer from Glaxo, conveniently located at RTP, to head RD&M in the US. He resigned from BW&Co. at the end of 1985.[28]

One of Little's firm recommendations was that there should be greater integration of research activities in Beckenham and RTP. On Jones's appointment as the new R&D director in the UK, Shepperd told him that he likened the relationship between the UK and the US as a bicycle, "not as a well-oiled machine in motion but them on the front and us on the back."[29] Cresswell had no doubt that the long-standing lack of cooperation between scientists at Beckenham and RTP had hampered the progress of the business. He found that after almost two decades working in the American company, once he moved to the UK, Sullivan and his former research colleagues at RTP had viewed Cresswell with suspicion because he was identified as a UK person.[30] It soon became apparent to Jones, too, that in his new role at times "it seemed that the US company was more of a threat to, rather than one of our own company."[31] Cresswell identified a significant difference between the approach to R&D by senior scientists at RTP and those at Beckenham, in particular with respect to bringing new drugs to market. Cresswell was critical of the ultra-conservative mindset prevailing at Beckenham where the emphasis on doing no harm to patients had become a justification for delay in the research process. Later, he compared this with the slogan espoused by scientists in the laboratories of Warner-Lambert/Parke-Davis (which he joined ar research director in 1988) which reflected the pro-active philosophy prevailing, "the patient is waiting."[32]

Following the resignation of Black and Vane, Schaeffer declined Shepperd's invitation to become group director R&D, preferring to remain domiciled in the US. Cresswell was removed from animal health, although he retained the chairmanship of Wellcome Bio Tech Ltd of which William Castell became managing director. He had joined the company as a commercial trainee apprentice in 1966 at the age of nineteen, subsequently acquiring accountancy qualifications, and had become financial controller of the company's sales organization supplying Europe, Asia, and the Far East. In 1980, Shepperd had appointed him as managing director of Wellcome Biotechnology at Beckenham where Castell believed that Shepperd expected him to introduce "some commercial sense" to guide the activities of the scientists at Beckenham.[33] The appointments of both Castell and Cresswell were intended to introduce a degree of accountability and commercial orientation, concepts which had been foreign to Sir James Black. Cresswell also became director of group R&D with responsibility for rationalizing through international integration. He also became Shepperd's immediate lieutenant with direct access to the chairman's office.

Cresswell's first steps towards rationalization attracted comment from the *Economist.* The commentator expressed appreciation of his achievements during nineteen years experience in the American company and welcomed his determination to rationalize R&D in an organization which was described as possessing a "rather reserved and academic air ... [with] a habit of employing eminent boffins to run its research teams ... [who] do not always make happy managers." The business in the UK was contrasted with the American organization which was "widely believed to have a snappier image."[34] The article suggested that the company's researchers

William F. Castell began as a commercial apprentice at WFL in 1966, left to qualify as an accountant and returned to WFL as regional controller of European operations. He became chairman of Wellcome Biotechnology Ltd in 1981 and in 1984 commercial director of WFL with a seat on the main board. The appointment of Robb, formerly marketing director at the Beecham Group, as CEO at Wellcome plc in 1989, led shortly to Castell's resignation. He became chairman of the Wellcome Trust in 2006. Wellcome Library, London.

were unlikely to welcome the prospect of rationalization, and so it proved. Cresswell remained with WFL for two years, joined Laporte Industries briefly in 1987, and subsequently became director of R&D at Warner Lambert to which he lured both Cuatrecasas and BW&Co.'s medical director, George Lyon. Cresswell's departure, the sixth senior director to leave the organization in two years, attracted another item in the *Economist*, headed "Wellcome – queuing for the door." It referred to the damaging exodus from the organization which left the chairman and managing director as the sole long-standing survivor at the top of an international business and raised the question, "What went wrong?"[35]

Cresswell (who had been regarded by the *Economist* commentator as Shepperd's heir apparent) explained his departure from WFL as his sheer frustration resulting from Shepperd's continuing "rule and divide" approach to management in an organization consisting of competing regional, R&D, and commercial baronies; if "barons showed allegiance to the King they could get away with anything."[36] This analysis, which implied limited control by the board, was identical to that offered by William Castell.[37] Castell also attributed the disharmony between senior managers in the company to a lack of leadership from Shepperd and to the competition between the "robber barons" on the board to become Shepperd's successor.[38] Cresswell described Shepperd's tactic of holding separate private dinners either for executives or for non-executive members of the board, setting each against the other. Shepperd's combined roles as chairman and managing director placed him in the position of adjudicator.[39] As managing director of BW&Co. (which Shepperd privately referred to as a cash cow), Coe, who knew Shepperd well, believed that he couldn't make a decision in his life.[40] A mantra which Shepperd repeated many times was that "no decision was a decision in itself," which Castell interpreted as the chairman's method of maintaining control

Table 17.3 *Numbers employed at BW&Co., WFL/Welcome plc, 1946–1994*

	BW&Co.	*WFL/Wellcome plc (UK)*	*Total WFL/ group*	*US employees as % of group*
1946	876			
1950	740	3,466	4,779	16
1955	842	3,077	4,514	19
*1960	1,040	3,225	12,300	8
1965	1,197	4,700	13,400	9
1970	1,377	4,230	13,242	10
1975	2,203	7,123	15,832	14
1980	3,403	6,764	18,491	18
1985	4,088	6,589	18,342	36
1990	4,773	6,910	18,853	25
1994	5,399	5,163	17,182	31

*Marks the acquisition of Cooper, MacDougal and Robertson Ltd and other overseas subsidiaries.

Sources: GWHC, BW&Co. (USA) Inc., 107.07/11, Public affairs, "Brief analysis"; Data supplied by Fred Coe Jr, by fax, 9 May 2002; GSK/WF/SCS/798, WFL and Wellcome plc accounts and annual reports.

by enabling him to strike "al fresco deals" with the feuding barons.[41] This is consistent with the perception expressed by Cresswell and by Gabriel Cipau, director of engineering and production at RTP, who later masterminded the production of Retrovir. After a period in London while seconded temporarily as advisor with regard to reorganization, Cipau described Shepperd as a politician even on a personal face-to face basis, "You never knew when you left his office which way to go. He really left it up to you and if you screwed it up you were in trouble."[42] Shepperd's reign was characterized by a tactic of compromise and division among competing directors and managers which consolidated his position, but resulted in a lack of decisiveness in the company's interest. The difficulties presented by management failure prevented the rationalization of the UK operations as recommended by successive management consultants. The numbers employed peaked in 1975 at 7,123 and fluctuated around the level of roughly one-third of all group employees and more than three times that of BW&Co. (which accounted for 14 per cent of the group). In 1990, the figure for the UK was 6,910, compared with 4,773 in the US. Only after 1990, when Shepperd's successor began to rationalize the company on a global basis, did the UK workforce drop substantially, falling below numbers employed in the US which represented 31 per cent of group employment by 1994.

The recently appointed non executives on the board, Lever and Sir Alistair Pilkington, the glassmaker industrialist who was also a non-executive on the board of BP, witnessed the upheavals at Wellcome with mounting concern. One consequence of the crisis was to highlight the lack of preparation for management succession, including that of chairman and managing director hitherto combined in Shepperd's role. Significantly, both Lever and Pilkington expressed criticism of this lack of career development, planning, and preparation for filling the most senior positions in the company.[43] The exposure of a failure of leadership at WFL and damaging internal strife prompted closer monitoring by the trustees who by 1981 were led by a vigorous and committed new leader who decided to intervene in the review process prior to devising new plans for the future of WFL and subsequently pressing for the implementation of the recommendations.

CHAPTER 18

The turning point: policy innovation at the Wellcome Trust, the formation of Wellcome plc, and the first public share issue in 1986

The Little review had begun shortly after a change in leadership at the Wellcome Trust. Just as Shepperd had sought to manage the review through his steering committee, the new chairman of the Trust ensured that secretly, the trustees also became engaged in the process. This would have been unthinkable during the chairmanship of Lord Franks. He had been due to retire from the Trust in 1980 and had named his successor as Lord Armstrong, formerly head of the civil service, who had been a trustee for six years during which he had accompanied Lord Franks in discussing matters affecting WFL. When serious illness prevented him from taking office, Lord Franks remained as chairman until April 1982 when Sir David Steel, a trustee since 1978, though largely an absentee member until his retirement from BP in 1981, took his place as chairman. The strengths exercised by Lord Franks had been those of an experienced civil servant, diplomat, and banker. These skills and a forceful personality had enabled him to dominate his fellow trustees who consisted of a lawyer and five distinguished members of the medical profession, for the most part appointed during his period in office.[1] His friendly relationship with Shepperd appears to have predisposed him to accept Shepperd's judgments and reassurances about the business. However, his introduction of Lord Armstrong and Sir David Steel as trustees suggests that as his retirement approached he recognized the need for intervention in the affairs of the business. Unlike Lord Franks, Sir David Steel had been trained as a solicitor and had spent most of his career with BP, both in the UK and in the US, before becoming its chairman until 1981. His achievements as chairman of BP included a successful resistance to a takeover by the state-owned British National Oil Co. which had been strongly supported by Energy Minister, Tony Benn, and for which Steel had subsequently received a knighthood.[2] The determined approach which he adopted in the independence campaign, however, contrasted with his style of chairmanship in the boardroom which, by repute, was restrained,

Sir David Edward Charles Steel, formerly chairman of BP who during his chairmanship of the Wellcome Trust, together with Roger Gibbs initiated the process of converting WFL into Wellcome plc and the first public share issue in 1986. Wellcome Library London.

consensual, and convivial – a reputation which Shepperd may have misinterpreted as a soft touch.[3]

Steel's first step as Trust chairman was to establish a collegial relationship with the trustees, familiarizing himself with their views and aspirations for the Trust which even then had become the largest charity in the UK funding medical research. Steel encouraged the participation of all trustees in discussions of policy, including relations with WFL, an opportunity largely denied to them in the past, except at the annual general meetings. The former cozy relationship between Franks and Shepperd, which the latter had cultivated to the company's advantage for so long, was replaced by a business-like relationship between the Trust as the sole owner and WFL's chairman and managing director. Shepperd's presumption that he would continue to be the dominant influence at the interface between the Trust as sole share-owner and the company proved to be a serious misjudgment.[4] As the company's financial performance was vital to the Trust's mission, which was about to be pursued with vigor, the new chairman soon familiarized himself with the state of the business. Between 1980 and 1983 group sales had increased by 82 per cent, capital employed had risen by 52 per cent. while profit rose by 22 per cent; however the rate of profit on capital employed fell from 14.6 to 11.9 per cent.

Table 18.1 *WFL net profit, capital employed, and rate of return, 1980–1985*

	Net pbrofit before tax (£million)	*Capital employed (£million)*	*Profit as % of capital employed*
1980	49.3	338.0	14.6
1981	50.1	403.0	12.4
1982	55.1	450.2	12.2
1983	61.2	513.8	11.9
1984	89.5	592.8	15.1
1985	121.7	607.8	20.0

Source: GSK/WF/SCS 798, Annual accounts and annual reports.

In addition to this worrying trend, Steel was critical of a dividend policy which had limited levels well above the normal cover by the company's profits which at BP and other similar companies were two or threefold.[5] When he complained to Shepperd that the Trust was not receiving "a fair whack" of the profits, Shepperd disagreed in a manner which gave Steel the impression that he was unused to being questioned on the company's financial performance in relation to dividends.[6] Steel demanded higher dividends in future, while offering reassurance that consideration would be given should future trading conditions become unfavorable. No such undertaking was given by the board to comply with Steel's demand.[7] Reports submitted by the chairman of WFL to the annual joint meetings of the board provided some evidence that the business in the UK was experiencing difficulties, though serious personal differences affecting management decisions were for a time concealed from the trustees.

Table 18.2 *WFL profits after tax and dividends (£million), 1970–1981*

	WFL profit after tax	*WFL dividend*
1970	4.7	2.1
1971	4.5	2.1
1972	4.6	2.9
1973	6.4	2.9
1974	9.3	3.4
1975	10.8	3.9
1976	11.0	4.6
1977	19.7	7.9
1978	25.0	7.7
1979	30.9	8.8
1980	31.9	12.2
1981	37.1	13.6

Source: GSK/WF/SCS 798, Annual accounts and annual reports.

Oil painting by Andrew Festing of Sir Roger Gibbs, 2000. Formerly chairman of Gerrard & National and of the London Discount Market, he was chairman of the Wellcome Trust. Together with Sir David Steel, Gibbs was responsible for the first public share issue by Wellcome plc. After the second share issue in 1992, he negotiated a merger with Wellcome plc to Glaxo to form Glaxo Wellcome, thereby ending completely the dependence of the Trust primarily upon dividends issued by the company. Wellcome Library, London.

The investigations conducted by Little gave Steel an opportunity to obtain independent expert evaluation regarding the management of the business. With the intention of gaining advantage for the board when the report was discussed with the trustees in January 1984, Shepperd monitored the review process through briefings from Faulkner, the consultant who was in charge of the process. Steel arranged his own secret briefings, deputing two of the trustees, Peart and Paton, to monitor progress also through Faulkner. Of particular concern among the medical trustees was the need to resolve the difficulties presented by the company's two senior scientists. In November 1983, Steel initiated a meeting attended by the two trustees and Faulkner. They were joined by the three protagonists, Vane, Black, and Cresswell in an attempt to secure agreement before Little's final report was submitted to the board.[8] The endeavour failed. Alarmed by Peart's report of the depth of the rift between Vane and Black and the crisis affecting the laboratory staff, and fearful of the prospect of resignations which (in view of Sir John Vane's Nobel Prize and recent elevation) might reflect badly on the Trust, Peart conveyed to Shepperd the trustees' wish for urgent action in confirming Vane as group director as well as for the creation of a new R&D director in the UK to carry out detailed management. Copies of the final draft were distributed initially to Peart, Paton, and Steel. Steel circulated it to all trustees, thereby undermining Shepperd's plan which had been to establish the board's own position before the report had been absorbed by the trustees and crucially, before discussion of Little's recommendations with Steel and the trustees.[9]

Despite the efforts of the Trust to secure full implementation of the recommendations in the Little report, the evident difficulties surrounding implementation that became clear during the ensuing months led to a more radical approach by the Trust to WFL's problems. Since the Trust had been formed in 1936, successive chairmen had interpreted clause 17 of Wellcome's will as prohibiting the issue of shares in the business, other than in exceptional circumstances, and in any case requiring approval from the UK Charity Commission through the High Court should the company wish to vary the terms of the trust deed.[10] The resulting exclusion of the business from the Stock Exchange as a source of funding became a serious handicap; first, because since World War II the absence of innovative commercially successful drugs had failed to provide profits sufficient to meet the company's requirements for capital investment; second, because the long-term loan market in the UK virtually disappeared until the 1980s. Until the that time, the Trust had accepted low dividends but, whilst acknowledging WFL's long record of low profits since World War II, remained adamant that investment in the business must be financed from internal funds and bank loans only. This situation had frustrated the board's aspiration to improve the company's competitiveness and profitability by growing through diversification by acquisition. Shepperd had raised the question of the capital structure of the business at a corporate strategy meeting of the board in 1982 when he had expressed his frustration with the Trust's traditional objection to parting with a proportion of the current holding in the company, "even though by doing so it could increase its earnings."[11]

The Trust had shown no interest in preliminary overtures made by other companies wishing to explore some form of collaboration with WFL that might involve capital reorganization.[12] In 1983, a £10 million loan for twenty-one years was raised from the UK government's Finance for Industry initiative. Subsequently in 1983, the Midland Bank rejected a request for a more substantial fifteen to twenty year loan to finance an acquisition.[13] In the same year, secret meetings of the board received Shepperd's reports on an informal approach from ICI with respect to the Cooper's animal health business owned by BW&Co. as well as his reports on two other approaches originating in the US. SmithKline Beckman, Merck, Sharp & Dohme sought discussion of "future relationships" with WFL specifically regarding BW&Co. Attracted by a higher than anticipated return on Wellcome capital, some main board directors favored pursuing a joint venture with ICI. Shepperd, however, feared that collaboration would develop into a complete takeover by ICI. His preference (subject to the Trust's concurrence) continued to be perpetuation of Trust control (and the Trust's protection) and a strictly limited equity issue, a formula which he believed would ensure both "group identity" and fund an acquisition.

His return to the possibility of a share issue was prompted by the recent appointment of a new chairman of the Trust who appeared to be introducing a business perspective to the conduct of the Trust's affairs. Shepperd informed the directors that Steel, who became chairman in February 1982, might be more receptive than Franks to the argument that expanding the company through acquisition could advance the Trust's own long-term financial interest.[14] Shepperd's hopes were soon to be confounded. During an initial period of familiarization with the affairs of the business, which coincided with investigations conducted by the Little consultants, Steel became alarmed by the crisis involving the senior scientists at Beckenham and by the widespread managerial malaise prevailing throughout the company in the UK. Steel made it clear to Shepperd that in future he was determined to secure sufficient income from WFL to fulfil the Trust's "financial and philanthropic ambitions"[15] through substantially greater funding of the advancement of medical research in accordance with Sir Henry Wellcome's wishes.

Steel's familiarity with the history of business and the city of London gave him a perspective against which to compare the company's performance and practices and to identify those which needed to change to enable the Trust to fulfil its aspirations. Later, Lawrence Banks, asset manager for Robert Fleming & Co. (Flemings), merchant bankers in the city of London who subsequently advised the Trust on its relations with the company, described Shepperd's attitude to the Trust (shared by the directors) as an intrusion, "a boring interference with the business of getting on and managing the company ... they did not consider the Trust in the light of being owners right up until the very end."[16] Within months of deciding that the state of affairs at WFL would have to be addressed and relationships between the Trust and the company would have to be changed and even before Little reported the full extent of WFL's weaknesses, Steel sought an additional trustee. As the sole non-science trustee, Steel chose another who was younger, energetic, and well-equipped to assist him with the task ahead. Already known to Steel, Roger Gibbs was appointed as a Wellcome trustee in February 1983.[17] He was an experienced stockbroker who was approaching the end of a long and distinguished career in the City of London where he was Chairman of Gerrard & National and well-connected with City financial institutions, eventually becoming chairman of the London Discount Market. Steel ensured that, following his own term of office which would terminate at the same time as Gibbs's city career, Gibbs would succeed him as Trust chairman in 1989.[18]

Gibbs's knowledge, skills, and connections were vital to the implementation of Steel's policy, as was his commitment, derived partly from family experience, to the direction in which Steel was intending to take the Trust. Gibbs's father, Sir Geoffrey Gibbs, had been a director of Barclays Bank and had handled the Nuffield Foundation account. Set up by its entrepreneur founder, Viscount Nuffield (William Morris) in 1943, the Nuffield Foundation had depended on income with which to fund philanthropic, mainly social and health-related research and experimentation, solely from the automobile business, the source of his considerable personal wealth.[19] During the 1950s and early 1960s, Lord Nuffield had resisted Geoffrey Gibbs's attempts to persuade him to diversify assets by selling shares in his privately-owned British Motor

Company (BMC). Pressure exercised by senior partners of the Cazenove merchant bank finally persuaded Lord Nuffield to sell 20 per cent of the BMC holding which remained virtually the sole asset base of the Nuffield Foundation after the collapse of BMC in 1967.[20] The resulting reduction in funding had drastically diminished the Nuffield Foundation's capacity to advance social wellbeing, its overarching objective. Steel and Gibbs were determined that the Trust should be prevented from suffering a similar disastrous fate.

Although before he had enlisted Gibbs's support as a trustee Steel had sensed that important changes were needed to alter the relationship between the Trust and WFL, it was only after conversations with Gibbs that strategic possibilities of establishing a new relationship between the Trust and the company began to take shape. Diversification of assets seemed to be one way of shaking up the company and diversification (though not public scrutiny) was favored by the board, but any strategy which involved a change in the status of the Trust would require legal advice and permission from the Charity Commission. Any alteration in the company's status would require advice on the practicalities of such changes and the services of merchant bankers to assist with implementation. Both permission and practicalities began to be explored towards the end of 1983 when, unknown to Shepperd, the first approach to the Charity Commission was made by Steel, Gibbs, and Trust secretary Williams.[21]

Discussions with the Charity Commission continued until shortly before preparations for flotation were completed at the end of 1985.[22] Meanwhile, in the autumn of 1984 in preparation for the case which would need to be presented to the trustees and to the board, they sought advice from Flemings with whom Gibbs had been associated in the past. The adviser who conducted the exercise, Lawrence Banks, recalled that the initial inquiry from the Trust did not concern corporate transactions but the evaluation of WFL as an asset which would provide a measure of the rate of return received by the Trust in the form of dividends. This reflected Steel's determination that, in the short term, the company would increase dividends. Banks's tentative estimate of the value of WFL was £500 million from which, between 1980 and 1984, the company's average pre-tax group profits were £61 million. Banks therefore concluded that average dividends during the same period of £13 million, could not be justified by Shepperd's insistence that a higher level would be unaffordable because of a low cash flow. Banks drew attention to WFL's possession of a large stream of dollar earnings yielding annual profit levels of between £50 million and £60 million. On the basis of comparisons with other companies' financial records, Banks also disputed Shepperd's claim that WFL was unable to raise long-term debt without resulting in an unacceptably high gearing ratio.[23] Steel's next step was to commission Flemings to prepare a report on the finances of WFL concentrating on the Trust's interest as sole shareholder. He also sought their expert advice on the financial implications of the current relationship between the Trust and the business. Although Shepperd was left in the dark regarding early meetings with the Charity Commission, twice during the winter of 1984, Steel, Gibbs, and Banks met him to inform him of their thinking.[24] He was required to observe complete confidentiality until the strategy had been decided when the Trust agreed that he was free to apprise other directors of the impending flotation.[25]

The analysis presented in the Flemings report emphasized the Trust's lack of control or influence over the asset which it owned. This baffled Banks. Poor commercial management of the company was criticized as was the large R&D expenditure which, in the UK, had been largely unproductive and had left the company dependent on a narrow range of products in a highly competitive industry. As a result, because it was the sole owner of its only asset, the Trust was as vulnerable as the company. The Trust was strongly advised to end the inertia which it had shown in the past and to diversify, either by selling the company altogether or by floating part of it through the Stock Exchange. One result of floating would be to open the company to market pressures and expose it to the glare of analysts which, as a consequence, would compel directors to "take a more commercial attitude to life and ... shake up the management."[26] Banks's analysis and prescription for a remedy confirmed Steel's perceptions of the state of the business and the urgency of proceeding with the abandonment of the Trust's historic sole-ownership policy, the introduction of transparency into the company's activities, and a transformation of the corporate culture.[27] Russell Dunoon Duncan of Cameron Markby, and legal adviser to the Trust recalled Steel's case to the other trustees. That it was vital for the Trust's future "not to have too many eggs in one basket however good the basket might be."[28] More problematical was the challenge to enlist Shepperd's support which was vital to ensure an uncomplicated flotation which a public rift between the company and the Trust would jeopardize.[29]

On the first occasion when Shepherd was made aware of preparations for a possible flotation, he displayed annoyance that "upstart bankers" should be advising the trustees to sell some of the company. Steel and Gibbs applied gentle pressure on Shepperd by reminding him that John Harvey Jones, chairman of ICI, was still waiting in the wings and that they were considering whether to invite him to visit the Trust with his cheque book. This proved a sufficient threat to obtain Shepperd's grudging cooperation at least to investigate the possibility of flotation with the board.[30] A document prepared by Flemings entitled "Trust ownership of the Wellcome Foundation and its implications" presented detailed justification for proposals culminating in the implementation of a share issue.[31] Shepperd reported to the board, outlining the trustees' concerns and his own apprehension regarding a loss of control the company had enjoyed in the past. Not all directors were sympathetic to Shepperd's reservations. Lord Greenhill (the non-executive director on whose recommendation Steel had been appointed to the Trust)[32] expressed understanding of the Trust's dilemma. He warned that as a consequence the Trust might reasonably decide that by selling the group entirely and investing the proceeds, the Trust might enable it to secure a substantially higher income and fulfil its mission.[33]

That possibility may have increased following a visit to Beckenham in July 1984 by the scientific Trustees, together with Shepperd, Copestake (a director of WFL), and

Lever (a non executive director), the latter two being new to the company. The purpose of the visit, which followed the issue of the Little report and subsequent discussions by both the board and the Trust, was to enable those present to inform themselves at first hand of the troubled R&D division. Exchanges between the visitors and senior scientists working at Beckenham revealed a cultural divide within the company as they listened to Vane describing "the rift between R&D and the business side of the company."[34] Lever was so dismayed by the experience that on the delegation's return to London, he requested permission from Shepperd to report on the visit to other board members. Lever had been especially impressed by the response of the scientific trustees to the question posed by a senior director (probably Vane himself) when he asked the trustees to declare what they wanted of the company. Their unanimous reply was that the Trust's "sole interest" was "to make money", that R&D personnel should not pursue research into "inefficacious drugs," and that they should be "motivated in the same way as any other pharmaceutical company," though they should also adhere to "the highest ethical standards."[35] Though some trustees harbored reservations regarding the ethics of seeking specific powers which they believed Sir Henry Wellcome had not given,[36] such remarks suggest that Steel's influence in moving the Trust towards adopting his flotation policy was succeeding. The Beckenham visit strengthened Steel's conviction that the dysfunctional corporate culture was fundamental and posed a threat to the potential for greatly enhanced income for the Trust.

Final formal advice communicated by Flemings (confirming Steel's initial conviction) was that the company should be sold either in its entirety or in part. The effect would be to force the company to adopt a more commercial approach, being subject to market discipline; public shareholders would re-enforce the Trust's desire for higher dividends. An initial issue of 25 per cent was considered to be acceptable, perhaps in the short-term, but it was thought probable that exposure to the market would result in higher prices to be obtained from subsequent share issues.[37] Hoare Govett was the firm appointed as brokers to the initial share issue.

The major obstacle facing the Trust was the requirement under clause 17 of Wellcome's will that the Trust should "hold the shares of the company as a permanent investment," which several Trustees interpreted as a complete block against flotation for all time. Unknown to Shepperd, together with Duncan, and Williams (secretary to the Trust), Steel sounded out the Charity Commission on the feasibility of a share issue despite clause 17. The reputation among the financial community of the Charity Commission as an anachronism out of touch in financial matters in the 1980s did not bode well.[38] However, relatively recently-appointed Chief Charity Commissioner, Denis Peach, not only accepted the Trust's argument but showed an unusually liberal approach to the degree of divestment he was willing to sanction. Duncan described the Charity Commission team which became responsible for the project as "cooperative, even enthusiastic."[39] Further evidence of this was the solution of the problem how to deal with the reference in Wellcome's will that made any sale of shares conditional on the existence of "exceptional and unforeseen circumstances" to justify proceeding to the court for approval.[40] The Commissioner's solution was to proceed under the Trustees Act of 1967 which had created a specific requirement that all trustees should give serious consideration to a policy of divestment and diversification so long as it was demonstrably in the interests of the Trust, which Flemings confirmed.[41] On advice from the Charity Commission, however, the decision was taken not to proceed under clause 17. Instead, whatever the will might indicate, it was decided that an application should be made for an order of the court or the Charity Commission (which had concurrent jurisdiction) to permit the sale, offering as justification the requirements contained in the 1967 legislation: to advance the paramount interest of the trustees.[42] This circumvented the exceptional circumstances test.

Although Shepperd knew of the Trust's general intention and had begun to prepare the ground for public listing, he reckoned flotation would take place within five years and assumed that public issue would not exceed 25 per cent of capital and would enable the Trust to release perhaps up to £200,000, sufficient for WFL to make an acquisition.[43] Following formal notification in April 1985 Shepperd briefed the board, in Steel's presence, of the Trust's intention to float in January 1986. Steel explained the Charity Commissioners' view that not only was it in the interests of the Trustees, but that the Trust was under an obligation to diversify its investment portfolio. Moreover, the Commissioners had urged the Trust to obtain complete discretion to dispose of equity in the future, subject to the consent of the Charity Commission, for the sale of each tranche (an indication that such consent would be given "on the nod"). On the Commissioners' advice, a draft scheme had been submitted on 1 April under the 1967 Charities Act, as a method of avoiding the courts and facilitating a more flexible approach to the testator's will.[44]

Representatives of the board's legal advisers, Slaughter & May, who were also present at the meeting, joined the chorus of directors, those present unanimous in expressing their opposition to the Trust's intentions. Specifically, there was dismay at the "unnecessary haste" in fixing the flotation date; concern was expressed that by securing unrestricted powers to divest shareholdings bidders might be attracted and pressure thereby imposed on the Trust even though its declared intention was not to concede control completely. Steel's response underlined the much greater threat to undermine the company if it delayed implementation of Little's recommendations. He viewed flotation as a spur to action which would be in the group's financial interest.[45] The other principal argument presented by the directors concerned the welfare of Wellcome employees, one element within the spirit of Wellcome's will to maximize benefit to mankind,[46] to which Steel's response was: "our only duty as trustees is to maximize income."[47]

The final agreement with the Trust, negotiated by Shepperd with assistance from Lever and Pilkington, vocal non-executive critics of the Trust, included a reassurance that the Trust would not embark on a further issue within two years without consultation, discussion, and "reasonable endeavors" to agree with WFL on any proposed sale.[48] The merchant bank, Barings, continued to advise the company which proceeded to prepare a prospectus for the Stock Exchange. The "pathfinder prospectus" prior to the flotation in 1986 was described in the *Economist* as "having the appeal of a placebo … [seeming] to be trying to put off investors."[49] The context in which the prospectus had been drawn up was the difficult negotiation between the respective advisers to the Trust and the company in which the company was anxious to keep the issue price low (considerably below the eventual price). Banks adduced two possible explanations for the WFL directors who sought a large premium when the shares were issued. One was the prospect of securing more resources for the company (still Shepperd's ambition);[50] the other (which he admitted was purely speculative) concerned individual company directors' stock option values. The ordinary share price eventually agreed was 120p.[51] Wellcome Pharmaceuticals Ltd was registered as a private limited company in November 1985 for the purpose of acquiring the whole of the issued capital of the WFL, thereby becoming the holding company of the Wellcome group. Wellcome plc was registered in January 1986 with an authorized capital of £260 million (c. $312 million) though WFL remained as the main operating company. The Trust retained a 71 per cent shareholding. The issue was oversubscribed seventeenfold when the company was valued at slightly more than £1 billion.[52] The timing of the issue was fortuitous. Within months, the share price had risen more than fourfold following the announcement of the accelerated FDA approval process for AZT, a new anti-viral drug in the US. This degree of volatility became characteristic of the company's shares.[53]

Shareholders were evidently more impressed by the news from the US than by the distinctly downbeat commentaries in the *Economist* which referred to recent "damaging internal struggles" within the WFL organization resulting in the departure of several senior scientists, including two Nobel Prize-winners, and senior managers (including the President of BW&Co.), losses which were damaging to corporate strategy.[54] Two of the interested parties – the Trust and the investors outside Wellcome plc – received far more value from the flotation than had been anticipated. Both secured increases in asset value, while the Trust's income also began to rise steeply. Even before the flotation, Shepperd had finally acceded to Steel's insistence on higher dividends. In 1983/4 the figure was £17 million on a pre-profit tax of £90 million (a cover of 2.8). The figure for 1984/5, agreed for a further four years was £21 million.[55] This marked a reversal of the widening divergence, which had developed during Shepperd's chairmanship, between the pre-tax profits of the business and the dividend payments to the Trust. During the 1980s, the Trust's income rose sixfold in direct relation to the rising pre-tax profits of Wellcome plc.[56] In 1987, the Trust obtained revised investment powers beyond those limited to equities quoted on the London and New York Stock Exchanges and allowed investment in "devices yet to be discovered,"[57] a step signaling a possibility that the Trust might assume a wider investment role in the future.

In response to the request from WFL, the Trust permitted the company to benefit from shares issued to the value of £100 million, far below Shepperd's expectations and deemed by the board to be insufficient to fund a substantial acquisition. Shepperd's target had been CDC Life Sciences Inc. (a Canadian vaccine business valued at £200 million) which he regarded as the last chance to enter the US market and to prop up the continuing unprofitable vaccine business of WBL in the UK. Shepperd's renewed request, made to the Trust in 1987, for permission for Wellcome plc to issue more shares was rejected because the trustees were not confident that diluting the Trust's ownership further, in order to finance an acquisition, would yield an adequate return from such an investment.[58] In effect, this was a vote of no confidence in the management of the company three years after the Little report.

The Trust's divestment policy again raised the question of Anglo-American control and independence at two levels; among American directors, especially the company's senior scientists, and separately by the president himself. Although no formal notification was received from London, the discovery by American directors that discussions had taken place with a view to a public flotation of WFL were well-advanced, prompted a small group, led by Barry at RTP, to prepare a proposal to the Trust which would detach BW&Co. from the new organization, Wellcome plc. The confidence behind the bid was based on the anticipated sales and profits expansion which would follow the anticipated entry of Zovirax in tablet form into the market, and the launch of the antiretroviral drug, Retrovir, in 1987. The plot to mount a management buyout first came to Shepperd's notice at a meeting with the trustees in May 1985. They also notified Sullivan of the plot which had not envisaged a senior role for him in a new, completely independent wholly American BW&Co.[59] The trustees' negative response to the plotters was conveyed in "an understanding letter."[60] Although hitherto Sullivan was not privy to the plot he had attempted to secure detachment of the American company from the chaotic UK business at the beginning of his presidency. Sullivan had approached the chairman of the Trust with a request that instead of reporting to the chairman of WFL, the president of BW&Co. should report directly only to the Trust. Steel dismissed the proposal. When news of this approach reached Shepperd, he regarded it as evidence of Sullivan's ambition to escape from WFL control which he interpreted also as representing a threat to the future of the business in the UK.[61]

Friction between the two also occurred when in 1982 when, in Sullivan's presence, the WFL board discussed a proposal that in addition to the dividend, BW&Co. should pay a further £4 million as 40 per cent of the construction costs of a new building for the Trust.[62] Although this item was not formally passed to the board of BW&Co., Sullivan reported the possible consequence to the board at RTP when he highlighted the threat of a reduction in American funding of RD&M. Shepperd accused Sullivan of breaching confidentiality which membership of the WFL board dictated. The nadir in their relations – and between Sullivan and the trustees – occurred at a crucial WFL board meeting on 6 January 1986, attended by the company's legal and financial advisers on the final day before the announcement of the first sale of shares in Wellcome plc. Aware of the company's recent management upheavals involving three senior research directors, the advisers drew the board's attention to the importance, as the organization approached the stock market, to provide corporate support by maintaining continuity among senior figures. However, to the astonishment of his co-directors and the advisors, Sullivan declared that he could not actually commit to stay with WFL should he be presented with alternative opportunities.[63] The meeting was adjourned after which a fierce exchange between Sullivan and Shepperd outside the boardroom ended in the immediate termination of Sullivan's contract which was subsequently endorsed by the Trust.[64]

Sullivan's successor as president was Ted Haigler. A chance encounter with Garth Quinn, BW&Co.'s long-serving director and vice president who was close to Coe, had led to Haigler filling the vacant position of financial controller in 1970, returning to his home state, North Carolina, where the company was about to relocate.[65] His appointment as president and CEO in 1986 coincided with the imminent launch of the new anti-viral, AZT which would present issues which were ethical, social, and political, as well as medical and financial. These were to thrust BW&Co. into the international limelight-for the better and for the worse.

PART FIVE:

"What price is life?" Profiting from AIDS and responding to public outrage

CHAPTER 19

Breakthrough: Burroughs Wellcome & Co., AZT-Retrovir, and the AIDS epidemic

Vital outcomes of antimicrobial research at BW&Co. in the 1980s resulted from investigations initiated by Hitchings in the late 1940s. In collaboration with Gertrude Elion and Elvira Falco, Hitchings's research led in 1962 to the production and marketing of Marboran, a drug for use in the prevention and treatment of smallpox. Research by the same team during the 1970s led to the discovery of the antiviral drug trifluorothymidine, a topical solution to treat herpes eye infections which the company marketed as Viroptic.[1] Among several related compounds, to which BW&Co acquired the rights at that time, was zidovudine, a compound first isolated and tested in 1964 by Jerome Horwitz of the Michigan Cancer Research Foundation.[2] Further experimentation had been abandoned when tests related to cancer showed the compound to be ineffective; there had been no patent application.[3] During the 1970s, scientists at RTP had studied zidovidune as an antibacterial by testing for toxicity and identifying a similarity in molecular structure to that of the antiviral drug acylovir.[4] However, because of insufficient antibacterial activity, the research was discontinued and shelved. Increasing resources were required for RD&M regarding acyclovir as a treatment for herpes which would be launched as Zovirax in 1982, and Wellbutrin, the company's first attempt to enter the area of psychiatric illness, for which a launch was envisaged in 1985/6. Table 19.1 shows the rising proportion of expenditure on RD&M related to profit during the 1980s.

Immediately after Zovirax entered the market, the principal research focus began to shift in a new direction as a consequence of the emergence of a new and deadly disease which in 1981 began to arouse concern among some general practitioners. The acquired immunodeficiency syndrome (AIDS as it came to be called), was first recognized as a lethal multisystem disease and rapidly assumed proportions which seemed likely to present a major public health problem. The discovery of the disease by practising physicians in California and New York revealed vulnerable populations of gay men residing in San Francisco, Los Angeles, and New York City. Sexual intercourse and needle-sharing intravenous drug use were seen to be the cause of a

Table 19.1 *WFL/Wellcome plc R&D as percentage of sales and profit after tax, 1980–1990*

	R&D/sales	*R&D/profit*
1980	11	150
1981	10	158
1982	11	180
1983	12	212
1984	12	201
1985	12	188
1986	13	216
1987	13	146
1988	13	124
1989	13	110
1990	15	112

Source: GSK/WF/SCS 798, WFL/Wellcome plc accounts and annual reports.

disease perceived to be spreading rapidly. Unlike the hepatitis B virus which was a known microscopic pathogen mostly transmitted through blood or sexual contact, the HIV virus is known as a retrovirus (rather than a virus) because the process of replication is effected through transcribing its RNA (unique genetic material) into DNA after entering a host cell. This process, which is the reverse of usual genetic transcription, damaged the immune system to a degree that proved fatal. The new disease was transmitted by a human retrovirus through blood and sexual activity.

The disease spread rapidly, especially among those young gay men who inhabited "gay ghettoes" which originated during the 1970s.[5] Important organizing features of gay male life in those cities where the ghettoes evolved included patterns of "sexual availability, erotic apparel, reciprocity in sexual technique,"[6] characteristics of "erotic liberation" which became associated with high rates of STDs. A formalization of serious concern among the gay population in New York City led to the formation of the Gay Men's Health Crisis Group in 1981, a body intended to offer support to communities and which provided a model for similar bodies formed in San Francisco, Los Angeles, Boston, and Baltimore. Whereas primarily such groups were concerned with providing support and trying to ensure welfare, as the disease began to assume an epidemic scale, from the mid 1980s overtly political active bodies emerged to engage in campaigning, lobbying, and exercising pressure on national and state governments, the pharmaceutical business, scientific bodies, and medical and social work professionals.[7] This trend towards more militant campaigning, however, could emerge only after recognition of the seriousness of the problem within the offices of politicians at national and State level (and, not least important, the White House).

Advertising poster: "AIDS DON'T DIE OF IGNORANCE." The concern shared by governments across the world prompted efforts in the form of arresting poster campaigns intended to ensure that potential sufferers were informed of symptoms and how to avoid further infection the form of poster campaigns. Wellcome Trust, AIDS Poster collection: 1986, Wellcome Library, London.

That learning process awaited scientists' ability to offer some hope of treatment that would at least alleviate the suffering of those afflicted which would then raise questions of cost, access to treatment, and the development of an administrative strategy; those organizations involved in these processes became potential targets for criticism and action. As scientists began to make progress towards explaining the character, origins, and modes of transmission of infection, the possibility of its spread among a wider population prompted increased public concern, hence the prevailing sense of crisis surrounding the new disease.[8]

The threat was regarded as so serious that in April 1982, Congressman Henry Waxman convened meetings of the House of Representatives Subcommittee on Health and Environment to take stock of the imminent risk to public health. At the time when expert witnesses were cross-examined by the committee, more than five hundred cases had been reported to the US Centre for Disease Control (CDC), the government agency responsible for responding to communicable diseases through remedial action. Multiple deaths had occurred, evidence which led the *Washington Post* to refer to an epidemic.[9] One expert witness emphasized the urgency for scientists to discover a successful treatment for the disease which should not be underestimated. "Iceberg"[10] was a recurrent image used by witnesses to convey apprehension that an unknown disease afflicted a vulnerable, rapidly growing population of uncertain size. The immediate outcome of the proceedings was a bill introduced by Waxman that appropriated $15 million to fund research at the clinical centers of the National Institute of Health (NIH).[11] The CDC created a task force to gather information and investigate the findings published in a report in 1982. This was followed in the Spring of 1983 by an expression of confidence by public health officials that a transmissible agent that interfered with the immune system's ability to resist opportunistic infections and cancers was responsible for AIDS; even in the absence of any knowledge of a cause, guidelines were issued relating to sexual behavior among males and drug users in the hope of assisting with disease prevention.

During this early period, the search for a cause of AIDS was concentrated in the laboratories and clinics of the US National Institutes of Health (NIH). Once AIDS was classified as an infectious disease, the National Institute for Allergy and Infectious Diseases (NIAID) became the institutional center for coordinating research. The National Cancer Institute (NCI) had an active program in virological research where Robert C. Gallo, who was chief of the Laboratory of Tumor Cell Biology, began to direct attention to the search for human retroviruses. Henceforward, the NCI became the most important public body in the history of AIDS research. Outside the US, the Pasteur Institute in Paris, France, was the most important location where in 1982, virologists in the oncological unit led by Luc de Montagnier first turned their attention to AIDS. The work by both groups resulted in seminal publications. In May 1983, the French group was the first to report evidence of a viral protein with antibodies in AIDS patients that turned out to be the human immunodeficiency virus (HIV). A year later, Gallo's group at the NCI presented evidence that a single retrovirus caused AIDS, thereby providing researchers with a single target for blood-screening tests. This process of separate but "co-discovery"[12] was a significant turning-point in the progress towards a treatment and a product.

Although the NCI would shortly become a collaborator with BW&Co. in the next phase of investigation, the trigger, in part serendipitously, which had already sparked interest in AIDS research among scientists at RTP was a report on current research conducted at the Pasteur Institute in Paris shortly before publication of the findings in *Science* in May 1983. Francoise Berre-Sinoussi was a member of the group led by Luc Montagnier at the Pasteur Institute, but she was also the daughter of a friend of Cuatrecasas's mother. While on Berre-Sinoussi's visit to see her mother in the US, Cuatrecasas managed to arrange for her to visit Raleigh where she briefed senior scientists on the research in Paris.[13] This informal presentation proved to be sufficient to persuade Cuatrecasas and Barry, head of virology, to commit resources to AIDS-related investigations.[14]

Barry possessed a substantial record of clinical research into viral vaccine and antivirals in addition to equally relevant experience inside government-funded institutions before he joined BW&Co. in 1977. He had trained as a physician and spent five years as an employee of the NIH. He had also worked with the FDA, partly as a researcher (specifically related to the Yellow Fever vaccine) and partly as a regulator. Barry's recent practical experience of cooperation with the FDA, which had culminated in the commercially successful Zovirax IND, was another factor favorable to the formation and management of an unprecedented degree of corporate-government collaboration throughout the investigative process.[15] This breadth of experience was acknowledged by Waxman's Congressional subcommittee, convened in 1982, when Barry had appeared as an expert witness to report on viral research. As vice president research, once Cuatrecasas had decided to prioritize a search for a treatment for HIV/AIDS, he appointed Barry as the leader of a group at RTP consisting of a matrix of departments. Reporting to Barry were the heads of molecular biology, biochemical pharmacology, pharmacology, medicinal chemistry, experimental therapy, microbiology, and virology.[16]

The company's program on AIDs retrovirals was the subject of criticism by McKinsey consultants who considered that the research would be unlikely to result in products sold to populations of greater than a limited size and therefore would be financially undesirable.[17] Despite endorsement of this analysis by the president of BW&Co. (and by the marketing department), Cuatrecasas allowed the program to proceed in secret as a SKUNK project, of which the research committee and all staff involved in RD&M were aware, but which was unknown to marketing personnel and to senior managers outside RD&M, including Sullivan himself.[18] A screening program had commenced during the summer of 1984 when selected compounds previously synthesized from among the three hundred of those "on the shelf" at RTP, were tested.[19] Whereas, however, hitherto the normal practice had been to screen large numbers of compounds at random in search of antiviral activity, advances in molecular biology had increased the possibility of identifying precisely which enzymes the virus required to reproduce itself in the cell and which of its genes were coded for those proteins. The study of the AIDS virus at the Pasteur Institute and at the NIC, published in the current literature, demonstrated the advantages of adopting this "rational" approach which was now embraced by researchers at RTP in a systematic attempt to design a drug possessing specific viral functions.[20]

While the initial impetus for AIDS-related research at RTP originated with work at the Pasteur Institute, the pace and scale of the search was transformed by collaboration between BW&Co., Duke University, and the NCI, beginning in October 1984. The figure who initiated this development was Dr Sam Broder who in 1980 had become head of the clinical oncology program at NCI, an institution charged with protecting public health and whose laboratories were well-equipped to test potential anti-retroviral agents. The organization possessed substantial experience of screening chemicals for anti-cancerous properties and an extensive record of conducting clinical trials. As head of the oncology program, Broder had participated in an innovative intramural clinical undertaking, the distinctive feature of which was the integration of laboratory with clinical activities such as to promote a free flow of information and which enabled individuals "to traffic in both scientific and clinical ideas."[21] Alongside this culture of inter-disciplinary exchange of knowledge, was the record of the NCI in focusing heavily on searching for new cancer drugs and, in effect, behaving "as a pharmaceutical company" working for the public in a difficult area "where the private sector either could not, or would, not make a commitment." However, while the NCI possessed an outstanding record in cancer research, Dr Robert Yarchoan, one of Broder's principal clinical investigators, acknowledged the limitations of NCI scientists with respect to drug *discovery* which he regarded as the special province of pharmaceutical companies.[22]

Broder devised an innovative plan intended to accelerate the search for an effective treatment for the disease, by now named HIV/AIDS. Compounds which had been tested in relation to other medical conditions, but had been discarded either because of showing low activity or high toxicity, might offer a more productive line of investigation in the context of the AIDS-related research then gathering momentum at the NCI. Broder envisaged the role of the NCI as undertaking tests for anti-HIV activity using promising compounds, regardless of source, acknowledging that some pharmaceutical companies might be in possession of potential drug candidates unlikely to receive the corporate investment necessary for transforming a chemical into an acceptable treatment. He also believed that a commercial partner or partners in the private sector would enable his team to circumvent an NHI bureaucracy which could slow down the process of finding an effective treatment. Initially, Broder approached several leading companies, including Pfizer, to propose a joint strategy intended to combine efforts to speed the process of developing a promising compound into an NDA. Such an arrangement would include support and advice from the NCI. Protection for a company's proprietary rights was to be assured by delivery of the drugs to the NCI under code to ensure concealment of the drug's identity. In return for testing and the circumvention of federal bureaucracy, any company agreeing to collaborate was expected to commit to developing and commercializing potentially effective drugs. None responded positively.[23] Yarchoan, from Broder's group, described the lack of interest by paraphrasing the general response attributed to the companies which had been approached thus, "Look it is an epidemic, but there are only 50,000 people with the disease and we cannot justify a big program to our shareholders for 50,000 people."[24] Initial failure of Broder's overtures to the large leading companies was followed by an initiative undertaken in October 1984 after a positive response from RTP to Broder's general appeal. Dr Dani Bolagnesi, a senior researcher at Duke University Medical Centre, whom Yarchoan decribed as an expert medicinal chemist/pharmacologist, convened a meeting between Broder and senior scientists at RTP.[25] He was connected to BW&Co.'s network of researchers and would have been familiar with the antiviral research insights obtained during the research and development which had led to Zovirax in 1982, described by Elion as the "platform on which the development of the AIDS drug was built."[26] Bolagnesi would also have been acquainted with staff possessing nucleoside expertise and doubtless with the recent screening program introduced by Barry only months previously during the summer of 1984.[27]

Having failed to enlist one of the industry's large manufacturers, Broder had visited senior scientists at RTP, later recalling that "to their credit they were the first to make a serious commitment".[28] By the time Broder visited RTP, scientists in the microbiology department had already chosen twelve compounds to take down from the shelf for further study, one of which was azidothymidine, or 509 US1 (initially known as AZT) which was discovered to be active against an animal virus.[29] Samples were sent to Duke University where Kent Weinhold, a cellular immunologist who had collaborated with Phillip Furman in the virology department at RTP, had begun to work with the human AIDS virus in his own laboratory shortly before the samples were received.[30]

In an informal meeting, Broder explained the NCI's aims and capabilities, reported results from recent screening, and outlined his vision for public-private collaboration in a program designed to find a cure for HIV. The NCI could supplement BW&Co.'s murine retrovirus experience with its own expertise regarding HIV to form an effective basis for collaboration. On behalf of the NCI, Broder guaranteed that in the event that a joint venture was agreed, then the company would have ownership of any resulting product. The outcome of the meeting, albeit through an informal agreement, was a partnership between the company and the NIH, committed to a common objective: to find a compound active against HTLV-III with which to tackle HIV/AIDS, and to file a successful NDA.[31] Henceforward, the company, scientists at the NCI and at Duke, and officials of the FDA were in continuous communication at every stage of development and testing.[32] Broder had been impressed by members of BW&Co. staff who "were willing to do things, to develop products, and not just to talk. They were willing to exchange information and provide drugs that could be tested … they were pretty clear that they would make a commitment to try to develop and commercialize a product that looked good."[33]

The *in vitro* studies of HIV positive samples presented a potential personal risk which analysts at BW&Co. were not prepared to undertake because the laboratories at RTP did not offer the highest levels of biosafety. The NCI also lacked such facilities, but Broder decided to proceed nonetheless, at some risk to himself and to Yarchoan.[34] In March 1985, screening demonstrated that AZT had significant *in vitro* activity against HIV which enabled the NCI to report to BW&Co. that the compound was the most active against human AIDS virus of any compound tested hitherto. After ten weeks during which the necessary animal toxicity data were collected, the company, in collaboration with the NCI, filed a submission to the FDA which after only seven days, on June 22nd 1985, received approval for IND exemption.[35] The speed of this process reflected the widespread concern within the FDA at the rapid pace of the spread of AIDS infection in the US.[36]

Phase I trials involved humans and were intended to establish dosage levels by testing rather than to measure efficiency. They began on 3 July 1985, some at the clinical center of the NCI where Yarchoan and Broder administered a dose of the drug to the first patient, and some at Duke laboratories conveniently located which enabled the company's scientists also to be involved.[37] Of the thirty-five patients selected, eleven died in the course of the six months' study as a result of the level of toxicity.[38] In addition to certain clinical improvements registered by the survivors was the discovery that zidovidune penetrated the blood barrier and was therefore potentially effective in treating HIV infection of the nervous system.[39] This marked a crucial stage in transition to a phase II trial which tested the strength of the collaborative arrangement. Phase II trials would establish both the efficacy and safety of the drug necessary to cross the bridge from research to therapy and its delivery as a marketable product. A 1982 report issued by the US President's Commission had produced evidence of conventions and bureaucracy associated with publicly-funded bodies which Cuatrecasas and Barry believed would result in delays towards the agreed objective, which was to deliver a product in the shortest time possible. For that reason, they decided to avoid placing the phase II trial under the control of NIH, thereby preempting anticipated endless arguments within the scientific community.

Unlike phase I, the phase II trial was a multi-center, double-blind, placebo-controlled study aimed at examining the effectiveness of zidovudine in a larger patient population. Initially, the population consisted of one hundred and sixty AIDS patients and one hundred and twenty-two AIDS-related complex (ARC) patients, each displaying multiple signs and symptoms of severe illness. The phase II trial was conducted at twelve medical centers across the country where the NIH had created "AIDS treatment evaluation units".[40] In addition to thirty investigators from within BW&Co., participants in the planning process for phase II included Broder, Yarchoan, and Hiroaki Mitsuya, a postdoctoral fellow working with Broder, who together comprised a self-styled "War Council against AIDS."[41]

One particular feature of phase II was highly controversial. Neither patients nor those administering medication knew which dosage was the placebo and which the drug. This feature of the trial aroused furious debate over the ethics of such a procedure (the most rigorous form of trial which in 1982 the President's Commission had advocated banning "whenever possible"[42]). Critics argued that the toxicity of the drug was too great to justify administering it to already weakened AIDS patients; they also accused the company of limiting the availability of the drug.[43] Despite criticism, phase II proceeded as planned on 3 July 1985, including the placebo-controlled double-blind trials. They attracted the attention of patient advocacy groups and other watchdog organizations whose rising expectations led to attempts to intervene in the normal process of drug approval. Their activities and the progress of the trials themselves were widely reported in the media. Partly as a response to the high level of interest within the AIDS community and the criticism leveled at phase II, NIAID, (the federal research group involved in the study) assumed responsibility for an intensified coordination of AIDs related drug development. NIAID convened an independent board, the Data and Safety Monitoring Board (DSMB), which was charged with reviewing all patient data at frequent intervals and with submitting reports on identifiable trends.[44] In September 1986, within seven months of the trial's launch in March, none of the one hundred and forty-five patients receiving AZT had died, whereas sixteen deaths had occurred among the one hundred and thirty-seven placebo patient cohort. This stark contrast led to the immediate termination of the trial, only seven months after it had begun.[45] In consideration of the ethical issues arising, all patients receiving the placebo were transferred to the AZT regime forthwith.[46] The phase II trial had achieved speedy and relatively unambiguous results. Meanwhile, as toxicologic pharmacologic testing proceeded, scaling-up began at RTP in preparation for manufacture on a commercial scale.[47]

Broder's admission of a degree of acquiescence when the company took control of phase II implies some reservations at NCI. However, in retrospect, both he

David Barry, at a press conference announcing the premature termination of the placebo-controlled Retrovir trial. Barry was a Yale graduate in medicine whose experience while employed by the NIH and the FDA and at his research at Rockefeller Foundation preceded his appointment at BW&Co. in 1977 to lead clinical investigations into viral vaccine and antiviral research. A central figure in the SKUNKWORKS project which led to the development of Retrovir, later Barry joined with Cresswell in an attempt to secure a merger of WFL with Warner Lambert, of which, by that time, Cresswell was research director. Wellcome News, Wellcome Library, London.

and Yarchoan acknowledged that the decision to proceed quickly (and to adopt a controversial method of trialling) proved to have been justified. They believed that their own approach to drug development was closer to that of the company's scientists than to that of many other scientific researchers (colleagues working in public institutions) of whom Broder was critical for adopting "skepticism as the format of science."[48] He believed that the pursuit of perfection tended to delay implementation of a new therapy.[49] Yarchoan expressed a similar view and approved the preparedness of the company's scientists to proceed with clinical testing even in the presence of a little toxicity because "they really felt that they only had one shot to show that it was working."[50]

By the time the phase II trial had ended, even President Reagan had been persuaded of the serious threat presented by AIDS. In 1981, he had appointed C. Everitt Koop, a pediatric surgeon, as Surgeon General. Amidst growing concern among medical practitioners, as well as sufferers, Koop was well aware of the threat to public health posed by AIDS, but party political considerations and a sceptical President prevented him from addressing the issue until 1986, when (within a year of the death from AIDS of the Hollywood film star, Rock Hudson, a personal friend of Reagan), the President ordered Koop to prepare a special report on the nature and causes of the epidemic. By that time, WHO was predicting that the epidemic would assume global proportions. In October, Koop's findings were incorporated in an explicit report which explained the causes and characteristics of AIDS, highlighted the seriousness of the threat and outlined methods of avoidance, including condom use. Twenty million copies were distributed through members of Congress, public health organizations, and parent teacher associations.[51] In the same month, an early morning meeting of the research committee at RTP ended abruptly when members were informed of an urgent summons to attend a meeting in Washington beginning at noon the same day. Others attending the meeting were the under-secretary of health and the assistant secretary of health who were joined later by the FDA commissioner. President Reagan kept in touch with progress from the White House by telephone. The outcome of nearly 20 hours of vigorous discussion resulted in agreement that the company should proceed to construct an NDA within four months, the fastest considered possible by the delegation; on behalf of the FDA, the commissioner undertook to ensure approval within four months of receipt of the NDA documentation.

The FDA also agreed to relax its usual most stringent requirements prior to approving a drug even for limited release. The declared purpose of the new policy was not to implement a clinical trial but to expand clinicians' limited knowledge of the drug, its safety, effectiveness, and the way in which the AIDS syndrome might respond to other therapeutic interventions, whether conventional or innovative. This was to be achieved through a new FDA category of "treatment IND" (investigational new drug) which was immediately applied to AZT. The new treatment IND program was accompanied by conferral by the FDA of "orphan status" on the drug (normally reserved for important drugs in relation to public health with small market potential and therefore not deemed to be a commercial; proposition). The effect of this was to reduce pre-clinical and clinical requirements normally necessary for drug approval; orphan status also gave the company 72 per cent tax subsidy for its clinical trials and a 25 per cent tax credit for increased research and development, benefits which later became subjects of controversy.

A more contentious issue arising at the October White House meeting was the health officials' strongly expressed view that the US government must be in a position to announce that the drug would be available immediately. Cresswell recalled the company delegation being told "very plainly that we had to...begin to put this drug out there on a compassionate use basis".[52] This presented the company with a problem. Because the drug was not a cure, continuous treatment would be necessary to reduce the viral load and maintain patients in a steady state. Added to this requirement was the fact that the supply of thymidine, the raw material from which the drug was made,[53] was strictly limited, consequently rationing needed to be imposed. The delegation estimated the number of patients receiving treatment should not exceed four thousand candidates in the US and one thousand in the UK, a formula adopted by health officials and the FDA representative. The remaining contentious proposal from health officials was that inquiries regarding entitlement to enrol on the new program should be submitted via the company's telephone line at RTP. Alarmed by the prospect of switchboard meltdown, the company delegation successfully resisted the proposal. Furthermore, mindful of anticipated media criticism damaging to the company's image, the delegation also succeeded in securing a compromise which avoided the company shouldering sole responsibility for allocation.[54] A new committee formed for the purpose included representatives of BW&Co., the FDA, and NIAID. The resulting protocol was based on the model already used for the distribution of cancer drugs not available for purchase. In addition to choosing those in the greatest need, the application of carefully specified eligibility criteria also formed the starting point for an analysis of a computerized data base constructed from data compiled from requests for patients submitted by those physicians who were participating in the program. The co-ordinating committee also controlled the actual distribution of the drug.[55]

Without proceeding to a phase III trial therefore, between October and December 1986, the company prepared an NDA, filing data and information to the FDA; the final tranche was delivered on 2 December 1986. On 16 January 1987, the FDA advisory committee recommended approval of AZT for selected patients. During the period covered by the treatment IND between September 1986 and March 1987, 4,500 AIDS patients, estimated to be roughly one-third of all living AIDS patients in the US, had received AZT. To enable the patients to receive the treatment free of charge, BW&Co. incurred costs of roughly $10 million which were supplemented by government subsidy.[56] As the number of reported cases rose to 71,000 and associated deaths reached 41,000,[57] the advisory committee recommended dispensing with a phase III trial and extending approval for use in a wider population of AIDS and ARC sufferers, though still limited to the treatment of the most severely affected HIV patients.[58] The completed NDA was reviewed by the anti-infective drugs committee in February 1987 when, despite reservations regarding the length, scope, and methodology used in the application and the long-term risks of AZT due to high toxicity, almost unanimously and with unprecedented speed (barely one hundred days), the committee recommended approval.[59] Complementary to the commitment and energy applied by Barry and his team was Broder's ability to cut through the usual bureaucratic procedures. This was instrumental in accelerating the process of development.[60]

The intention of the FDA to recommend formal approval on 19 March 1987 had been communicated to BW&Co on 6 March and announced at a meeting of managers and scientists by George Lyon, M.D., director of drug regulatory affairs at BW&Co.[61] The press conference that followed was attended by Broder and Donna Mildvan (chief of infectious diseases at the Beth Israel Medical Centre in New York). Mildvan pronounced the toxicity of the drug to be manageable, an opinion based on her experience from which she was able to draw examples of patient care. Broder referred to "probably the fastest drug development in the history of ethical pharmacology."[62] The FDA's approval of AZT for distribution was forthcoming only twenty-eight months after the first clinical trial began. From its existence as a compound on the shelf at RTP in 1984, within three years AZT had become available for distribution to pharmacists throughout the US. This compared with an average eight-year process for other major drug innovations to move from discovery to marketed product. Formal approval was accompanied by a press statement from the FDA announcing the release of AZT, a declaration which attracted major publicity, not least because such a public endorsement of a drug by the FDA was unprecedented.[63] On 17 September 1987, in preparation for normal marketing, the company filed for a patent on the product AZT-Retrovir. By this time, in order to avoid confusion with a different product, the name of the drug, hitherto widely- known as AZT, had been superseded by the trade name Retrovir, a trademark already registered and available for use.[64] In addition to the US and the UK, the drug was registered in twelve other countries where the company had received licenses to supply.[65] This enlargement of potential demand coincided with a further stimulus from within the US. In 1988, the Surgeon General's office issued a seven-page pamphlet based on his 1986 report entitled *Understanding AIDS*, which was circulated to all 107 million households, the largest mailing in American history.[66]

Between March and September, the company was free to market the drug to physicians who were now able to prescribe Retrovir as the first approved treatment for AIDS. The continuing limited available supply necessitated prolonging the protocol which was applied to patients who had been selected to participate in the IND treatment program, though access to the drug was extended to include others outside the program judged by the same criteria.[67] The announcement that rationing would continue because of short supply met with immediate criticism from within the AIDS community. The company took steps to deflect this by entering into a contract with Biospherics Inc. This organization was experienced in managing the allocation of medical services for the NCI through physicians employed by the NCI who determined which patients met the selection criteria and qualified for treatment. The same model was applied to Retrovir under the treatment IND until adequate supplies became available from September 1987 when arm's length distribution arrangements became unnecessary and the contract with Biospherics redundant.[68] During the interim period, the functions of the Retrovir center were complementary to those of Biospherics and continued to exist after the Biosphere contract had been terminated. The center was managed by the epidemiology, information, and surveillance divisions within the company's medical department. Physicians enrolled eligible patients to whom the center assigned coded numbers to facilitate anonymous monitoring. Pharmacists who received prescriptions for the drug placed orders with the center where checking occurred before arranging for the dispatch of prescription orders from Greenville within two weeks of a patient's initial enrolment.[69] The center also responded to telephone calls regarding AIDS, Retrovir, and to inquiries concerned with the criteria for eligibility to receive the drug.

FDA approval of Retrovir was contingent on an assurance of continuing close collaboration between BW&Co. and the FDA. The company was required to continue to research the drug with a view to improving safety and efficacy in the long-term and its suitability for the treatment of different and diverse patient populations; the results of each study were to be reported to the FDA for discussion. The company introduced a two-year study to follow up all patients who had been enrolled under the treatment IND program as well as a three-year study of 1,500 AIDS patients at several major treatment centers.[70] In March 1987, having already been approved for use with patients suffering the most severe manifestation of HIV, attention had turned to determine the usefulness of Retrovir at earlier stages of HIV infection and its efficacy in different types of populations. Monitors continued to follow patients who had entered the first placebo-controlled study in 1986 to accumulate data on the long-term use of the drug. In addition to pediatric studies, the company embarked on an investigation to determine the effect of treatment of asymptomatic patients in the earliest stage of HIV, a study which was funded by the NIH. Clinical trials combining Retrovir with Zovirax were the first of several investigations into combination therapies intended to reduce toxicity and improve the efficacy of AIDS therapy. One result was the adoption of lower prescription levels of AZT dosage which was a success for the researchers, the effect of which, from 1988, was to moderate demand and depress BW&Co.'s sales.[71]

However, an offsetting factor resulted from the August 1989 report of the first national study, begun by NIAID in 1987, which provided significant evidence of the safety and efficacy of Retrovir. The study had involved 2,000 AIDS patients, some presenting severe AIDS-related complex, others showing only early symptoms. The new drug and a placebo were administered in roughly equal populations until the study was brought to an abrupt halt in August 1989 when the Data and Safety Monitoring Board broke the code, thereby terminating the trial. A review of the data revealed evidence that the drug had been effective in delaying the development of full-blown AIDS in people who displayed early symptoms of the disease, that side effects were at a low level, and that the drug could be regarded as safe. Those receiving the placebo were given Retrovir forthwith. The consequent approval extended to the drug enabled patients who, hitherto had met the criteria for serious illness, to be treated with AZT in the US to rise immediately from 30,000 to 45,000.[72] From September, when normal marketing of the drug would begin, the effect of the FDA's release of Retrovir for use in treating a wider patient population over and above those who had met the serious illness criteria for limited use was to expand the potential market for Retrovir to levels estimated at 200,000 in the US alone and to 600,000 worldwide.[73]

Retrovir represented an important therapeutic breakthrough, but Broder believed that it was also significant in providing the model for corporate-government relations which could ensure greater efficiency and speed in the delivery of drugs in the future.[74] AIDS protest groups drew the same conclusion and sought to secure the incorporation of Broder's methods of circumventing the normal process into FDA regulations. Beginning in 1987, pressure from the AIDS lobby secured relaxation of the regulations. Henceforward, all terminal patients (not limited to AIDS sufferers) were permitted to receive an experimental drug on condition that no other treatment was available and that the drug was deemed to show "promise." For their part, during the experimental phase, drug companies were required to charge no more than "cost price" and to ensure that recipients were limited to those in most need.[75] A further innovation was NIAID's adoption of a new role similar to that taken in the development of Retrovir. Following the precedent established by Broder in 1985, in his tiny laboratory at the NCI, the network of physicians that had been established and mobilized by NIAID in the course of clinical testing offered opportunities for those pharmaceutical companies which were considered to be experimenting with drugs showing promise.[76] One effect of the FDA's ruling to relax regulations regarding patient eligibility was to place pressure on the supplier.

An enlarged level of demand would be the result, but predicting how large the scale of expansion might be, and its effect on costs, complicated the economics of the production of Retrovir.

CHAPTER 20

The economics of AZT: The supply, costs, and pricing of Retrovir, the AIDS drug

The initial problem affecting the supply of Retrovir in the earliest stage of development was caused by the limited availability of the natural base from which the drug was produced. This was because thymidine was a nucleoside derived from the DNA of the sperm of herring and salmon and therefore difficult for the company to obtain.[1] Broder solved the problem by arranging for the shipment of a sufficient supply from the NCI's own stock to allow the phase I clinical trial to begin.[2] However, even securing supplies of thymidine in sufficient quantity to release Retrovir for treating only the most severe AIDS cases during the eighteen months of the IND presented further difficulties. The responsibility for increasing production at Greenville fell to Gabriel Cipau, formerly head of chemical and plant development and engineering at RTP who since 1979, had been vice president in charge of manufacturing before being elevated to the board of BW&Co. in 1984. He soon discovered that Pfizer had already succeeded in synthesizing thymidine and possessed technology and plant in Germany capable of a production process. This involved a complex multi-step, time-consuming sequence which included ten chemical reactions.

The initial supply of the raw material from Heinrich Mack, the German subsidiary of Pfizer, was purchased for $750 per kilo, the purpose of which was not known by the small supplier. However, all was revealed once it became necessary to approach Pfizer with a view to an adequate supply of synthesized thymidine to meet the requirements of full scale production at Greenville. Pfizer justified more than doubling the price of larger scale production by the costs involved in the complex and therefore expensive process which was dangerous and required changing the production schedules of several plants.[3] In December 1986, Cipau negotiated a complicated non-exclusive ten-year licensing agreement with Pfizer which involved a combination of guaranteed volumes purchased and, once commercial production began under license, royalties to be paid on a reducing sliding scale. In return for an initial monopoly, the contract between Pfizer and BW&Co. gave the Wellcome group non-exclusive worldwide rights and license to use the technology, patented or unpatented, for the commercial

George Hitchings and Gertrude Elion. The FDA's approval of ATZ coincided with the joint award in 1988 of a Nobel prize to Hitchings and Elion for their record of research and development which laid the foundations for the successful outcomes of the company's anti viral programmes during the 1980s. *Wellcome News.*

scale organic synthesis of thymidine. Should, as envisaged, BW&Co. establish its own capacity for production, Pfizer would receive a royalty-free, non-exclusive worldwide license covering all improvements to the technology, patented or unpatented, made by BW&Co. or its third party subcontractors during the ten-year agreement.[4] The agreement allowed for annual re-negotiation, an option which encouraged a rapid search for an alternative, competitive source of supply.[5]

In December 1987, BW&Co. reached agreement with the ChemGen Corporation to fund a research program intended to develop a microbial process for producing thymidine from sugar. It was envisaged that ChemGen would patent the know-how and BW&Co. would receive an exclusive worldwide license with a right to sub-license, either to produce or to enable a third party to produce thymidine.[6] Mindful of the frustration within the AIDS community because of rationing even before the commercial production of Retrovir began, a decision was made not to adopt an optimal efficiency just-in-time inventory model, but to build sufficient stock to meet predicted demand at the time of the launch. This was acknowledged to be a costly policy requiring cash to meet interest on accumulated stocks, but some directors expressed a fear that should stocks of the drug run out, they would face the risk of being "lynched as murderers" by AIDS campaigners.[7]

The unavoidable continuance of restricted availability of the drug following final FDA clearance was not the only constraint to occasion antagonism within the AIDS community. The pricing of Retrovir presented the company with a particular dilemma at a time when sufferers, medical professionals, politicians, and journalists awaited the decision. Inevitably, the price was determined by the company's physical capacity to supply and its ability to balance costs against expected demand. Measuring predicted demand was highly problematical. Statistical estimates available to the company were those issued by WHO; 200,000 worldwide in 1988. The ARC population was assumed to be a multiple of this figure[8] but in the US alone, WHO estimated the number between 150,000 and 200,000.[9] Yet from the company's standpoint, numbers of those afflicted was a flawed basis for estimating the level of effective demand. The lack of public awareness of sexually transmitted diseases and the taboo surrounding the contraction of the condition had presented a problem which the company had already encountered in the marketing of Zovirax. Unlike herpes, however, AIDS was a completely new condition, was terminal, and was believed to be transmitted under circumstances that attracted even greater and more widespread social disapproval than those associated with heterosexual promiscuity. The company sponsored a survey which showed that in a population aged between eighteen and forty years, 52 per cent were somewhat or very concerned about STDs, thought most did not feel at risk of infection; 62 per cent had never enquired of a sexual partner about having an STD. Only if patients presented themselves to medical practitioners or other health professionals for testing, diagnosis, and prescription, would demand for Retrovir grow beyond those in whom the symptoms and condition of HIV/Aids were advanced. One implication was that early attention to methods of communicating with health professionals would be as crucial as pricing to the level of demand and commercial success of the drug. The timing of the preparation of plans for marketing therefore took precedence before taking a decision on price.

Gabriel Cipau, formerly head of chemical and plant development and engineering at Greenville since 1970, he became vice president in charge of manufacturing and board member of BW&Co. He bore most responsibility for planning and organizing the new Greenville factory and for the large scale commercial production of Septra, Zovirax and, most challenging of all, Retrovir.

Until Retrovir was launched into the market, the company's priority was to inform health professionals of the research which lay behind the development of the drug. In January 1987, building on previous experience of sponsoring symposia focused on the herpes simplex virus and Zovirax, the company entered into a $0.6 million contract with World Health Communications to plan and implement a teleforum focused on antiviral research and AIDS which was conducted simultaneously in fourteen American cities.[10] This was the first of a series of smaller symposia, seminars, and presentations at hospitals which formed the core of the program which also included the dissemination of publications resulting from such meetings. On an altogether different scale, the Wellcome International Antiviral Symposium held in Monte Carlo in December 1987, attracted seven hundred antiviral specialists from forty-six countries. Clinical investigators and scientists from eighteen countries reported on findings from clinical trials and post-epidemiological surveys; much of the information and many of the findings reported were hitherto unpublished. Teleconferences organized by Biospherics Inc. enabled members attending a meeting of the American Academy of Dermatology in San Antonio and those at the meeting of the American Society of Hematology in Washington DC to participate interactively with those assembled in Monte Carlo. The *American Journal of Medicine* devoted a special issue to the drug which included more than fifty articles provided by participants in the symposium.[11] At the same time, in San Francisco and New York, where AIDS and ARC patients were concentrated, sales representatives received specialized preparation for updating physicians individually.

A lack of awareness among the public, either of the risk of infection or of the possible consequences of contracting STDs, or how and when to seek treatment, explains why, in addition to informing the researchers and other health professionals, the company also focused on educating the public. The messages, directed towards those at risk of contracting diseases (whether transmitted sexually or through drug use), described the symptoms, the consequences, and the necessity of testing for diagnosis and treatment. Composing promotional literature proved to be problematic as TV networks baulked at the use of the word "genital" in the BW&Co.'s self-examination advertisements which the agency was compelled to prepare without even mentioning the relevant products.[12]

Whereas AIDS activists were divided in their opinions about rationing, distribution methods, and advertising, the company's pricing policy attracted universal condemnation among patient advocates, lobbyists, and many leading politicians. The price of Retrovir became a major political issue attracting extensive coverage in the media nationwide. Little detailed financial evidence on the precise formula employed has survived to explain how the figure was reached. Although Sullivan was no longer president when Retrovir was launched, his remarks on pricing relating to Zovirax suggest the approach to pricing decision-making at RTP during the 1980s was to "... price a drug the same way you price any other commodity: what you think the customer would pay for it ... you look at what is already being sold, and see how much that cost the patient ...; determine are we as good as, or better, than that other commodity? ... for example with the first anti-herpes treatment you ask yourself: how much, given the alternative, how much is someone willing to pay in order to get relief from the condition? ... you would have a base of cost, but in prescription pharmaceuticals the cost of production was always in a range that was not a determining factor in what you charge."[13] The view expressed by his successor, Haigler, was similar, though when he was interviewed by a journalist for the *Pharmaceutical Executive* at the time when the price of AZT had attracted the interest of Congress (including a letter signed by fifty-four members) as well as pressure groups, Haigler posed the question "What price is life?"[14] to which an anticipated response that life is priceless might imply the possibility of justifying a range anywhere between production cost and infinity. The responsibility for preparing a proposal for pricing the new drug for board discussion fell to Gabriel Cipau, head of manufacturing. His parameters consisted of a combination of costs, opportunity costs, and what the market would bear.

Uncertainty surrounding ongoing trials and, at least in the short run, the prospect of a limited patient base provided the immediate context for discussions about the price of Retrovir, by the board of BW&Co. at RTP in December 1986 for recommendation to the WFL board in January 1987. Four Americans attended the London meeting: Haigler the new president and CEO of BW&Co., Schaeffer the vice-president research, and Cresswell who had moved from RTP to London as group development director and was a member of the main board. Cipau's explicit starting assumption was that the main objective of the pricing strategy should be to maximize revenue and to ensure that after all expenditure related to Retrovir had been recouped, an additional margin must ensure a return for shareholders.[15] However, whereas production costs were measurable, the ability of patients to pay was not. Cipau interpreted the Californian legislature's preparation of an AIDS strategy as evidence which suggested that patients might be assisted by government and insurance organizations. The Californian legislature had already authorized Medi-Cal to provide full reimbursement for any drug approved by the FDA for the treatment of AIDS patients (in March 1987 it would announce state Medi-Cal funding specifically for Retrovir). Therefore, Cipau assumed that contributions towards funding the treatment would be forthcoming from government and insurance organizations and would mitigate the burden on some patients. None the less, until Retrovir secured FDA approval for the treatment of patients at early stages of HIV, the potential numbers of patients who might qualify, possess the financial resources, and elect to submit for testing to obtain a prescription, would remain limited. The other assumption included among Cipau's general corporate concerns, was the period of patent protection that would be secured for Retrovir which, he assumed, would enable the company to monopolize HIV/AIDS therapy for at least two years.

Cipau argued that it was "reasonable to begin with a reasonably high price which could be reduced if this was thought appropriate."[16] He also believed that it would be advantageous to limit supplies available to those patients who were seriously ill. He explained justification for a reasonably high cost of Retrovir in terms of opportunity cost because it was "easy to demonstrate that the cost of treatment with Retrovir on any realistic basis of pricing was cheaper for the patient/community than treatment without ... taking into consideration such factors as morbidity and mortality."[17] When these factors were taken into account, it became clear that Retrovir could claim to offer an enormous additional advantage, upon which corporate affairs vice president Kennedy elaborated. He emphasized the cost-effectiveness of Retrovir from the standpoint both of patients and their funders, maintaining that the treatment could reduce the direct medical costs of AIDS patients in the first year by at least 25 per cent of the palliative care costs needed, and of those required for ARC patients by 60 per cent.[18] Similar considerations were explored in the marketing division of WFL in London where a group convened to consider the promotion and marketing of the drug in the UK and elsewhere outside North America. The group was advised by an (unnamed) economics professor who was regarded as a pioneer in the development of health economics. It seems probable that his cost benefit analysis which impressed those who had hired him, indirectly affected the board's attitude towards pricing.[19] The conclusion reached by the group was that, even at an unprecedentedly high price, the formula which focused on the prevention of the hospitalization of the patient at £X per day would enable the company to demonstrate to the National Health Service in the UK the potential for substantial cost savings.[20]

If supply costs of Retrovir provided a floor for pricing, opportunity cost related to palliative care appears to have been accepted as an upper limit. The cost of thymidine set a floor at a relatively high level. Expenditure on inventories amounted to 46 per cent of total cost expenditure, capital investment was 16 per cent, RD&M 10 per cent, and sales and distribution costs 7 per cent.

This was the financial exposure which resulted from incremental expenditure only, i.e. before apportioning overheads. The cost of thymidine was approximately $300 per kilo before the expensive six-step conversion into Retrovir which included capsuling and packaging costs. The ex-factory cost of Retrovir was estimated at $15,000 per kilo (equivalent to a cost of $5,500 per patient per year assuming a daily dose of one gram). Based on WHO estimates and uncertain predictions for take-up, anticipated sales of Retrovir during the first year of production were $123 million.[21] Cipau recommended an initial wholesale price of $188 for one hundred capsules, an amount adequate for treatment for seventeen days. Because in 1987, the required dose for chronic patients was unusually high, eight capsules daily at four hourly intervals, the wholesale price for annual treatment was $7,000. These would be required as a lifetime treatment, unlike Zovirax which treated genital herpes. This unprecedentedly high price, which excluded hospital and other care costs, implied an annual cost of treatment for the patient of between $8,000 and $10,000.[22] Even the $8,000 represented nearly one-third of the median US household income in 1987.[23]

Other members of the WFL board also favored a high price, mainly because for many years the return on capital in the UK had been low and revenue from sales and profits from old products had declined.[24] There was agreement on the general principle that price should take account of the R&D cost of the parent company's past failure.[25] Shepperd sympathized with the view, expressed by the manager responsible for preparing pricing proposals in the UK, that the new drug should be charged "at a high price and then let it creep up."[26] Haigler's impression was that Shepperd appeared

Table 20.1 *Initial estimated costs and revenues relating to Retrovir*

RETROVIR (£million)	*GROUP Nov. 1987 INC*	*EXPOSURE FABS*	*Nov. 1987 INC*	*Aug. 1991 Projected FABS*
R&D				
USA	9.4	19.8	29.6	59.2
ROW	1.5	4.6	10.4	19.8
WF Group	10.9	24.4	40.0	79.0
CAPITAL INVESTMENT				
USA	8.0			
ROW	9.5			
INVENTORY				
USA	33.8			
ROW	16.0			
Group	49.8			
INTEREST	8.0			
COST OF SALES				
USA	5.1			
ROW	2.0			
TOTAL Expenditure	107.7	121.2		
Less REVENUE				
USA Sales	32.1	21.5		
ROW Sales	7.4	4.2		
	39.5	39.5		
Exposure	68.2	81.7		

INC = Incremental Expenditure wholly or mainly on research
FABS = Full absorption: incremental expense plus apportionment of overheads.
Source: GSK/WF/SCS 1274, Chairman's marketing and R&D committee, 11 Nov. 1987.

to have been comfortable about an even higher price than that proposed by Cipau.[27] However, Cipau's proposal, unanimously supported by the BW&Co. board, was accepted. The price for the UK market was set at 20 higher and even more higher in other European markets at levels perceived to be "what the local market would bear."[28]

Unlike the WFL directors, Cipau had left open the possibility of reducing the price in the US "if appropriate." This pragmatic approach showed his sensitivity to the mood in the US. He correctly anticipated media criticism of the company for delaying supply of the drug (a consequence of the decision to accumulate sufficient stocks to avoid disappointment for patients when the normal release of Retrovir commenced) and for excess profit-making. On Cipau's recommendation, the main board created a task force to consider how to protect the company's reputation, to coordinate and develop information strategies designed for specific audiences (patient interest groups and the professional medical and healthcare community), and to devise the most efficient way of communicating information to the various interest groups. The small task force, which was chaired by Cresswell and included representatives from RTP and Beckenham, concentrated on practical ways of avoiding excessive adverse publicity. At the same time, a firm of public relations consultants was engaged to act for the Wellcome group as a whole.

The solution proposed by the task force was a scheme which, through collaboration through a consortium with three other major companies, might divert the full force of the anticipated public condemnation directed towards the Wellcome organization However, the board rejected the proposal as unworkable because it would create legal and managerial problems. Criticism was inevitable.[29] The price of Retrovir in the US, the UK, and other European countries in which licenses had been issued was announced to the public in March 1987. The reaction was as dramatic as had been feared; the company faced fierce and widespread public criticism, became a target for direct action, and was threatened with government intervention.

CHAPTER 21

Public and political backlash

Shortly after the price of Retrovir was announced, Congressman Henry Waxman re-convened a meeting of the Subcommittee on Health and the Environment. The agenda of the re-convened committee in 1987 was much more specific than in 1982 and included an investigation of "the cost and availability of AZT" in which Barry would again play an important role. Waxman introduced the hearing by posing several questions for committee members and witnesses representing BW&Co. to consider "Is this a fair price? Who will pay for the people who are now being treated for free? Who will pay for the people who become ill after the drug is approved? Who is responsible for those who cannot pay?"[1] These questions were to persist in the minds of professionals, patients, and activist groups throughout the remainder of the decade and beyond. Waxman observed that because AZT had been shown to prolong life for patients suffering the most severe forms of HIV and had reduced the risk of opportunistic infections, eventually the drug must be made available to all AIDS sufferers. This implied two, though not mutually exclusive, possibilities – that federal and state governments and the insurance industry should ensure that the health care system funded treatment for all AIDS sufferers, and that BW&Co. should reduce the price of Retrovir to alleviate the burden otherwise placed on governments and insurers when the drug was prescribed.[2]

Questions surrounding the payment of costs for the use of new medical technology and treatments which could save lives were not new. In the 1970s, private insurers and government healthcare providers had been faced with costly organ transplants; by 1985, 85 per cent of major medical insurers undertook to reimburse for heart transplants. The comparable figure for the costlier combined heart-lung transplant was 69 per cent. Acquired immunodeficiency syndrome presented a problem because of the order of magnitude of treating an epidemic and of including treatment to try to protect those affected by HIV.[3] In 1989, the cost of Medicare's kidney dialysis program for the nation's 110,000 patients suffering end stage renal failure was costing taxpayers $2 billion according to the Health Care Financing Administration. One health economist predicted that by 1989, assuming that a national program would be in place to monitor medically and to treat those affected with HIV before they developed full-blown AIDS, the estimated cost of treating upwards of 200,000 patients would be between $2.5 billion and $10 billion.[4]

The two witnesses who represented the company at the Waxman committee hearings were Ted Haigler Jr, chief executive officer of BW&Co. since 1986, and David Barry. According to one witness present at the hearings, the calm demeanor of Haigler who had retained the accent of the stereotypical "dignified southern gentleman" from North Carolina, had surprised the assembled representatives who hailed principally from the north-east, the west, and the mid-west.[5] Kennedy (director of corporate affairs) and Barry collaborated in preparing a statement and script to aid Haigler's presentation of evidence. Barry's input was important because of his previous encounter with Waxman's committee in 1982 which enabled him to anticipate a characteristically robust cross-examination and to prepare Haigler accordingly. Early in the hearing, Waxman suggested that the company's profit for the year 1987/8 would be $250 million which he believed was excessive.[6] Market analysts believed the price of AZT (as it was still known) was intended to yield margins of up to 40 per cent, representing three times the company's existing average margins.[7] In response to Waxman's description of the price of Retrovir as "quite high," Haigler replied that the price was justified in the light of costs, uncertainty, and the margins customarily generated by significant new medicines.[8]

Waxman accepted the need for the company to make "a fair profit" but questioned whether the price yielded more than that because of the unprecedented level of support the company had received from the NHI and FDA. Through their actions, the company had been able to achieve an exceptionally swift screening process. Clinical trials had involved hundreds, rather than the usual thousands of people normally required. One effect had been to reduce considerably the time between development and commercial return from the market. He also noted the cost-offsetting benefits which the company had enjoyed as a result of the FDA conferral of orphan drug status for AZT. This was a concession normally limited to encourage companies to develop drugs for the treatment of relatively rare disorders, usually defined as those affecting fewer than 200,000 people, which seemed likely to be a substantial underestimate of demand resulting from AIDS drugs in the long-term. Orphan status allowed a 72 per cent tax subsidy for clinical costs and 25 per cent tax credit for increased RD&M; it also conferred an additional seven-year exclusive marketing license for the drug.[9] Haigler would not be drawn on exact costs in determining price and refused to speculate about future sales, prices, or profits. He rejected Waxman's accusation of profiteering, insisting that the price of AZT was reasonable under the circumstances.[10]

Unsuccessful in eliciting the detailed information he sought, Waxman's cross examination of Haigler moved from the narrow economics of AZT to the morality of the company's conduct. He suggested that the company had behaved irresponsibly by placing corporate profit above public interest and therefore had a moral obligation to moderate price and profit. Waxman asked whether AZT was available to other researchers outside the company, thereby enabling them to investigate combination studies using competitors' drugs with AZT. Barry emphasized the limited supply of the compound, was careful to refer to "ongoing discussions" (without specifying with whom) and mentioned a recent agreement to supply AZT for a study using interferon with AZT. Barry's reply lacked detail and gave the impression that cooperation was only now about to begin. It did not allay Waxman's concern that the company had maintained sole control of the allocation of the drug for research purposes. He argued that the NIH, which had enabled the company to develop and trial the drug, should have a continuing role in ongoing research into the drug.[11]

This was a line of argument which was not new. Evidence in support of Waxman's concern was provided by Dr Fauci of the NIH who expressed in the *New York Times* his frustration with the company's decision as to which trial should be supplied with AZT, thereby exercising complete control over the testing process.[12] He criticized the company for filing a use patent in 1985, accusing it of "taking a chance on AZT" by exercising a monopoly over testing the drug.[13] From the NHI perspective, "taking a chance" was unethical. Other critics were outraged by the economic rationale for price policy presented by company spokespeople: that the price level was justified by production costs, by the necessity to earn sufficient return on investment to enable the company to continue to invest in RD&M, and by the requirement to sustain dividends for shareholders.

In addition to these imperatives, spokespeople drew attention to the expectation that within a couple of years BW&Co.'s profits would suffer erosion as a result of competing antiviral medications entering the market.[14] In 1986, Merck and Hoffman La Roche had entered the retroviral field in search of a new class of drugs intended for the treatment of AIDS. In 1987, NHI scientists filed a patent for the use of HIV protease inhibitors on behalf of the federal government.[15] Although it was not until 1992 that new drugs received FDA approval (though used in combination with AZT), it is not surprising that the intense activity during the mid 1980s focused on a search for competing drugs. This was interpreted by managers at RTP as an imminent threat to an assumed short-term monopoly necessary for financial reward for investment.

Other critics of the company drew attention to the contributions which other agencies and individuals had made to the development of AZT. One was Dr Jerome P. Horowitz who had been funded by the NCI at the Michigan Cancer Foundation and who, in 1964, had been the first to synthesize the compound.[16] Another key figure was Sam Broder who had developed a special screening system which established the effectiveness of AZT to inhibit the duplication of the AIDS virus *in vitro* which had resulted in the FDA's clearance of the drug for clinical testing.[17] After reviewing the history of AZT-Retrovir, the *New York Times* correspondent pointed to the company's use patent in 1985 and the product patent for Retrovir in 1987 which ensured all benefit accrued to BW&Co. and asked readers, "Why shouldn't its reward be to charge whatever the market will bear?" To which the answer provided was "because profit should be related to risk and Burroughs Wellcome did not bear the full risk of developing AZT from scratch."[18] Similar criticisms were voiced in the UK. In April, an article appeared in the *Economist* in London, entitled "The awful cost of AIDS." The author accused the company of exploiting its monopoly and threw doubt on the justification of the Retrovir patent because of previous government collaboration and federal funding; the company had shouldered a fraction of the risk yet gathered in the full reward. Such allegations caused particular consternation among the directors in London.[19] The company's defense against the charge of unethical conduct was that both undertaking risk and insuring against risk were necessary to secure profit and future investment in RD&M and justified taking an early chance through patent protection.[20] In time, this would become a matter for the courts.

Meanwhile, the uproar surrounding the price of Retrovir continued into the summer of 1987, two months before normal marketing would proceed. At a BW&Co. board meeting convened by Haigler in July, the unanimous view was that in the light of adverse comments made by AIDS sufferers and sympathizers and because of pressure from government bodies which aroused concern that government intervention might be a possibility, the initial price should be reviewed and a possible reduction, for which agreement in London would be required, considered.[21] In July, Cipau took this resolution to the Wellcome board in London where he argued the case. He emphasized that a price cut would create goodwill among patients, government, and sick fund organizations. He conceded that because of an assumed absence of price elasticity of demand for Retrovir, a price reduction might result in a substantial fall in sales revenues below those forecast and would require a downward revision of profits for 1987/8. However, recent and continuing improvements in efficiency, yield, and cost in processing thymidine allowed scope for some reduction in price without a proportionate fall in group profits.[22] Directors continued to be worried about removing the substantial cash deficit incurred by RD&M attributable to the AZT-Retrovir project and to previous R&D failures. They did not share Cipau's view (soon to be exposed as over-optimistic) that criticism of the costs of treatment appeared to be abating. They were not reassured by the current absence of competitors. The Wellcome board in London opted for no immediate change.[23]

Haigler, meanwhile, declined repeated invitations from the New York State legislature to meet Assembly representative Nadler with either a consumer protection representative or accompanied by an attorney. A new bill was intended to enable a committee of the legislature to subpoena BW&Co. to produce witnesses and papers which, under the relevant current statute on price control, did not cover the case raised by the pricing of AZT-Retrovir.[24] Neither the attempts of Congress nor the New York State Assembly succeeded in eliciting cost or other precise financial detail from the company.[25]

In September, the WFL chairman's marketing and R&D committee returned to consideration of the relevant financial commitments associated with the development of AZT-Retrovir (see Table 20.1). They showed inventories held in the US valued at $54.1 million (£33.8million). Across all Wellcome companies the total was $59.7

million (£49.8 million) which implied a heavy burden of interest. Capital investment in the US dedicated wholly or mainly to the production of Retrovir was $12.8 million (£8 million) in the US. Dedicated RD&M costs were $15 million (£9.4 million) in the US and $17.4 million (£10.9 million) for Welcome plc. The RD&M figure included $10 million expenditure on the treatment IND in the US. Because commercial marketing of the 100 mg and subsequently the 250 mg capsules had hardly begun, sales costs were $6.6 million in the US.[26]

Set against this financial exposure was the revenue from sales which depended not only on price per milligram but also on the number of prescriptions. Depending on a patient's precise condition and therapy requirements, figures relating to the annual cost of treatment, often quoted in the press of between $7,000 and $8,000, were based on the initial recommended dosage in the US of 1200mg daily. The BW&Co. board was asked by directors in London to reconsider the matter "taking into consideration the moral, commercial, political, and other arguments canvassed in the course of discussion" before re-submitting a proposal to the December meeting.[27]

Cipau's July judgment that criticism of the company was beginning to diminish was entirely misplaced. In October 1987, the head of the New York State Consumer Protection Board announced an investigation into whether pharmacies and the manufacturer of the only federally-approved drug for treating AIDS were charging excessive prices. Should this be the case, the board's executive director threatened to "invoke state statutes concerning price gouging … to go after them."[28] In December 1987, Haigler drew attention to moves under way by the New York State legislature to institute inquiries into the price of Retrovir, and to the fact that the US President had established a commission to investigate the high costs of AIDS therapy which might lead to legislation affecting the private control of pharmaceuticals.[29] For the second time, the American directors agreed unanimously to recommend to the Wellcome board a reduction in the price of Retrovir by 20 per cent.

At a subsequent meeting in London, Haigler warned the board that the US government authorities would be most unlikely to accept a defense based on the estimated financial exposure of the company prepared by the company and would be likely to compel provision of all detailed figures of Wellcome's projected revenues as well as costs. Jones, director of R&D in the UK, expressed sympathy with Haigler's view, emphasizing how the price of Retrovir had become a "highly emotive and political issue" in the US; he endorsed Haigler's claim that the US government might compel BW&Co. to act.[30] Most of the London directors remained strongly in support of resisting any reduction which, it was estimated, would reduce group profits by around 10 per cent.[31] However, by the time the board met again in London in December, two new developments had influenced the outcome of the meeting. One was that during the preceding months pressure on BW&Co. had intensified and government intervention seemed imminent; the other was a renegotiation of the contract with Pfizer which had resulted in a reduction in the price of thymidine by 15 per cent per kilo. The Wellcome board agreed to a 20 per cent price cut in the

US market, to be applied to the UK and EEC markets at current sterling exchange rates. This left existing differentials unchanged.[32] The outcome is shown in estimates of international comparative costs of treatment with Retrovir prepared by Castell for the chairman's marketing committee in December 1988.

Table 21.1 *International comparative estimates of annual price of treatment with Retrovir, Zovirax, and combination in the US and Europe in 1988 (£)*

	Retrovir dose 4x800mg tabs	*Index*	*Zovirax dose 4x800mg tabs*	*Index*	*Combination R&Z dose 4x800mg*	*Index*
USA	3807	100	1292	100	5099	100
UK	4563	120	4343	336	8906	175
France	4143	109	2891	224	7034	138
Germany	4267	112	4070	315	8337	164

Source: GSK/WF/SCS 1274, Chairman's marketing and R&D committee, 9 Dec. 1988.

A carefully worded announcement issued to the Stock Exchange and to the press attributed the company's decision to its ability to pass on the benefit of improvements in production efficiency.[33] Improved productivity and material costs facilitated the price cut by reducing opportunity cost. However, the major consideration which exercised the American company was the threat of state intervention in some form which would affect adversely the business in the US. This, rather than manifestations of outrage among activists as has been claimed,[34] provided the impetus for the Americans' insistence on reducing the price of Retrovir.

In 1988, political pressure on the company for a second price reduction came from Lowell Weiker, the Republican senator from Connecticut, regarded as a liberal, whose proposal to the company was supported by the Democrat Senator Edward Kennedy. The existing Federal program, which had financed the purchase of the drug for individuals who failed to qualify for Medicaid or who lacked health insurance, would soon end. So far, Congress had made available $30 million to enable patients to purchase Retrovir. This was reflected in the company's sales. Weiker proposed requesting Congress to grant and extend the program for six months which would require a further $19 million for the purchase of the drug. A second price reduction, he maintained, would strengthen his argument with Congress.[35] Reickert, BW&Co.'s marketing vice-president, expressed the view that should the Congressional program end, the prospect of 6,000 patients being unable to undertake treatment "whether justifiably or not" would result in Wellcome receiving blame and therefore justified support for Weiker's proposal.[36] Haigler suggested a counter-proposal, a one-off tax-deductible donation by the company of $5 million, in return for Congressional agreement to a $15 million contribution to an extended program. A modified version which included a reduced request to Congress of $10 million, was given the green light by the board in London, despite reservations regarding a company contributing to US national health care funding. North Carolina Governor J. G. Marks, Senator Sanson and Congressmen Price and Valentine were briefed on the proposal with a view to gaining support.[37] However, within days of the counter-offer, the company received a letter signed by fifty-one congressmen and eight senators demanding a second price reduction.[38]

Meanwhile, momentum behind the campaign for a second price reduction had been gathering force among activists outside the formal political system, the origins of which lay in the early 1980s when, in New York and San Francisco, the movement to promote gay rights began. Among these groups, the Lavender Hill Mob emerged as a militant organization which during the mid 1980s had campaigned to press New York City to pass legislation to ban landlords from discrimination against tenants suffering from AIDS. A pattern emerged of demonstrations against bodies believed to be hindering the process of treating AIDS sufferers. US Centers for Disease Control and the FDA attracted criticism for a perceived slowness in approving and releasing drugs that might be effective in treating the afflicted. In March 1987, Larry Kramer, a playwright and AIDS activist, had formed the AIDS Coalition to Unleash Power (ACTUP) which quickly established groups in New York, Boston, and Chicago, while on the west coast, beginning with San Francisco and Los Angeles, a parallel group, Project Inform, was established as a non-profit education and advocacy organization.[39] This marked a new stage in AIDS activism in which demonstrations and events were aimed to attract the attention of national media and the wider public.[40] Measured by coverage in the newspapers, the strategy succeeded.

ACTUP accused the company of excessive profitability from Retrovir sales by securing a yield of 80 per cent. BW&Co.'s spokeswoman, Kathy Bartlett, denied the general charge, maintaining that the company had not revealed profits and that she had had no knowledge of the source of the alleged figure.[41] However, at a board meeting in London in July 1988, Castell had referred to an 80 per cent margin. This was a result primarily of an increase in productivity and increased yield had risen from 65 per cent when the drug was first available in 1987.[42] Bartlett's tactic was to emphasize the company's "compassionate policy," referring to the millions of capsules of AZT which the company had distributed freely for clinical trials and its financial donations to government AIDS programmes.[43] Barry defended the current price, emphasizing the RD&M cost of searching for new treatments which had amounted to $269 million in 1988/9. Another factor of concern was when physicians had recommended a reduction in the daily dosage for treating those who had contracted the virus but were yet to develop symptoms, the effect of which was to affect demand. Since 1987, when the initial recommended dose had been 1,200 mg, by September 1988, the average daily dose administered by physicians was 700 mg.[44] Castell calculated that the resulting annual cost of treatment fell from between $7,000 and $8,000 to $4,500.[45] This lower figure, however, still represented almost one-fifth of the median US household income in 1988.[46]

Radical gay AIDS activists intensified their campaigns for a second price cut. In January 1988, a demonstration at the company's distribution center in Burlingham, California, described in the *New York Times* as "the first civil disobedience protest against a drug price," led to the arrest of nineteen people.[47] The company issued a statement rejecting the demand for a further price cut but also invited representatives from AIDS advocacy groups to meet the vice president corporate affairs and vice president RD&M to discuss allegations of profiteering. The meeting ended without agreement.[48] On 21 April 1989, Peter Staley, a former bond salesman who was HIV positive, and three other members of ACTUP[49] were charged with first-degree trespassing and damage to property after they had evaded security and entered the building at RTP wearing city suits and ties and carrying brief cases. They gained access to the executive floor where, with the use of steel plates and rivets, they manacled themselves to the building. Their plan had been to gain access to the roof and unfurl a banner conveying a message critical of the company which would be visible from the nearby highway.[50] To ensure maximum publicity the media, including ABC and NBC, had been alerted. The stocks of drugs, medicines, water, and food left behind suggested that the event had been planned to last for several days.[51] The occupation of the executive floor lasted for eighteen hours, ending after the Durham County Sheriff's deputies (whom Barry had reassured that AIDS was not infectious through non-sexual contact) cut through a wall, severed the chains of the protestors and removed handcuffed activists from the building. The company dropped all charges.[52]

Waxman renewed his calls for a further price reduction.[53] In September 1989, the *New York Times* reported "a wave of protests developing on profits from AIDS drug" and that government lawyers were considering invoking a 1910 law (last invoked in the 1950s when the military had sought a lower than current market price for tetracycline) that would allow Federal officials to override the company's patents. This would enable other companies to attempt to produce the drug at a lower cost with a view to increasing the supplies available. A dozen groups of AIDS activists were reported to be planning a national boycott of the company's products.[54] In the same month, five members of ACTUP, carrying placards bearing the message "sell Wellcome," chained themselves to a banister at the New York Stock Exchange on Wall Street.[55] In New York, San Francisco, and London, protesters mounted sticker campaigns against the company. In the US, OTC products on drugstore shelves were defaced and affixed with a label: "AIDS profiteer."[56]

Kennedy, who was in charge of public relations, justified the perceived high price by quoting high production costs.[57] He continued the campaign which included lobbying senior members of Congress in an attempt to explain the company's dilemma. Other public relations initiatives were directed at the hot spots where the incidence of AIDS and AIDS-related conditions and the concentration of AIDS activism were at their greatest. In addition to the services of BW&Co.'s existing PR advisers in Washington and retainer agreements with Ogilvie and Mather in New York, the company enlisted the advice of a San Francisco company dealing specifically with AIDS related issues.[58]

The company sought support from individual pharmaceutical companies and from the Pharmaceutical Manufacturers' Association on the issue of corporate freedom from government, but without success. Haigler described the company as isolated and embattled.[59]

A letter from Waxman in which he renewed demands for detailed costings and a price reduction to be discussed at a meeting on 18 September 1989 alerted Haigler to the pressing need to establish WFL's position before the encounter. The board of BW&Co. agreed unanimously that a second reduction of at least 20 per cent in the US market should be recommended to the board of Wellcome plc. In London, Shepperd convened an extraordinary meeting of the board at short notice in order that they should be briefed on the accumulating pressure being exercised on BW&Co. in the US by Waxman and his committee, by AIDS activists, and by other diverse groups (politicians, medical health professionals, journalist critics, and campaigners).[60] Even the *Wall Street Journal*, hitherto sympathetic to the company, had joined the *New York Times* in publishing critical articles. At the board meeting on 16 September, Haigler argued that despite all the company's efforts in the US, the public image of the entire Wellcome group was at risk; this made a further price reduction imperative. Barry reminded the board that, although under government health schemes hospitalization and some other costs were subsidized, patients must pay for drugs. Godfrey warned that a price-cut would be interpreted as an admission of guilt and would invite further demands for reductions.[61] Both Godfrey and Jones were critical of BW&Co.'s public relations and believed that professionals and the public should be educated to understand that the company had invested heavily in research and development, that because of the previous price reduction and reductions in dosage, the true cost of annual treatment had dropped by about one half from an initial $8,000, and that so far, the company's sales were small and had yet to make a profit.[62] Shepperd also registered reservations in anticipation of criticism from investors who, he believed, would probably ask why a propaganda campaign had not been more vigorous. Haigler insisted that the climate of hostility in the US was so intense that no such messages would be heard by the public. Barry agreed that no-one was listening to the efforts of public relations to present the company's case. He expressed his fear that government might obtain powers to intervene, perhaps to amend the Orphan Drugs Act and possibly to allow challenges to the AZT-Retrovir patent in the courts which, in the current climate of opinion, the company could not be confident would produce a favorable outcome.[63]

The UK directors were divided over the American recommendation; two were adamantly opposed, three accepted with reluctance, and two expressed unease. The non-executives were also divided. From the chair, Shepperd drew the board's attention to the unanimous resolution by BW&Co. and secured unanimity among the Wellcome plc directors who agreed that "something must be done." On 16 September, the board approved a reduction of 20 per cent.[64] This did not, however, apply outside the US where, although the presence of HIV/AIDS did not compare in scale to that in other countries by 1986, the Royal College of Nursing predicted one million cases would exist in the UK by 1991. The UK government was the first among European countries to organize a publicizing and prevention strategy which, in 1986, included a national media advertising campaign in which images of tombstones and icebergs were accompanied by doom-laden messages. Other European governments followed this lead, but none could stem the spread of the disease thereby creating a significant market for Retrovir. As regulatory regimes in each country applied only to drugs developed and manufactured in those countries, companies supplying drugs from overseas were free to exercise price discrimination. This was the strategy adopted by Wellcome plc. as a method of offsetting the effects of price reductions in the US market.

The attacks on Wellcome plc, of which BW&Co. bore the brunt, were damaging to staff morale. Clifford Parrish, advertising director, captured the resentment shared by the American directors towards the WFL board in London for having resisted price reductions which the board of BW&Co. had advised under government and public pressure. The effect of this resistance was the intensification of criticism aimed against the American company, "Price was the biggest stumbling block … Everyone was gleeful to hear that we had come out with this wonder drug, but when they heard the price they thought we were a bunch of crooks."[65] Kennedy, corporate affairs director, summed up the problem of sustaining the company's image, "We were heroes for the research; we were villains for … pricing."[66] Rebuilding trust became a priority through reforming the company's approach to marketing and refocusing public relations by developing links to engage with the AIDS community.

CHAPTER 22

Marketing Retrovir and rebuilding trust through public relations

The second price reduction announced on 18 September 1989 (hours before Haigler's critical meeting with Waxman was due to begin) reduced the wholesale price of Retrovir from $1.50 to $1.20 per capsule. The retail price dropped from $1.75/1.85 to $1.47.[1] However, the second price-cut failed to silence the company's critics. The decrease in the estimated cost of annual treatment to the average AIDS patient from $8,000 to $6,400[2] did not satisfy the *New York Times* critic who castigated the company for continuing to abuse its monopoly power by charging an "extortionate price," compelling sufferers to "pay top dollar for the drugs that keep them alive."[3] He dismissed the company's defense that innovation justified the reward as spurious, "it did not invent AZT and, contrary to its claims, it was not the first to discover AZT's activity against AIDS-type viruses. Government took the risk of working with the AIDS virus, proved AZT was effective, and at first provided all the necessary thymidine, a rare ingredient. To avoid any delay over legal and commercial rights, Burroughs Wellcome was allowed to claim a use patent as well as exclusive right under the Orphan Drug Act. Yet still charging a price which made AZT the most expensive drug in history ... Burroughs Wellcome took a fraction of the usual risk yet grabbed for even greater reward than usual."[4]

The cost to patients dropped further following the positive 1989 NIAID findings which meant a widening of the spectrum of ant-viral conditions to which Retrovir might be applied with benefit, to include patients at relatively low risk. In January 1990, the FDA decreed that the dosage required to treat those patients who had the virus, but who did not show symptoms of the diseases associated with AIDS, should be reduced by one half. The effect of this decree was to reduce the annual cost of treatment for such patients from about $6,400 to $2,200[5] which rendered the drug affordable for more of the patient population. The price elasticity of demand for the drug, however, was unknown. More sales might be expected, but other influences which limited demand were as important as cost to the patient. General practitioners residing outside the city hot spots tended to display skepticism regarding treatment with Retrovir. Furthermore, even within the cities, prevailing taboos and ignorance surrounding STDs among the general population meant that a high proportion of the

Philip Tracy, formerly in legal practice in Washington DC who became general counsel at BW&Co. before becoming the last president of the American company in 1989.

anticipated increased number of potential patients (which were presumed to follow the price-cuts and the favorable NIAID results) did not present themselves to medical practitioners for testing. Without testing, potential patients remained undiagnosed and, regardless of the attitudes of GPs, no treatment could be prescribed. The company's experience with Zovirax had alerted it to problems associated with selling products to the public for the treatment of STDs. A well-trained and energetic sales force had been supported by advertising campaigns carefully devised by professional agencies. The embarrassment associated with a herpes condition (which could in any case be more easily concealed) could not compare with the stigma attached to AIDS sufferers during the early history of the disease. By comparison with Zovirax, therefore, because of the character of the illness for which Retrovir was the only treatment and because the cost to patients and organizations of the life-long therapy required was so much higher, the task of expanding sales presented a greater challenge. Medical practitioners needed to be persuaded to prescribe and to overcome critics of the company's pricing policy; potential patients needed to be educated about the disease and the importance of testing. Initially, many medical practitioners who treated AIDS displayed at least skepticism towards personal visits made by sales representatives seeking to detail Retrovir.

Michael McMullan was a senior sales representative in New York City where reportedly roughly 20 per cent of all AIDS infected patients in the US resided. It was

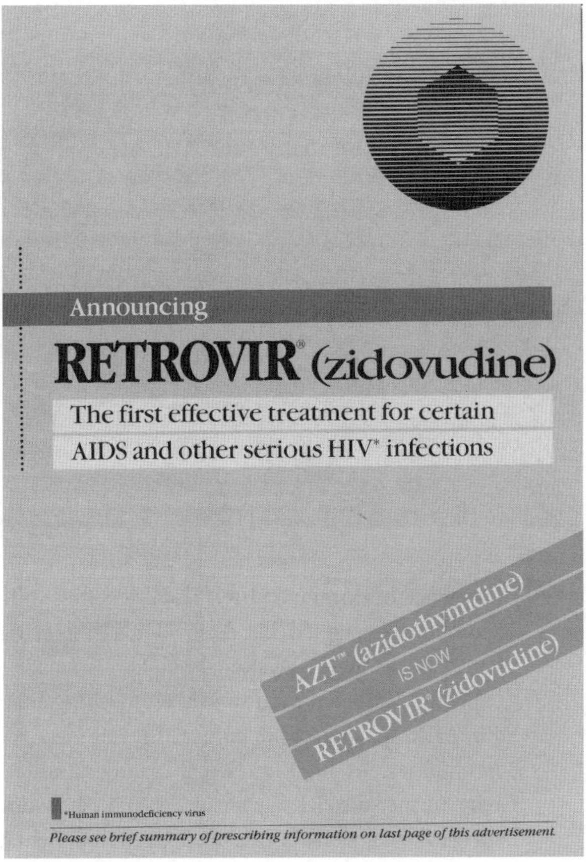

Retrovir was the first effective treatment for AIDS.

the location of the first pharmacy to dispense Retrovir and the center of the most effective organization of AIDS activists. He reported that initially, shortly before the second price reduction when AIDS activism was at its height, his visits to many medical practitioners had been received either in silence or with hostility. One doctor used a thirty second sand-timer to limit his visit. Many among the AIDS community were similarly unreceptive to his initial overtures.[6] Tadd Lazarus, director of early intervention with the HIV program at St Vincent's Hospital in New York and who had been a principal investigator for Retrovir in clinical trials from the start, described the problem facing the company and the medical community between 1987 and 1990, "We had a powerful drug but patients distrusted it. AZT was the focal point for the anger against the disease … You can't detail a drug like Retrovir that has so much emotionalism."[7] Under those circumstances he believed that detailing was widely perceived to be self-defeating. Although McMullan's early visits to medical practitioners as a Retrovir salesman in New York City proved difficult, advice from one of the few who specialized in treating AIDS patients led him to modify his approach to doctors and to establish a mode of behavior intended to eliminate or reduce their suspicion and establish trust. McMullan alerted the company to the

BW&Co. also created advertisements which instead of promoting the product directly provided informational promotion which here focused on the necessity of genital self-examination.

importance of distancing itself from detailing and proposed devising a new strategy. The company adopted his design for a systematic policy to replace detailing with promotion through educational public relations.[8]

Energy was directed towards establishing links to general practitioners dealing with AIDS patients and cultivating improved relations with the AIDS and gay communities. In 1990, an AIDS community advisory group was chaired by Fred Gregg, former district sales manager and newly-designated "AIDS community liaison manager." Membership included sales representatives, representatives from AIDS service organizations, and others from outside the company who possessed extensive knowledge and/or personal experience concerning every aspect of disease, issues, and trends concerning HIV.[9] The board's aim was to "to build a sustained and pro-active relationship with the HIV community on a national basis."[10] Twenty-two sales representatives who were considered as having already established positive relationships with the HIV communities in their respective territories were designated anti-viral representatives (AVRs) under McMullan's leadership.[11] Their role was to sell the anti-viral product line (including Zovirax) and to pay special attention to developing the long-term possibilities of securing Retrovir prescriptions. Unlike other representatives, AVRs enjoyed complete freedom to decide how much time to spend on visits.[12] Their responsibilities included relaying information about new HIV treatments to doctors, community health clinics, and counselors, to meet with AIDS service and advocacy groups, and to communicate outcomes to BW&Co.

Set up at a time when treatment was at an early stage and inevitably on a trial and error basis, a key organization with which the company became closely involved was the Community Health Project in New York City, the epicenter of AIDS and AIDS activism. The community clinic served over 15,000 gay and lesbian clients with medical services in a year and became a valuable source of information on all aspects of the disease and treatment. By monitoring carefully the treatment of such a large number of clients, many of whom were participants in several different trials and who shared experiences, the director of the clinic was able to detect trends in advance of the research and to communicate these to the AVRs. This connection enabled AVRs to keep senior directors of the company informed of the needs of patients afflicted by HIV, to advise the vice-president of marketing and sales on the appropriate content of communications, and to recommend through which channels information and promotion should be directed.[13] In addition to the leading doctors treating AIDS, these channels included the medical directors of city AIDS service organizations, the leader of the Gay Men's Health Crisis, and the leader of the Clinical Trials Group. Body Positive, an HIV service organization which issued a newsletter with a circulation of around 15,000, enlisted the company's assistance in securing access to medical and other information from the International AIDS Conference.[14] The company also became a major supporter of the American Foundation for AIDS Research from which it received advice on suitable recipients of funds, such as the Centre for Children and Families, a non-profit organization concerned for the welfare of street children, among whom were many youths addicted to drugs, some having already tested HIV positive. The company agreed to the agency's request for $25,000 to be used to fund a joint program of medical testing, counseling, and outreach.

Lazarus regarded the pioneering leadership and activities of McMullan in New York to have created an effective alternative to detailing. By reaching out to all parties involved (whether treating patients or counseling via the AIDS hotline and other channels), he believed that the efforts of McMullan's team of AVRs "made the drug usable."[15] Complementing the new methods adopted by AVRs to obtain prescriptions, the company's agents devised an alternative advertising campaign. The problem to be solved was how to avoid the charge of advertising drugs directly to consumers while at the same time persuading those in the early stages of AIDS and AIDS-related diseases to seek medical advice. The model for a new public service campaign, adopted by the Rolf Weiner Rosenthal agency, was that which it had planned for an earlier Zovirax campaign when the drug was promoted widely without mentioning the product by name. Proceeding along similar lines, under the banner headline "Living with HIV," the advertisements carried the message: "Early medical intervention could put time on your side," accompanied by the advice that "proper diet, exercise, and stress management" might also help. Although ACTUP and the Gay Men's Health Crisis activists were critical of the company which was accused of trying to push the drug, local and national health organizations and many other AIDS advocates for treatment welcomed the campaign.[16] Moreover, most gay publications agreed to carry the advertisements,[17] a significant breakthrough for the strategy. Some respected members of the activist community favored the company's attempt to educate the public on the benefits as well as the risks associated with Retrovir and also on the importance of testing which, for many, was a sensitive issue.[18] These developments reflected a growing division within the gay community between militant activists and others who favored a more constructive approach. In 1992, a group of ACTUP activists broke away to form the Treatment Action Group whose members emphasized the need to participate in the policy-making process.[19] This implied cooperation with public authorities, professional organizations, and indeed with the pharmaceutical industry.

Evidence that the company's public relations had begun to make progress was the agreement of Marty Levine, a gay clinical sociologist from New York (who was also an AIDS sufferer), to accept an invitation to become a member of the BW&Co. HIV community advisory board. Levine was a respected academic, active in the gay community, who regarded the adversarial history of relations between the AIDS community and the company to have been counterproductive for both sides. He explained his decision to become involved in policy as an opportunity to assist in repairing those relations.[20] ACTUP had been formed in the same month that AZT had been approved and he believed that the resulting outrage at the price and the animosity and action directed at the company were partly attributable to the perception among the AIDS community that BW&Co. was a small, unknown, faceless entity which they believed had just struck lucky with the drug.[21] Levine's mission was to remove fears of the drug among the AIDS community and to encourage its use, thus trying to extend the quality of life and survival of sufferers. Before this could be achieved, however, he believed that "the HIV community needed a corporate partner" and that the priority should be to "put a face on the company" which he believed to be a necessary precondition for establishing its credibility at a national level. His strategy was to assemble leading members of the mainstream gay community and company representatives to serve together on the advisory board. According to Gregg, his contribution marked an important development in the restoration of the company's public image. Seminars, small group meetings, and dinners with speakers were arranged. McMullan initiated a program within the company which Levine believed contributed further to a change in corporate culture and policy between 1987 and 1992. Levine described how BW&Co. emerged as "a major pioneer in advancing the rights of people with HIV … People who represent the company have to be comfortable with gay men, lesbians, people of color." All were included in the membership of the AIDS advisory board.[22] Gregg described Levine's leadership in that process as the driving force behind the company's outreach program, attributing to him the emergence of BW&Co. as "a significant player in HIV community advocacy."[23]

In 1992, Peter Staley, another AIDS sufferer and early member of ACTUP (he was among those arrested for the occupation of RTP in 1989), attended a "day of dialogue" arranged as part of the company's formal outreach program. Reflecting on the changes in corporate relations towards the AIDS community, and specifically to himself and other patients, he remarked on the "great deal of maturity" shown by the company in looking beyond the animosity and activism of the past. He referred to an unambiguous positive change in the company's approach to HIV and the gay community which had "moved on in a way that will help all people with AIDS … BW&Co's actions are speaking loudly these days."[24] Tangible evidence of the new orientation of public relations, managed through the advisory board, took the form of targeted donations; for example, a $4 million contribution to AIDS service and referral organizations and annual funding in support of a $10 million HIV patient assistance program to provide free medicines and treatment for people lacking adequate financial means. Even more significant, in Staley's view, in this new commitment to a "truly cooperative relationship" was the creation of a panel of treatment advocates. The role of the panel was to offer expertise and experience to advise the company's project team on the design of a treatment IND for ataovaqune, 566C80 (Acuvel), a new therapy for pneumocystis carinii pneumonia (PCP) and toxoplasmosis, by anticipating how the proposed protocol would be likely to be received by the HIV community. Mike Rogers, the Acuvel project leader, found that in formulating step-by-step answers to the panel's questions, it became possible to avoid misunderstandings, discuss potential issues of substance, and to resolve them. He concluded that the result was "a more effective protocol, more HIV community understanding and support for Acuvel, and potentially faster marketing approval and introduction."[25] Staley expressed his conviction that through discussion within the panel and by the influence of panel members from outside the company, the wider HIV community had reached a greater understanding of how much time, effort, and investment the company had expended in developing the new drug. He predicted, "Burroughs Wellcome will have a much easier time pricing Acuvel because the community understands."[26]

Whereas after 1989, relations between the company and the HIV community were transformed for the better, such was not the case with respect to the company's relations with the NCI, the Duke scientists who had been involved in the early development of AZT, or with the press. In response to critical correspondence appearing in the *New York Times,* Haigler defended the company's position and questioned the accuracy of the alleged role of scientists at the NCI and at Duke University in the development of AZT.[27] The scientists' angry reaction was expressed in a letter to the *New York Times* in which they insisted that the government-funded contribution had been vital to the drug's discovery and development. Moreover, they accused the company of having delayed the development process by refusing to work with the live AIDS virus and declining to receive samples from AIDS patients.[28] The allegation was justified. However, the 1988 Report of the President's Commission on the Human Immunodeficiency Virus Epidemic had expressed concern regarding the cost of protection or of liability actions arising from the risk to researchers which witnesses reported had deterred institutions from undertaking AIDS-related research.[29] Later, despite some reservations, Broder praised the company's serious commitment to the joint development of the drug; they exchanged information and supplied compounds that could be tested by the NCI. He also admitted that reliance solely on scientists in the public sector would have slowed the process down. He believed that commercial collaboration had been vital in ensuring a more rapid development and trialling towards the successful outcome. He described the AZT venture as "a successful example of a public/private collaboration" which "stimulated a lot of science and laid the foundation for better drugs in the future."[30]

Prompted by Broder at the NCI, the AZT patents came under scrutiny by counsel engaged by the NIH. Evidence of the government's substantial contribution was considered to be insufficient to justify the Commercial Litigation Branch of the Justice Department in filing a lawsuit against the company. In 1991, however, Public Citizen, a non-profit public interest litigation group, filed a lawsuit alleging a failure to disclose relevant and material facts in the patent application with the intention of invalidating the patent and blocking potential competition from generic manufacturers. The NHI threw its weight behind this initiative to undermine BW&Co's monopoly. In 1991, Barr Laboratories, an American manufacturer, filed an Abbreviated NDA to market a generic version of AZT. Another generic drug manufacturer, Novopharm, filed a similar suit. Both received support from the NIH which supplied two of its own lawyers. Meanwhile, Broder and his colleagues spent many hours giving testimony in court, challenging the company's patent.[31] None of these or other lawsuits succeeded. They were either dropped or failed after appeal and such challenges ended in 1994 as the date of patent expiry approached.[32] From the company's standpoint, the decision to secure early use patent was vindicated.

In an interview in 1998, Broder admitted to having displayed naivety in his early dealings with the company because he and his colleagues at the NCI had focused entirely on developing an effective product and securing rapid FDA approval for use of the drug while ignoring issues surrounding patenting and pricing.[33] On the charge of BW&Co.'s alleged guilt by profiteering, Broder accepted that there was room for disagreement, but that determining a precise level of financial reward that might be considered reasonable by all interested parties was problematic. Some level of financial return was necessary in order to incentivize private corporations to invest in such difficult areas of national concern where the risks of failure are high, a necessity implied in the provisions of the Technology Transfer Act of 1986 designed to promote private/public collaboration.[34] Contemporary perceptions of likely outcomes of retroviral research and the level of financial returns explain why, during the early years of AIDS-related research, scientists at Merck, Abbott, and Roche were limited to being no more than interested observers, though "following the AZT story intensely."[35] The impetus behind the search for a drug effective against AIDS at RTP was not driven primarily by an anticipated high rate of financial return, but by the confidence shared by Barry and Cuatrecasas in solving the problem. Despite criticism of the commercial prospects for viral research from the McKinsey investigators, the marketing division, and the American President of BW&Co., the scientists were convinced that their secret quest would succeed. Broder believed that the partnership between the NCI, Duke, and BW&Co. was both a scientific and a commercial success. The result of early commitment to the AIDS project collaboration was a reduction of prolonged suffering and saved thousands of lives.[36] The large corporations which initially had declined to collaborate, only embarked on research in this area after the triumvirate had demonstrated success.

PART SIX:

City businessmen and bankers, the Wellcome Trust, and Wellcome plc

CHAPTER 23

Management renewal and a reversion to core activities at Wellcome plc

The formation of Wellcome plc in 1986 and the associated share issue heralded unprecedented scrutiny of the company's affairs by investors, financial commentators, and other observers of the pharmaceutical industry. The management turbulence of the mid 1980s became public knowledge. The exodus of its most senior scientists from Beckenham and of the CEO of the American subsidiary conveyed an impression of Wellcome plc which was described in the *Economist* as "lacking direction where it is needed most."[1] An apparently well-informed reporter had welcomed the promotion of Cresswell, first from development director at RTP to become head of Wellcome Biotechnology at Beckenham in 1981 and, following Vane's departure in 1985, to group director of R&D with a seat on the main board; Cresswell was judged to possess the capacity to carry out the long overdue rationalization of the entire Wellcome Group that Shepperd had failed to effect.[2] In his new group main board director's role, Cresswell had embarked upon a policy intended to "make commercial an equal partner with science" by showing scientists that "there was no point in a certain area of research which would yield a product the company would not be able to sell … and persuading them that resources must be focused in areas that would result in marketable products, a process which required a cultural change which he described as "an uphill struggle."[3] He encountered similar resistance to rationalization through integration, a policy interpreted at RTP as implying a loss of independence for the American company. Neither with respect to bridging the Anglo-American divide nor to the reconciliation of deep-seated divisions which still existed at Beckenham, did Shepperd give active support. These difficulties, to which was added unhelpful interference from Shepperd (for example by establishing an office for his own use at Beckenham) led Cresswell to resign early in 1987.[4] Like the *Economist* commentator, the chairman of the Trust had assumed that Cresswell would succeed Shepperd as chief executive on his retirement and had expressed surprise when Cresswell left the company, first to join Laporte Industries and a year later to become chairman of pharmaceutical R&D at Warner-Lambert/Parke-Davis.[5]

Sir Alistair Frame was a professional engineer who created the RTZ international mining company which under his executive management became the world's largest mining company. After a period as non-executive chairman of British Steel., in 1990 he became non-executive chairman of Wellcome plc until 1993. He recruited new board members, increased dividends, and supported the new CEO's policy of thoroughgoing reform and rationalization. Ill health caused his retirement in 1993.

In the process of considering the appointment of Cresswell's successor, the issue re-emerged as to whether it was desirable to appoint a single group R&D director, rather than continue with separate US and UK directors which was the current arrangement. Jones, who had been appointed UK director of R&D, favored integration.[6] In his capacity as vice president RD&M at BW&Co., and group main board director until 1989 Schaeffer expressed alarm at the prospect of BW&Co. without an American vice president RD&M after his own retirement in 1989. He pointed out that Anglo-American relations had been at their worst when the parent company had been "in even nominal control and central direction of BW&Co."[7] Wrangling continued over a possible compromise but the matter continued unresolved on Shepperd's retirement in 1990.

The unexpected resignation of the heir apparent once more exposed the lack of formal procedure for preparing a successor to chief executive. The power to appoint resided with the Trust, but since the appointment of Bennett in 1940 when he was chosen by the Trust, successive chief executives had been appointed by the Trust only on a recommendation made by the board. The new chairman of the Trust ensured that he and his fellow trustees would take the initiative in preparing for and selecting Shepperd's successor. He insisted upon separating the role of CEO from that of chairman and setting the process of recruitment in motion two years before

Shepperd's retirement would take place. Both a non-executive (but substantially engaged) chairman and a CEO should be sought outside the company and both should be deemed acceptable to the board as well as to the Trust.[8]

Steel was influential in the appointment of Sir Alistair Frame as the new non-executive chairman, taking office in July 1990.[9] A professional engineer, Frame had been chief executive of RTZ, the world's largest mining company during the 1970s, and non-executive chairman between 1983 and 1989 when he also became non-executive chairman of British Steel. Regarded in business circles as a shrewd forceful figure[10] and described by Gibbs as a marvelous leader though "a touch cavalier,"[11] his style as chairman was in marked contrast to that of the secretive and indecisive Shepperd. From the outset, Frame's approach to Wellcome plc was as critical as that adopted by Steel.[12] He supported Steel's belief that the Trust should receive higher dividends. Under pressure from Steel and the trustees, the dividend during Shepperd's last year in office in 1989/90 had been 5.5p per share. Although under Frame's chairmanship the dividend rose to 6.5p per share in 1991, he told Steel that he required more time to change the culture of the board and to counter the influence of non-executive directors who had served for too long under Shepperd's chairmanship. Frame appointed Sir Graham Hearne, chairman of Enterprise Oil, as non-executive director.[13] In 1991/2 a dividend of 10 per cent was followed by 13 per cent in the following year, by which time Frame had been forced to retire owing to ill health.[14]

As Shepperd approached retirement the "barons" on the board jostled to succeed him, though it was the young Castell, a newcomer to the main board, who emerged as a possible successor.[15] At the age of thirty-three, Castell, qualified accountant, had become responsible for managing one-third of the R&D site at Beckenham as well as all biological manufacturing. In 1987, Shepperd had promoted Castell to group commercial director at the age of forty who, especially following Cresswell's departure, was poised to become a key figure in senior management.[16]

However, Steel was determined to make an external appointment introducing a suitably experienced manager completely foreign to the enduring Wellcome corporate culture. Receiving strong support from Frame and non-executive directors, Pilkington, Clausen, and Hearne, John Robb became deputy chief executive to Shepperd in July 1989 before assuming the office of CEO one year later.[17] At the age of fifty, Robb possessed long-standing practical experience as a salesman, managerial experience of marketing, and had been until 1985, chairman of Beecham's Products, the consumer division of the Beecham group, the large British food and drugs business. At a time when the Beecham group's financial performance was facing serious criticism in the financial press, one consequence of a boardroom coup was the resignation of the group CEO and Robb's assignment as acting CEO. During the subsequent three years, Robb had been instrumental in keeping the troubled Beecham group afloat by implementing a vigorous re-structuring, cutting costs by disposing of non-core activities, and re-invigorating management by replacing some existing directors with others possessing mature experience.[18] However, machinations

John Robb was formerly chairman of Beecham's Products division and subsequently acting CEO of the Beecham organization until 1989 when he was chosen by the Wellcome Trust to succeed Shepperd as CEO of Wellcome plc, to which Robb added the chairmanship in 1993.

occurred among Beecham's executives which created management upheavals, and McKinsey management consultants were introduced to review the group's activities. An impending merger with SmithKline implied a relegation of Robb's position in the new American corporate hierarchy. He had left Beecham in 1988.[19]

Robb's task at Wellcome plc was to restructure and reform the company's 40 operating companies throughout the world which manufactured and sold into 120 different markets. In the early 1980s, group output and sales of pharmaceuticals had been heavily concentrated on systemic antibacterials (16 per cent), cough and cold preparations (15 per cent), anti-gout preparations (12 per cent), and topical anti-infectives (11 per cent).

The width of the product range had been criticized in the 1984 Little report. The consequent recommendation had been severe rationalization and, looking to the future, the introduction of an effective process of managerial control and a systematic prioritization of R&D expenditure.[20] Even though the recommendations had been endorsed by the board in London, management turbulence, resignations, and retirements among the most senior figures in the company (both in the US and the UK) during the mid 1980s had contributed to the delay in implementing Little's reforms. Such was the situation facing Robb when he assumed responsibility for the group's future in 1990 although, since Little's report, the composition of sales had altered considerably. Most dramatic was the rise in sales of antivirals from 4 per cent of sales in 1984 to 37 per cent by 1990. Apart from "other pharmaceuticals" (which remained at 13 per cent) and other "non-pharmaceuticals," only cough and cold

Table 23.1 *WF/Wellcome plc sales by therapeutic market area as a percentage of group sales, 1984–1990*

	1984	*1986*	*1988*	*1990*
Antivirals	4	12	28	37
Cough and cold preparations	15	16	12	10
Cardiovascular	6	8	7	6
Anti-gout preparations	12	9	7	6
Topical and anti-infectives	11	10	7	5
Muscle relaxants	3	5	4	5
Systemic antibacterials	16	11	6	4
Diagnostics	2	3	3	3
Other pharmaceuticals	13	12	14	13
Other non-pharmaceuticals	20	16	12	11

Source: GSK/WF/SCS 798, WFL/Wellcome plc accounts and annual reports.

Table 23.2 *Wellcome plc sales, net profit, capital employed, and rate of return, 1986–1994*

	Sales	*Net profit before tax (£million)*	*Profit as % of sales*	*Capital employed (£million)*	*Profit as % of capital employed*
1986	1,005	125	14	683	18.
1987	1,132	169	15	754	22
1988	1,251	221	18	843	26
1989	1,408	283	20	994	28
1990	1,469	315	21	992	32
1991	1,456	403	28	1,232	33
1992	1,669	457	27	1,363	34
1993	2,052	667	33	1,778	38
1994	1,976	680	34	2,020	34

Source: GSK/WF/SCS 798, WFL/Wellcome plc accounts and annual reports.

preparations contributed more than 6 per cent to total sales. The success of antivirals and cough and cold preparations were attributable to the American company. Measured by financial performance, primarily the result of the rapidly rising sales of antivirals, the record of WFL from the early 1980s showed trading profit before R&D rising from 20 per cent (10 per cent after R&D) as a percentage of sales in 1981 to 24 per cent (12 per cent after R&D) by 1985. Between 1986 and 1990, profits rose to 37 per cent (21 per cent after R&D).[21]

Table 23.3 *WFL/Wellcome plc dividend per share (£million) and times covered and return on shareholders' equity, 1981–1994*

	Dividend (£m)	*Dividend per share (p)*	*Dividend cover*	*Return on shareholders' equity*
1981	10.5	(1.3)	3.2	11
1982	13	(1.6)	2.8	11
1983	14	(1.8)	2.6	10
1984	17	(2.1)	2.7	11
1985	23.8	(2.9)	2.9	15
1986	17.4	2.11	3.7	12
1987	23.7	2.81	4.0	17
1988	30.4	3.60	4.2	20
1989	42.8	5.05	3.9	21
1990	55.2	6.5	3.5	22
1991	85.7	10	2.9	23
1992	111.9	13	2.8	22
1993	149.8	17.3	2.6	26
1994*	(198.8)	(30.4)	(2.2)	23

*Based on reported 16 month figure only.
Source: GSK/WF/SCS 798, WFL/Wellcome plc accounts and annual reports.

In some respects (financial performance and expenditure on R&D) Wellcome plc's record during this period was on a par with that of Glaxo.[22] A comparison with that company's history is particularly relevant because of its competition with Wellcome plc in seven of the main market segments (including antivirals and cough/cold treatments, Wellcome's two largest segments).[23] However, divergence between the two companies during the 1980s is also apparent. Their relative size altered substantially over the decade. In 1981, sales parity existed. Wellcome generated £500 million compared with £537 million generated by Glaxo; by 1990, Glaxo's sales of £2,854 million were more than double those of Wellcome which were worth £1,469 million.[24] Wellcome's post-tax net profit earned per employee was £1,784 in 1981 compared with £2,162 for Glaxo; equivalent figures in 1985 were £3,533 for Wellcome and £10,806 for Glaxo and for 1990, £10,465 for Wellcome and £25,314 for Glaxo which showed Wellcome's lower and falling levels of labor productivity.

The most relevant measure of performance for the company's shareholders was the rate of return to equity which revealed Wellcome as having fallen well below Glaxo's record even though the company had improved under pressure from the Trust and as a consequence of the flotation of Wellcome plc in 1986. Comparative percentages in 1981 were 17 per cent for Wellcome's equity shareholders and 16 per cent for Glaxo's. The figure for Wellcome remained below 20 per cent until 1988 while that for Glaxo

Table 23.4 *WFL/Wellcome plc trading profits (£million) by location of company, 1981–1994*

	UK	*North America*	*Continental Europe*	*Rest of World*
1981	50.1	41.9	2.2	19.6
1982	60.0	46.8	1.5	23.5
1983	52.7	74.8	4.4	22.9
1984	49.5	114.9	5.2	27.0
1985	53.0	167.4	5.7	32.4
1986	65.3	163.7	10.1	30.8
1987	77.5	193.4	13.7	35.1
1988	109.5	225.3	17.7	44.1
1989	131.5	266.0	16.5	0.4
1990	164.7	291.0	22.4	0.0
1991	202.9	315.1	18.0	53.9
1992	251.0	389.9	35.3	56.7
1993	326.3	499.3	49.9	80.3
1994	423.2	477.4	40.5	135.6

Source: GSK/WF/SCS 798, WFL/Wellcome plc accounts and annual reports. The North America category includes the BW&Co. subsidiary company in Canada where sales and profits were insignificant by comparison with those in the US.

averaged 33 per cent between 1985 and 1989. Following three years when the figure climbed to barely 20 per cent, returns for Wellcome's shareholders reached a peak of 23 per cent in 1990 which compared with 29 per cent for Glaxo. Thus, though at a lower level than Glaxo, returns on equity none the less marked one area in which Wellcome plc gained ground on Glaxo. This was not the case with respect to the proportion of sales represented by expenditure on R&D during the 1980s when Glaxo almost achieved parity with Wellcome plc. During the early 1980s, the percentage spent by Wellcome (12 per cent) had been twice the level invested by Glaxo which placed Glaxo in the "medium degree of research intensity." By 1990, however, the figure for Wellcome was 15 per cent and for Glaxo 14 per cent which placed R&D expenditure in both companies in the "high degree" category, above the norm set at 9 per cent for the industry.[25]

Within Welcome plc, the superior performance of BW&Co. measured by sales growth, manufacturing productivity and costs, R&D expenditure and profitability during the 1980s, created increasing tensions across the organization and complicated the formulation and agreement of a strategy for the group. In 1981, whereas 16 per cent of group sales were consumed in the UK, 15 per cent were directed to the rest of Europe and 28 per cent consumed in North America. The remaining exports to the rest of the world went primarily to developing markets. By 1990, 45 per cent of sales were in North America and 10 per cent in the UK, the remainder were divided between Europe and the rest of the world. The trend of trading profit reveals a similar contrast. In 1981, UK trading profit was 44 per cent of group profit compared with 37 per cent in North America; by 1990, 61 per cent of trading profit originated in North America compared with 34 per cent in the UK.[26] The short-term future of Wellcome plc depended on products which were experiencing high and rising demand, the antivirals (Zovirax and Retrovir) which were manufactured in the US. Products already off-patent were Zyloric (Zyloprim), the anti-gout drug (£99 million), and Lanoxin which was for cardiovascular treatment (£92 million). Like Zyloric (Zyloprim) and Lanoxin, other niche products with limited sales potential were the anticancer drugs Tracrium, a muscle relaxant (£58 million), and Leucoverin.

At the time Robb joined Wellcome plc, concerns expressed by financial observers following the flotation persisted. Robb's capacity to reform the company became a matter for speculation. During his first year as CEO, pre-tax group profits represented a return on sales of 21 per cent which compared with 40 per cent at Glaxo. The contrast attracted comment in the *Economist* in an item entitled "Looking for profits not kudos" which underlined Wellcome plc's struggle to meet the expectations of investors and pundits since flotation in 1986 and concluded, "It has failed."[27] Another article referred to Wellcome plc as the twentieth largest pharmaceutical organization in the world, "one of the worst managed in the industry." Managers were accused of having bungled the marketing of AZT and having spent millions on biotechnology with little return.[28] Expressing skepticism regarding Robb's ability to transform Wellcome into a competitive drug firm, the columnist suggested that "his best bet may be to convince the Wellcome Trust to reduce its stake to 50 per cent. It is time to escape the dead hand of charity and trust the invisible hand of the market."[29] In 1991 when, for the first time, the Wellcome plc accounts separated BW&Co.'s results from those of the group, the disparity in performance of BW&Co. and WFL was revealed. From only a slightly larger asset base than that in the UK, US sales accounted for 44 per cent of the worldwide turnover of Wellcome plc; sales by the UK business amounted to 26 per cent. RD&M expenditure in the US exceeded that in the UK by 31 per cent. Operating profits of BW&Co. were 50 per cent greater than those generated by the business in the UK and the rest of the world.

After only six months at Wellcome plc, one financial observer detected early signs of the new CEO's determination to "inject some commercial realism into the company" which he considered to be long overdue.[30] The *Economist* judged other initiatives undertaken to have signaled a strategic shift in the company's direction, heralding "an injection of good old-fashioned market discipline."[31] Robb was assisted by internal and external recruits to the main board who replaced several of the retiring old guard. From within Wellcome plc, David Barry (director of RD&M at RTP and later to become Robb's choice as group R&D director) was a key promotion to the main board. Phil Tracy, the newly promoted president and CEO of BW&Co. who had replaced Haigler, also assumed membership. A British replacement from within

James Cochrane, a main board director in charge of European operations, he was the only director who remained in post at Glaxo Wellcome.

the organization was Keith Merrifield, formerly the overseas ROW group commercial director who had a long history of employment at WFL. He succeeded Robert Devereux, the long-standing director of manufacturing whom Hobbs, the personnel director, described as having harbored "a cordial hatred" for Vane. Devereux "ruled Dartford with … an increasingly iron hand" and had become more "tribal" towards other departmental heads over the years until Vane departed from the company.[32] Two of the most influential members joining from outside the Wellcome group were James Cochrane in 1987 and John Precious in 1989.

Cochrane became one of the most influential figures during Robb's period in office. An MBA graduate of London Business School, he had been an oil sales representative for Shell and a pharmaceuticals salesman for Bristol Myers. Subsequently, he became commercial operations manager for Bristol-Myers Squibb in charge of the company's European operations.[33] He was approached by head-hunters seeking a main board director for Wellcome plc. As Bristol-Myers Squibb's policy was to restrict directorships to American citizens, Cochrane accepted the directorship and became responsible for the operations of Wellcome companies throughout Europe. Cochrane brought to Wellcome plc knowledge and experience of implementing best commercial practice across large organizations. He believed that introducing an American results-based approach offered him an opportunity "to transform a Victorian company and bring it into the twentieth century."[34]

John Precious, finance director of Wellcome plc from 1989 to 1995.

John Precious was the second new main board director head-hunted to succeed the retiring finance director, R.M. Brookman of WFL since 1977. Precious was a chartered accountant by profession and previously finance director on the main board of the multinational chemical company Tioxide Group plc.[35] Like Cochrane, he too was critical of many aspects of the organization and practices at Wellcome plc, notably of the flawed systems of management and financial control. Financial data delivered to the board were six weeks out of date and devoid of financial information necessary for any meaningful analysis of business performance.[36] Consequently the board was ill-equipped to monitor, question, and exercise control over cash flow. Data supplied were aggregated for each region but omitted any detail of RD&M expenditure in the US which, by 1989, far exceeded that in the UK.[37] As a consequence, main board directors (none of whom, except the CEO, was represented on the board of the American company) were unable to monitor, question, and control financial input into specific projects or other areas of activity in the US.[38] The application by Precious of orthodox management financial criteria fully justifies his criticism of the group's structural weakness of the MNE, the consequence of which was a lack of effective control of the American company by the board of directors in London. The disappointing record of R&D in the UK, however, did not result from inadequate financial investment, but by a culture which hampered pharmaceutical innovation and commercial development. From the standpoint of managers at RTP, the degree

Table 23.5 *BW&Co. Sales, Profits and RD&M ($million), 1970–1994*

	Sales	*Pre-tax profit*	*Profit/sales*	*R&D*	*R&D/sales*
1970	60	12	20	7	12
1971	68	16	24	9	13
1972	79	19	24	10	13
1973	95	26	27	10	11
1974	111	27	24	11	10
1975	143	37	26	14	10
1976	167	44	27	18	11
1977	184	37	20	23	12
1978	202	45	22	28	14
1979	238	46	20	34	15
1980	262	33	13	43	16
1981	274	34	12	46	17
1982	310	24	8	54	18
1983	429	48	13	62	18
1984	415	78	19	72	17
1985	581	136	23	82	14
1986	665	141	21	105	16
1987	765	221	29	126	16
1988	891	401	45	140	16
1989	974	425	44	151	16
1990	1,186	524	44	209	22
1991	1,242	575	46	212	17
1992	1,304	690	53	230	18
1993	1,516	749	49	269	17
1994	1,366	759	56	282	21

Sources: GWHC, BW&Co. (USA) Inc., 107.01/02, President's annual reports; data provided by Fred Coe Jr, by fax, 9 May 2002. GSK/WF/SCS 798, WFL/Wellcome plc accounts and annual reports.

of independence which they enjoyed, including the high level of financial support for RD&M, was vital to the success of the American company and therefore to Wellcome plc as a whole.

Precious believed the flotation of Wellcome plc had been successful as a financial transition but he was critical of Shepperd and other main board directors for having forfeited the potential benefits that flotation offered through market discipline. Evidence of this was his perception of a corporate culture in which the ethos among researchers was to suspect commercial objectives. He blamed Shepherd and the directors of dereliction for having failed to explain to staff, especially to the Beckenham

Table 23.6 *BW&Co. Sales and Profits, 1970–1994 ($ million adjusted by price index for prescription drugs in the US: 1982–1984=100)*

	Sales	*Profit*		*Sales*	*Profit*
1970	124.6	25.3	1983	428.6	47.9
1971	143.0	33.8	1984	378.3	71.1
1972	167.4	40.3	1985	483.8	113.2
1973	201.7	55.2	1986	509.9	108.1
1974	230.3	56.0	1987	543.3	156.9
1975	279.3	72.3	1988	586.2	263.8
1976	309.8	81.6	1989	589.6	257.3
1977	321.7	64.7	1990	652.7	288.4
1978	327.9	73.1	1991	621.9	287.9
1979	358.4	69.3	1992	607.4	321.4
1980	361.4	45.5	1993	679.8	335.9
1981	339.1	47.1	1994	592.4	324.8
1982	346.7	26.6			

Source: Susan B. Carter et al., *Historical statistics of the USA*, Vol. 3, *Economic structure and performance* (Cambridge University Press, Cambrige, 2006), Table Cc 6–48.

scientists, the significant consequences of their behavior once WFL had become a limited company and therefore open to scrutiny by shareholders from outside the Trust and to critical examination by financial analysts. Laboratory staff had not been informed that after flotation "they would have to pursue research according to what would ... satisfy shareholders and the Stock Exchange."[39] Precious was also critical of the existence within the organization of "empires ... permanently at war with each other." He adduced the existence of separate directors of R&D, RD&M, and IT in the UK and the US as symptomatic of an international dysfunction.[40]

Precious was especially critical of the management of the company's peripheral activities, the financial results of which revealed that they had been conducted largely without cost control.[41] His cost benefit analysis approach lay behind one of Frame's first initiatives. Frame had commissioned a former head of R&D at Glaxo to conduct a review of Wellcome's portfolio, the purpose of which was to identify a set of priorities that might be employed as a framework for deciding upon immediate selective cuts and guidance for future policy. Once the resulting report had been studied by senior scientists at Wellcome plc, Frame's initiative stalled. Precious concluded that "the establishment managed to see him off."[42] However, when Robb assumed command, he took note of the report, ignored objections, persisted with this approach, and focused on the development of profitable core business. One step had already been taken when, in 1989, after almost thirty years of barely profitable activity, Cooper's veterinary drug division had finally been sold, though this was attributable to Sullivan's initiative at BW&Co., started several years before. Robb decided to sell the company's historic vaccine business and in 1990/91, Wellcome Biotechnology was disbanded.[43] Though Welcome Biotechnology was not peripheral it, too, was unprofitable. Successive directors, and latterly Precious, believed the company had suffered from under-investment relative to the parent company's expectations in terms of commercially rewarding medical innovation, and had been hampered by a consequent lack of scale. Cresswell had also been critical of Vane and subsequently, of Moncada, for having refused to release clinical resources to facilitate biological testing, thereby crippling activities intended to lead to innovation.[44] Under the new regime, the company was closed, staff disbanded, and the vaccine business (the historic basis of the original Burroughs Wellcome &Co.'s reputation and growth in London and Dartford from the 1890s) was sold.[45]

The next casualty of rationalization applying market criteria was tissue plasminogen activator (tPA), a heart attack treatment, which over the years had absorbed a substantial proportion of R&D expenditure at Beckenham. Even so, its commercial pay-off had remained uncertain. Robb made use of an independent international study of heart attack drugs which provided a clear justification for terminating the project. The investigation showed that the efficacy of tPA was not superior to that of Streptokinase, the established market leader.[46] Moreover, tPA would have to be priced at ten times the existing treatment to secure what Robb reckoned to be a "reasonable" return. Resources for further research were withdrawn. The *Economist* observer was impressed by the decision, "the company is unaccustomed to such naked profit-oriented management," a policy which, by March 1991, had resulted in a 10 per cent reduction in staff."[47]

Calmic was the most peripheral of all of Wellcome's subsidiary companies. It had been acquired in 1966 and although later renamed Wellcome Environmental Health was popularly referred to as a "men and women's washroom business." Calmic's activities, which were international as well as bewilderingly diverse, also included the production of pesticides, the manufacture of hospital trolleys, and modular operating theatre equipment. It also provided printing services to the pharmaceutical industry and in Australia, supplied paint finishing to the automobile industry. All were discontinued in 1992. Wellcome Diagnostics, which Precious described as another financial "black hole," was an additional casualty, sold to International Murex Technologies also in 1992.[48] Closure or disposal of these businesses, a matter of cutting losses, occurred in tandem with concentration on core activities, a strategy designed to transform the traditional horizontal, diverse product portfolio by replacing it with a vertically-integrated organization focused on human pharmaceuticals, prescription, and OTC medicines[49] – essentially the long-established model strategy pursued effectively by BW&Co. in the US.

A comparative review of the world pharmaceutical industry published in 1993[50] assessed the future prospects of leading companies, including Wellcome plc. Taggart's verdict was that Wellcome plc, which he described as "a major force in the global pharmaceutical industry", would survive beyond the millennium as a second rank producer, behind Astra and Glaxo which were predicted to dominate and lead the industry. This assumed that the company succeeded in resolving its dilemma which Taggart perceived to arise from pressure applied by the Wellcome Trust to obtain dividends at levels sufficiently high to fulfill the charity's ambition in its role as a major funder of medical research.[51]

Robb's managerial approach contrasted with that of Shepperd. Whereas although Shepperd had been respectful of senior scientists, he was indecisive and at times devious; Robb's style was open, robust, and even abrasive.[52] However, when forced by ill-health, Frame resigned in 1993, Robb took the opportunity to secure his own election by the board as chairman. By doing so, he ignored the Trust's deliberate separation of the two roles on Shepperd's retirement.[53] Precious criticized the Wellcome plc non-executives for failing to prevent Robb's coup which had given him the opportunity to dominate the company, a situation which the Trust had sought to avoid.[54] Robb's actions did not contribute to a sound relationship between the board and the Trust at a time when the company's future depended upon achieving a commercial performance sufficent to satisfy the dividends levels sought by the Trust.

CHAPTER 24

A global integration strategy

Transforming Wellcome plc into an integrated, global, profit-oriented pharmaceutical organization was a long-term process which would require cultural as well as structural and strategic changes. Structure and strategy affecting marketing (his specialty), financial control, and IT became Robb's immediate priorities. Although in charge of European operations of the Wellcome group, one of Cochrane's first initiatives followed his discovery of the limited scope and poor quality of Wellcome IT in the UK which lagged well behind IT services at BW&Co. With Robb's support, Cochrane ensured that global responsibility for IT passed to the American director.[1] R&D and cultural change were also seen to need reform, but were less amenable to rapid change and more susceptible to an incremental approach. Although Zovirax was the company's largest selling anti-viral, he believed that the global sales potential had yet to be realized, a failure which he attributed to a fragmented approach to marketing. This responsibility had resided with the group marketing directorate until 1987 and thereafter (following Vane's departure) with the joint R&D and marketing committee in London.[2] Robb was particularly critical of the process by which separate product development, data assembly, and drug approval were conducted by country.[3] Even Jones, previously director of development, admitted that the process of getting drugs to markets took too long.[4] A decision (following Vane's departure) by the newly-formed joint R&D and marketing committee in 1987 to move the marketing division from London to Beckenham had signaled a recognition of the need for interaction between scientists and commercial managers beyond director level. Relocation, however, appeared to have had minimal effect. The *Economist's* company profile of Wellcome plc in December 1990, referred to an abysmal record of marketing and a low rate of return on R&D. The development of Wellferon, a form of interferon used to combat rare cancers and other diseases, was adduced as an example.

The history of R&D investment into developing interferon originated in the WFL board's commitment to build on the company's traditional strength in vaccine research after World War II. In 1957, Isaacs and Lindenmann discovered the viral inhibitor, interferon, and in 1959 the Medical Research Council in the UK (MRC) had formed a committee whose members included biological scientists from Beckenham. The market for vaccines (in which historically since the 1890s Burroughs Wellcome had been a leader in the UK) was reliant to a high degree on the unpredictable demand,

Table 24.1 *Wellcome plc sales of Actifed/Sudafed, Zovirax, and Retrovir, 1987–1994 (£million)*

	Group sales	*Sudafed/Actifed*	*As %*	*Zovirax*	*As %*	*Retrovir*	*As %*
1987	1,132	127	11	248	22	25	2
1988	1,251	126	10	380	30	158	13
1989	1,408	148	10	492	35	225	16
1990	1,469	151	10	634	43	287	20
1991	1,456	140	10	838	58	315	22
1992	1,699	132	8	1,067	63	388	23
1993	2,052	141	7	1,140	56	372	18
1994	1,976	138	7	1,287	65	402	20

Source: GSK/WF/SCS 798, WFL/Wellcome plc accounts and annual reports.

often initiated by governments, for the treatment of foot and mouth disease. Patent protection was not available and, as a consequence, the vaccine business was regarded as a low-tech, low-profit activity. Shortly after Vane's appointment as research director in 1973, other board members expressed concerns over the commercial prospects of biologicals and the lack of innovative biological products. They questioned whether costs, which outweighed benefits, threatened the future of the company's activity in this area. Vane opposed abandonment of the company's traditional commitment to animal and human vaccines and to pesticides. Instead, he proposed investment in the production of interferon. Subsequent attempts at purification of human beta interferon had not proved to be successful; considerable skepticism existed in the scientific community.[5] However, Vane proposed that he should establish a new research project intended to use genetic manipulation to change the genetic content of a bacterium to make it usable. By investigating transformed cells, the intention was to produce lympho-blastoid interferon for clinical use. He envisaged the re-invigoration of biologicals following an outcome which would lead to the production of a high value product which would provide a major biological profit source.[6]

In 1976, the board committed funding for the project which was initiated when responsibility for its management was passed to a small group of senior staff chaired by Vane; the project team leader was Norman Fintner.[7] The first report of successful purification of human beta interferon in 1978 emerged from the laboratory of Y. H. Tan at the University of Calgary and paved the way for viral replication. Fintner joined biologists at Warwick University as a visiting professor where, aided by materials and technical assistance provided by WFL, he collaborated with scientists pursuing the genetic engineering route to interferon involving the use of recombinant DNA technology. In 1979, Wellferon received a UK clinical trial certificate which permitted trials on cancer patients.

The first substantial contract for which the company decided to tender was

Trevor Jones was a pharmacy graduate recruited from Boots to head technical development at WFL's Dartford factory where his responsibility was to ensure that all products conformed to local regulatory requirements in the UK and in other markets outside the North American region. Jones was one of the few senior scientists at WFL adept in negotiating relations within R&D, a division riven by rivalries. In 1984, he was appointed director of R&D in the UK and was a main board director of Wellcome plc between 1987 and 1994, Wellcome Library, London.

that posted by the NCI in the US. Organization and delivery of supply on the scale of requirement envisaged by the NCI necessitated the conversion of the large manufacturing and sterile processing plant at Torrino in Spain from the production of vaccine to that of interferon.[8] The responsibility for this was given to Castell who, in 1981, had assumed the role of general manager of WBL, of which Cresswell, formerly in charge of development at RTP, was chairman.[9] Both faced the challenge of transforming a historically loss-making biological products activity into a profit-making enterprise. Even as this initiative got underway, however, both in the UK and the US, directors expressed skepticism regarding the commercial potential because of high manufacturing costs, and criticized the company for being a laggard in the development of genetic engineering.[10] Non-executive director Greenhill was critical of the company's loss of its long-standing leadership in biological products having missed the opportunity to embark on genetic engineering sooner.[11] In 1980, two recently established small biotechnology companies in the US, Genentech (1976) and Biogen (1978), became the first to produce recombinant proteins using genetic technology to make human interferon. Shortly after, Schering Plough was the first pharmaceutical company to acquire the commercial rights to a recombinant product.

Negotiating prices also presented WBL with problems. This emerged in the negotiations with the NCI in the US. Setting a price required approval by Warlock. At that time the WFL group marketing director expressed his conviction that no interferon preparation would secure commercial success and that therefore, all accumulated costs since 1959 should be reflected in the price. The price quoted turned out to be substantially above the costs of interferon made from tanks of Namalwa cells, although, as this was intended only for chemical studies, there had been no necessity to provide the expensive manufacturing and sterile processing facilities required for the production of Wellferon. Even more of a setback for WFL was the NCI's insistence that, as required by all US government contracts, the standard reprocurement clause (intended to ensure value for money) must be adhered to at tendering and contractual stages. One implication of the clause was that WFL might become vulnerable to underwriting the costs of another manufacturer. This would occur in the event of WFL's withdrawal from supplying the NCI with Wellferon at an agreed price which might subsequently prove to be too low in relation to manufacturing costs. As this would probably necessitate an invitation to another manufacturer to supply interferon to the NCI, the clause would commit WFL to a subsidy. The second problem was a clause in the NCI contract which required "know-how" to become public property, a condition which WFL deemed unacceptable.

Problems of agreeing a contract were compounded in 1980 by the announcement that interferon had been made in genetically-manipulated bacteria. The seemingly imminent prospect of limitless quantities of interferon being available at trivial cost strengthened the NCI's negotiating position, prompting an insistence on a substantially lower price than that contained in the original Wellcome tender. Although recombinant interferons did not become readily available for several years, the expectation was that an alternative cheaper supply was imminent. The anticipated decision by Scherer and Roche to supply the NCI for clinical purposes at no cost, plus the improved efficiency of WBL's production process, enabled the NCI to negotiate reductions in price on each annual renewal of contracts. The result was to undermine the prospect for Wellferon's profitability.[12] Furthermore, the NCI lowered the amount of Wellferon contained in the initial tender by half, thereby reducing potential scale economies. Despite these setbacks, Vane resisted any budget reduction for vaccine research in which the company had enjoyed a long-standing leadership; he also secured a commitment for a new plant at Beckenham.[13] Meanwhile a series of clinical trials were initiated in a desperate search for uses for Wellferon. In 1986, Wellferon became the first interferon in the UK to receive a product license for use in the treatment of hairy cell leukemia.[14] In the same year, Schering secured FDA approval for the first Biogen-developed product for the same purpose for use in the US.[15]

Acknowledgement of the lead established by the American biotech companies prompted a plan to effect an immediate alliance with the Genetics Institute Inc. through a new, wholly-owned joint subsidiary company. Castell was the director deputed to negotiate with the Genetics Institute and to organize the formation of Wellgen. The purpose of this new organization was to construct a large production facility for the manufacture of proteins of value in human medicine by utilizing various cell systems, notably interferon and tPA.[16] However, the project was short-lived as a result of a failure by the Genetics Institute to provide the requisite finance with which to pay for the large factory that was constructed on Rhode Island. This was the consequence of the loss of a patent suit. Even more serious setbacks that left Wellcome further behind were Genentech's successful development of tPA and the success, by both Merck and SmithKline, in genetically engineering hepatitis B vaccine.[17] In 1989, employing Biogen technology, SmithKline Beecham launched a hepatitis B vaccine.[18] By this time, Vane and Shepperd had left Wellcome plc and, under a new chairman, the company's vaccine activity had fallen victim to Robb's rationalization of the company based on comparative costs, profits, and realistic research and market projections. Many years of heavy expenditure on the development of the hepatitis B vaccine had occurred at a time when Wellcome plc had been among the leaders in the search for a marketable drug. However, indicative of the company's failure was a comparison between the annual sales value of Wellferon in 1990 of $8.1 million and the annual sales value of Schering-Plough's version of the drug of $150 million[19]

Robb's earliest reforms tackled the financial, commercial, IT activities, and human resource management. He introduced a policy of developing and selling global medicines for global markets and extending the company's OTC business. For the first time at group level, marketing managers became involved with scientists in the process of prioritizing therapeutic areas for R&D expenditure and in planning product development[20] (an interaction already well-established at RTP) Robb also introduced an annual product portfolio review across the group.[21] An international regulatory team became responsible for preparing and monitoring the implementation of guidelines to satisfy regulatory authorities in all countries.[22]

Transforming R&D presented a more intractable problem, as his predecessor chairman had discovered. Frame's perception of the corporate culture of the company, which no doubt he would have shared with Robb when he was first appointed, was that staff regarded the organization, first and foremost, as a research portfolio rather than as a business. Frame had been critical of the level of expenditure on R&D which he had described as outrageous in the light of business performance.[23] In fact, an R&D expenditure of roughly 15 per cent of sales revenue (18 per cent of ethical drug sales) was only marginally above the industry average, though the 35 per cent devoted to research only (excluding development) was higher.[24] The difference between Wellcome and other companies among the world's twenty largest firms, however, was the absence of commensurate, commercially successful products other than those originating at RTP. Both Precious and Cochrane were particularly critical of the lack of any detailed breakdown of R&D expenditure in the UK and especially of RD&M undertaken in the US which both regarded as particularly serious. Cochrane criticized the presence of "a huge independence factor" which he believed undermined the coherence of the Wellcome group.[25] Similarly, of Wellcome plc, Precious believed that "One of the great lies … was to say it was one company [whereas] … it was always the US company and the rest."[26] Evidence of the lack of central control of R&D expenditure by the group main board is provided by Schaeffer's observation that, regardless of committee procedure throughout Shepperd's reign during the 1980s, the Americans could rely on him to agree to "just about everything we ever asked for"[27] at a time when fewer resources were allocated to Beckenham. The explanation lies in Shepperd's expressed perception of the American company as the UK's "cash cow."[28]

Cochrane believed that the representation of an R&D director from the UK and of an RD&M director from the US on the main board was one of the most serious weaknesses in the organization of Wellcome plc. Shortly before Shepperd's retirement, the appointments of Jones as research director in the UK and Schaeffer and subsequently, Barry as vice presidents RD&M at RTP (both main board directors), had perpetuated Anglo-American tension at the highest level. This arose from the duplication of research activities and difficulties in terminating projects.[29] When Phil Tracy became president of BW&Co., succeeding Haigler in 1990, he was fully accustomed to the American company's culture of independence. Like Cochrane, Tracy detected similar stresses and strains existing between scientists in the US and the UK. This arose from their contrasting achievements, their resources, and the existence of two research directors.[30] He shared a widespread frustration with the bureaucratic centralization of management functions imposed from London and then superimposed on the regional structure. Group marketing was a case in point; the group marketing function located in London "had very little to do with the US, but always wanted somehow to be more involved."[31] He summed up the attitude of marketing personnel at RTP as "We're working pretty well here; we don't need another level of bureaucracy getting involved."[32] The same applied to RD&M.

Robb grasped the nettle in 1990 when he appointed a single group R&D director whose brief was to rationalize and integrate activities in the US with those in the UK.[33] Jones, the UK director, was respected as a knowledgeable pharmacist primarily because of his experience of managing development. As a manager, he had been adept in conducting human relations under challenging circumstances, especially during the 1980s. However, with Robb in command in 1990, the new RD&M group directorship was given to Barry whose outstanding achievements as both a drug researcher and a "drug hunter"[34] were widely acknowledged. The confidence which his reputation was expected to give to scientists throughout the Wellcome organization commended him to main board directors who were prepared to overlook Barry's challengingly direct approach to human relations.[35] Referring to his own role and that of his scientific colleagues, Barry was reported as having informed other main board directors, "We are here to find the molecules. When we have found the molecules you guys in commercial are there to sell it."[36] Barry was openly critical of the low productivity at Beckenham which stemmed from the absence of commercial orientation to R&D displayed by most scientists. Tackling low productivity was his first declared priority. Closely related to this was a concern to raise prevailing low morale at Beckenham which he linked to poor performance. Another priority was ending the competitive tension between scientists in the UK and those in the US. Functional liaison groups brought together technical, clinical, and development managers from both US and the UK.

The goal established for group R&D in 1991 was to introduce one new chemical entity each year and one major extension of an existing product.[37] However, in the context of the need to develop new extensions for the use of Zovirax, developing a replacement for Retrovir, and legal challenges to the patents, it was not until 1994 that Barry convened a series of major review meetings attended in roughly equal numbers by British and American scientists and by representatives from manufacturing and marketing.[38] Without their collaboration, the goal laid down by Robb and the Wellcome plc board, was considered to be beyond the capacity of group RD&M.[39] The urgency of reaching the goal set in 1991 was underlined by the setback encountered by Wellbutrin and the group's increasing reliance for sales on anti-virals about which, in 1992, Robb had first expressed publicly his concern at the group's level of dependency.[40] Observing that the sales of Retrovir had consistently fallen below the levels anticipated by the board in the past, he described future prospects for the drug as "shaky."[41] He also regarded the future of Zovirax, which hitherto had exceeded expectations, to be problematical; it would depend partly on obtaining approval for wider uses to which the drug could be applied and partly on securing OTC status. The two substantial potential markets to which development was directed were as effective treatments for shingles and for chicken pox; the potential market for the latter was reckoned to be worth $150 million annually. Low dosage tablets for the treatment of shingles were introduced in 1991, and in 1992, a treatment for children who had already contracted chicken pox received endorsement by the American Academy of Pediatrics Committee on Infectious Diseases, though the recommendation did not include routine treatment of varicella in healthy children. In order to maximize sales, the company entered into a co-marketing arrangement with Wyeth-Ayerst, the dominant specialist in the pediatric market.[42] This was the first of several such co-marketing arrangements adopted to offset the company's handicap of lacking sufficient scale.

Securing OTC status for Zovirax, especially as a treatment for genital herpes, was more important than extending the range of treatments for which the drug could be marketed. Wellcome plc's first success occurred in New Zealand in 1992 when Zovirax cold sore cream achieved OTC status, as it did later in the UK and still later in countries in Continental Europe. After FDA approval in 1993, and in anticipation of FDA approval for OTC status as a cold sore treatment in the US, BW&Co. entered into an alliance with Warner Lambert, the leading OTC pharmaceutical company (where Cresswell was chairman of R&D), in the form of a joint marketing organization. Warner-Wellcome became the organization which sold Zovirax in worldwide markets wherever the drug enjoyed OTC status. It also sold BW&Co.'s other non-prescription drugs.[43] The promotion of Zovirax by Warner-Wellcome concentrated on a belief that UV light could reduce cold sores and focused on holiday use in both summer and winter. A special Christmas trade campaign featured a catch-line "be kissable." A 55 per cent increase in Zovirax sales was recorded in 1994 (at a level four times those of Retrovir) when the product accounted for 86 per cent of the entire cold sore treatment market in the US and for 43 per cent of the company's prescription-drug revenue.[44]

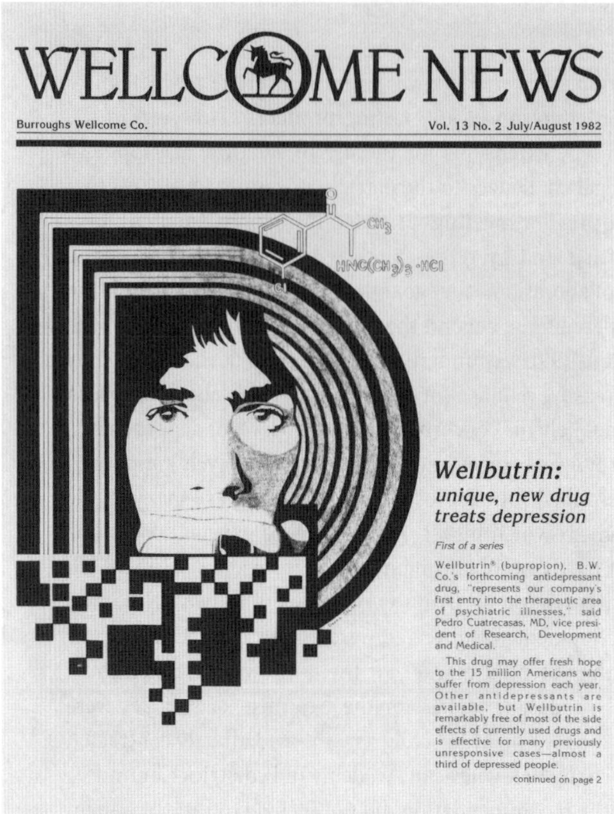

WELLCOME NEWS

Burroughs Wellcome Co. Vol. 13 No. 2 July/August 1982

Wellbutrin: unique, new drug treats depression

First of a series

Wellbutrin® (bupropion), B.W. Co.'s forthcoming antidepressant drug, "represents our company's first entry into the therapeutic area of psychiatric illnesses," said Pedro Cuatrecasas, MD, vice president of Research, Development and Medical.

This drug may offer fresh hope to the 15 million Americans who suffer from depression each year. Other antidepressants are available, but Wellbutrin is remarkably free of most of the side effects of currently used drugs and is effective for many previously unresponsive cases—almost a third of depressed people.

continued on page 2

Wellbutrin was the company's first anti-depressant drug. In conformity with FDA requirements, this advertisement includes a warning against seizure as a possible side-effect, Rescue from a resulting relative commercial failure occurred several years later through further development of other side effects which led to a re-launch as an anti-narcotic drug and as a stimulant affecting the female libido. *JAMA*. Wellcome Library London.

In other co-marketing agreements, Glaxo licensed its entire portfolio of OTC products to the newly-formed Warner-Wellcome Health Products group in return for a contribution to the development costs of Zantac.[45] Glaxo also formed an alliance with Warner-Lambert to market Zantac prescription drug alongside Wellcome's OTC products through the Warner-Wellcome Health Products group. One effect of the extensions and the marketing alliances was to increase further the dependency of BW&Co. (and of the group) on anti-virals which, by 1994, accounted for 49 per cent of all Wellcome plc sales of which Zovirax secured roughly three times those of Retrovir, though Retrovir accounted for almost half the group's operating profits.[46] Time was running out as, beginning in 1993, product by product and country by country, first Zovirax then Retrovir began to lose patent protection which would be removed altogether in the US by the end of 1997.[47] In 1995, another serious setback was a refusal by the FDA to extend OTC status for Zovirax as a treatment for genital herpes.[48]

Robb rang alarm bells which found echoes at RTP where the emergence of competition, even before the imminent lapse of anti-viral patents, had caused concern. In 1992, the BW&Co. directors undertook an internal review of the new competition facing the company's antivirals from firms described as "big, well-financed, and hungry."[49] Most of these were products of mergers between long-established

competitors. BW&Co. was ranked seventeenth in the US drug industry (twenty-fourth in the world) possessing a 2.2 per cent market share. Pfizer's total sales of anti-virals in 1991 exceeded those of BW&Co. ($2696 million) by 2.6 times. Sales by Bristol-Myers-Squibb, the largest of the rivals, were four times those of BW&Co.[50] The absolute scale of expenditure on advertising and promotion was dwarfed by the levels expended by the large firms with which BW&Co. competed, notably Bristol-Myers-Squibb, SmithKline Beecham, Hoffman La Roche, Eli Lilly, and Pfizer.[51] Inroads into the anti-viral market also depended upon innovation; by Bristol Myers Squibb which in 1991 had begun to market Brovovir in a competitor with Retrovir., and, which Roche developed Hivid (ddc), a drug marketed as a second-line therapy which testing showed to be effective as a first-line therapy when administered in combination with Retrovir.[52] BW&Co. also explored combination therapy, in 1994 combining acyclovir with zidovidune.[53]

Not only large companies entered the market for ant-virals. In 1990, Pharmatec Inc. had received FDA designation as an orphan drug, signaling a future threat from generics once the Retrovir patent expired. In 1993, two Canadian generic manufacturers, Barr Manufacturing and Novopharm Laboratories, began to supply zidovidune in competition with Retrovir.[54] BW&Co. challenged them in the US

District Court in North Carolina on the basis of patent rights and secured a legal ruling that infringement of patent had taken place. In 1994, successful legal action was also taken against SmithKline alleging patent infringement by manufacturing Famvir which BW&Co. claimed to be virtually identical to Zovirax.[55]

The status of Retrovir in the market experienced a serious setback in 1994 when an extensive international investigation into anti-virals, begun in 1992, was completed. The Concorde study concluded that while Retrovir had been shown to prolong the lives of some patients, the drug showed high toxicity and exhibited considerable side effects. Reiterating doubts he had expressed regarding the methodology underlying the Concorde study, Barry urged the board to allow him time to prepare a reasoned critique following his own statistical analysis of the results which, he hoped, would be accepted by editors of *The Lancet* for inclusion with the journal's own report of its findings.[56] Instead Robb opted for rapid reaction in an attempt to defend Wellcome plc's share price by reassuring investors. He convened a meeting of financial journalists to whom he offered reassurance that the company would not suffer commercial damage by the Concorde conclusions. Precious described the documentation presented in support of Robb's address as "sketchy and unconvincing" and the entire episode as a "public relations disaster."[57] Retrovir sales dropped 20 per cent and triggered a sharp fall in the share price of Wellcome plc.[58]

The futures of both relatively new and long-established products were also problematical. Lanoxin, the company's product with the longest history, faced competition from ACE inhibitors marketed by Merck and Bristol-Myers-Squibb. Sudafed had held the top position in the US analgesic market throughout the 1980s, but by 1992 Wellcome plc ranked tenth in the OTC market through Actifed and Sudafed sales. Competition in the market for medication for colds included four competitors from Schering-Plough, Sandoz, A. H. Robins, and Richardson-Vicks. Among neuromuscular blockers, Tracrium had been the market leader since its introduction in 1986, though by 1991, Wellcome plc shared the market evenly with Organon, the two firms together accounting for 80 per cent of sales.[59] Two products that were leaders were Neosporin in the topical first aid market and Nix in the treatment of head lice, though actual sales values were relatively small.[60]

Although the hopes for bupropion to become a blockbuster drug in the $1.2 billion market for anti-depressants (the largest and rapidly expanding therapeutic category) had been dashed in 1986/7 by a flawed clinical trial,[61] scientists at RTP had persisted with further development of the drug. The resulting Wellbutrin eventually secured FDA approval to market the drug as an anti-depressant, but by that time Eli Lilly's Prozac had quickly captured 55 per cent of the market. Pfizer's Zoloft entered the market in 1992, followed by SmithKline Beecham's Paxil.[62] Despite these setbacks experimental trialling at RTP led to the unexpected discovery, in 1994, that a side-effect of the bupropion drug was to inhibit nicotine addiction and might have a future as an anti-smoking treatment for which purpose the provisional trade name was Zidebeme[63] (later changed to Zyban). Subsequently, the drug was discovered to effect women patients as a libido stimulant, though it was not marketed as such until after 1995 when the drug became a significant revenue-generator from sales for all three conditions – depression, addiction, and low libido. It was limited to the US market.[64] By that time, however, neither BW&Co. nor Wellcome plc existed as separate entities.[65]

When Robb had joined the company in 1989, the public image of BW&Co. in the US and Wellcome plc in the UK had been damaged not only by concern regarding competition and the lack of replacements for the blockbuster products, but also by the furore over the pricing of Retrovir. He detected a widespread perception of a failure to strike the right balance between compassion and profitability which also attracted accusations of unethical conduct. By 1992, first in the US and subsequently in the UK, sufficient steps had been taken to elicit praise from the *BMJ* for the Wellcome organization's "positive action" outreach programs involving the HIV/AIDs communities.[66] Robb interpreted this as proof that the company had restored its "somewhat tarnished image" by having redressed the balance between concern for sufferers and the pursuit of profit,[67] a question re-opened publicly in 1994 by a critic of the company's ethical record.[68]

Meanwhile, other commentators began to question the vulnerability of the Trust which arose from Wellcome plc's indifferent financial performance. Since the first share issue in 1986 and especially following a second issue in 1992, the respective interests of the Trust, as interpreted by its new regime and Wellcome plc, increasingly diverged. Taggart's study of international competitiveness with respect to Wellcome plc concluded that it was imperative that the company should embark upon reforms which would result in a truly globalised company, the resources of which would be concentrated within the developed markets of the US, Europe, and Japan, "... if the Wellcome Trust wishes to have a continuing stream of dividends from its major shareholding in Wellcome plc in the long term, it must recognize [this] inescapable economic and strategic imperative ... In an ideal world, the Trust might even see its way to encourage this vital strategic thrust, as the alternative for Wellcome plc is inevitable stagnation."[69] Other observers expressed concern at the lack of progress in reforming the company to meet competition in an era of mergers and consolidation in the pharmaceutical industry across the world. However, neither Taggart nor other analysts envisaged the Trust adopting an alternative, more pro-active strategy. Since the 1986 flotation, however, and more so following a second flotation in 1992, stock market investors' behavior had begun to provide an environment which initiated momentum towards a more radical policy beyond direct intervention by the Trust into the internal affairs of Wellcome plc.

CHAPTER 25

The second share issue in 1992: A pathway to corporate revival or nemesis for Wellcome plc?

When the initial flotation occurred in 1986, the Trust had undertaken not to proceed with a further share issue for at least two years, an undertaking intended to reassure the market as well as allaying apprehension among the company's directors regarding the future of the business.[1] The growth in income received by the Trust after Steel became chairman, which immediately after flotation rose from £20 million to £35 million, demonstrated the company's capacity to sustain higher dividends, thanks largely to profits generated in the US (see Table 23.4). This evidence of the Trust's new muscular approach to the company and the prospect of anticipated reforms under market pressure provided no immediate incentive for the Trust to proceed further with divestment or to disregard the agreement with the board of Wellcome plc that, at least in the short term, the Trust should continue to retain roughly 75 per cent ownership. In 1986, therefore, the Trust had not formulated a long-term strategy that would culminate in the complete disposal of the company.[2]

For the first time, investors and financial analysts were able to scrutinize the company's affairs when its future was surrounded by uncertainty and attracted speculation. The share price spiralled initially. The final approval of the drug for treatment in March 1987 was the occasion for "hoopla and hullaballoo," according to the *Economist* which reported a fourfold increase in the share price of Wellcome plc as a result of excitement among public investors surrounding the prospects for the Wellcome AIDS drug.[3] Thereafter, whether communicated officially or by individuals, reports of clinical trials in progress on the highly toxic drug influenced investors' perceptions of its likely commercial significance and therefore the share price. Between 1986 and 1989, the company had attempted to manage the dissemination of results of other short-term trials conducted by international researchers by funding and organizing a series of international AIDS conferences both in North America and Europe. In addition to medical and health professionals, these were attended by thousands of patients, lay people, press, and analysts and provided an opportunity for

Wellcome scientists and those from other countries to report on the state of research and development relating to AIDS.

In 1988, BW&Co. organized an international conference in Stockholm, one of the largest devoted to an exchange of findings by researchers in the field of antiviral therapy. In addition to researchers, however, sixty of the company's managers were also in attendance, thoroughly briefed by expert staff from group commercial directorate RD&M, and US/UK public relations. In an attempt to control communications, press briefings were confined to specific times, supplemented by daily question and answer sessions. Shepperd instructed organizers and participants to avoid discussion of the economics of AZT and local company representatives were not allowed to deal with analysts from the financial press.[4] Despite careful management of the conference, however, not all of the discussion of AZT was favorable.[5] Two German scientists revealed evidence (not yet in the public domain or peer-reviewed) that indicated some reduction in the sensitivity of the AIDS virus to Retrovir. Shepperd conveyed this information to a meeting of the Wellcome board convened at short notice to decide whether and how the company should respond. Both he and Schaeffer favored no response. Schaeffer argued that, should a statement be issued to the effect that viruses were now shown to be less sensitive to AZT, experts would readily conclude that resistance to the drug had been discovered, a conclusion that risked alarming patients and their physicians (as well as stockbrokers). Jones concurred, emphasizing that, despite uncertainty, the drug's record showed that treatment with AZT had prolonged life. It was known that roughly 50 per cent of patients receiving AZT had died after two years and also that most, or perhaps all of those without such treatment, would have died within that period.[6]

However, the company secretary advised the board that in the light of information conveyed to the board, share dealing by employees would be contrary to the code for securities transactions on the London Stock Exchange and, therefore, should be suspended. Lever agreed that the information was price sensitive and justified the suspension of trading. Godfrey was not persuaded by the medical argument and urged that a statement be produced to protect the company. The board found it impossible to agree a statement because of the conflict between the perceived imperative of avoiding giving cause for alarm to patients and physicians and yet, at the same time, of observing a degree of transparency required under Stock Exchange rules which might have implications for trading in the shares of Wellcome plc. It was left to the chairman to receive careful briefing to enable him to answer questions at the forthcoming AGM "in such a form as to avoid raising alarm."[7]

A characteristic of the company's shares was their volatility. The media coverage of the outcomes (or anticipated outcomes) of clinical trials, of FDA decisions affecting the application of Retrovir, and the progress (or rumored progress) of the development programs of potential competitors became subjects for speculation.[8] Exposure of the uncertainties surrounding the company's commercial prospects led to financial analysts' speculations regarding the vulnerability of Wellcome plc in an era of mergers in the industry. Public exposure produced an environment which destabilized relationships between Wellcome plc and the Trust and the relationship of both with stock market investors.

On flotation, the company's shares had been underwritten at 120p and were heavily oversubscribed, soon rising rapidly to exceed 200p before the end of the year and doubling again in 1987. The share price climbed further on the tide of profits generated largely by sales of Zovirax, but they fluctuated sharply as the uncertainties surrounding the commercial prospects for the sales of Retrovir became a dominant influence on the share price. A price of 860p in December 1989 prompted the Trust to consider the sale of a further 10 per cent of equity, but by the time consultation with Flemings and legal advisers had taken place during 1990, the share price had dropped back to 400p. A second issue did not proceed, but remained a possibility as a resurgence in the share price during 1991 to 970p culminated in a spiral to 1,200p at the end of the year when the market reacted sharply to a dubious statement originating from within University College London that, taken in combination with other drugs, Retrovir would cure AIDS (a claim assiduously avoided by the company).[9] Underlying the logic of a second issue was the effect of the spectacular rise in the share price on the Trust's asset distribution which reverted to the highly concentrated ownership which had been the principle justification for the flotation in 1986.[10] Throughout 1991, Flemings provided a continuing stream of advice to the Trust (since 1989 under Gibbs's chairmanship) recommending a second sale, a reduction of ownership to below 50 per cent, and the most suitable time for a public announcement of an issue.[11]

The second issue was first under consideration in 1990, since when Duncan (the Trust's legal adviser) and Gibbs had cultivated relations with the commissioner whom they kept informed of the Trust's thinking through a series of unminuted meetings. Informal confidential meetings between Gibbs, Duncan (the Trust's legal advisor), and the charity commissioner, in preparation for the second divestment, culminated in advice that the Trust should seek permission to divest up to 75 per cent of its holding which would give the Trust greater flexibility. The sympathetic approach by the commissioner also contributed to the ease with which, in the spring of 1992, the High Court granted permission to the Trust to proceed.[12]

Rising profits and the board's new policy of distributing higher dividends resulted in a steady increase in the return to shareholders' equity as the Trust's pressure for further dividend increases intensified. The momentum building towards a second issue had coincided with Frame's announcement of a 10 per cent dividend for 1991/2, a level which exceeded the Trust's expectations.[13] None the less, Gibbs, accompanied by Peter Cazalet (a former deputy chairman of BP and newly appointed as a trustee), visited Frame and Robb to warn them that, notwithstanding the impressive dividend, the Trust was once again "looking seriously" at its shareholding.[14] From the time he became chairman, Frame's view was that the Trust would sell the entire company some day and for that reason he believed the directors should direct attention towards selecting a corporate partner to avoid having one imposed.[15] However, according to

Table 25.1 *Wellcome plc share price highs and lows, 1986–1994*

	1986	*1987*	*1988*	*1989*	*1990*	*1991*	*1992*	*1993*	*1994*
High	234	514	570	860	785	746	1,173	1,063	845
Low	156	178	292	400	423	357	704	604	499

Source: GSK/WF/SCS/798, WFL and Wellcome plc accounts and annual reports.

Table 25.2 *Wellcome Trust income; principal categories and WFL/Wellcome plc profit, 1985–1992 (£million)*

	Wellcome plc net profit after tax	*Trust income from Wellcome plc dividend*	*Investments*	*Deposits, and interest*	*Total Trust income*
1985	64.8	*25.3	3.4	–	28.9
1986	61.3	**12.7	7.3	5.1	25.4
1987	97.7	18.8	12.5	3.2	48.3
1988	131.8	25.7	11.6	3.7	41.5
1989	172.3	32.9	26.1	2.5	61.9
1990	197.3	44.2	22.2	4.2	71.2
1991	255.8	67.4	13.7	9.7	90.9
1992	264.6	†92.7	21.6	10.4	165.2

*Includes effect of restructuring of the Trustees' investment in creating Welcome plc.
**Plus proceeds of share sale of £199 million.
† Plus proceeds of share sales of £2.5 billion. Wellcome Trust and Wellcome plc annual accounts.
Source: GSK/WF/SCS/798, WFL and Wellcome plc accounts and annual reports.

Gibbs, Robb was stunned by the news of another share issue[16] and alarmed by the prospect of the Trust reducing its shareholding below 50 per cent thereby removing its protection from the company against possible predators. When finally Robb was informed that the Trust intended to seek permission from the Court to make a second issue scheduled for July (information subsequently conveyed to the board), concern was expressed that more time was needed to complete his planned reforms which were already in progress. The argument presented to the Trust was that a reformed business would allow higher dividends to the Trust and render a further issue unnecessary.

Frame's conviction that further divestment would occur perhaps within 5 years was based on the logic of financial expediency. Duncan's similar expectation of an eventual complete divestment was based only partially on financial considerations; he had detected a change in the mindset of trustees after the 1986 flotation. Hitherto, from time to time trustees had visited WFL head office and the Wellcome Laboratories at Beckenham and RTP to review developments in the knowledge that the company belonged to the Trust. Since the formation of Wellcome plc, Shepperd, quite properly, had discontinued the visits in order to avoid appearing to extend privileges to just one of many shareholders in the public company. Duncan believed one effect had been to diminish the trustees' identification with the business and therefore, their potential objection to further share sales. Moreover, trustees appointed since the 1986 flotation had no history of contact at all with the company, its directors, or scientists. As a result, they regarded Wellcome plc as no more than one investment among many and were content to accept advice on the disposition of Trust assets from the Trust chairman, merchant bankers and legal advisers.[17]

Once the Trust had settled legal and financial arrangements, the remaining challenge was to persuade the company to acquiesce in the face of "forcibly expressed concerns of management" against selling below 50 per cent without corresponding protections. The board sought a confidential undertaking which would preclude the Trust taking any initiative that involved a bid for the company which would inhibit, if not actually prevent, a takeover.[18] Two meetings of the board ended without agreement. A final meeting was convened. It was attended by Gibbs, Cazalet, Duncan, and Banks for the Trust and Frame, Robb, the lawyers and merchant bankers for the company.[19]

The company's position remained unchanged, and in anticipation of the issue's not being resolved, Duncan drafted a negotiating position which he had discussed with Gibbs on the previous evening. Duncan proposed that the Trust offer an apparent concession to the board. This was contained in a non-binding Memorandum of Understanding (MOU) and Deed of Covenant which, in retrospect, Duncan described as "legally … an oddity," though he believed it might break the deadlock.[20] The terms of the MOU were that the Trust would undertake neither to solicit takeovers, nor to sell further shares without first consulting the company, nor to facilitate any one investor or group of investors to buy a 10 per cent stake in Wellcome plc. In presenting the documents, Duncan explained that the significance of the non-binding nature of the MOU was that it enabled the Trust to preserve its ultimate obligation to act in its own best interests (in effect, freeing the Trust from the undertakings regarding future share issues).[21] Gibbs agreed that, should the meeting with the company's representatives produce stalemate, Duncan would deploy his tactic. After deliberation in private, the negotiators committed the board to accept both the undertakings and the trustees' right to act in the best interests of the Trust, however defined by the trustees. At a meeting with the Governor of the Bank of England Gibbs informed him that "something was going on."[22] The leading counsel for the Charity Commission approved the MOU and covenant which was signed later that evening, thus enabling the 1992 sale to proceed.[23]

On the initial announcement of the sale, Sir John Harvey Jones, chairman of ICI, telephoned Steel to find out whether the Trust might consider the purchase of all Wellcome shares on offer. Whereas the Trust showed no interest,[24] the possibility of an alliance with Zeneca (hived off from ICI and of comparable size to that of

Table 25.3 *Wellcome Trust income; principal categories and Wellcome plc profit, 1992–2000 (£million)*

	Wellcome plc net profit after tax	*Trust income from Wellcome plc dividend*	*Investments and interest*	*Total Trust income*
1992	264.6	*92.7	72.5	165.2
1993	426.6	62.9	136.1	199.0
1994	414.8	120.9	244.9	249.9
1995			321.3	322.7
1996			323.9	344.7
1997			280.9	312.1
1998			258.5	289.0
1999			276.5	313.5
2000			270.6	311.0

*Plus proceeds of share sales of £2.5 billion.
Source: GSK/WF/SCS/798, WFL and Wellcome plc accounts and annual reports.

Wellcome plc) was one of the possibilities pursued at a strategy conference held by the board a few months later. Precious was the advocate who sought to persuade his co-directors to give it serious consideration. By presenting comparative inter-company financial data in graphic form, he attempted to demonstrate that, from the standpoint of an investment fund manager, Zeneca was a preferred investment compared with Wellcome plc and that trend indicators also favored Zeneca for the future. However, the potential commercial benefits to which the analysis pointed, did not attract support for a merger, either from Robb or from his co-directors. Precious attributed his failure to persuade the board to the attitude shown by research scientists whom he believed torpedoed the idea by expressing skepticism regarding the content and potential value of Zeneca's pipeline.[25]

The sale reduced the Trust's shareholding from 73.6 per cent to 39.6 per cent.[26] Reinvestment of 93 per cent of the proceeds of the sale in August resulted in a 20 per cent rise in value, though this was attributable mainly to a sharp devaluation of sterling. The Trust's annual income rose from £25 million in 1986 to £165 million in 1992.[27] One-quarter of the shares was offered in Wellcome plc's first listing in the US when the Trust's portfolio was valued at almost $4.5 billion and total assets were valued at $8.25 billion.[28] The Trust's income increased by 50 per cent between 1992 and 1994.

Surprisingly reassured by the MOU that the company would continue to be protected by the Trust after the second share issue, Robb (who had persuaded the board to elect him as chairman following Frame's retirement on health grounds), Cochrane, Precious, and their co-directors stepped up the process of reform, details

Table 25.4 *Net worth of the Wellcome Trust, 1990–2000 (£billion)*

1990	0.2
1991	0.3
1992	2.5
1993	5.2
1994	5.5
1995	7.0
1996	8.5
1997	10.4
1998	10.2
1999	11.7
2000	15.0

Source: Wellcome Trust annual accounts. Even after adjusting for inflation (1987=100) net worth rose almost fivefold between the second issue in 1992 and 2000. Annual abstract of statistics, 2001.

of which, over the next five years, were outlined at the 1992 strategic conference.[29] The main board was strengthened by the addition of two more American directors, Cipau (who was now also Japanese operations director and president of Nippon Wellcome KK based in Kobe) and in 1994, Barry as group director research, development and medical affairs. Against a background of speculation among financial journalists on the most likely targets for merger or acquisition, most ruled out Wellcome plc because of its known historic relation to the Trust and because of the existence of the MOU, reference to which was necessarily included in the 1992 prospectus. Throughout 1993, Wellcome plc shares drifted down with the trend share prices of pharmaceutical companies and remained well below the 1992 issue price in the middle of 1994.[30]

Doubts were raised in the *Economist* regarding the company's ability "to thrive alone in the new industry dominated by giants."[31] Flemings shared this skepticism and conveyed the same reservation to the Trust following an analysis carried out by Banks in May 1994 which concluded that the directors' attention should be drawn to the danger that "the world was going to pass them by" with damaging consequences for the Trust. Banks proposed that, rather than a direct approach by the Trust, Flemings should contact the company to arrange a meeting with senior directors.[32] At a meeting held a month later, Banks conveyed the same message to them as that which he had given to the trustees, complete with a statistical analysis of the industry, showing inter-company trends including comparisons between Wellcome plc and its competitors. He concluded that without product leaders present within between four and six of the major therapeutic categories the company would be unlikely to secure a long-term future as an independent entity. The alternative options were either to make an acquisition, enter into a merger, or to be bought out. According to Banks, the directors listened extremely politely, but neither at the end of the meeting nor during the following six months did they make any response.

Fearing a collapse in the share price and in the absence of any reaction from the directors, Flemings urged the Trust to take the initiative before the company found itself in serious difficulties.[33] In private, Banks told Robb that he expected the Trust to receive a bid for the company within two years at which time, he was confident that the trustees would abide by the strict fiduciary duty to maximize its income and thus, fulfill its *raison d'être* in accordance with Wellcome's will. He deemed that as a result, the 1992 MOU and covenant would count for nothing. Banks pointed out that ultimately Robb and the company would probably be answerable to Flemings as the Trust's advisers who, in the event of a bid, would be asked by the Trust what action to take. He assured Robb that the answer from Flemings would be "a cold-blooded calculation as to whether the Trust would be better off selling."[34] Gibbs's representation of his own and the trustees' view at that time was that in the event of a bid "if the price was very high we'd have to accept."[35]

The Flemings initiative appears to have had the desired, if belated, effect. A report to the board in October 1994 referred to action having been taken with "a degree of urgency because of the ongoing consolidation in the industry." A strategy group was formed comprising two internal members: Keith Merrifield, main board director of Wellcome plc, and Sir Anthony Tennant, a recent addition to the board as non-executive deputy chairman of Wellcome plc. Tennant was formerly CEO and chairman of Guinness, the large drinks company, and a leading figure in the City of London and in the US where he was a director of J. P. Morgan. External members of the strategy group were two management consultants, one from McKinsey and the other from Morgan Stanley. The group's task was specific and arose from the continued conviction that the future of the Wellcome plc lay in maintaining independence which required a strategy that would persuade both the market and the Trust that this was a viable policy. The group's undertaking was two-fold: first, to apply tests against financial, business, and market criteria as the basis for drawing up a list of six potential targets for acquisition and second, to prepare defense arguments in anticipation of possible action by predators.[36]

The first interim report of the strategy group, produced in October 1994, exposed the unrealistic expectations of Robb and the majority of his co-directors. It revealed internal financial projections for the company over the next five years which implied a failure to meet management's aspirations of annual double digit earnings growth. It also indicated that the company's cost base needed to be further reduced by raising efficiency. The product mix was found to show strategic gaps in targeted therapeutic areas: anti-infectives, treatments for the central nervous system (CNS), and oncology. The penetration of the company's drugs overseas was also considered inadequate, notably in Japan. Measures introduced since Robb's appointment had begun to achieve results, but the report revealed fundamental problems. Because of these shortcomings, the group concluded that the company's ability to survive in competition with the industry's first tier companies was problematical. Furthermore, in the light of the company's inability to raise sufficient funding (as long as it was constrained by the Trust), the report's verdict on the board's aspiration to acquire a first tier company to form an alliance of its own choosing was that it was unrealistic.[37]

At the same time as the strategy group was reaching its pessimistic conclusions, an initiative was under way to offer the company a lifeline. The moving spirit was Cresswell, former main board director of Wellcome plc who had been a central figure in attempts to reform R&D during the 1980s, but who by 1994, was chairman of R&D at Warner Lambert. The advocate for the rescue plan within Wellcome plc was Barry, formerly Cresswell's colleague at RTP and at Beckenham and who was also, by this time, a Wellcome plc main board director. Already Wellcome plc and Warner Lambert were partners in a co-marketing organization, but the plan developed by Cresswell and Barry was for a full merger between Warner Lambert and Wellcome plc. Although Gibbs was apprised of the plan he was non-committal regarding the view which the Trust might take of such a proposal. From the Americans' standpoint, this was a discouraging response to a development that would require the Trust's support.[38] None the less, Cresswell succeeded in persuading the directors of Warner Lambert to agree in principle to create a new *British* company, leaving the occupancy of the post of CEO as the final barrier to successful implementation of the plan. Initially, Robb had agreed to the proposal that he should serve for a short period before making way for Mel Goodes, the CEO of Warner Lambert. However, during the course of negotiations, disagreement arose over the actual length of the "short period." This destroyed the hopes of Barry and Cresswell for securing a consensual merger. Barry conveyed his perception of the cause of the failure of their project to Cresswell as "We're hung up on two inflated egos."[39] The significance for Wellcome plc of the failure of this initiative became clear in 1996. The Parke Davis Research Laboratories, owned by Warner Lambert, completed the development of atorvastation calcium which was co-marketed with Pfizer as Lipitor, a blockbuster drug which would have filled the gaps left by Wellcome's anti-viral; Pfizer acquired Warner Lambert in the year 2000.

Meanwhile, after negotiations with Warner Lambert broke down, despite the limited choices offered by the strategy group, Robb and, it seems, most other directors believed that they would still have time to effect a gradual transformation of the business with "no sense of imminent threat to the company."[40] Cochrane attributed this optimistic view to the ethos inhabited by managers and staff throughout the company which continued to be rooted in an assumption of a continued undisturbed and protected status guaranteed by the Trust as largest shareholder at round about the 40 per cent level.[41] In December 1994, a *New York Times* financial columnist drew attention to renewed speculation among analysts regarding Welcome plc's survival as an independent company. He believed that in the short term it would survive hostile takeover bids because the Trust was still overwhelmingly the dominant shareholder and because of the MOU which he understood to commit the Trust not to sell more shares for at least five years. Other American commentators were less sanguine. In a column headed "Rocky road for Wellcome ahead," one observer predicted that without a re-invigorated product line after the anti-viral patents expired in 1997, the company would struggle to survive and would face dire consequences with serious implications for the Trust.[42] However, even in January 1995, a list of potential targets for takeover published in the *Times* financial column in the UK ruled out Wellcome plc because of the existence of the 1992 MOU.[43]

While the company was pressing on with reform and preparing a defense against any prospective bidder, the Trust continued to be under pressure from Flemings to take the initiative to find a partner or a buyer for Wellcome plc before the company was left behind with potentially disastrous effects on the share price and on the Trust's income. Gibbs was well aware of the merger trend in the industry, having received luncheon invitations from the heads of several large international pharmaceutical companies during the previous four years. Glaxo, whose $8.5 billion turnover was almost three times that of Wellcome plc, was known to have been "sniffing around" the company since March 1994.[44] Since 1984, Glaxo's rapid growth was attributable to the introduction of ranitidine (Zantac) an anti-ulcer treatment which competed effectively and overtook sales of Tagamet, SmithKline's blockbuster drug and hitherto world market leader.[45] So successful was Zantac that revenues generated led to a transformation of Glaxo during the 1980s which, by the 1990s, became one of the world's largest pharmaceutical companies in possession of resources wherewith to grow further through acquisition. The recently appointed chairman and chief executive of Glaxo Holdings in 1994 was Sir Richard Sykes, formerly a senior microbiologist at Glaxo and subsequently (before returning to Glaxo) director of biological sciences at Squibb's Princeton laboratories in the US.[46] He was regarded as possessing a sharp intellect combined with formidable communication skills, enthusiasm, and a "terrier-like" persistence.[47] When he had become chairman of Glaxo Holdings in 1994, the company possessed ample liquid financial resources for acquisitions. The possibility of an alliance with Zeneca did not materialize, but even in April 1994, Sykes pledged publicly that Glaxo would be "completely transformed within a year."[48] Beginning in May, he began preparations for a bid to the Trust to effect a merger with Wellcome plc.[49]

The prospects for a successful bid by Glaxo were in some ways greater than they had been in 1985 when such an alliance was first considered by previous chairmen of the two companies who did not proceed because both boards regarded an association as insufficiently rewarding. The fundamental change from complete to incomplete ownership (even though it would still own 75 per cent of the assets) by the Trust breached an historic principle. A reduction in ownership to 40 per cent following the second share issue in 1992 further simplified the task of persuading the trustees to sell more.[50] In 1985, when takeover had been seriously considered at Glaxo, the status of the Trust in relation to the company had been assumed but never tested; the rules and regulations applying to charitable bodies, which had been interpreted both

Sir Richard Sykes was appointed in 1972 as head of the antibiotic research unit of Glaxo Laboratories. He became R&D director of Glaxo Holdings, head of Glaxo Group research, and in 1993 deputy chairman and chief executive of Glaxo Holdings. His successful overture to the chairman of the Wellcome Trust with a view to takeover was central to Sykes's strategy to diversify Glaxo's product range which was heavily dependent on a single product, Zantac. In 1995, he became the first chairman and chief executive of Glaxo Wellcome and was instrumental in the formation of GlaxoSmithKline. Wellcome Library London.

inside and outside the company as providing the Wellcome company with absolute protection from takeover, had deterred potential predators. The prevailing perception among these and among financial commentators in 1994 was that since 1992, the ownership of 40 per cent of the company's assets as well as the MOU and deed of covenant continued to protect the company from takeover.[51] Sales of Zantac had fallen for the first time in 1994, while the important US patent on Zantac, which accounted for 43 per cent of Glaxo's sales, would expire in 1997. Equally worrying was the success of SmithKline's Tagamet, a drug of almost identical structure to that of Zantac, in overtaking Glaxo's dominance in the market for ulcer treatment.[52] Sykes anticipated post-patent expiry competition from generics which would flood the market and result in a possible loss of 90 per cent of Zantac sales within a year.[53] No new drug was in the pipeline to replace Glaxo's sales leader.[54]

The logic for a merger of the two companies in 1994, referred to by Sykes, was based partly on structural factors, a complementarity in R&D, product range, and partly on his belief that Glaxo had developed a culture of complacency at a time when global rationalization of the industry required greater competitiveness. The acquisition of Wellcome plc would be expected to supplement Glaxo's product range, offer economies from the process of rationalizing Wellcome plc begun by Robb, and strengthen Glaxo's American operations. However, Sykes's own declaration, delivered at the first meeting of roughly one hundred Glaxo managers six months after the merger with Wellcome plc, indicates a further motive. Cochrane, the only Wellcome plc director to remain on the board of the merged Glaxo Wellcome, later recalled Sykes's speech in which Sykes explained that his reason for acquiring Wellcome plc was not primarily to obtain the company's assets but to administer "a sudden sharp shock." By this, he meant putting everybody's job on the line and "creating a lot of uncertainty within Glaxo … to make it ready for the new world post-Zantac patent expiry."[55] In order to achieve this objective, however, Sykes had to overcome the barrier presented by the Trust's position as the dominant owner of Wellcome plc which, since the 1970s, had consistently resisted mergers and had deterred potential predators from mounting a bid. Sykes was to put this historic resistance and the MOU to the test.

CHAPTER 26

Ethics and economics, betrayal or moral obligation? The Wellcome Trust, the sale of Wellcome plc, and the formation of Glaxo Wellcome plc.

The involvement of Wellcome plc and the Wellcome Trust in the realization of Sykes's aspiration for Glaxo's future development began with a sequence of events in December 1994. An informal dinner, apparently unrelated to the affairs either of Wellcome plc or of the Trust, was attended by, among others, Sykes and two asset managers from Flemings, John Manser and Bernard Taylor, both of whom were colleagues of Lawrence Banks who handled the Trust's financial affairs.[1] The two Trust advisers were surprised by Sykes's casual after-dinner question, "What do you know about the Wellcome Trust?" In the contemporary environment of consolidation in the pharmaceutical industry and no doubt aware of Sykes's public statement of his ambition for Glaxo's future, Manser and Taylor interpreted Sykes's apparently innocent query as the earliest expression of an interest in Wellcome plc as a possible target for some form of alliance or even acquisition Days later, Sykes contacted Taylor to inform him that he wished to pursue the possibility of "an absolutely logical" merger between Glaxo and Wellcome plc, but that he had "no means of making any reasonable contact with the new chairman [of Wellcome plc] because he simply will not contemplate any such idea."[2]

Although the Fleming advisors were already aware that Robb and the board were determined to maintain the independence of Wellcome plc through a corporate acquisition which should be of the board's choice, Taylor offered to arrange a private luncheon attended only by Gibbs and Sykes. The purpose of the lunch was to enable Sykes to repeat his declaration of intent to the Trust chairman that a merger would be mutually beneficial for both companies and that he wished to explore the possibility through the Trust as the major shareholder. In preparation for the meeting on January 10th 1995, Banks and Taylor conducted "a little stage management" in the form of a scripted response for Gibbs's guidance when replying to Sykes's anticipated expression of interest; it was suggested that Gibbs should say the following: "If you come forward with an offer, the trustees will consider it. We are not seeking an offer, we are not encouraging an offer, but we are advised … that if you make an offer we couldn't refuse it. Should an offer be forthcoming our financial advisers would discuss with you the basis but without any commitment on the part of the Trust and ultimately the Trust would decide whether to accept."[3]

During a wide-ranging discussion over luncheon, Sykes expressed his conviction that no more than eight companies would survive in the global pharmaceutical industry by 2000 and that a merger between Wellcome and Glaxo could be one. Gibbs accepted Sykes's analysis but presented three reasons why the trustees might not favor a change in the status of Wellcome plc. These were: contentment with the current degree of portfolio diversification, confidence in the new management of the business, and probably the trustees' understanding of the existing 1992 MOU agreement with the company as precluding any action by the Trust towards further divestment before 1997, either on the Trust's initiative or in response to approaches from other companies. Furthermore, even if the trustees set aside these reservations and agreed to a merger in principle, a further difficulty could be anticipated because in the event of an approach from Glaxo (or any other company) the Trust would be required to inform the company first. It was also well known that the chairman was hostile to any alliance which was not of the board's own choosing.

The conversation ended with a question. Sykes asked Gibbs "Do you have your fiduciary duties?" (i.e. over and above duty to the company). Gibbs replied in the affirmative, re-iterating the Trust's ultimate right to act in the best interests of the charity it represented and of its beneficiaries.[4] Lying behind the question was the discovery by Glaxo's lawyers of a loophole in the arrangement between the Trust and the company. This was included in the detail of the MOU and covenant of 1992 which (as the creator of the document and the Trust chairman were aware) contained an inherent contradiction between the interest of the Trust, to which a higher priority should ultimately be accorded, and the company's interest. Glaxo's lawyers believed that, by persuading the trustees that the interest of the Trust had an overriding priority, the path towards negotiation could be cleared.[5] The Trust's proclaimed aim, as laid down in Sir Henry Wellcome's will, was to fund and promote medical research, but as this depended still to a large extent upon the company's performance, the current restructuring of the global industry in progress posed a threat to the future of both organizations. Sykes's leading question in January was crucial to Gibbs's acceptance of the logic of a merger in the interests, as he perceived the situation, of all three parties, Glaxo, the Trust, and Wellcome plc.[6]

Although Banks and Taylor acted without the Trust's formal authority, they met Sykes and representatives from Lazards, Glaxo's advisers, to negotiate a hypothetical price in the event of a bid. Sykes and his advisers assumed that Robb, and at least some of his co-directors, would regard a bid as hostile and feared that a spoiling action might be attempted. In anticipation of such an eventuality, even though Sykes declined to mention an actual offer price, he sought an undertaking that the Trust would not accept a higher offer than the actual one about to be made. Fleming objected that this proviso was contrary to the requirement that the Trust must observe its own fiduciary interest[7] which was in accordance with the provisions of the Charities Act of 1967.[8] Thus, the argument which Sykes had employed on his first meeting with Gibbs to persuade him to proceed with merger discussions in the first place was deployed to undermine an attempt to avoid competitive bids. Sykes dropped the demand that the Trust should only accept the informally agreed Glaxo offer price. However, an equally nimble response from Glaxo, which was intended to hobble Robb and his co-directors in any attempt they might make to attract a "white knight," was to replace the first condition suggested for another.[9] The Trust must make an "irrevocable commitment" to sell to Glaxo *before* the chairman and the board were informed of the bid; unless confidentiality surrounding the bid were observed, the offer would be withdrawn.[10]

The deal depended on the Trust's willingness to sell the remaining 39.6 per cent of the shares in Wellcome plc and to meet two further conditions: to disregard the 1992 MOU and deed of covenant, and to ignore the clause referring to the need to inform and consult with the company before considering any proposals from other companies that might affect the future of Wellcome plc. Gibbs later explained why the Trust decided to accept the confidentiality condition despite the widespread belief, shared by Robb and the board, that prior discussion of an approach regarding merger or acquisition, such as that by Glaxo, was a requirement under the 1992 agreement. Gibbs set out the Trust's position: "… in the documents we signed in 1992, we said that whatever is in these documents what has got to be understood, and understood clearly, is that we reserve the right to act in the best interests of our charity and in no other way even if it overrides everything in these documents."[11] Even though Banks had warned Robb months earlier that the MOU and covenant had no legal force, Robb and the board had continued to misinterpret the significance of both; Sykes and the Glaxo lawyers had not.

Immediately after the meeting between Sykes and Gibbs on 10 January 1995, Glaxo's advisers contacted the Trust's advisers conveying the intention to make a formal bid. Glaxo's starting price was 800p, but the level finally accepted by Fleming to be sufficient to justify recommending the Trust to sell was 1,040p, although as yet, the informally agreed price was provisional. Soon after, Sykes and a small support team met the trustees who, since the first flotation, had changed in composition. In 1995, it included leading figures from the financial community in London and scientists with whom Sykes was already personally acquainted through his own scientific career. Sykes presented a detailed case for the merger. The trustees agreed that the company had reached a critical point when both Zovirax and Retrovir had probably reached their peak sales before coming off patent and that. Wellcome plc shares had been under pressure. They acknowledged that an affordable acquisition of a second-ranked company might adversely affect the share price.[12] Therefore they accepted that a merger with Glaxo would be in the Trust's fiduciary interest. Sykes reassured the trustees that the name of Wellcome would continue to be associated with "true R&D activity" in the merged organization and that Wellcome employees would be treated "fairly and properly." A commitment was also undertaken to offer a board appointment to the chairman of Wellcome plc.[13] Both Sykes and Gibbs sought to reassure the trustees that the agreement contained in the MOU and deed of covenant of 1992 did not amount to an unqualified guarantee that no further sale would occur before 1997 because the signed document also included a declaration that the Trust "reserved the right to act in the best interests of our charity and our beneficiaries and in no other way."[14] Legal advice confirmed that the directors of Wellcome plc should have known and understood that neither the 1992 MOU nor the provision included in the covenant in response to forceful representation by the board compromised the right of the Trust to act in its best interests; these were left to the trustees to determine.

Immediately preceding an extraordinary meeting of the board held on 19 January, Tennant met Gibbs to report progress made by the Wellcome strategy group. Gibbs responded that he would like to see the Wellcome name continue, but did not wish to be briefed on any specific strategy the company had under consideration. He assured Tennant that the Trust would consider any recommendations that the board wished to make and emphasized that "the Trust did not have its own agenda."[15] At a meeting of the board, Robb informed the directors of Glaxo's impending offer to the Trust; £722 million in cash and forty-seven new Glaxo shares for every one hundred Wellcome shares, for which it was the Trust's intention, subject to High Court approval, "to enter into an irrevocable commitment to accept Glaxo's proposed offer in respect of the entire shareholding of Wellcome plc."[16]

The Trust formally entered into the commitment late on Sunday, 21 January, when arrangements were made to communicate the deed to the company as required by 07:30 a.m., before London Stock Exchange trading commenced at 08:00 a.m. on Monday, 22 January. An early morning meeting was planned at the Trust's Euston Road office when Gibbs, accompanied by Cazalet, would brief Robb on the position before meeting Sykes in the same building to discuss future plans. However, no such encounter occurred, because Robb's car broke down which delayed his arrival at Euston Road.[17] By the time Robb arrived at the office where he met Sykes, the markets had opened and desktop screens at Euston Road were showing a spike in Wellcome's share price.[18] Barry, who was in Beckenham, learned of the deal from the television news and telephoned Tracy, CEO of BW&Co. in North Carolina who was woken in the middle of the night to hear the news of the sale.[19] The share exchange was announced to all Wellcome shareholders on 23 January, a mixture of cash and shares.

The offer document, issued by Lazard Bros. (Glaxo's advisers) on 7 February, allowed twenty-one days to gain acceptance from more than 50 per cent of Wellcome shareholders. However, if the merger was to proceed smoothly the Trust needed the acceptance of the directors. At a meeting of the board joined by the strategy group advisers, directors insisted that the offer undervalued the company and criticized the Trust's "irrevocable commitment" to Glaxo which was seen as a discouragement to bids from other companies and therefore damaging to the company's chance of securing a superior deal.[20] A press release by the company declared that Glaxo's proposed offer was inadequate and that Wellcome plc was seeking an offer of a higher value in order to achieve "the best outcome for shareholders and the best possible future for Wellcome's business and employees."[21] In fact shares had hovered around 550p during the previous year, though they were quoted at close of business on Friday 19 January, at 688p.[22] This compared with the price offered by Glaxo of 1,025p (a 49 per cent premium on Wellcome shares). The bid represented a market capitalization of £8.9 billion. In addition to a cash payment of £6.3 billion from a position of high liquidity, the cost to Glaxo was the issue of shares to the value of 11.8 per cent of its share capital.

Before the sale could proceed, however, the Trust required permission from the High Court acting under its inherent charitable jurisdiction. The application raised the question as to when can an "irrevocable commitment" entered into by the Trust with Glaxo be revocable? The Court sanctioned the sale of the Trust's holding in Wellcome plc, though two changes included in the judgement were significant. First, the Court extended the final date by which the Trust had to accept the offer from 28th February to 8th March. Second, the Court ruled that the Trust should have the right to withdraw its acceptance of any higher bid submitted at any time until the Glaxo offer became unconditional.[23] In effect, the High Court diluted the benefits of the Trust's irrevocable commitment to Glaxo and thereby increased slightly the possibility for Robb and the directors of Wellcome plc to seek an alternative bidder.

The quest for a "white knight" focused on three companies identified by the strategy group as potential corporate suitors. Pfizer, Roche, and Zeneca had each been involved in previous collaborative or contractual transactions with Wellcome.[24] In the event, Pfizer did not bid. Roche considered but decided against making an £11 billion offer.[25] Zeneca remained interested at about the same level, but sought to pre-empt further bidding by insisting upon guaranteed acceptance of its higher offer. Because of the company's size relative to that of Wellcome plc an alliance might be regarded as a merger rather than a takeover, the Wellcome board requested the Trust to return to the High Court for advice on relaxing the arrangement with Glaxo.[26] The Trust declined because Zeneca refused to reveal the actual price to be offered. Two days before the deadline of 3rd March, Zeneca withdrew from further discussion.[27] The Wellcome board had no alternative but to recommend acceptance of Glaxo's bid. Glaxo Wellcome was valued at three times the amount of any previous bid made for a UK company and was among the world's five largest bids.[28] The assets of Wellcome plc became one-quarter of the world's largest pharmaceutical company with global sales approaching $12 billion.[29]

Outcomes for the company's employees and their reactions were very different. Although as part of the agreement between the Trust and Glaxo Robb was offered the position of non-executive deputy chairmanship of the new company he declined. He described the Trust's sale of the company as "much less than admirable ..."[30] This was a judgment echoed by directors and managers of BW&Co. who had failed to appreciate the implications of the 1992 MOU and covenant and who, like those in the UK, had remained completely in the dark over the sell-off until the bid had been announced. Immediate reaction to the deal in the financial press was cautious. The scope for rationalization was acknowledged to exist because of duplication of facilities for manufacturing and R&D in the US as well as in the UK, and of distribution facilities there and in other smaller markets overseas. There was also some overlap in the work in specific medical areas, notably cancer, AIDS, and migraine treatments. Wellcome was strong in anti-virals, whereas Glaxo led in the application of genetics research to drug discovery through a network of research alliances with both US and British biotech companies. Complementarity existed in marketing strategies, Glaxo focusing on prescription drugs while Wellcome had been developing the OTC trade, especially in the US.

However, reservations regarding the product lines of both companies raised doubts surrounding the future competitiveness of the new giant company. Forty-three per cent of Glaxo's worldwide sales depended on Zantac which was matched by Wellcome's 40 per cent reliance for sales of Zovirax. Both drugs were open to increased competition in the near future because the patents of both expired within two years of the formation of Glaxo Wellcome. In both companies improved replacement drugs were at the development stage, but neither had received approval for marketing. A further weakness shared in common was the lack of success in developing the Japanese market which, in 1995, accounted for 18 per cent of world pharmaceutical sales.[31] The most immediate opportunity was for cost reduction through rationalization, a process which revealed the extent to which the merger was in fact a takeover by Glaxo. Banks's view was that Robb's unwavering opposition to merger during the weeks after Glaxo's intention had been announced, compounded by the board's attempts to find an alternative bidder during the interim, removed the likelihood of a collaborative restructuring and reorganization of the merged companies. Robb and the board had decided upon a battle which, as Banks concluded, "The Wellcome board lost … and what happens to generals on losing sides is that they lose their heads."[32]

Robb's attitude is easily understandable. When he had been Beecham's CEO, within barely one year he had begun to implement a major reorganization of the company: slimming down, cutting costs, and the new chairman's priority – re-focusing activity around pharmaceuticals. Despite Robb's success in tackling the task which drew praise from the financial press, he felt compelled to resign once the incoming American chairman insisted on also occupying the chief executive role.[33] Robb's experience of Wellcome was, therefore, an uncanny repeat of his former ill-fortune, unseated not by a new chairman, but by the elimination of a chair to occupy. The process of implementing rationalization began within a year of the takeover when 7,500 jobs (representing 11 per cent of Wellcome's workforce) were cut. The factory at Dartford and the Wellcome research establishment at Beckenham and the research and manufacturing sites in France, Italy, and Spain, were closed and the large manufacturing plant at Greenville, where a sense of betrayal was at its most extreme, was sold.[34] Three months after the sale, the Trust set on record regrets that the bid had generated so much hostility from Wellcome plc.[35]

In the process of integration that followed, wherever duplication existed, senior managers from both the former Wellcome plc and Glaxo were required to compete. Cochrane, the only Wellcome director to survive the rationalization and to serve from the outset on Glaxo Wellcome's main board, described the process. He maintained that the criterion applied was merit, regardless of previous corporate affiliation; those appointed were deemed to possess the most appropriate experience and skills to fill each re-advertised post. The actual process was conducted by senior directors. One of them, Cochrane, assumed responsibility for implementing rationalization through integration of the two companies across Europe. Every choice made at management level was subject to the considered approval of the CEO's office before confirmation.[36] The upshot was that between 70 and 75 per cent of management posts were filled by Glaxo personnel. From Cochrane's perspective, the high attrition level suffered by Wellcome employees was a fair reflection of the comparative competences of people in the two pre-existing organizations.[37] An internal review of the entire assets of Glaxo Wellcome during the months after its formation led to the conclusion that the Wellcome business in the UK was the worst operating company with respect to culture and competence across the entire Wellcome Group.[38]

Whereas strong resentment against the takeover was shared by the directors of Wellcome plc and staff in London, Beckenham, Dartford, and elsewhere in the UK, feelings of betrayal at RTP and Greenville were even more intense. The takeover was perceived to have occurred, not because of the history of BW&Co. but because of the evident abysmal failure of management at Wellcome in the UK. Barry and Tracy were among the most outspoken of the Americans, but none was more vehement than the company's former long-serving president, Coe. He described the takeover as terrible, accusing the chairman of the Trust of failing to realize that in BW&Co. "he had a real gem."[39] Coe described the $400 million which the Trust gave to the Burroughs Wellcome Fund after the takeover as "a slap in the face" in view of the billions of dollars raised as a result of the sale of the American assets.[40] Barry was critical of the Trust for not giving Robb wholehearted support since his appointment and of the secretive manner in which the takeover had occurred.[41] Robb's verdict two years after the event was admiration for Glaxo which, together with Lazards had been very clever, but he added "… I can't say the same for our major shareholder. To have sold its interest in the company without talking to management is something many employees in the company will never forgive the Trust for … The Trust should have called Glaxo's bluff and asked them to make a full bid for the company, following which the Trust would seriously consider its position."[42] This was a view which was echoed by non-executive director Sir Jeremy Lever, who described the events of 1994/5 as "unedifying," particularly the exclusion of the company from any discussion, and he accused the trustees of combining "financial ineptitude with a course of conduct that I personally would not have been comfortable with."[43]

While not condoning the procedure by which the sale had occurred in 1995, on later consideration most critics grudgingly accepted the rationale and justification for the Trust's policy of divestment and diversification of its asset base.[44] Most directors, both British and American, agreed that Wellcome would probably not have survived without having made more alliances or a "friendly merger" initiated by Wellcome plc., the conclusion reached by the company's strategy group. The group's final recommendation to this effect were not due to be presented to the board until six months after the Trust had accepted Glaxo's bid,[45] though the potential suitors had been identified by the group during investigations prior to its report. The abortive last-minute involvement of Zeneca deemed to be unsatisfactory by the Trust meant that Wellcome's strategic plan ran out of time. Sir William Castell, who had left the company shortly after Robb's appointment (and who later became chairman of the Wellcome Trust), has described himself, after almost a lifetime as a Wellcome employee, as "very much part of the [Wellcome] family." After the final sale, he detected among employees in the UK "an enormous sense of betrayal," though he also believed that many years of mismanagement of the company finally gave the Trust no alternative.[46] On reflection, he would have made the same decision as the chairman of the Trust at that time.[47]

Perhaps Tracy, the last of BW&Co.'s presidents, best articulated the reasons for the universal shock experienced by staff in the US in reaction to the *fait accompli* presented by the Trust. He acknowledged that the former Wellcome plc was not large enough to compete in the consolidating market of the 1990s, that its future lay in some form of partnership with another company and that ultimately, as the major owner, the Trust possessed the power to decide with whom any such merger or joint venture should be pursued.[48] He accepted that technically, the 1992 agreement between the Trust and Wellcome plc was probably unenforceable. However, he also strongly believed that it conveyed a moral understanding among managers and directors that in the event of an approach received by the Trust, the main board of Wellcome plc, of which he and Barry were members, would be involved in preliminary discussion.[49] In effect, by failing to do this, the Trust had betrayed the faith which directors and senior managers had invested in it. Five years after the formation of Glaxo Wellcome, the Wellcome name ceased to exist, following a merger with SmithKlineBeecham to form GlaxoSmithKline.

PART SEVEN:
Epilogue

CHAPTER 27

Themes and Perspectives

This study provides new, archive-based evidence which supports some prevailing generalizations, hypotheses, and theoretical analyses based upon stylized facts, but qualifies or challenges others. The framework for the analysis is the concept of the firm as an organization affected by inherited resources. The most important areas of wider interest explored are as follows: the history of multinationals and management across borders, networks in the pharmaceutical industry, drug discovery and innovation, organizational cultures and corporate governance, interactions between business and government, and ethics.

The combined conclusions relating to each of these aspects explain the dynamics of the enterprise and add up to an endorsement of the view that diverse forms of coordination and relations between economic units or with social, cultural, and political institutions or groups, are more important than either formal ownership or managerial structure. The relatively small size of firm is not the key determining variable.[1]

Managing across MNE borders: a study in semi-detachment of a dominant subsidiary

The history of the relationship between BW&Co. in the US and its British parent company, known as WFL between 1924 and 1985 when it became Wellcome plc, reveals the complexity of the task of managing a multinational organization, a common feature of which is the potential for multiple competitive management perspectives.[2] Bartlett and Ghoshal conclude that the manner in which managements in different countries interact is influenced strongly by corporate history, by a company's "unique and ingrained administrative heritage … its way of doing things."[3] This perspective is similar to that of the concept of "inherited resources" to which Edith Penrose attaches such importance in her analysis of *The Theory of the Growth of the Firm* first published in 1959.[4] Penrose's thesis is especially relevant to explanations of innovation and firms' capacities for survival in competitive markets. A more recent analysis of market structure and competition in relation to advertising presented by Sutton also concludes that inherited resources are critical to understanding the dynamics of competition. In a chapter entitled "How history matters" he signals the importance of irregularities in affecting industrial structure and the significance of historical experience in explaining firms' capabilities, "the need to come to grips with historical influence is palpable."[5] Emphasis on the evolutionary dimensions of business processes becomes central to studies following the publication of Nelson and Winter's exposition of *An Evolutionary Theory of Economic Change*, in 1992.[6]

Of particular relevance to the historical experience of BW&Co. as an MNE subsidiary is Bartlett and Ghoshal's investigation of the problems and methods which companies employ in search of transnational solutions to organizational complexity associated with MNEs. They conclude that the determining influences on whether outcomes are successful include "the impact of leadership on corporate norms and priorities, influence of home country culture on underlying values and practices, and the powerful influence of organizational history."[7] Their stress on evolutionary influences to understand the dynamics of MNEs implies that structural and organizational factors possess limited explanatory capacity. They caution against acceptance of a market-oriented transaction cost rationale for the existence of MNEs. Yet hitherto, the basis for explaining this organizational form has been internalization theory which explains the existence of the MNE as a corporate form and the embodiment of a superior means by which knowledge can be transferred across borders most efficiently. Empirical evidence to support this proposition, however, is in short supply and has been described as a supposition rather than a factual observation based on empirical evidence.[8] In *Local Players and Global Games*, Kristenson and Zeitlin also find a lack of empirical evidence regarding knowledge flows between parent and subsidiary firms,[9] a finding echoed by Jones in a survey of globalization in 2005.[10] All three authors draw attention to the need for more research at the level of subsidiary companies in the ownership of MNEs, and particularly to the significance of sometimes conflicting tensions between parent and subsidiary.

This potential for divisions is observed by Bartlett and Goshal who highlight difficulties facing managers operating units across geographical boundaries, especially where cultural differences are significant. They raise the possibility of local managers developing limited perspectives and parochial interests, thereby producing tensions between centre and periphery resulting in the evolution of highly-skewed organizational capabilities and management perspectives.[11] They allude to the risk arising from tensions in relations between the headquarter-hub and the subsidiary, manifested in attempts by the latter to "protect turf and autonomy" exacerbated by blocked communications and strained, even adversarial, relations.[12]

The importance of institutional and cultural influences on the dynamics of the firm, particularly knowledge transfer and innovation, is also explicit in Jones's recent survey of the evidence from histories of multinationals. He emphasizes that these phenomena can be understood only by exploring historically evolving interactions between corporate strategies adopted by parent organizations and responses and policies pursued by subsidiary companies.[13] The history of BW&Co. provides a rich empirical demonstration of the relevance of differences in culture, aspirations, and objectives resulting in tensions between managers of the parent MNE and (in this case) its American subsidiary. This narrative documents the effects of differences with respect to knowledge creation and transfer and highlights disparate corporate performance between the two organizations.

The origins of Anglo-American tensions within the Wellcome organization are to be found in Henry Wellcome's withdrawal from active executive management of the multinational company which he had handed over to Pearson, his deputy, in London, who until he was removed from the company in 1940 had hindered the development of the American subsidiary which he regarded as a competitor to the business in the UK. A similar disregard for research conducted by American scientists was the basis for a mainly uncooperative and subsequently competitive relationships between senior scientists in the US and the UK. Mutual suspicions among managers and scientists contrasted with Wellcome's confident predictions from the outset, greatly reinforced during the 1920s and 1930s through investment in factory and laboratory plant and equipment and managers, that the American company was destined to achieve a prosperous future. Wellcome's personal (sometimes secretive) role was critical in the creation of an eventually productive research culture within a commercial environment such as was unusual before World War II.[14] His support for successive American presidents also strengthened BW&Co.'s establishment of a quasi-independence from the parent company in the UK. The evolution of separate and distinctively different corporate cultures and approaches, whether towards governance, capital depreciation and investment, R&D, innovation, marketing, or strategic policy regarding acquisitions and diversification, brought about a widening gap between the two companies after World War II.

From 1936, ultimate ownership by a charitable Trust had been an important differentiating feature that influenced a perception among employees (encouraged by senior managers) which contributed to a continuing sense of identity within the company. Shared values of integrity and trust proved resilient over the long term. However, unlike successive regimes at WFL, ownership by the Trust was not employed as a shield from market discipline by BW&Co.'s managers who applied their own discipline within an intensely competitive American market, but their approach was also influenced by the adoption of more advanced American business practices; differences between the companies in the US and the UK were cultural (accounting systems and methods of using information, for example) as well as personal. From the 1970s, BW&Co. began to make its voice known in an attempt to escape from the reputation of WFL which was an old-fashioned organization lagging behind the competition. The research in its laboratories, "the University of Beckenham," was dedicated to the pursuit of excellent science rather than to both excellence *and* innovation, twin priorities pursued in the US. Its American subsidiary projected the clear and contrasting image of a coherent *American* organization without capitalist stockholders, focused on the development of human medicines, and in command of capabilities which the parent company lacked. The success of the American business was achieved despite its status as a subsidiary of an MNE which was, to a considerable extent, dependent for that success on BW&Co. In many respects BW&Co. behaved as a dominant subsidiary.

A delicate balance: the scientific ethic and commercial imperatives

Themes explored in the scholarly literature focused on the analysis of organizations, administration, and management include the characteristics and dynamics of science-based elites in modern industrial society; specifically, the relationship between managers who shared an organizational structure with scientists but who were divided by philosophies and objectives.[15] The contrast has been drawn between the essence of management, which is seen to involve the exercise of some degree of control in pursuit of formulated strategic aims, and the fundamental nature of creative scientific activity which requires a high level of individual autonomy. Managing an R&D organization has been described as "essentially the art of integrating the efforts of diverse, creative and rather intelligent and autonomous individuals."[16] Autonomy in the context of laboratory environments has been defined as "...the freedom to choose the problems on which to work, to pursue them independently of directives from anywhere except the precepts of a discipline, and to publish freely the results of research,"[17] Bailyn drew a further distinction between "strategic autonomy" and "operational autonomy" to which Pahl and Winklers' notion of "strategic control" and "operational control"[18] represents a counterpoint. Within the context of industrial laboratories these concepts explain the existence of a potential conflict resulting from the simultaneous pursuit of managerial goals and the implementation of managerial procedures, which differ from the quest for creativity and innovation, for which scientists regard a degree of autonomy to be imperative.

The principal clash of cognitive styles occurred between scientists and commercial managers within the UK business and between presidents and managers in the UK and the US; and between scientists in the US and the UK.[19] From the beginning, both privately and in public, Wellcome had designated all laboratories as his own and not as an integral part of a business organization, although in reality, the laboratories had played an important role in the company's commercial success. In Wellcome's absence, senior scientists employed his confusing rhetoric to justify distancing themselves from commercial activity and to protect personal basic research as their principal endeavor. The resulting anti-commercial ethos which evolved in the laboratories persisted under successive directors after World War II. An evident lack of product innovation in the UK resulted in the company's relative decline in the industry.

This was in sharp contrast to the research culture and record of commercially significant pharmaceutical innovations in the American company beginning in the 1960s. Howsam's account of his visit to the Wellcome laboratories in Beckenham after his recent appointment as vice president of marketing and sales at BW&Co. provides evidence of a significant difference between approaches shown by scientists at Tuckahoe and later at RTP in the US, and those in the UK. George Hitchings, distinguished research director in the US, had invited him to join the RD&M committee, though on condition that Hitchings's committee would decide which drugs should proceed to development. Perceiving the opportunity for his own committee to accumulate information to enable it to plan how to market a product two years before the company filed for an NDA, Howsam readily accepted his role in relation to RD&M. However, when he visited the UK research laboratories, he recalled, "nobody wanted to talk to me. I was interested in profits, in sales, as opposed to being interested in science ... I was the capitalist beast."[20]

Attempts to reform the historically stultifying prevailing relations and to resolve the Anglo-American issue finally began under the new chairman of Wellcome plc who was appointed in 1990. Robb possessed experience of corporate reform and of restructuring a large consumer products and pharmaceutical manufacturer. The involvement of American managers and scientists at main board level in London began to exercise influence on the entire Wellcome organization. The new chairman soon discovered the existence of major competing constituencies within the organization. One was the American company which displayed a thriving culture shaped by historically de-facto independence from the parent. Unlike the UK organization, BW&Co. possessed the "distinctive capabilities"[21] of an innovative RD&M and product development system, a commercially productive research network, a marketing strategy, and a modern infrastructure. An important step towards the reinvigoration of the company in the UK was the first appointment in 1992 of a single research director who was charged with the task of creating a coherent, integrated, global research strategy across Wellcome plc. Barry, the senior American scientist from RTP who had led the team which developed Retrovir, became a main board director of Wellcome plc and relocated to London. Americanization of the company, which had retrieved the fortunes of the Beechams group, was now in progress. However, this development was unable to save the company in time; within three years, the merger of Wellcome plc with Glaxo heralded a rapid process of rationalization and global integration under the direction of the Glaxo chairman, Sir Richard Sykes, and the Glaxo board.

Underlying the contrasting relationships between managers and scientists in the UK laboratories and those in the US are differences in the attitudes of their respective research directors and senior managers, towards commercial strategy, to R&D, and to scientists' autonomy. In the UK, a succession of research directors regarded the strategic and operational autonomy of scientists to be inviolable and virtually non-negotiable. In the US, an accommodative approach adopted by senior managers elicited a more pragmatic attitude towards autonomy from R&D directors and other senior scientists, whose understanding of their role was to conduct research and development directed towards drug discovery and the production of marketable products. A brief interlude in the history of management of the American company during which a new president of BW&Co. attempted to impose strict board control over R&D priorities resulted in a clandestine pursuit of strategic and operational autonomy by scientists. In their interpretations of the management role, Coe and Sullivan were at opposite ends of the spectrum, as were Hitchings and Vane regarding their respective philosophies of science and their attitudes to R&D. The historical experience of relations between scientists and managers in the Wellcome organization, therefore underlines the fragility of adopting a rigid dichotomy that separates the outlooks of managers and scientists with respect to differences in perceptions of the degree of control or of autonomy regarded as necessary.

Organizational culture and networks of innovation

The failure of the Wellcome laboratories in the UK to innovate in ways resulting in substantial commercial rewards contrasts with the successful record of pharmaceutical innovation and associated profitable business achieved in the US. The explanation is partly historical. It includes Wellcome's own, somewhat misleading presentation of the role of the early laboratories in the UK, his withdrawal from business management, and the dominance within the organization acquired by senior scientists who defined their role almost entirely in terms of the scientific ethic as distinct from commercial considerations.

A brief recapitulation of the emergence of the American culture helps to explain why, despite its relatively small size, BW&Co. succeeded in becoming an internationally acknowledged centre of scientific research and a significant source of innovation in the market for medicines. The origins of BW&Co.'s research-driven strategy, established by Henry Wellcome and the company's American president after 1928, coincided with similar developments during the 1920s and 1930s at some leading old-line pharmaceutical companies, notably Eli Lilly & Co., the Squibb Corporation, Pfizer, SmithKline & French, Abbott Laboratories, and Merck.[22] Although smaller than these companies, BW&Co. also introduced in-house research programs and hired scientists from academia to lead research.[23]

An important difference between the history of R&D in the UK and RD&M in the US was that although early R&D in the American laboratories began with a template developed in the UK, an unrestrained scientific ethic was challenged by successive American presidents anxious to find new products in an increasingly competitive market during the 1930s and 1940s. After Wellcome's death, Nevin and subsequently Creasy attempted to impose policies requiring American directors of research to ensure that most research conducted in the laboratories was directed towards commercial objectives. This challenge to academic freedom and the threat of prescriptive research to be directed by other than the scientists themselves provoked resignations among senior figures. However, the tension between a research-oriented cognitive style and the profit-oriented approach was gradually eroded following the appointment of George Hitchings in 1942. His appointment marked the beginning of important scientific achievements by the small company.

Whereas in the UK scientists succeeded in challenging encroachment on their activities, the senior American scientists opted for a more subtle strategy. Hitchings did not challenge directly Creasy's interpretation of the role of research in the organization and the balance which Creasy favored between time spent on basic research and that which seemed likely, in the short term, to result in marketable products. Hitchings ignored it while at the same time speaking the language of commercial innovation. The result was the emergence in the US of a culture among scientists which was research-oriented yet focused, albeit long-term, on drug discovery and product innovation. In both organizations research leaders, and ultimately the chief executives, were influential in creating the context in which scientists, engineers, and commercial managers interacted, either forming dissimilar, even competing organizational cultures which occurred at WFL, or resulting in a cooperative, creative and productive system, such as that at BW&Co. Hitchings believed that the company would benefit if he succeeded in capturing the interest of the scientific community in the research that he led at Tuckahoe. His strategy for achieving recognition and the subsequent experience of BW&Co. also underline the importance of networks.

Rosenberg and Gombardella have analyzed the distinctive features of networks which they regard as peculiar to the pharmaceutical industry in the twentieth century. Both identify network participation, and therefore membership of the scientific community, as having enabled pharmaceutical companies to secure access to science research as a public good. Both regard this access as having had a strong influence on the commercial success or failure in the industry.[24] Historians of Merck emphasize the importance to its development of research leadership and the construction of research networks.[25] On the evidence from 20 case studies of US companies during the 1980s, Gombardella concluded that innovation and markey performance, were linked to the presence of an internally organised R&D which was "scientifically creative through open research and linkages with the scientific community."[26] The history of BW&Co. provides further evidence from a relatively small company to support the analysis by Rosenberg and Gombardella.

Competition and resource constraints during the 1940s and 1950s provided the context in which Hitchings's research led to a rapidly growing reputation for his team among the scientific community. These were instrumental in resolving the inherent tension between academic freedom, profitable activity, and resources wherewith to expand research at Tuckahoe. A striking demonstration of the significance of networking is the ten year collaborative agreement with the Sloan-Kettering Institute, which focused on cancer research, which included funding additional scientific staff engaged on Hitchings's research program and making the institute's laboratory and clinical facilities available to Tuckahoe scientists. The agreement was renewed and then terminated in 1957, by which time the company's financial position had improved and the greater number of researchers could be absorbed as employees of BW&Co. Thus, tangible gains from reputation and networking accrued to the company during that period.

The partnership with Sloan Kettering appears to make BW&Co. unusual for that time. Swann identifies a decline in the US of links between researchers in universities and institutes and those located in companies between the 1940s and 1970s.[27] The link with this prestigious scientific organization, an endorsement of the quality of research at Tuckahoe, enabled the company's scientists to increase their output of journal publications. This led to increasing mutual exchange of information with external bodies and placed Tuckahoe scientists firmly within a knowledge network.

Unlike the approach adopted by research directors in the UK, those in the US accepted a degree of urgency when balancing certainty regarding the outcome of the discovery of new compounds against patients' benefit from novel therapeutic developments. The underlying rationale for this approach was encapsulated in Cresswell's phrase: "the patient is waiting."[28] BW&Co.'s success in achieving this balance lay in the exercise of scientific leadership, the roles of enlightened business leaders, and networking. The model which allowed the spirit of the academic community to emerge and flourish in a commercial environment remained unchallenged until the 1980s, when the new president of BW&Co. attempted unsuccessfully to impose modish managerial methodologies in the direction of RD&M. His skepticism regarding the likely commercial outcome of continuing anti-viral research led the scientists to proceed in secrecy. Within the decade this research was to lead to Retrovir, the company's second largest selling drug in its history.

The above account of the creation of a knowledge-based culture, established at Tuckahoe and perpetuated at RTP, fits well with an ambitious speculative model of technology, science, and innovation in the US from 1945. In a wide-ranging review of the literature, Scranton argues that the deeply-rooted preoccupation of historians with mass production and the large modern corporation has crowded out identification of alternative paths to creativity and innovation.[29] He suggests that since World War II, trends can be discerned which might be described as indicative of a transition "from a society of structures to a society of flows, from an environment of knowledgeability," in which refining the known and the familiar characterized competition, "to an environment of performance and propulsive innovation"[30] in which experimentation and learning through failure became central in growing areas of business activity.[31] Under conditions of uncertainty, "forward learning capabilities" became more important than efficiency as the route to significant technical and scientific innovation and therefore to business dynamism.[32] Quoting the organizational theorist Karl Weick,[33] Scranton underlines the importance in the new economic environment, of managers' capacity for "managing the unexpected mindfully." This capability, attributed to the "learning organization", needed to be exercised by scientists and engineers, acknowledging that they could not presume to know whence or when significant learning would originate.[34] Managers should avoid narrowly prescriptive and rhetorical approaches and be prepared to learn from the wisdom of their colleagues in searching for effective ways of overcoming persistent uncertainty.[35]

Drug discovery and drug development

An important implication of Scranton's analysis is that in a prevailing environment of uncertainty, scale of organization becomes less important than flexibility. This is consistent with one of the conclusions drawn by Takuji Hara, the author of a recent review of the literature concerning innovation and the process of drug discovery and drug development in the international pharmaceutical industry.[36] Empirical evidence led him to suggest that the type of organization most conducive to paradigmatic innovation and application (of the kind forthcoming from BW&Co.)[37] is not a strongly integrated corporate organization. This is because of the improbability that more than a few members would accept the unfamiliar concept accompanying this type of innovation. Hence, the importance of the role of scientific leaders within a business in shaping compounds and, through clinical trials and drug applications, in shaping the market.[38] With the exception of a brief period during the 1980s, BW&Co. was an organization displaying an optimal, mutually supportive corporate and research leadership. Hitchings's encouraging, though occasionally critical, approach to the work of those whom he recruited, nurtured the knowledge and skills of a research team respected by both corporate management in the American company and the academic research community. Hitchings's early rational drug design approach allowed for trial and error (this involved discarding compounds in the process), and serendipitous influences on the direction and, at times, outcomes of research and development. In this respect, the balance between a rational approach and a serendipitous advance conforms to Hara's model of successful drug discovery and development in the industry.[39]

For the most part, influences are not entirely random. The reciprocity inherent in research networks is an important source from which originates unanticipated influences in the form of clues and cues offered by other researchers. The material significance of the network in the longer term lies in scientific innovation and new medicines resulting from subsequent collaboration, mainly with external institutions and individual academic researchers and clinicians. By influencing the directions of research initiated in the laboratories of BW&Co., network connections had substantial results that affected eventual outcomes of research. After World War II cooperation with WFL scientists in the UK was limited. Collaboration with the Sloan Kettering Institute during the late 1940s and 1950s culminated in the leukemia drug, Purinethol brand 6-Mercaptopurine, the first of several related developments. During the 1960s, Imuran, the important immunosuppressive drug which soon became associated with kidney and heart transplantation, resulted from interest and cooperation with scientists at The New England Medical Centre and The Peter Brent Brigham Young Hospital in Boston. The result of a visit to Tuckahoe by Dr Roy Calne, renal specialist from St Mary's Hospital in London and Dr Joseph Murray from Brigham Young, led to collaboration with Hitchings and his team in developing and testing the immunodepressant drug for kidney transplants which resulted in the company launching Imuran. Zyloprim, developed from a novel purine path to chemotherapy which was successfully applied to the treatment of gout and similar blood disorders, owed much to collaboration between Elion and Hitchings, and hematologists at Duke University.[40]

The first important collaboration with another company, Hoffmann La Roche, led to the development of the initial concept of a broad spectrum anti-bacterial. Scientists at the Wellcome Laboratories in the UK conducted a screening program for American researchers (a rare example of Anglo-American collaboration conducted between WFL scientists) which led to the development of Septrin being placed on the UK market in 1969. Further research in collaboration with Roche to develop a drug to meet FDA standards resulted four years later in Septra which was a major commercial success in the US. Attracrium, a neuromuscular blocking agent marketed by BW&Co in the 1980s as Tracrium, also originated outside the company. In 1974, Dr J. B. Stanlake, of the University of Strathclyde, Scotland, synthesized the compound, but was unable to obtain funding for sufficient development and testing in the US to demonstrate a toxicity low enough to meet FDA standards. Cresswell was familiar with the research carried out by his fellow Scot whom he respected, and secured funding from within the company to facilitate testing and developmental collaboration between the Scottish researchers and those at RTP. Following FDA approval, Tracrium was launched in the UK in 1981 and in the US in 1984, successfully challenging Organon, the market leader.[41]

Research by Schaeffer and Elion which eventually led to the marketing of Zovirax (the antiviral treatment for genital herpes) in 1982 was influenced by the intervention of research into cancer treatment some twenty years before conducted by Dr Charles Heidelberger while holder of an American Cancer Society Fellowship at the University of Wisconsin. His suggestion to researchers at RTP that they seek a treatment for corneal lesions caused by herpes was the stimulus to which Schaeffer, Elion, and Falco responded. Unprecedented multiple cooperation between universities, institutes, government, and BW&Co. culminated in the development of AZT, placed on the market in 1989 as Retrovir. The award of a joint Nobel Prize to Hitchings and Elion in 1988 recognized the cumulative contribution of "their discoveries of important principles of drug treatment."[42]

A tabulation of the corporate sources of drugs considered to have had the most impact upon therapeutic practice between 1965 and 1992 highlights the record of BW&Co.'s scientists by comparison with their competitors.[43] The authors of the study divided the drugs into three categories: in the first category four drugs resulted from the empirical, pharmacological screening of compounds using *in vitro* methods; none originated from BW&Co. Four drugs fell into the category of those discovered through fundamental science, one of which was Acyclovir/Zovirax which originated from BW&Co. Ten were the result of "mechanically-driven" screening of known agents or suspected disease targets and included BW&Co.'s AZT/Retrovir. Underlining the significance of the breakthrough resulting in the first antiretroviral therapy for AIDS which this represented was the time taken (sixteen years compared with the average of 24.4 for drugs within the same category) between the enabling discovery and the product launch into the market. Collaboration and close interaction with government agencies were crucial in this development, a process which had a wide significance for government-industry relations. The history of innovation at BW&Co.between 1942 and 1995 underlines the centrality of diverse paths to innovation.

Government, business, and pressure groups; price, politics, and public relations

The history of Retrovir, the culmination of decades of anti-viral research, was significant in the history of modern medicine. However, the collaboration which underpinned the development also marked a turning point in the history of relations between government and science-based companies. Since World War II, the pharmaceutical industry in the US had been a focus for political controversy and was subjected to a succession of Congressional hearings.[44] During the 1940s and 1950s, BW&Co. remained outside the elite group of large pharmaceutical companies favored by the US government through the activities of the Office of Scientific Research and Development. Tobell has emphasized the strategic importance of government initiatives promoting inter-firm cooperation and knowledge transfer between industry, universities and other research organizations.[45] However, BW&Co. developed its own research networks without such support. The connection with Sloan Kettering established a firm foundation for subsequent collaboration between the company's scientists and those in universities and other research institutes thereby forming an enduring network.

In 1962, the Thalidomide tragedy added to the momentum for reform and closer regulation of the industry. Hitherto, the FDA had been concerned with the safety of drugs; proof of efficacy was an issue only with respect to certain specific prescription drugs, such as insulin and antibiotics. After the Kefauver-Harris Amendments in 1962, efficacy was required before any new drug could receive FDA approval for marketing. New standards were set for methods of production and testing directed towards ensuring the efficacy as well as safety of medicines. BW&Co. was only marginally affected in the short-term by the resource requirements, though the added delay before approval had some effect and the bad-tempered battle with the FDA over Empirin soured relations between the FDA and BW&Co.

Relations were transformed during the 1980s. The catalyst was the AIDS epidemic. The attention of scientists at BW&Co. was first drawn to the possibility that their experience might enable them to find a treatment for the disease in 1984. The source was an informal communication by one of the participants in research then being conducted at the Pasteur Institute in Paris. Zovirax had demonstrated the company's capacity for viral research and with full support from Cuatrecasas, vice president research, Barry assembled an inter-disciplinary anti-viral team to which funds were committed to meet the challenge set by HIV/AIDS. The long-established reputation of RD&M enjoyed by BW&Co. justified the company's inclusion in a list of several (mostly large) firms which the National Cancer Institute approached to invite discussion with a view to possible collaboration. The NCI was already cooperating with scientists at Duke University who also shared a history of collaboration with BW&Co. scientists. The growing national concern that an epidemic was gripping the nation when no remedy appeared to be in sight led to the FDA also becoming part of a tripartite institutional matrix in search of a treatment.

The NCI represented public health; a purely scientific interest was represented by scientists at Duke; a commercial interest was the prime concern at BW&Co. The negotiating process and outcome by which these bodies came together to form a partnership assumed national significance. During the 1980s, a reconfiguration of relations between research institute, university, the regulator, and the company brought together equal partners in a successful national quest. The continuing negotiations over the next few years involved the process of defining the respective roles and responsibilities of the participants in this unusual partnership and culminated in recriminations and court hearings arising from disputes over the origins of AZT and patent rights. However, the material product of collaboration was the availability of a drug which could at least postpone death for AIDS sufferers, though as yet, not cure.

The experiences and the problems which such an alliance presented led to legislation. One effect of regulation since the 1960s had been to reduce the effective period of protection offered by patents from 13.6 years with respect to drugs coming off patent in 1966 to 9.5 years for an equivalent cohort in 1979.[46] In 1984, the Drug Price Competition and Patent Term Restoration (Hatch-Waxman) Act extended the effective length of patent protection by roughly five years. However, the innovative element in the Act was a reduction of barriers to entry for manufacturers of generic drugs for which restoring patent life was compensation for non-generic producers. Reliance on an adequate period of exclusive selling in a market, the size of which was impossible to gauge with any certainty, was an important consideration for BW&Co. Likewise, those who framed the Technology Transfer Act of 1986 acknowledged the need to provide sufficient incentives for those in the public sector in order to encourage private/public collaboration. This Act did, indeed, assist the continuing tripartite collaboration involving the NCI between 1986 and 1990.[47] The significance of the legislation was that, for the first time, government-owned government-operated laboratories were allowed to enter into cooperative research and development agreements with universities and the private sector. Henceforward, federal laboratories were required to undertake initiatives in transferring scientific advancements or technology to industry and universities leading to commercialization. Provisions under the act included the right to patent licenses and enabled federal employees to receive royalties (rather than returning them to the Treasury).

Marketing pharmaceuticals: selling, detailing etiquette, and education

The marketing of pharmaceuticals in the US has received relatively little attention from historians.[48] The exception is Greene's analysis of a transition in methods of selling which he asserted occurred in the 1940s and 1950s and which he explains in terms of two contemporary parallel developments. One was industrial and structural and is consistent with the relation between size, organization, structure, and strategy which Friedman related to a transformation in sales methods generally (without dealing specifically with drug salesmen). This applied to the period between the 1880s and the 1930s. His thesis is that during the 1940s and 1950s, the growth of large-scale, mass-producing pharmaceutical companies established powerful sales departments which exercised close management control, directing salesmen's selling activities and monitoring their performance.[49]

The other new development adduced by Greene to explain a transition in selling drugs was medical innovation. Innovations in medicine saw the emergence of new classes of more complex therapeutic compounds, notably sulfa drugs and antibiotics. The combined results of which, he argues, was a decline in the hard-selling practices of the detail man widespread before World War II, but which were superseded by the emergence of the professional sales representative, increasingly a pharmacy college graduate, whose role became that of educator and negotiator rather than that of the traditional detail man. A manifestations of the tactical and behavioral changes associated with these developments was the projection of salesmen's activities by their invasion of doctors' consulting rooms and hospitals which, before the 1940s, had been regarded as private social spaces restricted to medical staff. This development he perceived to have introduced a new dynamic resulting from tension arising from the conflicting interests of salesmen whose objectives were to secure prescription orders, and physicians who needed to obtain information regarding the relative merits of new treatments as they became available for treating patients.[50]

The history of BW&Co. before the 1940s cast doubt on the validity of each of these aspects of Greene's generalization regarding the chronology and therefore, the causes and consequences which contributed to developments in the history of selling and of detailing etiquette between 1940 and the 1960s. Henry Wellcome was a pharmacy graduate who had worked as a detail man for Wyeth & Brother in the 1870s and together with his partner Silas Burroughs, who possessed similar qualifications, introduced detailing to the British pharmaceutical industry which was replicated at the New York sales branch from the beginning.

As in the UK, the company's detail men in the US were not independent; they were subject to management supervision regarding territory, sales methods, and campaigns, and their performance was monitored. They were supported by advertising which was limited to professional, medical, and trade journals. Even before 1940, many of BW&Co.'s detail men were pharmacy graduates, several having accumulated experience in the retail drug trade before undergoing training with the company. A confidential monthly newsletter entitled "Points for Propaganda" was circulated to all detail men to apprise them of effective selling methods to be employed in a variety of situations, The company had introduced an educational dimension to selling from the 1920s onwards when salesmen in the US were required to detail advanced therapeutic products supplied from the Wellcome Research Laboratories in Beckenham, England. The "social spaces" which Greene assumes to have been the exclusive preserve of doctors and patients until the 1940s had been invaded by BW&Co.'s representatives decades before.[51]

Greene regards the evolution of market research during the 1940s and 1950s as a systematic process and part of the pivotal transition in selling. It is true that the increasing application of quantitative methods to market research and subsequently, the application of more sophisticated computerized data collection and analysis marked a major step forward. However, long before 1940, BW&Co.'s approach was neither unsystematic nor anecdotal. Information gathered by salesmen was cross-checked with pharmacists before managers compiled physician profiles which listed specialties and the actual prescribing behavior of medical practitioners. Greene's analysis of the transformation in selling is valid inasmuch as growing "scientific complexity" beginning in the 1940s, associated with the R&D of large firms, led to the development of new therapies and a necessarily greater emphasis upon the education and training of pharmaceutical representatives. However, the history of BW&Co. provides evidence which contradicts both Greene's chronology of such a selling transformation and his emphasis on the role of large organizations as essential to that process. The company's formal training program established in the 1930s was referred to by the author of a contemporary manual for selling pharmaceuticals as one of only a few companies to have introduced systematic training which was adequate to equip salesmen with a proper qualification before calling on doctors.[52]

Greene's emphasis on the importance of corporate size and extensive organization in enabling large sales departments to transform selling methods finds no support from the history of BW&Co. "Modern sales techniques and procedures," as defined by Friedman, include route planning for sales representatives, assignment of specific territories, profiling and evaluation of customers, the requirement for reports after salesmen's visits, allocation of monthly quotas, issuance of detailed instructions for salesmen on how to sell, the existence of a systematic training program, and the assembling of primitive research data gathered by detail men.[53] Each was an element in the company's strategy long before 1940.[54]

Inter-related institutional governance and policies: lessons from history

A recent review of the literature concerned with corporate governance ends inconclusively, emphasizing that, in order to distil generalizations, much more historical work on the variety of organizational mechanisms for the government of industrial enterprise is necessary.[55] The history of the governance of BW&Co., WFL, and the Wellcome Trust and the relations between them, is unlikely to contribute to any search to identify explanations for the variation or performance of different forms of governance. Henry Wellcome was an eccentric, though hugely successful entrepreneur during twenty years as partner and owner-manager of a company which, for a brief period, led the pharmaceutical industry in Britain.

However, his creation of the Wellcome Trust, which was to assume ownership of the business after his death, was the result of a will accompanied by separately expressed wishes which were ambiguous regarding the powers and role of the body responsible for the multinational company. Wellcome had specified the competencies to be required of each of five trustees to be appointed, among whom only one was required to have had experience of business (other than accountancy and estate management). In the short term, these wishes hampered immediate reform of the weakening business empire. Wellcome designated his long-time former deputy Pearson as his successor with the right to choose his own retirement date. He had presided over the decline of WFL in Wellcome's absence. During the early years of the Trust solicitors and academics possessing distinguished records in medical research dominated the board. Established figures from the world of business were introduced but remained the exception. Their presence did not mark any departure from the interpretation of the Trust's primary responsibility which was to disburse anticipated dividend income from WFL to fund medical research in accordance with Wellcome's wishes. The competencies shared by the trustees were to remain unchanged as were most of the aged trustees until in 1966 the High Court approved a request by the Trust to add two to the existing five trustees, one of whom should possess an understanding of finance and the city of London. The justification offered to the court was that WFL presented numerous problems of increasing complexity.[56] The opportunity to make such an appointment, however, did not occur until the 1980s.

The significance of Trust ownership changed over time and was interpreted differently in the UK and the US. During the 1940s the Trust had intervened to replace chairmen and managers whom the trustees deemed to be incompetent with others. Financial collapse of WFL was thereby avoided and therefore the threat to the Trust's income, except for forcing the resignation of the president of BW&Co. in 1969. During the period between 1948 and 1980 compliant trustees presided over the appointment of ineffectual chairmen and managers of WFL who persuaded successive Trust chairmen to agree to moderate claims for dividend income. The effect was to protect the company from market discipline and allow an increasingly centralized though bureaucratic organization to stagnate within a sclerotic corporate culture. A change in personnel at the Trust heralded a renewed policy of intervention in the form of a phased flotation with the intention of applying market discipline. Protection was withdrawn from WFL which under new management was compelled to restructure to meet competition.

Whereas successive chairmen and managers had regarded Trust ownership as a guarantee of independence and protection from takeover, in contrast successive presidents and directors of the American company had viewed Trust ownership differently. From the formation of the Trust, successive presidents articulated appreciation of Trust ownership as its role as a charity enabled BW&Co. to claim that its purpose in marketing ethical medicine was to advance medical research for the public benefit, the effect being to enhance the company's image. In his dealings with the Trust during the 1950s and 1960s intended to protect BW&Co.'s profits from the WFL board, Creasy referred to the American company having "a unique opportunity to be of service to mankind" because of the special relationship with the Trust and emphasized the company's dedication to executing the altruistic purposes of Sir Henry Wellcome's will.[57] He alluded to the dedication of those employed at Tuckahoe who had "faith in the unique character, traditions, and high aims of the company."[58] Policies and practices at BW&Co. exemplify the implications of the theoretical literature concerned with trust as a tangible asset.[59] Internal relations were also managed with a view not only to promote harmonious relations rooted in an essentially family-oriented approach, but also to create a corporate identity focused on the company's aims.

Creasy's presidency coincided with a revival in 1975 by the WFL chairman of an idea first discussed by the board in 1950, which envisaged a public share issue to sell the overseas subsidiary companies for the purpose of raising capital for investment in the UK business. The response by the American directors is significant inasmuch that in the course of protecting the independence of BW&Co. (envisaged to be one of the companies sold off) a case against was advanced against the proposal. Creasy articulated a coherent philosophy relating the values and aspirations held by all employed in the American company directly to ownership by the Trust. He emphasized the exceptional character of BW&Co. in the US which promoted itself as a business whose single stockholder was devoted to medical research. Fearful of a loss of the quasi-independence enjoyed by BW&Co., Creasy insisted that in addition to undermining the special reputation of both WFL and BW&Co. because of the special relationship with the Trust, a public share issue would contravene the founder's intentions.[60] The Trust rejected the proposal.

However, in 1973 Creasy raised the possibility that because the company was not "pressed by angry stockholders" the company might in future succumb to inertia.[60] The same fear had been expressed by Howsam, who joined the company as vice president responsible for marketing in 1972, and by Sullivan, BW&Co.'s counsel who became its president in 1980. Both Howsam and Sullivan possessed experience of large companies each with a diversified shareholder base. Coe's view, however, was completely different. The slogan he adopted for the company from 1970, "research is our only stockholder," which was incorporated in the company's literature and advertising, underlined the absence of capitalist stockholder control and associated the company with ethical research. Until 1982, exceptionality conferred by Trust ownership was a regular point of reference in his communications to employees. Like Creasy before him, Coe infused his annual addresses conveyed through Wellcome News with the message that all employees should be motivated in their work by the knowledge that they were ultimately employed by a philanthropic organization which was dedicated to funding research intended to advance the health and wellbeing of mankind. In the US, the protection afforded by trust ownership was deployed in support of internal corporate control, effective management, and innovative research within a coherent organization which enabled the company to survive the managerial administration introduced briefly – though incompletely – in the 1980s. In the UK, protection by the Trust allowed the business in the rest of the Wellcome Group outside North America, to be mismanaged almost beyond control, and lacking in direction. Thus, differences between the corporate significance of trust ownership in the US and the UK were determined neither by structure, nor by the philosophy and aspirations of the Wellcome Trust which were the same in both countries. Divergence between the significance of trust ownership in the two organizations is attributable primarily to contrasting histories of organizational cultures.

In the 1980s, by which time the Trust had begun to conduct its affairs under a new regime, the initiative for divestment originated with the Trust. The moving spirit initially was a new chairman experienced in the affairs of multinational companies, aided by his successor whose experience was in the workings of the London financial market. The Trust's primary motive to float the entire Wellcome organization in 1986 was to diversify shareholding in order to reduce risk for the Trust; the share issue increased resources available to the Trust from which to fund medical research. At the same time, flotation exposed the company's management to public scrutiny in the hope that a rapid strategic response would be forthcoming from the board of WFL. Meanwhile, the appointment of John Robb, a new chief executive from outside the company was a second part of the Trust's strategy which offered the company an opportunity to begin to transform the business in the UK and overseas. However, a combination of impatience with the pace of restructuring and reform and movement in share prices led the trustees to follow the flotation in 1986 with a second share issue in 1992, culminating in merger with Glaxo in 1995. The future of Wellcome plc was resolved by the Trust's sale of the company, a decision in which the board was given no choice.

The history of governance requires the analysis of evolving power relationships. The many struggles within the Wellcome organization present fertile ground for such study. Paradoxically, although the Wellcome Trust was sole owner of WFL, except for the financial crises of the 1940s the trustees showed reluctance to exercise control. WFL, for its part, proved incapable of implementing control over its subsidiary BW&Co. in the US, thus adding a further dimension to the complicated relationships between the three bodies. Despite the structural relationships between the three organizations, the dynamic which explains their history is not that of structures, but of powerful personalities. Between the 1950s and 1980s, the trustees' perception of their responsibility as owners was minimal, limited almost entirely to receiving dividends for disbursement. Virtually freed thereby from accountability to the Trust, WFL was in a position to exploit its structural dominance in relation to subsidiary companies, including its American "cash cow." However, structural dominance was almost completely undermined by BW&Co. in the US. Successive presidents pursued a consistent and independent path. Partly by stealth, sometimes in secret, partly by argument, sometimes appealing to the Trust for support, the Americans developed a culture of corporate independence underpinned by economic successes attributable to the discoveries and developments made by the company's leading scientists who acted within an enlightened and constructive management environment. In the 1980s, the balance of power between the Trust and WFL underwent radical change, a consequence, yet again, of forceful personalities who altered the culture of the Trust, adopted an aggressive approach towards the board of WFL, and introduced a strategy which exposed the business to the exercise of market discipline. The initial flotation of Wellcome plc in 1986 also represents a rare example of a lesson learned from history based on the personal experience and informed observation of business and the financial market by the Trust chairman, Sir David Steel, and by Roger Gibbs, second in command and his successor as chairman. After a second issue of shares in 1992, the logic of a further and complete divestment of the company's shares became increasingly clear. The patents on Zovirax and Retrovir rapidly approached termination and heralded a resulting intensification of competition in the market, both from imitative and improved products from "big pharma" and from generics. Presented with this impending scenario, the progress of restructuring of the business seemed unlikely to be sufficient to achieve an independent survival of Wellcome plc.

When, in the year 2000, Glaxo Wellcome merged with SmithKline to become GlaxoSmithKline (GSK), the Wellcome name finally disappeared from the world of business altogether. The Wellcome Trust, however, ensured that the name of Wellcome would be perpetuated in association with the largest non-governmental funder of biomedical research in the UK and one of the world's three most wealthy charities, far exceeding the net wealth possessed by the remainder. The name of the founder survives into the twenty-first century as the creator of an enduring, globally-important legacy. Before 1995, the realization of Sir Henry Wellcome's vision depended mainly on the wealth created by BW&Co. Wellcome had established the American company in 1906 and during the 1920s he had set it on a path towards scientific distinction and commercial success. The irony surrounding the events of 1995 was that only by the Trust's sale of Wellcome plc, including its dominant American subsidiary, was the full extent of Sir Henry Wellcome's bequest achieved.

Promotion, prices, profits, and principles: Wellcome corporate ethics

The image of the pharmaceutical industry has long been surrounded by controversy arising from a perception among the public and professional critics that profits from the industry have not been matched sufficiently by contributions to the common good; widespread mistrust and resentment has at times bordered on outright hostility[62]

Divergent interests between profit-seeking companies and those seeking to promote or receive affordable public health provision has created an environment in which tension is inherent. Such a conflict between objectives has inevitably attracted extensive scrutiny by the media which has been a powerful influence affecting the industry's public image and that of particular corporations. Wellcome plc was no exception.

In February 1994, the first of three substantial articles appeared in the *Sunday Times* in London entitled respectively: "Hard Sell",[63] "The Pill that Killed",[64] and "The Money Spinners."[65] The author was Brian Deer, an investigative journalist whose principal interest was the pharmaceutical industry. The interpretation which he presented amounted to a critique of policies and practices at Wellcome plc, questioning its corporate ethics and accusing the Wellcome Trust of duplicity and hypocrisy. The main thrust of his thesis was that the company pursued marketing strategies which elevated profit above the interests of patients; specifically, that the company's most profitable drugs: Septrin/Septra, Zyloprim/Zyloric, Zovirax, and Retrovir had been "promoted beyond the best medical opinion", with the result that "much of their yield has come from use by patients for whom they may be of trivial benefit, inappropriate, or sometimes even a danger".[66]

The criticisms focussed not only on the marketing methods employed by the company, which he compared with those applied to any commercial product, but also to a preceding stage of the process that required decisions regarding the introduction of new drugs to the market which he believed showed a lack of concern for patients. Deer believed the history of Septra/Septrin, the broad spectrum antibiotic introduced in 1973, justified his criticisms. He referred to a series of research-based reports published in reputable journals and to the conclusions of Britain's Committee on the Safety of Medicines which, in the 1970s, had thrown doubt on the seriousness of side-effects, some which had resulted in deaths. The author alleged that Wellcome had ignored evidence of side effects, issuing robust, massively-funded advertising to counteract its critics as recently as 1991. He acknowledged that since acyclovir was released in 1982, the lives of many patients in intensive care or undergoing transplant procedures had been saved. Due to immune suppression they were at special risk from herpes. For people with common genital conditions, acyclovir had been shown to suppress symptoms. The virus often continued to "shed" even in the drug's presence. This allowed continued infection and the risk of further transmission.[67]

Deer was especially critical of the company's reformulation of acyclovir for sale as a cosmetic lip cream for cold sores or "herpes labialis," an application which, as reported in the *BMJ* did not receive endorsement by researchers. The drug's use for the treatment of chicken pox in children, an infection rarely complicated and possibly a normal part of the body's training to fight infection, drew further criticism after the results of a large study published in the *NEJM* revealed that acyclovir had no effect on the transmission of the virus. The incentive to broaden the range of indications for which a drug might be used was, of course, that of extending the market and the life of a drug; in 1994, the estimated value of the market for a drug approved by the regulators to treat chicken pox was $150 million. Deer also condemned the company's efforts to extend prescribing Retrovir to include a much wider range of people well beyond those for whom drug treatment was effective in the short term by prolonging life for a few months to include those who were HIV positive but otherwise apparently well. The author quoted the *Lancet's* verdict that no evidence existed "to suggest that clinicians should be encouraged to give Zidovidune to most symptom-free patients".[68]

The Trust did not escape the author's criticism either. Deer asked: "How is it that a giant respected organization that is granted charitable status to relieve human suffering and which is taking a commanding position in medical science be historically and financially rooted in the sale of drugs which may be of trivial use and may be inappropriate or even dangerous?"[69]

Both the company and the Trust adopted their traditional policies when dealing with the media. They refrained from engaging in public debate with critics, leaving the company's scientists to respond to issues around safety and efficacy through scholarly exchanges in journal publications. Privately, the company's brief response to Deer's critique was to insist that responsibility for prescribing and protecting patients lay firmly with the medical profession and that in addition to government regulations, journals and journal editors were also important influences on medical practice. In defence of the Trust's hands-off position, officers underlined the independence of the Trust from the company except as investors. Therefore, it had no involvement with the company's products, limiting its own activity to promoting independent medical research. Such a feeble response could not be expected to reassure investors of the role which continued to be played by the company's largest shareholder at a time when the ethical reputation of Wellcome plc, a particularly important asset in the past, was under scrutiny. A qualifying observation might have conceded that the increased pressure from competition had altered the balance between Wellcome scientists' search for complete efficacy and safety of a highly toxic drug and the risk of adverse affects on relatively small numbers of the population. Regarding this balance between doing no harm to the patient and seeking new treatments for waiting patients, the approach adopted by Wellcome scientists appears to have been closer to meeting the needs of patients suffering from AIDS than to attaining scientific perfection of the drugs which they developed.[70]

The responsibility of the regulators, particularly of the FDA, in establishing and applying criteria for safety and efficacy was to ensure the safety of patients. The evidence on which judgements on approval were based derived mainly from clinical testing. These depended on the observance of ethical principles, widely observed among clinicians before the 1990s, though guides to the ethical conduct of trials were not the subject of international agreement until the 1990s.[71] The methodologies adopted by clinicians, however, were open to question, by other clinicians engaged in trials which produced different results and by researchers employed by companies motivated to justify the integrity and clinical utility of a new drug. However, beyond clinical trials, the ultimate decision on whether a drug should be used on a particular patient or class of patients resided with physicians, "gatekeepers for the medical system as a whole."[72] While judgements and decisions made by clinicians and regulators were vital before a new drug and subsequent variants entered the market signalling permission for the drug to be prescribed, judgements made by practicing physicians responsible for prescribing were even more crucial to the commercial success of a new drug because they determined sales. The analysis of the ethics involved in prescribing presented by Charles L. Bardes, Professor of Clinical Medicine at Cornell University, reveals the complexities involved in making a judgement as to whether to prescribe treatment or not and if so, which of the competing available drugs should they prescribe? Few drugs are entirely risk-free. Most involve some risk due to different levels of toxicity, each possessing pros and cons regarding the treatment of individual patients exhibiting different medical conditions and histories and therefore, necessitating a succession of separate risk/benefit analyses. Bardes described the essential dilemma facing the practicing physician which arose because "joined to the potential to do great good is the potential to do great harm."[73]

Prescribing new drugs posed additional problems. Typically during the early life of a new drug, the risk of side effects could be high. Such was the case with AZT which raised the ethical question whether depriving the many who might benefit from an opportunity to receive it because of personal adverse effects in only a few sufferers would be as unjust as selling a drug associated with high risk.[74] HIV sufferers preferred high risk to a high probability of death without retroviral treatment and lobbied the FDA to reduce testing and release the drug despite the uncertainty surrounding its effects because it prolonged life. Jurgen Drews, a physician and formerly research director at Hoffman La Roche, referred to the "compassionate use programs" whereby non-approved drugs against AIDS were permitted by the FDA in response to pressure from patient groups. He cited this as an example of conflict between the scientific ethic (which required the application of formal scientific criteria) and therapeutic needs for the purpose, if possible, of curing patients, or at least relieving suffering.[75] He characterized the reconciliation of medical and scientific ethics as "a balancing act between the interests of the many and the needs of the few."[76]

Underlying Deer's critique of Wellcome was an implicit elevation of scientific criteria to ensure minimal risk surrounding drugs before use above that of the physician's therapeutic imperative which was to cure or relieve the suffering of patients. An important difference of perspective comparing these approaches is time; drug research, development, and testing required time to achieve the lowest toxicity possible and minimal risk in the interest of the general population, whereas physicians were presented with individual patients needing instant treatment. These divergent perspectives were evident in the contrasting approaches by Wellcome scientists in the UK and those in the US. As group director R&D, Cresswell contrasted the philosophy which guided research and drug development at Beckenham – to do no harm – with the approach of scientists at RTP which was patient-centred and for this reason, prepared for relatively higher levels of risk acceptable to individual physicians and their patients who sought treatment at the time that a drug became available.

BW&Co. was vulnerable to the accusation that aggressive marketing may have persuaded some physicians to prescribe a drug for patients without specifying the levels of risk involved. This applied particularly to the 1970s campaign to promote Septra which resulted in deaths. This occurred during the company's transitional phase. From being mainly a pill-promoting business, albeit presented through ethical advertising, and employing sales staff practicing traditional detailing methods, BW&Co. became an organization offering important medical therapies which received international acclaim from the scientific and medical professions. Methods of promotion changed to self-styled educational approaches to marketing, an evolution common to the industry though retaining elements of traditional detailing methods (the provision of free samples and gifts) as inducements to prescribe. From the 1980s, honoraria, conference travel, and research funding assumed increasing importance.

Wazana's review of peer-reviewed journals[77] concluded the involvement of pharmaceutical companies was most influential in continuing medical education sponsorship (in which BW&Co. was heavily involved) with which was associated the provision of company speakers and the provision of conference expenses. In these respects, the company is exposed to criticisms similar to those levelled against the international pharmaceutical industry by sceptical contemporary observers from outside the industry, particularly by healthcare practitioners and academics from medical-related sciences.[78] Such methods of selling and promotion are widely believed to have resulted in non-rational prescribing behaviour, an increasing prescription rate, and a tendency for novelty to bias prescribers against generics.[79]

Wellcome plc was equally vulnerable, however, regarding the pricing of Retrovir which provoked criticism of the company condemned as an exploitative, opportunist organization, a notorious price-gouger and profiteer. Such was the implication of the questioning of the company's leaders by Congressman Henry Waxman of the sub-committee on health and environment in 1987. Although there is a history of government intervention in the US, principally with regard to the safety and efficacy of drugs and anti-competitive behavior, confrontation between a government body and an individual company over the price of a new product was unusual and possibly unprecedented. BW&Co. was not accused of any illegal action. Waxman's Congressional sub-committee's strictures on the company's pricing policy were based on an implied notion of an ethical pricing policy which required a considerably lower price than that set by the company.

The initial price which the board of BW&Co, recommended to WFL directors was based on the profit-maximization principle, though the American director responsible acknowledged that, depending on public reaction, downward revision could be made. It is significant that the president's evidence to the Congressional Committee avoided requests for financial information that might justify the price announced by the company. Meanwhile a presidential commission to investigate the high cost of AIDS therapy and a threat of legal action by the New York State legislature over pricing was interpreted by the company as representing a serious challenge to private control. WFL directors in London showed a reluctance to acknowledge the importance of these threats, focusing instead on the profitability they demanded to compensate for the past and present commercial failure of the parent company in the UK. A prolonged resistance to BW&Co.'s recommendation of price reductions revealed a board of directors who, with few exceptions, appeared to be devoid of sound judgement.

Under increasing pressure exerted by activists among patients and medical professionals and consumer protection groups who created a whirlwind of criticism and caused serious reputational damage to the company the first price reduction occurred followed soon, bringing the total effective reduction to 36 per cent within two years. At the same time the company embarked on a strategy aimed at corporate rehabilitation and a restoration of trust through an outreach program in which leading activists participated fully. The program included donations to AIDS service, referral organizations, and annual contributions to an HIV patient assistance program. The role of an advisory panel of treatment advocates, which also included activists as well as professional specialists, was to offer advice and expertise to the company's project team in developing an improved treatment IND. By 1992, favorable judgments on the policy, intended to advance mutual understanding between the company and the wider HIV community, were forthcoming from both sides. Economics rather than ethics posed a greater threat to Wellcome plc.

The charge against Wellcome directors and managers of having adopted an unethical approach relating to the issuance and promotion of drugs, especially new ones, omits examples where the evidence does not support the generalization. An important case in point is that of Wellbutrin. Under the same direction and management responsible for the development and promotion of Retrovir during the 1980s and 1990s, Wellbutrin was the company's first anti-depressant that had been in development at RTP for even longer than Retrovir and was expected to become another blockbuster therapy. Yet after receiving FDA approval for the drug to enter the market, on the eve of implementation of a costly nationwide marketing plan, the American directors cancelled the conference launch and withdrew the plan. The reason for the decision was the report of a clinical trial (not one of the company's own) which appeared to question the drug's safety. By the time it transpired that clinicians had employed a flawed research methodology, Prozac had become the anti-depressant of choice and left Wellbutrin, although its safety had been confirmed, well behind. The history of the Wellcome companies suggest that judgements regarding ethical or unethical behavior are attributable to specific decisions rather than to a corporate philosophy or approach. Decisions resulted from the balancing of risks and choices arising from competing priorities. Safety and short-term betterment of patients required judgement of risk. Considerations of profit and competition were balanced against efficacy and safety within the terms of approval of a treatment set by the FDA. Ultimately, the decision to prescribe lay with the practitioner. The scientific ethic focused on advancement of knowledge was not always in harmony with the patient-centred ethic of medical and clinical research. Such complexity is not more easily understood by applying notions of ethical and unethical behavior.

Table 27.1 *Wealthiest Charitable Foundations in 2012*

	Founded	*Headquarters*	*Endowment ($USD)*
Bill and Melinda Gates Foundation	1994	US	$37 billion
Stichting INGKA Foundation	1982	Netherlands	$36 billion
The Wellcome Trust	1936	UK	$22 billion
Howard Hughes Medical Institute	1953	US	$15 billion
Ford Foundation	1936	US	$14 billion
Church Commissioners of England	1948	UK	$11 billion
J. Paul Getty Trust	1982	US	$10 billion

Total value of invested donations of non-profit foundations only.
Source: www.ranker.com/list/richest charities.

With the formation of Glaxo Wellcome in 1995 when the Trust sold its remaining holdings in Wellcome plc, the Wellcome name continued as a part of the UK's largest pharmaceutical manufacturer, though both manufacture and research in the UK and production in the US were drastically reduced during the ensuing process directed by Glaxo. The sale of the entire company to Glaxo in 1995 secured for the Trust the ultimate diversification of assets of which shares in the pharmaceutical industry formed a tiny part. Thereafter, the Trust's income depended entirely on a handful of financial institutions which managed a combination of investments in UK gilts, listed equities in the UK and the US, property, private equity, and venture capital. Income rose to unprecedented levels, as did net wealth. In 2012, the Wellcome Trust ranked third among the world's largest charitable foundations[66] demonstrably fulfilling Henry Wellcome's ambitions for the Trust. However, the price was the end of the multinational business enterprise which he had founded with Silas Burroughs in London in 1880. After the acquisition of Glaxo Wellcome by GlaxoSmithKline in 1995, the Wellcome name was no longer associated with a business but only with the Wellcome Trust and the Burroughs Wellcome Fund.

APPENDIX

The Burroughs Wellcome Fund

In addition to the Wellcome Trust, a second beneficiary from the sale of shares was the Burroughs Wellcome Fund, the American medical charitable foundation created in 1955 with an annual endowment from the company of $160,000.[1] Neither of the two historians of the Burroughs Wellcome Fund referred to the grudging manner in which the initial donation was made.[2] The context was WFL's continuing financial weakness and dependency upon dividends and transfers from the American subsidiary. Creasy resented what he perceived to be exploitation by the WFL board and proposed the formation of an American charitable foundation dedicated to advancing medical research and education based on the model established by the Wellcome Trust in London. Such a proposal had become more attractive following a recent provision in the US which rendered a proportion of charitable incomes tax deductible. Wheeler, managing director of WFL, had opposed Creasy's proposal and dissuaded the trustees, whose approval was required to release funds for that purpose, from agreeing to Creasy's plan. An angry response from Creasy was followed by a meeting between Sir Henry Dale (a longtime friend of Creasy and conscious of the important contribution made by the American company to the financial history of WFL) and Wheeler. The outcome was an agreement between the WFL board and the Trust to the formation and financing of the Burroughs Wellcome Fund. Funding was not guaranteed but depended on BW&Co.'s profits of the company; it was, therefore, a corporate foundation.[3]

Although annual income fluctuated, the Fund's average annual income from WFL rose slowly from $160,000, not exceeding $1 million until the 1980s when the annual figure varied between $5 million and $7 million. The second significant addition to funding occurred in 1992 shortly before the second Wellcome plc share issue. A proposal for enlarged funding followed an informal conversation in midsummer 1992 between John Robb, the chairman of Wellcome plc, and Martha Peck, who had been executive director of the Burroughs Wellcome Fund since 1981, when Peck expressed the view that the Fund's potential was limited by income and that "probably $100 million" would remedy this. This was the basis on which the Fund President, Howard Schaeffer (who had succeeded George Hitchings in 1990) prepared a proposal for securing increased funding from the Trust which coincided with the Trust having raised $4.4 billion dollars.[4]

Schaeffer's personal contribution to the development of Zovirax and Retrovir reinforced the case and his close relationship with Gibbs eased the process of persuading the Trust to support the proposal. However, the strongest champion for Schaeffer's initiative was Stan Peart, a Wellcome Trustee between 1975 and 1993 and Deputy Chairman at the time of the second issue. Gibbs referred to a feeling among the Trustees that "we really ought to do something for medical research in the country of Henry Wellcome's birth."[5] Perhaps significantly, Peart must have been very familiar with the major role which the American company had played in the history of WFL and Wellcome plc and therefore of the Trust; Gibbs was familiar with the relationship between BW&Co. and the Trust since joining the Trust in the early 1980s, while Julian Jack, the third trustee, who also favored the proposal, had become a Trustee only in 1987. The other four trustees, recent appointees who therefore lacked a corporate memory, initially resisted the proposal, arguing that medical research in the US received superior funding by comparison with the UK research community which received the lowest per capita funding of the five major medical research nations.[6] However, the chairman and deputy chairman, supported by Jack, persuaded the others to support the endowment.[7] On his return to the US, Schaeffer was elated at the response to his proposal.[8] Later, Peart described the Trust's contribution as "only simple justice."[9] From a longer term American perspective, longtime President of BW&Co. Coe regarded the $400 million transfer over five years as "a slap in the face" in view of the billions of dollars raised as a result of the sale of the American assets.[10]

One significant effect on the Fund was that by becoming completely independent of BW&Co., it was no longer a corporate foundation, an important consideration in view of UK tax liabilities relating to the donations.[11] Furthermore, although income was still small compared with that of the Trust, the donations immediately placed the among the fifty wealthiest foundations in the US. From assets of $35 million in 1992, when the final tranche was released by the Trust in 1997, the Fund's assets rose to $600 million. During that time, grants in aid of research increased fivefold.[12] The trustees were aware of the strength of feelings among staff at BW&Co., especially those of Nobel Prize winner Gertrude Elion, a Wellcome Fund Director, and Howard Schaeffer, its chairman. However, when in 1995, for a second time, Schaeffer requested the Trust to make an additional grant, presumably on the basis of the justice argument pressed by Peart in 1992 which at the time the Trustees had accepted, the Trust did not regard the endowment as a precedent that must be followed and rejected the request. The Wellcome Fund's independence since 1993 rendered the justice argument technically redundant. Furthermore, Peart's retirement in 1993 removed the Fund's principal advocate from the Trustees who rejected the request in 1995. The composition of the Trust had changed since 1992, enlarged because of the huge increase in the funds which the Trust now administered. It included two new appointees in 1994 and 1995. In the new, enlarged Trust were six distinguished academic scientists from among the medical elite who occupied professorships at Oxford, Cambridge, and Imperial College London. Perhaps it is not surprising that the counter argument presented in 1992 regarding funding support for medical research in the UK prevailed in 1995. Recognition of Schaeffer's personal contribution to the company, particularly with respect to his work on Zovirax, took the form of a £1 million endowment to fund the Howard Schaeffer Chair at the University of Arizona College of Pharmacy, a fellowship intended to enable academic scientists in the UK to spend time in the US.[13] Nobel Prize winning Elion was awarded $110,000 towards the production of a film of her life and work.[14] Since that time the Fund has been dedicated to the advancement of biomedical sciences by supporting basic research and other scientific and educational activities.

Notes

Introduction

1 Ralph Landau, Basil Achilladelis, and Alexander Scriabine (eds), *Pharmaceutical Innovation: Revolutionizing Human Health* (Chemical Heritage Foundation, Philadelphia PA, 1999), p. 328; A. D. Chandler Jr, *Shaping the Industrial Century* (Harvard University Press, Cambridge MA, 2005), chap. 7; Viviane Quirke and Judy Slinn (eds), *Perspectives on Twentieth Century Pharmaceuticals* (Peter Lang, Oxford, 2010), p. 7.

2 The exception was the brief presidency of William N. Sullivan between 1982 and 1986. See chapter 15.

3 "The Nobel Prize in Physiology or Medicine 1988" 1 Oct. 2012 www.nobelprize.org/nobel_prizes/medicine/laureates/1988/.

4 See barely a page devoted to WFL which includes only a single mention of the American company and is misleading in its account of the relationship between R&D, innovation, and finance in relation to the Wellcome Trust. Chandler, *Shaping the Industrial Century*, pp. 246–48.

5 Roy Church and E. M. Tansey, *Burroughs Wellcome & Co.: Knowledge, Trust, Profit, and the Transformation of the British Pharmaceutical Industry, 1880–1940* (Crucible Books, Lancaster, 2007), pp. 55–66.

6 James Taggart, *The World Pharmaceutical Industry* (Taylor & Francis, London, 1993), p. 287.

7 Ibid., p. 288.

8 Ibid.

9 Viviane Quirke, "Drug discovery from 1945 to 1995," in Stuart Anderson (ed.), *Making Medicines: A Brief History of Pharmacy and Pharmaceuticals* (Pharmaceutical Press, London, 2005), p. 192, Box 10.2.

10 The Burroughs Wellcome Fund was incorporated in the State of New York in 1955 for the purpose of financing charitable projects in medical science. The Fund was financed from a regular transfer of a proportion of the profits of Burroughs Wellcome USA (Inc.). See appendix.

Chapter 1: The origins of Burroughs Wellcome & Co. in the US

1 Chapters 1 and 2 consist of a heavily abbreviated version of chapters 1, 4, 8, 13, and 15, of Church and Tansey, *Burroughs Wellcome & Co.*, where full references can be found.

2 WF, Wellcome LB 30, 768, BW&Co., to NY, 28 Feb. 1907.

3 WF, F/FA/328, Report on NYB accounts, 30 June 1910.

4 Ibid.

5 WF, Wellcome LB 32, 14–17, BW&Co., 27 Jan. 1906.

6 WF, Acc 82/1 Box 38, Pearson to Nevin, 26 Oct. 1914.

7 Quoted in Church and Tansey, *Burroughs Wellcome & Co.*, p. 249.

8 Ibid., p. 248.

9 WF, F/FA/328, Report on NYB accounts, 15 Dec. 1909.

10 Quoted in Church and Tansey, *Burroughs Wellcome & Co.*, p. 250.

11 WF, Acc 87/56, Wellcome to Pearson, 12 Dec. 1927.

12 Ibid.

13 WF, Acc 82/1 Box 38, Wellcome to Pearson, 19 Oct. 1917.

14 Ibid.

Chapter 2: Americanisation of a UK Subsidury

1 Quoted in Church and Tansey, *Burroughs Wellcome & Co.*, p. 393.

2 WF, Acc 82/1 Box 19, Wellcome to Pearson, 23 Oct. 1926.

3 WF, Acc 82/1 Box 19, Nevin to Wellcome, 1 July 1927.

4 Nevin quoted in Church and Tansey, *Burroughs Wellcome & Co.*, p. 466.

5 Confidential correspondence between Nevin and Pearson between 1928 and 1940 is reproduced in C. H. Kellaway, "Review of the US laboratories, 1928–1946" (typescript, 1954), WFA/E/10/15, Nevin to Pearson, pp. 1–5.

6 Ibid., p. 3.

7 GWHC, BW&Co. (USA) Inc., 107.07/11, Public affairs, "History of the Wellcome Research laboratories" (typescript n.d.), pp. 1–2; 107.08/05, Phoenix, 6, 1929, p. 5; 1, 1930, pp. 8–9; 4, 1930, pp. 6–7.

8 Church and Tansey, *Burroughs Wellcome & Co.*, pp. 412–14.

9 GWHC, BW&Co. (USA) Inc., 107.07/01, *Wellcome News*, Spring 1964, p. 3.

10 Confidential correspondence between Nevin and Bennett between 1940 and 1946 is reproduced in C. H. Kellaway, "Review of the US laboratories, 1928–1946" (typescript, 1954), WFA/E/10/15, Nevin to Bennett, 30 July 1941, pp. 19–21.

11 Ibid.

12 Ibid.

13 Ibid.

14 GWHC, BW&Co. (USA) Inc., 107.07/05, Public affairs, Monthly letter, May 1936, p. 156.

15 GWHC, BW&Co. (USA) Inc., 107.07/01, *Wellcome News*, Winter 1968, pp. 3–4.

16 Johnson-Saint to Robert Wallace Nevin, 7 Jan. 1965, reproduced by e-mail from Mrs Linda Nevin 23 July 2002.

17 Email to author from Mrs Linda Nevin, 11 July 2002.

18 Ibid.

19 Church and Tansey, *Burroughs Wellcome & Co.*, pp. 448–49.

20 Ibid.

21 The first chairman of the Trust was George Lyall who died after a year in office.

22 A. R. Hall and B. A. Bembridge, *Physic and Philanthropy: A History of the Wellcome Trust, 1936–1986* (Cambridge University Press, Cambridge, 1986), pp. 48–49.

23 Ibid., p. 34.

24 Robert Rhodes James, *Henry Wellcome* (Hodder and Staughton, London, 1994), pp. 371–72.

25 Quoted in ibid., p. 43.

26 Elliott provided a moral justification for intervention which was Sir Henry's will which envisaged that "Man is to benefit, not the private shareholder."

27 Church and Tansey, *Burroughs Wellcome & Co.*, p. 470.

28 Hall and Bembridge, *Physic and Philanthropy*, p. 48.

29 Ibid., p. 52.

30 Ibid., pp. 548–49.

Chapter 3: Adapting to peacetime markets after World War II

1 GWHC, BW&Co. (USA) Inc., 107.01/02, President's annual report, 1946/7.

2 WF/M/AV/O/02/03, Collins/Church interview with Coe, April 2001, p. 13.

3 GSK/WF/SCS 283, Board minutes, 7 July 1948, 2046.

4 GSK/WF/SCS 283, Board minutes, 20 June 1946, 1273.

5 See below chapter 6

6 GWHC, BW&Co. (USA) Inc., 107.01/02, President's annual report, 1945/6; BWFL, Private papers, Creasy to Hitchings, 29 April 1974.

7 *American Druggist*, Feb. 1945, p. 17.

8 *American Druggist*, Feb. 1945, p. 149.

9 WF/M/AV/O/02/03, Collins/Church interview with Coe, April 2001, p. 6; *American Druggist*, 14 Feb. 1946, p. 13.

10 WF/M/AV/O/02/06, Collins interview with Baker, April 2001, p. 6.

11 GSK/WF/SCS 283, Board minutes, 28 June 1945, 80.

12 *Wellcome News*, Spring 1968, p. 3; WF/M/AV/O/02/03, Collins/Church interview with Coe, April 2001, p. 3.

13 WF/M/AV/O/02/03, Church/Collins interview with Coe, April 2001, p. 3.

14 WF/M/AV/O/02/03, Church/Collins interview with Coe, April 2001, p. 11.

15 Ibid.

16 H. Helfand, B. Woodruff, K. M. H. Coleman,

and D. L. Cowen, "Wartime Industrial Development of Penicillin in the United States," in J. Parascandola (ed.), *A History of Antibiotics: A Symposium* (American Society for the History of Pharmacy, Madison WI, 1980), pp. 31–56.
17 GWHC, BW&Co. (USA) Inc., 107.01/02, President's annual report, 1948/9.
18 James C. Wharton, "'Antibiotic abandon': the resurgence of therapeutic rationalism," in Parandascola (ed.), *A History of Antibiotics*, p. 126.
19 Ibid.
20 GWHC, BW&Co. (USA) Inc., 107.01/02, President's annual report, 1944/5.
21 Ibid.; *Wellcome News,* Nov. 1945, p. 3.
22 GWHC, BW&Co. (USA) Inc., 107.07/11, Public affairs, "Brief analysis," n.p.
23 GWHC, BW&Co. (USA) Inc., 107.01/02, President's annual report, 1944/5.
24 GWHC, BW&Co. (USA) Inc., 107.07/11, Public affairs, Tanner interview with Elion, c. 1977.
25 GWHC, BW&Co. (USA) Inc., 107.01/02, President's annual report, 1947/8.
26 Ibid.
27 GWHC, BW&Co. (USA) Inc., 107.07/11, Public affairs, "Brief analysis," n.p.
28 Ibid.
29 GWHC, BW&Co. (USA) Inc., 107.07/11, H. Pollinger, "Research" (c. 1955), p. 9.
30 WF/M/AV/O/02/22, Collins interview with Krenitsky, 14 May 2001, p. 3. For biographical details of Dr George Hitchings see below, chapters 8–9.
31 GWHC, BW&Co. (USA) Inc., 107.01/02, President's annual report, 1944/5.
32 Ibid., President's annual report, 1948/9.
33 Ibid., President's annual report, 1946/7.
34 Ibid., President's annual report, 1948/9.
35 Ibid., President's annual report, 1947/8.
36 GWHC, BW&Co. (USA) Inc., 107.07/11, Public affairs, "Brief analysis," n.p.; GWHC, BW&Co. (USA) Inc., 107.01/02, President's annual report, 1946/7.
37 GWHC, BW&Co. (USA) Inc., 107.01/02, President's annual report, 1947/8; Ibid., President's annual report, 1948/9.
38 Ibid., President's annual report, 1947/8.
39 GWHC, BW&Co. (USA) Inc., 107.07/11, Public affairs, Tanner interview with Elion, c. 1977.
40 Though compounds received from London and external sources are excluded from this figure. GWHC, BW&Co. (USA) Inc., 107.01/02, President's annual report, 1947/8.
41 See chapter 7.
42 GWHC, BW&Co. (USA) Inc., 107.01/02, President's annual report, 1959/60.
43 WF/M/AV/O/02/03, Church/Collins interview with Coe, April 2001, pp. 15–16.
44 See Karl E. Weick and Kathleen M. Sutcliffe, *Managing the Unexpected* (Josey-Bass, John Wiley, San Francisco, 2001), chapters 1 and 5.

Chapter 4: Empirin a dominant leader in the US market for analgesics

1 GWHC, BW&Co. (USA) Inc., 107.07/11, Public affairs, "Brief analysis," n.p.
2 GWHC, BW&Co. (USA) Inc., 107.01/02, President's annual report, 1957/8.
3 WF/M/AV/O/02/15, Collins interview with Parrish, 15 March 2001, p. 7.
4 *American Druggist,* 21 Jan. 1952.
5 BWFL, Private papers, Creasy to Hitchings, 29 April 1974.
6 Ibid.
7 *American Druggist,* 21 Jan. 1952.
8 BWFL, Private papers, Creasy to Hitchings, 29 April 1974.
9 *American Druggist,* 21 Jan. 1952.
10 GWHC, BW&Co. (USA) Inc., 107.07/11, Public affairs, "Brief analysis," n.p.
11 GWHC, BW&Co. (USA) Inc., 107.01/02, President's annual report, 1959/60.
12 Federal Trade Commission Report to Congress, July 1958. "Economic report on the antibiotics industry," p. 136.
13 *American Druggist,* 24 March 1958, pp. 5–7.
14 Ibid.
15 GWHC, BW&Co. (USA) Inc., 107.01/02, President's annual report, 1957/8.
16 Ibid.
17 Ibid.
18 *Wellcome News,* Nov. 1954, p. 4; GWHC, BW&Co. (USA) Inc., 107.01/02, President's annual report, 1960/1.
19 Ibid.
20 GWHC, BW&Co. (USA) Inc., 107.01/02, President's annual report, 1961/2.
21 *American Druggist*, 31 Jan. 1955, p. 17.
22 GWHC, BW&Co. (USA) Inc., 107.01/02, President's annual report, 1952.
23 *American Druggist*, 4 Aug. 1952, p. 5.
24 *American Druggist*, 31 Jan. 1955, p. 13.
25 GWHC, BW&Co. (USA) Inc., 107.01/02, President's annual report, 1962.

26 Louis Lasagna, "Congress, the FDA, and New Drug Development: before and after 1962," *Perspectives in Biology and Medicine* 32:3, Spring 1989, pp. 323–30.
27 Ibid., pp. 329–32.
28 Ibid.
29 *American Druggist,* 14 Sept. 1964, pp. 50–51.
30 Ibid., p. 52.
31 Ibid.
32 *American Druggist*, 3 April 1960, p. 12.
33 WF/M/AV/O/02/06, Collins interview with Baker, April 2001, p. 17.
34 *American Druggist*, 8 July 1963, p. 39.
35 WF/M/AV/O/02/05, Collins interview with Sullivan, April 2001, p. 15.
36 WF/M/AV/O/02/12, Collins interview with Howsam, 11 May 2001, p. 16.
37 GWHC, BW&Co. (USA) Inc., 107.01/02, President's annual report, 1965/6.
38 *American Druggist*, Oct. 1970.
39 *American Druggist,* 1 Sept. 1977, p. 36, Oct. 1977, p. 47; 1 Jan. 1980, p. 67.
40 *Wellcome News*, Sept./Oct. 1982, p. 7.
41 See chapter 15.
42 WF/M/AV/O/02/05, Collins interview with Sullivan, April 2001, pp. 5–6.
43 WF/M/AV/O/02/06, Collins interview with Baker, April 2001.
44 WF/E/19, Creasy to Cresswell, 5 March 1972.
45 WF/M/AV/O/02/06, Collins interview with Baker, April 2001, pp. 7–8.
46 In 1974 Lanoxin held 90 per cent of the generic market. *American Druggist*, 15 May 1974, pp. 26–27.

Chapter 5: Development and "detailing" in the prescription drug market

1 B. Spilker, *Multinational Drug Companies: Issues in Drug Discovery and Development* (Raven Press, New York, 1989), p. 6 Table 1.
2 Paul de Haen annual reports published in *American Druggist*, 1955–1968 (de Haen was a pharmaceutical industry consultant).
3 *American Druggist*, 1 March 1954, p. 7.
4 Historically, those who sold pharmaceutical goods in the US were known as "detail men" which referred to their direct face-to-face approach which involved explaining and promoting products. As a result of a process of professionalization beginning in the 1970s the term was gradually superseded by "sales representatives." The two are employed interchangeably in the text.
5 *Wellcome News*, Oct./Nov. 1958, p. 4.
6 GWHC, BW&Co. (USA) Inc., 107.01/02, President's annual report, 1951.
7 WF/M/AV/O/02/25, Collins interview with Regan, 17 May 2001, p. 19.
8 See below, chapter 11.
9 *Wellcome News*, 8 April 1954, pp. 6–7; June 1957, p. 7; 10 Sept. 1957, pp. 3–4.
10 *American Druggist*, 31 Aug. 1952, p. 41.
11 GWHC, BW&Co. (USA) Inc., 107.01/02, President's annual report, 1951.
12 Ibid., President's annual report, 1951.
13 Ibid., President's annual report, 1953, 1962. *Wellcome News*, Oct./Nov. 1958. The turnover rate for the pharmaceutical representatives was reported to be one in four.
14 GWHC, BW&Co. (USA) Inc., 107.01/02, President's annual report, 1955.
15 WF/M/AV/O/02/16, Collins interview with Donelson, May 2001, p. 16.
16 Ibid., pp. 3–5, 12–14.
17 *Wellcome News*, Oct./Nov. 1958, p. 5.
18 GWHC, BW&Co. (USA) Inc., 107.01.02, President's annual report, 1956.
19 Ibid., President's annual report, 1954.
20 GSK/WF/SCS 556, Group organisation report, 1966/7.
21 GWHC, BW&Co. (USA) Inc., 107.01/02, President's annual report, 1967.
22 Author's transcript: Coe diaries, 30 Sept. 1967.
23 See below, chapter 17
24 GWHC, BW&Co. (USA) Inc., 107.01/02, President's annual report, 1967.
25 Ibid., President's annual report, 1960.
26 Ibid., President's annual report, 1968.
27 Ibid., President's annual report, 1968. This program may be compared with that of Geigy, whose annual sales were $50m and which in 1969 employed 500 'professional service representatives (detailers), of whom 25 per cent were qualified pharmacists. The training period was four weeks at a special centre over a period of six months plus two weeks of 'indoctrination' by division managers. In the field they visited doctors on average 6 or seven times a year. *American Druggist*, 22 Sept. 1969, p. 13.
28 GWHC, BW&Co. (USA) Inc., 107.01/02, President's annual report, 1967.
29 Ibid., President's annual report, 1960.
30 Ibid., President's annual report, 1968.
31 *American Druggist*, 4 Sept. 1961, p. 69.

32 GWHC, BW&Co. (USA) Inc., 107.01/02, President's annual report, 1968.
33 Ibid., President's annual report, 1960.
34 Ibid., President's annual report, 1962.
35 Ibid., President's annual report, 1953.
36 Ibid., President's annual report, 1953, 1954.
37 Ibid., President's annual report, 1953.
38 Ibid., President's annual report, 1953, 1954.
39 Ibid., President's annual report, 1953, 1954.
40 Ibid., President's annual report, 1968.
41 Ibid., President's annual report, 1968.
42 WF/M/AV/O/02/15, Collins interview with Parrish, 15 March 2001, p. 9.
43 *Wellcome News*, Sept. 1957, pp. 3–5.
44 GWHC, BW&Co. (USA) Inc., 107.01/02, President's annual report, 1961.
45 Ibid., President's annual report, 1967.
46 Ibid., President's annual report, 1965.
47 *Wellcome News*, Dec. 1968, p. 5.
48 *American Druggist*, 15 Nov. 1971 p. 32.
49 Ibid.
50 *American Druggist*, 22 Nov. 1971 p. 13.
51 GWHC, BW&Co. (USA) Inc., 107.01/02, President's annual report, 1968.
52 *American Druggist*, 21 Feb. 1972, p. 24.
53 Ibid., 15 May 1974, pp. 26–27.
54 Ibid., 17 Feb. 1964, p. 10; 7 Sept. 1970, p. 34.
55 Ibid., 7 Sept. 1970, p. 34.

Chapter 6: Anglo-American relations

1 Edgar Jones, *The Business of Medicine* (Profile Books, London, 2001), pp. 65–66.
2 Hall and Bembridge, *Physic and Philanthropy*, pp. 48–54; Jones, *The Business of Medicine*, chapter 3.
3 GSK/WF/SCS 284, Board minutes, 15/16/17 June 1948.
4 WT/TRU/Min/1–2, 1452, 22 March 1948. p. 550.
5 Hall and Bembridge, *Physic and Philanthropy*, pp. 53–55.
6 GSK/WF/SCS 283, Board minutes, 15–17 June, 1948, 2029.
7 GSK/WF/SCS 283, Board minutes, 3 Nov. 1948, 2213.
8 Even after these remittances, however, the American company's account showed a surplus of $1.9m. GSK/WF/SCS 283, Board minutes, 3 Nov. 1948, 2213.
9 GSK/WF/SCS 284, Board minutes, 26 Oct. 1948, 2207.
10 Ibid.
11 GWHC, BW&Co. (USA) Inc., 107.07/11, Public affairs, "Brief analysis."
12 This was Sier's characterization of the essence of the approach adopted by managers of the Wellcome Foundation. GSK/WF/SCS 283, Board minutes, 2 Dec. 1948, 2228.
13 GSK/WF/SCS 283, Board minutes, 2 Dec. 1948, 2228.
14 BWFL, Private papers, Creasy to Sier, 7 Feb. 1950; Creasy to Sier, 1 March 1950.
15 BWFL, Private papers, Creasy to Sier, 1 March 1950.
16 BWFL, Private papers, Creasy to Sier, 1 March 1950.
17 See chapter 11.
18 GSK/WF/SCS 284, Board minutes, 7 July 1948, 2046; 6 Oct. 1948, 2174.
19 GSK/WF/SCS 284, Board minutes, 6 Oct. 1948, 2174.
20 GSK/WF/SCS 283, Board minutes, Dec. 1948, 2229.
21 Contrary to the observation made by Hall and Bembridge, *Physic and Philanthropy*, p. 72.
22 GSK/WF/SCS 284, Board minutes, 9 Jan. 1950, 2493.
23 GSK/WF/SCS 284, Board minutes, 9 Jan. 1950, 2403; 24 Jan. 1950, 2503; Coe diaries, 25 Jan. 1950, p. 2.
24 GSK/WF/SCS 264, Board minutes, 5 April 1952, 2853.
25 WF, Acc 82/1 Box 19, Nevin to Pearson, 28 Jan. 1926; Rhodes James, *Henry Wellcome*, p. 291.
26 Hall and Bembridge, *Physic and Philanthropy*, pp. 70–71.
27 Ibid., pp. 72–73.
28 Ibid., p. 113.
29 Ibid., p. 72.
30 GSK/WF/SCS 285, Board minutes, 16 Sept. 1954, 3332.
31 GWHC, BW&Co. (USA) Inc., 107.01/02, President's annual report, 1952/3.
32 GSK/WF/SCS 285, Board minutes, 8 July 1953, 3025.
33 Ibid.
34 Ibid.
35 *Wellcome News*, May 1959, p. 3.
36 GWHC, BW&Co. (USA) Inc. 107.01/02, President's annual report, 1955/6.
37 GSK/WF/SCS 285, Board minutes, 15 March 1956, 3759.

38 GWHC, BW&Co. (USA) Inc., 107.07/11, Public affairs, "Brief analysis," n.p.
39 GSK/WF/SCS 285, Board minutes, 4 April 1955, 3495.
40 GWHC, BW&Co. (USA) Inc., 107.01/02, President's annual report 1955/6.
41 Ibid.
42 GSK/WF/SCS 285, Board minutes, 20 Jan. 1955, 3429.
43 Ibid.; Coe diaries, 14 Jan. 1955; 10 Feb. 1955.
44 GSK/WF/SCS 285, Board minutes, 20 Dec. 1956, 3993.
45 Ibid.
46 GSK/WF/SCS 285, Board minutes, 18 Oct. 1956, 3907.
47 GSK/WF/SCS 285, Board minutes, 9 Dec. 1957, 4301; Coe diaries, 22 Nov. 1959, p. 30.
48 GSK/WF/SCS 285, Board minutes, 20 Dec. 1956, 3991.
49 Coe diaries, 7 May 1953, p. 3.
50 A draft letter of resignation (the first of three in succeeding years), which Coe described as 'nasty', was toned down on Coe's request. Coe diaries, 12 and 27 Jan. 1956, p. 6.
51 Ibid.
52 Ibid., 16 Feb. 1955.
53 Ibid., 5 April 1955.
54 *American Druggist,* 1960s trade advertisements.
55 WF/M/AV/O/02/37, Collins interview with David Godfrey, 27 Aug. 2001, and WF/M/AV/O/02/38, Collins interview with John Bowler, 27 Aug. 2001.
56 WF/M/AV/O/02/38, Collins interview with Bowler, 27 Aug. 2001.
57 GWHC, BW&Co. (USA) Inc., 107.01/02, President's annual report, 1957/8.

Chapter 7: Conflict, crisis, and the end of a presidency

1 *Wellcome News,* Oct./Nov. 1957, p. 2.
2 Iris B. Evans, *The Burroughs Wellcome Fund, 1955–1985. Investment in Research* (Burroughs Wellcome Fund, Henderson, NC, 1985), pp. 16–17.
3 WF/M/AV/O/02/09, Collins interview with Evans, 28 April 2001, pp. 21, 27–28.
4 *Wellcome News,* Oct./Nov. 1957, p. 2.
5 GSK/WF/SCS 286, Board minutes, 9 Dec. 1957, 4301.
6 Ibid.
7 Ibid.
8 Church and Tansey, *Burroughs Wellcome & Co.*, chapter 2.
9 GSK/WF/SCS 286, Board minutes, 9 Dec. 1957, 4301.
10 Ibid.
11 Coe diaries, Feb. 1958.
12 Coe diaries, Jan. 1954.
13 Coe diaries, 25 May 1955.
14 Coe diaries, 29 June 1961.
15 GWHC, BW&Co. (USA) Inc., 107.07/11, Public affairs, "Brief analysis," n.p.
16 WF/M/AV/O/02/38, Collins interview with Bowler, 27 Aug. 2001.
17 See chapter 8.
18 Coe diaries, 7 Oct. 1959.
19 Coe diaries, 30 April 1964.
20 In this instance, the pull factor may have been at least as important as troubled relations in the laboratories at Tuckahoe. GWHC, BW&Co. (USA) Inc., 107.01/02, President's annual report, 1966/7.
21 He also displayed erratic behavior when attending social functions and events with colleagues. Coe diaries, 14 Oct. 1953.
22 WF/M/AV/O/02/25, Collins interview with Regan, 17 May 2001, p. 4.
23 Even in 1957, Coe had been critical of Creasy's condescending treatment of the directors intended to convey superiority; "I can't stand it." A year later, when Coe received an offer from Denver Chemical Co. to manage a newly-acquired subsidiary company, Coe gave it careful consideration. Salary and prospects would be attractive and Coe reflected that "If Creasy puts enough heat on, he'll drive me to do it." Coe diaries, 3 July 1957.
24 Coe diaries, 25 Jan.; 24 March 1960.
25 Coe diaries, 16 Aug. 1965.
26 See appendix.
27 Coe diaries, 28 Oct. 1965.
28 GSK/WF/SCS 556, Group organisation report, 1965–67.
29 Coe diaries, 23 Sept. 1966.
30 The context for the review was the postwar record of minimal dividends received by the Trust (See Table 7.1).
31 Coe diaries, 22 Sept. 1966.
32 See chapter 9.
33 Coe diaries, 4 Oct. 1966.
34 WF/M/AV/O/02/35, Collins interview with Williams, 14 Aug. 2001, p. 4.
35 Coe diaries, 7 May 1968.
36 Ibid., 6 Jan. 1967.

37 Ibid., 6 Jan. 1967.
38 Ibid., 8 April 1967.
39 Ibid., 9 April 1967.
40 Ibid., 22 April 1967.
41 Ibid., 26 April; 2 June 1967.
42 Ibid., 6 Dec. 1967, 25 Jan. 1968. For an assessment of Creasy's contribution to the history of the company see below p. 124.
43 Coe diaries, 25 Jan. 1968.
44 Ibid., 27 June 1967.
45 Ibid., Christmas 1968.
46 The consultants visiting Tuckahoe appear to have been sufficiently impressed by the performance of Coe and Dowling as the senior managers in control that the report included no reference to Creasy's exasperating behavior.
47 GSK/WF/SCS 1583, Chairman's marketing committee, 28 Aug. 1973.
48 Ibid.
49 GSK/WF/SCS 556, Group organisation report, 1965–67.
50 Ibid.
51 GSK/WF/SCS 367, Corporate image: A reappraisal, November 1972. The survey was conducted by MIPAL, a British organisation in collaboration with Lea Inc., an American company.
52 See above p. 85.

Chapter 8: Drug discovery and networks of innovation

1 GWHC, BW&Co. (USA) Inc., 107.01/02, President's annual report, 1944/5.
2 Ibid., President's annual report, 1962/3.
3 GWHC, BW&Co. (USA) Inc., 107.01/02, D. S. Searle to B. Halloby, 7 Sept. 1949, contained in medical department report annexed to President's annual reports, 1948/9; 1954/5.
4 BWFL, Private papers, Creasy to Hitchings, 29 April 1974.
5 Ibid.
6 GWHC, BW&Co. (USA) Inc., 107.07/11, Public affairs, Jan Tanner, "Burroughs Wellcome & Co. History" (unpublished typescript, 1979), pp. S6K-1-3; BWFL, Private papers, Creasy to Hitchings, 29 April 1974.
7 "George H. Hitchings," in Tore Frängsmyr (ed.), *Les Prix Nobel. The Nobel Prizes 1988* (Nobel Foundation, Stockholm, 1989).
8 Sara Hunter, "Lifting chemotherapy out of limbo: The man who made immunosuppressive drugs a clinical reality", interview with George H. Hitchings by Sara Hunter PhD, *Modern Medicine*, 1 July 1975, pp. 98–99.
9 *Wellcome News*, May 1949, p. 3; Hunter, "Lifting chemotherapy out of limbo," pp. 90–104.
10 John P. Swann, "Universities, industry, and the rise of biomedical collaboration in America," in J. Liebenau, G. J. Higby, J. Gregory, and E. C. Stroud (eds), *Pill Pedlars: Essays on the History of the Pharmaceutical Industry* (American Institute of the History of Pharmacy, Madison WI, 1988), pp. 73–80.
11 John Parascandola, "The 'preposterous provision:' The American Society for Pharmacology and Experimental Therapeutics' ban on industrial pharmacologists, 1908–1941," in Liebenau, Higby, Gregory, and Stroud (eds), *Pill Pedlars*, pp. 37–42.
12 K. H. George, "George H. Hitchings, 1905–, American pharmacologist," in E. J. McMurray, J. K. Kosel, and R. M. Valada (eds), *Notable Twentieth Century Scientists,* Vol. 2 (Gale Group, Reading, 1996), pp. 933–34.
13 Quoted in Hunter, "Lifting chemotherapy out of limbo," p. 93.
14 WF/E/19, Quoted by Cresswell, Castell interview with Cresswell, 3, Aug. 2012, p. 2.
15 Quoted in Clealand F. Baker, "Burroughs Wellcome: Pioneer in pharmaceutical research," *Private Practice*, Jan. 1980, pp. 38–39.
16 Quoted in Hunter, "Lifting chemotherapy out of limbo," p. 93.
17 GWHC, BW&Co. (USA) Inc., 107.07/11, Public affairs, Tanner interview with Elion, *c.* 1977.
18 GWHC, BW&Co. (USA) Inc., 107.07/11, Historical reference material, Gertrude B. Elion, "Historical perspectives" (typescript, 1968), pp. 1–5; Frängsmyr (ed.), *Les Prix Nobel*, n.p.; Mary Ellen Avery, "Gertrude Belle Elion, 23 January 1918–21 February 1999," *Biographical Memoirs of Fellows of the Royal Society* 54, 2008, p. 161.
19 GWHC, BW&Co. (USA) Inc., 107.07/01, *Wellcome News*, May 1949, p. 3.
20 Hitchings, "Autobiography," 1988, Nobelprize.org Log.
21 Frängsmyr (ed.), *Les Prix Nobel*, n.p.
22 Ibid.
23 G. H. Hitchings, G. B. Elion, P. B. Russel, and H. Van der Werff, "Studies on analogs of purines and pyrimidines," *Annals of the New York Academy of Sciences* 52, 1950, p. 1318.

24 Christopher R. Flowers, and Kenneth L. Melmon, "Clinical champions as critical determinants of drug development," in Landau, Achiladelis, and Scriabine (eds), *Pharmaceutical Innovation*, p. 339.
25 G. B. Elion, "Historical perspectives", in *Design and achievements in chemotherapy: A symposium in honour of George H. Hitchings at Research Triangle Park, NC* (Sciences and Medicine Publishing, NC, 1976), p. 337.
26 Quoted in Flowers and Melmon, "Clinical champions," p. 339.
27 G. H. Hitchings, "Selective inhibitors of dihydroflate reductase," In vitro cellular and developmental biology, Nobel lecture in physiology or medicine, 1988, in Frängsmyr (ed.), *Les Prix Nobel*, n.p.
28 *Wellcome News*, Nov. 1953, p. 3; April 1954, p. 11.
29 Flowers and Melmon, "Clinical champions," p. 342.
30 Interview with Hitchings and Elion by Katherine Boulton (ed.), *New York Times*, 29 Jan. 1989, p. 28.
31 *American Druggist*, 2 Dec. 1957, p. 11.
32 Ibid., 24 March 1958, pp. 5–7.
33 *Wellcome News*, Nov. 1954, p. 3.
34 Ibid., Aug. 1958, p. 4.
35 Ibid.
36 GWHC, BW&Co. (USA) Inc., 107.07/11, Public affairs, Tanner interview with Elion, *c.* 1977.
37 Coe diaries, Dec. 1953; GWHC, BW&Co. (USA) Inc., 107.01/02, President's annual report, 1956/7; GWHC, BW&Co. (USA) Inc., 107.07/11, Public affairs, "Brief analysis."
38 This included Gertrude Elion, Dr Marion Sherwood, H. Van der Werf, Dr Peter Russell and Elvira Falco.
39 *Wellcome News*, June 1951, pp. 9–11.
40 GSK/WF/SCS 285, Board minutes, 25 July 1956, 3862.
41 WFL decided against the company's embarking on specific research in abortiffacient or contraceptive fields or to an issuance of abortiffacient products. GSK/WF/SCS 285, Board minutes, 17 Dec. 1953, 3141.
42 *Wellcome News*, Spring 1965, p. 9.
43 *American Druggist*, 1 July 1968, p. 38.
44 *Wellcome News*, Spring 1965, p. 7; *American Druggist*, 1 July 1968, p. 38.
45 See below p. 122.
46 Flowers and Melmon, "Clinical champions", pp. 349–51.
47 *American Druggist*, 1 July 1968, p. 38.
48 WF/E/19, Castell interview with Cresswell, 2, Aug. 2012, p. 5.
49 Hunter interview with Hutchings, "Lifting chemotherapy out of limbo," pp. 90–104.
50 *Wellcome News*, 2 Feb. 1972, pp. 100–1.
51 Ibid., 6 Feb. 1976, p. 11.
52 Ibid., 3 April 1976, p. 15.
53 Hunter, "Lifting chemotherapy out of limbo," pp. 90–104.
54 The award was also bestowed on James Black, formerly employed during a brief, unproductive and conflictual period during the 1980s by WFL, though in recognition of his prize for physiology and medicine was in recognition of his development of histamine H2 antagonist cimetidine, marketed as Tagamet for the treatment of peptic ulcers, while he was employed by Smith Kline & French.

Chapter 9: Investment in RD&M, laboratory reorganisation, and the FDA

1 See Lasagna, "Congress, the FDA, and New Drug Development," pp. 322–43.
2 Coe diaries, December 1953; GWHC, BW&Co. (USA) Inc., 107.01/02, President's annual report, 1956/7; GWHC, BW&Co. (USA) Inc., 107.07/11, Public affairs, "Brief analysis."
3 GWHC, BW&Co. (USA) Inc., 107.01/02, President's annual report, 1955/6.
4 GWHC, BW&Co. (USA) Inc., 107.01/02, President's annual report, 1956/7.
5 Ibid., President's annual report, 1959/60.
6 Ibid., President's annual reports, 1959/60, 1962/3.
7 Ibid., President's annual reports, 1959/60, 1962/3.
8 Ibid., President's annual reports, 1959/60, 1962/3.
9 Ibid., President's annual report, 1960.
10 Ibid., President's annual report, 1960.
11 Ibid., President's annual report, 1962.
12 Ibid., President's annual report, 1963.
13 Ibid., President's annual report, 1961.
14 *American Druggist*, annual series 1956–1965. The other main categories were hormones and antihistamines (both 9 per cent), vitamins and narcotics (both falling from 8 to 4 per cent), and sulfas (falling from 5 to 4 per cent).

15 The main drugs were Neosporin, Lubasporin, and Cortisporin, the antibiotic-steroid.
16 GWHC, BW&Co. (USA) Inc., 107.01/02, President's annual report, 1966/7.
17 Lasagna, "Congress, the FDA, and New Drug Development," pp. 330–32.
18 See chapter 3.
19 Lasagna, "Congress, the FDA, and New Drug Development," pp. 330–31.
20 GWHC, BW&Co. (USA) Inc., 107.01/02, President's annual report, 1965/6.
21 GSK/WF/SCS 556, Group organisation report, 1965–67.
22 GWHC, BW&Co. (USA) Inc., 107.01/02, President's annual report, 1966/7.
23 He was consultant to the National Institute of General Medical Services of the National Institute of Health (NIH), which contracted with the company to carry out fundamental studies of interactions between drugs and chemical compounds. He was one of three US representatives on the WHO section of pharmacology and toxicology, a member of the Council of Pharmacology and Experimental Therapeutics, and one of the industry's two representatives included on the Drug Research Board of the National Academy of Science. He was also chairman of the Pharmaceutical Manufacturers' scientific advisory body.
24 GWHC, BW&Co. (USA) Inc., 107.01/02, President's annual report, 1962/3.
25 Ibid., President's annual report, 1965/6.
26 Ibid., President's annual report, 1962/3.
27 Ibid., President's annual report, 1970/1.
28 Ibid., President's report, 1965/6.
29 Hitchings signed a new contract agreeing to work for a further five years, which meant postponing his own retirement.
30 WF/M/AV/O/02/44, Collins interview with Cresswell, 14 Sept. 2001, pp. 1–2.
31 Cresswell's qualities had been drawn to Creasy's attention when he was first appointed, because his curriculum vita had been drawn to his attention by his private secretary whose husband had attended the same Glasgow school where Cresswell had been captain.
32 GWHC, BW&Co. (USA) Inc., 107.01/02, President's annual report, 1970/1.
33 Ibid., President's annual report, 1960.
34 WF/M/AV/O/02/22, Collins interview with Krenitsky, 14 May 2001, pp. 3–4.
35 GWHC, BW&Co. (USA) Inc., 107.07/11, Public affairs, Tanner interview with Elion, *c.* 1977.
36 Ibid.
37 WF/E/19, Creasy to Cresswell, 20 Feb. 1973.
38 Ibid.

Chapter 10: Relocation from Tuckahoe to Research Triangle Park

1 GWHC, BW&Co. (USA) Inc., 107.07/11, Historical reference material.
2 Coe diaries, 20 June 1967, p. 12.
3 Ibid., 26 June 1967, p. 12.
4 WF/USA/01/01/01, Coe typescript, 24 Feb. 1969; Jan Tanner, "American story," part 2, *Wellcome News,* July 1981, pp. 13–14.
5 Tanner, "American story," part 2, pp. 14–15.
6 Ibid.
7 GWHC, BW&Co. (USA) Inc., 107.01/02, President's annual report, 1947/8.
8 Ibid., President's annual report, 1948/9.
9 Ibid., President's annual report, 1946/7.
10 WF/M/AV/O/02/08, Collins interview with James Feathers, 27 Aug. 2001; WF/M/AV/O/02/13, Collins interview with Harry Leslie, 2 May 2001.
11 GWHC, BW&Co. (USA) Inc., 107.07/11, Jan Tanner, "Burroughs & Wellcome History" (unpublished typescript, *c.* 1981), p. 5.
12 GWHC, BW&Co. (USA) Inc., 107.01/02, President's annual report, 1955/6.
13 WF/M/AV/O/02/22, Collins interview with Krenitsky, 14 May 2001, p. 2.
14 WF/M/AV/O/02/04, Collins interview with Kennedy, 25 April 2001.
15 WF/M/AV/O/02/13, Collins interview with Don Duff, Harry Leslie, and James Murphy, 2 May 2001.
16 GWHC, BW&Co. (USA) Inc., 107.01/02, President's annual report, 1960/1.
17 Ibid., President's annual report, 1966/7.
18 Ibid., President's annual report, 1966/7.
19 GWHC, BW&Co. (USA) Inc., 107.01/02, President's annual report, 1966/7.
20 Coe diaries, 16 May 1967.
21 Coe diaries, 18 July 1968. It may be significant that shortly after the announcement of the move to North Carolina in 1969 Coe recorded in his diary that managers of the US Vitamin Company wished to meet him and Dowling "to discuss the *real* reasons behind our move." Ibid., 30 July 1969.
22 S. D. Williams, "Introduction," in S. D. Williams, *Park Guide: The 1994 Guide to*

Research Triangle Park, 8 (Research Triangle Park, NC, 1994), pp. 15–16.
23 Michael Binyon, "Research Park where the grass is already greener," *Times Higher Education Supplement*, 306, 9 Sept. 1977, p. 1.
24 Coe diaries, 19 Aug. 1968.
25 GSK/WF/SCS 299, General meetings, 26 Jan. 1967.
26 Ibid., General meetings, 21 Jan. 1969.
27 Ibid., General meetings, 15 Jan. 1970.
28 Ibid., General meetings, 26 Jan. 1971.
29 Tanner, "American story," p. 6.
30 Coe diaries, 31 Jan. 1969.
31 Tanner, "American story," p. 6.
32 The cost was 8.25 per cent for two years and thereafter prime rate plus 0.25 per cent. Repayment was required in three installments no later than the end of years four, five, and six. GSK/WF/SCS 299, General meetings, 15 Jan. 1970.
33 Leslie recalled that he told Barry that this promotion was on the understanding that should the union make any attempt to organise the workers at Greenville, he should inform Leslie immediately. Two years later, the Chemical Workers' Union did contact Barry, who explained that he was unable to assist in any way as he was supervisory staff. He told Leslie: "... there is no effort at the present time and if you keep handling people the way you're doing down here now there is no need for a union." WF/M/AV/O/02/13, Collins interview with Harry Leslie, 2 May 2001.
34 GWHC, BW&Co. (USA) Inc., 107.01/02, President's annual report, 1969/70.
35 WF/M/AV/O/02/13, Collins interview with Harry Leslie, 2 May 2001.
36 WF/M/AV/O/02/08, Collins interview with James Feathers, 27 Aug. 2001.
37 Tanner, "American story," part 2, pp. 7–8.
38 GWHC, BW&Co. (USA) Inc., 107.01/02, President's annual report, 1969/70.
39 Ibid., President's annual report, 1969/70.
40 Ibid., President's annual report, 1971/2.
41 Ibid., President's annual report, 1968/9.
42 WF/USA/01/01/01, *Herald Statesman*, 7 Aug. 1969.
43 GWHC, BW&Co. (USA) Inc., 107.01/02, President's annual report, 1969/70.
44 Ibid., President's annual report, 1969/70.
45 WF/M/AV/O/02/13, Collins interview with Harry Leslie, 2 May 2001.
46 GWHC, BW&Co. (USA) Inc., 107.01/02, President's annual report, 1971/2.
47 Coe diaries, 23 Jan.; 4 Feb.; 24 Feb.; 27 Feb. 1969.
48 Tanner, "American story," part 3, *Wellcome News*, Aug. 1981. pp. 13–15.
49 GWHC, BW&Co. (USA) Inc., 107.01/02, President's annual report, 1971/2.
50 Tanner, "American story," part 3, *Wellcome News*, Aug. 1981, p. 15.
51 Coe diaries, 22 May 1972; 25 Jan. 1973.
52 GWHC, BW&Co. (USA) Inc., 107.01/02, President's annual report, 1971/2.
53 Ibid., President's annual report, 1968/9.
54 Ibid., President's annual report, 1971/2.

Chapter 11: Reorganization, recruitment, corporate image, and marketing

1 WF/M/AV/O/02/04, Collins interview with Kennedy, April 2001, p. 55.
2 *American Druggist*, 11 Aug. 1969, p. 43.
3 Ibid.
4 Ibid.
5 GWHC, BW&Co. (USA) Inc., 107.01/02, President's annual reports 1966 and 1967.
6 Ibid., President's annual report, 1972.
7 *Wellcome News*, 17:1, 1986, p. 4.
8 WF/M/AV/O/02/12, Collins interview with Howsam, 11 May 2001, p. 8.
9 The interview consisted of two four hour sessions. Both Howsam and Donelson believed this was explained by Creasy's previous history of showing a reluctance to bring in senior outsiders and that as a new President Coe was anxious to make no mistake. In fact on learning of Howsam's appointment Creasy did complain to Coe that this was misguided as suitable candidates were available from within BW&Co. WF/M/AV/0/02/12, Collins interview with Howsam, 11 May 2001, p. 2; WF/M/AV/O/02/16, Collins interview with Donelson, 7 May 2001, p. 13; Coe diaries, 21 April 1970.
10 WF/M/AV/O/02/12, Collins interview with Howsam, 11 May 2001, pp. 3–5.
11 GWHC, BW&Co. (USA) Inc., 107.01/02, President's annual report, 1973.
12 WF/M/AV/O/02/04, Collins interview with Kennedy, April 2001, p. 2.
13 GWHC, BW&Co. (USA) Inc., 107.01/02, President's annual report, 1971.
14 WF/M/AV/O/02/12, Collins interview with Howsam, 11 May 2001, pp. 3–4. He excluded Coe

from a charge of not regarding profit to be central to prioritising activity.

15 GWHC, BW&Co. (USA) Inc., 107.01/02, President's annual report, 1972.

16 GWHC, BW&Co. (USA) Inc., 107.07/11, Public affairs, Tanner interview with Howsam, 1979, p. 6.

17 GWHC, BW&Co. (USA) Inc., 107.01/02, President's annual report, 1968.

18 GSK/WF/SCS 367, "Corporatc image: A reappraisal," Oct. 1972, see also chapter 16.

19 Howsam was comparing marketing at BW&Co. with best practice of Warner Lambert. A few years earlier, Urwick Orr had been so impressed by marketing and training at BW&Co. that this had been held up as a model for the parent company to follow. See above, chapter 5.

20 WF/M/AV/O/02/12, Collins interview with Howsam, 11 May 2001, pp. 1–2.

21 Ibid., pp. 3–4, 6. Howsam later expressed his pride to be in the presence of the distinguished Vice President-Research, Hitchings. Howsam contrasted his own welcome by Hitchings with that which he, Howsam, received on a visit to the Wellcome Laboratories at Beckenham where he was introduced as the new vice president of marketing and sales to the researchers; no-one spoke to him.

22 Ibid.

23 WF/M/AV/O/02/12, Collins interview with Howsam, 11 May 2001, pp. 1–2; *Wellcome News*, Nov. 1971, p. 34; WF/M/AV/O/02/15, Collins interview with Parrish, 15 March 2001, p. 6.

24 GWHC, BW&Co. (USA) Inc., 107.07/11, Public affairs, Tanner interview with Howsam, 1979, p. 2.

25 WF/M/AV/O/02/15, Collins interview with Parrish, 15 March 2001, p. 27.

26 WF/M/AV/O/02/12, Collins interview with Howsam, 11 May 2001, p. 6; WF/M/AV/O/02/16, Collins interview with Donelson, 7 May 2001, p. 20.

27 *Advertising Age*, 13 Feb. 1978, p. 66.

28 *American Druggist*, 4 Oct. 1971, p. 5.

29 Ibid., 1 Sept. 1974, p. 61.

30 Ibid., 1 Nov. 1974, p. 34.

31 *Advertising Age*, 13 Feb. 1978, p. 66.

32 Peter Howsam, "Product planning at Burroughs Wellcome," *Medical Marketing Media*, June 1976, p. 10.

33 *American Druggist*, 7 March 1960, p. 35.

34 GWHC, BW&Co. (USA) Inc., 107.01/02, President's annual report, 1972.

35 Ibid., President's annual report, 1972.

36 GWHC, BW&Co. (USA) Inc., 107.07/11, Public affairs, Tanner interview with Howsam p. 6.

37 Howsam, "Product planning."

38 *Wellcome News*, March/April 1976, n.p.

39 GWHC, BW&Co. (USA) Inc., 107.07/11, Public affairs, Tanner interview with Howsam, p. 11.

40 Ibid.

41 Howsam, "Product planning."

42 WF/M/AV/O/02/16, Collins interview with Donelson, 7 May 2001, p. 19.

43 *American Druggist*, 2 Jan. 1972, p. 25.

44 *Wellcome News*, March/April 1976, n.p.

45 GWHC, BW&Co. (USA) Inc., 107.01/02, President's annual report, 1971.

46 Ibid.

47 Ibid.

48 WF/E/19, Creasy to Cresswell, 18 March 1973.

49 WF/M/AV/O/02/16, Collins interview with Donelson, May 2001, p. 16.

50 GWHC, BW&Co. (USA) Inc., 107.07/11, Public affairs, Tanner interview with Howson, pp. 4–5.

51 Ibid.

52 Ibid., p. 3.

53 Ibid.

54 *Wellcome News*, March/April 1976, n.p.

55 WF/M/AV/O/02/25, Collins interview with Regan, 17 May 2001, p. 28.

56 Ibid., p. 29.

57 Howsam, "Product planning," p. 10.

58 GSK/WF/SCS 367, "Corporate image: A reappraisal," Oct. 1972.

59 WF/M/AV/O/02/12, Collins interview with Howsam, 11 May 2001, pp. 7–8.

60 GWHC, BW&Co. (USA) Inc., 107.01/02, President's annual report, 1972.

61 *Product Management*, April 1974, p. 31.

62 WF/M/AV/O/02/12, Collins interview with Howsam, April 2001, p. 6.

63 WF/E/19, Creasy to Cresswell, 18 March 1973.

64 *Medical World News*, 24 Jan. 1983, p. 61.

65 GWHC, BW&Co. (USA) Inc., 107.01/02, President's annual report, 1972.

66 *American Druggist*, 2 Nov. 1970, p. 56.

67 *Wellcome News*, June/July 1976, n.p.; GWHC, BW&Co. (USA) Inc., 107.01/02, President's annual report, 1971.

68 *Product Management*, April 1974, p. 31.

69 *Wellcome News*, Jan. 1975, n.p.

70 *Wellcome News*, 16, 1985, p. 16.

Chapter 12: Septra: product innovation and consumer marketing

1 *Foundation News,* April 1985, p. 8; GWHC, BW&Co. (USA) Inc., 107.07/11, Jan Tanner, "Burroughs Wellcome history" (typescript, 1979), p. S6K-8.
2 WF/M/AV/O/02/44, Collins interview with Cresswell, 14 Oct. 2001, p. 1.
3 Ibid., p. 9.
4 GWHC, BW&Co. (USA) Inc., 107.01/02, President's annual report, 1953.
5 WF/M/AV/O/02/44, Collins interview with Cresswell, 14 Oct. 2001, p. 9.
6 WF/M/AV/O/02/37, Collins interview with Godfrey, 27 Aug. 2001, p. 31.
7 WF/M/AV/O/02/38, Collins interview with Bowler, 27 Aug. 2001, p. 24.
8 WF/M/AV/O/02/44, Collins interview with Cresswell 14 Sept. 2001, pp. 3–4; WF/M/AV/O/02/22, Collins interview with Krenitsky, 14 May 2001, p. 9. See below.
9 WF/M/AV/O/02/38, Collins interview with Bowler, 27 Aug. 2001, p. 24.
10 *Wellcome News,* Dec. 1968, p. 4.
11 Ibid.
12 Ibid.
13 GWHC, BW&Co. (USA) Inc., 107.07/11, Public affairs; *Wellcome News,* 4 Aug. 1973, pp. 1–3.
14 *Wellcome News,* Dec. 1968, p. 7.
15 GSK/WF/SCS 299, General meetings, 2 Jan.; 15, Jan. 1970.
16 *Wellcome News,* 4 Aug. 1973, pp. 3–4.
17 WF/E/19, Castell interview with Cresswell, 3, Aug. 2012, p. 2.
18 See below pp. 161–62.
19 *Wellcome News,* 7 Aug. 1973, p. 3.
20 GWHC, BW&Co. (USA) Inc., 107.07/11, Public affairs, Tanner interview with Howsam, 1979, p. 8; WF/M/AV/O/02/38, Collins interview with Bowler, 27 Aug. 2001, p. 25.
21 WF/M/AV/O/02/12, Collins interview with Howsam, pp. 6–7.
22 Coe diaries, 29 May 1972, p. 5.
23 WF/M/AV/O/03/33, Burton interview with Cipau, 7 March 2002.
24 *Wellcome News,* 7 Aug. 1973, p. 1.
25 Coe diaries, 29 May 1972, p. 5.
26 Ibid.
27 *Wellcome News,* Nov. 1974, n.p.; GWHC, BW&Co. (USA) Inc., 107.01/02, President's annual report, 1972.
28 WF/M/AV/O/02/12, Collins interview with Howsam, April 2001, p. 6.
29 GSK/WF/SCS 1583, Chairman's management committee minutes, 29 Nov. 1978, fn. 179.
30 *Product Management,* April 1974, p. 31.
31 *Wellcome News,* Oct. 1976, n.p.
32 Ibid., 4 Aug. 1981, p. 2.
33 Ibid., 3 July 1985, p. 1.
34 *American Druggist,* 7 March 1960, p. 53.
35 Lasagna, "Congress, the FDA, and New Drug Development," pp. 322–43.
36 GSK/WF/SCS 1583, Marketing committee minutes, 20 July 1973, 94.
37 *Advertising Age,* 16 June 1978, p. 31.
38 *Medical World,* 24 Jan. 1983, pp. 60–61.
39 WF/M/AV/O/02/12, Collins interview with Howsam, April 2001, p. 22.
40 Ibid.
41 This process of "cannibalization" (a term used by James Balog, vice-president of D. Willer & Co., New York, brokers specializing in drug investment) was adopted by Bristol Myers, for example, which began to produce a version of penicillin hitherto associated with Lilly, and Upjohn which introduced erythromycin, originally developed by Abbott. The cannibalized product was supported by intensive advertising and promotion supported by discounting by up to 25 per cent. *American Druggist,* 22 Feb. 1971, p. 13.

Chapter 13: Personalities, policies, dividends, Anglo-American relations

1 Hall and Bembridge, *Physic and Philanthropy.* p. 56.
2 Peter Williams, "The Wellcome Trust Story, 1960–1991: Personal Reminiscences" (unpublished memoir, 1992), pp. 19–20.
3 Ibid.
4 Of whom it was said by a contemporary "behind that chest of steel beats a heart of ice," ibid., p. 21.
5 WA, Peter Williams in interview with Francis Tufton and Richard Hodges, 6 July 1966, p. 264.
6 WF/M/AV/O/02/46, Collins interview with Hobbs, 29 Oct. 2001, p. 5.
7 GSK/WF/SCS 556, Group organization report, 1965–67.
8 Wrigley had expected to be appointed as his successor, as did many others who respected his

dynamic managerial qualities. He received only a single vote by from fellow directors on the board of WFL, which one contemporary director attributed to Wrigley's capacity to alienate colleagues, though a perception also existed that Wrigley was "past his prime". Coe diaries, 20 Nov. 1974; WF/M/AV/O/02/37, Collins interview with Godfrey, 27 Aug. 2001, p. 32.

9 Ibid., p. 17.

10 Coe also observed that everyone except Gray appeared to have enjoyed the post board meeting cocktail party and banquet. Socializing was a frequent activity among the directors and senior Managers. Coe diaries, 11 Nov. 1971.

11 Coe diaries, 9 April 1972.

12 GSK/WF/SCS 556, "Group organisation," draft statement by Chairman Perrin, 23 Jan. 1967.

13 *Foundation News*, 25 May 1975, p. 2.

14 Ibid., 25 July 1975, p. 3.

15 Ibid., 25 May 1975, p. 3.

16 Ibid., 26 Sept. 1975, pp. 2–3.

17 Ibid., 25 April 1975, pp. 4–5.

18 Obituary, *The Independent*, 26 Oct. 2007.

19 GSK/WF/SCS 1583, Chairman's marketing committee, 9 June 1977.

20 GSK/WF/SCS 1583, Chairman's marketing committee, 9 June 1977. Coe concluded that 'the meeting came to no real conclusion', but that he had succeeded in getting "a few digs into Worlock," though he described the three-person attack on him as gentle and Worlock's response meek. However at a private dinner with the Committee later, Coe described Shepperd as having "really ripped into Worlock." Coe diaries, 9 June 1977.

21 "Marketing in London seems to have the thing all screwed up as usual," was Coe's diary entry referring to this. Coe diaries, 20 Jan. 1977.

22 Coe diaries, 27 Jan. 1976.

23 GSK/WF/SCS 1583, Chairman's marketing committee, 28 Sept. 1977.

24 Coe diaries, 15 May 1977.

25 *Foundation News*, 26 Sept. 1975, pp. 2–3.

26 Ibid.

27 Ibid., 25 July 1975, p. 4.

28 Ibid., May 1975, p. 2.

29 Coe diaries, 22 March 1977.

30 WA, Peter Williams in interview with Max Blythe, 1995, p. 124.

31 Williams, "The Wellcome Trust Story," pp. 21–22.

32 WA, Peter Williams in interview with Francis Tufton and Richard Hodges, 6 July 1966, p. 264.

33 WA, Peter Williams in interview with Max Blythe, 1996, p. 166.

34 Ibid.

35 Ibid., pp. 28, 146.

36 WT/TRU/Min/10 P 2271, 11 March 1975, 494: 7.

37 WF/M/AV/O/03/17, Connolly interview with A. J. Beale, 7 March 2001.

38 Nobelprize.org, Sir John R. Vane, "Autobiography".

39 WF/E/19, Creasy to Cresswell, 15 June 1972, 18 March 1973.

40 Cresswell observed that relations between Hitchings and Adamson were 'quite good' only 'as long as George was left alone.' WF/M/AV/O/02/44, Collins interview with Cresswell, 14 Oct. 2001, p. 6; Coe diaries, 26 July 1975, p. 6.

41 Coe diaries, 26 July 1975, p. 6.

42 WF/M/AV/O/02/44, Collins interview with Cresswell, 14 Oct. 2001, p. 6.

43 Coe diaries, 26 July 1975, p. 6.

44 Vane insisted that the post must be advertised in London. Coe diaries, 7 Feb. 1973, p. 3; 21 March 1973, p. 4; 24 May 1973, p. 5.

45 Coe persuaded Hitchings not to carry out his threat to leave and to "sit on his butt." Coe diaries, 24 May 1973, p. 5.

46 WF/M/AV/O/03/48, Burton interview with Cuatrecasas, 2002.

47 Coe diaries, 23 Nov. 1977, 24 Aug. 1978.

48 Ibid., 23 Nov. 1977, p. 11.

49 Ibid., 25 June 1981, p. 3.

50 WT, Wellcome Trust Board of Management, BOX A001 Book 1, 26 Oct. 1964, p. 1208.

51 Coe diaries, 15 Dec. 1966.

52 In 1975 the merger was finalized and became known as Wellcome Vaccines, seen as an integral part of the Animal Health division. *Wellcome News*, 6:8, Sept. 1975, pp. 8.

53 GSK/WF/SCS 105, Board minutes, 9 Sept. 1970, 7554.

54 Ibid., Board minutes, 19 July 1972, 1507.

55 Ibid., Board minutes, 16 Sept. 1970, 7571.

56 Coe recorded that "The more I hear about Jen-Sal the less I am interested in it." Coe diaries, 22 Nov. 1978.

57 GWHC, BW&Co. (USA) Inc., 107.01/02, President's annual report, 1979.

58 Coe diaries, 10 April 1980; 23 May 1980.

59 See chapter 12.

Chapter 14: Zovirax, blockbuster drug, and expansion at RTP and Greenville

1 WF/M/AV/O/02/07, Collins interview with Schaeffer, 26 April 2001, p. 1.
2 Ibid., pp. 2–5.
3 Hitchings no longer commanded a laboratory but remained in active service as a mentor.
4 WF/M/AV/O/02/10, Collins interview with Barry, 30 April 2001, p. 7.
5 WF/M/AV/O/02/07, Collins interview with Schaeffer, 26 April 2001, p. 4.
6 Church and Tansey, *Burroughs Wellcome & Co.*, pp. 468–74. See also below, chapter 15.
7 WF/M/AV/O/02/07, Collins interview with Schaeffer, 26 April 2001, p. 4.
8 Ibid., p. 7.
9 Baker, "Burroughs Wellcome," p. 40.
10 WF/M/AV/O/02/07, Collins interview with Schaeffer, 26 April, p. 8.
11 Ibid., p. 10.
12 Ibid.
13 *Wellcome News*, March/April 1983, p. 4.
14 See p. 185.
15 WF/M/AV/O/02/10, Collins interview with Barry, 30 April 2001, p. 7.
16 Ibid., pp. 3–5.
17 WF/M/AV/O/02/17, Collins interview with Walton, 21 April 2001, pp. 7, 14.
18 Ibid., p. 37.
19 WF/M/AV/O/03/30, Burton interview with Schaeffer, 12 Feb. 2002.
20 Schaeffer described him as "a nice guy but pretty tough." WF/M/AV/O/02/07, Collins interview with Schaeffer, 26 April 2001, pp. 22–23.
21 Coe diaries, 17 June 1977, p. 10.
22 Ibid., p. 11.
23 BWFL, Schaeffer's private papers.
24 GSK/WF/SCS 2179, Board minutes, AGM, 8 June 1981.
25 GSK/WF/SCS 2179, Board minutes, AGM, 3 Feb. 1981.
26 GSK/WF/SCS 299, WFL General meetings, 2, 1975–1994, 1981.
27 Ibid.
28 *Wellcome News*, 4 Aug. 1981, pp. 4–5.
29 Flowers and Melmon, "Clinical champions," p. 353.
30 WF/E/19, Castell interview with Cresswell, 2, Aug. 2012, p. 2.
31 WF/M/AV/O/02/07, Collins interview with Schaeffer, 26 April 2001, pp. 22–23.
32 *Wellcome News*, 12 Aug. 1981, p. 3.
33 *JAMA* 236:5, 29 Oct. 1973, p. 527.
34 Ibid.
35 *Newsweek*, 12 April 1982, pp. 75–76.
36 *Science* 216, June 1982, p. 14.
37 Whitney Shaw, "Acyclovir," *Business, North Carolina*, Oct. 1982, p. 31.
38 *Wellcome News*, June/July 1981, p. 7.
39 Shaw, "Acycylovir," p. 31.
40 *Wellcome News*, June/July 1982, p. 7.
41 *Medical Marketing and Media*, Sept. 1982, pp. 18–19.
42 Shaw, "Acyclovir," p. 29.
43 *Medical World News*, 24 Jan. 1983, p. 61.
44 Ibid., p. 66.
45 GSK/WF/SCS 796, Board minutes, 23 Feb. 1984, 10457.
46 *Wellcome News*, Dec. 1981, p. 3; Jan./Feb. 1982, pp. 2–5.
47 WF/M/AV/O/02/10, Collins interview with Barry, 30 April 2001, pp. 25–27.
48 *Drug Topics* 129, Feb. 1985 p. 59.
49 GSK/WF/SCS 1585, Chairman's marketing and R&D committee, 1989.
50 *Boston Globe*, 30 Jan. 1985, p. 3; Wellcome plc accounts 1989.
51 GSK/WF/SCS 1274, Chairman's RD&M and Marketing Committee, 9 Dec. 1988.
52 *Wellcome News*, March/April 1983, p. 4.
53 Ibid.
54 WF/M/AV/O/03/48, Burton interview with Cuatrecasas, 2002.
55 *Wellcome News*, Sept./Oct. 1982, p. 9.
56 Ibid., p. 28.
57 *Wellcome News*, March 1986, pp. 1–2.
58 WF/M/AV/O/03/33, Burton interview with Cipau, 7 March 2002.
59 Coe diaries, 28 Oct. 1953; 25 Jan. 1960; 24 March 1960.

Chapter 15: Mckinsey's review of Burroughs Wellcome & Co.

1 Coe diaries, 20 May 1980, p. 11; 7 May 1981, p. 3.
2 "Businessman in the news," *Business, North Carolina*, May 1982.
3 Coe diaries, 10 June 1980, p. 3.
4 Ibid.
5 Coe diaries, 20 May 1980, p. 11.
6 Coe diaries, 11 Dec. 1980. The exception was

Cuatrecasas who congratulated Sullivan, though the values and management style quickly turned Cuatrecasas into an outspoken critic.

7 WF/M/AV/O/02/05, Collins interview with Sullivan, 23 April 2001, pp. 2, 14.

8 WF/M/AV/O/02/04, Collins interview with Kennedy, 23 April 2001, p. 44.

9 GSK/WF/SCS 461, Board minutes, 3 Nov. 1982, McKinsey, "US strategy study."

10 Ibid.

11 Ibid.

12 GSK/WF/SCS 461, Board minutes, 3 Nov. 1982, McKinsey, "US strategy study"; GWHC, BW&Co. (USA) Inc., 107.07/01, *Wellcome News*, Sept./Oct. 1982, p. 3.

13 GSK/WF/SCS 461, Board minutes, 3 Nov. 1982, McKinsey, "US strategy study."

14 WF/M/AV/O/02/05, Collins interview with Sullivan, 23 April 2001, pp. 4, 8.

15 WF/M/AV/O/02/05, Collins interview with Sullivan, 23 April 2001, p. 26.

16 GWHC, BW&Co. (USA) Inc., 107.07/01, *Wellcome News*, Aug. 1981, p. 2.

17 WF/M/AV/O/02/05, Collins interview with Sullivan, 2 April 2001, p. 31.

18 GSK/WF/SCS 1708, Secret board minutes, 1883–89, 6 June 1983.

19 Ibid.

20 *Wellcome News*, March/April, 1983, p. 4.

21 WF/M/AV/O/02/05, Collins interview with Sullivan, 23 April 2001, p. 27; GSK/WF/SCS 1707, General meeting minutes, 31 Jan. 1984.

22 *Wellcome News*, Sept./Oct. 1983, pp. 10–11; WF/M/AV/O/02/15, Collins interview with Parrish, 15 March 2001, p. 43.

23 *Wellcome News*, Sept/Oct. 1983, p. 10.

24 GSK/WF/SCS 2179, Board minutes, AGM, 3 Feb. 1981.

25 *Wellcome News* 17:5, 1986, pp. 1–2.

26 WF/M/AV/O/02/25, Collins interview with Regan, 15 March 2001, p. 32.

27 GWHC, BW&Co. (USA) Inc., 107.07/01, *Wellcome News* 17:5, 1986, p. 3.

28 Ibid.

29 GWHC, BW&Co. (USA) Inc., 107.07/01, *Wellcome News* 17:5, 1986, p. 2.

30 GSK/WF/SCS 591, BW&Co., Board minutes, June 1981, 5422; GWHC, BW&Co. (USA) Inc., 107.01/02, President's annual report, 1981.

31 *Wellcome News*, Sept./Oct. 1983, p. 13.

32 *Wellcome News*, Sept/Oct. 1983, p. 12.

33 *Wellcome News*, Oct. 1988, p. 20.

34 WF/M/AV/O/02/05, Church/Collins interview with Sullivan, 23 April 2001, pp. 25–26; WF/M/AV/O/02/15, Collins interview with Parrish, 15 March 2001, pp. 16, 35.

35 WF/M/AV/O/02/05, Church/Collins interview with Sullivan, 23 April 2001, pp. 31–33.

.36 *Medical World*, 24 Jan. 1983, pp. 60–61.

37 Ibid., pp. 61–62.

38 GSK/WF/SCS 591, BW&Co., Board minutes, 1980–83, 22 July 1982, 5552.

39 Sidney Wolfe and Christopher M. Coley, *Pills that Don't Work* (Farrar, Strauss, & Giroux, New York, 1981 edition).

40 Ibid.

41 *Wellcome News*, Jan./Feb. 1982, pp. 1, 12.

42 Ibid.

43 WF/M/AV/O/02/05, Church/Collins interview with Sullivan, 2 April 2001.

44 GWHC, BW&Co. (USA) Inc., 107.07/01, *Wellcome News* 15:2, 1984, p. 23.

45 WF/M/AV/O/02/05, Church/Collins interview with Sullivan, 2 April 2001; WF/M/AV/O/02/12, Collins interview with Howsam, April 2001, p. 6.

46 WF/M/AV/O/02/15, Collins interview with Parrish, 15 March 2001.

47 Ibid.; GWHC, BW&Co. (USA) Inc., 107.07/01, *Wellcome News* 16:4, 1985, p. 15.

48 GWHC, BW&Co. (USA) Inc., 107.07/01, *Wellcome News* 16:4, 1985, p. 15.

49 Ibid.

50 GWHC, BW&Co. (USA) Inc., 107.07/01, *Wellcome News* 17:3, 1986, pp. 14–15.

51 Ibid., p. 2.

52 Ibid., p. 16.

Chapter 16: Clashing cultures: conflicts at BW&Co. and WFL

1 WF/M/AV/O/02/05, Church/Collins interview with Sullivan, 23 April 2001, p. 23.

2 WF/M/AV/O/02/07, Collins interview with Schaeffer, 26 April 2001, p. 15. See chapter 13.

3 WF/M/AV/O/02/04, Collins interview with Kennedy, 23 April 2001, p. 24.

4 GWHC, BW&Co. (USA) Inc., 107.07/01, *Wellcome News* 15, 1984, p. 14.

5 WF/M/AV/O/02/04, Collins interview with Kennedy, 23 April 2001, p. 24.

6 WF/M/AV/O/02/05, Collins interview with Sullivan, 23 April 2001, p. 10.

7 Ibid., p. 23.
8 *Wellcome News*, Sept./Oct. 1982, p. 3.
9 WF/M/AV/O/02/04, Collins interview with Kennedy, 23 April 2001, p. 24.
10 *Wellcome News* 15:2, 1984, p. 14.
11 WF/M/AV/O/02/07, Collins interview with Schaeffer, 26 April 2001, p. 12.
12 See pp. 185–86.
13 WF/M/AV/O/02/10, Collins interview with Barry, 30 April 2001, p. 11.
14 WF/M/AV/O/02/04, Collins interview with Kennedy, 23 April 2001, p. 24; WF/M/AV/O/02/10, Collins interview with Barry, 20 April 2001, p. 11.
15 WF/M/AV/O/02/07, Collins interview with Schaeffer, 26 April 2001, p. 12.
16 *Wellcome News* 16:3, 1985, p. 10–11.
17 Reproduced as Businessman in the news, *Business, North Carolina*, May 1982.
18 *Wellcome News*, Sept./Oct. 1983, pp. 14–17.
19 Tom Peters and Robert Waterman Jr, *In Search of Excellence* (Profile Books, New York, 1982). Beginning in 1984, subsequent critiques, mainly by academics who focused on methodology, culminated in 1993 with the publication by Merrill R. Chapman entitled *In Search of Stupidity* (Apress, New York, 1993).
20 WF/AV/M/O/02/15, Collins interview with Parrish, 15 March 2001, p. 34, 37; WF/AV/M/O/02/17, Collins interview with Agyapong, pp. 14–15. Comparing Coe's approach to communications with that adopted by Sullivan, Agyapong recalled that "if Fred Coe showed up in your lab or office, people didn't die of shock. He was known to walk around and get to know people ... [he] wasn't untouchable ... The cafeteria was for everyone."
21 WF/M/AV/O/02/04, Collins interview with Kennedy, 23 April 2001, p. 32.
22 WF/M/AV/O/02/07, Collins interview with Schaeffer, 26 April 2001, pp. 11–12.
23 WF/M/AV/O/02/10, Collins interview with Barry, 30 April 2001, p. 8.
24 WF/M/AV/O/02/44, Collins interview with Cresswell, 14 Oct. 2001, p. 7.
25 WA, Max Blythe interview with Peter Williams, 1995/6, p. 170.
26 GSK/WF/SCS 2179, Board minutes, 15 Nov. 1981, 10, 128.
27 Coe diaries, 23 Dec. 1980.
28 WF/M/AV/O/02/33, Collins interview with Sir John Vane, 7 Aug. 2001, p. 9.
29 Jones, *The Business of Medicine*, pp. 333–34.
30 WF/M/AV/O/02/33, Collins interview with Sir John Vane, 7 Aug. 2001, p. 11.
31 Ibid., p. 12.
32 WF/M/AV/O/02/44, Collins interview with Cresswell, 14 Oct. 2001, p. 8.
33 Ibid.
34 *Wellcome News*, March 1993, p. 7.
35 WF/M/AV/O/02/33, Collins interview with Sir John Vane, 7 Aug. 2001, p. 9.
36 GSK/WF/SCS 1114, Biologicals review, report to Biologicals committee, 7 Oct. 1980.
37 Ibid.
38 Ibid.
39 GSK/WF/SCS 2179, Board minutes, 30 July 1981, 10047.
40 GSK/WF/SCS 2179, Board minutes, 8 Jan. 1981, 9889; 11 Nov. 1981, 10127.
41 GSK/WF/SCS 1114, Biologicals review, report to Biologicals committee, 7 Oct. 1980.
42 WF/E/19, Castell interview with Cresswell, 3, Aug. 2012, p. 3.
43 Sir James W. Black, *Autobiography* (Nobel Foundation, Stockholm, 1988), p. 3.
44 GSK/WF/SCS 2179, Board minutes, 15 Nov. 1981, 10131.
45 WF/M/AV/O/02/33, Collins interview with Sir John Vane, 7 Aug. 2001, p. 12.
46 GSK/WF/SCS 461, Board minutes, US strategy study meeting, Singapore, 31 Oct. 1982, 10361.
47 WF/E/19, Castell interview with Cresswell, 3, Aug. 2012, p. 3.
48 GSK/WF/SCS 461, Board minutes, US strategy study meeting, Singapore, 31 Oct. 1982, 10361.
49 Ibid.
50 Ibid.
51 GSK/WF/SCS 711, A. J. Shepperd to A. D. Little, re: *International Management* article entitled "Dilemma and decision," Dec. 1984. This was an anonymous spoof account of the troubled company written in the form of an Italian operatic narrative featuring the two scientists in the leading roles clearly recognisable by those aware of the company's problems. Legal advice to Shepperd was against proceedings against the author for defamation on grounds of proof and cost. Instead, a "stiff letter" was addressed to A. D. Little accusing the firm of unprofessional conduct in allowing the use of information gathered in confidence. The substantive report of A. D. Little relating to the WFL organisation is considered in Chapter 16.
52 The description was applied to the anonymous

combatants in the article published in the above journal in 1984. It was later also used with disarming percipience by Vane to describe his relationship with Black. WF/M/AV/O/02/33, Collins interview with Vane, 2001.

Chapter 17: A. D. Little's review, recommendations, and consequences

1 GSK/WF/SCS 774, R&D strategy, Little Report, 1983/4, pp. 5–7.
2 GSK/WF/SCS 774, R&D strategy, Little Report, 1983/4.
3 GSK/WF/SCS 1274, Chairman's R&D committee, 26 Sept. 1984, 30.
4 GSK/WF/SCS 713, R&D problems, general 1983–86.
5 Ibid.
6 Ibid.
7 Ibid.
8 GSK/WF/SCS 774, R&D strategy, Little Report, 1983/4, pp. 1–30.
9 GSK/WF/SCS 2181, Board minutes, Jan. 1984, 10701.
10 GSK/WF/SCS 774, R&D strategy, Little Report, 1984, pp. 30–38.
11 See chapter 18.
12 GSK/WF/SCS 2181, Board minutes, A. D. Little Report received by the board, 27 Jan. 1984, 10701.
13 GSKWF/SCS 2181, Board minutes, 30 Jan. 1984, 10704.
14 Ibid., Board minutes, 31 Jan. 1984, 10719.
15 Ibid., Board minutes, 30 Jan. 1984, 10704.
16 GSK/WF/SCS 797, Board minutes, 29 March 1984, 10752.
17 GSK/WF/SCS 2181, Board minutes, 1984–86, 30 Jan. 1984, 10704.
18 Vane's response to Sullivan was that "if Black was subjected to too much rigorous control it might well inhibit his inventiveness." GSK/WF/SCS 2181, Board minutes, 30 Jan. 1984, 10704.
19 GSK/WF/SCS 2181, Board minutes, 30 Jan. 1984, 10704.
20 "... This company needs hard-nosed commercial people making positive decisions for the benefit of this company ... We do not need theoreticians and academics whose main objective seems to be the pursuit of glory." GSK/WF/SCS 2181, Board minutes, 31 Jan. 1984, 10719, letter from D. Robinson, Manual workers' central shop stewards committee, D. Robinson to Shepperd, 8 Feb. 1984.
21 GSK/WF/SCS 2181, Board minutes, 30 Jan. 1984, 10719.
22 Ibid.
23 WF/M/AV/O/02/44, Collins interview with Cresswell, 14 Oct. 2001, p. 13.
24 GSK/WF/SCS 712, Executive directors, Little Report to Wellcome Trust 1984/1985 re research implementation, 14 Jan. 1985. Those present were A. J. Shepperd, M. R. Brookman, H. Copestick, R. C. Devereux, D. Godfrey, P. T. G. Hobbs, and C. Matons.
25 Ibid.
26 WF/M/AV/O/02/41, Collins interview with Castell, 26 Sept. 2001, p. 14.
27 *Economist*, 297, 18 May 1985, p. 181.
28 Cuatrecasas was appointed with a brief to build a basic research facility related to cell growth and regulation.
29 WF/M/AV/O/03/15, Tansey interview with Jones, 15 March 2001, p. 20.
30 As an example, Cresswell mentioned the attitude towards and limited investment into interferon as a casualty of the Anglo-American divide. WF/M/AV/O/02/44, Collins interview with Cresswell, 14 Oct. 2001, p. 7.
31 WF/M/AV/O/03/15, Tansey interview with Jones, 15 March 2001, p. 22.
32 WF/M/AV/O/02/44, Collins interview with Cresswell, 14 Oct. 2001, p. 8.
33 Ibid., pp. 8–10.
34 *Economist,* 297, Dec. 1985, p. 74.
35 *Economist*, 303, 18 March 1987, p. 17. The article was discussed the at a board meeting when Shepperd rejected the allegation and requested (and received) unanimous support for a rebuttal. GSK/WF, SCS 1290, Board minutes, 5 Aug. 1987, 11385.
36 The *Economist's* source is unknown, but un-named insiders were reported to have blamed Shepperd's policy of "divide and rule." Castell also referred to Shepperd's approach to management as that of divide and rule. WF/M/AV/O/02/41, Collins interview with Castell, 26 Sept. 2001, p. 12; WF/M/AV/O/02/44, Collins interview with Cresswell, 14 Oct. 2001, p. 14.
37 WF/M/AV/O/02/41, Collins interview with Castell, 26 Sept. 2001, pp. 9–10.
38 Ibid., p. 12.
39 Vane also referred to Shepperd's isolating tactic which was also remarked upon by Little

consultants. WF/M/AV/O/02/33, Collins interview with Vane, 7 Aug. 2001, p. 13. He observed that between board meetings Shepherd "only talked to one person at a time … that was his method of dealing with things, isolating people." Non-executive Lever described Shepperd's approach as "fiendish clever." WF/M/AV/O/02/44, Collins interview with Cresswell, 14 Oct. 2001, pp. 14, 20.

40 WF/M/AV/O/02/44, Collins interview with Cresswell, 14 Oct. 2001, p. 22.

41 Typescript memoir referred to in supplementary interview by the author, 19 Oct. 2009.

42 WF/M/AV/O/03/33, Burton interview with Cipau, 2002.

43 GSK/WF/SCS 1290, Board minutes, 9 April 1987, 11359.

Chapter 18: Policy innovation and the formation of Wellcome plc

1 WA, Peter Williams, Blythe interview with Lord Franks, 15 May 1991, pp. 10–14.

2 Obituary, *Independent*, 21 Aug. 2004.

3 WA, Max Blythe interview with Peter Williams, 1995/6, p. 169.

4 Church supplementary interview with Sir Roger Gibbs, 8 Jan. 2009.

5 WA, Max Blythe videos, Williams's transcript interview with Steel and Gibbs, 1 April 1996, p. 22.

6 Steel quoted in WA, Blythe videos, Williams's transcript interview with Steel and Gibbs, 1 April 1996, p. 22.

7 GSK/WF/SCS 796, Minutes of Board meeting, 17 Nov. 1983, 10668.

8 WF/M/AV/O/02/33, Collins interview with Sir John Vane, 14 Oct. 2001, p. 12.

9 GSK/WF/SCS 1274, Board minutes, 30 Jan. 1984, 19703.

10 WA, Blythe videos, Williams transcript interview with Francis Hufton and Richard Hodges, 6 July 1996, p. 275–78.

11 GSK/WF/SCS 61, Board minutes, 31 Oct.; 5 Nov. 1982, 10631.

12 Ibid.

13 GSK/WF/SCS 796, Board minutes, 27 Jan. 1983, 10432.

14 GSK/WF/SCS 1708, Secret board minutes, 1983–89, 27 Jan. 1983; 24 Feb. 1983.

15 WA, Blythe videos, Williams transcript interview with Steel and Gibbs, 1 April 1998, p. 22.

16 WA, Blythe videos, Williams transcript interview with Lawrence Banks, 30 Aug. 1996, p. 300.

17 WA, Blythe videos, Williams transcript interview with Steel and Gibbs, 1 April 1996, pp. 23–26.

18 WF/M/AV/O/02/52, Collins interview with Gibbs, 9 Nov. 2001, pp. 5–6.

19 Williams, "The Wellcome Trust Story," pp. 171–72; WA, Blythe videos, Williams transcript interview with Steel and Gibbs, 1 April 1996, pp. 22–23.

20 Church supplementary interview with Gibbs, 8 Jan. 2009. In an earlier interview Gibbs observed that in 1948 the value of the Nuffield Foundation was roughly 40 times larger than the Wellcome Trust; after diversification of the Trust's portfolio was 60 times larger than that of the Nuffield Foundation.

21 WA, Blythe videos, Williams transcript interview with Steel and Gibbs, 1 April 1996, pp. 25–26.

22 See below, pp. 265.

23 WA, Blythe videos, Williams transcript interview with Lawrence Banks, 30 Aug. 1996, pp. 298, 302.

24 WA, Blythe videos, Williams transcript interview with Steel and Gibbs, 1 April 1996. pp. 27–28.

25 GSK/WF/SCS 1078, Secret board minutes, 1983–89, 27 Jan. 1985; 24 Feb. 1985.

26 WA, Blythe videos, Williams transcript interview with Lawrence Banks, 30 Aug. 1996, pp. 301–2.

27 WA, Blythe videos, Williams transcript interview with Steel and Gibbs, 1 April 1996, p. 22.

28 WA, Blythe videos, Williams transcript interview with Russell Denton Duncan, 13 Sept. 1996, p. 279; WA, Blythe videos, Williams transcript interview with Steel and Gibbs, 1 April 1996, pp. 21–22.

29 WA, Blythe videos, Williams transcript interview with Steel and Gibbs, 1 April 1996, pp. 27–28.

30 WA, Blythe videos, Williams transcript interview with Lawrence Banks, 30 Aug. 1996, pp. 305–7.

31 Ibid., p. 303.

32 WA, Blythe videos, Williams transcript interview with Steel and Gibbs, 1 April 1996, p. 20.

33 GSK/WF/SCS 796, Board minutes, 17 Nov. 1983, 10668.
34 GSK/WF/SCS 796, Board minutes, 29 March 1984, 10828.
35 GSK/WF/SCS 797, Board minutes, 12 July 1984.
36 WA, Blythe videos, Williams's interview with Macgregor, 28 Nov. 1996, p. 212.
37 WA, Blythe videos, Williams's transcript interview with Duncan, 13 Sept. 1996, p. 302.
38 Ibid., p. 275.
39 Ibid., p. 277.
40 Ibid., p. 278.
41 WA, Blythe videos, Williams's transcript interview with Steel and Gibbs, 1 April 1996, pp. 26–28.
42 Ibid., pp. 26–28.
43 GSK/WF/SCS 797, Board minutes, 15 Sept. 1984, 10855.
44 GSK/WF/SCS 1289, Board minutes, 3 April 1985, 10964.
45 GSK/WF/SCS 1289, Board minutes, 2 May 1985, 10975.
46 WF/M/AV/O/02/48, Collins interview with Sir Jeremy Lever, 7 Nov. 2001, p. 7.
47 GSK/WF/SCS 1289, Board minutes, 2 May 1985, 10975.
48 GSK/WF/SCS 1289, Board minutes, 3 April 1985, 10969.
49 *Economist,* 298, 18 Jan. 1986, p. 68.
50 WA, Blythe videos, Williams's transcript interview with Lawrence Banks, 30 Aug. 1996, p. 308.
51 Ibid., pp. 308–9.
52 GSK/WF/SCS 1368, Wellcome plc Board minutes, 14 Nov. 1985.
53 *Economist*, 298, 18 Jan. 1986, p. 68; 301, 28 Feb. 1987, p. 93; 303, 18 March 1987, p. 15.
54 *Economist*, 298, 18 Jan. 1986, p. 68.
55 GSK/WF/SCS 797, Board minutes, 2 May 1985, 10970; Ibid., 27 June 1985, 10828.
56 Peter Williams, private papers, "History of medicine" (chart, 1996).
57 WA, Blythe videos, Williams's transcript interview with Macgregor, 28 Nov. 1996, p. 223.
58 WT, 69:11:87, Discussions by trustees, 10 Nov. 1987; GSK/WF/SCS 1570, Wellcome plc Board minutes, (4), 25 Feb. 1988, 233.
59 WF/M/AV/O/02/35, Collins interview with Williams, 14 Aug. 2001, p. 25.
60 WT, Box A0009, Meeting minutes, 13/14 May 1985, 174.
61 Coe diaries, 10 Feb. 1981; WF/M/AV/O/02/03, Church/Collins interview with Coe, April 2001, pp. 27–28.
62 GSK/WF/SCS, Board minutes, 23 June 1982, 10273.
63 I am grateful to Mr Peter Hobbs, at that time personnel director, for clarification of the events at this meeting. Private correspondence, Hobbs to Church, 9 March 2012.
64 WF/M/AV/O/02/46, Collins interview with Hobbs, 29 Oct. 2001, p. 12.
65 Interview with Ted Haigler, *Pharmaceutical Executive*, 7:8, Aug. 1987, p. 24.

Chapter 19: AZT-Retrovir and the AIDS epedemic

1 Baker, "Burroughs Wellcome," pp. 36–40. GWHC, BW&Co. (USA) Inc., 107.07/11, Historical reference material.
2 Victoria A. Harden, *AIDS at 30: A History* (Potomac Books, Washington, 2012), p. 129.
3 Victoria Harden and Caroline Hannaway interview with Dr Samuel Broder, 1997, NIH, "In their own words," n.p.
4 *Wellcome News,* 17 Aug. 1986, pp. 1–2.
5 M. Levine, "Gay Ghetto," in M. Levine, *Gay Men: The Sociology of Male Sexuality* (Harper Row, New York, 1979), pp. 182–204.
6 R. Jonsen and Jeff Stryker (eds), The Social Impact of AIDS in the United States (National Academic Press, Washington DC, 1993), p. 262.
7 Ibid., pp. 5–9. See also chapter 21.
8 Harden, *AIDS at 30,* chapter 1.
9 Philip Hilts, *Protecting America's Health: The FDA, Business, and One Hundred Years of Regulation* (University of North Caroilna Press, Chapel Hill NC, 2003), p. 237.
10 Harden, *AIDS at 30*, p. 36.
11 Henry Waxman, Subcommittee on Health and Environment, Committee on Energy and Commerce, House of Representatives, 100th Congress, Los Angeles CA, 13 April 1982.
12 Harden, *AIDS at 30*, p. 67.
13 WF/M/AV/O/02/10, Collins interview with Barry, 30 April 2001.
14 Ibid.
15 Ibid.
16 GSK/WF/SCS 1124, BW&Co. USA, Meeting minutes, 18 March 1986, 5997; Among the heads of these departments, Dannie King (director of

the department of infectious diseases), Sandra Lehman (senior clinical research scientist), and later Paul Dreyer (product manager for AZT) also played major roles. *Wellcome News*, 18 March 1987, p. 1

17 WF/M/AV/O/02/22, Collins interview with Pagano, 11 May 2001, p. 9. The marketing staff reckoned that the limit might be a few hundred thousand dollars.

18 WF/M/AV/O/03/48, Burton interview with Cuatrecasas, 2002; see above chapter 15.

19 *Wellcome News*, 17:6, 1986, pp. 1–2.

20 *Wellcome Journal*, August 1988, p. 10.

21 Harden and Hannaway interview with Broder, NIH, "In their own words," n.p.

22 Harden and Hannaway interview with Yarchoan, p. 19.

23 Harden and Hannaway interview with Broder, NIH, "In their own words," n.p.

24 Harden and Hannaway interview with Robert Yarchoan, NIH, "In their own words," p. 19.

25 Harden and Hannaway interview with Broder, NIH, "In their own words," n.p.

26 *Wellcome News*, Aug. 1992, p. 6.

27 See chapter 19.

28 Harden and Hannaway interview with Broder, NIH, "In their own words," n.p.

29 *Wellcome News*, Aug. 1986, pp. 1–2.

30 Ibid., pp. 4–5.

31 Ibid.

32 *Wellcome News*, Aug. 1986, pp. 6–8; WF/M/AV/O/03/32, Burton interview with Robert Maxwell, 13 Feb. 2001; *Wellcome News*, March 1987, p. 5; Harden and Hannaway interview with Broder, NIH, "In their own words," n.p.

33 Harden and Hannaway interview with Broder, NIH, "In their own words," n.p.

34 Ibid.

35 Harden and Hannaway interview with Yarchoan, NIH, "In their own words," n.p.

36 *Wellcome News*, June 1985, pp. 1–3. Dr Harry Meyer, director of the FDA Centre for Drugs remarked that "no drug … has moved as fast as AZT through the drug development system. It is moving literally like a greased pig." *Wellcome News*, June 1986, p. 6; *Wellcome News*, March 1987, p. 5.

37 Harden and Hannaway interview with Yarchoan, p. 22.

38 *Wellcome News*, Aug. 1986, p. 4.

39 *Wellcome News*, March 1987, p. 5.

40 *Wellcome News*, 6 June 1985, pp. 1–3.

41 Mark Yarchoan, "The story of AZT: partnership and conflict," pdf at http.omsj.org/22010/History of AZT, p. 12.

42 *Report of the President's Commission on the Immuno-defficiency Virus Epidemic*, 24 June 1982, pp. 35–37.

43 BW&Co. People, The Retrovir Story (internal pamphlet, NC, 1987).

44 Ibid.

45 Evidence of Ted Haigler, House Committee on Energy and Commerce, Subcommittee on Health and the Environment, 100th Congress, 10 March 1987, pp. 8–9.

46 Linda J. Wastilla and Louis Lasagna, "The history of Zidovidine (AZT)," *Journal of Clinical Research and Pharmacoepidemiology* 4:4, 1990, pp. 25–27.

47 *Wellcome News*, March 1987, p. 5.

48 Harden and Hannaway interview with Broder, NIH, "In their own words," n.p.

49 Ibid.

50 Harden and Hannaway interview with Yarchoan, NIH, "In their own words," p. 27.

51 Koop, C. Everett, "The C. Everett Koop Papers: AIDS, the Surgeon General, and the Politics of Public Health," *Profiles in Science*, National Library of Medicine, Washington DC, 23 Feb. 2012.

52 WF/E/19, Castell interview with Cresswell, 2, Aug. 2012, pp. 4–5.

53 See below p. 371.

54 Ibid.

55 BW&Co., People. The Retrovir story (internal pamphlet, NC, 1987).

56 Evidence of Ted Haigler, House Committee on Energy and Commerce, Subcommittee on Health and the Environment, 10 March 1987, pp. 8–9.

57 Hilts, *Protecting America's Health*, p. 245.

58 The following paragraphs draw heavily on Wastilla and Lasagna, "The history of Zidovidune." Wastilla was formerly an employee of BW&Co. The article was received by the company for cpmment before publication.

59 *Wellcome News*, March 1987, p. 1.

60 Ibid.

61 Ibid., pp. 1–5.

62 Ibid., p. 1.

63 David G. Adams, FDA Assistant Chief Counsel for Drugs is referred to as the source. GSK/WF/SCS 1637, Board minutes, 28 April 1987, 675.

64 The explanation was the need to avoid

confusion in the UK and elsewhere, as AZT was already used to designate azothyaprine, an immuno suppressant drug. GSK/WF/SCS 1290, Board minutes, 2/4 Oct. 1986, 11257; 11 Dec. 1986, 11293.

65 GSK/WF/SCS 1637, Board minutes, 28 April 1987, 675.

66 Koop, "The C. Everett Koop Papers."

67 Wastilla and Lasagna, "The history of Zidovidunc," pp. 25–37.

68 GSK/WF/SCS 1124, BW&Co. USA, Board minutes, 18 Feb. 1987, 6122; 2 Sept. 1987, 6182.

69 *Wellcome News*, March 1987, p. 3.

70 Ibid., p. 4.

71 *Wellcome News*, Jan./Feb. 1988, p. 4.

72 *Washingon Post*, 4 Aug. 1989, p. 6; GWHC, BW&Co. (USA) Inc., 107.07/11, Public affairs; BWFL, Schaeffer's private papers.

73 *New York Times*, 16 Sept. 1989, p. 1.

74 Yarchoan, "The story of AZT," p. 12.

75 *Economist*, 303, 20 June 1987, p. 15.

76 Yarchoan, "The story of AZT," p. 12.

Chapter 20: The economics of AZT: supply, costs, and pricing of Retrovir

1 Evidence of Ted Haigler, House Committee on Energy and Commerce, Subcommittee on Health and the Environment, 100th Congress, 10 March 1987, pp. 8–9.

2 Yarchoan, "The story of AZT," p. 8.

3 WF/E/19, Castell interview with Cresswell, 2, Aug 2012, p. 5.

4 GSK/WF/SCS 1124, BW&Co. USA, Meeting minutes, 19 Dec. 1986, 6102; GSK/WF/SCS 1637, Board minutes, 12 Jan. 1987, 1308.

5 *Wellcome News*, Jan./Feb. 1988, p. 4.

6 GSK/WF/SCS 1124, BW&Co. USA, Meeting minutes, 18 Dec. 1987, 6224.

7 *Pharmaceutical Executive* 10:7, July 1990, p. 34, interview with Shepperd.

8 GSK/WF/SCS 1567, Board minutes, 26 July 1988, 11584.

9 GSK/WF/SCS 1290, Board minutes, 12/4 Oct. 1986, 11257; 12 Jan. 1987, 11305.

10 GSK/WF/SCS 1124, BW&Co. USA, Meeting minutes, 19 Jan. 1987, 6110.

11 *Wellcome News*, Jan./Feb. 1988, pp. 4–5.

12 WF/M/AV/O/03/30, Burton interview with Schaeffer, 12 Feb. 2002.

13 WF/M/AV/O/02/05, Collins interview with Sullivan, 23 April 2001, pp. 16–17.

14 "Profile of Thomas Haigler Jr," *Pharmaceutical Executive* 7:8, p. 27.

15 GSK/WF/SCS 1637, Board minutes, 12 Jan. 1987, 11310.

16 GSK/WF/SCS 1637, Board minutes, 12 Jan. 1987, 11310.

17 Ibid.

18 This was also the policy applied to pricing Zovirax. *Wellcome News*, March 1987, p. 1.

19 WF/M/AV/O/03/26, Collins/Connolly interview with L. Petty, 28 Feb. 2001, p. 68.

20 Ibid., p. 69.

21 GSK/WF/SCS 1274, Chairman's marketing and R&D committee, 11 Nov. 1987.

22 Evidence of Haigler, House Committee on Energy and Commerce, Subcommittee on Health and the Environment, 10 March 1987, pp. 8–10.

23 Robert Sutch and Susan Carter (eds), *History of Statistics in the US*, Vol. 2, *Work and Welfare* (Cambridge University Press, Cambridge, 2006), Table Ba 4485; *US Census Bureau*.

24 GSK/WF/SCS 1637, Board minutes, 12 Jan. 1987, 11310.

25 GSK/WF/SCS 1290, Board minutes, 21 Jan. 1987, 11319.

26 WF/M/AV/O/02/54, Collins interview with Shepperd, 24 Nov. 2001, p. 40.

27 WF/M/AV/O/02/02, Collins interview with Haigler, 27 April 2001, p. 24.

28 WF/M/AV/O/02/54, Collins interview with Shepperd, 24 Nov. 2001, p. 40.

29 GSK/WF/SCS 1637, Board minutes, 12 Jan. 1987, 11312.

Chapter 21: Public and political backlash

1 Waxman, Subcommittee on Health and the Environment, House Committee on Energy and Commerce, 100th Congress, 10 March 1987, p. 1.

2 Ibid., pp. 1–2.

3 Victor F. Zonana, "AIDS care: Who'll pick up the bill?", *Los Angeles Times*, 7 Aug. 1989.

4 Peter Arno's estimates to appear in *Journal of the American Medical Association,* quoted by Victor Zonana in Zonana, "AIDS care."

5 WF/M/AV/O/02/04, Collins interview with Kennedy, 9 April 2001, p. 43.

6 Zonana, "AIDS care."

7 Barnaby J. Federer, "Drug expected to spur

growth of profit," *New York Times*, 21 March 1987, p. 32.

8 Haigler, evidence to Subcommittee on Health and the Environment, pp. 8–10.

9 Zonana, "AIDS care."

10 Haigler, evidence to Subcommittee on Health and the Environment, pp. 25–27.

11 Waxman, Subcommittee on Health and the Environment, p. 16.

12 Philip M. Boffey, "Experts find lag on testing drugs in AIDS patients," *New York Times*, 12 April 1987.

13 "Forcing poverty on AIDS patients," *New York Times*, 30 Aug. 1988.

14 GSK/WF/SCS 1673, Board minutes, 12 Jan. 1987, 11310; Peter Arno and Karyn Feiden, *Against the Odds: The Story of AIDS Drug Development, Politics, and Profits* (HarperCollins, New York, 1992), pp. 137–41.

15 Harden, *Aids at 30*, p. 136.

16 Philip J. Hilts, "Experimental drug AZT was designed for tumors: skill, luck led to promising tests on AIDS," *Washington Post*, 19 Sept. 1986.

17 "Forcing poverty on AIDS patients," *New York Times*, 30 Aug. 1988.

18 Ibid.

19 *Economist*, 303, 11 April 1987. The initial reaction had been to write a letter rejecting the allegations. However, Shepperd was advised against any written response which might risk encouragement to other parties who might wish to attack the patent. A subsequent article entitled "Wellcome – queuing for the door" (18 April 1987), the subject of which was the hemorrhage of senior managers and scientists which the author suggested was attributable to Shepperd's failure to manage, led to a meeting between Wellcome representatives and the editor, business editor, and pharmaceutical correspondent who visited the Wellcome building, where a complaint of "unfair treatment" by the *Economist* formed the subject of a private exchange of views. GSK/WF/SCS 1290, Board minutes, 24 April 1987, 11353; 28 May 1987, 11385; 29 July 1987, 11400.

20 Haigler, evidence to Subcommittee on Health and the Environment, pp. 8–10.

21 WF/M/AV/O/02/02, Collins interview with Haigler, 27 April 2001.

22 GSK/WF/SCS 1290, Board minutes, 29/31 July 1987, 11405.

23 Ibid.

24 GSK/WF/SCS 1567, Board minutes, 18 Jan. 1988, 11491.

25 "Protest over AZT price led to the arrest of 19," *New York Times*, 9 Feb. 1988.

26 GSK/WF/SCS 1274, Chairman's marketing and R&D committee, 11 Nov. 1987; *Wellcome News*, 18 March 1987, pp. 1–2.

27 GSK/WF/SCS 1290, Board minutes, 29 Oct. 1987, 11450.

28 Thomas Morgan, "State studies pricing of AIDS drug," *New York Times*, 9 Oct. 1987.

29 GSK/WF/SCS 1567, Board minutes, 10 Dec. 1987, 11475.

30 GSK/WF/SCS 1290, Board minutes, 29 Oct. 1987, 11450.

31 WF/M/AV/O/02/02, Collins interview with Haigler, 27 April 2001, p. 24.

32 GSK/WF/SCS 1567, Board minutes, 10 Dec. 1987, 11475.

33 GSK/WF/SCS 1567, Board minutes, 10 Dec. 1987, 11741.

34 Harden, *AIDS at 30*, p. 136.

35 GSK/WF/SCS 1567, Board minutes, 16 Sept. 1988, 11606.

36 Ibid.

37 Ibid.

38 GSK/WF/SCS 1567, Board minutes, 20 Sept. 1988, 11612.

39 Martin Delaney, "AIDS activism and the pharmaceutical industry," in Michael A. Santoro and Thomas M. Gorrie (eds), *Ethics and the Pharmaceutical Industry* (Cambridge University Press, Cambridge, 2005), p. 306.

40 Craig A. Rimmerman, "ACTUP," in Raymond A. Smith (ed.), *Encyclopedia of AIDS* (Penguin, New York, 2001), pp. 2–7.

41 Kim Painter, "AIDS activists protest price of AZT drug," *USA Today*, 15 Sept. 1989.

42 GSK/WF/SCS 1567, Board minutes, 26 July 1988, 11584.

43 Painter, "AIDS activists protest price of AZT drug."

44 GSK/WF/SCS 1567, Board minutes, 26 July 1988, 11584.

45 Ibid.

46 Sutch and Carter, *History of Statisticsin the US*, Vol. 2, Table Ba 4485; *US Census Bureau.*

47 *New York Times*, 9 Feb. 1988.

48 Ibid.

49 Hilts, *Protecting America's Health*, p. 247.

50 Ibid.

51 WF/M/AV/O/02/27, Collins interview with Whitehead, 18 May 2001.

52 Ibid. Those arrested included one on horseback inside the building. Dennis Patterson, "AIDS protest ends in 4 arrests," *Charlotte Observer*, 26 April 1989.
53 GSK/WF/SCS 1568, Board minutes, 16 Sept. 1989, 11785.
54 Philip Hilts, "Wave of protests developing on profits from AIDS drug," *New York Times*, 16 Sept. 1989.
55 Painter, "AIDS activists protest price of AZT drug."
56 Hilts, "Wave of protests developing on profits from AIDS drug."
57 WF/M/AV/O/02/04, Collins interview with Kennedy, 9 April 2001, pp. 42–43.
58 GSK/WF/SCS 1503, Chairman's marketing committee, 14 Nov. 1989, 8792; WF/M/AV/O/02/04, Collins interview with Kennedy, 9 April 2001, pp. 42–43.
59 GSK/WF/SCS 1568, Board minutes, 16 Sept. 1989, 11785.
60 Ibid.
61 Ibid.
62 Ibid.
63 Ibid.
64 Ibid.
65 WF/M/AV/O/02/15, Collins interview with Parrish, 15 March 2001, p. 22
66 WF/M/AV/O/02/04, Collins interview with Kennedy, 9 April 2001, p. 42.

Chapter 22: Marketing Retrovir and rebuilding trust

1 GSK/WF/SCS 1503, Chairman's marketing committee, 14 Nov. 1989.
2 In January 1990, the FDA reduced the dosage which reduced the average cost to $2,200. *Charlotte Observer*, 17 Jan. 1990, p. 5.
3 *New York Times*, 29 Sept. 1989, p. 34.
4 *New York Times*, 29 Sept. 1989.
5 *Charlotte Observer*, 17 Jan. 1990, p. 5.
6 "BW&Co. & the HIV community," *Wellcome News*, June/July 1992, pp. 10–11.
7 Ibid., p. 11.
8 Ibid., pp. 10–11.
9 Ibid.
10 Ibid., p. 6.
11 Ibid., pp. 10–11.
12 Ibid., p. 11.
13 Ibid., pp. 10–12.
14 Ibid., p. 12.
15 Ibid., p. 11.
16 Philip H. Dougherty, "Burroughs Wellcome places Anti-AIDS drug," *New York Times*, 15 Oct. 1989.
17 Kim Folz, "The media business: advertising," *New York Times*, 15 Nov. 1990, p. 19.
18 "BW&Co. and the HIV community," p. 12.
19 Ronald Medley, "Demonstrations and direct action," in Smith, *Encyclopedia of AIDS*, p. 201.
20 Marty Levine, "A voice of reconciliation," *Wellcome News*, June/July 1992, p. 13.
21 "BW&Co. and the HIV community," p. 7.
22 Levine, "A voice of reconciliation," p. 13.
23 "BW&Co. and the HIV community," p. 12.
24 Ibid., pp. 5, 8.
25 Ibid., p. 8.
26 Ibid.
27 *New York Times*, 16 Sept. 1989.
28 "Credit government scientists with developing anti-AIDS drug," *New York Times*, 28 Sept. 1989. The signatories were Broder, Mitsua and Yarchon (NCI), and Bolognesi (Duke).
29 *Report of the President's Commission on the Human Immunodeficiency Epidemic*, 24 June 1988, p. 38.
30 Harden and Hannaway interview with Broder, NIH, "In their own words," n.p.
31 Ibid.
32 Richard Stevenson, "Market place: Wellcome may be past the worst," *New York Times*, 28 Feb. 1994, p. 4.
33 Harden and Hannaway interview with Broder, NIH, "In their own words," n.p.
34 Harden and Hannaway interview with Yarchoan, NIH, "In their own words," p. 20.
35 Harden and Hannaway interview with Broder, NIH, "In their own words," n.p.
36 Ibid.

Chapter 23: Management renewal and a reversion to core activities

1 *Economist*, 298, 18 Jan. 1986.
2 *Economist*, 303, 18 March 1987.
3 WF/M/AV/O/02/44, Collins interview with Cresswell, 30 April 2001, p. 15. The worst example of a mismatch between R&D and a commercially marketable product was Semprex acrivastine, a non-sedative antihistamine. The direct R&D costs during the years before "the scientists had presented the molecule and expected the salesmen to sell it" had amounted to roughly

£80m; the peak sales of the product reached £2m.

4 WF/M/AV/O/02/44, Collins interview with Cresswell, 14 Oct. 2001, pp. 7–13.

5 Ibid., pp. 14–15.

6 Godfrey had first joined to WFL in 1956 leaving in 1963, but rejoined WFL in 1966 to complete the acquisition of Calmic. WF/M/AV/O/02/37, Collins interview with Godfrey, 27 Aug. 2001, p. 22.

7 GSK/WF/SCS 1567, Board minutes, 23 March 1989, 11711.

8 GSK/WF/SCS 1567, Board minutes, 25 Feb. 1988, 11507.

9 WF/M/AV/O/02/52, Collins interview with Gibbs, 9 Sept. 2001, p. 15.

10 Roger Moody, *The Gulliver File: Mines, People and Land: A Global Battlefield* (Pluto Press, London, 1992).

11 WF/M/AV/O/02/52, Collins interview with Gibbs, 9 Sept. 2001, p. 15.

12 WA, Blythe videos, Williams transcript interview with Steel and Gibbs, 1 April 1996, p. 31.

13 Frame had known him as a formidable adversary during RTZ's unsuccessful attempt to takeover Enterprise Oil, an association which had resulted in mutual respect WF/M/AV/O/02/47, Collins interview with Hearne, 7 Nov. 2001, pp. 1–2.

14 WA, Blythe videos, Williams transcript interview with Steel and Gibbs, 1 April 1996, pp. 31–32.

15 WF/M/AV/O/02/41, Collins interview with Castell, 26 Sept. 2001, pp. 9–10, 15.

16 Ibid, pp. 9–10, 15.

17 WF/M/AV/O/02/48, Collins interview with Sir Jeremy Lever, 7 Nov. 2001, pp. 14–15; WF/M/AV/O/02/46, Collins interview with Peter Hobbs, 29 Oct. 2001, p. 15; WA, Blythe videos, Williams transcript interview with Steel and Gibbs, 1 April 1996, p. 31.

18 Ibid., pp. 239–40, 246.

19 T. A. B. Corley, *Beecham's: From Pills to Pharmaceuticals, 1848–2000* (Crucible Books, Lancaster, 2011), pp. 237–38, 246.

20 GSK/WF/SCS 2181, Board minutes, A. D. Little Report to the board, 27 Jan. 1984, 10701. The range remained virtually unchanged in 1990. Taggart, *The World Pharmaceutical Industry*, p. 290.

21 Ibid., p. 306.

22 Ibid.

23 Taggart, *The World Pharmaceutical Industry*, p. 309. Table 7.19. Fison competed in four; both ICI and Beecham competed in three segments though not in the antiviral market.

24 Ibid., pp. 254, 302, Tables 7.6 and 7.18.

25 Ibid., p. 37.

26 Ibid.

27 *Economist*, 318, 2 March 1991, p. 74.

28 *Economist*, 317, 22 Dec. 1990, p. 90.

29 Ibid.

30 Ibid.

31 *Economist*, 318, 2 March 1991, p. 74.

32 WF/M/AV/O/02/46, Collins interview with Hobbs, 29 Oct. 2001, pp. 6–7.

33 *Economist*, 318, 2 March 1991, p. 74

34 WF/M/AV/O/02/36, Collins interview with Cochrane, 17 Aug. 2001, p. 2.

35 WF/M/AV/O/02/50, Collins interview with Precious, 17 Nov. 2001, pp. 1, 7.

36 Precious had been used to working with data 10 working days old.

37 WF/M/AV/O/02/50, Collins interview with Precious, 17 Nov. 2001, p 7.

38 Ibid, p. 7.

39 Ibid., pp. 3–4.

40 Ibid., p. 41.

41 Ibid., pp. 18–19.

42 Ibid., p. 37.

43 *Economist*, 318, 2 March 1991, p. 74.

44 WF/M/AV/O/02/44, Collins interview with Cresswell, 14 Oct. 2001, pp. 10–11.

45 *Economist*, 318, 2 March 1991, p. 74. Castell, formerly managing director of Wellcome Biotechnology and since 1987 main board group director of marketing, was regarded as one of the few possible internal successors to Shepperd from a very limited younger generation of main board members. Shortly after Robb's appointment (and the closure of Wellcome Biotechnology) Castell resigned, critical of the philosophy and style that Robb introduced into the company. Church interview with Castell, 14 Oct. 2009.

46 *Economist*, 318, 16 March 1991, p. 112.

47 *Economist*, 318, 2 March 1991, p. 74.

48 WF/M/AV/O/03/15, Tansey interview with Jones, 19 Oct. 2001, p. 12; WF/M/AV/O/02/50, Collins interview with Precious, 17 Nov. 2001, p 18.

49 GSK/WF/SCS 1831, Strategic conference: Chewton Glen, 10 Sept. 1992.

50 Taggart, *The World Pharmaceutical Industry*, p. 293,

51 Ibid., pp. 422–37.

52 Particularly irksome to colleagues was his apparent delight in contrasting his personal history as a salesman selling Brylcreem in Singapore with the polite, gentlemanly ethos prevailing among senior Wellcome staff, many of whom were university graduates, postgraduates, or postdocs. WF/M/AV/O/02/41, Collins interview with Castell, 26 Sept. 2001, pp. 15–16.

53 WF/M/AV/O/02/48, Collins interview with Sir Jeremy Lever, 7 Nov. 2001, pp. 14–15; WF/M/AV/O/02/46, Collins interview with Peter Hobbs, 29 Oct. 2001, p. 15.

54 WF/M/AV/O/02/50, Collins interview with Precious, 17 Nov. 2001, p. 7.

Chapter 24: A global integration strategy

1 WF/M/AV/O/02/36, Collins interview with Cochrane, 17 Aug. 2001, p. 31.

2 Geoffrey Foster, "How to make yourself Wellcome," *Management Today*, July 1992, p. 3.

3 Ibid.

4 Ibid.

5 See Tone Pieters, *Interferon: The Science and Selling a Miracle Drug* (Routeledge, New York, 2006).

6 GSK/WF/SCS 1511, Board minutes, 22 July 1977, 9000; WF/M/AV/O/03/15, Connolly interview with Jones, 7 March 2001; WF/M/AV/O/03/17, Connolly interview with Beale, 7 March 2001.

7 Norman Fintner, "Wellferon: Disappointment and Success," *Wellcome World*, Jan./Feb. 1994, pp. 6–7.

8 Ibid.

9 WF/M/AV/O/02/41, Collins interview with Castell, 26 Sept. 2001, p. 9.

10 GSK/WF/SCS 2179, Board minutes, 30 July 1981, 1047.

11 Ibid.

12 GSK/WF/SCS 2179, Board minutes, 11 Nov. 1981, 10127.

13 WF/M/AV/O/03/15, Connolly interview with Jones, 7 March 2001.

14 Fintner, "Wellferon," pp. 6–10.

15 *Economist*, 317, 22 Dec. 1990, p. 74.

16 GSK/WF/SCS 1709, Board minutes, 17 July 1991.

17 WF/M/AV/O/03/15, Connolly interview with Jones, 19 Oct. 2001, p. 10.

18 Fintner, "Wellferon," pp. 6–10.

19 *Economist* 317, 22 Dec. 1990, p. 90.

20 Foster, "How to make yourself Wellcome," p. 2.

21 *Economist*, 318, 2 March 1991, p. 74.

22 Ibid.

23 WF/M/AV/O/02/50, Collins interview with Precious, 17 Nov. 2001, p. 18.

24 Foster, "How to make yourself Wellcome," p. 69.

25 WF/M/AV/O/02/50, Collins interview with Precious, 17 Nov. 2001, pp. 7–8; WF/M/AV/O/02/36, Collins interview with Cochrane, 17 Aug. 2001, pp. 21–22.

26 WF/M/AV/O/02/50, Collins interview with Precious, 17 Nov. 2001, p. 9.

27 WF/M/AV/O/02/07, Collins interview with Schaeffer, 26 April 2001, p. 17.

28 Schaeffer recalled a request for 19 new senior appointments in medical, development, and toxicology at RTP in mid-financial year ("an awful lot"), to which Shepperd signalled his agreement *within 20 minutes*. WF/M/AV/O/02/07, Collins interview with Schaeffer, 26 April 2001, p. 17.

29 WF/M/AV/O/02/36, Collins interview with Cochrane, 17 Aug. 2001, pp. 22, 30. This division, of course, only institutionalized at group level the long-standing competition for resources by R&D in the UK and the US.

30 WF/M/AV/O/02/36, Collins interview with Tracy, 10 May 2001, p. 30.

31 Ibid.

32 Ibid.

33 WF/M/AV/O/02/36, Collins interview with Cochrane, 17 Aug. 2001, pp. 22–28, 30. Shepperd had tried to achieve the single directorship on Vane's resignation when Shepperd asked Howard Schaeffer to become overall director of R&D. Schaeffer declined, preferring to stay at RTP in the US. Jones became the UK director of R&D.

34 A distinction drawn by Jones was between drug researchers, like Vane and Cuatrecasas and drug hunters, like Hitchings and Schaeffer, who were crucial to the production of commercial product. WF/M/AV/O/03/15, Connolly interview with Trevor Jones, p. 4.

35 WF/M/AV/O/02/36, Collins interview with Cochrane, 17 Aug. 2001, pp. 22–26. Jones left the company, subsequently becoming chairman of the Association of British Pharmaceutical Manufacturers' trade association.

36 WF/M/AV/O/02/36, Collins interview

with Cochrane, 17 Aug. 2001, pp. 22–28. This contrasted with the philosophy articulated by his American predecessor at RTP, Howard Schaeffer (who had declined the directorship of R&D throughout the Wellcome organisation when Vane had retired), Schaeffer had insisted that R&D should be directed towards areas with a view to discovering a treatment that would be useful and would lead to the development of a drug – a product for which there would be a demand. He believed this approach was alien to the ethos at Beckenham. WF/M/AV/O/02/07, Collins interview with Schaeffer 26 April 2001, p. 4.

37 *Economist* 318, 2 March 1991, p. 74.

38 WF/M/AV/O/02/10, Collins interview with Barry, 30 April 2001, p. 19.

39 *Economist*, 318, 2 March 1991, p. 74.

40 Foster, "How to make yourself Wellcome," p. 2.

41 *Economist*, 318, 2 March 1991, p. 74. Though a marginal increase in sales in 1991 was followed by roughly 20 per cent growth between 1991 and 1994.

42 GSK/WF/SCS 1831, Wellcome plc Strategic conference: Chewton Glen, 10 Sept. 1992.

43 A similar arrangement already existed between Warner Lambert and Glaxo plc. "Market place: Wellcome may be past the worst," *New York Times*, 28 Feb. 1994, p. 4; OTC news & market report, 80, June 1995, p. 205.

44 "Market place: Wellcome may be past the worst," p. 4; OTC news & market report, 80, June 1995, p. 205; *Wellcome World*, Sept/Oct. 1993, p. 15.

45 GSK/WF/SCS 1710, Wellcome plc Board minutes, 29 June 1993, 655.

46 Richard Stevenson, "Rocky road lies ahead for Wellcome," *New York Times*, 11 Dec. 1994, p. 4.

47 Foster, "How to make yourself Wellcome," p. 3.

48 *Antiviral Agents Bulletin* 8:2, Feb. 1995.

49 *Wellcome News*, Dec. 1992, pp. 10–11.

50 Ibid.

51 Ibid.

52 *Wellcome News*, Dec. 1992, p. 7.

53 "Old drug holds new hope for increasing HIV survival," *AIDS Alert* 9:9, Sept. 1994, p. 124.

54 Yarchoan, "The story of AZT," pp. 15–18.

55 *Economist*, 332, 20 Aug. 1994, p. 7.

56 GSK/WF/SCS 1708, Secret board minutes, 24 Feb. 1994.

57 WF/M/AV/O/02/50, Collins interview with Precious, 17 Nov. 2001, p. 12.

58 Stevenson, "Rocky road lies ahead for Wellcome," p. 4.

59 *Economist*, 325, 7 Nov. 1992, p. 116; *Wellcome News*, Dec. 1992, p. 7.

60 *Wellcome News*, Dec. 1992, p. 7.

61 See chapter 14.

62 *Wellcome News*, Dec. 1992, p. 7.

63 GSK/WF/SCS 798, Chairman's statement, AGM Wellcome plc, 1994.

64 WF/M/AV/O/02/11, Collins interview with Tracy, 10 May 2001, pp. 19–20.

65 At an early stage of feedback from patients, the apparently unique versatility of Wellbutrin was described by a spokesman for GlaxoWellcome thus: "… if you take this, when you have had sex you won't want a cigarette after you finish and you won't feel depressed." WF/M/AV/O/03/32, Burton interview with Maxwell, 13 Feb. 2002, p. 5; WF/M/AV/O/02/07, Collins interview with Schaeffer, 26 April 2001, pp. 32–33. For an early scholarly confirmation of the effects, see R. Taylor Seagraves, Harry Croft, Richard Kavoussi, John A. Ascher, Sharyn R. Batey, Vicky J. Foster, Carolyn Bolden-Watson, Alan Metz, "Bupropion sustained release (SR) for the treatment of hypoactive sexual desire disorder (HSDD) in non-depressed women," *Journal of Sex & Marital Therapy* 27:3, 2001, pp. 303–16.

66 GSK/WF/SCS 1831, Wellcome plc Strategic conference: Chewton Glen, 10 Sept. 1992.

67 Ibid.

68 See chapter 27.

69 Taggart, *The World Pharmaceutical Industry*, p. 315.

Chapter 25: Corporate revival or nemesis for Wellcome plc?

1 Had Shepperd been more amenable to Steel's initial request that WFL pay a higher dividend, flotation may not have taken place until 1988. WA, Blythe videos, Williams transcript interview with Duncan, 13 Sept. 1996, p. 283.

2 Ibid.

3 *Economist*, 303, 18 March 1987, p. 17. The article was discussed the at a board meeting when Shepperd rejected the allegation and requested (and received) unanimous support for a rebuttal. GSK/WF/SCS 1290, Board minutes, 1986–87, 25 Aug. 1987, 11385.

4 GSK/WF/SCS 1503, Chairman's marketing and R&D committee, 1 June 1988, 8.1.

5 Stockholm was the last conference when the company's monopoly was unchallenged. At the international conference held in Montreal in 1989 more scientists expressed doubts concerning the drug's safety while evidence was presented showing that a half dozen anti-viral drugs were being prepared to enter into clinical trials, by Bristol Myers, Repligen/Merck, British Biotechnology, and by the NIH.

6 GSK/WF/SCS 1708, Secret baord minutes, 18 Jan. 1989.

7 Ibid.

8 Steve Lohr, "Market place: Wellcome's bet on AIDS drug," *New York Times,* 12 Jan. 1987, p. 6. "Big AZT study says drug slows onset of AIDS," *Wall Street Journal,* 4 Aug. 1989.

9 WA, Blythe videos, Williams transcript interview with Lawrence Banks, 30 Aug. 1996, pp. 309–10.

10 Ibid., pp. 309–12.

11 WA, Blythe videos, Williams transcript interview with Duncan, 13 Sept. 1996, p. 285.

12 Ibid., p. 285.

13 See chapter 23.

14 See chapter 26.

15 WF/M/AV/O/02/47, Collins interview with Hearne, 7 Nov. 2001, p. 12.

16 WA, Blythe videos, Williams transcript interview with Steel and Gibbs, 1 April 1996, p. 32. WF/M/AV/O/02/50, Collins interview with Precious, 17 Nov. 2001, p. 12.

17 WA, Blythe videos, Williams transcript interview with Duncan, 13 Sept. 1996, p. 283.

18 Ibid., pp. 286–87.

19 Ibid.

20 Ibid.

21 Ibid.

22 Ibid.

23 Ibid., pp. 287–88.

24 WA, Blythe videos, Williams transcript interview with Steel and Gibbs, 1 April 1996, p. 36.

25 Subsequently Glaxo did seek a merger with Zeneca but was rebuffed, which explains why early in 1994 Glaxo began to turn its attention to Wellcome plc. WF/M/AV/O/02/50, Collins interview with Precious, 17 Nov. 2001, pp. 34–35.

26 WA, Blythe videos, Williams transcript interview with Lawrence Banks, 30 Aug. 1996, pp. 311–12.

27 WA, Blythe videos, Williams transcript interview with Steel and Gibbs, 1 April 1996, p. 33.

28 WT/TRU/MIN/24, 7/8 June 1993. The timing of the flotation, which was also delayed by court hearings, a general election, and a major AIDS conference, proved to be fortunate because Clinton's subsequent election as President introduced his proposed health care plan. This, together with under-performance by pharmaceutical companies in 1993 sparked a general fall in the shares of pharmaceutical companies. WA, Blythe videos, Williams transcript interview with Lawrence Banks, 30 Aug. 1996, p. 313.

29 WF/M/AV/O/02/36, Collins interview with Cochrane, p. 18; WF/M/AV/O/02/50, Collins interview with Precious, 17 Nov. 2001, pp. 31, 36.

30 WA, Blythe videos, Williams transcript interview with Lawrence Banks, 30 Aug. 1996, p. 313.

31 Welcome ranked 23rd in the world drug industry in 1992. *Economist,* 323, June 1992, p. 118.

32 WA, Blythe videos, Williams transcript interview with Lawrence Banks, 30 Aug. 1996, p. 314. Banks recalled "... we said to the trustees look, shall we have a go?"

33 Ibid., p. 314.

34 Ibid., p. 316

35 WF/M/AV/O/02/49, Collins interview with Gibbs, 9 Nov. 2001, p. 12.

36 WF/GSK/SCS 1710, Wellcome plc Board minutes, 26 Oct. 1994, 746.

37 Ibid.

38 WF/M/AV/O/02/10, Collins interview with Barry, 30 April 2001, p. 19.

39 WF/M/AV/O/02/44, Collins interview with Cresswell, 30 April 2001, p. 31.

40 WF/M/AV/O/02/36, Collins interview with Cochrane, p. 18; WF/M/AV/O/02/50, Collins interview with Precious, pp. 31, 36.

41 WF/M/AV/O/02/36, Collins interview with Cochrane, p. 18; WF/M/AV/O/02/50, Collins interview with Precious, pp. 31, 36.

42 Stevenson, "Rocky road ahead for Wellcome," p. 4; WA, Blythe videos, Williams transcript interview with Steel and Gibbs, 1 April 1996, p. 34.

43 WF/M/AV/O/02/10, Collins interview with Barry, 30 April 2001, p. 19.

44 The possibility of some form of alliance had been discussed in 1979, when both decided that as neither had promising products in the pipeline

such a step would not be productive. WF/M/AV/O/02/46, Collins interview with Hobbs, 29 Oct. 2001, pp. 5–6.
45 Jones, *The Business of Medicine*, pp. 334–36, 401–5.
46 Ibid., p. 342.
47 Corley, *Beecham's*, p. 253.
48 *Financial Times*, 24 Jan. 1994, p. 18.
49 Robert Lilja, *International Equity Markets: The Art of the Deal* (Euromoney Books, London, 1997), p. 373.
50 WF/M/AV/O/02/45, Collins interview with Sir Richard Sykes, 22 Oct. 2001, pp. 2, 4–5.
51 WF/M/AV/O/02/10, Collins interview with Barry, 30 April 2001, p. 19.
52 Corley, *Beecham's*, p. 243.
53 WF/M/AV/O/02/45, Collins interview with Sykes, 22 Oct. 2001, p. 8.
54 *Financial Times*, 24 Jan. 1995, p. 18.
55 WF/M/AV/O/02/36, Collins interview with Cochrane, 17 Aug. 2001, p. 49.

Chapter 26: Sale of Wellcome plc, formation of Glaxo Wellcome plc

1 WF/M/AV/O/02/45, Collins interview with Sykes, 22 Oct. 2001, pp. 1, 3.
2 WA, Blythe videos, Williams transcript interview with Banks, 30 Aug. 1996, pp. 318–19.
3 Ibid., p. 316.
4 WA, Blythe videos, Williams transcript interview with Steel and Gibbs, 1 April 1996, p. 34.
5 WF/M/AV/O/02/10, Collins interview with Barry, 30 April 2001, p. 22.
6 WF/M/AV/O/02/49, Collins interview with Gibbs, 9 Nov. 2001, p. 9.
7 WA, Blythe videos, Williams transcript interview with Banks, 30 Aug. 1996, p. 319.
8 See above, chapter 20.
9 WF/M/AV/O/02/45, Collins interview with Sykes, 22 Oct. 2001, p. 6.
10 WA, Blythe videos, Williams transcript interview with Banks, 30 Aug. 1996, p. 319.
11 WA, Blythe videos, Williams transcript interview with Steel and Gibbs, 1 April 1996, p. 34.
12 Communication from Gibbs to Church, 14 Jan. 2009.
13 WF/M/AV/O/02/45, Collins interview with Sykes, 22 Oct. 2001, p. 6.
14 WA, Blythe videos, Williams transcript interview with Steel and Gibbs, 1 April 1996, p. 34.
15 GSK/WF/SCS 1710, Wellcome plc Board minutes, 19 Jan. 1995, 769.
16 Ibid.
17 To meet the Stock Exchange deadline, Tenant was informed by telephone at his home where he was having an early morning bath. WF/M/AV/O/02/10, Collins interview with Barry, 30 April 2001, p. 23; WA, Blythe videos, Williams transcript interview with Cazalet, 4 April 1996, p. 103.
18 Sykes described Robb's reaction as "shocked" but also "composed." WF/M/AV/O/02/45, Collins interview with Sykes, 22 Oct. 2001, p. 6.
19 WF/M/AV/O/02/10, Collins interview with Barry, 30 April 2001, p. 23.
20 GSK/WF/SCS 1710, Wellcome plc Board minutes, 25 Jan. 1995, 775.
21 Ibid.
22 WF/MV/AV/O/02/49, Collins interview with Gibbs, 9 Nov. 2001, p. 9.
23 *PLC Magazine* (UK), 1 March 1995.
24 GSK/WF/SCS 1710, Wellcome plc Board minutes, 28 Jan. 1995, 783; WA, Blythe videos, Williams transcript interview with Steel and Gibbs, 1 April 1996, p. 37.
25 *Economist*, 333, 11 March 1995.
26 *Financial Times*, 8 March 1995, p. 27.
27 WA, Blythe videos, Williams transcript interview with Banks, 30 Aug. 1996, p. 317–18.
28 *Financial Times*, 24 Jan. 1995, p. 18.
29 *Financial Times*, 8 March 1995, p. 27.
30 Ibid.
31 Glaxo ranked 44th and Wellcome 77th, *Financial Times*, 24 Jan. 1995, p. 18.
32 WA, Blythe videos, Williams transcript interview with Banks, 30 Aug. 1996, pp. 320–21.
33 Corley, *Beecham's*, p. 239.
34 "The painful path from hostility to synergy: GlaxoWellcome integration," *Financial Times*, 9 April 1996, p. 27.
35 WT/TRU/min/182, Trustee minutes, June 1995, p. 27.
36 WF/M/AV/O/02/36, Collins interview with Cochrane, 17 Aug. 2001, p. 57.
37 Ibid., pp. 51–53.
38 Ibid., p. 54.
39 WF/M/AV/O/02/03, Collins/Church interview with Coe, 19 April 2001, p. 50.
40 Ibid.

41 WF/M/AV/O/02/10, Collins interview with Barry, 30 April 2001, p. 20.
42 Ibid.
43 WF/M/AV/O/02/48, Collins interview with Lever, 17 Nov. 2001, pp. 10–11.
44 WF/M/AV/O/02/36, Collins interview with Cochrane, 17 Aug. 2001, p. 44; WF/M/AV/O/02/11, Collins interview with Tracy, 30 April 2001, pp. 37–38; WF/M/AV/O/02/10, Collins interview with Barry, 30 April 2001, p. 23.
45 WF/M/AV/O/02/36, Collins interview with Cochrane, 17 Aug. 2001, pp. 33–34; WF/M/AV/O/02/11, Collins interview with Tracy, 30 April 2001, pp. 37–38; WF/M/AV/O/02/03, Collins/Church interview with Coe, 19 April 2001.
46 Castell had joined WFL as a junior at the age of 19, rising through the ranks after qualifying in accountancy to become managing director of Wellcome Biotech, group commercial and main board director, and regarded by some as potential candidate to become CEO at the age of 42. He resigned shortly after Robb's arrival (by which time Castell had married the daughter of the personnel manager). WF/M/AV/O/02/41, Collins interview with Castell, 26 Sept. 2001, p. 19. On Gibbs's decision in 1994, he observed: "I think overall if I had been in his position as chairman of the Trust I would make that decision." Ibid., p. 16.
47 WF/M/AV/0/41, Collins interview with Castell, 26 Sept. 2001, p. 16.
48 WF/M/AV/O/02/11, Collins interview with Tracy, p. 38–39.
49 Ibid., pp. 36–37.

Chapter 27: Themes and perspectives

1 See Jonathan Zeitlin, "The historical alternatives approach," in Geoffrey Jones and Jonathan Zeitlin (eds), *Oxford Handbook of Business History* (Oxford University Press, Oxford, 2008), p. 121.
2 Christopher A. Bartlett and Sumantra Ghoshal, *Managing across Borders, the Transnational Solution* (Harvard Business School, Boston MA, 1998), pp. 35–36.
3 Ibid., p. 81.
4 Edith M. Penrose, *The Theory of the Growth of the Firm* (Johns Hopkins, New York, 1959).
5 J. Sutton, *Sunk Costs and Market Structure: Price Competition, Advertising and the Evolution of Concentration* (Bellknapp Press, Cambridge MA, 1992), p. 324.
6 Richard R. Nelson and Sidney G. Winter, *An Evolutionary Theory of Economic Change*, (Harvard University Press, Cambridge MA, 1982).
7 Ibid., p. 38.
8 Geoffrey Jones, *Multinationals and Global Capitalism from the Nineteenth to the Twenty-First Century* (Oxford University Press, Oxford, 2005), pp. 191–93.
9 P. H. Kristensen and J. Zeitlin, *Local Players and Local Games: the Strategic Constitution of a Multinational Corporation* (Oxford University Press, Oxford, 2005).
10 Jones, *Multinationals and Global Capitalism*.
11 Bartlett and Ghoshal, *Managing across Borders*, pp. 77–79.
12 Ibid, pp. 38–40, 87.
13 Geoffrey Jones, "Globalization," in Jones and Zeitlin (eds), *The Oxford Handbook of Business History*, p. 160.
14 John P. Swann, *Academic Scientists and the Pharmaceutical Industry. Cooperative Research in Twentieth-Century America* (Johns Hopkins University Press, Baltimore MD, 1988).
15 D. C. Coleman, "Gentlemen and players," *Economic History Review* 26:1, Feb. 1973, pp. 92–98; Andrew Pettigrew, *The Awakening Giant: Continuity and Change in ICI* (Basil Blackwell, Oxford, 1985); Ronald R. Kline and Thomas Lassman, "Competing research traditions in American industry: uncertain alliances between engineering and science at Westinghouse Electric, 1886–1935," *Enterprise and Society* 6:4, 2005, pp. 601–45.
16 R. K. Jain and H. C. Triandis, *Management of Research and Development Organisations: Managing the Unmanageable* (John Wiley, New York and London, 1990), p. xiv.
17 I. Bailyn, "Autonomy in the industrial R&D lab," *Human Resources Management* 24, 1985, p. 132.
18 R. Pahl and J. T. Winkler, "The economic elite," in P. Stanworth and A. Giddens (eds), *Elites and Power in British Society* (Cambridge University Press, Cambridge, 1974), pp. 102–22.
19 Raelin, J. A., "The basis for the professionals' resistance to managerial control," *Human resource Management* 24:2, 1985, pp. 147–75; E. Greenberg, "The importance of autonomy in encouraging creativity: managerial implications from a study

in fashion design," *Creativity and Innovation Management* 3:3, September 1994, pp. 167–76.
20 WF/M/AV/O/02/12, Collins interview wih Howsam, 13 April 2001, p. 11.
21 John Kay, *Foundations of Corporate Success* (Oxford University Press, Oxford, 1993), chapter III.
22 Chandler Jr, *Shaping the Industrial Century*, pp. 192–211.
23 Swann, *Academic Scientists and the Pharmaceutical Industry*, p. 6.
24 Nathan Rosenberg, "Why do firms do basic research (and with their own money)?" *Research Policy* 19:2, 1990, pp. 165–74; Alfonso Gambardella, *Science and Innovation: the US Pharmaceutical Industry: Trends, Problems and Achievements* (Cambridge University Press, Cambridge, 1995), chapter 3.
25 Paul Galambos and Jane E. Sewell, *Networks of Innovation: Vaccine development at Merck, Sharpe & Dohme and Mulford, 1895–1995* (Cambridge University Press, Cambridge, 1995), pp. 243–46.
26 Gombardella, *Science and Innovation*, p. 61.
27 Swann, *Academic Scientists and the Pharmaceutical Industry*, p. 170.
28 WF/M/AV/O/02/44, Collins interview with Cresswell, 14 Oct. 2001, p. 8.
29 Philip Scranton, "Technology, science, and American innovation," *Business History* 48:3, July 2006, p. 316.
30 Ibid p. 326
31 Ibid.
32 Ibid p. 313.
33 Karl Weick, "Organisational Redesign and Improvisation," in Karl Weick, *Making Sense of the Organization*, Vol. 1 (Blackwell, Oxford, 2000); Weick and Sutcliffe, *Managing the Unexpected*, chapters 1 and 5.
34 Ibid., p. 316
35 Ibid., p. 320. The Sullivan presidency at RTP validates this particular dimension of Scranton's analysis.
36 Takuji Hara, *Innovation in the Pharmaceutical Industry: The Process of Drug Discovery and Drug Development* (Edward Elgar, Cheltenham and Northampton MA, 2003).
37 The company was not included in the survey.
38 Hara, *Innovation in the Pharmaceutical Industry*, p. 104.
39 Ibid.
40 G. B. Elion, "The purine path to chemotherapy," *Science* 244, 1989, pp. 41–47.
41 GSK/WF/SCS 2179, Board minutes, 8 Jan. 1981; WF/M/AV/O/02/12, Collins interview with Howsam, 1 May 2001, p. 20. Howsam implied that despite Coe's skepticism in view of current developments in the field at RTP, Cresswell was keen to support a fellow Scot whom he liked.
42 "George Hitchings" and "Gertrude Elion," in Frängsmyr (ed.), *Les Prix Nobel*, n.p.
43 Mark Beggs, V. Emerick, and Richard Arthur, "High therapeutic screening," in Jeffrey S. Handen (ed.) *Industrialization of Drug Discovery* (Taylor & Francis, London, 2005), pp. 103–37, Table 5.1.
44 D. Mowery and Nathan Rosenberg, "Twentieth Century Technological Change," in S. Engerman and Robert Gallman (eds), *Cambridge Economic History of the United States* Vol. III (Cambridge University Press, Cambridge, 2000), pp. 863–64.
45 Dominique A. Tobbell, *Pills, Power, and Policy: The Struggle for Drug Reform in Cold War America and its Consequences* (University of California Press, Berkeley CA, 2012), chapter 8.
46 Henry G. Grabowski and John M. Vernon, *The Regulation of Pharmaceuticals: Balancing the Benefits and Risks* (American Enterprise Institute for Public Policy, Washington DC, 1983), p. 10.
47 See Harden, *AIDS at 30*, chapter 5.
48 Little space was found for discussion of the detailing of pharmaceuticals either in Friedman's history of selling or in Chandler's survey of the global pharmaceutical industry. See Walter A. Friedman, *Birth of Salesman: The Transformation of Selling in America* (Harvard University Press, Cambridge MA and London, 2004); A. D. Chandler, "The chemical and pharmaceutical industries," in Chandler, *Shaping the Industrial Century.*
49 Jeremy Greene, "Attention to 'details': etiquette and the pharmaceutical salesman in post-war America," *Social Studies of Science* 34, 2004, pp. 271–92.
50 Ibid., p. 285.
51 Church and Tansey, *Burroughs Wellcome & Co.*, pp. 396–402; Roy Church, "Salesmen and the transformation of selling in Britain and the US in the nineteenth and early twentieth centuries," *Economic History Review* 61:3, Aug. 2008, pp. 695–725.
52 Thomas Jones, *Detailing the Physician* (Romaine Pearson, New York, 1940), p. 46.
53 Friedman, *Birth of a Salesman*, pp. 10–12.
54 This strategy had been employed by the British parent company since the 1880s. The method was

introduced by the American subsidiary from its formation in 1906. Church and Tansey, *Burroughs Wellcome & Co.*, pp. 240–51.

55 Gary Herrigel, "Corporate governance," in Jones and Zeitlin (eds), *Oxford Handbook of Business History*, pp. 470–92.

56 Hall and Bembridge, *Physic and Philanthropy*, pp. 80–81.

57 GWHC, BW&Co. (USA) Inc., 107.01/02, President's annual report, 1955/6.

58 Quoted by Hall and Bembridge, *Physic and Philanthropy*, p. 112.

59 See Bruce Lyons and Judith Mehta, "Contracts, opportunism, and trust: Self interest and social orientation," *Cambridge Journal of Economics* 21, 1997, pp. 237–57; Roy Church, "Trust, Burroughs Wellcome & Co. and the foundation of a modern pharmaceutical industry in Britain, 1880–1914," *Business History* 48:3, July 2006, pp. 376–98.

60 Ibid., p. 117.

61 WF/E/19, Creasy to Cresswell, 18 March 1973.

62 There is a considerable literature which is critical of the industry. See, for example, Jeffrey Robinson, *Precription Games. Money, Ego, and Power: Inside the Global Pharmaceutical Industry* (Simon & Schuster, London, 2001); Merrill Goozner, *The $800 Million Pill* (University of California Press, Berkeley CA, 2004); John Abramson, *Overdosing America: The Broken Promise of American Medicine* (Harper perennial, New York, 2004); Ray Moynihan and Alan Cassels, *Selling Sickness: How the World's Biggest Pharmaceutical Companies are Turning us all into Patients* (Nation Books, New York, 2005).

63 Brian Deer, "News Review," *Sunday Times*, 6 March 1994, p. 1.

64 Ibid., p. 2.

65 Ibid.

66 Ibid., p. 1.

67 Ibid., 27 Feb. 1994, p. 2.

68 Ibid.

69 Ibid.

70 A particularly illuminating collection of essays which explore various aspects and implications of the tensions analysed from different scholarly and professional standpoints is to be found in Michael A. Santoro, "Introduction: Charting a sustainable path for the twenty-first century Pharmaceutical Industry," in Santoro and Gorrie (eds), *Ethics and the Pharmaceutical Industry*, pp. 1–5.

71 Juliana E. Idanpaan-Heikkila and Sev Fluss, "Emerging international norms for clinical testing: Good clinical trial practice," in Santoro and Gorrie (eds), *Ethics and the Pharmaceutical Industry*, p. 39.

72 Michael A. Santoro, "Introduction, Part II," in Santoro and Gorrie (eds), *Ethics and the Pharmaceutical Industry*, p. 131.

73 Charles L. Bardes, "Ethics and prescribing: The clinician's perspective," in Santoro and Gorrie (eds), *Ethics and the Pharmaceutical Industry*, p. 136.

74 Edward Greg Koski, "Renegotiating the grand bargain: Balancing prices, profits, people, and principles," in Santoro and Gorrie (eds), *Ethics and the Pharmaceutical Industry*, p. 396.

75 Jurgen Drews, "Drug research: Between ethical demands and economic constraints', in Santoro and Gorrie (eds), *Ethics and the Pharmaceutical Industry*, pp. 24–25.

76 Ibid., p. 36.

77 A. Wazana, "Physicians and the pharmaceutical industry: Is a gift ever just a gift?" *JAMA* 238:3, 19 Jan. 2000, pp. 373–80.

78 See J. Lexchin, "Doctors and detailers: Therapeutic education or pharmaceutical promotion?" *International Journal of Health Services* 19, 1989, pp. 663–79; Wazana, "Physicians and the pharmaceutical industry," pp. 373–80.

79 M. Adani, "Thick prescriptions: Towards an interpretation of pharmaceutical sales practices," *Medical Anthropology Quarterly* 18, 2004, pp. 325–38.

Appendix: The Burroughs Wellcome Fund

1 Iris B. Evans, *The Burroughs Wellcome Fund, 1955–1985: Investment in Research* (The Burroughs Wellcome Fund, NC, 1985), xii.

2 The authors are Mirinda J. Kossoff (ed.), *History of the Burroughs Wellcome Fund, 1955–2005: Celebrating 50 years of Advancing the Biomedical Sciences* (Buroughs Wellcome Fund, NC, 2005) and Evans, *The Burroughs Wellcome Fund*. Both refer only to the Trust's enthusiastic support for the 1954 proposal; Kossoff also overlooked resistance to the 1992 proposal shared by several trustees.

3 Coe diaries, 3 May 1954.

4 Kossoff (ed.), *History of the Burroughs Wellcome Fund*, pp. 32–34.

5 Gibbs quoted in Peter Williams, Transcript

of a round table discussion about the Burroughs Wellcome Fund, RTP, NC, 30 Oct. 1997, p. 409.

6 Julian Jack, in Peter Williams, Transcript of a round table discussion about the Burroughs Wellcome Fund, RTP, NC, 30 Oct. 1997, p. 412.

7 Ibid.

8 Kossoff (ed.), *History of the Burroughs Wellcome Fund*, p. 34.

9 Peart, in Peter Williams, Transcript of a round table discussion about the Burroughs Wellcome Fund, RTP, NC, 30 Oct. 1997, p. 408.

10 WF/M/AV/O/02/03, Church and Collins interview with Coe, 13 April 2001, p. 50.

11 Kossoff (ed.), *History of the Burroughs Wellcome Fund*, p. 34.

12 Martha Peck in Peter Williams, Transcript of a round table discussion about the Burroughs Wellcome Fund, RTP, NC, Oct. 30 1997, p. 410.

13 WT/TRU/MIN/284:9:95; 28:11:96, 13 Nov. 1996.

14 WT/TRU/MIN/284:25:10: 9 Oct. 1996.

Bibliography

Abrams, Thomas, "The regulation of prescription drugs: a policy dilemma," in Santoro and Gorrie (eds), *Ethics and the Pharmaceutical Industry*, pp. 153–68.

Abramson, John, *Overdosed America: The Broken Promise of American Medicine* (Harper Perennial, New York, 2004).

Adani, M., "Thick prescriptions: towards an interpretation of pharmaceutical sales practices," *Medical Anthropology Quarterly* 18, 2004, pp. 325–38.

Anderson, Stuart (ed.), *Making Medicines: A brief history of pharmacy and pharmaceuticals* (Pharmaceutical Press, London, 2005)

Arno, Peter S., and Karyn Feiden, *Against the Odds: The Story of AIDS Drug Development, Politics, and Profits* (HarperCollins, New York, 1992).

Avery, M. E., "Gertrude Belle Elion, 23 January 1918–21 February 1999," *Biographical Memoirs of Fellows of the Royal Society* 54, 2008, p. 161.

Bailyn, I., "Autonomy in the industrial R&D lab," *Human Resources Management* 24, 1985, pp. 129–46.

Baker, Clealand, "Burroughs Wellcome: Pioneer in pharmaceutical research," *Private Practice*, 1980, pp. 36–40.

Balance, R.J. Pogany and H. Forstner, *The World's Pharmaceutical Industries* (Edward Elgar, Cheltenham and Northampton MA, 1992).

Bardes, Charles L., "Ethics and prescribing: the clinician's perspective," in Santoro and Gorrie (eds), *Ethics and the Pharmaceutical Industry*, pp. 136–52.

Bartlett, Christopher A., and Samantha Ghoshal, *Managing Across Borders, the Transnational Solution* (Harvard Business School, Boston MA, 1998).

Bayer, R., and M. Oppenheimer, *Voices from the Epidemic: Oral History* (Oxford University Press, New York, 2000).

Beggs, Mark, V. Emerick and Richard Arthur, "High throughput screening," in Jefferey S. Handen, *Industrialization of Drug Discovery* (Taylor & Francis, London, 2005), pp. 103–37.

Berridge, V., "AIDS: contemporary history," in E. Fee and D. Fox (eds), *AIDS: Contemporary History* (University of California Press, Berkeley CA, 1990), pp. 41–64.

Berridge, V., *Aids in the UK: The Making of Policy 1981-1994* (Oxford University Press, Oxford, 1996).

Bonin, H., and P. de Goey (eds), *American Firms in Europe, 1880–1980: Strategy, Identity, Perception, and Performance* (Librairie Droz, Geneva, 2008).

Brandt, A. M., *No Magic Bullet: A Social History of VD in the US* (Oxford University Press, Oxford, 1987).

Bud, Robert, *The Uses of Life: A History of Biotechnology* (Cambridge University Press, Cambridge, 1994).

Carter, Susan B. et al., *Historical statistics of the USA*, Vol. 3, *Economic structure and performance* (Cambridge University Press, Cambrige, 2006).
Castagno, William G., *Medicine Avenue: The Story of Medical Advertising in America* (Medical Advertizing Hall of Fame, Hartington NY, 1999).
Caves, Richard E., Michael D. Winston and Mark A. Hurwitz, "Patent Expiration, Entry and Competition in the US Pharmaceutical Industry," *Microeconomics*, 1991, pp. 1–66.
Chandler, A. D. Jr, *Shaping the Industrial Century* (Harvard University Press, Cambridge MA, 2005).
Church, Roy, "Trust, Burroughs Wellcome & Co. and the foundation of a modern pharmaceutical industry in Britain, 1880–1914," *Business History* 48:3, July 2006, pp. 376–98.
Church, Roy, "Salesmen and the transformation of selling in Britain and the US in the nineteenth and early twentieth centuries," *Economic History Review* 61:3, August 2008, pp. 695–725.
Church, Roy, and E. M. Tansey, *Burroughs Wellcome & Co.: Knowledge, Trust, Profit, and the Transformation of the British Pharmaceutical Industry, 1880–1940* (Crucible Books, Lancaster, 2007).
Coleman, D. C., "Gentlemen and players," *Economic History Review* 26:1, Feb. 1973, pp. 92–98.
Colvin, M., "G. Belle Elion, 1918–1999," *Science* 284, 1999, p. 1480.
Corley, T. A. B., *Beecham's: From Pills to Pharmaceuticals, 1848–2000* (Crucible Books, Lancaster, 2011).
Delaney, Martin, "AIDS activism and the pharmaceutical industry," in Santoro and Gorrie (eds), *Ethics and the Pharmaceutical Industry*, pp. 300–25.
Di Masi, J. A. Hansen, R. W. Grabowski, and L. Lasagna, "The cost of innovation in the pharmaceutical industry," *Journal of Health Economics* 10, 1991, pp. 107–42.
Drews, Jurgen, "Drug research: between ethical demands and economic constraints," in Santoro and Gorrie (eds), *Ethics and the Pharmaceutical Industry*, pp. 21–36.
Drumwright, M. E., "Company advertising with a social dimension: the role of non-economic criteria," *Journal of Marketing* 60, October 1996, pp. 71–87.
Elion, Gertude M., "The purine path to chemotherapy," *Science* 244, 1989, pp. 41–47.
Evans, Iris B, *The Burroughs Wellcome Fund, 1955–1985: Investment in Research* (Burroughs Wellcome Fund, Henderson NC, 1985).
Fildes, Paul, "A rational approach to research in chemotherapy," *Lancet* 235:6091, 1940, pp. 955–57.
Flowers, Christopher R., and Kenneth L. Melmon, "Clinical champions as critical determinants of drug development," in Ralph Landau, Basil Achilladelis, and Alexander Scribine (eds), *Pharmaceutical Innovation: Revolutionizing Human Health* (Chemical Heritage Foundation, Philadelphia PA, 1999), pp. 331–72.
Frängsmyr, Tore (ed.), *Les Prix Nobel: The Nobel Prizes, 1988* (Nobel Foundation, Stockholm, 1989).
Friedman, Walter A., *Birth of a Salesman: The Transformation of Selling in America* (Harvard University Press, Cambridge MA and London, 2004).
Galambos, Paul, and Jane E. Sewell, *Networks of Innovation: Vaccine development at Merck, Sharpe & Dohme and Mulford, 1895–1995* (Cambridge University Press, Cambridge, 1995).
Galambos, Paul, and Jeffrey Sturchio, "Pharmaceutical Firms and the Transition to Biotechnology," *Business History Review* 72, 1998, pp. 250–78.
Gambardella, Alfonso, *Science and Innovation in the US Pharmaceutical Industry: Trends, Problems, and Achievements* (Cambridge University Press, Cambridge, 1995).
George, K. H., "George Hitchings, 1905–, American pharmacologist," in E. J. McMurray, J. K. Kosel, and R. M. Valada (eds), *Notable Twentieth Century Scientists*, Vol. 2 (Gale Group, Reading, 1996), pp. 933–34.
Goozner, M., *The $800 Million Pill: The Truth behind the cost of New Drugs* (University of California Press, Berkeley CA, 2004).
Grabowski, Henry G., and John N. Vernon, *The Regulation of Pharmaceuticals: Balancing the*

Benefits and Risks (American Enterprise Institute for Public Policy, Washington DC, 1983).
Greenberg, E., "The importance of autonomy in encouraging creativity: managerial implications from a study in fashion design," *Creativity and Innovation Management* 3:3, September 1994, pp. 167–76.
Greene, Jeremy A., "Attention to details: the etiquette and the pharmaceutical salesman in post war America," *Social Studies of Science* 34, 2004, pp. 271–92.
Greene, Jeremy and Elizabeth Sieger Watkins (eds), *Prescribed: Writing, Filing, Using, and Abusing the Prescription in Modern America* (Johns Hopkins University Press, Baltimore MD, 2012).
Hall, A. R., and B. A. Bembridge, *Physic and Philanthropy: A History of the Wellcome Trust, 1936–1986* (Cambridge University Press, Cambridge, 1986).
Hannaway, Caroline, Victoria A. Harden, and John Parascandola (eds), *AIDS and the Public Debate: Historical and Contemporary Perspectives* (IOS Press, Amsterdam and Washington, 1995).
Hara, Takuji, *Innovation in the Pharmaceutical Industry: The Process of Drug Discovery and Drug Development* (Edward Elgar, Cheltenham and Northampton MA, 2003).
Harden, Victoria A., *AIDS at 30: A History* (Potomac Books, Washington, 2012).
Hardy, Anne, *Health and Medicine in Britain, since 1960* (Palgrave, Basingstoke, 2001).
Hawthorne, Fran, *The Drug Juggernaut: The Inside Story of a Pharmaceutical Giant* (Wiley & Son, Hoboken NJ, 2003).
Helfand, H., B. Woodruff, K. M. H. Coleman, and D. L. Cowen, "Wartime Industrial Development of Penicillin in the United States," in J. Parascandola, *History of Antibiotics: A Symposium* (American Society for the History of Pharmacy, Madison WI, 1980), pp. 31–56.
Herrigel, Gary, "Corporate Governance," in Geoffrey Jones and Jonathan Zeitlin (eds), *Oxford Handbook of Business History* (Oxford University Press, Oxford, 2008), pp. 470–500.
Hilts, Philip, *Protecting America's Health: The FDA, Business, and One Hundred Years of Regulation* (University of North Carolina Press, Chapel Hill NC, 2003).
Hounshell, D., and J. K. Kenley Smith, *Science and Corporate Strategy: Du Pont R&D 1902–1980* (Cambridge University Press, Cambridge, 1998).
Hull, F., "Inventions from R&D: organisational designs for efficient research performance," *Sociology* 23:3, 1998, pp. 393–415.
Idanpaan-Heikkila, Juhana E., and Sev Fluss, "Emerging international norms for clinical testing: Good clinical trial practice," in Santoro and Gorrie (eds), *Ethics and the Pharmaceutical Industry*, pp. 37–47.
Jain, R. K., and H. C. Triandis, *Management of Research and Development Organisations: Managing the Unmanageable* (John Wiley, New York and London, 1990).
Javetz, W., "Antibiotics Revisited: Problems and Prospects after 2 decades' *British Medical Journal*, ii, 1963, pp. 951–55.
Jones, Edgar, *The Business of Medicine* (Profile Books, London, 2001).
Jones, Geoffrey, *Multinationals and Global Capitalism from the Nineteenth to the Twenty-First Century* (Oxford University Press, Oxford, 2005).
Jones, Geoffrey, "Globalization", in Geoffrey Jones and Jonathan Zeitlin (eds), *The Oxford Handbook of Business History* (Oxford University Press, Oxford, 2008), pp. 141–70.
Jones, Thomas, *Detailing the Physician* (Romaine Pierson, New York, 1940).
Jonsen, R., and Jeff Stryker (eds), *The Social Impact of AIDS in the United States* (National Academic Press, Washington DC, 1993).
Katz, R. (ed.), *Managing Professionals in Innovative Organisations* (Ballinger, Pensacola FL, 1988).
Kay, John, *Foundations of Corporate Success* (Oxford University Press, Oxford, 1993).
Khan, Arthur D., *AIDS: The Winter War* (Temple University Press, Philadelphia PA, 1993).

Kirp D. L., and R. Bayer (eds), *Aids in the Industrialized Democracies* (Rutgers University Press, New Brunswick NJ, 1992).

Kline, Ronald R., and Thomas Lassman, "Competing research traditions in American industry: uncertain alliances between engineering and science at Westinghouse Electric, 1886–1935," *Enterprise and Society* 6:4, 2005, pp. 601–45.

Koop, C. Everett, "The C. Everett Koop Papers: AIDS, the Surgeon General, and the Politics of Public Health' (Profiles in Science – National Library of Medicine, Washington DC, 23 Feb. 2012)

Koski, Edward Greg, "Renegotiating the grand bargain: balancing prices, profits, people, and principles," in Santoro and Gorrie (eds), *Ethics and the Pharmaceutical Industry*, pp. 393–404.

Kossoff, Mirinda J. (ed.), *History of the Burroughs Wellcome Fund, 1955–2005: Celebrating 50 years of Advancing the Biomedical Sciences* (Burroughs Wellcome Fund, Henderson NC, 2005).

Kristenson, P. H., and J. Zeitlin, *Local Players and Local Games: The Strategic Constitution of a Multinational Corporation* (Oxford University Press, Oxford, 2005).

Lamoreaux, Naomi, Daniel M. G. Raff, and Peter Temin, "Beyond markets and hierarchies: Towards a new synthesis of American business history," *American Historical Review* 106, April 2003, pp. 404–43.

Landau, Ralph, Basil Achilladelis and Alexander Scriabine (eds), *Pharmaceutical Innovation: Revolutionizing Human Health* (Chemical Heritage Foundation, Philadelphia PA, 1999)

Lasagna, Louis, "Congress, the FDA, and New Drug Development: before and after 1962," *Perspectives in Biology and Medicine* 32:3, Spring 1989, pp. 322–43.

Lauritson, John, and Peter Duesberg, *AZT: Poison by Prescription, the AZT Story* (Asklepois Press, Hamburg, 1990).

Lawrence, G. (ed.) "Research, industry, commerce, and the state: the politics of AIDS research in the UK, 1982–1993," in G. Lawrence (ed.), *Technologies of Modern Medicine: Proceedings of a Seminar Held at the Science Museum, London, March 1993* (Science Museum, London, 1994).

Levine, M., "Gay Ghetto," in Levine, M., *Gay Men: The Sociology of Male Sexuality* (Harper Row, New York, 1979), pp. 182–204.

Lexchin, J., "Doctors and detailers: Therapeutic education or pharmaceutical promotion?" *International Journal of Health Services* 19, 1989, pp. 663–79.

Liebenau, Jonathon, *Medical Science and the Medical Industry: The Formation of the American Pharmaceutical Industry* (Macmillan, Basingstoke, 1987).

Liebenau, Jonathon, G. H. Higby, J. Gregory, and Elaine C. Stroud (eds), *Pill Pedlars: Essays on the History of the Pharmaceutical Industry* (American Institute of the History of Pharmacy, Madison WI, 1988).

Lilja, Robert, *International Equity Markets: The Art of the Deal* (Euromoney Books, London, 1997).

Lindebaum, S., "Knowledge and action in the shadow of AIDS," in G. Herdt and S. Lindebaum (eds), *The Time of AIDS: Social Analysis, Theory, and Method* (Sage, Thousand Oaks CA, 1992).

Lyons, Bruce and Judith Mehta, "Contracts, Opportunism, and Trust: Self Interest and Social Orientation," *Cambridge Journal of Economics* 21, 1997, pp. 239–57.

McQuillan, Rufus L., *Is the Doctor in? The Story of a Drug Detail Man's Fifty Years with Doctors and Druggists* (Exposition Press, New York, 1963).

Mahoney, Tom, *The Merchants of Life* (Harper Bros, New York, 1959).

Marra, Linda, *Prescription for Profits* (Scribner, New York, 1997).

Marshall, L., "Gertrude Bell Elion, 1918–, American biochemist," in E. J. McMurray, E. J. Kosel, and J. K. Valeda (eds), *Notable Twentieth Century Scientists*, Vol. 1 (Gale Group, Reading, 1996), pp. 583–84.

Mazzucato, Mariana, and Giovanni Dosi (eds), *Knowledge Accumulation and Industry Evolution: The Case of Pharma-biotech* (Cambridge University Press, Cambridge, 2006).
Medley, R., "Demonstrations and direct action," in R. A. Smith (ed.), *Encyclopedia of AIDS* (Penguin, New York, 2001), pp. 199–202.
Moody, Roger, *The Gulliver File: Mines, People and Land: A Global Battlefield* (Pluto Press, London, 1992).
Morgan, E. J., "Innovation and merger decisions in the pharmaceutical industry," *Review of Industrial Organisation,* 19, 2001, pp. 184–86.
Mowery, D., and Nathan Rosenberg, "Twentieth century technological change," in Stanley Engerman and Robert Gallman (eds), *The Cambridge Economic History of the United States*, Vol. III (Cambridge University Press, Cambridge, 2000).
Moynihan, Ray, and Alan Cassels, *Selling Sickness: How the World's Biggest Pharmaceutical Companies are Turning us all into Patients* (Nation Books, New York, 2005).
Nelson, Richard R., and Sidney G. Winter, *An Evolutionary Theory of Economic Change* (Harvard University Press, Cambridge MA, 1982).
Nightingale, Paul "The economies of scale in experimentation: the knowledge and the technologies of pharmaceutical R&D," *Industrial and Corporate Change* 9:2, June 2000, pp. 315–59.
Pahl, R., and J. T. Winkler, "The economic elite," in P. Stanworth and A. Giddens (eds), *Elites and Power in British Society* (Cambridge University Press, Cambridge, 1974), pp. 102–22.
Parascandola, J., "The 'preposterous provision:' The American Society for Pharmacology and Experimental Therapeutics' ban on industrial pharmacologists, 1908–1941," in J. Liebeneau, G. J. Higby, J. Gregory, and E. C. Stroud (eds), *Pill Pedlars: Essays on the History of the Pharmaceutical Industry* (Institute of the History of Pharmacy, Madison WI, 1988), pp. 29–47.
Parascandola, J. (ed.), *A History of Antibiotics: A Symposium* (American Institute of the History of Pharmacy, Madison WI, 1980).
Parker, R. Stephen and Charles E. Pettijohn, "Pharmaceutical drug marketing strategies and tactics: a comparative analysis of attitudes held by pharmaceutical representatives and physicians," *Health Marketing Quarterly* 22:4, 2005, pp. 27–43.
Parker, R. S., and C. E. Pettijohn, "Ethical considerations in the use of direct to consumer marketing and pharmaceutical promotions: the impact on pharmaceutical sales and physicians," *Journal of Business Ethics* 48:3, 1999, pp. 279–90.
Penrose, E. M. *The Theory of the Growth of the Firm* (Johns Hopkins, New York, 1959).
Peters, T. J., "A skunkworks tale," in Katz, *Managing Professionals in Innovative Organisations*, pp. 433–41.
Pettigrew, Andrew, *The Awakening Giant: Continuity and Change in ICI* (Basil Blackwell, Oxford, 1985).
Pieters, Tone, *Interferon: the Science and Selling of a Miracle Drug* (Routledge, New York, 2006).
Quirke, V., "From alkaloids to gene therapy: a brief history of drug discovery in the twentieth century," in Stuart Anderson (ed.), *Making Medicines: A brief history of pharmacy and pharmaceuticals* (Pharmaceutical Press, London, 2005), pp. 175–202.
Quirke, V., "Anglo-American relations and the co-production of American hegemony in pharmaceuticals," in H. Bonin and P. de Goey (eds), *American Firms in Europe, 1880–1980: Strategy, Identity, Perception, and Performance* (Librairie Droz, Geneva, 2008), pp. 363–84.
Quirke, V., and Slinn, J. (eds), *Perspectives on Twentieth Century Pharmaceuticals* (Peter Lang, Oxford, 2010).
Raelin, J. A., "The basis for the professionals' resistance to managerial control," *Human resource Management*, 24:2, 1985, pp. 147–75.
Rasmussen, N., "The drug industry," *Bulletin for the History of Medicine* 79:2, 2005, pp. 116–31.
Reisel, W. D., and L. M. Sama, "The distribution of life-saving pharmaceuticals: viewing the

conflict between social efficiency and economic efficiency through a social contract lens," *Business and Society Review* 108:3, 2008, pp. 365–87.
Rhodes James, Robert, *Henry Wellcome* (Hodder and Staughton, London, 1994).
Rimmerman, C. A., "ACTUP," in R. A. Smith (ed.), *Encyclopedia of AIDS* (Penguin, New York, 2001), pp. 2–7.
Robinson, Jeffrey, *Prescription Games, Money, Ego, and Power: Inside the Global Pharmaceutical Industry* (Simon Schuster, London, 2001).
Rosenberg, Nathan, "Why do firms do basic research (and with their own money)?" *Research Policy* 19:2, 1990, pp. 165–74.
Santoro, Michael A., and Thomas M. Gorrie (eds), *Ethics and the Pharmaceutical Industry* (Cambridge University Press, Cambridge, 2005).
Scranton, Philip, "Technology, science, and American innovation," *Business History* 48:3, July 2006, pp. 311–31.
Shadlen, K. C., "Challenges to treatment: the price infrastructure trap and access to HIV/AIDS drugs," *Journal of International Development* 16:8, 2004, pp. 1169–80.
Silverman, M., and P. R. Lee, *Pills, Profits, and Politics* (University of California Press, Berkeley CA, 1974).
Slinn, J., "The development of the pharmaceutical industry," in S. Anderson (ed.), *Making Medicines* (Pharmaceutical Press, London, 2005), pp. 155–74.
Slinn, J., "Research and development in the UK pharmaceutical industry from the nineteenth century to the 1960s," in Roy Porter and M. Teich (eds), *Drugs and Narcotics in History* (Cambridge University Press, Cambridge, 1996), pp. 168–86.
Slinn, J., "Price controls or control through prices? Regulating the cost and consumption of prescription pharmaceuticals in the UK, 1948–1967, *Business History* 47:3, July 2005, pp. 352–366.
Smith, R. A. (ed.), *Encyclopaedia of AIDS* (Penguin, New York, 2001).
Spilker, B., *Multinational Drug Companies: Issues in Drug Discovery and Development* (Raven Press, New York, 1989).
Sturchio, Jeffrey L., *Values and Visions: A Merck Century* (Merck & Co., Rahway NJ, 1991).
Sutch, Robert, and Susan Carter (eds), *History of Statistics in the US,* Vol. 2, *Work and Welfare* (Cambridge University Press, Cambridge 2006).
Sutton, J., *Sunk Costs and Market Structure: Price Competition, Advertising, and the Evolution of Concentration* (Bellknap Press, Cambridge MA, 1992).
Swann, John P., *Academic Scientists and the Pharmaceutical Industry: Cooperative Research in Twentieth-Century America* (Johns Hopkins University Press, Baltimore MD, 1988).
Taggart, James, *The World Pharmaceutical Industry* (Taylor & Francis, London, 1993).
Taguire, R., "Value orientations and the relationship of managers and scientists," *Administrative Science Quarterly* 10:1, 1965, pp. 39–51.
Tansey, E. M., and L. A. Reynolds (eds), "Post penicillin antiobiotics," *Wellcome Witness to Twentieth Century Medicine* 6, 2000, pp. 25–39.
Temin, P., *Taking Your Medicine: Drug Regulation in the US* (Harvard University Press, Cambridge MA, 1980).
Thompson, I. D., *Organisation and Action: Social Science Bases of Administrative Theory* (McGraw Hill, New York, 1967).
Tobbell, Dominique A., *Pills, Power, and Policy: The Struggle for Drug Reform in Cold War America and its Consequences* (University of California Press, Berkeley CA, 2012).
Turney, Jon, *Rational Drug Design: Gertrude Elion and George Hitchings* (Wellcome Trust, London, 2001).
Wastilla, Linda J., and Louis Lasagna, "The history of Zidovidine (AZT)," *Journal of Clinical Research and Pharmacoepidemiology* 4:4, 1990, pp. 25–37.
Wazana, A., "Physicians and the pharmaceutical industry: is a gift ever just a gift?" *JAMA* 238, 2000, pp. 373–80.

Weatherall, M., *In Search of a Cure: A History of Pharmaceutical Discovery* (Oxford University Press, Oxford, 1990).

Wharton, James C., "'Antibiotic abandon:' the resurgence of therapeutic rationalism," in J. Parascandola (ed.), *A History of Antibiotics: A Symposium* (American Society for the History of Pharmacy, Madison WI, 1980), pp. 125–36.

Whittington, R., "Changing control strategies in industrial R&D," *R&D Management* 21:1, 1991, pp. 125–39.

Whittington, Richard, and Michael Mayer, *The European Corporation: Strategy, Structure, and Social Science* (Oxford University Press, Oxford, 2000).

Williams, Peter O., *Evolution and Work of the Wellcome Trust* (Quiller Press, Shrewsbury, 2010).

Williams, S. D., *Park Guide: The 1994 Guide to Research Triangle Park*, 8 (Research Triangle Park, North Carolina, 1994).

Wolfe, Sidney, and Christopher M. Coley, *Pills that Don't Work* (Farrar, Strauss, & Giroux, New York, 1981 edition).

Yarchoan, Robert and Samuel Broder, "Development of antiretroviral therapy for the acquired immunodeficiency syndrome and related disorders," *New England Journal of Medicine* 316:9, 1987, pp. 557–65.

Young, James Harvey, *Toadstool Millionaires: A Social History of Patent Medicines in America before Federal Regulation* (Princeton University Press, Princeton NJ, 1961).

Internal publications

Wellcome News, Wellcome World, Foundation News

Official

House Committee on Energy and Commerce, Hearings before the Subcommittee on Health and the Environment, 100th Congress first session, 10 March, April 27, 1987, serial number 110–68.

Report of the Presidential Commission on the Human Immuno-deficiency Virus Epidemic submitted to the President of the United States (Watkins Commission), Washington DC, 24 June 1988.

Newspapers and trade journals

American Druggist, Times, Financial Times, Sunday Times, Investors Chronicle, Economist, Management Today, New York Times, Boston Globe, Los Angeles, Washington Post, Times, Charlotte Observer, Pharmaceutical Business, Pharmaceutical Executive, Medical Marketing Media, Advertising Age, Private Practice, Business North Carolina, International Management, USA Today, Wall Street Journal

Index

Abbott Laboratories, 27, 29, 40, 54, 74, 139, 290, 344, 346
acquisitions/takeovers, 74, 88, 167–8, 181–2, 218, 229, 240, 322, 326–8, 332
Actidil, 56, 107, 115, 163, 178, 203
Actifed, 53, 56, 66, 107, 115, 123, 146, 163–4, 197, 202–11, 308, 315
ACTUP, (AIDS Coalition to Unleash Power), 279–80, 287–8
Acyclovir, 186, 191, 251, 314, 350, 359, 382, *see also* Zovirax
Adamson, K., 84–5, 87, 124, 131–2, 157, 163, 170–1, 178–9
addiction, 53–4, *see also* phenacetin
A.D. Little, management consultants, 224–5.
advertizing, *see also* Burroughs Wellcome & Co., Burroughs Wellcome (USA) Inc. and Wellcome plc
  advertisements, 48, 58–9, 72–3, 152–4, 161–2, 164, 194, 208, 211, 268, 286–7, 373
  agencies, 8, 11, 72, 144, 152, 275, 284
  ethical, 48, 194, 353
  expenditure, 31, 42–3, 48, 68, 141, 146, 185, 194
  "gifts", 362
  policy, 24, 28, 31–2, 40, 42, 48, 54, 59–60, 66, 73, 78, 93, 134, 145,-6, 149, 151–5, 162–4, 194, 205, 210, 214, 268, 284
  space-oriented campaigns, 210–11
  television, 93, 148, 150, 154–6, 205, 208–12
Aerosporin, 53, *see also* antibiotics
agencies/branches *see* Burroughs Wellcome & Co., agencies and branches, by country
AIDS (acquired immunodefiency syndrome), 251, 253–70, 273–90, 317–61 *see also* HIV, AZT, clinical trials, Retrovir
  costs of treatment, 270–3
  "epidemic", 252–3, 6, 260
  estimates of infected population, 192–3, 267, 270
  government prevention campaigns, 253, 262, 282
  medical insurance, 269 273, 278, 304
  national bodies, *see* NHI, NCI
  protest related to, *see* ACTUP
  vulnerable populations, 251–3
  "war council" against, 258
allopurinol, 103, 109, 204–5
American Druggist, 54, 57, 59, 65, 74, 107, 367
American Federation for AIDS Research, 259–260
American Society for Pharmacology and Experimental Therapeutics, 102
Americanization, 21–5, 345, *see also* Nevin
analgesics, 47, 51–61, 72, 148, 150, 162, *see also* Aspirin, Empirin, Tylenol
Anectine, 53, 60, 66, 71, 101, 114, 146
anesthiologists, 149
Anglo-American relations, 236, 241, 75–87, 93–7, 166–88, 232, 247, 293–4, 312–14, 343–50
  friction between managers, 13–20, 84–9, 200, 277
  friction between scientists, 82–3, 179–80, 188–9, 227, 230
  ownership issues, 81–2, 247, 326
Antepar, 53
Anstey, M., 191
antibiotics, 3, 45, 51–4, 59, 65, 73, 116, 351, 353, *see also* Sporins
anti-trust and monopoly Senate sub-committee, 56
antivirals, 2, 180–248, 254, 296–8, 300, 314
antihistamines, 100, 107, 375
Armstrong, Sir William (subsequently Lord), 176, 236
aspirin, 19, 58–9, 178, 204, 219, *see also* Empirin
assets, *see* capital, investment
Atebrin, 108
Australia, Burroughs Wellcome & Co., 36, 76–7, 83–4, 141, 167, 169–73, 306
Avadio, Dr D. M., 107
Avicap, 42
Avimal, 42
Ayer, N. W., 148
azidothymidine/AZT, 180, 203, 215, 246, 256–90, 300, 319, 352, 361, *see also* Retrovir
  clinical trials, 256–61, 263, 274, 279, 285, 319, 361
  ethics of research questioned, 274, 289

FDA approval, 262
"orphan status" conferred by FDA, 260, 274, 281, 283, 314
rationing, 260, 266–8
trade name changed to Retrovir, 262, *see also* Retrovir

Bacitracin, 53
Bactrim, 158, 160–2
Banks, Lawrence, 241–2, 330, *see* Flemings
Barcroft, Prof., 159
Barings, 246
Barnard, Dr Christian, 109
Baron, Shirley, Dr, 55
Barr Laboratories, 290–313
Barry, David, *see also* SKUNKWORKS
as expert witness before Congressional sub-committee regarding anti-viral research, 254
as head of virology, 188
as principal investigator in SKUNKWORKS anti-viral research, 215–16, 290
as Wellcome plc group director of RD&M, 300, 312–13, 324
as witness before Congressional sub-committee regarding AZT/Retrovir, 273–5
collaboration with NIH, 256–7, 261
conducts phase II trial of AZT independently, 256
early career, 185–6, 254
failure of secret attempt to detach BW&Co. from WFL before flotation of Wellcome plc, 247
failure of secret attempt to secure merger of Wellcome plc with Warner Lambert, 326
former connections with FDA and NIH, 254
leads HIV/AZT research group, 254–9
Barry, George, 133
Bartlett, Kathy, 279, 339
Bauer, Dr John, 190–1
Bayer A. G., 18–20, 58
Bayer Aspirin, 23 *see also* Compbayer, Empirin
Beauchamp, Lillia, 191
Beckenham, 52, 60, 78, 80, 82, 85, 93, 97, 107, 140, 157–9, 163, 178–191, 219–32, 241–4, 293, 295, 303–12, 326, 333, 335–6, 343–5, 354, 361, 378, 395, *see also* Wellcome Foundation Ltd (WFL)
Beecham Group, 169, 225, 233, 295–6, 310, 313, 315, 334, 336, 343, 391
Bennett, T. R. G., 13, 38–41, 75–82, 89, 294
Bentley, Dr P. H., 230
Berre-Sinoussi, Francoise, 254
Beth Israel Medical Center, 261
Biogen, 309–11
Biospherics Inc, 262, 268
biotechnology, *see* Wellcome Biotechnology Ltd
Black, Sir James
as chairman of biological committee, 221
as drug discoverer, 219
denied resources, 220
engages in personality clashes, 224
receives ultimatum, 230
head-hunted by Vane, 219
knighted, 229
resignation with independent funding from WFL through Rayne Institute, 231
unmanageable colleague, 222
Blaiberg, Philip, 109
Body Positive, 287
Bolagnesi, Dani, 256
Borofax, 47
branches, *see* Burroughs Wellcome & Co. agencies and branches, by country
brands, 12, 16, 19, 28–31, 44, 50, 53, 58–61, 66, 73–4, 101, 107, 123, 205, 207, 349 *see* trade names, Kepler, Tabloids, Wellcome Brand Chemicals, Empirin etc
Brewin, P. K., 173
Bristol Myers, /Squibb 74, 155, 301, 314–15, 327, 346
Broder, Sam, 255–65, 275, 289–90
as NCI head of clinical oncology program, 255
creates model for corporate-government relations, 263–4
initiates collaborative search for HIV/AIDS treatment with corporate leaders, 256
secures informal partnership between NCI and BW&Co., 257
undertakes high risk *in vitro* studies at NCI laboratories, 257
view of the role of Burroughs Wellcome/Wellcome plc. in retroviral R&D, 289–90
Brookman, R. M, 303
Buck, Johannes S., Dr, 26, 31, 100, 134
Bufferin, 54, 58
Bullock, L. C., 35, 89–90, 92–3
bulimia, 198
Burns, John, 28, 95, 113–14, 118–20, 123, 140
Burroughs, Silas Mainville/ S. M. Burroughs & Co.
deteriorating relations with Wellcome, 2, 8, 10
early career, 7
premature death, 10
Burroughs Wellcome & Co.
agencies, 10–11
employment, 10
formation and early history in London and Dartford, 9–12
management, 14, 16, 35, 38
marketing, 10–11
partnership, 8–9
products, 9–10
takeover of Kepler Malt Extract Co., 10
Burroughs Wellcome & Co., agencies and branches:
Burroughs Wellcome & Co. Australia (Melbourne), 11, 76–7, 83–4, 141, 167, 171, 173, 305 (BW&Co. Sydney), 17, 38

Burroughs Wellcome & Co. Canada (Montreal), 13–14, 36, 81, 87, 89, 92, 118, 141, 165
Burroughs Wellcome & Co South Africa (Cape Town), 11, 76
Burroughs Wellcome & Co. USA (New York), 1906–1924
  accounting practices applied disadvantageously from London., 15–17
  business/management culture, 14
  "detailing", 7–8, 13
  effects of First World War, 17
  formation, 11
  management, 17, 22–4
  manufacturing, 9, 17
  perception of relation to parent company by Wellcome, 16–17
  products, 12, 17–18
  policy controlled from London, 21
  profits, 26 table 2
  sales, table 2.1
  transfers and dividends, table 2.2
Burroughs Wellcome (USA) Inc. (1924–1972)/ Burroughs Wellcome & Co. (1972–1985),
  advertising, 48, 59, 72–3, 152–6, 161, 164, 194, 208–11, 268, 286–7, table 5.2
  agencies, 12, 144, 152, 284, 351
  agreement with Chemgen, 266
  American model conceded by md of WFL to be superior to that in the UK, 70
  Americanization of product development policy, 22, 24–5, 345
  business and statistics department, 32
  candidates for presidency, 200
  centralization, 213
  collaboration with other companies, 158–64
  contract with Pfizer for supply of thymidine, 266, 277
  corporate/management culture, 70, 85, 94–7, 129, 138, 144, 155, 157, 188, 199, 200–1, 212–23, 288, 312, 342
  corporate image, 107, 133, 136–182, 198, 200, 210, 232, 253, 261, 281–2, 343, 356
  corporate structure, 41, 120, 122, 139, 143, 145, 154, 187, 189, 202, 345, fig. 3
  cost control, 40, 47, 98, 144
  data processing, 73
  depreciation policy, 189
  "detailing", 48, 65–73, 162, 285–7, 353 *see also* marketing
  distribution, 47–8, 55, 66, 69, 73, 78, 82, 94, 112, 153–4, 193
  dividends, tables 2.2, 6.1, 13.1
  drug development program, 159
  employment, 22, 32, 40, tables 4.1, 5.2, 9.1, 12.1
  equal employment policy, 70
  equity release opposed, 82, 178
  expenditure, tables 5.3, 11.1, 12.2, 15.3, 23.5
  financial support for WFL in London, 86–7, 95
  formation, 21–2
  government contracts, 31, 40–1, 57, 70, 75
  Great Depression policies, 25, 31
  high rates of depreciation, 189
  impact of WWII, 43, 66–7
  investment, 44, 46, 49, 113, 115–24, 202, 212–17, 277, 356
    return on, table 15.2
  management
    buyout rejected, 247
    laboratories, 30
    mergers pursued, 259
    recruitment, 30, 139, 139–44
    structure, 21, fig. 2.1
    styles, 40, 138, 187, 199, 346–7, *see also* Nevin, Creasy, Coe, Haigler, Tracy
    succession, 94, 200
    training, 136, 144, 152
  manufacturing policy, 21–3, 25, 27–31, 46, 98, 188, 195–6, 266–7
  marketing, 28–9, 31, 40, 48–9, 67, 113, 193, 353–4,
    anti-virals, 1935, 285
    co-marketing, 165, 313–14, 326
    costs, table 3.1
    employment, tables 5.2, 9.1, 11.3, 11.4
    exhibitions/exhibits, programs, 31, 48–9, 72–3
    expenditure, tables 5.2, 11.1
    organization/ reorganization, 46–7, 67, 137, 141–8, 154, 187, 202–7, 226–7, fig. 11.2.
    market research, 66, *see also advertizing*
  medical department, 42, 49–50, 69, 71-3
    growth of, 139. 160
    monitors advertizing copy, 71, 155
    organizes clinical trials, 101–2, 107, 115, 211
    prepares publicity literature, 72-3
    prepares NDAs for submission to FDA, 100, 115

psychiatric section, 198
role in the distribution of Retrovir through the Retrovir Center, 262
visits medical faculty in ''centers of influence.119
role in training sales representatives, 69, 71
packaging, 48, 73, 115–16, 142, 162, 183, 189, 270
product development/ planning, 151, 163
sales, tables 2.1, 3.1, 5.1, 5.2, 6.1, 9.2, 12.2, 13.1, 15.3, 23.5, 23.6
salesmen, recruitment, 68–71, 120, 151, 153–4
salesmen, training, 29, 31, 46–9, 68–70, 193–4
sampling, 48
selling to doctors, 51, 68, 73, 153–4, 193–6, 285, 253–4, *see also* "detailing"
selling to hospitals, 49–50
veterinary products, 94
veterinary marketing advisory group, 174
organizational restructuring, 46–7, 137–47, 187, 202–7, 216–17, fig. 11.1
ownership issues, 73, 78
pricing policy, 24, 31
premises, 22–3, 54, *see also* Tuckahoe, Research Triangle Park
pressure on WFL board to reduce price of Retrovir, 270-1, 281-2
price maintenance, 56
products, 12, 16–32, 41–58, 61–7, 71–6, 86, 115–24, 144,-55, 163, 165, 205–14, 300, 308, tables 4.1, 5.1, 9.2, 15.1, *see also* individual products, brand
product development, 47–9, 65, 150, 191, 202, 204, 206
public image, 154-6, 198
relations, 133-4, 149, 194, 198, 202, 205, 210-11
relations department, 133
profits, tables 2.1, 12.2, 13.1, 15.3, 23.5
RD&M,
clinical testing facilities and MD staff expansion, 106, 139–41
collaboration with external researchers, 104, *see also* Sloan-Kettering
with other university scientists in the US, 107–8, 137, 191, 257
with NCI scientists, 256–9
with WFL scientists, 82, 85, 157–9, 163, 190–2
comparison of laboratory cultures in US and UK, 188
culture in laboratories, 30, 80, 100–3, 105–11, 186–8, 216–17
effect of FDA regulation, 115–17
employment, table 5.2, 9.1
expenditure, tables 11.1, 19.1
Experimental Research Laboratories, 25–6, 49, 102, 117, 124
investment, *see* expenditure
management, structure, 113–114, 120–1
methodology, 104–12
networks, 55, 85, 111, 118–19, 346–51
organization/ reorganization, 8, 30, 102, 113, 139, figs 9.1, 9.2, 114
recruitment of academic scientists, 122–3
relations with AIDS community, 286–7
reputation, 110, 123, 154–5, 188, 193, 282, 289, 347–9
staff, 146
relations with WFL, 89–94, 188, 282, *see also* Anglo-American relations
relations with FDA, 56–8 116, 260–2, 264, 274
relations with the Wellcome Trust, 81–2, 89–93, 95–7, 154–5, 247–8, *see also* Burroughs Wellcome Fund
relocation, *see* Tuckahoe, Research Triangle Park
reputation, 154–5, 214
retail trade, 205, 207
Burroughs Wellcome Fund, *see* appendix
Bushby, Stanley, R., 85, 157–9, 188
"Buy American first" campaign, 25

Calmic, 173, 306
Calne, Roy, 108
Cameron Markby, 243
Canada, Burroughs Wellcome & Co., 12–14, 36, 81, 92, 118, 141
Cardilate, 53
Carnegie Illinois Steel, 44
Castell, William, 232–3, 278–9, 309–10, 337
early career, 232
group commercial director, 295
manager of Torrino processing plant conversion to production of interferon, 309
managing director Wellcome Biotech. Ltd, 295, 309
negotiates with Genetics Institute regarding formation of Welgen, 310
reveals divisive management culture, 237
verdict on sale of Wellcome plc, 310
Cazalet, Peter, 320
CDC Life Sciences Inc., 247

Center for Children and Families, 287
Center for Disease Control (CDC), 191–3, 247, 253
Charity Commission, 237, 240–5, 300, 321–2, 331
Charities Act (1867), 245
Chemical Workers' Union, 129–30, 133, 191
Chemgen Corporation, 266
Chicago Exposition 1933, 31
CIBA-Geigy, 122, 141, 200–1
Cipau, Gabriel, 199, 234, 276–7, 324
  early career, 161–2
  director and president of Wellcome Nippon, 324
  establishes manufacturing at Greenford, 162, 189
  expansion in technical capacity, 195
  formulates price for AZT/Retrovir, 266–71
  introduces project system at Greenville, 188–9
  negotiates thymidine contracts with Pfyzer, 265–6
clinical trials, 55, 107, 109, 115, 164, 192, 198–9, 211, 220, 255, 257, 260, 263, 268, 274, 279, 285, 287, 307–10, 318–19, 349, 360–1, *see also* under specific compounds
Clinical Trials Group, 287
Cochrane, J. M. T., 301, 307, 310–11, 323, 326, 328, 336
Codeine, 43, 47–59, 146, 150, 162, 164, 203, 205, *see also* products
cod liver oil, *see* Kepler
Coe, Jr, Fred,
  appointment and early career, 43–4
  conceals profit, 189
  deputy president, 225
  distribution manager, 48–51, 66
  executive committee chairman, 94
  expansion planning, 117–19
  group chairman of North, South, and Central Americas, 171
  managerial style, 136, 138, 143, 199–200, 356
  opposition to diversification into veterinary medicine, 94, 181; *see* CMR, Denver
  production manager, 44
  president, 43, 59, 69–7
  relations with Vane, 179–80
  relocation policy, 124, 127–8, 130–4, *see* chapter 12
  training intitiatives, 66, 70, 144, 151–3
  vision for BW&Co., 74, 124, 155–6
Compbayer, 19–20
Committee on Medical Research (CMR), 45, 52, 94
Community Health Project, 286
competition/competitors, 25, 27, 40–1, 55–61, 73–4, 87, 108, 116, 148, 156–62, 178, 182, 185, 202, 205, 220–1, 229, 233, 290, 298, 313–14, 328, 335, 341–3, 347–8, 351, 355, 358, 360, 363
compressed medicines, *see* Tabloids
Concorde study, 314
Condensed Beer Company, 10
Cooper, McDougall and Robertson (CMR), 45, 72, 78, 93–5, 171–4, 181, 234, 303
Coopers Animal Health, 173, 232
Copestick, Henry, 172
corporate governance, 341–3, 354–7
corporate ethics, 358–63
corporate image, 84, 98, 124, 136, 154–8, 162, 356, 359
Cortisporin, 146, 204
Creasy, William N.,
  early career, 32, 34
  balances product innovation with research, 100
  builds structure of sound employee relations and welfare provision, 128–9
  commitment to support research, 49, 101, 106–7, 115, 118–19, 122, 124
  critical review of WFL for the Wellcome Trust, 89–95
  differences with the FDA, 57–8
  early efforts to initiate R&D projects, 47, 52, 54–5, 346
  fractious relations with board of WFL over dividends, 77–81, 86–9, 90–5
  grooms successor, 94
  initiates development of antibiotics, 52–3
  initiates development of antihistamines, 55
  management style, 32, 40, 95, 123–4, 199
  opportunistic Neostam contract initiative, 46
  opposes acquisition of Denver Serum, 181
  policy of interim innovation, 51
  rapid managerial promotions, 40
  rationalization policy, 46–9
  relations with Sir Henry Dale, 89
  resists sale of BW&Co. by WFL, 81–2
  resignation in ill health and under pressure, 95–7
  spearheads campaign to promote and defend Empirin, 54–9
  supportive of scientists, 106, 103
  surprised by Hitchings's initiative involving Roche, 158
Cresswell, Ronald M.,
  and development of Zovirax, 192
  anomalous role within WFL group R&D, 225–7, 293
  as chairman of Wellcome Biotechnology Ltd, 232
  as head of development research, 179, 188
  as WFL group technical director, relations with BW&Co. 218
  attempts at R&D rationalization and cultural change at WFL, 232
  chairs "reputation" task force, 272 , *see also* separate companies
  critique of R&D of WFL, 219, 222, 4, 232–4

early career, 122
initiative leading to Tracrium, 350
philosophy underlying R&D, 220, 348
regarded as heir apparent at Wellcome plc, 233, 293
relations with Hitchings, 122, 179–80
resigns to join Warner Lambert, followed by Cuatrecasas, 233
review of biological R&D and recommendations for reform, 220–2, 230, 305
secret attempt, with Barry, to negotiate merger with Warner Lambert, 259, 326
cross-licensing, 119, 158, 174
Cuatrecasas, Pedro, 141, 179–80, 185–88, 191–3, 198–9, 215–18, 223, 227, 231–3, 254–8, 290, 351
attacks short-term priorities in corporate research, 216–17
early career, 179–80
initiates SKUNKWORKS project, 215
interdisciplinary approach to research, 187–8
proceeds to development stage with anti-depressant, 198
joins Glaxo, 231
rancorous relations with Vane, 180, 218, 227
culture, business/management/organizational, 2, 70, 97, 129, 144, 155, 173, 186, 199–201, 216, 218, 243–4, 288, 295, 302, 311–12, 328, 336, 339–42, 344, 353–6
culture, scientific, 4, 14, 85, 157, 212–15, 219, 255, 345–6, *see also* research
customer service, 67

Dale, Sir Henry Hallet, 34–5, 39, 77–80, 84, 89–90, 95–6, 124, 166, 178, 181
Dameshek, William, 108
Daraprim, 33, 108, 110, 114, 157
Dartford, UK factory, 10, 12, 16, 20, 22, 24, 38, 55, 78, 92–3, 97
Darvon, 54
Data and Safety Monitoring Board, 258, 263
Davee, Koehlin& Keating, 144
de Beer, Edwin J., 49, 52, 83, 87, 100–2, 107, 113, 117–18, 163
de Montagnier, Luc, 254
decongestant, 3, 55, 107, 145, 163–4, 205, 209–10, *see also* Actifed, Sudafed
Deer, Brian, 357–9
Deltakos advertising agency, 152
Denver Serum Company, 181–2, 372
"detailing", 7, 48, 65–73, 162, 230, 285–7, 353, 362, *see* salesmen, sales representatives and also under separate companies
Devereux, R. C., 173, 175, 302
Dexin, dietary supplement, 28, 31, 41, 43–4, 47–50
diagnostics, 141, 168, 297, 306
Digitalis/Digoxin, 29, 59–60, 74, 80, *see also* Lanoxin
distribution, 12–13, 17, 26, 47–52, 66–7
diversification, 41, 83, 88, 93–4, 100, 165, 167, 181–2, 240–5, 331, 337, 343, 364
dividends, 26–7, 38, 77, 79–87, 95, 113, 154–5, 166–181, 238–46, 275, 294–5, 306, 317–21, 357, 365, *see also* Burroughs Wellcome & Co., WFL, Wellcome plc.
doctors, 51, 65, 68, 73, 139, 153–4, 193–6, 209, 285–7, 353
Donelson, D., 69
Drug discovery/innovation, 51, 100, 104–12, 159, 186, 190, 216–20, 251, 255–62, 289, 316, 335, 341, 345–51
Drug Efficacy Amendment to the Federal Food, Drug, and Cosmetics Act, 1962, 56, 112
Drug Efficiency Study Review, 164, 209, 263
Drug Price Competition and Patent Term Restoration (Hatch-Waxman) Act, 207, 350
drug safety, *see* clinical trials, 109–17, 160, 192, 206, 209, 220, 257–63, 351, 360–3
drugs, ethical prescription, versus OTC, 2, 17, 23–6, 72–4, 139, 155, 164, 181, 194, 354
Druggists, *see* pharmacists
Duke University, 26, 109, 131, 137, 140, 255–7, 289–90, 324, 350–2
Dunbar, Guy, 32
Duncan, Russell Dunoon, 243–4, 320–1

Economist, 233, 246, 276, 293, 300, 305, 307, 318
Eli Lilly, 45, 102, 158, 199, 314, 316, 346
Elion, Gertrude B.,
adjunct Professor, University of North Carolina, 137
approachable and supportive to young researchers, 188–9
early career, 104
awarded Nobel Prize jointly with Hitchings, 110
collaborates with Hitchings's purine research, 105–9, 123, 251
collaborates with Schaeffer's anti-viral research leading to acyclovir (Zovirax), 191, 350
as head of new experimental therapy department, 120, 190
inhabits sympathetic laboratory environment, 105
obtains joint patent for aziothioprine (Imuran) with Hitchings, 108–9
opposed to relocation to North Carolina, 132, 136
reputation, 118
Elixoid, 47
Elliott, T. R., 34–5, 38, 367
Empirin, 3, 18–20, 28–9, 32, 43–61, 66, 92, 111, 115, 123, 146–64, 203–8, 351 *see also* Compbayer Aspirin, Bayer Aspirin

employment, 67, 70, 90–2, 104, 120, 129–31, 135, 140, 144, 185, 234, tables 4.1, 5.1, *see also* contract, labor, trade unions
Emprazil, 53
entrepreneur/entrepreneurship, 10, 40, 106, 138, 201, 217, 241, 355, *see also* Burroughs, Silas; Wellcome, Henry; Nevin, Thomas; Creasy, William; Coe, Jr, Fred
epidemic, *see* Herpes, AIDS, 19, 27, 192–3, 251–6, 260, 273, 289, 351–2.
Ernutin, 29
ethical/unethical conduct, 24–5, 117, 194, 198, 244, 258, 261, 275–6, 317, 356, 360, 339, 361–2, *see* culture, reputation
Ethidol, 29
exhibitions/expositions, 12, 48–9
Experimental Research Laboratories, *see* Tuckahoe
exports *see* overseas trade
extracts,
  malt, 10, 12, 17, 20, 27
  adrenal, 29
Europe, 110, 118, 141, 161, 170–3, 197, 233, 271–2, 278, 282, 300–1, 307, 313, 336

Fair Trade, 56
Fairchild agency, 17
Falco, Elvira, 103–6, 109, 157, 251, 350
Family Health, 191
Famvir, 313
Fantus, 127–8, 133
Food and Drug Administration, 49, 52–61, 74, 96, 100, 106–23, 139–42, 158–64, 185–92, 195–202, 206–9, 246–83, 290, 310, 313–18, 351, 360, 363
Food, Drug and Cosmetics Amendment Act (1962), 100, 112, 115–120, 159–60, 202
Fedrazil, 71
finance, *see* assets, capital, profit, dividends
Finance for Industry, 240
Fintner, Norman, 307
First national City Bank & Trust Co., 133
First World War, effects of, 17, 26, 29
Fleming, Robert & Co.241–5, 319–333
Fonda, Howard, 30, 40, 44, 85, 87, 93–5, 102
Frame, Sir Alistair, 294–5, 302–5, 310, 320–1
Franks, Lord, 90, 166–7, 176–7, 200, 218, 336–7, 241
free samples and "gifts", 67, 289, 362
Freestone, Dr D. S., 230
Funk, D. Casimir, 26
Furman, Philip, 256

Gallo, Robert C., 254
Gauch, Ronald, 113
gay communities, 251–2, 279–80, 286–8
Genentech, 309–10
generic drugs, 61, 74, 150, 162, 202, 204–7, 290, 315, 328, 352, 358, 362
Genetic Institute, 310
Germany, 265
Gibbs, Sir Geoffrey, 241
Gibbs, Sir Roger,
  affirms Trust's "fiduciary issue," 331–23
  approach to sale of Wellcome plc to Glaxo, 325–6
  as Wellcome trustee, 241
  early career, 241
  influenced by salutary history of Nuffield Foundation, 241–2
  instrumental in the first share issue, 242–3
  meetings with Sir Richard Sykes regarding merger possibility, 327
  meets Wellcome plc strategy group, 333
  orchestrates second share issue, 320–2
  relations with Charity Commissioner, 320
Gillette, 208
Glaxo Laboratories/Holdings, 1, 4 75–6. 225, 231, 239, 298, 306, 314, 327–38, 345, 357–8, 364
Glaxo Wellcome, 328–9, 332–6, 345, 357, 364
GlaxoSmithKline, 321, 358, 364
Goddard, James L., 116, *see also* FDA
Godfrey, David, 173–4, 223, 281, 319
Goodall, Chesney, 140
Goodwin, L. G., 108
Gosselin, 72, 144
gout, treatment of, 72, 103, 109–10, 123, 149–52, 204, 296–7, 300, 350, *see also* Zyloprim
Governance, 2, 341–3, 354–7
Government contracts, 31, 40–1, 45–7, 71, 75, 310
Gray, A. A., 170–3, 176–8, 181
Great Depression, impact on BW&Co. (USA) Inc., 25, 31
Greenhill, Lord, 221, 229–30, 243, 309
Greenville,
  collaboration with Dartford, 198-9
  local recruitment, 135–6
  introduction of project system, 188, 265
  planning non-unionized, racially integrated plant, 133–4
  quality circles, 189, 198
  reorganization, 134
  transfer of manufacturing, development, and medical departments to, 133–4
  see also Cipau

Haigler, Theodore Jr, 142–4, 198, 200, 248, 269–70, 274–8, 281, 283, 289
  cancels launch of Wellbutrin, 143–4
  defends company's record regarding development of AZT, 289
  early career, 142
  gives evidence to House Subcommittee on health and Environment, 274–6

negotiates with Congressmen, 278–9
pricing AZT/Retrovir, 269–77
reforms finance, 143–4
second price reduction, 281–3
Harfenist, Morton, 216
Hazeline Snow cosmetics, 31
health care, 270, 278–9
Health Maintenance Act, 206
Health Policy Advisory Center, 194
Health Research Group, 209
Hearne, Sir Graham, 295
Heidelberger, Dr Charles, 190, 350
herpes, 3, 190–8, 251, 267–70, 284, 314–15, 350, 359
herring, sperm of as natural raw material, see thymidine, 265
Hitchings, George H.,
adjunct professor, Duke University, 137
as joint director of research, 95
as director of chemotherapy, 102, 113
as vice president RD&M, and first scientist main board member, 120
attitude towards McKinsey review of the laboratories, 213
awards/honors, 110
collaborative research/networks, 108, 110, 137, 140
collaboration with Elion, *see* Elion
creates laboratory culture, 186–8
designs scientific exhibit for promotion, 72
early career, 102–3
explains switch from academe to industry, 102–4
obtains joint patent on 6-MP with Elion, 106
opposes relocation to North Carolina, 132, 136
prepares 5-year investment plans for laboratories, 96, 117, 139
pursues unfashionable areas of research, 102–3, 123
receives support for research from Creasy, 113, 124
recruits Elion, 104
recruits Cresswell, 122
recruits Schaeffer, 123, 185, 189
relations with Sullivan, 215, 217
reorganization of laboratories, 120
reputation, 118
research committee decides on drug development, 345
research leads to Daraprim, 107–8
research leads to Zyloprim, 123
research philosophy/methodology, 105–6
secret joint agreement with Hoffman La Roche to develop anti-bacterial, Septra, 157–8
secures medium-term funding from the Kettering Sloan Institute, 106
uneasy relations with Vane, 179
HIV, *see* AIDS, 252, 254–63, 273–5, 280–9, 317, 322, 341, 352, 360, 363
Hjort, Axel, Dr, 26, 31, 100
Hodgson Rubber Company, 22
Hoffman la Roche, 95, 157, 275, 314, 350, 361
Horowitz, Jerome, 275
Hospital management organizations (HMO), 206
House of Representatives Subcommittee on Health and Environment, 253, 273–4
Howsam, Peter,
adopts new approach to marketing Zyloprim, 149, including by film, 149
as head of distribution committee, 143
as marketing director, 142
ceases sales through wholesalers, 152
creates ambitious Septra marketing campaign, 162
dismissed by Sullivan, 205
early career, 141–2
embarks on OTC initiative with Actifed, 163
favoured by BW&Co. directors to become president, 200
initial impression of BW&Co., 144–5
introduces new product planning system, 150–2
joins research committee, 187
licensing activity blocked by WFL, 165
new Empirin sales campaign, 148
prepares for marketing Zovirax, 193–4
reforms product range, 146–7
sceptical of effect on motivation by association with Wellcome Trust, 155
transforms marketing strategy, 154
14165, 187, 193–4, 199–200, 205, 208, 344–5, 356
Hudson, Rock, 259
Hudson Street premises NYC, 12, 22, 127

IBM, 129, 192
ICI, 3, 122, 173, 219–20, 243, 322
Imuran, 100, 109–10, 114, 203, 349–50
Industrial and Commercial Finance Corporation, 89, 166
industrial pharmacologists, 102
industrial relations, 20, 128–137, see also labor
Influenza epidemic, 19, 27
Infundin, 29
Inglis, A. B., 41
innovation, *see* marketing, R&D, technology, networks, and individual companies
Insulin, 30, 75, 179
Interferon, *see* Wellferon
International Chemical Workers' Union ICWU), 130, 133

Jawetz, Ernest, 52
Jensen Serum Company, 169, 172
Johnson & Johnson, 38, 58–9, 104, 157, 173, 208

Johnson-Saint, Capt. Peter, 33
Jones, Sir John Harvey, 243, 321
Jones, Trevor, 231, 309
Jowett, A. D., 22

Kala-azar, 46
Karsten Bill, 53–4
Katsiskis, Elli, 157
Kefauver-Harris Amendments to the Food, Drugs, and Cosmetics Act (1962), effects on Burroughs Wellcome & Co. in the US, 56, 351
Kellaway, C. H., 83, 101, 124
Kennedy, President J. F., 56, 111
Kennedy, Senator Edward, 149, 278
Kennedy, Thomas E., 143, 202, 270, 274, 280, 282
Kepler Malt Extract Company, 8, 10, 17
Kepler products, 10, 12, 17–18, 27–8
Kettering, Charles F., 106, *see also* Sloan-Kettering Institute
Kirkpatrick, D. L., 13–14
Klemme, Carl J., 30
Knight, A, 123
"knight, white", 332
Koehnlein & Keating, 144
Koop, C. Everitt, 259–60
Kramer, Larry, 279
Krenitsky, Dr T., 123

labor *see also* employment, industrial relations, trades unions
  contracts, 130–1
  policy, 128–30, 133–6
  welfare, 12
  recruitment 136
Lamictal, 220
Lancet, 314, 358
Landers, Ann, 194
Lang, J. S., 14, 24
Lanoxin, 53, 59–61, 66, 73–4, 123, 152, 155, 202, 204–5, 300, 315, 371
Lavender Hill Mob, 279
Lazard Bros, 331, 334, 337
Lazarus, Ted, 285, 287
Leonard, Clifford S., Dr, 25–6, 30
Lever, Sir Jeremy, 229–30, 234–5, 244–5, 317, 336
Levine, Marty, 288
licensing, 119, 158, 174, 182, 265
Lilly, Eli, 3, 29, 45, 54, 102, 158, 199, 202, 314, 316, 346
Lister Centenary and Clinical Congress, 24
Little, A. D., management consultants, 221–29, *see* Wellcome Foundation Ltd (WFL)
lobbying, 224, 252, 280
Lockwood Greenee & Associates, 127
Los Angeles, 251–2, 279
Luc de Montagnier, 254
Lyall, George, 35
Lyon, George, 217, 233, 261
Mack, Heinrich, see also Pfizer, 265
Malt extract *see* Kepler
Manser, John, 329
management, *see* by name of company
manufacturing, 2, 14,–22, 44–6, 49, 55–8, 117, 131–6, 167, 182, 265–9, 301, 309–10, 336, *see also* Dartford, Greenville, Tuckahoe
Marboran, 190–1, 251
Marezine, 55, 107, 115
Marketing, *see* under separate companies; see also, advertising, sales representatives
market by therapeutic area, 267, table 23.1
McAdams, William Douglas, 152, 161
McKesson & Robbins, 19
McKinsey management consulting, 200–15, 255, 290, 296, 325
McMichael, Sir John, 159
McMullan, Michael, 285–8
McNeil Laboratories, 208
malarial disease, 53, 108, 157, 219, 221
Manser, John, 329
Marboran, 190–1, 251
Marezine, 107, 115
Matons, Claude, 173–4
medical department, 42, 55, 68, 71–3, 80, 96, 100–7, 112–20, 139, 141, 155, 160–1, 198, 211, 220, 262
Medical Research Committee (MRC) UK, 307
Medicare, 71, 73, 206, 273
MEDCOM, learning systems, 149
MEDIX films, 150
Mehta, Nari, 198
Melbourne, Australian agency, 11, 76
Memorandum of understanding (MOU), 322–5, *see also* second share issue, Glaxo Holdings.
Menthofax, 28, 47
Mercaptopurine, 53, 106–7, 349
merchant bankers, see Flemings, Barings, 241–2, 321
Merck, 12, 74, 102, 155, 185, 192, 202, 208, 240, 275, 290, 315, 346–7
Merrifield, Keith, 346–7
Mexico, 168, 172, 182
Michigan Cancer Research Foundation, 251, 275
Midland Bank, 76–7, 176, 240
Mildvan, Donna, 261
Mitsuya, Hiroaki, 258
Monsanto, 132
Montagnier, Luc. de, 254
Montreal, Canadian agency, 11, 13–14, 24, 79, 81, 87, 141
Moore, G. Leslie, 13, 15
Moore, Thomas Henry, 13–14
multinational companies, 3, 7, 122, 341–64
Munro Forbes, Dr, 220
Myers Infoplan International Inc., 133
muscle relaxants, 47, 53, 71, 101, 206, 297, 300

National Cancer Institute, 233, 254, 281, 324, 352
National Labor Relations Board, 130
National Prescription Audit Services Inc., 72, 144
National Institute for Allergy and Infectious Diseases (NIAID), 254, 258, 261, 263–4, 283–4

National Institutes of Health (NIH), 119, 185, 253–9, 263, 275, 290
Neosporin, 146, 149–50, 162, 204–5, 211, 316
Nelson, Erwin E., 100
Neostam, 46–7
networks, 27, 55, 85, 111, 118–19, 346–9
Nevin, Thomas, 13–16, 19–34, 39–41, 48, 82, 99, 101, 104, 115, 200–1, 346
 as manager of Burroughs Wellcome & Co. New York branch, 14
 as salesman at Burroughs Wellcome & Co. Canadian branch, 14
 as vice president and general manager of Burroughs Wellcome & Co., New York branch, 14
 critical of strict management control of American company from London, 14–16, 22
 discordant relations with Pearson, 22–3
 ensures rapid promotion of Creasy, 32
 overlooked for post of general manager of WFL, 33
 impresses Wellcome, 13
 receives Wellcome's personal support for investment in manufacturing at Tuckahoe, 25–6
 shared vision with Wellcome for BW&Co., in the USA, 24
 struggles with competing priorities, between research and new product development, 30–1
 vision of laboratory research at Tuckahoe fulfilled by Wellcome, 25–6
New Drug Application (NDA), 100, 105, 113, 117, 123, 349
Newsweek, 192
New York branch1–2, 7, 11, 13–17, 27, 353, *see also* overseas branches
New York City, 251–2, 261, 280, 285–7
New Drug Indications (NDI), 116, 159, 359
New York State legislature, 276, 363
New York State Consumer Protection Board, 277
New York Stock Exchange, 246, 280
New York Times 275, 283, 289, 326–7
Nippon Wellcome, 168, 324
Nobel Laureate, 101, 103, 110, 178, 220, 230, 239, 246, 266, 350, 366
Non-executive board members, 221, 229–30, 233–5, 243 245, 281, 295, 306, 309, 325
North Carolina State University, 131–2, 137
Novopharm, 290, 315
Nuffield Foundation, 241–2

Oakes, C. G., 36, 38, 41, 77, 87
Odum, Howard, 131
Ogilvie & Mather, 280
organization, 152, 204, 213, 225, 227–8, 342–8, 354, 357
Organon, 173
OTC (over-the –counter) drugs, 24, 31, 55, 163,-4, 199, 203, 205–8, 211–112, 280, 306, 311–15, 333
ownership, 29, 33, 155, 204, 243, 318, 320, 327–8, 343, 354–8

packaging, 48, 73, 92, 115–16, 142, 162, 189, 270
Parke Davis & Co. US, 27, 29, 40, 74, 102, 232, 293, 326
Parrish, Clifford, 142, 210, 282
Pasteur Institute, 254–5, 349
patents, 10, 36, 110, 143, 158, 165, 202, 280, 290, 313–14, 327, 375, 352, 358, *see also* trademarks/names, impending expiration of Zovirax and Retrovir
Paton, Julia B., Dr, 26
Paton, Sir William, 190, 239
Peach, Dennis, 244
Pearson, George E., 15-26, 30, 33–8, 75, 89
 as chairman and governor of WFL, 33
 as deputy governor of Burroughs Wellcome & Co., 15
 assumes responsibility for New York branch, 13
 early career, 11
 fails to block introduction of manufacturing at New York branch or Tuckahoe, 26-8
 fails to prevent creation of the Experimental Laboratories at Tuckahoe, 25
 prejudiced against American subsidiary company's activities, 16-19
 resigns under pressure, 38
Peart, Prof. W. S., 190, 239, 368
penicillin, 44, 51, 73, 75–6, 191
Perazil, 53, 55, 100, 107, 114–15
Perrin, Sir Michael, 83–7, 90, 93–7, 132, 159, 170
Phenacetin, 57–9, 148
pituitary extracts, 29
Pfizer, 44, 52, 74, 81–2, 155, 208, 256, 265–6, 277, 313–16, 326, 335, 346
Pharmaceutical Executive, 265
Pharmaceutical Manufacturers' Association, 149, 281
pharmaceutical industry,
 in the UK, 300
 in the US, 25, 30, 45, 56, 73–4, 102, 115–119, 217, 256, 327, 351–3
 international, 1–3, 305–6, 317, 324, 327, 331
pharmacists, 44, 49, 58–9, 69, 156, 193–4, 207, 262, 354
Pharmacy education program, 156
Pharmatec, 313
Phenacetin, 57–9, 148
Philadelphia College of Pharmacy, 7, 9, 13, 69
Piercy, Lord, 84, 89–93, 96, 166
Pilkington, Sir Alistair, 234–5, 245, 295
Pitt Community College, 136
plasminogem activator (tPA), 306

Polymixin, 52–3
Polysporin, 205
Precious, John, 301,-5, 311, 315, 323
prescription medicines, 3, 25, 54, 56, 65, 67, 69–74, 104, 115–16, 139, 144, 149, 153, 156, 163–4, 193–6, 203–10, 219, 243, 262–3, 267–9, 277, 286–7, 306, 313–14, 351
President's Commission (US),
  on cost control, 1984 (the Grace commission), 289, 362
  on the Human Immunodeficiency Virus Epidemic, 1988, 254, 289
Price, Martin, 34–5, 76, 89
price, 16–18, 22–32, 45–7, 55–8, 61, 80, 87–92, 110, 134, 143–6, 162–4, 192, 197–8, 204–5, 219, 244–6, 264–5, 267- 85, 305, 309–10, 362–3, table 21.1
price maintenance, 56
products, 7–12, 16, 21, 23, 25, 27–31, 41, 43, 47–50, 53, 55–63, 71, 74, 76, 90, 92–100, 115, 117–36, 146–8, 163–5, 175, 202, 204–8, 221, 280, 300, 308–9, 316, 345–7, tables 4.1 14.1, 15.1
  absence of new from WFL, 83, 88, 190, 230, 317
product development, 65–6
  diversification, 41, 74, 83, 93–4, 100, 167, 181–2, 240
  innovation, 144, 152–7, 188, chapter 12
  planning/rationalization, 152, 181, 293, 305, 335
Product Management, 154
production, 44–5, 75–6, 92, 115–16, 120, 127, 134, 161–2, 175, 188–9, 195, 265–7, 308–9
profit, *see* assets, capital, dividends
Prontosil, 104
proprietary drugs, 24, 74, 199, 256
Prozac, 199, 316, 363
Pseudoephodrine, 53
psychiatric illness, 198, 251
public image, 154–6, 198, 210, 281–2, 317, 356–9, *see separate companies*
public relations, 133–4, 142, 149, 198, 288, *see separate companies*
Purinethol, 53, 100, 106–7, 110, 114, 349

Quinn, Garth, 248

R&D/RDM *see separate companies*
Rayne Institute, 231
Reagan, President Ronald, 259–60
Regulation, *see* FDA
Reiff, Douglas, 206
Reiner, Dr Lazlo, 26, 30–1
relocation of manufacturing to Greenville,
  non-union plant, 134
  recruitment and training of production workers, 134–5
Research Triangle Park (RTP),
  BW&Co. building administration and R&D building, 133
  architecture 133, 137
  Fantus, 127–8
  labor difficulties minimal, 131
  management of relocation, 133–4
  opposition to relocation, 132, 134
  origins, 127–33
  researching locations, 127
  purposes for removal, 128, 131,- 132
Retrovir, *see* AZT
  avoids clinical phase III trial, 261
  clinical phase I trial, 257, 265
  clinical phase II trial, 257–9
  combination therapies, 275
  Concorde study of, 316
  cost to patients, 274, 276–7, 283
  costs, 265–6, table 20.1
  first price reduction, 277–8
  marketing, 267, 284–6
  NIAID report on safety and efficacy, 263
  patents challenged, 290
  price of criticized, 273, 275–8
  pricing, 267–72
  production difficulties, 234, 265, 271
  projected revenues, 265–6, table 20.1
  revenue, 271
  sales, 197
  selling strategy, 284–6, 286
  second price reduction, 278–83
  subject of cross examination by Congressional committee, 274–5
Rhoads, C. P., 106, see also Sloan Kettering Institute
Rigg, Earl, 40
Ringle, Stata Norton, Dr, 120
Robb, John, 233, 295–6, 300–37, 345, 357, 365
  early career, 295
  accepts MOU as reassurance of medium term independence for Wellcome plc, 322–3
  appointed CEO at Wellcome plc, 296
  appoints single group director of R&D, 312
  believed to harbour unrealistic expectations regarding speed of reform strategy, 325
  closes unprofitable R&D activities, 305, 308
  declines offer of non-executive deputy chairman of Glaxo Wellcome, 330, 334–5
  elected chairman of Wellcome plc, 306
  impresses financial observers, 300
  initiates reform of IT, 307
  initiates reform of product development, 307, 311
  leads opposition to takeover by Glkaxo, 330
  leads opposition to second share issue, 321
  management style, 306
  rationalization focuses on "core business", 300–1, 325
  seeks white knight, 332, 334–5
  sells Calmic, 305
  sets annual goal for product innovation, 313

sells vaccine business, 305
set task of wholesale restructuring and reform, 296
terminates negotiations for merger with Warner Lambert, 326
verdict on takeover by Glaxo, 336
warned by merchant bankers of strong likelihood of sale by the Trust, 325
Robinson, Dudley, 77
Roche, Hoffman La, 95, 157, 275, 315, 350, 361
Rogers, Mike, 289
Rollo, I, 108
Rosenthal, Rolf Werner
advertising agency, 152, 161, 193–4, 287
Ross Roy/Compton advertising agency, 208
Roth, Dr Barbara, 157
Rudolph, Paul, 133
Rundles, R. W., 109

sales, sales representatives, and detailing *see separate companies*
San Francisco, 32, 49, 55, 129, 251–2, 268, 279–8
Sciarpelletti, John, 129
Schaeffer, Howard J., 103, 123, 141, 185, 191, 199, 215–17, 230–2, 269, 294, 311–12, 319, 350, 365–7
anti-viral research leading to acyclovir compound and to Zovirax, 189–91
collaborates with Heidelberger, 109
declines offer to become WFL group director of research, 232
describes the laboratory culture at RTP, 186–7
early career, 123, 185–9
resigns from task force investigating R&D at WFL, 230–1
vice president RD&M at BW&Co., 293
Schering and Chemische Industrie Basel (CIBA), 55, 74, 87, 122, 141, 163, 200–1, 210, 309
Schering-Plough, 311, 316
Schirra, Wally, 210
Schwarz, Robert, 108
Science, 192
scientific ethic, 344–64
second share issue, *see* WFL and Wellcome plc, 317–27, *see* chapter 25
Second World War, effects of, 40–7, 71, 93, 101, 108, 182, 182, 306, 347, 349
Seed, John C., 54
Senate Subcommittee on Anti-Trust and Monopoly, 56, 115
Septra, 157–65, chapter 12,
competition with Hoffman La Roche, 161–2
enters market for anti-bacterials, 160
implications for future scale of production and marketing at RTP, 160
outcome of joint agreement with Hoffman La Roche, 159
R&D leading to development of compound, 157
role of WFL scientists, 157
marketing cricized, 359
sales, 162
"Septra Pink Day", 160
Septrin, launch in the UK 1968, 159–60, 188, 350, *see* Septra
Seth Thomas Clock Company, 43
sexually transmitted infections, 183, 191, 194, 267–8, *see also* herpes, AIDS
share prices, 316–27, 331–4, 357
Sharpe & Dohme, 40
Shepperd, Alfred, 173–80, 189–201, 218–48, 270, 281, 293–6, 303, 306, 311–12, 319, 322
admits unsatisfactory management of WFL, 175, 231
concedes higher dividend payments to Trust, 177
disagrees with Steel over dividends to Trust, 238
early career, 173–4
fails to secure Trust approval for share issue, 218–19
fears libel arising from the Little management review of Beckenham laboratories, 228
gives brief to Cresswell to Americanize WFL, 221
grapples with problem from incompatible "prima donna" scientists, 224, 229
informed of proposed sale of shares by the Trust, 243, 245–7
initial opposition to price reduction for AZT/Retrovir, 270
maintains policy of long, low term dividends, 176
management style, 224, 233–4
opts for Sullivan as president of BW&Co., 200
redirects resources into RD&M at BW&Co., 178, 222
refers to 'upstart bankers', 243
resignation under pressure, 295
resists joint venture with ICI, 240
Shionogi, 157
Sier, H. H., 76–84
Singler Charles, 69–70, 142, 153
SKUNK WORKS project, 180, 215, 255, 259
Slaughter & May, 245
Sloan-Kettering Institute, 42, 106, 141
S. M. Burroughs & Co., 7, 10
SmithKline French, 139, 141, 143, 219–20, 254, 346
Smithkline Beecham, 4, 296, 315–16, 337
South Africa, Burroughs Wellcome & Co., 11, 36, 76, 171
South and Central America, 171, 182
Sporins, 52, 55–6, 123, see antihistamines

Squibb, 12, 27, 29, 40–1, 45, 74, 101–2, 178, 301, 315–16, 327, 346
Staley, Peter, 280, 288–9
Steel, Sir David, 229, 236–47, 294–5, 318, 322, 358
accepts highly critical management consultants' report on WFL, 225, 236
advised by merchant bankers, 242–3
appoints Roger Gibbs, 240
commitment to secure higher dividends from WFL, 258, 272, 295
disagreement with Shepperd over dividend levels, 238
discussions with Charity Commissioner, 244–5
early career, 236
influence on attitudes of trustees, 244
new approach to Trust chairmanship, 237
resolves to float WFL on Stock Exchange, 240–2
Strelnick, Dr Hal, 194
Streptomycin, 44–5, 51
Sudafed, 53, 55–6, 66, 107, 123, 145–6, 150, 162–3, 203, 205, 210–11, 308, 316, table 24.1
Sullivan, William N.,
accused of undermining morale through bureaucratic reforms, 215–16
attempts to reform RD&M frustrated, 214–15
attends Stanford Young Presidents' program, 202
commissions McKinsey consulting, 202
condfidentiality issue with Shepperd, 248
contract terminated, 248
debates research/business orientation divisions at RTP, 216–17
experiments with TV advertising, 209
fails in attempt to detach BW&Co. from WFL, 247
implements McKinsey reforms, 212–13
managerial style, 200–1, 218
perceptions of BW&Co. culture, 201
provokes SKUNKWORKS project, 215
questions respective powers of WFL group directors and senior managers of BW&Co., 223
reforms pricing policy, 204
reforms product planning system, 207
regards association of of BW&Co. with Wellcome Trust as demotivating, 204
WFL board intervention threatens uncertainty with potential effect on flotation of plc, 248
resigns, 248
Sulphonamides, 105, 157–8
Sydney, Australia agency, 11, 17, 38
Sykes, Sir Richard, 327–333, 345, *see also* Glaxo Laboratories/ Holdings
Syncurine, 101, 114

Tabloid brand compressed medicines, 9–12, 17–20, 27–32, 37, 43, 47–9, 54, 59, *see also* Empirin, products
Taft-Hartley law, effects on labor relations at BW&Co., 128
Tagamet, 219, 327–8
Taggart, James, 3, 305–6, 317
Tannafax, 28
Tan, Y. H., 308
Tanner, Jan, 128
Timofax, 47
Tariff, 1909, effect of, 15, 17
taxation, 75, 79, 86–7, 260, 273–4, 365
Taylor, Bernard, 330
Technology Transfer Act 1986, 290, 352
Tennant, Sir Anthony, 325, 333
thalidomide, 56, 111, 164, 351
Therapeutic Research Corporation, 75
Thymidine, 260, 265–6, 270, 276–7, 283
Three Bromides Effervescent, 17, 23, 27, 29 *see also* products
Timofax, 47
tPA, 305, 310–11
Tracrium, 203, 206–7, 300, 316, 350
Tracy, Philip, 200, 284, 300, 312, 333, 336–7
trade names, 21, 24, 60, 74, 159–60, 256, 262, 316, *see* brands, proprietary drugs
trade unions, 127–9, 130–1, 135, 201, 234
training, 13, 32, 49, 66, 70, 129, 136, 144–7, 151–3, 192, 194, 354
production workers, see also Greenville
see also detailing and separate companies
Treatment Action Group, 288, *see also* AIDS
Tricoloid, 158
Trifluorothymidine, 251
Trimethoprim, 109, 157–60, *see also* Septra/Septrin
tropical medicine, 46, 230
Trotte, Larry, 135
Trust, 14, 124, 143, 194, 282, 288–9, 317, 363
Trustees Act 1967, 245
Tubarine, 47
Tuckahoe, 21–32, 39–41, 44–6, 49–60, 69–70, 74, 80–120, 124, 187, 190–1, 198, 345, 347–9, 356
Tylenol, 58–9, 208

"Understanding Aids", 262
"University of Beckenham", 186–7, 228, 343, *see* WFL
University of North Carolina, 131, 137
UNRRA, 46
Upjohn, 27, 41, 45, 74, 102, 139, 164, 174, 202
Upton, J. H. Peter, 171, 173, 175
Urwick Orr & Partners Ltd, management consultants, 38, 95, 97–8, 117, 132, 170–1

Vaccines, 181–2, 221–3, 307–8
Vane, Sir John R., 178–82, 190–1, 195, 217–39, 244, 293, 301, 305–11, 346
acrimonious relations with Black, 219, 222, 224, 227
early career, 178
imposes unprofitable veterinary medicine business on BW&Co., 181–2
knighted, 293
managerial style, 278
opposes reforms to R&D, 221–2, 230–1
invites Black to lead biological research at Beckenham, 219
resignation under pressure, 293
uncooperative relations with scientists at RTP, 179–80, 218, 230
defends continued unprofitable, though historic, vaccines and interferon R&D, 221–2
proposes "solution" to R&D management strife at Beckenham, 230
Vasoxyl, 53, 100, 114
Veterans'Administration, 49, 71
veterinary medicine, 16, 63, 104, 118–20, 197, 200, 207–8, 330
Viroptic, 217, 229, 277
vitamin products, 52–3, 67–9, 148, 181, 232, 234

Wachovia Bank, 134
Wall Street Journal, 280
war, *see* First World War, Second World War
Warehousemens' Union, 129
Warlock, Arnold, 173
Warner Lambert, 74, 100, 141, 167–71, 181, 191, 258–9, 285, 319, 339–40, 352
Warner-Wellcome Health Products Group, 339–40
Waxman, Congressman Henry, 279–80, 300–1, 306–9, 362
Waxman/Hatch Act (1984), 207
Weiker, Lowell, 278
Weinhold, Kent, 256
Welfare Medical Assistance Program, 71
Wellferon, 219–22, 275, 307–10
Wellbutrin, 225, 230, 294, 371, 375–6
Wellcome Biotechnology/Biotech Ltd., 122, 168, 222, 232–3, 293, 300, 304, 308
Wellcome Brand Chemicals, 12, 46
Wellcome Bureau of Scientific Research, 37–8
Wellcome Chemical Research Laboratories, 37
Wellcome Chemical Works (Dartford) Pheonix Mills Factory, 62
Wellcome Diagnostics, 297, 305
Wellcome Foundation Ltd (WFL),
acquisitions/ diversification, 167, 180–2, 41, 83, 88, 93–4, 100, 167, 181–2, 240, 242, 245, 331–7, 343, fig. 13
assets, 76, 81, 218, 241–2, 322–3
bank loans, 75–86, 101–7, 112, 192, 240, 266
board directors, 2, 4, 10, 15, 34–5, 38, 75–98, 166–171, 174–5, 221–31, 234, 245–8
biologicals, report on 1980, 221–5, 232
boffins, 232
capital limitation, 82, 178
Coe's critique of, 174–6, 181–2
Creasy's critique of, 81–2, 89–93
Cresswell's critique of, 221–2
consideration of bids for acquisition of BW&Co. (USA) Inc., 81–2
consideration of the recommended price of Retrovir, 277, 281–2
corporate image, 98, 154, 232, 276, 293, 300, 359–60
corporate planning, 175
dividend policy, 94–5, 113, 176–8, 240, 242, 244, 246, table 7.1
employment, table 4.1
financial analysis, tables 7.1, 13.1, 15.2, 17.1, 17.2, 18.1, 23.2, 23.3
finance, 76–9, 81–6, 101–7, 112, 192, 240, 266
formation, 21
interferon/Wellferon, 219,–22, 275, 307–10
investment, 84, 178, 181, 190
licensing policy, 165
management culture, 4, 27, 173, 221–3, 228, 243, 295, 302–3, 311–12, 336, 342, *see also* under separate companies
management failure, 174–6, 229–35
management investigation by Urwick Orr, 167, 170
management review by A. D. Little, 224–35
management structure, 170–3, fig. 13.1
management succession, 235, 294–5
marketing, 4–5, 171, 221, 228, 300, 307, 311–12
non-executive directors, 221, 229, 230, 233–4, 243–5, 281, 295, 306, 309, 325, 336
organization, 225–35, figs 2.1, 6.1
products, 60, 76, 88, 91. 240, 311
profits, 75, 87, 90, 92, 97, 187, 240, 242, 247, tables 7.1, 13.1, 13.2, 18.1
R&D, discordant organization of, 178–80, 218–31, *see also* Little
regionalization, 182
relations with Wellcome Trust, *see* Wellcome Trust
research culture, 227–35
sales, tables 7.1, 13.1, 17.2, 23.2
Wellcome, Henry Solomon
business philosophy applied to BW&Co., 17–20
death, 32
establishes the Wellcome Trust, 34–5
early career, 7–10
enters into partnership with Silas Burroughs, 9
forms New York branch, 11

nominates Pearson as commanding deputy governor of WFL, 33
over-rules Pearson affecting the development of the American company, 21–6
shares Nevin's ambition for manufacturing and research at BW&Co., 21–6
sole owner-manager of BW&Co., 10
will, 34–5
withdraws from management, 16
see also Wellcome Trust
Wellcome Historical Museum and Library, 21, 35, 39, 77, 81
Wellcome plc,
adverse impact on of Concorde study, 316
Anglo-American relations, 311–13
appointment of CEO from Beecham plc, 295–6
assets, 327–9, 364
attractions of acquisition by Glaxo, 329–30
board of directors, 277–81, 294–5, 301–5, 312, 318–20, 322–6, 331–7, 344–8, 363
accept MOU as Trust's assurance of medium term independence, 322
criticize Trust procedure in negotiating with Glaxo, 334
elect to combine CEO with chairmanship, 306
fail to prevent to second share issue, 322
oppose Glaxo sale, 333
seek "white knight", 334
set product innovation objectives, 313
under pressure from Trust to distribute higher dividends, 295
views on pricing Retrovir, 281–2
warned by merchant bankers of inevitability of merger, 324
co-marketing agreements, 313–14, 326
comparison with Glaxo Holdings, 298–9
competition, 314–16
critical commentaries on management of in financial press, 300, 324
expansion of OTC trade, 313–14
failure of merger negotiations with Warner Lambert, 326
financial analysis, 298, 321
flotation of, 245–6
globalization of structure and organization, 307, 311
heavy dependence on anti-viral sales, 313
limited financial benefit from flotation, 246–7
management difficulties exposed to public, 293–4, 311, 323,
management renewal, 301–2
perception of by trustees, 321–2
profit, 298–9, table 25.2
public image, 317
rationalization of activities, 304–6
R&D reforms, 310–13
reorganization, 311–12
restructuring challenge for CEO, 296, 323–5
sales, 296–7, tables 14.2, 23.1, table 24.1
share price volatility, 311, 319–20, table 25.1
strategy group fails to produce convincing plan to protect independence, 325–6
transparency implications of plc status, 302–4, 318–19, 324
Wellcome tradition, 80, 82, 165, 175, 182, 201, 356
Wellcome Tropical Research Laboratories, 107
Wellcome Research Laboratories, 29, 35, 47, 84, 100–1, 178, 219, 224, 343
Wellcome Trust,
accepts Glaxo's bid, 333–4
advice from merchant bankers, 242–6, 327–30
assets, 323
concerns over R&D at WFL, 229–30
discussions with Charity Commission, 242–5, 320, 322
dividend policy, 166, 178, 189, 236–9, 318
dividends/income, tables 25.2, 25.3
endorses management consultants' report, on WFL, 170
exercizes "power of last resort", 38
fiduciary duties, 331
flotation of WFL, 241–3
formation, 34–5
funding research constrained, 177
income, tables 13.2, 25.2, 25.3
intervention in management of WFL, 89–93
"irrevocable commitment" condition by Glaxo, 322
"last resort" power, 35, 38
merger negotiations with Glaxo, 330–2
memorandum of Understanding (MOU), 322
ownership and control of WFL, 38–9
reinvigoration of "financial and philanthropic ambitions", 241
rejects American buyout, 247
replaces senior managers at WFL and Burroughs Wellcome, 38, 77, 96–7, 248
share issue opposed by WFL, 322–4
supports reform of WFL, 176–7
response to financial crisis at WFL, 76–7
response to Little management review, 239–40, 243
trustees, 34–5, 90, 236, 241
wealth, tables 27.1, 27.2

Wellcoverin, 203, 207
Wellferon, 307–1
Wenyon, C. K., 36–7, 82–3
Weston, Jean, 113–114
Weston, Kathleen 113–14
Wheeler, D. E., 41, 77, 87, 90–5, 167, 170–1, 181, 365
White House, 252, 260
"White knight", 332, 334
WHO Expert Committee on Narcotics, 57
William Douglas McAdam advertising agency, 272, 152, 161
Williams, Peter, O., 166, 176, 242, 244
Winthrop Pharmaceutical Company, 46
Wolfe, Sidney, 209
Wood, Brigadier General Dr John R., 102, 112
Worlock, Arnold, 173–4
Wrigley, Fred, 87–8, 90–6, 131–2, 141
Wyeth & Brother, 7–9, 54, 74, 313, 353

Yarchoan, Robert, 255–9
Yellow Fever, 37, 254

Zantac, 314, 327–9
Zeneca, 322–3, 327, 334, 337
Zidebeme, 316
Zidovudine, 251, 258
Zovirax,
  advertising account with Rosenthal, 193–4
  clinical trials, 196
  cost to patients, 198
  production, 195
  estimates of demand, 192–3
  FDA approval, 196
  production costs, 198
  prompts antiviral drug sales training, 192, 194
  sales, 194–5, 197
  treatment for herpes, 192, *see also* herpes
Zyban, 316
Zyloprim/Zyloric, 72, 109–10, 123, 146, 148–50